BRIEF CONTENTS

SECTION I *INTRODUCTION*

CHAPTER 1 *INTRODUCING STRAIGHT TALK ABOUT MANAGING BUSINESS ETHICS: WHERE WE'RE GOING AND WHY* 2

SECTION II *ETHICS AND THE INDIVIDUAL*

CHAPTER 2 *DECIDING WHAT'S RIGHT: A PRESCRIPTIVE APPROACH* 38

CHAPTER 3 *DECIDING WHAT'S RIGHT: A PSYCHOLOGICAL APPROACH* 70

CHAPTER 4 *ADDRESSING INDIVIDUALS' COMMON ETHICAL PROBLEMS* 110

SECTION III *MANAGING ETHICS IN THE ORGANIZATION*

CHAPTER 5 *ETHICS AS ORGANIZATIONAL CULTURE* 150

CHAPTER 6 *MANAGING ETHICS AND LEGAL COMPLIANCE* 207

CHAPTER 7 *MANAGING FOR ETHICAL CONDUCT* 251

CHAPTER 8 *ETHICAL PROBLEMS OF MANAGERS* 288

SECTION IV *ORGANIZATIONAL ETHICS AND SOCIAL RESPONSIBILITY*

CHAPTER 9 *CORPORATE SOCIAL RESPONSIBILITY* 318

CHAPTER 10 *ETHICAL PROBLEMS OF ORGANIZATIONS* 351

CHAPTER 11 *MANAGING FOR ETHICS AND SOCIAL RESPONSIBILITY IN A GLOBAL ENVIRONMENT* 400

INDEX 447

CONTENTS

PREFACE **XIII**

ACKNOWLEDGMENTS **XVII**

SECTION I
INTRODUCTION 1

CHAPTER 1 *INTRODUCING STRAIGHT TALK ABOUT MANAGING BUSINESS ETHICS: WHERE WE'RE GOING AND WHY* **2**

Introduction **2**

The Financial Disaster of 2008 **4**

    Borrowing Was Cheap **4**

    Real Estate Became the Investment of Choice **5**

    Mortgage Originators Peddled "Liar Loans" **5**

    Banks Securitized the Poison and Spread it Around **6**

    Those Who Were Supposed to Protect Us Didn't **7**

Moving Beyond Cynicism **9**

Can Business Ethics Be Taught? **14**

    Aren't Bad Apples the Cause of Ethical Problems in Organizations? **14**

    Shouldn't Employees Already Know the Difference between Right and Wrong? **15**

    Aren't Adults' Ethics Fully Formed and Unchangeable? **16**

This Book is about Managing Ethics in Business **19**

Ethics and the Law **21**

Why Be Ethical? Why Bother? Who Cares? **21**

    Individuals Care about Ethics: The Motivation To Be Ethical **22**

    Employees Care about Ethics: Employee Attraction and Commitment **23**

    Managers Care about Ethics **24**

    Executive Leaders Care about Ethics **25**

    Industries Care about Ethics **26**

    Society Cares about Ethics: Business and Social Responsibility **26**

The Importance of Trust **27**

The Importance of Values **29**

How This Book Is Structured **30**

Conclusion **31**

Discussion Questions **32**

Exercise **33**
   Your Cynicism Quotient **33**
Notes **34**

SECTION II
ETHICS AND THE INDIVIDUAL **37**

CHAPTER 2 *DECIDING WHAT'S RIGHT:*
           A PRESCRIPTIVE APPROACH **38**

Ethics and the Individual **38**
   Ethical Dilemmas **38**
   Prescriptive Approaches to Ethical Decision Making in Business **39**
   Eight Steps to Sound Ethical Decision Making in Business **51**
   Practical Preventive Medicine **58**
Conclusion **61**
Discussion Questions **61**
Exercise **62**
   Clarifying Your Values **62**
Introducing the Pinto Fires Case **63**
Case: Pinto Fires **63**
Short Cases **68**
Notes **68**

CHAPTER 3 *DECIDING WHAT'S RIGHT:*
           A PSYCHOLOGICAL APPROACH **70**

Ethical Awareness and Ethical Judgment **70**
Individual Differences, Ethical Judgment, and Ethical Behavior **74**
   Ethical Decision-Making Style **75**
   Cognitive Moral Development **76**
   Locus of Control **83**
   Machiavellianism **84**
   Moral Disengagement **85**
Facilitators of and Barriers to Good Ethical Judgment **87**
   Thinking about Fact Gathering **87**
   Thinking about Consequences **88**
   Consequences as Risk **89**
   Thinking about Integrity **90**
   Thinking about Your Gut **92**
   Unconscious Biases **93**
   Emotions In Ethical Decision Making **94**
Toward Ethical Action **96**
   Revisiting the Pinto Fires Case: Script Processing and Cost-Benefit Analysis **100**
   Cost-Benefit Analysis **102**
Conclusion **104**

Exercise   **104**
    Understanding Cognitive Moral Development   **104**
Discussion Questions   **105**
Short Case   **106**
Notes   **106**

CHAPTER 4   *ADDRESSING INDIVIDUALS' COMMON ETHICAL PROBLEMS*   110

    Identifying Your Values—and Voicing Them   **111**
People Issues   **113**
    Discrimination   **114**
    Harassment, Sexual and Otherwise   **118**
Conflicts of Interest   **122**
    What Is It?   **122**
    How We Can Think about This Issue   **124**
    Why Is It an Ethical Problem?   **125**
    Costs   **125**
Customer Confidence Issues   **126**
    What Is It?   **126**
    How We Can Think about This Issue   **130**
    Why Is It an Ethical Problem?   **130**
    Costs   **130**
Use of Corporate Resources   **131**
    What Is It?   **131**
    How We Can Think about This Issue   **135**
    Why Is It an Ethical Problem?   **136**
    Costs   **136**
When all Else Fails: Blowing the Whistle   **136**
    When Do You Blow the Whistle?   **139**
    How to Blow the Whistle   **140**
Conclusion   **144**
Discussion Questions   **145**
Short Cases   **145**
Notes   **147**

SECTION III
MANAGING ETHICS IN THE ORGANIZATION   149

CHAPTER 5   *ETHICS AS ORGANIZATIONAL CULTURE*   150

Introduction   **150**
Organizational Ethics as Culture   **151**
    What Is Culture?   **151**
    Strong versus Weak Cultures   **151**

How Culture Influences Behavior: Socialization and Internalization   **152**

Ethical Culture: A Multisystem Framework   **153**

Alignment of Ethical Culture Systems   **154**

Ethical Leadership   **156**

Executive Leaders Create Culture   **156**

Leaders Maintain or Change Organizational Culture   **157**

Other Formal Cultural Systems   **165**

Selection Systems   **165**

Values and Mission Statements   **167**

Policies and Codes   **168**

Orientation and Training Programs   **170**

Performance Management Systems   **171**

Organizational Authority Structure   **174**

Decision-Making Processes   **177**

Informal Cultural Systems   **178**

Role Models and Heroes   **179**

Norms: "The Way We Do Things around Here"   **180**

Rituals   **181**

Myths and Stories   **181**

Language   **182**

Organizational Climates: Fairness, Benevolence,
Self-Interest, Principles   **184**

Developing and Changing the Ethical Culture   **185**

How an Ethical Culture Can Become an Unethical Culture   **186**

Becoming a More Ethical Culture   **187**

A Cultural Approach to Changing Organizational Ethics   **189**

Audit of the Ethical Culture   **190**

A Cultural Systems View   **190**

A Long-Term View   **191**

Assumptions about People   **191**

Diagnosis: the Ethical Culture Audit   **191**

Ethical Culture Change Intervention   **193**

The Ethics of Managing Organizational Ethics   **195**

Conclusion   **195**

Discussion Questions   **195**

Case: Culture Change at Texaco   **196**

Case: An Unethical Culture In Need of Change: Tap Pharmaceuticals   **198**

Case: "Bad to the Bone"   **200**

Notes   **202**

CHAPTER 6   *MANAGING ETHICS AND LEGAL COMPLIANCE*   **207**

Introduction   **207**

Structuring Ethics Management   **208**

Making Ethics Comprehensive and Holistic   **211**

Managing Ethics: The Corporate Ethics Office **211**
Ethics and Compliance Officers **211**
The Ethics Infrastructure **213**
The Corporate Ethics Committee **214**
Communicating Ethics **215**
Basic Communications Principles **215**
Evaluating the Current State of Ethics Communications **218**
Multiple Communication Channels for Formal Ethics Communication **220**
Interactive Approaches to Ethics Communication **222**
Mission or Values Statements **225**
Organizational Policy **226**
Codes of Conduct **227**
Communicating Senior Management Commitment to Ethics **229**
Formal and Informal Systems to Resolve Questions and Report Ethical Concerns **235**
Using the Reward System to Reinforce the Ethics Message **238**
Evaluating the Ethics Program **239**
Surveys **240**
Values or Compliance Approaches **241**
Globalizing an Ethics Program **242**
Conclusion **245**
Discussion Questions **245**
Short Case **246**
Appendix: How Fines Are Determined under the U.S. Sentencing Guidelines **247**
Notes **249**

CHAPTER 7 *MANAGING FOR ETHICAL CONDUCT* **251**

Introduction **251**
In Business, Ethics is about Behavior **251**
Practical Advice for Managers: Ethical Behavior **252**
Our Multiple Ethical Selves **252**
The Kenneth Lay Example **253**
The Dennis Levine Example **255**
Practical Advice for Managers: Multiple Ethical Selves **255**
Rewards and Discipline **256**
People Do What Is Rewarded and Avoid Doing What Is Punished **256**
People Will Go the Extra Mile to Achieve Goals Set by Managers **257**
How Goals Combined with Rewards Can Encourage Unethical Behavior **258**
Practical Advice for Managers: Goals, Rewards, and Discipline **259**
Recognize the Power of Indirect Rewards and Punishments **260**
Can Managers Really Reward Ethical Behavior? **262**
What About the Role of Discipline? **263**
Practical Advice for Managers: Discipline **265**
People Follow Group Norms **266**
"Everyone's Doing It" **266**
Rationalizing Unethical Behavior **266**

Pressure to Go Along **267**
Practical Advice for Managers: Group Norms **267**
People Fulfill Assigned Roles **268**
The Zimbardo Prison Experiment **269**
Roles at Work **270**
Conflicting Roles Can Lead to Unethical Behavior **271**
Roles Can Also Support Ethical Behavior **271**
Practical Advice for Managers: Roles **272**
Obedience to Authority: People Do What They're Told **272**
The Milgram Experiments **273**
Obedience to Authority at Work **275**
Practical Advice for Managers: Obedience to Authority **275**
Responsibility is Diffused in Organizations **275**
"Don't Worry—We're Taking Care of Everything" **276**
Diffusing Responsibility in Groups **276**
Diffusing Responsibility by Dividing Responsibility **277**
Diffusing Responsibility by Creating Psychological Distance **278**
Practical Advice for Managers: Personal Responsibility **279**
Conclusion **280**
Am I Walking My Ethical Talk? **280**
Discussion Questions **281**
Case: Sears, Roebuck, and Co.: The Auto Center Scandal **281**
Short Case **284**
Notes **285**

CHAPTER 8 *ETHICAL PROBLEMS OF MANAGERS* **288**

Introduction **288**
Managers and Employee Engagement **288**
Managing the "Basics" **291**
Hiring and Work Assignments **291**
Performance Evaluation **292**
Discipline **295**
Terminations **297**
Why Are These Ethical Problems? **299**
Costs **299**
Managing a Diverse Workforce **300**
Diversity **301**
Harassment **302**
Family and Personal Issues **304**
Why Are These Ethical Problems? **306**
Costs **306**
The Manager as a Lens **306**
The Buck Stops with Managers **307**
Managers Are Role Models **309**

Managing Up and Across   **310**
   Honesty Is Rule One   **311**
   Standards Go Both Ways   **312**
Conclusion   **313**
Discussion Questions   **313**
Short Cases   **314**
Notes   **315**

SECTION IV

ORGANIZATIONAL ETHICS AND SOCIAL RESPONSIBILITY   **317**

CHAPTER 9   *CORPORATE SOCIAL RESPONSIBILITY*   **318**

Introduction   **318**
Why Corporate Social Responsibility?   **318**
Types of Corporate Social Responsibility   **325**
   Economic Responsibilities   **325**
   Legal Responsibilities   **326**
   Ethical Responsibilities   **326**
   Philanthropic Responsibilities   **327**
Triple Bottom Line and Environmental Sustainability   **330**
Is Socially Responsible Business Good Business?   **334**
   The Benefit of a Good Reputation   **334**
   Socially Responsible Investors Reward Social Responsibility   **335**
   The Cost of Illegal Conduct   **335**
   The Cost of Government Regulation   **337**
   What the Research Says about Social Responsibility and Firm Performance   **339**
   Being Socially Responsible Because It's the Right Thing to Do   **342**
Conclusion   **344**
Discussion Questions   **344**
Case: Merck and River Blindness   **345**
Short Case   **346**
Notes   **347**

CHAPTER 10   *ETHICAL PROBLEMS OF ORGANIZATIONS*   **351**

Introduction   **351**
Managing Stakeholders   **352**
Ethics and Consumers   **353**
   Conflicts of Interest   **354**
   Product Safety   **362**
   Advertising   **367**
Ethics and Employees   **372**
   Employee Safety   **372**
   Employee Downsizings   **377**

Ethics and Shareholders   **380**

Ethics and the Community   **385**

Why Are These Ethical Issues?   **388**

Costs   **388**

Conclusion   **389**

Short Cases   **390**

Discussion Questions   **395**

Notes   **395**

CHAPTER 11 *MANAGING FOR ETHICS AND SOCIAL RESPONSIBILITY IN A GLOBAL ENVIRONMENT*   **400**

Introduction   **400**

Focus on the Individual Expatriate Manager   **401**

  The Difficulties of Foreign Business Assignments   **401**

  The Need for Structure, Training, and Guidance   **401**

  Foreign Language Proficiency   **402**

  Learning about the Culture   **402**

  Recognizing the Power of Selective Perception   **404**

  Assumption of Behavioral Consistency   **405**

  Assumption of Cultural Homogeneity   **405**

  Assumption of Similarity   **406**

  How Different Are Ethical Standards in Different Cultures—Really?   **413**

  Development of Corporate Guidelines and Policies for Global Business Ethics   **414**

The Organization in a Global Business Environment   **418**

  Deciding to Do Business in a Foreign Country   **419**

  Development of a Transcultural Corporate Ethic   **426**

Conclusion   **431**

Discussion Questions   **431**

Short Case   **432**

Case: Selling Medical Ultrasound Technology in Asia   **432**

Case: Google Goes to China   **436**

Notes   **441**

INDEX   **447**

PREFACE
WHY DOES THE WORLD
NEED ANOTHER BUSINESS
ETHICS TEXT?

The popular business press is replete with feature stories describing ethical meltdowns and how those corporate misdeeds have eroded the public trust of business leaders and their organizations. As most of us learned at our parents' knees, trust and reputation are built over many years and take but an instant to be destroyed. So here we stand at a crossroads. Is it going to be business as usual for business? Or are businesspeople going to commit to regaining the trust of our peers, our families, and our fellow citizens?

In response to this crisis of trust, universities across the country are scrambling to design new courses that incorporate leadership, communication skills, the basics of human resources management, and ethics. That's why we wrote this book; we want to make the study of ethics relevant to real-life work situations. We want to help business-people regain the trust that's been squandered in the last few years. This book is different from other business ethics texts in several key ways: First, it was written by an unusual team. Linda Treviño is Distinguished Professor of Organizational Behavior and Ethics in the Management and Organization Department of the Smeal College of Business at the Pennsylvania State University. Her prolific research on the management of ethical conduct in organizations is published in the field's best journals and is internationally known and referenced. She has more than 25 years of experience in teaching students and executives in university and nonuniversity settings, and she also has experience as a corporate consultant and speaker on ethics and management issues. Kate Nelson is a full-time faculty member at the Fox School of Business at Temple University in Philadelphia, where she teaches management, business ethics, and human resources to undergraduates. Before joining Temple's faculty, Kate worked for more than 30 years in strategic organizational communication and human resources at a variety of companies including Citicorp, Merrill Lynch, and Mercer HR Consulting. She also has worked as a consultant specializing in ethics and strategic employee communications and has designed ethics programs for numerous organizations. We think that bringing together this diverse mix of theory and practice makes the book unique.

Second, the approach of this book is pragmatic, and that approach is a direct response to complaints and suggestions we have heard from students, employees, and corporate executives. "Make it real," they have said. "Tell us what we need to know to effectively manage people. Take the mystery out of this subject that seems so murky. Get to the point." This book starts with the assumption that ethics in organizations is about human behavior in those organizations. We believe that behavior results from a number of factors, many of which can be influenced by managers and the organizations themselves. As a result, this book is organized into sections about individuals, managing in an organizational context, and organizations in their broader environment, the ethical dilemmas managers face, and how they might solve them. It also features philosophical and psychological factors of decision making, ethical culture, how managers can influence employees' behavior through ethical leadership, what corporations are doing to encourage ethical behavior and corporate social responsibility, and international business ethics.

Third, we have used a different mix of examples than is found in conventional business ethics texts. Most texts focus on high-level, corporate dilemmas: "Should senior executives be paid at a particular level? Should this industry do business in China? Should American environmental laws apply to American companies operating overseas?" Although these are interesting issues, the vast majority of students and employees will never have to face them. However, they will have to hire, manage, assess performance, discipline, fire, and provide incentives for staff, as well as produce quality products and services and deal effectively and fairly with customers, vendors, and other stakeholders. As a result, although we do feature some classic corporate ethics cases, many of the cases in this book center on the kinds of problems that most people will encounter during the course of their careers. All of the "hypothetical" cases in this text are based on actual incidents that have happened somewhere—it's the real stuff that goes on every day in offices across the country.

Fourth, this book was developed with the help of students at a number of universities and with guidance from numerous managers and senior executives from various corporations and organizations. We have incorporated the latest research on ethics and organizational behavior into this text, and much of the material that appears within these pages has been tested in both university and corporate settings.

Fifth, we believe this book is easy to use because it is organized to be flexible. It can be used alone to teach an ethics course, or it can be used as a supplement to a more conventional, philosophical text. The sections in this book basically stand alone and can be taught in a different sequence than is presented here, and the book also has many cases and vignettes you can use for class discussion. Wiley will create custom versions of the text with selected chapters if requested to do so. To help teach this course, the instructor's guide provides resources such as outlines, overheads, discussion questions, and additional cases for class discussion; it also supplies references to many other resources that can be used to teach the course.

A NOTE TO STUDENTS

This book was written for you. We have listened to your complaints and your wish lists and have tried to pare this complicated subject down to a digestible size. The cases that appear in this book all happened to people just like you, who were not as prepared to deal with the dilemmas as you will be after taking this course. Before you get into this book, we have one suggestion: know that regardless of how large an organization you find yourself in, you're not some little cog in a giant wheel. You have the power to change not only your own behavior and knowledge of ethics but also the behavior and knowledge of the people you work with. Use that power: the job you save may be your own.

We also want to suggest that when interviewing for your next job, you try to make sure that you're joining an organization that values ethics. Are ethics and values described in the firm's recruiting materials? Do organizational representatives talk about ethics and values during their interviews with you? When you ask about how their organization demonstrates ethics and values, does your interviewer respond enthusiastically, or does he or she look like a deer caught in headlights so you instantly know that he or she has never even considered this question before? It's much easier to get into an ethical organization in the first place than try to get out of an unethical one later on.

ACKNOWLEDGMENTS

It takes a lot of work by a lot of people to make a project like this come together. We'll begin with some joint thank-yous. Then, because this process has been so meaningful for each of us, we will separately share our more personal thanks.

We both offer our heartfelt appreciation to current and former executives who helped us with this and previous editions, in particular, Larry Axline, Jeffrey Braun, Jacquelyn Brevard, Earnie Broughton, Craig Cash, Frank Daly, Srinivas Dixit, Ray Dravesky, Kent Druyvesteyn, Kim Ingham, Dennis Jorgensen, John O'Byrne, Kevin O'Connor, Joe Paterno, Robert Paul, Jo Pease, Shirley Peterson, Vin Sarni, Carl Skooglund, Phil Tenney, and George Wratney. All shared their valuable time and advice, some of them on multiple occasions. Their wisdom can be found throughout this book, but especially in Chapter 6. They helped bring the subject of managing business ethics to life.

We also wish to thank Gary Weaver (University of Delaware) for being our philosophy adviser for the first edition, and Dennis Gioia (Penn State faculty member and dear friend) for sharing his Pinto fire case and especially his reflections.

John Wiley & Sons, Inc. is a fine publisher with a superb team. These people encouraged, nudged, nudged, and nudged again. We have many Wiley people to thank for helping to make this book a success.

The book's past and present reviewers also contributed significantly to making this a better book, and we thank them as well. We also thank our students and particularly Penn State undergraduate, MBA, and Executive MBA students who provide us with excellent feedback and advice semester after semester.

SPECIAL ACKNOWLEDGMENTS—FROM LINDA K. TREVIÑO

I have always wondered what makes people do especially good and bad things. As the child of Holocaust survivors, I have a unique perspective on and curiosity about such issues. My parents and their families escaped Nazi Germany before Hitler began killing Jews en masse, but not before my maternal grandfather was severely beaten and not before my fraternal grandfather was taken to a concentration camp (euphemistically referred to as a work camp at the time). My father's family received papers allowing them to emigrate from Germany to the United States shortly before the war began (in spring 1939), allowing my grandfather to be released from the camp where he was being held (once they were able to find him!). Both families landed in New York, where they survived through sheer grit, perseverance, and belief in the American dream. Although my family never dwelled on their experiences in Germany, I grew up with a special sensitivity and concern for equality and fair treatment.

I traveled to Germany with my dad and brother about 35 years ago. We visited the tiny towns where Mom and Dad were born and met some wonderful German people who had helped them or at least tried to. I walked through a German village holding hands with the elderly woman who had been my maternal grandmother's best friend and who urged the family to leave Germany because she anticipated the worst. I met another elderly woman who had cared for my father and aunt when they were children and who tried to take care of their home when they were forced to leave everything behind. These were special people, and the opportunity to connect with them holds a special place in my heart. So my family and background influenced me in ways I can't fully grasp with my mind but in ways that I feel in my soul. And I know that my quest to understand what makes people do good and bad things has something to do with that influence.

Many special people have helped along the path that brought me to the writing of this book. I'll begin by thanking my mentors in the doctoral program at Texas A&M University's management department. Many thanks to Stuart Youngblood (now at Texas Christian University), Don Hellriegel, Richard Woodman, Dick Daft (now at Vanderbilt University), and Mary Zey, who encouraged my early theorizing and research in business ethics. They told me to go with my gut and to do what was important, and they supported my every step. My exceptional colleagues in the Management and Organizational Department at Penn State have also been supportive all along the way. They have read my papers and challenged me to think harder and make my work ever better.

My thanks also to the colleagues who have worked with me on ethics-related research over the years and who have been partners in learning about the management of business ethics: particularly Gail Ball, Michael Brown, Ken Butterfield, Derron Bishop, Niki den Nieuwenboer, James Detert, David Harrison, Laura Hartman, Jennifer Kish Gephart, Glen Kreiner, Don McCabe, Bart Victor, Gary Weaver, and more. This shared learning has contributed to the book in important ways.

Shortly after becoming a faculty member at Penn State, I had the good fortune to meet my friend and coauthor, Kate Nelson. I was intrigued by a brief Wall Street Journal article about Kate's work at Citibank (you'll read more about that later). We met and became fast friends, who (believe it or not) loved talking about business ethics. We decided to write an article together, and the rest, as Kate says, is history. Kate brought the real world into this book. She was also willing to tell me when I was getting too academic (not her words exactly). It became clearer and clearer to me that we were supposed to write this book together, and I'm very glad we did. Thanks, Kate!

The article became a book proposal that we first shared with publishers at the Academy of Management meeting in 1992 (almost 20 years ago now). Shortly thereafter, Bill Oldsey (formerly publisher at John Wiley & Sons, Inc.) showed up in my office at Penn State. His enthusiasm for the book was immediate and infectious, and he talked us into writing a textbook rather than a trade book. I want to thank Bill for the special part he played.

Over the years, Penn State colleagues, administrators, and donors have continued to support my efforts in the area of business ethics. I am grateful to the Cook family, especially the late Ann Cook, for supporting business ethics at Smeal and the Cook Fellowship that I held for a number of years. My thanks also to Mrs. Mercedes Shoemaker (and her late husband, Albert) for supporting the Shoemaker program in Business Ethics that has brought us wonderful speakers on the topic of business ethics year after year. Finally, I am especially grateful to Dean James Thomas for naming me Distinguished Professor of Organizational Behavior and Ethics. My association with the Ethics Resource Center Fellows program (see www.ethics.org) has connected me with executives who manage ethics in large business organizations as well as consultants and those in government who are interested in making the business world (and the rest of the world, for that matter) a more ethical place. I appreciate the relationships and the learning that have come from this association as well as the time these executives have shared with me. In particular, I appreciate the funding that this group has provided for research that has found its way into this book, especially research on executive ethical leadership.

My heartfelt thanks also go to family members, colleagues, and many dear friends not only for cheering me on (as usual) but also for their many contributions to this book. They have served as readers and interviewees. They have provided clipping services, helped me make contacts, and offered ideas for cases. They were there when I was overwhelmed. I can't thank them enough. Finally, I thank the light of my life, Dan, for the inspiration, love, and support he provides every day of my life and for being one of the most ethical human beings I know.

SPECIAL ACKNOWLEDGMENTS—FROM KATHERINE A. NELSON

I began to learn about ethics and integrity as a very young child in a family where "doing it right" was the only option. I was blessed to grow up hearing about how your reputation is priceless and you must always guard it and act in ways that enhance that reputation. As a result, my biggest debt is to my parents, the late Harry R. and Bernadette Prendergast Nelson (formerly of New Hartford, New York), and my brother, James V. Nelson of Pasadena, California. My parents worked tirelessly to set Jim and me on the right path, and Jim's generosity and enthusiastic support encouraged me not only to teach ethics but also to write this book. (Jim proved to me that one can be an investment banker and have high ethical standards, and I'm very proud of him.) I'm also grateful to Jim's wife, Susan, for her many encouraging words of support and for giving our family its two most precious additions, Conor Vincent and James Patrick Nelson.

Thanks to my dearest friends, for their friendship, love, and support: Debra Besch, Loren Hart, Rose Ciotta, Elizabeth Dow, Carol Dygert, Ann Frazier Hedberg, and Gail Martin. Thanks also to the educational institutions that provided me with a sound footing in values: Utica Catholic Academy in Utica, New York, and the College of Mount St. Vincent in Riverdale, New York.

If I had ever known how much fun it is to teach, I might have made the transition to academia much earlier. Many thanks to the deans at the Fox School of Business at Temple University—including Moshe Porat, Rajan Chandran, and Diana Breslin Knudson, who took a chance on my teaching ability—and thanks to my many students past and present, who have enriched my life in ways I could not have imagined. Sincere thanks also to my many colleagues at Temple, who were so welcoming to this corporate refugee and who made me feel so much a part of this wonderful institution, especially Norm Baglini, Gary Blau, Debbie Campbell, Deanna Geddes, Terry Halbert, and John McClendon.

Thanks go to the many executives who, each in his or her own way, taught me that business ethics need not be an oxymoron: Christopher York, Don Armiger, Peter Thorp, Judith Fullmer, Jerry Lieberman, and Jane Shannon—all formerly with Citicorp in New York City; and Eugenie Dieck, Charlie Scott, and Lea Peterson, all formerly with Mercer HR Consulting in Philadelphia and Boston. And thank you to Allan Kennedy, the coauthor of the groundbreaking book from the late 1970s, *Corporate Cultures*. While working at Citicorp as a McKinsey consultant back in 1985, Allan was the very first person who encouraged me to go into ethics by helping me germinate the idea of designing an ethics game for Citicorp.

The most important thank-you goes to my wonderful husband, Stephen J. Morgan— an honorable man if there ever was one—who inspires and loves me every day. This book and my teaching would not be possible without his support, wisdom, and encouragement.

Of course, a final thank-you goes to my coauthor, Linda Treviño, for her dear, dear friendship and for working with me to produce this book in what, in comparison to accounts from other writing teams, was an almost painless experience.

INTRODUCTION

INTRODUCING STRAIGHT TALK ABOUT MANAGING BUSINESS ETHICS: WHERE WE'RE GOING AND WHY

INTRODUCTION

Back in 1993, when we sat down to write the first edition of this book, people wondered if business ethics was just a fad. At that point, companies were just beginning to introduce ethics into new-hire orientations and management training programs. In academia, business ethics was just beginning to gain traction as a subject for serious academic study, and some business schools were going so far as to require a business ethics course to graduate.

Back then there was still the feeling among many experts that business ethics—like time management, quality circles, and other management buzzwords of the day— would soon become a footnote in texts that described business fads of the late twentieth century. Despite multiple waves of scandal over the years, these have often been portrayed as temporary blips. For example, one prominent business writer for *Fortune Magazine* wrote an article in 2007 entitled "Business is Back!" Here's a choice excerpt: "It must be said: The shaming is over. The $5^1/_2$ year humiliation of American business following the tech bubble's burst and the Lay-Skilling-Fastow-Ebbers-Kozlowski-Scrushy perp walks that will forever define an era has run its course. After the pounding and the ridicule, penance has finally been done. No longer despised by the public, increasingly speaking up and taking stands, beloved again by investors, chastened and much changed—business is back."[1] Could he have been more wrong? Business managed to outdo itself on the shame index yet again just about a year later. We've seen these ethical debacles occur regularly for the past 25 years. As a result, we're convinced that business ethics is far from a fad. It's an ongoing phenomenon that must be better understood and managed and for which business professionals must be better prepared.

We tell our students that serious ethical scandals often result from multiple parties contributing in their own small or large ways to the creation of a catastrophe. As you'll read later on in this book, Enron's collapse in 2001 was not just the failure of Enron executives and employees, but also the failure of Enron's auditors, the bankers who loaned the company money, and the lawyers who never blew the whistle on Enron's shenanigans. However, no scandal of recent years—not even Enron—matches the financial industry debacle in 2008. Like Enron, many players contributed to this colossal failure. But the financial crisis was unparalleled in its scope and has fueled public outrage like no other business disaster in our lifetime. The aftermath has people around the world angry and mistrustful of companies, governments, regulators, rating agencies, and the people who work in them. If there was ever a crisis of trust and confidence, this is it. It is also a textbook-perfect example of how numerous people's actions (and inactions) can conspire to spawn an almost unimaginable calamity.

Recent business history has proven beyond any doubt that divorcing business from ethics and values runs huge risks. Rushworth Kidder,[2] the highly regarded ethics writer and thinker who died in 2012, wrote about the financial debacle and the resulting public anger. He eloquently described how free marketers cite Adam Smith's *Wealth of Nations* to justify a breed of capitalism that abhors regulation and focuses on short-term profits over long-term stewardship. Kidder wisely noted that 17 years before his more famous book, Smith wrote another one entitled *The Theory of Moral Sentiments*. Smith's first book deserves more attention because he always presumed that the messages from these two books would go hand in hand. Smith's "moral sentiments" work rests on the assumption that human beings are empathetic; they care about others, and they derive the most joy from human love and friendship. His book opened with the following statement: "How selfish soever man may be supposed, there are evidently some principles in his nature, which interest him in the fortune of others. . . . "[3] Smith believed that a good life derives from the expression of "beneficence," not from material wealth. He proposed that self-love (which he also acknowledged) can spur the individual to better his own condition by besting competitors. But he argued that this must be done in a just manner and in the spirit of fair play as judged by an informed, ethical, and impartial spectator. We care what others think of us because we are first and foremost social beings. But we also are moral beings who want to do the right thing because it is the right thing to do (not just to win the praise of others). According to Smith, virtuous persons balance prudence (mature self-love), strict justice, and benevolence, and ideal societies are comprised of such persons. Finally, a flourishing and happy society is built upon a foundation of justice and rules of conduct that create social order. Smith was confident that humankind would progress toward this positive ethical state; he called on leaders to avoid the arrogance of power and, instead, to be virtuous statesmen. Kidder's point was that capitalism will succeed only when firmly tethered to a moral base, and he reminds us that Adam Smith—that hero of free marketers—knew this better than anyone.

We completely agree. We began this book almost 20 years ago with the firm belief that business isn't just "better" when companies and businesspeople are ethical, but rather that good ethics is *absolutely essential* for effective business practice. This is not just empty rhetoric. Work is essential to life, and most people work for a business of some kind. How we work and the standards we uphold while we are working affect much more than just commerce. Our business behavior also affects our personal and company reputations, politics, society at large, and even our national reputation. For example, the 2008 financial crisis, while global in scope, had its roots in the United States, and the nation's reputation has suffered because of the behavior of individuals and companies. Similarly, China's reputation has suffered because of contaminants found in Chinese exports such as infant formula, drywall (used in construction), and children's toys. So, corporate misbehavior does not happen in a vacuum, and it's not just corporate reputations that suffer as a result. These scandals cast long shadows, and they often affect entire industries and countries. In this complex and increasingly transparent world, where reputation influences everything from who wants to hire you or trade with you to who buys your products to who finances your debt—and much more—unethical behavior in business is a very big deal indeed. So, let's take a closer look at the elephant in the room: the near collapse of the financial markets in 2008 and what it has to do with business ethics.

THE FINANCIAL DISASTER OF 2008

The implosion of the financial markets in 2008 was largely not the result of illegal behavior. For the most part, the activities that brought down the U.S. economy and others around the world were not against the law, at least not yet (government regulators and the legal system often play catch-up after ethical debacles in business). Many of those activities, however, were unethical in that they ultimately produced great harm and were contrary to a number of ethical principles such as responsibility, transparency, and fairness. Let's start with some of the factors that laid the groundwork for the disaster in the United States.

Borrowing Was Cheap

First, borrowing money became really cheap. In 2000, stocks in high-technology companies had soared to unsustainable heights, and that bubble finally burst. To soften the effects on the U.S. financial markets, Alan Greenspan, who headed the Federal Reserve at that time, lowered the Federal Funds rate (the rate banks charge each other for overnight loans, which has a direct impact on short-term interest rates, including the prime rate) to almost zero. That move, seemingly innocent at the time, injected huge amounts of money into the U.S. financial system. It made the cost of borrowing so low that it fueled a glut of consumer borrowing. Suddenly, it was amazingly cheap to buy a new car, a wide-screen television, a backyard pool, a larger home, a second home, and all sorts of designer goodies. There was even encouragement to indulge. Following the terrorist attacks in September 2001, President George W. Bush told people that if they wanted to help the economy they should go shopping. And people did. Household debt levels rose to $13.9 billion in 2008, almost double what households owed in 2000, and savings dipped into negative territory. Responsible borrowers should have thought about what they could afford rather than what bankers would lend to them. And responsible lenders should have established that borrowers could actually afford to pay back the loans before lending them money.

Real Estate Became the Investment of Choice

Of course, people also want to invest in something safe, and what could be safer than real estate? There had been relatively few instances of real estate values declining, and when they did the declines were generally shallow and short-lived. A point of pride in the United States was the high percentage of Americans who owned their own homes. Investing in a home traditionally had been a very safe investment and one that was slow to appreciate in value. But suddenly in the early 2000s, real estate investing became a real moneymaker. With a backdrop of historically low interest rates, real estate became such a popular way to invest that demand soon outstripped supply and prices soared. The value of homes skyrocketed—homes that were selling for $300,000 in one year sold for $450,000 the next. Prices rose so fast that speculation grew tremendously. People bought houses with almost no down payment, remodeled them or waited a few months, and then resold the houses for a quick profit. A number of popular television programs showed viewers how to "flip" real estate properties for profit.

Since the cost of borrowing was so low and home equity had grown so quickly, many consumers borrowed on the equity in their homes and purchased additional real estate or a new car or financed a luxury vacation. For example, suppose someone purchased a house for $500,000 in 2003. By 2005, the home might have been worth $800,000. The home owner refinanced the mortgage—borrowing as much as the entire current worth of the house (because its value could only go up, right?), which resulted in a $300,000 cash infusion for the home owner. This practice was very popular, and it laid the groundwork for a huge disaster when the housing values fell off a cliff in 2008 and 2009. Imagine the home owner who refinanced the home just described. Imagine that he took the $300,000 and purchased a summer home and a sports car and paid for his children's college educations. Suddenly, home values plummeted and his house lost 30 percent of its value, which was common in markets such as California, Florida, Nevada, and Arizona, where the real estate bubble was particularly inflated. After the real estate bubble burst, his house was worth $560,000. Now suppose he loses his job and needs to sell his house because he can't afford the mortgage payments. He can't get $800,000 for his home, which is what he owes on his mortgage. His only choice is to work with the mortgage holder (probably a bank) to refinance (unlikely) or declare bankruptcy and walk away from the house. This is what a lot of home owners have done, and it is one of the factors at the heart of the current financial crisis. Lots of folks were in on this bubble mentality, getting what they could in the short term and not thinking very much about the likelihood (or inevitability) that the bubble would burst.

Mortgage Originators Peddled "Liar Loans"

In the early 2000s, as housing investments increased in popularity, more and more people got involved. Congress urged lenders Freddie Mac and Fannie Mae to expand home ownership to lower-income Americans. Mortgage lenders began to rethink the old rules of financing home ownership. As recently as the late 1990s, potential home owners not only had to provide solid proof of employment and income to qualify for a mortgage, but they also had to make a cash down payment of between 5 and 20 percent of the estimated value of the home. But real estate was so hot and returns on investment were growing so quickly that mortgage lenders decided to loosen those "old-fashioned" credit restrictions. In the early 2000s, the rules for obtaining a mortgage became way less restrictive. Suddenly, because real estate values were rising so quickly, borrowers didn't have to put any money down on a house. They could borrow the entire estimated worth of the house; this is known as 100-percent financing. Also, borrowers no longer needed to provide proof of employment or income. These were popularly called "no doc" (no documentation) or "liar loans" because banks weren't bothering to verify the "truth" of what borrowers were claiming on their mortgage applications.

This complete abandonment of lending standards opened the mortgage market to rampant fraud, and it was not exactly a secret. The FBI warned of an "epidemic" of mortgage fraud back in 2004, four years before that epidemic torpedoed the financial industry.[4]

Banks Securitized the Poison and Spread It Around

At about the same time liar loans were becoming popular, another new practice was introduced to mortgage markets. Investors in developing countries were looking to the United States and its seemingly "safe" markets for investment opportunities. Cash poured into the country from abroad—especially from countries like China and Russia, which were awash in cash from manufacturing and oil, respectively. Wall Street bankers developed new products to provide investment vehicles for this new cash. One new product involved the securitization of mortgages. (Note: structured finance began in 1984, when a large number of GMAC auto receivables were bundled into a single security by First Boston Corporation, now part of Credit Suisse.) Here's how it worked: Instead of your bank keeping your mortgage until it matured, as had traditionally been the case, your bank would sell your mortgage—usually to a larger bank that would then combine your mortgage with many others (reducing the bank's incentive to be sure you would pay it back). Then the bankers sold these mortgage-backed securities to investors, which seemed like a great idea at the time. Real estate was traditionally safe, and "slicing and dicing" mortgages divided the risk into small pieces with different credit ratings and spread the risk around.

Of course, the reverse was also true, as the bankers learned to their horror. This method of dividing mortgages into little pieces and spreading them around could also spread the contagion of poor risk. However, starting in 2002 and for several years thereafter, people couldn't imagine housing values falling. So much money poured into the system, and the demand for these mortgage-backed security products was so great, that bankers demanded more and more mortgages from mortgage originators. That situation encouraged the traditional barriers to getting a home mortgage to fall even farther. These investment vehicles were also based upon extremely complex mathematical formulas (and old numbers) that everyone took on faith and few attempted to understand. It looks like more people should have followed Warren Buffett's sage advice not to invest in anything you don't understand!

Add to that toxic mix the relatively new idea of credit-default swaps (CDS). These complex financial instruments were created to mitigate the risk financial firms took when peddling products such as securitized mortgages. CDS are insurance contracts that protect the holder against an event of default on the part of a debtor. One need not own the loan or debt instrument to own the protection, and the amount of capital tied up in trading CDS is very small compared to trading other debt instruments. That is a very significant part in the increase in the popularity of CDS at sell-side and buy-side trading desks. The insurance company AIG was a huge player in this market, and so were the large banks. The firms that were counterparties to CDS never stepped back from the trading frenzy to imagine what would happen if both the structured finance market and the real estate bubble burst (as all bubbles eventually do) at the same time. Both underwriters and investors would be left holding the bag when the music stopped playing—and the U.S. taxpayer has had to bail out most of the financially stressed firms to save the entire financial system from collapse. Please note that all of this happened in a part of the market that was virtually unregulated.

Those Who Were Supposed to Protect Us Didn't

One protection against financial calamity was thought to be the rating agencies, including Standard and Poor's and Moody's. They rate the safety or soundness of securities, including those securitized mortgage products. A credit opinion is defined as one which rates the timeliness and ultimate repayment of principal and interest. But, like everyone else, the rating agencies say they didn't foresee a decline in housing prices; and consequently, they rated the mortgage securities as being AAA—the highest rating possible, which meant that the rating agencies considered these securities to be highly safe.

The agencies are the subject of much criticism for their role in the crisis. If they had done a better job analyzing the risk (their responsibility), much of the crisis might have been avoided. But note that these rating agencies are hired and paid by the companies whose products they rate, thus causing a conflict of interest that many believe biased their ratings in a positive direction. So, people who thought they were making responsible investments because they checked the ratings were misled.

Another protection that failed was the network of risk managers and boards of directors of the financial community. How is it that one 400-person business that was part of the formerly successful insurance behemoth, AIG, could invest in such a way that it brought the world's largest insurance company to its knees? The risk was underestimated all around by those professionals charged with anticipating such problems and by the board of directors that didn't see the problem coming. The U.S. government (actually taxpayers) ended up bailing out AIG to the tune of $170 billion. The risk managers and boards of other financial firms such as Citigroup, Merrill Lynch, Lehman Brothers, Bear Stearns, and Wachovia were similarly blind.

On Wall Street, there were other contributing factors. First, bank CEOs and other executives were paid huge salaries to keep the price of their firms' stocks at high levels. If their institutions lost money, their personal payouts would shrink. As a result, bank executives focused on short-term financial results often to the exclusion of long-term planning or organizational strategy. Since their compensation packages were directly tied to the company stock price, they were paid handsomely for their efforts to bolster short-term profits. The Wall Street traders were similarly compensated—they were paid multimillion-dollar bonuses for taking outsized risks in the market. What seemed to matter most were the short-term profits of the firm and the short-term compensation of those making risky decisions. The traders took risks, the bets were at least temporarily successful, and the bankers walked off with multimillion-dollar bonuses. It didn't matter that the risk taking was foolish and completely irresponsible in the long run. The bonus had already been paid. Consequently, a short-term mentality took firm root among the nation's bankers, CEOs, and boards of directors.

If you thought that bankers' behavior would change as a result of the financial debacle, think again. In 2012, JPMorgan Chase—which in the wake of the financial crisis was described by many experts as being the best managed U.S. bank—suffered a huge loss at the hands of a rogue trader in its London office. The initial losses were estimated to be $2 billion, but later revised to be perhaps as high as $9 billion—in the same exact type of investments that created the financial catastrophe just a few years earlier.[5]

Finally, we cannot examine the financial crisis without questioning the role of regulatory agencies and legislators. For example, for a decade, investor Harry Markopolos tried on numerous occasions to spur the Securities and Exchange Commission to investigate Bernard L. Madoff. The SEC never did uncover the largest Ponzi scheme in the history of finance. The 65-billion-dollar swindle unraveled only when Madoff admitted the fraud to his sons, who alerted the SEC and the U.S. attorney's office in New York in December 2008.

Others who are culpable in the financial crisis are members of the U.S. Congress, who deregulated the financial industry, the source of some of their largest campaign contributions. Among other things, they repealed the Glass-Steagall Act, which had been passed after the U.S. stock market crash in 1929 to protect commercial banking customers from the aggression and extreme risk taking of investment bank cultures. The act created separate institutions for commercial and investment banks, and they stayed separate until the merger of Citicorp and Travelers to form Citigroup in 1998. The two companies petitioned Congress to eliminate Glass-Steagall, claiming that it was an old, restrictive law and that today's markets were too modern and sophisticated to need such protection. And Congress listened.

Those 1930s congressmen knew that if the two banking cultures tried to exist in the same company—the staid, conservative culture of commercial banking (our savings and checking accounts) and the razzle-dazzle, high-risk culture of investment banking—the "eat what you kill" investment bank culture would win out. Some said that staid old commercial banks turned into "casinos." But, interestingly, casinos are highly regulated and are required to keep funds on hand to pay winners. In the coming months, we expect to learn more about the behavior that led to this crisis. As we noted earlier, much if not most of it was probably legal because of the lack of regulation in the mortgage and investment banking industries. But look at the outcome! If only ethical antennae had been more sensitive, more people might have questioned products they didn't understand, or spoken out or refused to participate in practices that were clearly questionable. As just one tiny example, could anyone have thought it was ethical to sell a product they called a liar loan, knowing that the customer surely would be unable to repay (even if it was legal to do so)?

In 2010, the U.S. Congress passed the Dodd-Frank Financial Regulation Legislation—an attempt to rein in the most egregious practices in the financial industry. Financial institution lobbyists continue trying to water down the effects of this bill as regulators work to implement its complex regulations. Several European countries may be ahead of the U.S. when it comes to comprehensive financial regulation reform.[6]

What's increasingly clear is that corruption exists among the world's leading financial institutions and that sometimes they collude in that corruption. If you think that is an exaggeration, please read about the LIBOR scandal that broke during the summer of 2012. LIBOR, which stands for the London Interbank Offered Rate, is the interest rate by which banks can borrow from one another. LIBOR is important because so many of the loans around the world—mortgage rates, car loans, corporate debt, etc., are pegged to those LIBOR rates. Experts estimate that hundreds of trillions of dollars worth of financial contracts and derivatives are tied to LIBOR.

Regulators in several countries have accused a number of global financial institutions with cooperating with one another to rig LIBOR rates to make themselves appear healthier in the wake of the financial collapse of 2008–2009. As this book goes to press, two huge banks have already settled charges that they manipulated LIBOR rates. Barclays paid $450 million and UBS is paying $1.5 billion to U.S., U.K., and Swiss regulators for their part in the crisis. This crisis is far from over, because the UBS settlement not only charges that UBS manipulated rates to make itself look healthier, but also that it colluded with other global banks to make money from the manipulated rates. This is the equivalent of the big players admitting that the game is fixed. The banks under investigation include the largest firms in the world: Bank of America, JPMorgan Chase, Morgan Stanley, Citigroup, and Bank of England, among others.[7] One Wall Street veteran described the scandal this way: "It's like finding out that the whole world is on quicksand."[8]

Let's delve into the cynicism that this and previous scandals have created and then try to move beyond it so that *you* can do things differently in the future.

MOVING BEYOND CYNICISM

After multiple waves of business scandals, some cynicism (a general distrust) about business and its role in society is probably healthy. However, cynicism about business has truly become an epidemic in the United States. To be fair, we should note that although the financial industry screwed up royally, at the same time most other mainstream American companies were "running their companies with strong balance sheets and sensible business models."[9] Most companies were responsible, profitable, and prudent. Because they had serious cash reserves, many of them have actually managed to weather the recent crises reasonably well. But the attention has not been on these responsible companies. It's been on the financial sector and its irresponsibility.

How bad is the cynicism? According to the 2012 Edelman Trust Barometer[10]—a survey of almost 30,000 college-educated people around the world—it's very bad, especially in the United States. (Edelman is the world's largest independent public relations firm with 53 offices around the world. Its business is helping companies build and maintain reputations.) Edelman's study shows that consumer trust in corporations has declined precipitously. More than half of the respondents stated that they trust business less than they did four years ago (in 2008). The decrease is particularly acute in the United States, where citizens have traditionally had higher opinions of business than they do in Europe. For example, only 35 percent of Americans surveyed trust banks to be ethical—a 34-point drop since 2008. The only part of the world where trust levels have not declined is in the developing world—the so-called BRIC nations (Brazil, Russia, India, China).

The Edelman study also highlights the importance of consumer trust—the degree to which consumers trust organizations has a direct impact on their buying patterns and much more. Over a one-year period, 91 percent of consumers stated that they purchased a product of service from a company they trust, and 77 percent of consumers refused to purchase a product or service from a company that they mistrusted. These figures suggest that corporate reputations affect consumer buying patterns, and companies risk harming their bottom line when they do not act to protect their good name.

However, consistent with our idea that business ethics is not a fad, neither is public cynicism about business ethics new. We have written about it in every edition of our book (since 1995). Surely, the factor that has contributed the most to cynicism in recent years is the highly visible behavior of some of the nation's leading corporations and executives, whose activities have garnered so much space in the business press and on the evening news. How do you watch hour after hour of such reporting and not walk away jaded? In the last few years, all you had to do was read about or watch the news to feel cynical, and business school students are no exception. We also note that business is not alone in its scandalous behavior. In recent years, we've learned about government employees who stole or misused funds, academics who falsified their research results, ministers who stole from their congregations, priests who abused children, and athletes who took bribes or used performance-enhancing drugs. It seems that no societal sector is immune.

Many of our readers are business school students, the current or future managers of business enterprises. Surveys suggest that many business students are themselves surprisingly cynical about business (given that they've chosen it as their future profession). They may believe that they'll be expected to check their ethics at the corporate door or that they will be pressured to compromise their own ethical standards in order to succeed.[11] Consider this scenario that took place at a large university: A professor asked his class to name management behaviors that are morally repugnant. His class struggled to name one! In another of his classes, the professor asked if the students would dump carcinogens in a river. This time the class agreed that they would do so because if they didn't, someone else would. When the professor asked if they really wanted to live in such a cynical environment, the class insisted that they already did. The dismayed professor believed that the attitudes of his students were formed long before they landed in his classroom. He agreed with other observers that the problem goes way beyond business and business schools and that our society, with its emphasis on money and material success, is rearing young people who strive for achievement at any cost. One symptom: cheating is pervasive in many high schools and colleges.[12]

This scenario is enough to make anyone wonder about today's business students. But at the same time, we know that students at many colleges and universities, including business schools, are encouraging their own faculty and administrators to establish newly invigorated academic integrity policies and honor codes. In an honor code community, students take responsibility for implementing the academic integrity policy and for holding each other accountable to it. They manage study-run judiciaries that mete out serious discipline to their fellow students who tarnish the community by cheating. These efforts, which are gaining real traction at many schools, suggest that at least some students have had enough and are willing to turn from cynicism toward a proactive approach to change things.

A 2008 Aspen Institute study of nearly 2,000 MBA students from 15 leading international business schools provides some insight into MBA students' attitudes, which appear to be moving in a less cynical direction. Similar to the findings they obtained in a 2002 survey, the results of Aspen's 2008 survey of MBA students indicate that the students anticipate facing difficult conflicts regarding values in their jobs, and they suggest some cynicism about ethics in the workplace. However, about 40 percent of these students believe that their business education is preparing them to manage values conflicts "a lot," and another 50 percent believe that they're being prepared "somewhat." Also, more than a quarter of the respondents said they are interested in finding a job that gives them the opportunity to contribute to society (compared to only 15 percent in 2002). More than half believe that safe, high-quality products and responsible governance and transparent business practices are very important in a potential employer. In addition, more than half said they would advocate alternative values or approaches in response to values conflicts at work (many more than in 2002).[13]

The media may be largely responsible for students' cynical attitudes. Think about the depiction of business and its leaders in movies and on television. The Media Research Center conducted a survey of 863 network TV sitcoms, dramas, and movies in the mid-1990s. Nearly 30 percent of the criminal characters in these programs were business owners or corporate executives. Entrepreneurs were represented as drug dealers, kidnappers, or sellers of defective gear to the military.[14] *Fortune* magazine called this "the rise of corporate villainy in prime time."[15] Movies have abounded with negative messages about corporate America. Think *Arbitrage, Avatar, Inside Job, Up in the Air, The Constant Gardner, Gasland, Wall Street, Boiler Room, Civil Action, Glengarry Glen Ross, The Insider, Erin Brockovich, Supersize Me, The Corporation, Enron: The Smartest Guys in the Room, Michael Clayton, The International, Quiz Show, The Insider*, and *Bowling for Columbine*. And there are more such movies every year; we're sure you can add to the list. A much tougher exercise is to generate a list of movies and television shows that actually create a positive ethical impression of business. Can you think of any? The consistent negative representation of business in the media has its effects. Academic research suggests that cynicism toward American business increased after study participants viewed the film *Roger & Me*, which depicted ruthless plant closings and layoffs at General Motors.[16] Imagine the cumulative, daunting effect of viewing countless movies and television programs that portray business as corrupt and business leaders as ruthless and unethical.

To counter that media-fueled cynicism at least somewhat, we encourage you to think about your own life and the hundreds of reliable products and services you trust and depend on every day as well as the people and businesses that produce them. These good folks are businesspeople too, but it isn't nearly as exciting or sexy for the media to portray businesspeople who do the right thing every day. We also encourage you to talk with businesspeople you know, perhaps people in your own family who work for businesses. Do they feel pressured to compromise their ethical standards, or do they see their employer in a more positive light?

Interestingly, the Ethics Resource Center's 2011 National Business Ethics Survey found that only 13 percent of employees of for-profit enterprises report feeling pressured to compromise their ethical standards. That means that more than 87 percent say that they're *not* feeling such pressure. Also, nearly two-thirds of these employees said that their own company has a strong or strong-leaning ethical culture. What do these numbers mean? To us, it means that most Americans who work in business think that their own company and coworkers are pretty ethical. Still, they read the same media accounts and see the same movies and TV programs as everyone else, and these offerings influence cynicism about American business in general.[17]

Finally, we won't leave a discussion of cynicism without talking about the events of September 11, 2001. While the business scandals of 2001–02 left many cynical, the events of September 11, 2001, showed us some of the best in many individuals and businesses. We have read about the care, compassion, and assistance that countless American firms gave to those who were harmed by the terrorist attacks. Few firms were hit as hard as Sandler O'Neill & Partners, a small but profitable Wall Street investment bank that lost 66 of its 171 employees—including two of the firm's leading partners—on September 11. The firm's offices were on the 104th floor of the World Trade Center. Despite its dire financial straits, the firm sent every deceased employee's family a check in the amount of the employee's salary through the end of the year and extended health-care benefits for five years. Bank of America quickly donated office space for the firm to use. Competitors sent commissions their way and freely gave the company essential information that was lost with the traders who had died. Larger Wall Street firms took it upon themselves to include Sandler in their deals. The goal was simply to help Sandler earn some money and get back on its feet.[18] This is only one of the many stories that point to the good that exists in the heart of American business. In this book, we offer a number of positive stories to counterbalance the mostly negative stories portrayed in the media.

The bottom line is this. We're as frustrated as you are about the media portrayal of business and the very real, unethical behavior that regularly occurs in the business community. But we also know that the business landscape is a varied one that is actually dominated by good, solid businesses and people who are even heroic and extraordinarily giving at times. So, for our cynical readers, we want to help by doing two things in this book: (1) empowering managers with the tools they need to address ethical problems and manage for ethical behavior, and (2) providing positive examples of people and organizations who are "doing things right" to offset some of the media-fueled negativity.

In May 2009, something notable and quite positive happened. A group of 20 second-year students at Harvard Business School created *The MBA Oath* in an attempt to articulate the values they felt their MBA degree ought to stand for:

THE MBA OATH

As a business leader I recognize my role in society.

- My purpose is to lead people and manage resources to create value that no single individual can create alone.
- My decisions affect the well-being of individuals inside and outside my enterprise, today and tomorrow.

Therefore I promise:

- I will manage my enterprise with loyalty and care, and will not advance my personal interests at the expense of my enterprise or society.
- I will understand and uphold, in letter and spirit, the laws and contracts governing my conduct and that of my enterprise.
- I will refrain from corruption, unfair competition, or business practices harmful to society.
- I will protect the human rights and dignity of all people affected by my enterprise, and I will oppose discrimination and exploitation.
- I will protect the right of future generations to advance their standard of living and enjoy a healthy planet.
- I will report the performance and risks of my enterprise accurately and honestly.
- I will invest in developing myself and others, helping the management profession continue to advance and create sustainable and inclusive prosperity.

In exercising my professional duties according to these principles, I recognize that my behavior must set an example of integrity, eliciting trust and esteem from those I serve. I will remain accountable to my peers and to society for my actions and for upholding these standards.

This oath I make freely, and upon my honor.

This focus on positive values among business students and business in general received significant publicity and turned into something of a movement. More than 400 graduates of Harvard Business School signed the oath, and they were joined by more than 6,000 business students from 300 other colleges and universities globally. For more information, go to www.mbaoath.org.

CAN BUSINESS ETHICS BE TAUGHT?

Given all that has happened, you may be wondering whether business ethics can be taught. Perhaps all of the bad behavior we outlined earlier results from a relatively few "bad apples" who never learned ethics from their families, clergy, previous schools, or employers.[19] If this were so, ethics education would be a waste of time and money, and resources should be devoted to identifying and discarding bad apples, not trying to educate them. We strongly disagree, and the evidence is on our side.

Aren't Bad Apples the Cause of Ethical Problems in Organizations?

According to the bad apple theory, people are good or bad and organizations are powerless to change these folks. This bad apple idea[20] is appealing in part because unethical behavior can then be blamed on a few individuals with poor character. Although it's unpleasant to fire people, it's relatively easier for organizations to search for and discard a few bad apples than to search for some organizational problem that caused the apple to rot.

Despite the appeal of the bad apple idea, "character" is a poorly defined concept, and when people talk about it, they rarely define what they mean. They're probably referring to a complex combination of traits that are thought to guide individual behavior in ethical dilemmas. If character guides ethical conduct, training shouldn't make much difference because character is thought to be relatively stable: it's difficult to change, persists over time, and guides behavior across different contexts. Character develops slowly as a result of upbringing and the accumulation of values that are transmitted by schools, families, friends, and religious organizations. Therefore, people come to educational institutions or work organizations with an already defined good or poor character. Good apples will be good and bad apples will be bad.

In fact, people do have predispositions to behave ethically or unethically (we talk about this in Chapter 3). And sociopaths can certainly slip into organizations with the sole intent of helping themselves to the organization's resources, cheating customers, and feathering their own nests at the expense of others. Famous scoundrels like Bernie Madoff definitely come to mind. Such individuals have little interest in "doing the right thing," and when this type of individual shows up in your organization, the best thing to do is discard the bad apple and make an example of the incident to those who remain.

But discarding bad apples generally won't solve an organization's problem with unethical behavior. The organization must scrutinize itself to determine whether something rotten inside the organization is spoiling the apples. For example, Enron encouraged a kind of devil-may-care, unethical culture that is captured in the film *Enron: The Smartest Guys in the Room.* Arthur Andersen's culture morphed from a focus on the integrity of audits to a consulting culture that focused almost exclusively on feeding the bottom line (you'll read more about that in Chapter 5). In this book you'll learn that most people are not guided by a strict internal moral compass. Rather, they look outside themselves—to their environment—for cues about how to think and behave. This was certainly true in the financial crisis when the mantra became "everyone is doing it" (and making a lot of money besides). At work, managers and the organizational culture transmit many cues about how employees should think and act. For example, reward systems play a huge role by rewarding short-term thinking and profits, as they did in the recent financial crisis. In this book, you'll learn about the importance of these organizational influences and how to harness them to support ethical behavior and avoid unethical behavior.

So, apples often turn bad because they're spoiled by "bad barrels"—bad work environments that not only condone, but may even expect unethical behavior. Most employees are not bad to begin with, but their behavior can easily turn bad if they believe that their boss or their organization expects them to behave unethically or if everyone else appears to be engaging in a particular practice. In this view, an organization that's serious about supporting ethical behavior and preventing mis- conduct must delve deeply into its own management systems and cultural norms and practices to search for systemic causes of unethical behavior. Management must take responsibility for the messages it sends or fails to send about what's expected. If ethics problems are rooted in the organization's culture, discarding a few bad apples without changing that culture isn't going to solve the problem. An effective and lasting solution will rely on management's systematic attention to all aspects of the organization's culture and what it is explicitly or implicitly "teaching" organizational members (see Chapter 5).

This question about the source of ethical and unethical behavior reflects the broader "nature/nurture" debate in psychology. Are we more the result of our genes (nature) or our environment (nurture)? Most studies find that behavior results from both nature *and* nurture. So, when it comes to ethical conduct, the answer is not either/ or, but *and.* Individuals do come to work with predispositions that influence their behavior, and they should take responsibility for their own actions—but the work environment can also have a large impact. In this book, you'll learn a lot about how that work environment can be managed to produce ethical rather than unethical conduct.

Shouldn't Employees Already Know the Difference between Right and Wrong?

A belief associated with the good/bad apple idea is that any individual of good character should already know right from wrong and can be ethical without special training—that a lifetime of socialization from parents, school, and religious institu- tions should prepare people to be ethical at work. You probably think of yourself as an individual of good character, but does your life experience to date prepare you to make a complex business ethics decision? Did your parents, coaches, and other influential people in your life ever discuss situations like the one that follows? Think about this real dilemma.

You're the VP of a medium-sized organization that uses chemicals in its production processes. In good faith, you've hired a highly competent scientist to ensure that your company complies with all environmental laws and safety regulations. This individual informs you that a chemical the company now uses in some quantity is not yet on the approved Environmental Protection Agency (EPA) list. However, it has been found to be safe and is scheduled to be placed on the list in about three months. You can't produce your product without this chemical, yet regulations say that you're not supposed to use the chemical until it's officially approved. Waiting for approval would require shutting down the plant for three months, putting hundreds of people out of work, and threatening the company's very survival. What should you do?

The solution isn't clear, and good character isn't enough to guide decision making in this case. As with all ethical dilemmas, values are in conflict here—obeying the letter of the law versus keeping the plant open and saving jobs. The decision is complicated because the chemical has been found to be safe and is expected to be approved in a matter of months. As in many of today's business decisions, this complex issue requires the development of occupation-specific skills and abilities. For example, some knowledge in the area of chemistry, worker safety, and environmental laws and regulations would be essential. Basic good intentions and a good upbringing aren't enough.

James Rest, a scholar in the areas of professional ethics and ethics education, argued convincingly that "to assume that any 20-year-old of good general character can function ethically in professional situations is no more warranted than assuming that any logical 20-year-old can function as a lawyer without special education."[21] Good general character (whatever that means) doesn't prepare an individual to deal with the special ethical problems that are likely to arise in a career. Individuals must be trained to recognize and solve the unique ethical problems of their particular occupation. That's why many professional schools (business, law, medicine, and others) have added ethics courses to their curricula, and it's why most large business organizations now conduct ethics training for their employees.

So, although individual characteristics are a factor in determining ethical behavior, good character alone simply doesn't prepare people for the special ethical problems they're likely to face in their jobs or professions. Special training can prepare them to anticipate these problems, recognize ethical dilemmas when they see them, and provide them with frameworks for thinking about ethical issues in the context of their unique jobs and organizations.

Aren't Adults' Ethics Fully Formed and Unchangeable?

Another false assumption guiding the view that business ethics can't be taught is the belief that one's ethics are fully formed and unchangeable by the time one is old enough to enter college or a job. However, this is definitely not the case. Research has found that through a complex process of social interaction with peers, parents, and other significant persons, children and young adults develop in their ability to make ethical judgments. This development continues at least through young adulthood. In fact, young adults in their twenties and thirties who attend moral development educational programs have been found to advance in moral reasoning even more than younger individuals do.[22] Given that most people enter professional education programs and corporations as young adults, the opportunity to influence their moral reasoning clearly exists.

Business school students may need ethics training more than most, because research has shown they have ranked lower in moral reasoning than students in philosophy, political science, law, medicine, and dentistry.[23] Also, undergraduate business students and those aiming for a business career were found to be more likely to engage in academic cheating (test cheating, plagiarism, etc.) than were students in other majors or those headed toward other careers.[24] At a minimum, professional ethics education can direct attention to the ambiguities and ethical gray areas that are easily overlooked without it. Consider this comment from a 27-year-old Harvard student after a required nine-session module in decision making and ethical values at the beginning of the Harvard MBA program.

> Before, [when] I looked at a problem in the business world, I never consciously examined the ethical issues in play. It was always sub-conscious and I hope that I somewhat got it. But that [ethics] was never even a consideration. But now, when I look at a problem, I have to look at the impact. I'm going to put in this new ten-million-dollar project. What's going to be the impact on the people that live in the area and the environment. . . . It's opened my mind up on those things. It's also made me more aware of situations where I might be walking down the wrong path and getting in deeper and deeper, to where I can't pull back.[25]

In 2004, Harvard's MBA class of 1979 met for its 25-year reunion. The alumni gave the dean a standing ovation when he stated that a new required course on values and leadership was his highest priority and then pledged to "live my life and lead the school in a way that will earn your trust."[26]

It should be clear from the above arguments that ethics can indeed be taught. Ethical behavior relies on more than good character. Although a good upbringing may provide a kind of moral compass that can help the individual determine the right direction and then follow through on a decision to do the right thing, it's certainly not the only factor determining ethical conduct. In today's highly complex organizations, individuals need additional guidance. They can be trained to recognize the ethical dilemmas that are likely to arise in their jobs; the rules, laws, and norms that apply in that context; reasoning strategies that can be used to arrive at the best ethical decision; and the complexities of organizational life that can conflict with one's desire to do the right thing. For example, businesses that do defense-related work are expected to comply with a multitude of laws and regulations that go far beyond what the average person can be expected to know.

The question of whether ethics *should* be taught remains. Many still believe that ethics is a personal issue best left to individuals. They believe that much like proselytizing about religion, teaching ethics involves inappropriate efforts to impose certain values and control behavior. But we believe that employers have a real responsibility to teach employees what they need to know to recognize and deal with ethical issues they are likely to face at work. Failing to help employees recognize the risks in their jobs is like failing to teach a machinist how to operate a machine safely. Both situations can result in harm, and that's just poor management. Similarly, we believe that, as business educators, we have a responsibility to prepare you for the complex ethical issues you're going to face and to help you think about what you can do to lead others in an ethical direction.

DEFINING ETHICS   Some of the controversy about whether ethics can or should be taught may stem from disagreements about what we mean by ethics. Ethics can be defined as "a set of moral principles or values"—a definition that portrays ethics as highly personal and relative. I have my moral principles, you have yours, and neither of us should try to impose our ethics on the other.

But *our* definition of ethics—"the principles, norms, and standards of conduct governing an individual or group"—focuses on conduct. We expect employers to establish guidelines for work-related conduct, including such basic matters as what time to arrive and leave the workplace, whether smoking is allowed on the premises, how customers are to be treated, and how quickly work should be done. Guidelines about ethical conduct aren't much different. Many employers spend a lot of time and money developing policies for employee activities that range from how to fill out expense reports to what kinds of client gifts are acceptable to what constitutes a conflict of interest or bribe. If we focus on conduct, ethics becomes an extension of good management. Leaders identify appropriate and inappropriate conduct, and they communicate their expectations to employees through ethics codes, training programs, and other communication channels.

In most cases, individual employees agree with their company's expectations and policies. For example, who would disagree that it's wrong to steal company property, lie to customers, dump cancerous chemicals in the local stream, or not comply with regulations on defense contracts? At times, however, an employee may find the organization's standards inconsistent with his or her own moral values or principles. For example, a highly religious employee of a health maintenance organization may object to offering abortion as an alternative when providing genetic counseling to pregnant women. Or a highly devoted environmentalist may believe that his or her organization should go beyond the minimum standards of environmental law when making decisions about how much to spend on new technology or on environmental cleanup efforts. These individuals may be able to influence their employers' policies. Otherwise, the person's only recourse may be to leave the organization for one that is a better values match.

GOOD CONTROL OR BAD CONTROL?   Whether or not we like to admit it, our ethical conduct is influenced (and to a large degree controlled) by our environment.

In work settings, leaders, managers, and the entire cultural context are an important source of this influence and guidance. If, as managers, we allow employees to drift along without our guidance, we're unintentionally allowing them to be "controlled" by others. If this happens, we're contributing to the creation of "loose cannons" who can put the entire organization at risk. Guidance regarding ethical conduct is an important aspect of controlling employee behavior. It can provide essential information about organizational rules and policies, and it can provide explanations and examples of behavior that is considered appropriate or inappropriate in a variety of situations.

But should organizations be "controlling" their employees in this way? B. F. Skinner,[27] the renowned psychologist, argued that it's all right, even preferable, to intentionally control behavior. He believed that all behavior is controlled, either intentionally or unintentionally. Therefore what was needed was more intentional control, not less. Similarly, ethical and unethical behavior in organizations is already being controlled explicitly or implicitly by the existing organizational culture (see Chapter 5). Thus, organizations that neglect to teach their members "ethical" behavior may be tacitly encouraging "unethical behavior" through benign neglect. It's man-agement's responsibility to provide explicit guidance through direct management and through the organization's culture. The supervisor who attempts to influence the ethical behavior of subordinates should be viewed not as a meddler but as a part of the natural management process.

To summarize, we believe that educational institutions and work organizations should teach people about ethics and guide them in an ethical direction. Adults are open to, and generally welcome, this type of guidance. Ethical problems are not caused entirely by bad apples. They're also the product of bad barrels—work environments that either encourage unethical behavior or merely allow it to occur. Making ethical decisions in today's complex organizations isn't easy. Good intentions and a good upbringing aren't enough. The special knowledge and skill required to make good ethical decisions in a particular job and organizational setting may be different from what's needed to resolve personal ethical dilemmas, and this knowledge and skill must be taught and cultivated.

THIS BOOK IS ABOUT MANAGING ETHICS IN BUSINESS

This book offers a somewhat unique approach to teaching business ethics. Instead of the traditional philosophical or legalistic approach, we take a managerial approach. Between us, we have many years of experience in management, in consulting, and in management teaching and research. Based on this experience, we begin with the assumption that business ethics is essentially about human behavior. We believe that by understanding human behavior in an organizational context, we can better understand and manage our own and others' ethical conduct. Kent Druyvesteyn was vice president for ethics at General Dynamics from 1985 to 1993 and one of the first "ethics officers" in an American company. He made a clear distinction between philosophy and management in his many talks with students and executives over the years. As he put it, "I am not a philosopher and I am not here to talk about philosophy. Ethics is about conduct."

We agree with Mr. Druyvesteyn. After years of study and experience, we're convinced that a management approach to organizational ethics is needed. As with any other management problem, managers need to understand why people behave the way they do so that they can influence this behavior. Most managers want the people they work with to be productive, to produce high-quality products, to treat customers well, and to do all of this in a highly ethical manner. They also want and need help accomplishing these goals.

Therefore we rely on a managerial approach to understanding business ethics. We introduce concepts that can be used to guide managers who want to understand their own ethical behavior and the behavior of others in the organization. And we provide practical guidance to those who wish to lead their department or organization in an ethical direction.

We define *ethical behavior in business* as "behavior that is consistent with the principles, norms, and standards of business practice that have been agreed upon by society." Although some disagreement exists about what these principles, norms, and standards should be, we believe there is more agreement than disagreement. Many of the standards have been codified into law. Others can be found in company and industry codes of conduct and international trade agreements.

Importantly, we treat the decisions of people in work organizations as being influenced by characteristics of both individuals and organizations. We also recognize that work organizations operate within a broad and complex global business context. We will cover individual decision making, group and organizational influences, and the social and global environment of business. The first part of this perspective, the influences on individual decision making, is represented in Figure 1.1.

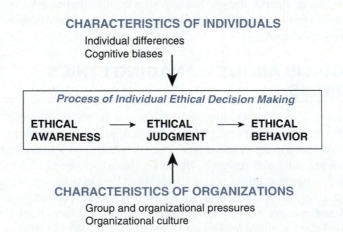

FIGURE 1.1 The Ethical Decision-Making Process

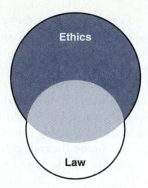

FIGURE 1.2   Relationship between Ethics and Law

ETHICS AND THE LAW

It's important to think about the relationship between the law and business ethics, because if one could just follow the law, a business ethics book wouldn't be necessary. Perhaps the easiest way to visualize the relationship between business ethics and the law is in terms of a Venn diagram (Figure 1.2). If we think of the law as reflecting society's minimum norms and standards of business conduct, we can see a great deal of overlap between what's legal and what's ethical. Therefore, most people believe that law-abiding behavior is also ethical behavior. However, many standards of conduct are agreed upon by society and not codified in law. For example, some conflicts of interest may be legal but are generally considered unethical in our society and are commonly prohibited in codes of ethics. For example, having an affair with someone who reports to you may be legal, but it is considered unethical in most corporate contexts.

As we said earlier, much of the behavior leading to the 2008 financial crisis was legal, but unethical. So the domain of ethics includes the law but extends well beyond it to include ethical standards and issues that the law does not address. Finally, there are times when you might encounter a law that you believe is unethical. For example, racial discrimination was legal in the United States for a long time. But racial discrimination was, and is, highly unethical. Similarly, many companies do business in developing countries with few, if any, laws regulating environmental pollution or labor conditions. They can "legally" pollute the air and water in these countries. Such companies have to choose between adhering to ethical standards that are higher than the legal standards in those countries and deciding that it's okay to harm the well-being of the people and communities there. The legal and ethical domains certainly overlap, but the overlap is far from complete.

WHY BE ETHICAL? WHY BOTHER? WHO CARES?

Assuming that you accept the notion that business ethics can be taught, and that as current or future managers you have a role to play in creating an environment supportive of ethical conduct, you may still wonder why you should care about being ethical. As workers, we should care about ethics because most of us prefer to work for ethical organizations. We want to feel good about ourselves and the work we do. As responsible citizens, we must care about the millions of people who lost retirement savings because of the greed of those at AIG, Citigroup, Lehman Brothers, Merrill Lynch, and other financial firms that brought down the global economy in 2008. These people are our parents, spouses, siblings, children, and friends—they're *us*! We live in a world community, and we're all inextricably connected to each other and to the environment that surrounds us. Our future depends on our caring enough.

Most important, it is the right thing to do.

Individuals Care about Ethics: The Motivation To Be Ethical

Classical economists assume that practically all human behavior, including altruism, is motivated solely by self-interest—that humans are purely rational economic actors who make choices solely on the basis of cold cost-benefit analyses. However, a new group of economists who call themselves behavioral economists have found that people are not only less rational than classical economists assumed, but more moral. Much evidence suggests that people act for altruistic or moral purposes that seemingly have little to do with cost-benefit analyses.[28] For example, people will mail back lost wallets to strangers, cash and all; help strangers in distress; and donate blood marrow for strangers or a kidney to a family member. Also, a large majority of people will refrain from stealing even if it's easy to do so.

In his book *The Moral Dimension*, Amitai Etzioni[29] cited many more examples and research evidence to document his claim that human action has two distinct sources: the pursuit of self-interest and moral commitments. Accordingly, most human decisions are based on ethical and emotional considerations as well as rational economic self-interest. People are motivated by both economic and moral concerns.

In a typical behavioral economics experiment, subject A in the experiment receives 10 one-dollar bills and can give subject B any number of them. Subject B can choose to accept or reject A's offer. They are told that if B accepts, they each get what was offered. If B rejects the offer, each gets nothing. From a pure economics perspective, A would do best offering B one dollar and keeping the rest. B should accept that offer because, in economic terms, getting one dollar is better than nothing. But most A subjects offer B close to half the total, an average of about four dollars. B subjects who are offered one or two dollars generally reject the offer.

Economists can't explain this result based upon rational self-interest. People's sense of fairness seems to be driving both subjects' behavior. Interestingly, when people play the game with a machine, they are more likely to play as classical economics would predict because they don't expect a machine to be "fair." Autistic A players (whose autism means that they don't take others' feelings into account) also play as the theory would predict. So, most people expect fair play in their interactions with other human beings, and the experiments demonstrate they will even forgo economic benefits in order to maintain a fair system.

Neuroscience is also beginning to substantiate the moral sense that develops in humans. New imaging technologies have allowed scientists to locate a unique type of neuron in the brain—spindle cells—that light up when people perceive unfairness or deception. Only humans and African apes have these cells. An adult human has over 82,000 of them, whereas a gorilla has around 16,000 (perhaps explaining why a gorilla might save a human child). A chimp has less than 2,000. In humans, these cells appear at around four months of age and gradually increase with moral development.[30]

In 2003, neuroscientists used functional magnetic resonance imaging (fMRI) to look inside the brains of people playing the ultimatum game, and they found that unfair offers were associated with heightened activity in parts of the brain associated with strong negative emotions, as well as in other parts of the brain associated with long-term planning. The subjects who rejected the unfair offers had more activity in the emotional part of the brain, which is the part that usually wins out.[31]

Given these research findings, we begin this book with an important assumption—that, as human beings and members of society, all of us are hardwired with a moral and ethical dimension as well as self-interested concerns. People care about ethics for reasons that stem from both of these sources.

Beyond being hardwired for fairness and altruism, employees are also concerned about their personal reputations. In today's work environment, success depends on an individual's ability to work effectively with others. Trust greases the wheels of working relationships with peers across departments and on project teams. We disagree with the old adage that "nice guys (or gals) finish last." If it looks like bad guys (or gals) come out ahead, this is generally a short-run result. A reputation for being difficult to work with, dishonest, or mean often catches up with you as coworkers withhold important information and promotions go to others. Given the importance of relationships to effectiveness in business today, your reputation for integrity is an essential ingredient for success and personal satisfaction. This is even truer in an age of social networking that can send news of bad behavior to a broad audience in seconds.

Employees Care about Ethics: Employee Attraction and Commitment

Organizations are concerned about their ability to hire and retain the best workers. The evidence suggests that employees are more attracted to and more committed to ethical organizations. "People who know that they are working for something larger with a more noble purpose can be expected to be loyal and dependable, and, at a minimum, more inspired."[32]

Graduating students at nearly 150 colleges and universities now sign or recite the "Graduation Pledge," in which they promise to "take into account the social and environmental consequences of any job" they consider. They also pledge to "try to improve these aspects of any organizations" where they work. Elite universities such as Harvard and Cornell are participating. Prospective employers should be very interested in these graduates and their concerns, which go beyond just making a living.[33] (Go to www.graduationpledge.org for more information.)

Recent surveys confirm that it may be important to consider how potential and current employees are affected by an organization's ethics. In a survey conducted by *Working Woman* magazine, "a strong majority of those polled said that they would not work for a company with a history of environmental accidents, insider trading or worker accidents, or a law firm that defends known racketeers."[34] In another survey conducted by a national opinion research firm, ethical corporate behavior, honest company communications, and respectful treatment ranked among employees' five top-ranked goals—before good pay, which was 11th on the list, and job security, which ranked 14th. Ethical corporate behavior was ranked so high because "workers translate the ethics of the company into how they're personally treated." People "want to be proud of where they work." They "don't want to work for bandits, and when companies get negative publicity for their activities, workers suffer."[35]

Managers Care about Ethics

Managers care about ethics in part because they face the thorny problem of how to prevent and manage unethical behavior in their ranks. Ask any manager for examples, and be prepared to spend the day listening. More than their jobs depend on this concern—managers can be held legally liable for the criminal activities of their subordinates. Further, the U.S. Chamber of Commerce estimates that workplace theft costs U.S. businesses between $20 billion and $40 billion each year, and employees are thought to be responsible for much of it.[36] In addition to such self-interested behavior, employees may engage in unethical behavior because they think (rightly or wrongly) that it's expected or that their behavior is justified because they've been treated unfairly. Or they simply may not know they are doing something that's considered to be unethical.[37]

Whatever its source, subordinates' unethical behavior is a management problem that won't go away. It becomes even more of a challenge as restructuring continues to reduce management layers, thus leaving fewer managers to supervise more workers. With more workers to supervise, the manager can't directly observe behavior. Restructuring also increases the number of part-time or contingency workers. These workers are likely to feel less loyalty to the organization and may be more prone to engage in unethical behaviors such as theft.

In addition, more workers may cross the line between ethical and unethical behavior in response to fierce business competition and a strict focus on the bottom line. Employees may believe that they can help the company succeed (at least in the short term) by fudging sales figures, abusing competitors, or shortchanging customers. Those who are potential layoff candidates are also more likely to flirt with impropriety.[38] Many perceive the message to be: "reaching objectives is what matters and how you get there isn't that important."[39] Therefore, today's managers may have to work even harder to communicate the idea that ethical conduct is expected, even in the midst of aggressive competition.

Moreover, many managers understand the positive long-term benefit a reputation for ethics can bring to business dealings. Carl Skooglund, former ethics officer at Texas Instruments, had this to say:

> There are very positive, even competitive, reasons to be ethical. If you walk into a relationship and somebody says, "I know you, I know your track record, I can trust you," that's important. Two years ago, in a survey that we sent out to employees, I received an anonymous comment from somebody who said, "A reputation for ethics which is beyond reproach is a silent partner in all business negotiations." I agree and it works in all personal and business relationships. An unethical company is very diffi-cult to do business with. You can't trust them. You're never sure if a commitment's a commitment. At TI, our customers have told us that they can be sure of one thing: Once TI commits, we're going to break our tail to make it happen. That's an easy company to do business with.

Executive Leaders Care about Ethics

Some of us are understandably cynical about CEO ethics after the widely publicized scandals, huge compensation packages, and CEO "perp walks" of recent years. But many business executives do care about ethics in their own organizations and about business's image in society.

John Akers, former chairman of the board of IBM, wrote: "No society anywhere will compete very long or successfully with people stabbing each other in the back; with people trying to steal from each other; with everything requiring notarized confirmation because you can't trust the other fellow; with every little squabble ending in litigation; and with government writing reams of regulatory legislation, tying business hand and foot to keep it honest. . . . There is no escaping this fact; the greater the measure of mutual trust and confidence in the ethics of a society, the greater its economic strength."[40]

Jeffrey Immelt, the CEO of General Electric, spoke powerfully about ethics at Columbia University in October 2008 (available for viewing on YouTube). Immelt described how, above all else, leaders had to consider their organizations and protect their organizations for shareholders, employees, and the greater good. "I believe that ethical behavior in 2008 starts first and foremost, as always, with a real sense of permanence, excellence, accountability, and safety, making sure that the enterprise endures no matter how tough the situation becomes."

Warren Buffett, the legendary investor and CEO of Berkshire Hathaway, had perhaps the best idea about ethics and integrity when he said, "Somebody once said that in looking for people to hire, you look for three qualities: integrity, intelligence, and energy. And if they don't have the first, the other two will kill you. You think about it; it's true. If you hire somebody without the first, you really want them to be dumb and lazy."[41]

We believe that organizational ethics is a distinct managerial concern that must be addressed by management at all levels of the organization.

Industries Care about Ethics

When companies get bad publicity for ethical scandals, whole industries suffer. So, in some industries, companies have joined together in voluntary efforts to promote ethical conduct among organizations in the industry. Prominent among these efforts is the Defense Industry Initiative. A cynic might say that these initiatives are aimed solely at preventing more intrusive government regulation and that companies in these industries don't truly "care" about ethics. Certainly, these types of initiatives have generally begun in response to a scandal or crisis. But over the years, they tend to take on a life of their own. Members internalize beliefs about appropriate conduct, hire support staff, and develop structures for enforcement that become institutionalized among member organizations.

The Defense Industry Initiative on Business Conduct and Ethics (DII) is a major voluntary industry initiative. It is described on the organization's website (www.dii.org) as "a consortium of U.S. defense industry contractors which subscribes to a set of principles for achieving high standards of business ethics and conduct." It developed out of the President's Blue Ribbon Commission on Defense Management (the Packard Commission), which was convened after a number of defense-industry scandals in the early 1980s. In 1986, the commission concluded that the industry could be improved by focusing on corporate self-governance. A number of companies voluntarily joined forces to "embrace and promote ethical business conduct," and their work together continues today. As of July 2012, over 85 companies were signatories; as such, they have agreed to live according to the following obligations:

- Adopt a written code of conduct.
- Conduct employees' orientation and training with respect to the code.
- Provide employees a mechanism to express concerns about corporate compliance with procurement laws and regulations.
- Adopt procedures for voluntary disclosure of violations of federal procurement laws.
- Participate in Best Practices Forums.
- Publish information that shows each signatory's commitment to the above.

The organization hosts a two-day Best Practices Forum each year, in which the industry's prime customer, the Department of Defense, participates. It also hosts workshops on specific topics, including an annual one-day workshop to train ethics professionals, and publishes an annual report to the public and government summarizing DII activities.

Society Cares about Ethics: Business and Social Responsibility

Business ethics also matters because society cares. From an economic perspective, businesses are powerful. Wal-Mart's size and profits make it a more powerful economic force than most countries. Business is learning that it must use its power responsibly or risk losing it. Using power responsibly means being concerned for the interests of multiple *stakeholders*—parties who are affected by the business and its actions and who have an interest in what the business does and how it performs.[42]

These stakeholders include many constituencies: shareholders, employees, suppliers, the government, the media, activists, and many more. Stakeholders have the power to interfere with a firm's activities. For example, employees can strike, customers can stop buying products, protesters can bring bad publicity, and the government can act to regulate a firm's activities. Consequently, it's a matter of paramount importance for organizations to consider all of their various stakeholders and what those stakeholders expect and require before they make decisions that will affect those various audiences. Increased regulation is an almost certain societal response to business scandal, and with new regulations comes increased costs and reduced power for business. In addition, organizations that do not act responsibly risk criminal liability and the resulting financial damage. Even without criminal liability, businesses that don't act responsibly risk their reputations, and a lost reputation is tough to rebuild. As business becomes more global and business practices more transparent, it's almost impossible to hide bad behavior. There is a growing emphasis worldwide on corporate social responsibility (CSR), and this emphasis and the reasons for it are covered in much more detail in Chapter 9.

THE IMPORTANCE OF TRUST

A more elusive benefit of ethics is trust. Although it's difficult to document, trust has both economic and moral value. Scientists are beginning to understand the "biology of trust." In trusting relationships, neuroscientists have found that the brain releases a hormone, oxytocin, that makes cooperating feel good.

Trust is essential in a service economy, where all a firm has is its reputation for dependability and good service. Individuals and organizations build trust accounts that work something like a bank account.[43] You make deposits and build your trust reserve by being honest and by keeping commitments. You can draw on this account and even make mistakes as long as the reserve is maintained. Having a trust reserve allows the individual or organization the flexibility and freedom to act without scrutiny, thus saving a great deal of time and energy in all types of relationships. Think of a marriage that is based on trust; the partners go about their daily business without feeling any need to check up on each other or to hire private detectives to confirm the other's whereabouts. The same is true of trust-based business relationships, where a handshake seals a deal and a business partner's word is considered to be a contract. Corporations also build trust with their customers.

Johnson & Johnson made a huge contribution to its trust account when it recalled all Tylenol from store shelves after the poisoning crisis in 1982 (a situation discussed in more detail in Chapter 10). Despite no recall requirement and huge recall costs, the company put its customers first. Trust may be even more important in efforts at global collaboration and alliances, and in cross-cultural management teams. Trust encourages the open exchange of ideas and information, reduces the need for costly controls, allows for rapid adjustment to change, and is associated with willingness to work through cultural differences and difficulties.[44]

Trust accounts are easily overdrawn, however. And when they are, all flexibility disappears. Every word and action is carefully checked and double-checked for signs of dishonesty. In organizations, lawyers are hired, contracts are drawn up and signed, and CYA (cover your you-know-what) memos fly. Recent corporate ethics scandals have created a huge gap in the public's trust. In an essay for *Businessweek* titled "Can You Trust Anybody Anymore?" Bruce Nussbaum wrote:

> There are business scandals that are so vast and so penetrating that they profoundly shock our most deeply held beliefs about the honesty and integrity of our corporate culture. Enron Corp. is one of them. This financial disaster goes far beyond the failure of one big company. This is corruption on a massive scale. Tremendous harm has befallen innocent employees who have seen their retirement savings disappear as a few at the top cashed out. Terrible things have happened to the way business is conducted under the cloak of deregulation. Serious damage has been done to ethical codes of conduct held by once-trusted business professionals . . . Investor confidence is critical to the success of our economic system . . . People increasingly feel the game is rigged . . . Who can come to the rescue? The reputations of many of the professionals who were counted on to safeguard the economic system lie in tatters . . . What's to be done? . . . The lesson from the Enron debacle should be to restore basic integrity to the bottom line, ethics to business professionals, and clout to overseers that even a deregulated economy need.[45]

The entire American business system relies on the public's faith and trust. That trust has been shattered in a manner that could be extremely costly to society. A decade ago, the public considered the debacles at companies such as Enron, Arthur Andersen, WorldCom, Tyco, and Adelphia not as an anomaly, but as an example of the workings of a business culture that has lost its way. Although some strides were made to correct that not-very-flattering image of business, the financial crisis of 2008 was truly devastating to public trust in business, government, finance, and the economy. Harris Interactive, a research company that regularly surveys the public to determine trust levels, uncovered astoundingly low levels of trust following the financial scandals of 2008. In a survey conducted in May 2009, Harris Interactive found that only 4 percent of the respondents said that Wall Street firms are honest and trustworthy. The percentage is higher, but still dismal, for banks in general; 25 percent of those surveyed would believe a statement made by someone who works for a bank.[46]

Normally after a crisis, reputations stabilize and improve over time, but Harris Interactive's research in 2012 is just as bleak. Four years after the crisis, they recorded a 35 percent jump in negativity in their research. Eight companies had excellent reputations in 2012, down from 16 with excellent reputations in 2011. The technology and automotive industries showed the greatest improvement, with technology leading all industries in public perception. The industries with the lowest reputations were financial services, banking, and government. The companies with the lowest reputations— with scores so low that in the past such scores indicated a real danger of the company's viability—were AIG, Goldman Sachs, Bank of America, BP (British Petroleum), and JPMorgan Chase.[47]

Unfortunately, all companies have been tainted by the scandals. Blue-chip companies now face even closer scrutiny and the skepticism of shareholders as they are being asked to open their books and reveal much more information than has been recent practice.[48] Meeting profit projections or beating them by a penny is being viewed suspiciously as evidence of accounting chicanery rather than reliability.[49] Confidence and trust in the system must be restored, or access to capital (the engine of the entire system) could be cut off.

The good news is that many corporations are responding. Boards of directors are replacing inside members with outsiders who are seen as more independent. Stock options are being expensed. CEO compensation packages that are seen as excessive are being cut. And executives are asking their people whether they are living by the "spirit of the law" as well as the letter of the law.[50]

The idea of trust, however, is bigger than business. One reason why so much of our society appears to be in disarray is that people have so little trust in institutions. Recent Gallup polls that measure such confidence show that institutional trust has eroded significantly over the last 25 years. For example, in 1987, 51 percent of those polled expressed "a great deal or quite a lot of" trust in banks. In 2012, that number had declined to 21 percent. Similar drops were reported for Congress, the Presidency, public schools, newspapers, and other institutions that form the basis for our society. This lack of trust is not a good thing, and the ethical debacles that have occurred over the last few decades have proven to be a blight on our civic landscape because so many people trust no one. It has also become increasingly difficult for people to engage in civil discourse. If people find it difficult to even talk to one another in civil tones, trust will become even more elusive.[51]

THE IMPORTANCE OF VALUES

As a theme even broader than trust, you can think of values as a kind of "glue" that guides our thinking across the book. Values are relevant to individuals, to organizations, and to societies. For individuals, values can be defined as "one's core beliefs about what is important, what is valued, and how one should behave across a wide variety of situations." For example, most of us agree that honesty, fairness, and respect for others are important values. Where individuals differ is in how they prioritize their values. For example, some people may believe that ambition is more important than other values. Others may feel that helpfulness predominates. Strongly held values influence important decisions such as career choices as well as decisions in particular situations. For example, someone for whom helpfulness is most important is more likely to choose a "helping" profession such as social work, while someone for whom ambition is most important may be more likely to choose a business career. In Chapter 2, you'll have the opportunity to think about your own values and how they influence your ethical decision making.

Values are also relevant at the organizational level. Many of you have seen organizational values statements that aim to create a shared sense of purpose among employees and to convey something about the organization's identity to outsiders. If you haven't, just look at company websites and you'll see that most of them include values statements. Values lists often include respect, integrity, diversity, innovation, teamwork, and the like. Just as individual values guide individual thinking and action, organizational values guide organizational thinking and action. And, just as with individuals, the key question is how the organization prioritizes its values. For example, at 3M Corporation, no value is more important and more ingrained in the culture than innovation. Innovation is encouraged in myriad ways and has been "baked" into the culture through the commitment of senior executives, thus creating a culture that rewards collaboration and teamwork and that views mistakes as opportunities to learn.[52]

You'll see in Chapter 5 that organizational values undergird the ethical culture of an organization and influence how its managers and employees behave. Thus, an organization that highly values diversity and respect is more likely to make efforts to hire and retain a diverse workforce and to take diversity into consideration when making supplier choices and other decisions. We know of an organization with a strong value for diversity that walked away from business when a customer insisted on dealing only with white males.

However, organizations don't always "really" value what they say they value. That's why values statements are often the butt of Dilbert jokes. For example, in Enron's values statement, the verbiage described an organization where excellence and respect and integrity were key values. The scandal at Enron showed that what Enron really cared about—maximizing profits at any cost—was a far cry from what appeared in print on its values statement. For organizational values to work in a positive way, the organization must live those values every day.

Societies and cultures also have shared values, and these an important part of the business environment and expectations of business and businesspeople. When we talk about cross-cultural values, we often focus on the differences. But, as you'll see in Chapter 11, values across cultures are often more similar than different. Even in corrupt cultures, if you ask people what they value, they'll tell you that they would prefer to live in an environment where everyone can be trusted to do business honestly and fairly. We'll return to a discussion of values again and again as a touchstone for ethical business practice.

HOW THIS BOOK IS STRUCTURED

Section II of this book deals with ethics and the individual. Chapter 2 presents the reader with an overview of some basic philosophical theories that have formed the underpinning for the traditional study of individual ethical decision making from a prescriptive viewpoint. Chapter 3 presents a more psychological approach to individual ethical decision making. It provides a "reality check" for Chapter 2 by suggesting that managers need to understand the individual characteristics that can influence employees' ethical decision making and the human cognitive biases that can interfere with the ideal decision-making process (see Figure 1.1). Chapter 4 categorizes the common ethical problems individuals face at work and provides an opportunity for you to apply what you've learned. Chapter 4 is also about finding your moral voice to raise or report ethical issues or to stand up for what you value. Despite the best of intentions and the most carefully reasoned ethical judgments, doing the right thing can be difficult.

Section III of the book focuses on the internal life of organizations, how they develop ethical (or unethical) cultures, and how culture influences employee behavior. Chapter 5 focuses on business ethics as a phenomenon of organizational culture. It provides a comprehensive overview of how an organization can build a culture that reflects a concern for ethics, and how it can change its culture to be more supportive of ethical conduct. This chapter also emphasizes the importance of executive ethical leadership in creating a strong ethical culture. Chapter 6 follows with more practical and specific advice on how organizations can design an ethics infrastructure as well as effective communications and training programs. It also includes examples of the programs various companies have implemented to encourage ethical conduct among their employees. Many of these examples resulted from interviews we conducted with top managers in these companies.

Chapter 7, "Managing for Ethical Conduct," introduces management concepts that can help explain the group and organizational pressures that influence people to behave ethically or unethically. We also provide practical advice for managers about how to use these management concepts to encourage ethical conduct and discourage unethical conduct in their employees. Finally, Chapter 8 explores how culture plays out at the manager's level and features a series of cases to test your knowledge of ethics and management skills.

After considering individuals and organizations, Section IV of this book looks at organizations in the broader social environment (see Figure 1.3). Chapter 9 focuses on corporate social responsibility and discusses the environment that organizations are part of—and what they must do to be considered "good citizens" of the broader world. Chapter 10 examines some of the classical organizational ethics cases using a stakeholder framework. Finally, Chapter 11 extends our discussion of business ethics to the global business environment. Although global examples appear throughout the book, this issue is important enough to warrant its own chapter.

CONCLUSION

This chapter was designed to pique your interest in business ethics. We hope we have done that. We also hope that reading this book gives you a better understanding of ethics from a managerial perspective, and of how you can encourage ethical business behavior in yourself and others. We aim to help you understand how this aspect of the

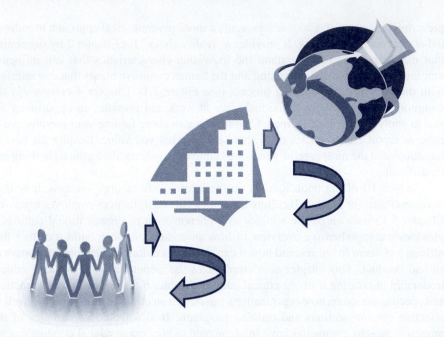

FIGURE 1.3   From Individuals to Organizations to Environments

organizational world actually works and what you can do to manage it. We also provide practical decision-making guidance for facing your own ethical decisions and for helping others do the same.

It's critically important that we all understand ethics, because good ethics represents the very essence of a civilized society. Each of us must understand that ethics is the bedrock for all of our relationships; it's about how we relate to our employers, our employees, our coworkers, our customers, our communities, our suppliers, and one another. Ethics is not just about the connection we have to other beings—we are all connected; rather, it's about the quality of that connection. That's the real bottom line and our society is threatened when we ignore it.

DISCUSSION QUESTIONS

1. Before reading this chapter, did you think of ethics as "just a fad"? Why or why not? What do you think now? Why?

2. Have you been cynical about business and its leaders? Why or why not? (See the following cynicism exercise.) How does cynicism affect you, as a business student or as a manager?

3. Can you think of something that is legal but unethical, or something that is ethical but illegal?

4. Do you think business ethics is important? Why or why not?

5. Identify reasons why a person would be interested in being ethical, and classify those reasons in terms of whether they represent moral motivation or economic motivation.

6. Think about the television programs and films you've seen recently that depicted business in some way. How were business and businesspeople portrayed? Is there anything business could or should do to improve its media image? Some businesses try to stay out of the limelight. Why might that be? What do you think of that strategy?

7. Do you believe that employees are more attracted and committed to ethical organizations? Are you? Why or why not? Make a list of the companies you would prefer to work for, and state the reasons why. Are there also companies that you would refuse to work for? Why? Are there ethically "neutral" companies that don't belong on either list?

8. Discuss the importance of trust in business. Can you cite examples? What happens when trust is lost?

9. What do you think the Harris Interactive research on corporate reputation means to the companies involved?

10. What can we learn about business ethics from the recent financial crisis?

11. How does a lack of trust in institutions affect us? Do you trust institutions? If not, what effect does that have on you?

EXERCISE

Your Cynicism Quotient

Answer the following questions as honestly as you can. Circle the number between 1 and 5 that best represents your own beliefs about business.

	Strongly Disagree	Disagree	Neither Agree nor Disagree	Agree	Strongly Agree
1. Financial gain is all that counts in business.	1	2	3	4	5
2. Ethical standards must be compromised in business practice.	1	2	3	4	5

	Strongly Disagree	Disagree	Neither Agree nor Disagree	Agree	Strongly Agree
3. The more financially successful the businessperson, the more unethical the behavior.	1	2	3	4	5
4. Moral values are irrelevant in business.	1	2	3	4	5
5. The business world has its own rules.	1	2	3	4	5
6. Businesspeople care only about making profit.	1	2	3	4	5
7. Business is like a game one plays to win.	1	2	3	4	5
8. In business, people will do anything to further their own interest.	1	2	3	4	5
9. Competition forces business managers to resort to shady practices.	1	2	3	4	5
10. The profit motive pressures managers to compromise their ethical concerns.	1	2	3	4	5

Add the total number of points. The maximum is 50 points. Total ___.

The higher your score, the more cynical you are about ethical business practice. Think about the reasons for your responses. Be prepared to discuss them in class.

NOTES

1. G. Colvin, "Business Is Back!" *Fortune*, May 14, 2007, 40–48.
2. Rushworth M. Kidder, "Must Capitalism Be Moral?" Commentary on Ethics Newsline, on Institute for Global Ethics website (www.globalethics.org), May 4, 2009.

3. Adam Smith, *The Theory of Moral Sentiments*, eds. D. D. Raphael & A. L. Macfie, based on 1790 edition in *The Glasgow Edition of the Works and Correspondence of Adam Smith*, (Vol. 1), eds. D. D. Raphael and Andrew Skinner (Oxford: Clarendon Press, 1790 [1976]).

4. T. Frieden, "FBI Warns of Mortgage Fraud 'Epidemic,'" *CNN Justice*, September 17, 2004. (www.cnn.com).

5. J. Silver-Greenberg and S. Craig, "JPMorgan Trading Loss May Reach $9 Billion," *The New York Times*, June 28, 2012 (www.nyt.com).

6. V. McGrane, "Senate GOP Leaders: Repeal Dodd-Frank," *Wall Street Journal*, April 1, 2011. (www.wsj.com).

7. H. Touryalai, "LIBOR Scandal Just Took a Nasty Turn, Collusion Findings Should Make Banks Very Nervous," *Forbes*, December 19, 2012.

8. M. Taibbi, "Why Is Nobody Freaking Out About the LIBOR Banking Scandal?" *Rolling Stone*, July 3, 2012.

9. F. Zakariah, "Greed is good (to a point)," *Newsweek*, June 22, 2009, 41–45.

10. 2009 and 2012 Edelman Trust Barometer, www.edelman.com.

11. J. A. Wood, J. G. Longenecker, J. A. McKinney, and C. W. Moore, "Ethical Attitudes of Students and Business Professionals: A Study of Moral Reasoning," *Journal of Business Ethics* 7 (1988): 249–57; D. N. DeSalvia and G. R. Gemmill, "An Exploratory Study of the Personal Value Systems of College Students and Managers," *Academy of Management Journal* 14 (1971): 227–38; M. S. Lane, D. Schaupp, and B. Parsons, "Pygmalion Effect," *Journal of Business Ethics* 7 (1988): 223–29; R. M. Fulmer, "Business Ethics: A View from the Campus," *Personnel Administrator* 45, no. 2 (1968): 31–39; T. M. Jones and F. H. Gautschi, "Will the Ethics of Business Change? A Survey of Future Executives," *Journal of Business Ethics* 7 (1988): 231–48.

12. Michael Skapinker, "Business Schools Focus on Making Money, Not Martyrs," *Financial Times*, January 5, 2005, 10.

13. "Where Will They Lead? 2008 MBA Student Attitudes about Business & Society" (Washington, D.C.: The Aspen Institute Center for Business Education, 2008).

14. L. Elber, "Bad Guys Wear Business Suits: Businessmen and Women Get a Bad Rap on Television," (State College, PA) *Centre Daily Times*, June 27, 1997, 22C.

15. "Villains of Prime Time: Business Is TV's Newest Bad Guy," *Fortune*, July 7, 1997, 32.

16. T. S. Bateman, T. Sakano, and M. Fujita, "Roger, Me, and My Attitude: Film Propaganda and Cynicism toward Corporate Leadership," *Journal of Applied Psychology* 77 (1992): 768–71.

17. Ethics Resource Center, *2011 National Business Ethics Survey.*

18. K. Brooker, "Starting Over," *Fortune*, January 21, 2002, 50–68.

19. L. K. Treviño and A. Youngblood, "Bad Apples in Bad Barrels: A Causal Analysis of Ethical Decision-Making Behavior," *Journal of Applied Psychology* 75, no. 4 (1990): 378–85.

20. Ibid.

21. J. R. Rest and S. J. Thoma, "Educational Programs and Interventions," In *Moral Development: Advances in Research and Theory*, ed. J. Rest (New York: Praeger, 1986), 59–88.

22. J. R. Rest, "Moral Judgment: An Interesting Variable for Higher Education Research," Paper for the Annual Convention for the Association for the Study of Higher Education, Baltimore, Maryland, November 21, 1987.

23. D. McCabe, and L. K. Treviño, "Academic Dishonesty: Honor Codes and Other Situational Influences," *Journal of Higher Education* 64 (1993): 522–38.

24. D. McCabe and L. K. Treviño, "Cheating among Business Students: A Challenge for Business Leaders and Educators," *Journal of Management Education* 19, no. 2 (1995): 205–18.

25. T. R. Piper, M. C. Gentile, and S. D. Parks, *Can Ethics Be Taught?* (Boston: Harvard Business School, 1993).

26. O. Ryan, "Class of '79: God and Man at Harvard Business School," *Fortune*, November 1, 2004, 52.

27. B. F. Skinner, *Beyond Freedom and Dignity* (New York: Knopf, 1971).

28. A. Etzioni, *The Moral Dimension: Toward a New Economics* (New York: Free Press, 1988).

29. Ibid.

30. S. Blakeslee, "Humanity? Maybe It's in the Wiring," *New York Times*, December 9, 2003, D1.

31. J. Lehrer, "Driven to Market," *Nature* 443 (2006): 502–04.

32. J. Channon, "Creating Esprit de Corps," In *New Traditions in Business*, ed. J. Renesch (San Francisco: Berrett-Koehler Publishers, 1992), 53–68.

33. "Get a Job, Save the Planet," *Businessweek*, May 6, 2002, 10.

34. R. Sandroff, "How Ethical Is American Business?" *Working Woman*, September 1990, 113–16.

35. C. Kleiman, "Heading the List of Worker Wishes Isn't More Money!" (Allentown, PA) *Morning Call*, October 2, 1989, B10.

36. R. Zemke, "Employee Theft: How to Cut Your Losses," *Training*, May 1986, 74–78.

37. J. Collins, "Why Bad Things Happen to Good Companies and What Can Be Done," *Business Horizons*, November–December 1990, 18–22.

38. B. Hager, "What's Behind Business' Sudden Fervor for Ethics," *Businessweek*, September 23, 1991, 65.

39. K. Labich, "The New Crisis in Business Ethics," *Fortune*, April 20, 1992, 167–76.

40. J. F. Akers, "Ethics and Competitiveness: Putting First Things First," *Sloan Management Review*, Winter 1989, 69–71.

41. Warren Buffett and Bill Gates at Columbia Business School, CNBC, Summer 2009; available at www.youtube.com/watch?v=tgbZzgyHZgI.

42. E. Freeman, *Strategic Management: A Stakeholder Approach* (Boston: Pitman/Ballinger, 1984).

43. S. R. Covey, *The 7 Habits of Highly Effective People* (New York: Simon & Schuster, 1989).

44. J. Child, "Trust—the Fundamental Bond in Global Collaboration," *Organizational Dynamics* 29, no. 4 (2001): 274–88.

45. B. Nussbaum, "Can You Trust Anybody Anymore?" *Businessweek*, January 28, 2002, 31–32.

46. Harris Interactive, "Ethics Newsline," July 6, 2009; available at http://www.globalethics.org/newsline/2009/07/06/banks-honesty-poll/.

47. Harris Interactive, "2012 Reputation Quotient." February 13, 2012; available at http://www.harrisinteractive.com/vault/2012_Harris_Poll_RQ_Summary_Report.pdf.

48. J. A. Byrne, "How to Fix Corporate Governance," *Businessweek*, May 6, 2002, 69–78.

49. J. Useem, "In Corporate America, It's Cleanup Time," *Fortune*, September 16, 2002, 62–72.

50. Ibid.

51. "Confidence in Institutions," *Gallup Polls,* June 7, 2012; available at www.gallup.com.

52. "3M's Seven Pillars of Innovation," *Businessweek*, May 10, 2006.

ETHICS AND THE INDIVIDUAL

CHAPTER 2

DECIDING WHAT'S RIGHT: A PRESCRIPTIVE APPROACH

ETHICS AND THE INDIVIDUAL

This chapter begins the part of the book that focuses on ethical decision making as something that individuals do. Many if not most ethical decisions in business organizations are made by individuals like you. In later chapters, we will address how the organizational context and the broader business environment also affect individual ethical decision making.

There are two ways to think about individual ethical decision making—the prescriptive approach and the descriptive approach. This chapter covers the prescriptive approach. It is derived from ethical theories in philosophy and offers decision-making tools (ways of thinking about ethical choices) that help you decide what decision you *should* make as a "conscientious moral agent" who thinks carefully about ethical choices[1] and who wants to make the ethically "right" decision. Our assumption is that your intentions are good and that your goal is to do the right thing. So, in this chapter we introduce ethical decision-making tools that can help you do just that, and we'll explain how you can integrate them and use them in a practical way.

We know, however, that people don't always make the best decision. Prescriptions aren't always followed. So it's helpful to understand how people's minds work—how people really make decisions. The descriptive approach, discussed in Chapter 3, relies on psychological research to describe how people actually make ethical decisions (rather than how they *should* make them). It focuses in particular on individual characteristics that influence how individuals think and on cognitive limitations that often keep people from making the best possible ethical decisions. Hopefully, if we understand both approaches, we can improve our ethical decision making. Now let's learn about the prescriptive approach.

Ethical Dilemmas

Many ethical choices are clear-cut enough that we can decide what to do rather easily because they pit "right" against "wrong." Is deciding whether to embezzle corporate funds a tough ethical dilemma? Not really, because embezzling is stealing and it's wrong, period. There's not much of a "dilemma" there. But things can get pretty murky in situations where two or more important values, rights, or responsibilities conflict and we have to choose between equally unpleasant alternatives. We define an *ethical dilemma* as a situation in which two or more "right" values are in conflict. Consider the following ethical dilemma.

THE LAYOFF

Pat is the plant manager in one of ABC Company's five plants. She's worked for the company for 15 years, working her way up from the factory floor after the company sent her to college. Her boss just told her in complete confidence that the company will have to lay off 200 workers. Luckily, her job won't be affected. But a rumor is now circulating in the plant, and one of her workers (an old friend who now works for her) asks the question, "Well, Pat, what's the word? Is the plant closing? Am I going to lose my job? The closing on our new house is scheduled for next week. I need to know!" What should she say? What would you say?

This is a true ethical dilemma because two values are in conflict. Two "right" values that can create significant conflict are truthfulness and loyalty. As illustrated in the case, telling the truth to your friend would mean being disloyal to the company that has treated you so well. The value of loyalty can even be in conflict with itself as you weigh loyalty to your friend against loyalty to your boss and company. In this chapter, we introduce conceptual tools drawn from philosophical approaches to ethical decision making that are designed to help you think through these tough ethical dilemmas from multiple perspectives. None of the approaches are perfect. In fact, they may lead to different conclusions. The point of using multiple approaches is to get you to think carefully and comprehensively about ethical dilemmas and to avoid falling into a solution by accident. At the very least, you can feel good because you've thought about the issue thoroughly, you've analyzed it from every available angle, and you can explain your decision-making process to others if asked to do so.

Prescriptive Approaches to Ethical Decision Making in Business

Philosophers have been wrestling with ethical decision making for centuries. We certainly don't intend to provide a philosophy course here, but we can distill some important and practical principles that can guide you toward making the best ethical decisions. In this section, we outline some of the major contemporary approaches that we think can provide you with the most practical assistance.[2] We then incorporate them into a series of steps that you can use to evaluate ethical dilemmas, and along the way, we apply these steps to the short layoff case as well as other examples.

FOCUS ON CONSEQUENCES (CONSEQUENTIALIST THEORIES)   One set of philosophical theories is categorized as consequentialist (sometimes referred to as teleological, from the Greek *telos* for "end" and *logos* for "reason"). When you're attempting to decide what's right or wrong, consequentialist theories focus attention on the results or consequences of the decision or action.

Utilitarianism is probably the best-known consequentialist theory. According to the principle of utility, an ethical decision should maximize benefits to society and minimize harms. What matters is the net balance of good consequences over bad for society overall.

A utilitarian would approach an ethical dilemma by systematically identifying the stakeholders in a particular situation as well as the alternative actions and their consequences (harms and/or benefits) for each. A *stakeholder i*s any person or group with a stake in the issue at hand. So who are the stakeholders in the layoff situation? Key stakeholders would include Pat's friend, her friend's family, Pat's boss, Pat, her family, other workers, and the company—quite a list! And, what would be the consequences (societal harms and benefits) for each stakeholder of a decision to tell or not tell? The consequentialist approach requires you to do a mental calculation of all the harms and benefits of these consequences, stakeholder by stakeholder. What would be the consequences if Pat tells her friend what she knows about the layoff? What would be the consequences (societal harms and benefits) if Pat doesn't share what she knows? A potential harm of telling her friend would be that he or she might tell other workers and send the plant into chaos. Perhaps more people would lose their jobs as a result. Another potential harm might be that Pat could lose the trust of her boss (another stakeholder), who provided information to her in confidence. Pat might even lose her job, which has consequences for her family. A potential benefit might be that Pat would retain the trust of a valued friend. Another potential benefit might be that her friend could use the information to make a decision about going through with buying the new house. After Pat conducts a thorough analysis that estimates these harms and benefits, the "best" ethical decision is the one that yields the greatest net benefits for society, and the "worst" decision is the one that yields the greatest net harms for society. So, if more people would be ultimately hurt than helped if Pat were to inform her friend of the impending layoff, a utilitarian would conclude that Pat shouldn't tell. Keep in mind that this perspective requires you to think broadly about the consequences for "society," not just for yourself and those close to you, as we are often inclined to do. When conducting such an analysis, you may want to create a table for yourself like the one below that can help you sort out the complexities by identifying the stakeholders and the anticipated harms and benefits. But arriving at a bottom-line conclusion about the action that will serve the greater good of society is easier said than done. It requires some way to "weight" the harms and benefits and that requires you to think hard about what you value more and less. We encourage you to attempt to account for this "weighting" in some way as you complete the table. It will help you decide where the consequentialist analysis leads in terms of a decision about what you should do.

Consequentialist Analysis

Stakeholder	Tell—Harms	Tell—Benefits	Don't Tell—Harms	Don't Tell—Benefits
1				
2				
3				
4				
etc.				

Bottom line: the best decision or action is the one that produces *the greatest net good and the least net harm for society overall.*

In 2005, Mark Felt, also known as "Deep Throat," revealed his identity as the source who secretly fed information to *Washington Post* investigative reporters Bob Woodward and Carl Bernstein. The information ultimately led to the 1974 resignation of President Richard Nixon over his involvement in the cover-up of the 1972 burglary at the Democratic headquarters in the Watergate building. Woodward and Bernstein turned the story into a book and later a film, *All the President's Men.* We can't get inside Felt's head to understand his ethical decision-making process at the time. We will never know his true motivation, because Felt became cognitively impaired in his later years. But we can imagine that, as the number two person at the FBI, he may have weighed the harms and benefits of leaking information about the Watergate break-in and the involvement of Nixon and his aides in criminal wrongdoing. Felt certainly took a huge personal risk and may have considered the costs to others. Several individuals went to prison as a result of the investigation, and their families suffered as a result. A president also resigned in disgrace. If Felt had been discovered, his career would probably have been ruined, and his family would have experienced the rippling effects. But those who believe that he did the right thing would say that Felt's decision served the long-term greater good and ultimately helped preserve democracy in the United States.

The consequentialist approach can be extremely practical and helpful in thinking through an ethical dilemma. Don't we generally look at the consequences of our own and others' actions in trying to decide what's right? And don't we consider who will benefit and who will be harmed? When the state decides to build a new highway through your property, aren't they using a utilitarian rationale when they argue that the benefits to the greater community (increased development and jobs, reduced traffic, fewer accidents, etc.) outweigh the harm to the few property holders who will be inconvenienced by an eyesore in their backyard?

However, a challenge involved in using a strictly consequentialist approach is that it is often difficult to obtain the information required to evaluate all of the consequences for all stakeholders who may be directly or indirectly affected by an action or decision. In business (or in life for that matter), when do you have *all* of the facts? Could Deep Throat have known what the outcomes of his decision would be? And even if you have all of the information, it can be extremely cumbersome to calculate all of the harms and benefits every time you encounter a new ethical dilemma. Try it. Can you list all of the potential harms and benefits for everyone who may be directly or indirectly involved in the layoff situation described above? It's relatively easy for Pat to list the potential harms and benefits to herself and those close to her. But can you envision all of the potential harms and benefits to all of the other people who may be involved? If you don't have a crystal ball that allows you to foretell the future (and most of us don't), you're unlikely to arrive at a completely accurate assessment of all future consequences. Nevertheless, with this approach, it's important to do your best to accurately assess the potential consequences. You have a responsibility to gather and use the best, most up-to-date information available. Remember, according to this approach, the most ethical decision maximizes benefits and minimizes harm *to society*. The challenge of making the best ethical decision is to step outside of oneself and think as broadly as possible about all of the consequences for all of those affected. Taking this step is guaranteed to widen your decision-making lens and allow you to take into account consequences that you otherwise might not consider.

Another difficulty with this type of approach is that the rights of a minority group can easily be sacrificed for the benefit of the majority. For example, slaveholders in the Old South argued that the greatest good for the greatest number would be served by maintaining the system of slavery. But hopefully we all agree that such a system did not respect the civil or human rights of the people who were enslaved (a deontological perspective we discuss next).

The consequentialist approach remains particularly important to ethical decision making in business for a variety of reasons. First, utilitarian thinking—through its descendant, utility theory—underlies much of the business and economics literature. Second, on the face of it, most of us would admit that considering the consequences of one's decisions or actions for society is extremely important to good ethical decision making. In fact, studies of ethical decision making in business have found that business managers generally rely on such an approach.[3] As we'll see, though, other kinds of considerations are also important.

FOCUS ON DUTIES, OBLIGATIONS, AND PRINCIPLES (DEONTOLOGICAL THEORIES)   The word *deontological* comes from the Greek *deon*, meaning "duty." Rather than focusing on consequences, a deontological approach would ask, "What is Pat's ethical duty now that she knows about the layoff?" Deontologists base their decisions about what's right on broad, abstract universal ethical principles or values such as honesty, promise keeping, fairness, loyalty, rights (to safety, privacy, etc.), justice, responsibility, compassion, and respect for human beings and property.

According to some deontological approaches, certain moral principles are binding, regardless of the consequences. Therefore some actions would be considered wrong even if the consequences of the actions were good. In other words, a deontologist focuses on doing what is "right" (based on moral principles or values such as honesty), whereas a consequentialist focuses on doing what will maximize societal welfare. An auditor taking a deontological approach would likely insist on telling the truth about a company's financial difficulties even if doing so might risk putting the company out of business and many people out of work. A consequentialist auditor would weigh the societal harms and benefits before deciding what to do. If convinced that by lying now he or she could save a good company in the long term, the consequentialist auditor would be more willing to compromise the truth.

Knowing what values are important to you and how you prioritize them is an important first step toward understanding and applying this approach in your own life (now is a good time to complete the end-of-chapter exercise, "Clarifying Your Values"). Which values are most important to you? Which ones are you willing to adhere to consistently, and how do you prioritize them if they conflict? Try to keep your list of values to just a few that you believe are truly the most important. In attempting to decide which values are most important to you, it's helpful to think back to recent ethical dilemmas you have faced. Which ones guided your behavior? Which ones trumped other conflicting values? Think carefully when selecting your ethical values. For example, students often select promise keeping as a value. But what if keeping a promise requires you to breach another more important value such as honesty or justice? If promise keeping is important to you, be careful what you promise. Should you promise to lie to authorities for a friend who has broken the law and harmed others? If you select loyalty, you'll need to think about "loyalty to whom," because multiple loyalties can conflict as they do in the layoff situation we've been discussing.

Some deontological theories focus on rights rather than duties, values, or principles. The concept of rights goes back to classical Greek notions of "natural rights" that emerge from "natural law." Rights can be thought of as "negative rights," such as the limits on government interference with citizens' right to privacy or the pursuit of happiness. Or rights can be thought of in more positive terms, such as the individual's rights to health and safety. The rights of one party can conflict with the rights of another party, as when the rights of a company to seek profits for its shareholders conflict with the rights of a community to clean air or water or the rights of a consumer to buy a safe product. Furthermore, the rights of one party are generally related to the duties of another. So, if we agreed that communities have the right to clean water, businesses would have the duty to protect that right.

How does a deontologist determine what rule, principle, or right to follow? One way is to rely on moral rules that have their roots in Western biblical tradition. For example, the *Golden Rule*, a basic moral rule found in every major religion, is familiar to most of us and provides an important deontological guide: The most familiar version tells us to "Do unto others as you would have them do unto you." In our layoff situation, the Golden Rule would suggest that Pat should tell her friend what she knows because she would want her friend to do the same for her if the situation were reversed. But note that the Golden Rule leads you to the best decision *only* if you're highly ethical. For example, do you think that the Golden Rule would expect you to lie for a friend who has broken the law because you would want the friend to do that for you? No, because a highly ethical person wouldn't ask a friend to lie. The ethical person would be responsible and would accept the consequences of his or her illegal actions.

The German philosopher Emmanuel Kant provided another useful moral rule with his *categorical imperative*: "Act as if the maxim of thy action were to become by thy will a universal law of nature." This rule asks you to consider whether the rationale for your action is suitable to become a universal law or principle for everyone to follow. For example, if you break a promise, the categorical imperative asks, "Is promise breaking a principle everyone should follow?" The answer is no; if everyone did this, promises would become meaningless. In fact, they would cease to exist.

A practical Kantian question to ask is, "What kind of world would this be if everyone behaved this way or made this kind of decision in this type of situation?" What kind of world would this be if everyone broke promises at will? Consider the following example:

A DRUG STUDY

A number of physicians are recruited to participate in a large-scale, multi-center study to investigate the survival rates of breast cancer victims who are being treated with a new drug. Strict rules are developed regarding inclusion of patients in the study. Only those who have had surgery within the last three months can be included. Dr. Smith has a patient who hears about the study and wants very much to participate. Because Dr. Smith thinks the drug could really help this patient, he agrees to include her even though her surgery took place six months ago. He changes the dates on her charts to conform with the study requirements and reasons that this one little change shouldn't affect the study results.

According to the categorical imperative, we must ask whether the rationale for Dr. Smith's action (helping his patient by breaking the study rules) is suitable to become a principle for all to follow. The answer is clearly no. What if other doctors did the same thing as Dr. Smith? What if those involved in medical research followed their own preferences or motives rather than the rules guiding the study? Society would be unable to rely on the results of medical research. What kind of a world would it be if researchers were routinely dishonest? It would be one where we simply couldn't depend on the integrity of scientific research, and most of us would deem that kind of world unacceptable. Interestingly, given the potential for societal harm of a decision to be dishonest and enroll the patient in the study, consequentialist thinking would lead to the same decision. Only the patient would potentially benefit, and society as a whole would be harmed.

Additional moral rules come from the work of the highly regarded American political philosopher John Rawls. Rawls proposed that decision makers use a *veil of ignorance* exercise to arrive at fundamental principles of justice that should guide ethical decision making. In his approach, imaginary people come together behind a hypothetical veil of ignorance. These imaginary people do not know anything about themselves, their identities, or their status. They don't know if they (or others they are thinking about) are male or female, young or old, rich or poor, black or white, the CEO or a janitor, intelligent or mentally retarded, physically fit or disabled, sick or healthy, patient or doctor. According to Rawls, rational people who use this veil of ignorance principle will be more likely to develop ethical rules that do not unfairly advantage or disadvantage any particular group.[4] Because humans are fundamentally risk averse and wary of being the worst off, such neutral people would arrive at fair principles that grant all individuals equal rights to basic liberties and equality of opportunity and that benefit the least advantaged in society. This approach was designed to be used as a guide in any ethical decision, but it may be most useful when fairness concerns are central to the decision at hand. It offers yet another way to broaden your view and urges you to consider the needs of those who are less advantaged than yourself. So, following Rawls, if a business needs to downsize, what kind of process would the group of imaginary people behind the veil of ignorance devise for deciding whom to lay off and when to tell employees? How would doctors decide who will be included in drug studies? How would lifesaving prescription drugs be priced? Would sweatshop working conditions ever be acceptable?

A major challenge of deontological approaches is deciding which duty, obligation, right, or principle takes precedence because, as we said earlier, ethical dilemmas often pit these against each other. What does the deontologist do if one binding moral rule clashes with another? Can it be determined which is the more important right or principle? Because the U.S. Constitution is based on a rights approach, many U.S. public policy debates revolve around questions such as these. For example, the abortion debate rests on the question of whether the rights of the mother or the fetus should take precedence. In ethical dilemmas at work, loyalty to your boss or organization can easily clash with other strongly held values such as compassion or fairness. What if your boss tells you that you must lay off a subordinate—an excellent performer—because he was hired last, and the principle guiding the layoff is "the last hired is the first fired"? But imagine that this subordinate will lose his health insurance with the layoff, and you know that his child is seriously ill. Another subordinate who has been with the company somewhat longer is also a good performer but is single and has no family obligations. What is the most ethical decision here?

Another difficulty of deontological approaches arises when they conflict with consequentialist reasoning. First, what happens when following a rule will have devastating consequences? For example, in World War II Germany, telling the truth to the Nazis about whether Jews were hiding in your attic would have devastating consequences—the Jews would be taken and killed. In response to such concerns, some philosophers argue that deontological principles (i.e., truth telling, promise keeping) don't have to be regarded as absolute. For example, one could violate a rule or principle for a good reason (according to Kant, a reason that you would be willing to accept for anyone in the same position).[5] In the Nazi scenario, Kant's categorical imperative would be helpful because most of us would not want to live in a world where people are expected to tell the truth when doing so means the death of an innocent human being. Respect for human life trumps honesty.

Consider yet another example of conflict between a consequences approach and a principles approach. In 2009, the owner of a shipping company had to decide whether to pay ransom to pirates who were holding his ship and its crew hostage and who threatened to kill everyone if the ransom were not paid. This business owner acknowledged that paying the ransom would reinforce the pirates' behavior and would likely lead to more kidnappings and hostage takings, an outcome that is clearly to the detriment of society overall. However, having considered this, he nevertheless concluded that he would pay the ransom because he felt strongly that his primary responsibility as an employer was to his people. His values of respect for human life and compassion for the employees' families were more important to him in this situation than the potential longer-term broader harm.

Sometimes, a decision with good consequences contradicts an important ethical principle. For example, the Commonwealth of Virginia in the U.S. developed a method for sentencing criminals that incorporates the risk of recidivism.[6] Using factors such as gender, age, employment status, and prior criminal record, the state learned that it can predict the likelihood of an individual's committing another crime. This calculation is designed to protect the public and save taxpayer money, and many felons are being released from jail and returned to the community successfully. The system works, and one could argue, based on consequentialist thinking, that it benefits most people. But some argue, based on principle, that those who commit a crime deserve to be punished and that it is unfair to treat offenders who committed the same crime differently. Under the system, a young, unemployed male is more likely to go to jail than an older woman who has a job.[7] The consequences are good for society, but is the system fair?

FOCUS ON INTEGRITY (VIRTUE ETHICS)   The virtue ethics approach focuses more on the integrity of the moral actor (the person) than on the moral act itself (the decision or behavior). The goal here is to be a good person because that is the type of person you wish to be. Although virtue ethics as a philosophical tradition began with Aristotle, a number of contemporary ethicists (including business ethicists) have returned it to the forefront of ethical thinking.[8]

A virtue ethics perspective considers the actor's character, motivations, and intentions (something we didn't discuss at all under the other two perspectives). According to virtue ethics, it is important that the individual *intends* to be a good person and exerts effort to develop him- or herself as a moral agent, to associate with others who do the same, and to contribute to creating an organizational context that supports ethical behavior.[9] This doesn't mean that principles, rules, or consequences aren't considered, just that they're considered in the context of assessing the actor's character and integrity. One's character may be assessed in terms of principles such as honesty, in terms of rule following (did this actor follow his profession's ethics code?) or in terms of consequences (as in the physician's agreement to, above all, do no harm).

Motivations and intentions are important to ethical decision making, as the law acknowledges. If a person harms another, society judges that person less harshly if he or she did not intend to commit harm; i.e., it was an accident. In thinking about Mark Felt's decision to provide information to Woodward and Bernstein in the Watergate affair, virtue ethics would ask us to think about his intentions and motivation. Was he motivated by revenge because he was passed over for the top job at the FBI (as some have suggested), or was he guided by broader concerns about doing the right thing as a conscientious moral agent who was concerned about sustaining the American system of government?

In virtue ethics, one's character may be defined by a *relevant moral community*, a community that holds you to the highest ethical standards. Therefore, it's important to think about the community or communities in which the decision maker operates. Mark Felt was an FBI man who was sworn to keep confidences. That makes it hard for some in the FBI community to accept his talking to journalists, even if the long-term consequences contributed to the greater good of the country. But the broader community, the U.S. public at large, likely judges Felt more kindly if they think of him as someone who took a great personal risk to do what he thought was right. Think about yourself. What community or communities do you look to for guidance in deciding whether you have acted as a person of integrity? Are you guided by the standards of your professional association, the regulatory community, your religious community, your family, your company's ethics office, the broader public? Note that unless you work in a highly ethical organizational context, the relevant moral community is not your own work group or your organization. A virtue ethics perspective requires that you look to the community that will hold you to the highest ethical standard and support your intention to be a virtuous person.

A virtue ethics approach is particularly useful for individuals who work within a professional community that has developed high standards of ethical conduct for community members. For example, the accounting profession has developed a code of conduct for professional accountants. Being a virtuous accountant would mean abiding by that code of professional responsibility. The same goes for certified financial consultants, engineers, lawyers, physicians, and psychologists who all agree to abide by their profession's rules and standards. Such professional codes are generally living documents that evolve with changing times. For example, building on 20 years of thinking about ethics and torture, a committee of the American Psychological Association (APA) developed new standards in 2009, consistent with its "do no harm" principle: without exception, the new APA standards prohibit professional psychologists from participating in torture. Psychologists are required to disobey orders to torture, intervene to stop torture, and report torture if they become aware of it.[10] A decision maker can often rely on such relevant community standards to guide decisions and actions. The assumption is that the professional community has already done this type of thinking and has done it carefully.

Consider this fascinating example from the U.S. legal profession. The rule of attorney-client privilege requires criminal defense lawyers to keep information shared by their clients completely confidential. This rule is based on the idea that, in order for defendants to get the best possible defense, they must feel free to be completely truthful with their lawyers. The underlying principle of the U.S. system of justice says that everyone deserves a vigorous defense and that defense lawyers must act in the interests of their clients. Then it is up to judges and juries to decide guilt and innocence. That all makes a lot of sense in the abstract. But a recent case in Illinois (profiled on *60 Minutes*)[11] was particularly challenging for nonlawyers to understand. Here's what happened. Two criminal defense lawyers went public to share information that their client had committed a murder for which another man, Alton Logan, was erroneously convicted. When the lawyers went public, Logan had already served

26 years in prison for a crime he did not commit! Most observers' immediate reaction was to say that the lawyers should have spoken up right away because it just isn't fair for someone to go to jail for a crime he didn't commit, and they could and should have stopped it. But because of attorney-client privilege, a central ethical principle in the legal profession, the lawyers were not allowed to share this private information. As lawyers, they understand that the larger system of justice depends on that principle, even if some individuals are harmed in the process of upholding it. Interestingly, they also noted that if they had shared the information, it would not have been admissible in court and could not have helped Alton Logan. The lawyers were able to finally come forward only because, years before, they had convinced their client to sign an affidavit saying that they could share the information about his admission of guilt after he died. That's what they did when their client died in prison (where he was serving a life sentence for committing a different crime), and Alton Logan was finally released. Interviews with the lawyers suggested that they understood and were guided by the ethics of the legal profession. However, importantly, they also went beyond professional community expectations when they asked their client to sign the affidavit that ultimately allowed them to share the information. So from a virtue ethics perspective, they followed their community's guidance. But as thoughtful moral agents who were motivated to do the right thing, they didn't completely surrender to legal community standards. Their intentions were good and they used their own thinking to devise a plan that ultimately resulted in Logan's release (although a deontologist might say that it was 26 years too late).

It's important to do your own thinking because some professional communities provide limited guidance or none at all. For example, management is not a "profession" with explicit ethical standards and acknowledged responsibilities to society (although some influential thinkers believe and argue that it could and should be).[12] In fact, the authors of a 2008 *Harvard Business Review* article[13] offer "A Hippocratic Oath for Managers" that calls on managers to commit to the following (adapted from the original):

1. *Service to the Public and Society.* Recognize the manager's responsibility to serve the public interest by creating sustainable value for society in the long term.

2. *Balance Multiple Stakeholders' Interests.* Recognize that managers must balance the often-conflicting needs of many stakeholders to enhance enterprise value in a way that is consistent with societal well-being. The authors note that "this may not always mean growing or preserving the enterprise and may include such painful actions as its restructuring, discontinuation, or sale if these actions preserve or increase value."

3. *Acting with Integrity in the Enterprise's Interest.* Put the interests of the enterprise ahead of personal interests while behaving as a person of integrity, consistent with personal values, and leading others to do the same. This means avoiding behavior that advances personal ambitions that harm either

the business or society. It also means reporting the ethical or legal violations of others.

4. *Adherence to the Law.* Make a commitment to adhere to the spirit and the letter of the law and contracts in personal and enterprise action.

5. *Accurate and Transparent Reporting.* Report enterprise performance accurately and transparently to all relevant stakeholders (e.g., investors, consumers, the public, etc.) so that they can make informed decisions.

6. *Respectful and Unbiased Decision Making.* Make decisions in an unbiased and respectful manner without considering race, gender, sexual orientation, religion, nationality, politics, or social status. The goal is to protect the interests of the less powerful who are affected by these decisions.

7. *Professional Development.* Commit to continuous professional development for the self and others with the goal of always using the best and most current available knowledge to make informed decisions.

8. *Responsibility to Protect the Profession.* Recognize that being considered a professional has privileges that come with responsibilities to uphold and protect the standards, and continue to develop them in a way that contributes to the trust, respect, and honor associated with them and with the profession.

Interestingly, if you study these principles carefully, you can find evidence of all three ethical decision-making approaches. Can you identify consequentialist thinking, deontological thinking, and virtue ethics thinking? Do you think management is ready to become a profession that requires its members to adhere to such a code? Should it?

Whether or not your own professional community provides guidance, it remains essential that you think for yourself, because a professional community can be wrong. For example, auditors are professional accountants with a fiduciary responsibility to the public. Their audits provide investors with assurance that public companies' financial statements can be trusted. The American Institute of Certified Public Accountants (AICPA) is the national, professional organization for all certified public accountants (www.aicpa.org). It has a code of conduct for members and a mission that includes establishing and enforcing conduct standards. But the institute also acts as a lobbying organization. During the 1990s, auditing firms got into the business of providing consulting to their audit clients; this was an ethically dangerous practice because of its potential for conflict of interest. The firms might feel pressure to go easy on their audit clients in order to gain these clients' consulting business. This is exactly what happened. Because consulting was more lucrative than auditing, firms lobbied hard to protect their relationships with these clients and their rights to both consult and provide audit services to the same firms. As a result, the AICPA was blamed for contributing to an environment that led to financial scandals at Enron, WorldCom, and other companies.[14] So if you're looking for solid ethical guidance, it's important to scrutinize the source and make sure that it is free of conflicts of interest.

When a professional community isn't available, doesn't provide good guidance, or seems wrong, you can turn to the broader community and societal standards for guidance. A useful decision-making shortcut based on the broader community as a guide is known as the disclosure rule. This practical shortcut is widely used by managers and executives. The disclosure rule asks, "How would you feel if your behavior appeared on ___? You fill in the blank of a particular media outlet. Is it the front page of the *New York Times*, the *Wall Street Journal*, your hometown newspaper, *60 Minutes*, CNN? The assumption behind the disclosure rule is that community standards do exist for most situations, and at a gut level, most of us know what those are. If our gut tells us it wouldn't look good to have our behavior appear in one of these media outlets, we simply shouldn't be doing it because it means that if we did, we wouldn't be considered persons of integrity in society's view.

If your goal is to be considered a person of integrity, another useful question to ask yourself is how your harshest moral critic or ethical role model would advise you. Who serves in that role for you? Is it someone in your family or a respected teacher, coach, or spiritual adviser? Identify your strongest ethical role model or harshest moral critic and consider what this individual would think of the behavior you're contemplating. Most of us have people in our lives whose integrity we respect and whose moral judgment of us we value.

Finally, a virtue ethics perspective assumes that your identity as a moral actor is important to you and that you are devoted to continuously developing that aspect of yourself. Being an ethical person is just an important part of who you are. Those of us who have made such a commitment know that life and careers present ongoing ethical challenges and opportunities to work on the ethical aspect of ourselves. Are you following an ethical fitness program by practicing good behavior over time and developing good habits? Just as an exercise program challenges your muscles, balance, and coordination, an ethical fitness program challenges your ethical thinking and leads to improvement. Such an ethical fitness program can help you develop your comfort with speaking up on behalf of your values. It can also reinforce your view of yourself as a person of integrity and contribute to improving your ethical fitness over time. Identifying ethical role models in your life, choosing to interact with people of integrity, and choosing to work in an ethical environment can all be ways to support this aspect of your personal development.[15] We've now considered consequentialist, deontological, and virtue ethics approaches. These are just a few of the philosophical approaches that may be applied in ethical dilemma situations. We've introduced the approaches we believe have the most practical benefit to business managers, and, admittedly, we've introduced them in a rather general way, without many of the nuances developed by philosophers over the years. We've suggested that all of the approaches have limitations. No one of them, by itself, provides perfect guidance in every situation. Obviously, if all of the approaches lead to the same solution, the decision is a relatively easy one. The tough ones arise when the approaches conflict. When that happens, it will be up to you to consider the situation as comprehensively as possible and make the best decision you can based upon societal good, your most important values and principles, and considerations of what a person of integrity would do. Stuart Youngblood, professor of management at Texas Christian University in Fort Worth, suggested the following example that he has used in his business ethics class:

THE BURNING BUILDING

Assume you approach a burning building and hear voices coming from both ends, each seeking help. Assume the fire is burning so rapidly you only have time to go to one or the other end of the building. Initially, you hear multiple voices at one end and a sole voice at the other end. Which way do you go? Why? Now include some additional information. The sole voice is that of your daughter (father, mother, etc.). Do you still choose to go to the end with multiple voices (to do the greatest good for society)? If not, why not? What has changed? What will the different approaches advise?

We certainly won't resolve the academic controversies over the "best" philosophical approach here. Even so, we believe that the approaches we've presented incorporate important factors that should guide ethical business decisions. All of them would have provided excellent ethical guidance to those whose actions contributed to the recent U.S. financial crisis, during which mortgage brokers sold NINJA (no income, no job or assets) loans to people who clearly couldn't afford the homes they were buying, investment bankers packaged these risky mortgages into securities they touted as safe, and rating agency employees rated the securities AAA (without fully addressing the underlying risks). A consequentialist perspective would have focused attention on the potential harms to multiple stakeholders (customers, society) of these risky mortgages and mortgage-backed securities. A deontological approach would have focused attention on the importance of responsibility, honesty, and transparency with customers about these products. A virtue ethics approach would have asked whether a person of integrity would sell mortgages to people with little or no income or rate these securities highly despite the lack of experience with them. A serious consideration of these factors by the actors involved could have averted a systemic crisis that has harmed all of us.

Next, we offer eight steps that aim to integrate the three types of analysis just discussed.[16] Before presenting them, we'd like to offer a caveat. The eight steps suggest a linear decision-making process that is necessarily inaccurate. Ethical decision making is often not linear. Still, it's helpful to cover all of these points, even if they don't always occur in this particular sequence.

Eight Steps to Sound Ethical Decision Making in Business

STEP ONE: GATHER THE FACTS   The philosophical approaches don't tell us explicitly to gather the facts. But they seem to assume that we'll complete this important step. You might be surprised at how many people jump to solutions without having the facts. Ask yourself, "How did the situation occur? Are there historical facts that I should know? Are there facts concerning the current situation that I should know?"[17]

Fact gathering is often easier said than done. Many ethical choices are particularly difficult because of the uncertainty involved in them. Facts may simply be unavailable. For example, in our layoff case, Pat may not have good information about the legal requirements on informing workers about layoffs. Also, she may not have enough information to determine how long it would take these 200 workers to find new jobs. It's important to recognize these limitations as you do your best to assemble the facts that are available to you.

In the financial crisis, decision makers not only failed to gather good information, but it appears that they may have explicitly avoided getting the facts. For example, mortgage lenders processed mortgages for unemployed people because they required no documentation to prove employment (as lenders had always done in the past). All the person had to do was claim to have a job, and the mortgage would be processed. The mortgage lender earned fees for creating and processing the loan and then sold it off in the secondary mortgage market, where it was packaged with other mortgages and sold to investors. The "fact" that the person with the mortgage was unemployed and would likely not be able to sustain payments was first ignored and then lost as the mortgage made its way through the mortgage market system.

STEP TWO: DEFINE THE ETHICAL ISSUES   Many of us have knee-jerk responses to ethical dilemmas. We jump to a solution without really thinking through the ethical issues and the reasons for our response. For example, in the layoff case, one person might say, "Oh, that's easy; promise keeping is the ethical issue. Pat has to keep her promise to her boss and protect her job." Another person might say that honesty is the key ethical issue: "Pat just has to tell the truth to her friend."

Don't jump to solutions without first identifying the ethical issues or points of values conflict in the dilemma. Also recognize that the toughest situations usually involve multiple ethical issues that go back to the philosophical approaches we just discussed. For example, in the layoff case, one ethical issue has to do with the rights of both the workers and the company. How would you define the workers' right to know about the plant closing in advance? How much advance notice is appropriate? What does the law say? Another ethical issue has to do with the company's right to keep the information private. Furthermore, what is the company's obligation to its workers in this regard? At a more personal level, there are the ethical issues related to principles such as honesty, loyalty, and promise keeping. Is it more important to be honest with a friend or to keep a promise to one's boss? Who is owed more loyalty? Think about the situation from a justice or fairness perspective: What would be fair to the company and to those who would be laid off?

Points of ethical conflict may go back to the conflict between consequentialist and deontological approaches. For example, if I tell the truth (consistent with the principle of promise keeping), bad things may happen (negative consequences). A consequentialist would think about the ethical issues in terms of harms or benefits. Who is likely to be harmed? Who is likely to benefit from a particular decision or action? And what is the bottom line for society overall? A virtue ethics approach would suggest thinking about the ethical issues in terms of community standards. Does your relevant moral community (the one that would hold you to the highest ethical standards) identify a particular action as wrong? Why or why not?

Especially when we're under pressure or in a rush, our inclination is to stop with the first ethical issue that comes to mind. For example, in our layoff case, we might be inclined to stop with the issue of loyalty to a friend. Challenge yourself to think of as many issues as you possibly can. Here's where talking about the problem with others can help. Present the dilemma to coworkers, to your spouse, or to friends you respect. Ask them whether they see other issues that you may have missed.

STEP THREE: IDENTIFY THE AFFECTED PARTIES (THE STAKEHOLDERS) Both consequentialist and deontological thinking involve the ability to identify the parties affected by the decision. The consequentialist will want to identify all those stakeholders who are going to experience harm and benefits. The deontologist might want to know whose rights are involved and who has a duty to act in the situation.

Being able to see the situation through others' eyes is a key moral reasoning skill. Lawrence Kohlberg, developer of a key theory of moral reasoning, called this skill role taking. It means putting yourself in others' shoes and being sensitive to their needs and concerns. Rawls's veil of ignorance exercise asks you to do this as well. Frequently, you have to think beyond the facts provided in a case in order to identify all affected parties. It often helps to begin with the individuals in the case who are immediately affected (e.g., in the layoff case, it would be Pat, the worker, and Pat's boss) and then progressively broaden your thinking to incorporate larger groups. For example, in this case, you might include the other workers, the rest of the company, the local community, and society in general. As you think of more and more affected parties, additional issues will probably come to mind. For example, think about the local community. If this is a small town with few other employers, fairness to the entire community becomes an important issue. Shouldn't they have as much time as possible to plan for the impact of this plant closing? Try to put yourself in their shoes. How would they argue their case? How would they feel?

Earlier, we introduced the concept of stakeholders, all of those individuals or groups who have a stake in the particular decision or action. In the context of ethical decision making in business, we should identify the stakeholders affected by the decision and ask how they are affected. Try to make your thinking as broad as possible here. Some of the stakeholders affected by the decision may not even be born yet. The best concrete example of unborn stakeholders might be "DES daughters." In the 1940s, DES, a synthetic estrogen, was prescribed for pregnant women who seemed to be in danger of miscarrying. By 1971, it became clear that DES produced a birth defect in the daughters of these women. Because of the birth defect, DES daughters were more likely to develop vaginal cancer, especially between the ages of 15 and 22. They also had a higher than normal rate of cervical cancer.[18]

Once stakeholders are identified, role-playing can help you see the issue from different stakeholder perspectives. In your classroom or your department, get individuals to seriously play the relevant roles. You may be surprised at how perspectives change based on this simple exercise. What decision would you reach if you were someone else (e.g., the customer?) in the situation? This step incorporates the Golden Rule to treat others as you would like others to treat you. Imagine yourself as each of the players in a decision situation. What decision would they reach, and why?

Another consideration may be to ask whether you can "test" a potential decision with affected parties before your prospective course of action is made final. The objective is to gauge how various audiences will react, so that you can adjust or fine-tune a decision along the way.[19] One question you could ask yourself is, how would this or that stakeholder react if this decision were made public? For example, imagine that ABC Co. (in our layoff case) had another thriving plant in another location. However, in the decision-making process, it was assumed that employees wouldn't want to relocate because of their ties to the local community. Wouldn't it be better to ask them their preferences than to assume what they would want to do?

STEP FOUR: IDENTIFY THE CONSEQUENCES After identifying the affected parties, think about the potential consequences for each party. This step is obviously derived from the consequentialist approaches. It isn't necessary to identify every possible consequence. You should, however, try to identify consequences that have a relatively high probability of occurring and those that would have particularly negative consequences if they did occur (even if the probability of occurrence is low). Who would be harmed by a particular decision or action? For example, in our layoff case, telling the truth to the worker might cause Pat to lose her job, which would have negative consequences for Pat and her entire family (especially if she's a major breadwinner in her family). However, it would give her worker (and presumably others who would be told) the benefit of more time to look for a new job and perhaps save many families from negative financial consequences. Can you determine which solution would accomplish the most net good and the least net harm for society?

Think about the drug thalidomide. It was prescribed to women in the late 1950s to treat morning sickness and produced devastating birth defects in 12,000 babies in Europe, Canada, Australia, and Japan (the Food and Drug Administration never approved it for use in the United States). Many of the babies died, but others were left to live with severe deformities. Randy Warren, a Canadian born in 1961, is the founder of the Thalidomide Victims Association of Canada. His mother took just two doses of thalidomide, but Warren is only a little over 3 feet tall and has no thumbs, arms that are 2 inches too short, and stumps for legs. The consequences of this drug when prescribed to pregnant women were obviously devastating; and shortly after Warren was born, the drug was banned in most places. But continued research produced renewed interest in thalidomide as an effective treatment for Hansen's disease (a painful skin condition associated with leprosy) as well as for "wasting" disease in AIDS patients, arthritis, blindness, leukemia, and other forms of cancer. This drug that had such terrible consequences for so many was being considered for approval because it also had the potential to help many people who were dealing with other devastating illnesses. As Warren put it, "When I heard . . . that thalidomide takes people out of wheelchairs and I think of myself and others that were put in wheelchairs . . . tell me we don't have the moral quandary of the century."

In the end, Warren was consulted and became involved in the decision to return the drug to the marketplace. In 1998, the FDA approved the drug to treat Hansen's disease under the highest level of restriction ever given to a drug. Doctors, pharmacists, and patients all must be registered with the manufacturer, Celgene. Two forms of birth control are required to prevent the possibility of pregnancy and resulting birth defects. Male patients are required to use condoms. No automatic refills of the drug are allowed. And Warren has become "something of a company conscience." Although extremely difficult, the decision to market thalidomide in the United States was made with input from those stakeholders most familiar with its potential for both devastating consequences and remarkable benefits. Regulators at the FDA and company officials got to know Randy Warren as a real person who continues to suffer consequences that they might not have been able to imagine just by reading reports and statistics.[20]

Long-Term versus Short-Term Consequences In business decisions, it's particularly important to think about short-term *and* long-term consequences. Are you confident that your behavior will be considered ethical over a long period of time, even if circumstances or people change? In the layoff case, is the long-term health of the company and the people who will remain employed more important than the short-term consequences to the 200 workers who will be laid off? In the U.S. financial crisis, if people had been thinking about long-term consequences, they would have been much more likely to question behaviors that focused primarily on short-term profits.

Symbolic Consequences In business, it's also extremely important to think about the potential symbolic consequences of an action. Every decision and action sends a message; it stands for something. What message will a particular decision or action send? What will it mean if it is misunderstood? For example, if Pat doesn't tell her worker the truth, and he finds out later that she knew, what will the symbolic message be to this worker and the others who work for Pat—that she's more interested in saving her own hide than in taking care of them? From a leader's perspective, what are the symbolic consequences of accepting tickets to a football game from a valued client when your organization has a rule against accepting gifts from clients? Although the leader may see going to the game as important for getting the big sale, the symbolic message it will likely convey to employees is that the rule doesn't apply to senior leaders. Such a symbolic message can have dire consequences for the organization because employees may then feel that the rule shouldn't apply to them either.

Consequences of Secrecy If a decision is made in private in order to avoid some negative reaction, think about the potential consequences if the decision were to become public. Think about the disclosure rule here. If you're inclined to keep it a secret, that should be a clue that something isn't right. For example, the public was outraged by the fact that tobacco executives secretly knew about the negative health effects of cigarette smoking and lied about it to the American people in testimony before Congress.[21]

STEP FIVE: IDENTIFY THE OBLIGATIONS   Identify the obligations involved and the reasons for each one. For example, in the layoff case, consider Pat's obligations toward the affected parties. When identifying Pat's various obligations, be sure to state the reasons why she has this duty or obligation. Think in terms of values, principles, character, or outcomes. For example, if you're considering Pat's obligation to keep her promise to her boss, your reasoning might go like this: "Pat shouldn't break her promise to her boss. If she does, the trust between them will be broken. Promise keeping and trust are important values in superior-subordinate relationships."

The obligations you identify will vary depending on the people involved and the roles they play. For example, our faith in our financial system depends in part on auditors' obligation to tell the truth about a company's financial difficulties and our faith in rating agencies to accurately grade financial instruments. Similarly, our faith in science as an institution depends on the integrity of the scientific data and how scientists report it. Individuals in these roles have a particularly strong obligation to tell the truth; and if they see themselves as moral actors, they will be motivated to do so.

STEP SIX: CONSIDER YOUR CHARACTER AND INTEGRITY   Here, think about yourself as a person of integrity. Ask yourself what a person of integrity would do in this situation. In attempting to answer this question, you may find it useful to identify the relevant moral community and consider what that community would advise. Begin by identifying the relevant professional or societal community. Then, determine how community members would evaluate the decision or action you're considering.

Remember the disclosure rule. It asks whether you would feel comfortable if your activities were disclosed in the light of day in a public forum like the *New York Times* or some other news medium. In general, if you don't want to read about it in the *New York Times*, you shouldn't be doing it. If you would be uncomfortable telling your parents, children, spouse, clergy, or ethical role model about your decision, you should rethink it.

Thomas Jefferson expressed it like this: "Never suffer a thought to be harbored in your mind which you would not avow openly. When tempted to do anything in secret, ask yourself if you would do it in public for all to see. If you would not, be sure it is wrong."

This kind of approach can be especially valuable when a decision needs to be made quickly. Suppose someone in your organization asks you to misrepresent the effectiveness of one of your company's products to a customer. You can immediately imagine how a story reporting the details of your conversation with the customer would appear in tomorrow's paper. Would you be comfortable having others read the details of that conversation? The ideal is to conduct business in such a way that your activities and conversations could be disclosed without your feeling embarrassed.

Another method might be to ask: "How will I be remembered when I'm gone?"[22] Many people don't often think about this question, but it's a good one. Will you be remembered as an individual of integrity? Students often don't realize how small professional communities can be. This is especially true in today's world of social networking. Although you'll likely change jobs and organizations multiple times over the years, many people remain in a single industry where they have developed industry-specific expertise. A reputation for trustworthiness, respectful interaction, and integrity will open doors to new clients and career opportunities. But the opposite is true as well. A stained reputation is extremely difficult to overcome.

STEP SEVEN: THINK CREATIVELY ABOUT POTENTIAL ACTIONS   Perhaps this should be Step One. Before making any decision, be sure that you haven't unnecessarily forced yourself into a corner. Are you assuming that you have only two choices, either A or B? It's important to look for creative alternatives. Perhaps if you've been focusing on A or B, there's another answer: C. In our layoff case, perhaps Pat could work with management to devise a fair system for alerting employees sooner, or at least she could advise them that information is forthcoming soon, and they should not make big financial commitments until the announcement is made. Perhaps she could advise her boss that she is hearing rumblings from the rumor mill and suggest moving up the timetable for telling employees. As another example, what if you received an extravagant gift from a foreign supplier? This situation could easily be conceptualized as an A or B quandary. Should you accept the gift (which is against company policy), or should you refuse it (which could be interpreted as a slap in the face by this important supplier, who is from a culture where gift giving is a valued part of business relationships)? A potential C solution might be to accept the item as a gift to the company that would be displayed in the headquarters entrance, explaining that large personal gifts are against company policy. Obviously, you would have to check with your company about the acceptability of this C solution. The idea here is to think outside the box.

Here is yet another example. In an overseas location, Cummins Engine Company was having difficulty with local children cutting through a wire fence and stealing valuable electronic components. The A or B solution was to arrest or not arrest these young children when they were caught. After involving the community, the managers were able to arrive at a C solution. They discovered that the children were stealing because there weren't enough classrooms at the local school, thus leaving the children with little to do but get into trouble. Cummins made classrooms available on their site. The mayor provided accreditation, books, and teachers. This C solution cost the company very little and accomplished a great deal. A total of 350 students were accommodated, the stealing problem disappeared, and Cummins became a valued corporate citizen.

STEP EIGHT: CHECK YOUR GUT   The emphasis in these steps has been on using a highly rational fact-gathering and evaluation process once you know that you're faced with an ethical dilemma. But don't forget your gut. We are all hardwired to be empathetic and to desire fairness. Empathy is an important emotion that can signal awareness that someone might be harmed, and intuition is gaining credibility as a source for good business decision making. We can't always say exactly why we're uncomfortable in a situation, but years of socialization have likely made us sensitive to situations where something just doesn't feel quite right. So, if your gut is sending up red flags, give the situation more thought. In fact, this may be your only clue that you're facing an ethical dilemma to begin with. Pay attention to your gut, but don't let it make your decision for you. Once you recognize that you're facing an ethical dilemma, use the rational decision-making tools developed here to help guide your decision making.

Practical Preventive Medicine

DOING YOUR HOMEWORK   There's no doubt that you'll encounter ethical dilemmas—every employee probably encounters hundreds of them during a career; the only thing in doubt is when. Your mission is to be as prepared as possible before you run into a problem. The more informed you are, the more effective you'll be in protecting yourself and your employer. The best ways to do that are to learn the rules of your organization and your profession, and to develop relationships that can help you if and when the need arises.

You can learn the rules in various ways. First, read your company's code of ethics (if it has one) and policy manual. Since most policy manuals are huge, you obviously can't memorize one. If you skim the contents, some of the rules will sink in—you may not remember the exact policy, but at least you'll probably remember that one exists and where to find it.

Second, ask questions. Managers, executives, and peers will admire your initiative when you ask what they think is "important around here." Since many organizational standards are unwritten, and they differ from company to company, the best way to find out about them is by asking. Query your coworkers (including management) about what kinds of ethical situations are most common in your organization and how your organization generally handles those issues. Ask your manager how to raise ethical issues within your organization. Since he or she will certainly tell you to raise an issue with him or her first, be sure to find out how you raise an issue in your manager's absence. This not only gives you a road map for raising issues, but it also sends a signal to your manager that ethics are important to you.

Finally, develop relationships with people outside of your chain of command. Get to know people in human resources, legal, audit, and other departments; they might be able to provide information, help you raise an issue or determine whether something is even an issue, or vouch for your credibility in a crisis. You might also want to join a professional group or association. Many professions have developed ethical standards apart from those that may exist in your company, and it can be helpful to know other people in your profession who can advise you if a crisis arises in your company. Some may say this is being political, but we think it's just plain smart to network with people outside of your immediate job and company. It's the difference between being a victim of circumstance and having the power, the knowledge, and the network to help manage circumstances.

After you've done your homework and learned about your company's standards and values, you may find that your values and your employer's values are in conflict. If the conflict is substantial, you may have no choice but to look for work in another organization. We'll be addressing issues of company values and codes more in Chapters 5 and 6.

WHEN YOU'RE ASKED TO MAKE A SNAP DECISION Many businesspeople place value on the ability to make decisions quickly; and, as a result, many of us can feel pressure to make up our minds in a hurry. This can be a particular issue when people are inexperienced for whatever reason—this may be their first job or a new company or industry—and they may feel a need to prove their competence by making decisions quickly. Obviously, that can be dangerous. The ethical decision-making tools described earlier in the chapter assume that you'll have some time to devote to the decision—to consider multiple sides of the issue and the inherent conflicts with any one course of action. Do your best to get the time to assess, think through, and gather more information. Also consider the following guidelines when a quick decision seems called for:

1. Don't underestimate the importance of a hunch to alert you that you're facing an ethical dilemma. Your gut is your internal warning system. As one senior executive at a multinational computer company said, "The gut never lies." When your gut tells you something's wrong, consider it a warning siren.

2. Ask for time to think it over. Most snap decisions don't have to be that way. Say something like, "Let me think about it, and I'll get back to you soon." Bargaining for time is a smart way to give yourself a break—then you can really think about the decision and consult with others. It's better to take the time to make a good decision than it is to make a bad decision quickly and have lots of time to regret it. Would you rather be known as cautious or reckless?

3. Find out quickly if your organization has a policy that applies to your decision.

4. Ask your manager or your peers for advice. You should consider your manager the first line of defense when you encounter an ethical dilemma. Regardless of your level within the organization, never hesitate to ask for another opinion. This is where a trusted network comes in handy. If you have friends in human resources or the legal department, you can float the issue with them on a casual basis to see if there even is an issue.

5. Use the quick-check *New York Times* test (the disclosure rule). If you'd be embarrassed to have your decision disclosed in the media or to your family, don't do it.

SHOULD JORDAN ACCEPT THE PRINTER DISCOUNT?

Jordan is upgrading his department's data processing capabilities and has just placed an order for four personal computers and two laser printers with a computer company representative. When he mentions that he wishes he had a printer at home like the ones he just ordered, the representative tells him that because of his large order, she can give him a 50 percent discount on a printer for his home. Jordan feels that this is not quite right, but he's not sure why and would like some time to think about her offer.

In this case, Jordan could have real doubt about whether or not to accept a 50 percent discount on a printer for his home. Even though he feels funny about the offer, he might be thinking that he does a lot of work at home, so accepting a discount on a personal printer could be justified. And since the computer representative made the offer after the order was placed, there's no conflict of interest—Jordan's decision to purchase obviously wasn't influenced by the offer of a discount.

But he should listen to his gut, which is feeling that this isn't quite right. He can first stall the computer representative by telling her he'll get back to her later in the day or tomorrow. He can find out what his company policy says about making purchases. (Many companies would equate the discount with a gift and forbid accepting it unless it's available to all employees.)

Suppose he finds nothing in the policy manual to prohibit the discount, and other workers have said "go for it." Then he can use the *New York Times* test. How would the public react to his decision? Some people would probably think that his order was influenced by the offer of a discount. He knows that's not true, but it might be difficult to convince other people of that. This is called an appearance of a conflict of interest, an appearance can be as damaging as an actual conflict. If someone could think your judgment has been affected by a relationship—or in this case, a discount—it could be viewed as the appearance of a conflict and should be avoided. Appearances are extremely important in business and may not be accounted for by the philosophical tools provided earlier in the chapter. Whether you appear to be fair may be as important as whether you're really fair.

Here's the bottom line: If you think that your decision could be misinterpreted or if someone could think the objectivity of your decision has been compromised, rethink the decision. In the example, Jordan can politely refuse the representative's offer by saying something like, "My company doesn't allow personal discounts," or "I just don't feel right about it."

If you ever feel that accepting a favor from a vendor will place you under an obligation to the vendor in the future, be very careful. For example, a public relations manager, Mary, described an incident with a printing company (we'll call it Type Co.) sales representative who was trying to get her business. Type Co. already did business with a number of departments within her company, but Mary was satisfied with her current printer and saw no reason to switch. Just before the holidays, Type Co. sent a popular electronic device (worth about $250) to Mary and to all of its customers in her company. Mary immediately felt that the gift was inappropriate; but to check out her judgment, she called one of Type Co.'s other customers in her company. Mary's colleague assured her that there was nothing wrong with accepting the gift and that it was simply a token of good will. (If Mary had been friendly with one of her company's lawyers or human resources managers, she probably would have received very different advice.) Mary listened to her internal warning system, despite what her colleague said. She sent back the gift.

When asked why she returned the gift, Mary said, "I felt like I was being bribed to do business with Type Co." A reader of the *New York Times* would probably agree.

CONCLUSION

This chapter has presented a prescriptive approach to individual ethical decision making. When you're confronted with an ethical dilemma, you should find it helpful to inform your choice by considering the ideas and steps offered in this chapter. The end-of-chapter questions and case should give you some practice in applying these ideas and steps to real ethical dilemmas.

DISCUSSION QUESTIONS

1. If you had to choose just one of the philosophical approaches discussed in this chapter to guide your decision making, which would you choose? Why? Or, if you had to rank them from most to least helpful, how would you rank them?

2. Some of the steps in the eight-step model might suggest very different courses of action for resolving your dilemma. How would you choose among these distinct courses of action? Why?

3. Think about situations where your values have been in conflict. How have you resolved those conflicts? Now that you have studied the ethical decision-making frameworks in this chapter, what should you have done?

4. Think about an ethical dilemma situation that you've faced. Apply the three approaches and the eight steps recommended in this chapter. Does it change your thinking about the situation? Would it change your action?

5. Some corporations and other organizations have designed ethical decision-making tests that incorporate some of the principles and systems described in this chapter. For example, Carl Skooglund, former vice president and ethics director at Texas Instruments, outlined the following Ethics Quick Test recommended for use by Texas Instrument employees:[23]

   - Is the action legal?
   - Does it comply with your best understanding of our values and principles?
   - If you do it, will you feel bad?
   - How will it look in the newspaper?
   - If you know it's wrong, don't do it, period!
   - If you're not sure, ask.
   - Keep asking until you get an answer.

Think about this list in terms of the decision-making guides discussed in the chapter. Which ones are being used here? Which are not? What recommendations, if any, would you make to alter this list? If you had to make up a list for your company, what would be on it? Why?

Do the same with the Rotary International Four-Way Test:

   - Is it the truth?
   - Is it fair to all concerned?

- Will it build goodwill and better relationships?
- Will it be beneficial to all concerned?

The Seneca (one of the five tribes of the Iroquois Nation) people's guidelines for self-discipline also include these questions:[24]

- Am I happy in what I'm doing?
- Is what I'm doing adding to the confusion?
- What am I doing to bring about peace and contentment?
- How will I be remembered when I am gone?

Could these tests serve as guides for ethical decision making in business? Why or why not?

6. The last question leads us to a useful exercise. If you had to write your own epitaph, what would it say? How would you like to be remembered? What kind of life do you hope to lead?

7. Albert Schweitzer (the philosopher and mission doctor) said, "Success is not the key to happiness. Happiness is the key to success. If you love what you are doing, you will be successful." What do you think? How does this relate to the prescriptive approaches discussed in the chapter?

8. What do you think of the proposed Hippocratic oath for managers?[25]

9. What limitations, if any, can you think of to the prescriptions provided in this chapter? Can you think of reasons why they might not work?

10. If you were to design an ethical fitness program for yourself, what would you include?

EXERCISE

Clarifying Your Values

If you wish to be better prepared to make tough ethical decisions at work or elsewhere in your life, it can be extremely helpful to clarify your personal ethical values *before* they're seriously challenged. Following is a selected list of values (in alphabetical order). Feel free to add one or more if you have a deeply held value that is not represented on this list (it is not meant to be exhaustive). In priority order (with 1 being the most important value), *list from three to six values that are most important to you personally in making decisions*. That's the easy part. Next, think seriously about what happens when two or more of these values conflict. For example, what happens if you value both honesty and success and they come into conflict? Are you willing to forgo financial success in order to be completely honest with customers or suppliers? Next, if you're working, *think about the values of your organization and how those are prioritized*. Are there serious conflicts between your personal values and the organization's values? *Finally, list those values that you would choose to serve as the basis for business dealings in an ideal society.* Be prepared to discuss.

Action orientation	Freedom	Responsibility
Altruism	Harmony	Risk taking
Authority	Helpfulness	Security
Compassion	Honesty/Integrity	Self-discipline
Competence	Honor	Status
Conformity	Humility	Success
Creativity	Initiative	Teamwork
Customer satisfaction	Innovation	Tradition
Diversity	Moderation	Wealth
Equality	Novelty	Winning
Excitement	Obedience	
Experimentation	Order	
Fairness/Justice	Power	
Family well-being	Promise keeping	
Flexibility/Adaptability	Respect	

INTRODUCING THE PINTO FIRES CASE

Next we'll discuss a case that chronicles events that took place over 30 years ago. You may ask, why study such an old case? We present this case because it is extremely important in American business history. In 2005, *Fortune Magazine* called it one of the 20 business decisions that "helped create the business world as it is today."[26] According to *Fortune*, the case and ensuing legal battles contributed to the development of consumer activism as well as to the consumer protections and class action lawsuits that we now take for granted. We have also seen aspects of the case play out in more recent product safety cases.

CASE

PINTO FIRES

by Dennis A. Gioia (used with permission)

On August 10, 1978, three teenage girls died horribly in an automobile accident. Driving a 1973 Ford Pinto to their church volleyball practice in Goshen, Indiana, they were struck from behind by a Chevrolet van. The Pinto's fuel tank ruptured and the car exploded in flames. Two passengers, Lynn Marie Ulrich, 16, and her cousin, Donna Ulrich, 18, were trapped inside the inferno and burned to death. After three attempts, Lynn Marie's sister, 18-year-old Judy Ann, was dragged out alive from the driver's seat, but died in agony hours later in the hospital.

They were merely the latest in a long list of people to burn to death in accidents involving the Pinto, which Ford had begun selling in 1970. By the time of the accident, the car had been the subject of a great deal of public outcry and debate about its safety, especially its susceptibility to fire in low-speed rear-end collisions. This particular accident, however, resulted in more media attention than any other auto accident in U.S. history. Why? Because it led to an unprecedented court case in which the prosecution brought charges of reckless homicide against the Ford Motor Co.—the first time that a corporation had been charged with criminal conduct, and the charge was not negligence but murder. At stake was much more than the maximum penalty of $30,000 in fines. Of immediate concern, a guilty verdict could have affected 40 pending civil cases nationwide and resulted in hundreds of millions of dollars in punitive damage awards. Of perhaps greater concern, however, were larger issues involving corporate social responsibility, ethical decision making by individuals within corporations, and ultimately, the proper conduct of business in the modern era.

How did Ford get into this situation? The chronology begins in early 1968 when the decision was made to battle the foreign competition in the small car market, specifically the Germans, but also the growing threat from the Japanese. This decision came after a hard-fought, two-year internal struggle between then-president Semon "Bunkie" Knudsen and Lee Iacocca, who had risen quickly within the company because of his success with the Mustang. Iacocca strongly supported fighting the competition at their own game, while Knudsen argued instead for letting them have the small car market so Ford could concentrate on the more profitable medium and large models. The final decision ultimately was in the hands of then-CEO Henry Ford II, who not only agreed with Iacocca but also promoted him to president after Knudsen's subsequent forced resignation.

Iacocca wanted the Pinto in the showrooms by the 1971 model introductions, which would require the shortest production planning period in automotive history to that time. The typical time span from conception to production of a new car was more than three and a half years; Iacocca, however, wanted to launch the Pinto in just over two years. Under normal conditions, chassis design, styling, product planning, advance engineering, component testing, and so on were all either completed or nearly completed prior to tooling of the production factories. Yet, because tooling had a fixed time frame of about 18 months, some of these other processes were done more or less concurrently. As a consequence, when it was discovered through crash testing that the Pinto's fuel tank often ruptured during a rear-end impact, it was too late (in other words, too costly) to do much about it in terms of redesign.

A closer look at the crash-test reports reveals that Ford was aware of the faulty fuel tank design. Eleven Pintos were subjected to rear-end collisions with a barrier at average speeds of 31 miles per hour to determine whether any fuel would be lost after impact. All eight of the Pintos equipped with the standard fuel tank failed. The three remaining cars, however, survived the test because special measures had been taken to prevent tank rupture or fuel leakage. These measures included a plastic baffle placed between the axle housing and the gas tank, a steel plate between the tank and the rear bumper, and a rubber lining in the gas tank.

It should be noted that these tests were done under guidelines established by Federal Motor Vehicle Safety Standard 301, which was proposed in 1968 by the National Highway Traffic Safety Administration (NHTSA), but not officially adopted until the 1977 model year. Therefore, at the time of the tests, the Pinto met the required standards. Standard 301 had been strenuously opposed by the auto industry, and specifically Ford Motor Co. In fact, the lobbying efforts were so strong that negotiations continued until 1976, despite studies showing that hundreds of thousands of cars burned every year, taking 3,000 lives annually; the adoption of the standard was projected to reduce the death rate by 40 percent. Upon approval of Standard 301 in 1977, all Pintos were provided with a rupture-proof fuel tank design.

But for the Pinto's 1971 debut, Ford decided to go with its original gas tank design despite the crash-test results. Because the typical Pinto buyer was assumed to be extremely price conscious, Iacocca set an important goal known as "the limits of 2,000": the Pinto could not cost more than $2,000 and could not weigh more than 2,000 pounds. Thus, to be competitive with foreign manufacturers, Ford felt it could not spend any money on improving the gas tank. Besides, during the late 1960s and early 1970s, American consumers demonstrated little concern for safety, so it was not considered good business sense to promote it. Iacocca echoed these sentiments when he said time and time again "Safety doesn't sell," a lesson he had learned after a failed attempt to add costly safety features to 1950s Fords.

Ford had experimented with placing the gas tank in different locations, but all alternatives reduced usable trunk space. A design similar to that of the Ford Capri was successful in many crash tests at speeds over 50 miles per hour, but Ford felt that lost trunk space would hurt sales too much. One Ford engineer, when asked about the dangerous gas tank said, "Safety isn't the issue, trunk space is. You have no idea how stiff the competition is over trunk space. Do you realize that if we put a Capri-type tank in the Pinto, you could only get one set of golf clubs in the trunk?"

The last of Ford's reasons for not making adjustments to the fuel tank design, however, was unquestionably the most controversial. After strong lobbying efforts, Ford and the auto industry in general convinced NHTSA regulators that a cost-benefit analysis would be an appropriate basis for determining the feasibility of safety design standards. Such an analysis, however, required the assignment of a value for a human life. A prior study had concluded that every time someone died in an auto accident there was an estimated "cost to society" of $200,725 (detailed in Table 2.1: What's Your Life Worth?).[27]

Having this value in hand, Ford calculated the cost of adding an $11 gas tank improvement versus the benefits of the projected 180 lives that would be saved (via an internal memo entitled "Fatalities Associated with Crash-Induced Fuel Leakage and Fires"). This is presented in Table 2.2: The Cost of Dying in a Pinto.[28] As is demonstrated, the costs outweigh the benefits by almost three times. Thus, the cost-benefit analysis indicated that no improvements to the gas tanks were warranted.

Ford decided to go ahead with normal production plans, but the Pinto's problems soon surfaced. By early 1973, Ford's recall coordinator received field reports suggesting that Pintos were susceptible to "exploding" in rear-end collisions at

Table 2.1 What's Your Life Worth?

Component	1971 Costs
Future productivity losses	
Direct	$132,300
Indirect	$41,000
Medical costs	
Hospital	$700
Other	$425
Property damage	$1,500
Insurance administration	$4,700
Legal and court	$3,000
Employer losses	$1,000
Victim's pain and suffering	$10,000
Funeral	$900
Assets (lost consumption)	$5,000
Miscellaneous accident cost	$200
Total per fatality	$200,725

The chart, from a 1971 study by the National Highway Traffic Safety Administration, is a breakdown of the estimated cost to society every time someone is killed in a car accident. The Ford Motor Company used the $200,725 total figure in its own cost-benefit analysis.

very low speeds (under 25 miles per hour). Reports continued to indicate a similar trend in subsequent years, but no recall was initiated despite the mounting evidence. At every internal review, those responsible decided not to recall the Pinto.

Prior to the Indiana accident, the most publicized case concerning the Pinto's gas tank was that of Richard Grimshaw. In 1972, Richard, then 13, was riding with a

Table 2.2 The Cost of Dying in a Pinto

Benefits

Savings: 180 burn deaths, 180 serious burn injuries, 2,100 burned vehicles

Unit Cost: $200,000 per death, $67,000 per injury, $700 per vehicle

Total Benefit: (180 × $200,000) + (180 × $67,000) + (2,100 × $700) = $49.5 million

Costs

Sales: 11 million cars, 1.5 million light trucks

Unit Cost: $11 per car, $11 per truck

Total Cost: (11,000,000 × $11) + (1,500,000 × $11) = $137.5 million

These figures are from a Ford Motor Co. internal memorandum on the benefits and costs of an $11 safety improvement (applicable to all vehicles with similar gas tank designs) that would have made the Pinto less likely to burn.

neighbor on a road near San Bernardino, California, when they were hit from the rear. The Pinto's gas tank ruptured, causing the car to burst into flames. The neighbor was burned to death in a crash that would have been survivable if there had been no fire. Richard suffered third-degree burns over 90 percent of his body and subsequently underwent more than 60 operations, with only limited success. A civil suit was settled in February 1978, when a jury awarded a judgment of over $125 million against Ford, most of which consisted of punitive damages (later reduced to $6 million by a judge who nonetheless accused Ford of "callous indifference to human life"). This judgment was based on convincing evidence that Ford chose not to spend the $11 per car to correct the faults in the Pinto gas tanks that its own crash testing had revealed.

The Pinto sold well until the media called special attention to the Pinto fuel tank story. As a consequence, in June 1978, in the face of pressure from the media, the government, pending court cases, and the potential loss of future sales, Ford ordered a complete recall of all 1.5 million Pintos built between 1970 and 1976. During the 1980 Indiana trial that resulted from the fatal accident of 1978, differing views continued to be expressed about the Pinto fires case. Ford representatives argued that companies must make cost-benefit decisions all the time. They claimed that it is an essential part of business, and even though everyone knows that some people will die in auto accidents, buyers want costs held down; therefore, people implicitly accept risks when buying cars.

In a scathing article accusing Ford of criminally mismanaging the Pinto problem, investigative reporter Mark Dowie framed the case in a different and rather more sensational way, with this often-quoted speculation: "One wonders how long the Ford Motor Company would continue to market lethal cars were Henry Ford II and Lee Iacocca serving twenty-year terms in Leavenworth for consumer homicide."[29]

Case Questions

1. Put yourself in the role of the recall coordinator for Ford Motor Co. It is 1973, and field reports have been coming in about rear-end collisions, fires, and fatalities. You must decide whether to recall the automobile.

    a. Identify the relevant facts.

    b. Identify the pertinent ethical issues and points of ethical conflict.

    c. Identify the relevant affected parties.

    d. Identify the possible consequences of alternative courses of action.

    e. Identify relevant obligations.

    f. Identify your relevant community standards that should guide you as a person of integrity.

    g. Check your gut.

    What will you decide?

SHORT CASES

As a counselor in an outplacement firm, you've been working with Irwin for six months to find him a new position. During that time, he has completed extensive assessment work to determine whether he's in an appropriate profession or if he might benefit from a career change. The results of the assessment indicate that Irwin has low self-esteem, probably could benefit from psychotherapy, and is most likely ill suited for his current profession. Irwin has been actively interviewing for a position that's very similar to two others he has held and lost. He desperately wants and needs this job. The company where he's interviewing happens to be one of your most important clients. You receive a call from the head of human resources at the company, who tells you that Irwin suggested she call you for information about his abilities, interests, and personality style as measured by the assessment process. She also asks you for a reference for Irwin. Since he has, in effect, asked that you share information with this woman, is it okay for you to give her an honest assessment of Irwin? What are your obligations to Irwin, who is your client in this case? Is there a way for you to be honest, yet not hurt Irwin's chances to obtain this job? Or is that important? What will you do?

You have worked in business for several years and you're now ready for some further education. You have applied to multiple prestigious MBA programs via a website called ApplyYourself.com that handles the application process for many of these programs. You're anxiously awaiting replies and expect to receive them in about a month. You're up late one night and, while surfing the Web, you discover instructions for a "back door" way to take advantage of a technical glitch on the website that would allow you to check the status of your application and find out if you've been accepted or rejected. Multiple steps are involved, but the instructions provide clear guidance. Would it be right to take advantage of this information? Why or why not? If you were the admissions director or dean of one of these schools and you learned that some applicants had taken advantage of the glitch, what would be the right thing to do?

NOTES

1. J. Rachels, *The Elements of Moral Philosophy* (New York: McGraw-Hill, 1983).
2. L. Peach, "An Introduction to Ethical Theory," in *Research Ethics: Cases and Materials*, ed. R. L. Penslar (Bloomington: Indiana University Press, 1994).
3. D. J. Fritsche and H. Becke, "Linking Management Behavior to Ethical Philosophy: An Empirical Investigation," *Academy of Management Journal* 27 (1984): 166–75.
4. J. Rawls, *A Theory of Justice* (Cambridge, MA: Harvard University Press, 1971).
5. J. Rachels, *The Elements of Moral Philosophy* (New York: McGraw-Hill, 1983).
6. E. Bazelon, "Sentencing by the Numbers," *New York Times Magazine*, January 2, 2005, 18.
7. Ibid.
8. R. C. Solomon, *Ethics and Excellence* (New York: Oxford University Press, 1988).
9. G. R. Weaver, "Virtue in Organizations: Moral Identity as a Foundation for Moral Agency," *Organization Studies* 17 (2006): 341–68.
10. "Saying It Again: Psychologists May Never Participate in Torture," American Psychological Association (APA) Press Release, April 22, 2009.

11. "26-Year Secret," CBS News.com (June 16, 2009), at www.cbsnews.com.
12. R. Khurana, *From Higher Aims to Hired Hands* (Cambridge, MA: Princeton University Press, 2007).
13. R. Khurana and N. Nohria, "It's Time to Make Management a True Profession," *Harvard Business Review* 86, no. 10 (2008): 1–8.
14. "Bloodied and Bowed," *Businessweek*, January 20, 2003, 56–57.
15. G. R. Weaver, "Virtue in Organizations: Moral Identity as a Foundation for Moral Agency," *Organization Studies* 17 (2006): 341–68.
16. M. Bebeau, "Developing a Well-Reasoned Moral Response to a Moral Problem in Scientific Research Ethics," Paper distributed at the Teaching Research Ethics conference, Poynter Research Center for the Study of Ethics and American Institutions at Indiana University, Bloomington, Indiana, May 1994.
17. L. Nash, "Ethics without the Sermon," in *Ethics in Practice*, ed. K. R. Andres (Boston: Harvard Business School Press, 1989).
18. D. E. Larson, *Mayo Clinic Family Health Book* (New York: William Morrow, 1990).
19. L. Nash, "Ethics without the Sermon," in *Ethics in Practice*, ed. K. R. Andres (Boston: Harvard Business School Press, 1989).
20. S. G. Stolberg, "Their Devil's Advocates: Thalidomide Returns with an Unlikely Ally: A Group of Its Original Victims." *New York Times Magazine*, January 25, 1998, 20–25.
21. D. M. Messick and B. Bazerman, *Ethics for the 21st Century: A Decision Making Perspective. MIT Sloan Management Review* 37, no. 2 (1996): 9–22.
22. B. Steiger, *Indian Medicine Power* (Atglen, PA: Whitford Press, 1984), 92.
23. C. Skooglund, "Ethics in the Face of Competitive Pressures," *Business Ethics Resource* (Fall 1992): 4.
24. B. Steiger, *Indian Medicine Power* (Atglen, PA: Whitford Press, 1984), 92.
25. R. Khurana and N. Nohria, "It's Time to Make Management a True Profession," *Harvard Business Review* 86, no. 10 (2008): 1–8.
26. J. Useem, K. Bonamici, N. D. Schwartz, and C. Murphy, "20 That Made History," *Fortune*, June 27, 2005, 58 (14 pages).
27. M. Dowie, "How Ford Put Two Million Fire Traps on Wheels," *Business and Society Review* 23 (1977): 51–55.
28. Ibid.
29. Ibid.

CHAPTER 3

DECIDING WHAT'S RIGHT: A PSYCHOLOGICAL APPROACH

C hapter 2 introduced prescriptive ethical theories, developed by philosophers, which are designed to help individuals decide what they *should* do in response to ethical dilemmas. But psychology teaches us that people often don't even recognize the ethical dimensions of the situation at hand. And, when they do, they often don't think about it in expected ways. So, this chapter is designed to help you understand how people *actually* think and what people *actually* do by introducing the psychological factors—the individual differences and mental processes that influence how people think and behave. It also explains some factors that can keep well-intentioned people from making good ethical decisions and suggests some ways to overcome them. Finally, this chapter introduces relevant new neuroscience research and research on the role of emotions in ethical decision making.

ETHICAL AWARENESS AND ETHICAL JUDGMENT

If a decision maker is to engage in ethical judgment processes (like those discussed in Chapter 2) that will eventually lead to ethical action, she or he must first recognize the ethical nature of the situation at hand.

Ethical Awareness → Ethical Judgment → Ethical Action

We refer to this initial step in the ethical decision-making process as ethical awareness. With ethical awareness, a person recognizes that a situation or issue is one that raises ethical concerns and must be thought about in ethical terms. It is an important step that shouldn't be taken for granted. Sometimes people are simply unaware that they are facing an issue with ethical overtones. And, if they don't recognize and label the issue as an ethical one, ethical judgment processes (like those we studied in Chapter 2) will not be engaged. In fascinating new research, parts of the brain that are associated with recognizing the ethical nature of an issue were differentiated from those involved in other kinds of thinking. Researchers used functional magnetic resonance imaging (fMRI) in a study showing that when Executive MBA students identified "an important point or issue" in scenarios, a different part of the brain was more active when the issue had ethical overtones compared to more neutral issues.[1] In a different study, a part of the brain associated with emotional processing was activated when participants viewed morally relevant pictures compared to more neutral ones.[2] So, it seems that something different happens in our brains when we begin thinking about an issue we recognize as having ethical overtones.

Consider the following ethical awareness example. Students are doing online research for classroom assignments. The technology makes it easy to find up-to-date information, download it, and cut and paste it right into a paper that then gets submitted to a professor for a grade. Perhaps you have done this without thinking too much about it. However, in this process, students often overlook the fact that they may be plagiarizing—"stealing" someone else's intellectual property. Intellectual property is protected by copyright and patent laws in the United States. These laws are important because there would simply be no incentive to write a book, publish a magazine, or develop a new product if anyone could simply reproduce it freely without any attention to the rights of the person or company that invested time and resources to create it. The education community has adopted academic integrity rules that guide how students can fairly use intellectual property. In keeping with those rules, students are expected to paraphrase and then carefully reference all sources of information. When you're quoting someone else's words, these words must be put in quotation marks, and the exact citation to the source must be provided. In the pre-Internet days, this kind of research meant physically going to the library, searching the shelves for information, copying pertinent information by hand, making careful notes about the sources, and then organizing the information into a paper that had to be typed from scratch. Plagiarism actually required conscious effort in those days. Now, information is so accessible and it's so easy to simply cut and paste that it can be harder to recognize the ethical issues involved. But if your college has an academic integrity policy or honor code, and your professor takes the time to explain the importance of academic integrity, the role of intellectual property in our society, the definition of plagiarism, and your responsibilities as a member of the higher education community, you should be more aware of the ethical issues involved. Under those circumstances, when you're tempted to just cut and paste, you'll be more likely to think about the ethical dimensions of your actions—the rights of the intellectual property owner, and whether your actions would be considered plagiarism by your professor and others in your academic community.

Now for a work-related example.

> You've just started a new job in the financial services industry. One afternoon, your manager tells you that he has to leave early to attend his son's softball game, and he asks you to be on the lookout for an important check that his boss wants signed before the end of the day. He tells you to do him a favor—simply sign his name and forward the check to his boss.

To a naive employee, this may seem like a straightforward and easily accommodated request. But if the company trained you well, you would immediately be aware of the ethical nature of the situation. Your manager has asked you to engage in forgery, a serious ethical lapse, especially in the financial services industry where the validity of signatures is essential to system functioning and trust. Recognizing the ethical nature of the situation would likely lead to some very different thinking about how to respond.

Research has found that people are more likely to be ethically aware, to recognize the ethical nature of an issue or decision, if three things happen: (1) if they believe that their peers will consider it to be ethically problematic; (2) if ethical language is used to present the situation to the decision maker; and (3) if the decision is seen as having the potential to produce serious harm to others.[3]

Let's take these factors one at a time. First, as we'll see later, most people look to others in their social environment for guidance in ethical dilemma situations. So, if you believe that your coworkers and others around you are likely to see a decision as ethically problematic, it probably means that the issue has been discussed, perhaps in a company-sponsored ethics training program or informally among coworkers or with your manager. Such discussions prime you to think about situations in a particular way. When a similar situation arises, it triggers memories of the previous ethics-related discussion, and you are more likely to categorize and think about the situation in ethical terms.[4] Using the forgery example, perhaps a company training program provided instruction on the importance of signatures in the financial industry and labeled signing for someone else as forgery. Perhaps the company even presented a similar problem to trainees and you all agreed that signing someone else's name to the check would be wrong. Having participated in such a discussion, you would recognize that signing the check would be ethically problematic and you would be more likely to see your boss's request as an ethical problem.

Second, situations can be represented or "framed" in different ways—using ethical language or more neutral language. Using ethical language (positive words like *integrity*, *honesty*, *fairness*, and *propriety*, or negative words such as *lying*, *cheating*, and *stealing*) will trigger ethical thinking because these terms are attached to existing cognitive categories that have ethical content. For example, if the manager in the example above had asked you to forge the check for him, the word *forge* would be more likely to trigger legal or ethics-related concerns than if he simply asked you to sign the check (more neutral language). In response to the term *forgery*, you would more likely wonder if signing the check was ethically wrong, if anyone was being hurt, and what the consequences would be if you did or didn't do it. The term *plagiarism* would likely trigger similar thinking.

Think about the power of the word *genocide*. If you've seen the film *Hotel Rwanda*, you know about the horrible killing in 1994 of some 800,000 Tutsi men, women, and children by Hutu extremists while the rest of the world, including the United States, did nothing to help. According to President Clinton's national security advisor, the administration refused to allow use of the word *genocide* for six weeks because "if you used the word, then you're required to take action."[5] Former President Clinton has said that failing to help in Rwanda is one of his "greatest regrets."[6]

Avoidance of the morally powerful term *genocide* likely contributed to the administration's inaction and the public's lack of support.

Neutral language can be used to make an unethical action seem less problematic. The use of *euphemistic language* can easily keep individuals from thinking about the ethical implications of a decision or action. With euphemistic language, we name or label actions in ways that minimize their ethical overtones. For example, troubled assets don't seem nearly as problematic as "toxic" assets. And the term *no-doc loans* (used to describe new high-risk loans that were made to mortgage customers who were not required to provide documentary evidence of their job security or income) raises ethical antennae much less than does the term *liars' loans*. The latter term (actually used by some in the mortgage industry before the meltdown) acknowledges that borrowers were lying about their incomes on their loan applications. The use of euphemistic language may not be intentionally unethical, but it certainly has the effect of allowing us to feel okay about what we're doing when perhaps we should be thinking much harder about the ethical overtones.

Here is a great business example of euphemistic language. In 2006, Hewlett-Packard's (HP) then chairwoman of the board of directors, Patricia Dunn, was upset about boardroom leaks to the press about HP's strategy. In an attempt to learn the leaker's identity, the company hired investigators who were allowed to misrepresent their identities to the phone company (they lied) in order to obtain cell phone records of board members and a journalist; they referred to this behavior as "pretexting." When the press learned about it, they (perhaps more properly) used ethically charged language to label the behavior as spying, and a high-profile scandal ensued. Dunn was replaced, along with two other board members and the executive heading the company ethics program (who knew about the investigation). The CEO testified in congressional hearings, and HP (a company that had long claimed privacy as a core value) had to scurry to try to overcome the company's association with spying, lying, and invasion of privacy.[7] If someone involved in approving this investigation had labeled the behavior using ethical language (lying, spying, invasion of privacy) instead of the more neutral-sounding pretexting, red flags would more likely have gone up to stop the investigators' behavior.

Finally, and perhaps most important, an issue or situation that has the potential to produce serious harm to others is more likely to be seen as an ethical issue. If HP executives could have imagined the potential damage to board members or the journalist, or the resulting scandal and implications for the company's reputation, they would have been more likely to raise ethical concerns. In the forgery example, if you see that forging the check could result in serious harm to customers, you would more likely see it as a serious issue than if no one would be harmed. Thomas Jones proposed that individuals are more likely to recognize the ethical nature of issues that are *morally intense*.[8] The moral intensity of an issue is higher when the consequences for others are potentially large, the consequences are relatively immediate and likely to occur, and the potential victims are psychologically or physically close to the decision maker. For example, a decision to allow toxic chemicals to leak into the local water supply is very likely to harm many people in one's own community. Such a decision is "morally intense," and therefore the decision maker is more likely to see it as an ethical issue. In contrast, a decision that might require laying off a few individuals in a foreign subsidiary would be less likely to trigger ethical awareness. Only a few people will be affected, the consequences will occur in the future, and these individuals are both psychologically and physically distant from the decision maker.

So, managers can encourage employees to be ethically aware by providing training and by talking with employees about the types of ethical issues they're likely to face and why these issues are ethically problematic. They can also encourage employees to have these discussions themselves, to use ethical language in such interactions, and to think about the consequences of their actions and take responsibility for the consequences of the decisions they make.

On the other hand, all of us should be on the lookout for situations that are likely to reduce our chances of seeing the ethical overtones in a situation. For example, downloading music from the Internet may seem benign if one doesn't recognize that the American economy loses an estimated $12.5 billion dollars a year from it. That includes jobs and tax revenues that are lost because of what the industry has termed "music piracy."[9] Investment bankers who pay for mutual fund managers to go to the Super Bowl and lavishly entertain clients are not likely to think that they are engaged in "bribery" or that their behavior is anything more than what "every one else does." Never mind that the average investor is likely disadvantaged by the wining and dining. If we think about issues in ethical terms, the ethical judgment processes we discuss next are more likely to be triggered.

INDIVIDUAL DIFFERENCES, ETHICAL JUDGMENT, AND ETHICAL BEHAVIOR

Once people are aware of the ethical dimensions of a situation or decision, they engage in ethical judgment processes that can contribute to ethical (or unethical) conduct. By ethical judgment, we mean making a decision about what is the right thing to do. As with ethical awareness, neuroscience (fMRI) research is finding that certain parts of the brain are activated more during ethical decision making compared to when the same individuals are making other kinds of decisions.[10] These findings suggest that ethical judgment is truly a unique form of decision making.

The next part of this chapter focuses on individual differences that influence ethical judgment and action. Much of this book will focus on situational pushes and pulls. For example, people follow leaders or their peers. They tend to do what's rewarded. Yet, despite these powerful pushes and pulls, people do bring something of their unique selves to situations. Heroes emerge when you least expect it. People blow the whistle despite fear of retaliation. Others embezzle funds or lie to customers despite all of management's efforts to support good conduct. One way to explain these ethical and unethical behaviors is to focus on characteristics of individuals that differentiate one person from another, making one person more predisposed to think and behave ethically while another is predisposed to think and behave unethically.

Research has uncovered a number of individual differences that influence the way people think and behave in response to ethical dilemma situations. In this section, we discuss several of these differences and how they influence ethical judgment and/or ethical action. They're illustrated below:

Individual Differences
Ethical decision-making style
Cognitive moral development
Locus of control
Machiavellianism
Moral disengagement

Ethical Awareness → Ethical Judgment → Ethical Action

Ethical Decision-Making Style

In Chapter 2, we introduced different frameworks for making ethical decisions and advised that individual decision makers should use these in combination if they wish to make the best decisions. But research suggests that individuals have preferences for particular prescriptive ethical theories. Forsyth proposed that we think about these individual preferences in terms of two factors: (1) *idealism* or the person's concern for the welfare of others; and (2) *relativism* or the person's emphasis on ethical principles being dependent on the situation rather than being applicable to all situations.[11] Idealism is related to what we referred to as thinking about consequences in Chapter 2. For example, individuals who are keen on idealism believe that one should always avoid harming other people in ethical dilemma situations, while non-idealists believe that "it depends" because "harm is sometimes . . . necessary to produce good."[12] Relativism is more related to deontological theories and our focus on principles in Chapter 2.

For example, individuals who are low on relativism believe that all situations are subject to universal ethical principles (such as honesty). On the other hand, individuals who value relativism believe that people should weigh the particular circumstances in a situation when making decisions, because there are no universal ethical principles that determine right action in every situation. Research suggests that those who focus on idealism are more likely to have ethical intentions and to be critical of unethical behavior.[13] This is probably because idealists are more concerned about anything they might do that would harm others.[14] By contrast, high relativism has been found to be associated with unethical intentions, perhaps because relativists who do not follow clear ethical principles find it easier to rationalize unethical behavior.[15]

You can discover your own style by taking a survey that your professor may make available to you. The relationship between ethical decision style and ethical action has not yet been tested, but it seems logical that the way an individual thinks about a situation and that person's ethical or unethical intentions will influence the action he or she takes. As we did in Chapter 2, we continue to strongly recommend systematically considering ethical dilemma situations from multiple perspectives. Still, it can be useful to understand that you (or the people who work with you or for you) likely have a preference for one approach over another. If so, you may be able to improve your own ethical decision making by forcing yourself to consciously consider all angles. You may also be able to influence ethical decision making in discussions with others by pointing them to these alternative perspectives.

Cognitive Moral Development

One important explanation for both ethical judgment *and* action based on individual characteristics comes from the moral reasoning research of Lawrence Kohlberg.[16] When people respond to ethical dilemma situations, they must, among other things, decide what course of action is ethically right (as we discussed in Chapter 2), and they must choose the ethically right path over others.[17] In other words, if they decide that blowing the whistle is the ethically right path, they must follow through and do it (take the ethical action).

Kohlberg's moral reasoning theory is a cognitive developmental theory that focuses primarily on how people think about and decide what course of action is ethically right. His research began by following 58 American boys ranging in age from 10 to 16 years old. He interviewed them regularly, asking for their open-ended responses to hypothetical moral dilemmas. Their responses were analyzed, and the findings contributed to our understanding of how moral reasoning in human beings gradually develops over time through brain development and life experience.

Kohlberg's cognitive moral development theory proposes that moral reasoning develops sequentially through three broad levels, each composed of two stages. As individuals move forward through the sequence of stages, they are cognitively capable of comprehending all reasoning at stages below their own, but they cannot comprehend reasoning more than one stage above their own. Development through the stages results from the cognitive disequilibrium that occurs when an individual perceives a contradiction between his or her own reasoning level and the next higher one. This kind of development can occur through training, but it generally occurs through interaction with peers and life situations that challenge the individual's current way of thinking. You can think of those conversations parents sometimes have with children at the dinner table as attempts to challenge the child's thinking and influence moral reasoning and moral development. According to Kohlberg, the actual decision an individual makes isn't as important as the reasoning process used to arrive at it. However, he argued—and this is an important concept—that the higher the reasoning stage, the more ethical the decision, because the higher stages are more consistent with prescriptive ethical principles of justice and rights (like those discussed in the deontological approach in Chapter 2).

Kohlberg's theory has been successfully applied to studies of adults in business settings.[18] For example, James Weber interviewed business managers about their responses to the following hypothetical dilemma:

> Evelyn worked for an automotive steel casting company. She was part of a small group asked to investigate the cause of an operating problem that had developed in the wheel castings of a new luxury automobile and to make recommendations for its improvement. The problem did not directly create an unsafe condition, but it did lead to irritating sounds. The vice-president of engineering told the group that he was certain that the problem was due to tensile stress in the castings. Evelyn and a lab technician conducted tests and found conclusive evidence that the problem was not tensile stress. As Evelyn began work on other possible explanations of the problem, she was told that the problem had been solved. A report prepared by Evelyn's boss strongly supported the tensile stress hypothesis. All of the data points from Evelyn's experiments had been changed to fit the curves, and some of the points that were far from where the theory would predict had been omitted. The report "proved" that tensile stress was responsible for the problem.[19]

A number of questions were presented to the interviewees. For example, they were asked whether Evelyn should contradict her boss's report and why. We will use this hypothetical dilemma to understand the theory and how responses to the above question (along with others) help identify an individual's placement in Kohlberg's moral reasoning stage framework. Table 3.1 outlines the levels and stages involved.

LEVEL I: PRECONVENTIONAL   A level I individual (labeled the preconventional level and including stages 1 and 2) is very self-centered and views ethical rules as imposed from outside the self. Unfortunately, a small percentage of adults never advance beyond this stage, and managers must be ready for that possibility. As you read the following descriptions, see if you know anyone who thinks this way.

Stage 1 individuals are limited to thinking about obedience to authority for its own sake. Avoiding punishment by authority figures is the key consideration. It's easy to imagine a child thinking, "I should share my toy because, if I don't, Mom will yell at me" (i.e., I'll be punished). A stage 1 response to the Evelyn situation might argue that it would be wrong to contradict her boss because she must obey her superiors, and she would certainly be punished if she disobeyed.

At stage 2, concern for personal reward and satisfaction become considerations in addition to a kind of market reciprocity. What is right is judged in terms of a "you scratch my back, I'll scratch yours" reciprocal relationship. A stage 2 child might think, "If I share my toy with my brother, he might share his with me later." A stage 2 response in the Evelyn situation might argue that Evelyn should support her boss because he is responsible for her performance appraisals; and, if she lets this one go, he

Table 3.1 Levels of Cognitive Moral Development According to Kohlberg

Stage	What Is Considered to Be Right
Level I: Preconventional	
Stage 1: Obedience and Punishment Orientation	Obedience to authority for its own sake. Sticking to rules to avoid punishment.
Stage 2: Instrumental Purpose and Exchange	Following rules only when it is in one's immediate interest. Right is an equal exchange, getting a good deal.
Level II: Conventional	
Stage 3: Interpersonal Accord, Conformity, Mutual Expectations	Stereotypical "good" behavior. Living up to what is expected by peers and people close to you.
Stage 4: Social Accord and System Maintenance	Fulfilling duties and obligations of the social system. Upholding laws and rules except in extreme cases where they conflict with social duties.
Level III: Postconventional or Principled	
Stage 5: Social Contract and Individual Rights	Upholding rules because they are the social contract if they are consistent with values such as fairness and rights and the greater good (not because of the majority opinion).
Stage 6: Universal Ethical Principles	Following ethical principles of justice and rights. Acting in accord with principles when laws violate principles.

Source: Adapted from L. Kohlberg, "Moral Stages and Moralization: The Cognitive-Developmental Approach," in *Moral Development and Behavior: Theory, Research, and Social Issues*, ed. T. Lickona (New York: Holt, Rinehart and Winston), 34–35.

might overlook some of her problems from the past. Also, if her boss has been kind or helpful to her in the past, she may consider her obligation to repay the favor.

In general, a level I person can be expected to consider questions like "What's in it for me?" At stage 1, the questions might be "Can I get away with it?" or "Will I get caught, punished?" At stage 2, the questions might be "How will I benefit or what will I get in return if I do this?"

LEVEL II: CONVENTIONAL At level II (labeled the conventional level and including stages 3 and 4), the individual is still externally focused on others but is less self-centered and has internalized the shared moral norms of society or some segment like a family or work group. What's ethically right is explained in terms of living up to roles and the expectations of relevant others, fulfilling duties and obligations, and following rules and laws.

At stage 3, what's right is thought to be that which pleases or helps others or is approved by those close to you. Interpersonal trust and social approval are important. For example, a stage 3 response to the Evelyn dilemma might say that Evelyn shouldn't contradict her boss because he would perceive her as disloyal, and she might lose the social approval and trust of her boss and peers. On the other hand, what if Evelyn shares her dilemma with close family members whose opinions are important to her, and they feel strongly that she must contradict her boss? In this case, she would likely reason that she should contradict her boss because the people she trusts and whose approval she values say that it's the right thing to do.

At stage 4, the perspective broadens to consider society. The individual is concerned about fulfilling agreed-upon duties and following rules or laws that are designed to promote the common good. A stage 4 person recognizes that rules and laws often exist for good reason, and she follows them because the social system works better when everyone does that. Therefore, a stage 4 response might say that Evelyn should contradict her boss because of her duty to society. What if the noises do represent a safety problem? She has a responsibility as a good member of society to report it. She would feel particularly strongly about this if she were aware of product safety laws that required her to report the problem.

So, a level II person is looking outside the self for guidance when deciding what to do. A stage 3 person would likely ask, "What would my peers do?" or "What would my trusted supervisor advise?" At stage 4, the considerations would be broader, such as "What do the rules or laws prescribe?" Kohlberg's research placed most American adults at this conventional level, and Weber's research found that most managers' responses to the Evelyn dilemma were at the conventional level as well.

LEVEL III: POSTCONVENTIONAL A level III (postconventional, sometimes called principled reasoning—stages 5 and 6) principled individual has developed beyond identification with others' expectations, rules, and laws to make decisions more autonomously. Such an individual looks to ethical principles of justice and rights (similar to the deontological principles we discussed in Chapter 2). Note that stage 6 is thought to be a theoretical stage only, so we focus below only on stage 5.

At stage 5, the emphasis is still on rules and laws because these represent the recognized social contract, but stage 5 thinkers are willing to question the law and to consider changing the law for socially useful purposes. A stage 5 individual would take into account moral laws above society's laws, such as considering what decision would create the greatest societal good. A stage 5 Evelyn might reason that she should contradict her boss because doing so would be consistent with the ethical principle of the greatest societal good, particularly if she considered the safety of the automobiles to be a potential problem. Her responsibility goes beyond that of a good law-abiding member of society and certainly beyond doing what her boss thinks is right. A stage 5 Evelyn is also responsible to principles of justice and rights. So, even if no law requires her to report what she knows, a stage 5 Evelyn would consider the automobile consumers' rights to safety as an important reason for her to tell. When deciding what to do, a stage 5 person would likely ask, "What does the law say?" and then "Is the law consistent with principles of justice and rights? and "What's best for society?"

Students sometimes get confused by this idea of what it means to be principled according to Kohlberg. We're often asked questions such as, weren't the 9/11 hijackers principled? Although a definitive answer would require probing interviews with the hijackers to determine the reasoning for their behavior (not possible now), the answer is that their thinking likely represented lower-level reasoning (e.g., the leader told me to do it; I did it to receive a reward in heaven, etc.). So, it's important to note that Kohlberg is quite precise about the kinds of principles that qualify as principled thinking. Broadly defined, level III principles are principles of justice and rights similar to the principles introduced in Chapter 2 under deontological theories. Wrongdoers often appeal to what they call principles, such as when the members of a violent Mexican drug cartel claimed to train its members in ethical principles. But the purpose of these principles (e.g., sobriety) was to keep members in line and obedient to cartel authorities. The ethical trainer in this case is accused of ordering murders and running prostitution rings with young girls; such behavior is not supported by principles of justice and rights.[20]

Finally, the principle "I always do what my religion tells me to do because the deity will punish me if I don't" would not qualify as principled thinking. In Kohlberg's model, this type of thinking actually represents a low level of cognitive moral development because it is based on unquestioning obedience and fear of punishment. Often religious prescriptions such as the golden rule are consistent with theories of justice and rights. To be considered a principled decision maker, an individual would have to be capable of thinking through the ethical situation on his or her own (reasoning according to principles of justice and rights), and not just blindly follow a particular religious authority.

So don't be confused just because someone uses the term *principled*. To be principled in terms of cognitive moral development theory, one must have arrived at the decision autonomously based on principles of justice, rights, and the greater good.

To understand Kohlberg's theory, you must also remember that it is a cognitive theory. What matters are the reasoning processes and considerations involved in a decision. Although these considerations are likely to affect the decision made, it is the reasoning process that counts.

The cognitive moral development exercise at the end of the chapter will test your understanding of cognitive moral development. You may want to try it now.

ARE WOMEN AND MEN DIFFERENT?   In 1982, the psychologist Carol Gilligan published *In a Different Voice*, a book about women's cognitive moral development. Gilligan claimed that Kohlberg's theory was flawed because he had studied only boys. Her research led Gilligan to question the almost exclusive focus on justice in Kohlberg's higher moral reasoning stages. She argued that females were more likely to use a "morality of care" that emphasized relationships—raising issues related to caring for others, responsibility to others, and the continuity of interdependent relationships.[21]

Gilligan's claims received a great deal of attention, but the applicability of her ideas to adults working in business organizations is quite limited. Gilligan's own research comparing the moral reasoning of male and female medical students found no significant difference between the genders, suggesting that both men and women are strongly influenced by the powerful socialization and cultural norms of medical practice.[22] Similarly, an interview study of business managers based on Gilligan's theory found no gender differences.[23] All but one of the managers (male and female) who described a moral conflict at work based their moral reasoning on rights, not care. Finally, many cognitive moral development studies based on Kohlberg's theory have found only small, if any, gender differences. Interestingly, when differences have been found, females generally have scored higher than men in justice-based reasoning.[24] Business ethics researchers now advise that additional research on the question of gender differences is likely unnecessary.[25]

We can now begin to address the second requirement for ethical behavior: doing what's right, or ethical action. Recall that to behave ethically, people must first decide what course of action is ethically right, probably depending to a large degree on their ethical awareness and ethical judgment (stage of cognitive moral development). Then they must choose the ethically right path over others.

LOOKING UP AND LOOKING AROUND   One reason understanding cognitive moral development is so important is that most adults are at the conventional level of cognitive moral development (level II). This means they're highly susceptible to external influences on their judgment about what is ethically right and their subsequent action. Their decision about what's ethically right, and therefore their likely action, is inextricably linked with what others think, say, and do. We call this "looking up and looking around" for ethical guidance.[26]

These individuals aren't autonomous decision makers who strictly follow an internal moral compass. They look up and around to see what their superiors and their peers are doing and saying, and they use these cues as a guide to action. Therefore most people are likely to do what's expected of them as a result of the reward system, role expectations, authority figure demands, and group norms. That's why the remainder of this book focuses so heavily on these external influences on ethical action and why it's so important that managers structure the work environment to support ethical conduct and lead followers in the right direction. The large majority of employees will be looking for guidance, and they'll do what's right if guided and supported along those lines by managers and peers.

AUTONOMOUS PRINCIPLED THINKING AND ACTION   Higher-stage thinking is more independent of these external influences. The postconventional principled thinker looks to justice and rights-based principles to guide ethical decision making. Research has demonstrated that these individuals are also more likely to behave consistently with their principle-based decisions—they're more likely to carry through and do what they think is right. More principled individuals also have been found to be less likely to cheat, more likely to resist pressure from authority figures, more likely to help someone in need, and more likely to blow the whistle on misconduct.[27] So the theory suggests that whistle-blowers such as Sherron Watkins, who tried to convince

Kenneth Lay (Enron's CEO) to address the company's financial shenanigans before it was too late, are likely principled thinkers. But it's important for managers to remember that level III individuals are in the minority in most organizations. Autonomous decision making based on principles of justice and rights is the exception rather than the rule.

Also keep in mind that cognitive moral development represents a cognitive "capacity" to reason about ethical dilemmas at a particular level, and that it is possible to act below one's capacity. However, cognitive moral development theory argues that this inconsistency would be difficult to sustain over time because of the cognitive strain that would come from thinking at one level and acting at another.[28] Such a person might think, "I know this is wrong—why am I doing it?" So a principled-level individual who found himself or herself in a situation that required unethical action would be more likely to try to change that situation or leave.

The bottom line for managers is this: Cognitive moral development theory and research tell us that most of the people you manage are going to be strongly influenced by what you do, say, and reward. They can be thought of as "good soldiers" who are looking up and looking around for guidance from you and their peers, and they're likely to mimic what they see around them. Therefore, it's the manager's responsibility to structure the work environment in a way that supports ethical conduct. If you avoid this responsibility, these people will look elsewhere for guidance, probably to their peers, and the guidance they receive may not support ethical conduct at all.

A small percentage of individuals may never advance beyond preconventional thinking. Such individuals can be thought of as "loose cannons." They will do whatever they can get away with. People like this require close supervision and clear discipline when they get out of line.

Those individuals who have reached principled levels of moral reasoning should be singled out to lead key decision-making groups, to manage situations where ethical ambiguities are likely to arise, and to lead organizations. Research on ethical decision making in groups has found that when less-principled individuals lead a group, the group's ethical decision-making performance decreases. On the other hand, groups with leaders higher in moral reasoning either improve or stay the same.[29] Also, when an organization's leader is high in cognitive moral development, the entire ethical climate of the organization is stronger. This is particularly true for leaders whose choices are consistent with their ethical reasoning capacity and for leaders who run young organizations that are more open to their influence. Finally, when employees and the organization's leader are similar in their level of cognitive moral development, the employees are more satisfied and more committed to the organization. Employee satisfaction and commitment are especially negative when the leader's cognitive moral development is lower than the moral development of employees.[30]

Cognitive moral development can be assessed by using instruments designed by cognitive moral development researchers. Moral reasoning can also be increased through training. Over the years, Kohlberg and his students and colleagues have designed training approaches based on cognitive moral development theory. In this type of training, facilitators give participants hypothetical ethical dilemmas for discussion. The facilitator promotes movement through ethical reasoning stages by challenging participants' thinking and by exposing individuals to reasoning higher than their own. This approach creates cognitive conflict, leading the participant to question and eventually revise his or her own reasoning upward. Research has supported the effectiveness of this type of training with adults in dental, medical, and business schools.[31] Managers may want to consider incorporating these ideas into their firms' ethics training.

Locus of Control

Another individual characteristic that has been found to influence ethical action is locus of control.[32] *Locus of control* refers to an individual's perception of how much control he or she exerts over life events. Locus of control can be thought of as a single continuum from a high internal locus of control to a high external locus of control. An individual with a high internal locus of control believes that outcomes are primarily the result of his or her own efforts, whereas an individual with a high external locus of control believes that life events are determined primarily by fate, luck, or powerful others.

External Locus of Control ◄————————► Internal Locus of Control

Locus of control develops over a long period of time through interactions with other people and the social environment. At any particular time, however, locus of control can be thought of as a stable individual characteristic that differentiates people from each other. Some individuals are more internal and others are more external in their locus of control. In that way, locus of control is similar to a personality trait that characterizes a person's thinking and action across situations. It does not shift from one situation to another. Therefore it's not appropriate to say, "My locus of control was external in this situation because my boss made me fudge the numbers." What has shifted in this situation is the control exerted by the boss, not the employee's locus of control.

An employee with an internal locus of control who has a controlling boss will be uncomfortable with the boss's request to do something inappropriate. So, due to that high internal locus of control, this employee will be more likely to resist the boss's influence and more likely to look for an opportunity to leave and find a more compatible boss and work situation. An employee with an external locus of control is more likely to see his or her fate in the boss' hands and simply do what the boss asks. You can test your own locus of control through a survey measure that your professor may make available to you.

A caveat: although locus of control does not shift easily, it can change over time due to strong life interventions or compelling situations. For example, if someone with a very high internal locus of control became a prisoner of war with little chance of escape, he or she would likely develop a more external locus of control over time.

RELATIONSHIP TO ETHICAL JUDGMENT AND ACTION   How is locus of control related to ethical judgment and action? It likely has a lot to do with taking responsibility for one's behavior. First, in their judgment, individuals with a high internal locus of control see the relationship between their behavior and its outcomes more clearly than do those with an external locus of control. Internals see themselves as being in control of things that happen in their lives. Thus they're more likely to take responsibility for the consequences of their actions. It would be more difficult for such an individual to say, "Well, it's not my responsibility; I just work here," or "I'm just following orders." If an individual takes personal responsibility for his or her behavior, it seems likely that person will also behave more ethically. For example, studies have found that internals are more likely to help another person, even if there's a penalty for doing so.[33]

Internals see themselves as being in charge of their own fates. Therefore, they should also be less willing to be pressured by others to do things they believe to be wrong. One interesting study asked subjects to complete a story in which the main character was pressured to violate a social norm.[34] The more internal the subject's locus of control, the more likely the story completion had the hero resisting the pressure. In an obedience-to-authority experiment (explained in more detail in Chapter 7), externals were more likely than internals to give apparently (but not truly) harmful electric shocks to someone if told to do so by the experimenter.[35]

For managers, it may be helpful to know where you stand and where your workers fit on the locus of control continuum. It can help you understand how they think and how they might react in a variety of situations, including ethical situations. For example, workers who constantly blame bad luck and other external factors for performance failures or ethical lapses may be doing so because of an external locus of control—that's the way they view the world. Managers can work with such individuals to help them see the relationship between their actions and the outcomes by consistently holding them responsible and accountable for what they do. As a result, their locus of control may shift over time, and they will take more responsibility for the consequences of their actions.

Machiavellianism

Whereas an internal locus of control and more principled thinking are generally associated with ethical action, another individual difference, *Machiavellianism*, has been associated with unethical action. Perhaps you have heard the term *Machiavellian* used to describe individuals who act in self-interested, opportunistic, deceptive, and manipulative ways to win no matter what the cost or how it affects other people. The personality trait known as Machiavellianism was named after Niccolò Machiavelli, a sixteenth-century philosopher, statesman, and political theorist who is associated with promoting a pragmatic leadership style that included amoral, if not clearly unethical, behavior with the aim of achieving self-interested outcomes. The idea that "the ends justify the means" is often associated with Machiavelli. In his most famous publication, *The Prince*, Machiavelli famously said that a ruler should "do good if he can, but . . . commit evil if he must."[36] Research using a survey that assesses an individual's Machiavellianism has found that individuals high on Machiavellianism are significantly more likely to have unethical intentions and to engage in unethical action such as lying, cheating, and accepting kickbacks.[37] Managers should be on the lookout for employees who they think might be Machiavellian because they are likely to engage in self-interested action that can put the entire organization at risk. Organizations may also want to consider including Machiavellianism among other personality characteristics when assessing job applicants.

Moral Disengagement

The idea behind moral disengagement[38] is that most of us behave ethically most of the time because we've internalized standards of good conduct and judge our behavior against these standards. If we consider behaving unethically, we feel guilty and stop ourselves. All of us probably recognize that process. But research has found that individual people have a higher (or lower) propensity to deactivate that self-control system through eight *moral disengagement* mechanisms. These moral disengagement mechanisms allow individuals to engage in unethical behavior without feeling bad about it.

Moral disengagement mechanisms can be organized into three categories. One of these categories involves ways of thinking about our behavior that makes bad behavior seem more acceptable. A mechanism in this category is the use of euphemistic language (discussed earlier in relation to ethical awareness). Another is called *moral justification*, whereby unethical behavior is thought to be okay because it contributes to some socially valued outcome. For example, mortgage lenders may have believed that it was okay to sell those no-doc loans to people because they were helping individuals who would otherwise not be able to purchase a home to take part in the "American dream." A related moral disengagement tactic is called *advantageous comparison*, whereby people compare their own behavior to more reprehensible behavior and thus make their own behavior seem more okay. For example, the same mortgage lender may feel okay about selling these loans because she counsels clients to be sure to pay the mortgage every month and avoid credit card debt, while colleagues in her office don't bother to do any counseling and care only about making their commissions.

A second category of moral disengagement mechanisms has to do with distorting consequences or reducing personal responsibility for bad outcomes. For example, with *displacement of responsibility*, individuals will reduce personal accountability by thinking of their actions as resulting from an authority figure's dictates ("my boss made me do it"). With *diffusion of responsibility*, individuals will reduce personal accountability by looking to others or the group ("it's not my job," or "my team made the decision"). With *distorting consequences*, individuals will think of negative consequences as less serious than they are (it's "no big deal" to fudge the numbers on my expense report).

The third category of moral disengagement mechanisms reduces the person's identification with the victims of unethical behavior. With *dehumanization*, individuals make those who would be harmed less worthy of ethical consideration because they're thought to be different, stupid, or not even human. This mechanism characterizes thinking among those who commit genocide. One can also imagine mortgage lenders thinking that people who took out loans they clearly couldn't afford were just dumb and not worthy of concern. *Attribution of blame* lays blame on the victims of harm for a variety of reasons ("it's their own fault").

Some of these mechanisms lend themselves to certain situations more than others. So if you have an authoritarian and unethical boss, displacement of responsibility ("my boss made me do it") may be used more than other tactics. Still, research does show that some individuals are more likely to engage in this kind of thinking overall, regardless of the situation. And those individuals with a high propensity to morally disengage have been found to have reduced empathy for other people, to be more cynical, to see their behavior as resulting from chance or fate (a more external locus of control), and to have a reduced moral identity relative to their other identities—a weaker sense of themselves as ethical beings. Most important, these individuals are more likely to behave unethically.[39]

You can test your own propensity to morally disengage with a short survey that your professor may make available to you. And you can reduce that propensity by being on the lookout for certain justifications that come up in your own mind or in discussions with others. When you find yourself thinking the following (or hear something like this in a meeting), "stop and think" about whether what you're doing is right:

It's not my responsibility—my boss told me to do it.

It's not my responsibility—my team decided this.

It's no big deal.

It's not as bad as (what someone else) is doing.

They deserve whatever they get.

They brought this on themselves.

FACILITATORS OF AND BARRIERS TO GOOD ETHICAL JUDGMENT

In the previous section, we discussed characteristics that distinguish individuals from each other. But individual differences aside, as human beings, we all share ways of thinking about the world that can facilitate or interfere with good ethical judgment. The steps offered in Chapter 2 assume a rational and ethical decision-making process that prescribes how an ethical decision should be made. However, studies have found that actual human decision making doesn't match this rational ideal. Although people generally intend to be rational in their decision making, they're often not.

In recent years, psychologists have discovered a number of weaknesses and biases in how human beings make decisions.[40] Some of these decision-making weaknesses have direct implications for ethical decision making in organizations and for the advice given in Chapter 2.[41] So think of this part of the chapter as a kind of reality check. If you're going to manage your own and others' ethical behavior, you need to understand how people really think in addition to how they should think.

As a backdrop, recognize that the cognitive weaknesses and biases we will be discussing operate primarily because people try to reduce uncertainty and simplify their world. Although uncertainty is a fact of organizational life, businesspeople want very much to deny the uncertainty they face. Therefore they tend to act as if the world is rational and they're in control. Being "in charge" and able to predict events is a highly valued characteristic, especially in business. But this focus on being in charge is an illusion that can get managers into trouble. What if you really don't know all of the facts about the risks, the potential affected parties, and all the consequences of your decisions? You'll see below that the best way to avoid decision-making weaknesses and biases is to become aware of them and to incorporate steps into your decision making that are explicitly aimed at reducing their impact.

Thinking about Fact Gathering

In Chapter 2, we advised you to "get the facts" as an important first step in good ethical decision making. Be aware, though, that your thinking about the facts is likely to be biased. Research evidence suggests that you may look for the wrong ones or stop looking too soon because you think you already have all the facts you need.

We know that most people, including business students and business executives, are overconfident about their knowledge of the facts. For example, in research studies, people were asked factual questions. Then they were asked to judge the probable truth of their answers. For example, in response to the question, "Is Rome or New York farther north?" most people chose New York, and they believed that the probability was about 90 percent that they were right. Actually, they were wrong. Rome is slightly north of New York. Being overconfident can make you fail to search for additional facts or for support for the facts you have.[42]

Even if you gather additional facts or support, another cognitive bias termed the *confirmation trap* may influence your choice of which facts to gather and where to look.[43] All of us have the tendency to look for information that will confirm our preferred answer or choice and to neglect to search for evidence that might prove us wrong. If you were an investment banker who wanted to believe that mortgage-backed securities were safe (because they were *so* profitable at the time), you were more likely to look for supportive information and ask a question like, "Historically, what percentage of mortgages have defaulted?" Given that question, the banker will probably underestimate the risk involved. Because of no-doc loans and other new and riskier subprime mortgages, relying on historical default patterns no longer made sense. The meeting might take a very different turn if the banker were to ask, "What future problems are possible with this type of new product? What has changed? What haven't we thought of?"[44]

In an attempt to overcome the confirmation trap, it's important that you consciously try to think of ways you could be wrong. Incorporate questions in your individual and group decision-making processes such as, "How could I/we be wrong?" "What facts are still missing?" and "What facts exist that might prove me/us to be wrong?" You may still miss some important facts, but you'll miss less of them than if you didn't ask these questions at all.

Thinking about Consequences

In Chapter 2, we also advised you to think about all the potential consequences of your decision for a wide variety of stakeholders. Who can argue with such sage advice? However, psychologists have found a number of problems with how people think about consequences.

REDUCED NUMBER OF CONSEQUENCES   One way people simplify their decisions and make them more manageable is to reduce the number of consequences they consider. They're especially likely to ignore consequences that are thought to affect only a few people. But consequences that affect only a few people can be serious. For example, a highly beneficial drug may have positive consequences for many and adverse consequences for only a few people, but what if those few people could die from side effects of the drug?[45] Obviously, you wouldn't want to ignore such serious consequences no matter how few people are affected. In attempting to consciously deal with this situation, it helps to consult a broad range of people who have a stake in the decision you're making. Invite input from all interested parties, especially those who disagree with you and those with the most to lose. Ask them what consequences they're concerned about and why. Then, incorporate these consequences in your decision making.

CONSEQUENCES FOR THE SELF VERSUS CONSEQUENCES FOR OTHERS   Consequentialist theories require us to think about costs and benefits for society—for multiple stakeholders. However, psychological research suggests people tend to make decisions in a self-interested manner. For example, they're inclined to give more weight to the consequences of a decision or action for themselves (or those close to them) than for others. That may be because consequences to the self are more immediate or more imminent. In addition, when the consequences of multiple alternatives are ambiguous, people tend to choose the alternative they personally prefer rather than the one that is more just. To make matters worse (from an ethics perspective), people underestimate the extent to which they are self-interested and the extent to which they rationalize their own behavior. They just aren't aware of their own cognitive biases. Again, it can help to consciously consider those outside of yourself who are going to be affected by a decision or action. As a manager, you can ask your people to make a list of those individuals or groups who might be affected and seek their input, or have your employees try to imagine themselves in the shoes of those stakeholders. How would they react?[46]

Consequences as Risk

One way to think about consequences is to think in terms of decision making about risk. Managers are in the business of assessing risk. But, research suggests that people tend to underestimate potential risks because of an *illusion of optimism*. They overestimate the likelihood of good future events and underestimate the bad. For example, even though around one-half of marriages end in divorce, newlyweds are highly optimistic that their own new marriages will be everlasting. And, although some analysts may knowingly have lied about the future prospects of mortgage-backed securities, it's likely that many were simply overly optimistic and believed that the housing market would never simultaneously crash everywhere in the country, bringing down an entire market and the U.S. economy with it.

People also generally believe that they're less susceptible to risks than other people are. This belief is supported by the *illusion of control*, the general belief that we really are in charge of what happens. And if we think we can control events, we also think bad things are less likely to happen. This illusion of control has been demonstrated to exist in MBA students from top U.S. business schools, suggesting that managers are certainly vulnerable.[47] Managers whose judgment is influenced by these cognitive biases are likely to underestimate the risk facing the firm as a result of a particular decision. But if managers ignore risks, they're also ignoring important consequences. So it's important to recognize this tendency to ignore risk, and design risk analysis into your decision-making processes.

Even if we attend to risks, we still have difficulty thinking about them in a completely rational way. One tendency that can contribute to downplaying risk was already discussed—the tendency to attend to information that will help confirm the decision we would prefer to make (confirmation bias). In the famous space shuttle *Challenger* disaster that killed all the astronauts on board, everyone knew that risk existed. The question was how much, and was it too much? Many economic and political factors were pushing NASA to launch this shuttle. The media were paying more attention to the launch than they usually would because a schoolteacher was on board. Researchers now believe that confirmation bias may have influenced decision makers to focus on the information that confirmed their preference, which was to launch, and to discount available information about risks that would have supported a delay.[48]

CONSEQUENCES OVER TIME: ESCALATION OF COMMITMENT The prescription to think about consequences also fails to account for the fact that decisions are not isolated choices, but often become part of a series of choices within the context of a larger decision or project. Consider the following scenario:

> You finally graduated from college and landed a great job, and you've invested most of your savings in the car of your dreams—a used BMW. But in a short time, the car begins having mechanical problems. Every time you bring it to the mechanic, he claims that it is fixed for good; but the problems continue and your bank account is being drained. Should you quit trying to fix the car?

Because you've already made the decision to buy the car, and you've already invested a lot of money in it, your tendency will be to continue your commitment to this previously selected investment. This tendency has been called "escalation of commitment to a losing course of action" or "throwing good money after bad."[49] A perfectly rational decision maker would consider the time and expenses already invested as "sunk costs." They aren't recoverable and shouldn't be considered in a decision about what to do. Only future costs and benefits should be considered. But this is difficult. Norms in our society and in our organizations support trying, persisting, and sticking with a course of action. Also, if others are involved, we're likely to feel the need to justify our original decision—whether it was to buy a car, a piece of equipment, or land.

So when you're in a situation that involves decisions about whether to continue to invest in an ongoing project, be careful! One way to overcome escalation of commitment is, as with many biases, to recognize that it exists and try to adjust for it. Ask yourself explicit questions about whether you're committed to a decision just because failure would make your original decision look bad. Ask yourself, "If I took over the project today, with no personal investment, would I support the project?" Another approach is to bring in outsiders and ask for their opinions, or turn the project over to them completely. That gets your own ego out of the decision-making process.

Thinking about Integrity

In Chapter 2, you were also advised to think about your own character and integrity— to ask yourself what a person of integrity in a highly ethical community would do in the particular situation. But cognitive biases can get in the way here too. First, if your thoughts about yourself are controlled by illusion rather than reality, how can you make a good decision about your integrity? The basic idea here is that individuals are likely to think positively about their own ethics. They will unconsciously filter and distort information in order to maintain a positive self image. Psychologists know that people have an *illusion of superiority* or *illusion of morality*. Surveys have found that people tend to think of themselves as more ethical, fair, and honest than most other people.[50] It's obviously an illusion when the large majority of individuals claim to be more honest than the average person, or more ethical than their peers. It's a little like Garrison Keillor's mythical Lake Wobegon, where all the children are above average. There isn't a whole lot you can do here except try to be honest with yourself. But this kind of illusion can lead to bad decisions—when physicians take gifts from sales-people because they're sure they're ethical and their decisions won't be affected,[51] or when mortgage lenders selling subprime loans convince themselves that what they're doing is contributing to the American dream.

Second, the virtue ethics approach suggests that you rely on the ethics of your profession (or other relevant moral community) to guide you. But consider the accounting professionals in recent cases, as when Arthur Andersen auditors signed off on audits that misrepresented the finances of companies such as Waste Management, Enron, and Adelphia Communications.

Certified public accountants are supposed to be guided by the AICPA code of professional ethics. The code says that, as professionals, auditors have a responsibility to act in the public interest to provide objective opinions about the financial state of the organization—be free of conflicts of interest, not misrepresent facts, or subordinate professional judgment to others. Given human cognitive limitations, however, this expectation is probably unrealistic. Consider what is likely to go through an auditor's mind when deciding whether to provide a negative audit opinion on the financial statements of a big client. Auditors work closely with their audit clients, often over a long period of time. By contrast, auditors have no personal relationship with the "public" they are supposed to represent. Therefore, as biased information processors, their thinking is likely to emphasize the potential negative consequences of a qualified (or negative) audit opinion for themselves and the client—not for the public. The negative consequences for themselves and the client are clearer and more immediate. The auditor who offers a qualified audit may very well lose the client (and the money associated with that client) as well as the personal relationships forged over time. On the other hand, the consequences for the public of a qualified audit opinion are more ambiguous and likely spread over more people and time. It isn't clear how much specific members of the public will gain or lose, especially if the misrepresentation is deemed to be small or unclear. So auditors can easily rationalize a decision that is consistent with their own and their company's self-interest and downplay the potential consequences to an ambiguous, unknown public.[52]

What is a professional organization to do? It is important to recognize that auditors (and other professionals) are human beings who are affected by cognitive limitations and biases. Given what we know about these biases, here are some potential solutions. First, auditors should be discouraged from developing personal relation-ships or socializing with their clients. Companies should change auditors every few years to avoid forging such personal ties. Second, audit firms should work hard to sensitize auditors to the likely negative consequences of financial misrepresentation for their own firms and the public. The Enron bankruptcy contributed to huge financial losses to its employees and investors and to the ultimate demise of Arthur Andersen. Regular attention to the importance of maintaining the integrity and long-term reputation of the audit firm is essential, as is the leader's role in creating a strong ethical climate. The reward system (discussed more fully in later chapters) can be used to send important signals about what's expected. For example, auditors who turn down client business or risk losing a client by providing a negative audit opinion should be supported and reinforced for doing so. Those auditors who risk the reputation of the firm should be disciplined.

Given the above discussion, we might suggest other "red flags" for you to be on the lookout for. If you find yourself thinking (or others saying) the following, consider whether your biases are showing!

The facts support our decision.

Nothing bad will happen.

We're ethical—we wouldn't do anything bad.

We've already invested so much—we can't afford to quit now.

Thinking about Your Gut

Our last piece of advice in Chapter 2 was to listen to your gut. But in this chapter, we've spent a great deal of time telling you that your gut may well be wrong—led by cognitive limitations and biased thinking.

Yet, your gut can still be useful in alerting you that something might be wrong—that you're facing an ethical dilemma—in the first place. But once that decision is made, you should temper your gut with careful analysis guided by the knowledge gained in this chapter and the rest of the book. Hopefully, the combination of your gut and an informed brain will help you make better decisions.

YOUR GUT—"AUTOMATIC" ETHICAL DECISION MAKING In Chapter 2, we treated ethical decision making mostly as a systematic and rational step-by-step process. Even in this chapter, we have thus far discussed how ethical awareness leads to ethical judgment, which then leads to ethical action in a seemingly systematic and deliberative way. But we suggested in Chapter 2 that your gut can be a useful way of waving a red flag at yourself. In fact, new research from moral psychology, which is often backed up by neuroscience and brain imaging studies, finds that ethical judgments are often more intuitive, impulsive, and automatic than deliberative. Jonathan

Haidt, a psychologist at New York University, has argued that much ethical judgment occurs "quickly, effortlessly, and automatically,"[53] often operating below conscious awareness. Haidt has been particularly interested in people's automatic reactions of disgust. For example, in his research, he has used a vignette about a family that accidentally runs over and kills the family dog and then reacts by cooking and eating it! Most of us recoil instantly at the thought. It seems disgusting to us and wrong to eat the family dog. When asked why, however, we can't explain our very strong gut reactions. After all, most of us eat other animals. So, clearly, something besides a purely rational process is at work—something that's more intuitive and emotional.

Even more intriguing is research suggesting that individuals who rely only on more conscious, deliberative approaches to ethical decision making may arrive at worse ethical decisions than do those who use moral intuition and who have strong emotional responses to ethical situations.[54] Much more research will be required to fully understand these important processes, when they operate, and when they interfere with good ethical decision making rather than actually improve it.

Unconscious Biases

One relatively new research tool that can help us understand the potential (often negative) role of the unconscious in a certain type of ethical thinking is the Implicit Association Test (IAT). Results reveal most people's preferences for young people over old, straight people over gay, able people over disabled, and a variety of other categories. For example, hundreds of studies with the "race IAT" lead to the conclusion that the large majority of us have an unconscious tendency to value white people more than black people even if we consciously disavow such views and truly believe that we have no racial bias. Here's how the race IAT works. Participants are asked to press a key on the computer keyboard when they see a black person's face or a word that has negative connotations (e.g., *rotten*, *bad*) and to press another key when they see a white person's face or a word with positive connotations (*love*, *good*). Then the task is reversed, and participants are told to press the same keyboard key in response to black faces and pleasant words or white faces and unpleasant words. It turns out that most of us respond more quickly when we're linking the black faces with negative words and white faces with positive words because such links are cognitively easier for us—they fit with our unconscious, implicit attitudes. Some have criticized these studies as simply representing higher familiarity with some groups than others, and as unable to predict behavior in real-life situations. Our goal is not to defend or criticize the IAT. Rather, we use it to point out that unconscious attitudes probably influence our behavior more than we think. Given the importance of fair treatment in all kinds of ethical decisions at work (hiring, performance appraisal, layoffs, compensation, etc.), understanding the potential impact of such unconscious bias should help us understand why we need to put organizational procedures in place that provide less opportunity for these unconscious biases to influence our decisions.[55] (To experience the IAT for yourself, go to https://implicit.harvard.edu/implicit/.)

Emotions In Ethical Decision Making

Age-old philosophical prescriptions assume cool, rational, ethical decisions, but we are also beginning to understand how important emotions are to the ethical decision-making process.[56] Importantly, emotions are not just an interference to good ethical judgment, as many used to believe. Instead, emotions often lead to right action.[57] For example, when we consider hurting someone, our brain reacts with a visceral negative emotion ("an internal alarm") that keeps violence in check.[58] And these reactions tend to happen very quickly, before we even have time to engage in rational thought.

Consider two classic philosophical dilemmas. In one, a runaway train is headed for five people who will die if nothing is done. You can save the five by diverting the train to a different track, where it would kill only one person. Should you divert the train?

In the second dilemma, you're standing next to a stranger on a bridge over the tracks. The only way to save the five people is to push the stranger onto the tracks, where his body would stop the train. Should you push the stranger?

To philosophers, the rational logic in these scenarios is similar; in both cases, you would be intentionally sacrificing one person in order to save five people. But, when asked, most people say that you should divert the train in the first dilemma but not push the stranger onto the tracks in the second. Psychologists now tell us that emotions explain the difference between the scenarios because the second scenario engages emotions more than the first. This hypothesis was supported in an experiment that used brain scans to track brain activity during decision making. In dilemmas like the second one, parts of the brain associated with emotional processing were more active, and those who decided that pushing the stranger would be right took longer to make a decision because emotions slowed down their thought processes.[59] Most normal people would find it difficult, if not impossible, to actually take another's life in such a situation. This reluctance is attributed to the strong feelings of revulsion that come up from just thinking about taking a human life. These reactions are likely hardwired into human beings through evolution because they aid our survival. Interestingly though, people who have damage to the prefrontal cortex of the brain have no such reaction. They are much more likely to simply make the utilitarian analysis and say they would kill one person to save the others.[60] (If you want to get a "feel" for this type of exercise, try taking the moral sense test at http://moral.wjh.harvard.edu. It presents complex ethical dilemmas that have no clearly right answer.)

So, emotions are clearly important in ethical decision making, and continuing research will help us more fully understand the process. It seems clear that emotions can aid us in doing the right thing when they alert us to ethical concerns, cause us to act to help others in need, or keep us from violent reactions (because of sympathy for another, pangs of guilt, or automatically triggered negative feelings).[61] Feelings of betrayal or moral outrage can also cause people to act in the interest of fairness.[62] For example, people may be more willing to speak up about the unfair treatment of a coworker if they feel moral outrage about it.[63] Interestingly, research has found that people will even forgo financial benefits if they feel they're being unfairly treated.

In some fascinating experiments, researchers have demonstrated that individuals will punish another individual they perceive to be unethical even if there is nothing for them to gain and something to lose. They will do this even if they don't know the person who has been offended.[64] Accordingly, research has shown that the parts of our brains associated with feeling satisfaction are activated when we consider retaliating against someone who has unfairly harmed us.[65]

The bottom line here is that we often act not because we have coolly and rationally decided on the best course of action, but rather because it "feels" like the right thing to do at the time. Often, emotions can lead us to act ethically. But emotions can also interfere with good decision making when they lead to a (perhaps irrational) desire for revenge. For example, when a competitor "poaches" one of your best people, do you try to recruit someone away from the competitor just to get even or to do damage to the competitor when you should be focusing more rationally on who is best prepared to do the job?[66]

Consider how General Motors managers handled a four-year legal battle with Volkswagen over their allegation that a 56-year-old GM executive, Jose Lopez, took 20 boxes of GM proprietary documents when he left GM to join Volkswagen in 1993. In 1992, Lopez was GM's worldwide purchasing czar, known for his ability to cut costs ruthlessly. The missing documents included information about GM's suppliers and their prices for auto parts, as well as information about upcoming Opel car models in the GM Europe division. *Fortune* magazine referred to the four-year legal battle that ensued as a tale of "betrayal" and "revenge." Lou Hughes, head of GM Europe, was furious that Lopez would take proprietary documents to its fiercest competitor. He insisted that there would be no settlement with VW as long as Lopez remained there. When asked what he hoped to gain from the litigation, Hughes replied, "Look, this is not a question of business. This is a question of ethics."[67]

Years of investigation yielded no hard evidence to suggest that anyone at VW had actually used the secret GM information. *Fortune* suggested that at the time, "one might have expected GM to act pragmatically, find some face-saving exit, and return its attention to the car business."[68] That might have been the "rational," coolheaded thing to do. Instead, GM escalated the fight, bringing a racketeering suit that was expected to drag on for years and cost tens of millions of dollars. When pragmatic board members questioned the action, the board chairman insisted that the company had to pursue the suit because it "had been terribly wronged." "Some things aren't measured in time and money. They're just who we are."[69]

Finally, in January 1997, the two companies settled the case. Lopez, who had already resigned from Volkswagen, was barred from doing any work for VW through the year 2000. Volkswagen paid GM $100 million and agreed to buy $1 billion worth of GM parts over seven years. *Fortune* asked, "But what, in the end did the long, bitter, and costly struggle accomplish? In the cold light of day, the answer seems simple and shocking: not much."[70] A huge company devoted years of attention and spent millions of dollars because its managers were morally outraged that their former friend had betrayed them. It was obviously an emotional reaction.

Clearly, anger and other emotions can influence thoughts and actions. Whether that is good or bad depends on whether the emotion leads to "right" or "wrong" action. If empathy or guilt lead you to recognize an ethical issue or think about the consequences of your actions for others, that's a good thing. If moral outrage leads you to seek justice, that's good as well. But moral outrage can also lead to a desire for revenge, and that may be the time to bring cooler heads to the decision to determine whether action based upon revenge is a good ethical (and business) decision. Those who are not as emotionally involved in the interpersonal issues may be able to offer a more rational and balanced assessment of the situation. In the GM–Volkswagen case, those pragmatic board members may have been right to support a quick settlement.

TOWARD ETHICAL ACTION

Most of this chapter has focused on ethical awareness and ethical judgment processes. We've seen that these also influence ethical action. For example, those with stronger ethical awareness are more likely to make ethical choices because they think about the harm they're doing, they use ethical language to label the situation, or they recognize that others would see an action as ethically problematic. Also, we know that some individuals are more prone to think in ways that make ethical action more likely. Individuals who score higher in cognitive moral development, internal locus of control, and idealistic decision-making style, and those who are lower in Machiavellianism and less prone to use morally disengaged thinking are all more likely to behave ethically.

But we've also seen that, as human beings, we're all prone to cognitive biases that can get in the way of good thinking and interfere with ethical action. Beyond that, it's sometimes hard to do what's right even for those of us with the best thinking and intentions. We may have an unethical boss who insists that we do inappropriate things, we may find ourselves in an unethical culture, or we may fear repercussions for speaking the truth. Next, you'll read an article that addresses some of these issues: Dennis Gioia's reflections on his involvement in the Pinto Fires case. In future chapters, we'll focus more on how you can find your moral voice and do what's right despite the challenges.

REFLECTIONS ON THE PINTO FIRES CASE (SEE CHAPTER 2)

by Dennis A. Gioia (used with permission)

Chapter 2 ended with the provocative Pinto Fires case, highlighting some of the sordid events in the history of the Pinto fires problem. As the authors indicate later in this chapter, I was involved with this infamous case in the early 1970s. They have asked me to reflect on lessons learned from my experience.

I take this case very personally, even though my name seldom comes up in its many recountings. I was one of those "faceless bureaucrats" who is often portrayed as making decisions without accountability and then walking away from them—even decisions with life-and-death implications. That characterization is, of course, far too stark and superficial. I certainly don't consider myself faceless, and I have always chafed at the label of bureaucrat as applied to me, even though I have found myself unfairly applying it to others. Furthermore, I have been unable to walk away from my decisions in this case. They have a tendency to haunt—especially when they have such public airings as those involved in the Pinto fires debacle have had.

But why revisit 20-year-old decisions, and why take them so personally? Here's why: because I was in a position to do something about a serious problem—and didn't. That simple observation gives me pause for personal reflection and also makes me think about the many difficulties people face in trying to be ethical decision makers in organizations. It also helps me to keep in mind the features of modern business and organizational life that would influence someone like me (me, of all people, who purposefully set out to be an ethical decision maker) to overlook basic moral issues in arriving at decisions that, when viewed retrospectively, look absurdly easy to make. But they are not easy to make, and that is perhaps the most important lesson of all.

The Personal Aspect

I would like to reflect on my own experience mainly to emphasize the personal dimensions involved in ethical decision making. Although I recognize that there are strong organizational influences at work as well, I would like to keep the critical lens focused for a moment on me (and you) as individuals. I believe that there are insights and lessons from my experience that can help you think about your own likely involvement in issues with ethical overtones.

First, however, a little personal background. In the late 1960s and early 1970s, I was an engineering/MBA student; I also was an "activist," engaged in protests of social injustice and the social irresponsibility of business, among other things. I held some pretty strong values that I thought would stand up to virtually any challenge and enable me to "do the right thing" when I took a career job. I suspect that most of you feel that you also have developed a strongly held value system that will enable you to resist organizational inducements to do something unethical. Perhaps. Unfortunately, the challenges do not often come in overt forms that shout the need for resistance or ethical righteousness. They are much more subtle than that, and thus doubly difficult to deal with because they do not make it easy to see that a situation you are confronting might actually involve an ethical dilemma.

After school, I got the job of my dreams with Ford and, predictably enough, ended up on the fast track to promotion. That fast track enabled me to progress quickly into positions of some notable responsibility. Within two years I became Ford's vehicle recall coordinator, with first-level responsibility for tracking field safety problems. It was the most intense, information-overloaded job you can imagine, frequently dealing with some of the most serious problems in the company. Disasters were a phone call away, and action was the hallmark of the office where I worked. We all knew we were engaged in serious business, and we all took the job seriously. There were no irresponsible bureaucratic ogres there, contrary to popular portrayal.

In this context, I first encountered the neophyte Pinto fires problem in the form of infrequent reports of cars erupting into horrendous fireballs in very low-speed crashes and the shuddering personal experience of inspecting a car that had burned, killing its trapped occupants. Over the space of a year, I had two distinct opportunities to initiate recall activities concerning the fuel tank problems, but on both occasions I voted not to recall, despite my activist history and advocacy of business social responsibility.

The key question is how, in the space of two short years, I could have engaged in a decision process that appeared to violate my own strong values—a decision process whose subsequent manifestations continue to be cited by many observers as a supposedly definitive study of corporate unethical behavior. I tend to discount the obvious accusations: that my values weren't really strongly held; that I had turned my back on my values in the interest of loyalty to Ford; that I was somehow intimidated into making decisions in the best interests of the company; that despite my principled statements I had not actually achieved a high stage of moral development, and so on. Instead, I believe a more plausible explanation for my own actions looks to the foibles of normal human information processing.

I would argue that the complexity and intensity of the recall coordinator's job required that I develop cognitive strategies for simplifying the overwhelming amount of information I had to deal with. The best way to do that is to structure the information into cognitive "schemas," or more specifically "script schemas," that guide understanding and action when facing common or repetitive situations. Scripts offer marvelous cognitive shortcuts because they allow you to act virtually unconsciously and automatically, and thus permit handling complicated situations without being paralyzed by needing to think consciously about every little thing. Such scripts enabled me to discern the characteristic hallmarks of problem cases likely to result in recall and to execute a complicated series of steps required to initiate a recall.

All of us structure information all of the time; we could hardly get through the workday without doing so. But there is a penalty to be paid for this wonderful cognitive efficiency: We do not give sufficient attention to important information that requires special treatment, because the general information pattern has surface appearances indicating that automatic processing will suffice. That, I think, is what happened to me. The beginning stages of the Pinto case looked for all the world like a normal sort of problem. Lurking beneath the cognitive veneer, however, was a nasty set of circumstances waiting to conspire into a dangerous situation. Despite the awful nature of the accidents, the Pinto problem did not fit an existing script; the accidents were relatively rare by recall standards, and the accidents were not initially traceable to a specific component failure. Even when a failure mode suggesting a design flaw was identified, the cars did not perform significantly worse in crash tests than competitor vehicles. One might easily argue that I should have been jolted out of my script by the unusual nature of the accidents (very low speed, otherwise unharmed passengers trapped in a horrific fire), but those facts did not penetrate a script cued for other features. (It also is difficult to convey to the layperson that bad accidents are not a particularly unusual feature of the recall coordinator's information field. Accident severity is not necessarily a recall cue; frequently repeated patterns and identifiable causes are.)

The Corporate Milieu

In addition to the personalized scripting of information processing, there is another important influence on the decisions that led to the Pinto fires mess: the fact that decisions are made by individuals working within a corporate context. It has escaped almost no one's notice that the decisions made by corporate employees tend to be in the best interest of the corporation, even by people who mean to do better. Why? Because socialization processes and the overriding influence of organizational culture provide a strong, if generally subtle, context for defining appropriate ways of seeing and understanding. Because organizational culture can be viewed as a collection of scripts, scripted information processing relates even to organizational-level considerations. Scripts are context bound; they are not free-floating general cognitive structures that apply universally. They are tailored to specific contexts. And there are few more potent contexts than organizational settings.

There is no question that my perspective changed after joining Ford. In retrospect, I would be very surprised if it hadn't. In my former incarnation as a social activist, I had internalized values for doing what was right, as I understood rightness in grand terms; but I had not internalized a script for applying my values in a pragmatic business context. Ford and the recall coordinator role provided a powerful context for developing scripts—scripts that were inevitably and undeniably oriented toward ways of making sense that were influenced by the corporate and industry culture.

I wanted to do a good job, and I wanted to do what was right. Those are not mutually exclusive desires, but the corporate context affects their synthesis. I came to accept the idea that it was not feasible to fix everything that someone might construe as a problem. I therefore shifted to a value of wanting to do the greatest good for the greatest number (an ethical value tempered by the practical constraints of an economic enterprise). Doing the greatest good for the greatest number meant working with intensity and responsibility on those problems that would spare the most people from injury. It also meant developing scripts that responded to typical problems, not odd patterns like those presented by the Pinto.

Another way of noting how the organizational context so strongly affects individuals is to recognize that one's personal identity becomes heavily influenced by corporate identity. As a student, my identity centered on being a "good person" (with a certain dose of moral righteousness associated with it). As recall coordinator, my identity shifted to a more corporate definition. This is an extraordinarily important point, especially for students who have not yet held a permanent job role, and I would like to emphasize it. Before assuming your career role, identity derives mainly from social relationships. Upon putting on the mantle of a profession or a responsible position, identity begins to align with your role. And information processing perspective follows from that identity.

I remember accepting the portrayal of the auto industry and Ford as "under attack" from many quarters (oil crises, burgeoning government regulation, inflation, litigious customers, etc). As we know, groups under assault develop into more cohesive communities that emphasize commonalities and shared identities. I was by then an insider in the industry and the company, sharing some of their beleaguered perceptions that there were significant forces arrayed against us and that the well-being of the company might be threatened.

What happened to the original perception that Ford was a socially irresponsible giant that needed a comeuppance? Well, it looks different from the inside. Over time, a reasonable value for action against corporate dominance became tempered by another reasonable value that corporations serve social needs and are not automatically the villains of society. I saw a need for balance among multiple values, and, as a result, my identity shifted in degrees toward a more corporate identity.

The Torch Passes to You

So, given my experiences, what would I recommend to you, as a budding organizational decision maker? I have some strong opinions. First, develop your ethical base now! Too many people do not give serious attention to assessing and articulating their own values. People simply do not know what they stand for because they haven't thought about it seriously. Even the ethical scenarios presented in classes or executive programs are treated as interesting little games without apparent implications for deciding how you intend to think or act. These exercises should be used to develop a principled, personal code that you will try to live by. Consciously decide your values. If you don't decide your values now, you are easy prey for others who will gladly decide them for you or influence you implicitly to accept theirs.

Second, recognize that everyone, including you, is an unwitting victim of his or her own cognitive structuring. Many people are surprised and fascinated to learn that they use schemas and scripts to understand and act in the organizational world. The idea that we automatically process so much information so much of the time intrigues us. Indeed, we would all turn into blithering idiots if we did not structure information and expectations, but that very structuring hides information that might be important—information that could require you to confront your values. We get lulled into thinking that automatic information processing is great stuff that obviates the necessity for trying to resolve so many frustrating decisional dilemmas.

Actually, I think too much ethical training focuses on supplying standards for contemplating dilemmas. The far greater problem, as I see it, is recognizing that a dilemma exists in the first place. The insidious problem of people not being aware that they are dealing with a situation that might have ethical overtones is another consequence of schema usage. I would venture that scripted routines seldom include ethical dimensions. Is a person behaving unethically if the situation is not even construed as having ethical implications? People are not necessarily stupid, ill-intentioned, or Machiavellian, but they are often unaware. They do indeed spend much of their time cruising on automatic, but the true hallmark of human information processing is the ability to switch from automatic to controlled information processing. What we really need to do is to encourage people to recognize cues that build a "Now Think!" step into their scripts— waving red flags at yourself, so to speak—even though you are engaged in essentially automatic cognition and action.

Third, because scripts are context-bound and organizations are potent contexts, be aware of how strongly, yet how subtly, your job role and your organizational culture affect the ways you interpret and make sense of information (and thus affect the ways you develop the scripts that will guide you in unguarded moments). Organizational culture has a much greater effect on individual cognition than you would ever suspect (see Chapter 5).

Last, be prepared to face critical responsibility at a relatively young age, as I did. You need to know what your values are, and you need to know how you think so that you can know how to make a good decision. Before you can do that, you need to articulate and affirm your values now, before you enter the fray. I wasn't really ready. Are you?

For a more thorough description and analysis of Dennis Gioia's experiences, see his article, "Pinto Fires and Personal Ethics: A Script Analysis of Missed Opportunities," *Journal of Business Ethics* 11, nos. 5, 6 (1992): 379–89.

Revisiting the Pinto Fires Case: Script Processing and Cost-Benefit Analysis

Dennis Gioia, management scholar and expert on social cognition, has provided us with a rare opportunity to look inside the head of someone who was involved in a widely publicized business ethics situation. He has analyzed his own thoughts and behavior as vehicle recall coordinator at Ford Motor Company shortly after the Ford Pinto was introduced in both an article in the *Journal of Business Ethics*[71] and in his "Reflections" that you just read.

In 1972, Gioia graduated with an MBA. His value system included opposition to the Vietnam War and deep concerns about the ethical conduct of business.

"I cultivated my social awareness; I held my principles high; I espoused my intention to help a troubled world; and I wore my hair long. By any measure I was a prototypical 'Child of the '60s.'"[72] A car enthusiast, Gioia was hired by the Ford Motor Company as a "problem analyst." Within two years he became Ford's field recall coordinator, in charge of organizing current recall campaigns and identifying developing problems.

SCRIPT PROCESSING   In analyzing his participation in the decision *not* to recall the Pinto, Gioia suggests that his behavior was highly influenced by script processing. *Scripts* are cognitive frameworks that guide human thought and action. Although they are generally not written down, scripts contain information about the appropriate sequence of events in routine situations. For example, most of us have a fairly complex script for how to behave in a fancy restaurant, from approaching the maître d' to tasting the wine to choosing a fork to use to leaving the appropriate tip. Information processing is made much more efficient because a cognitive script allows the individual to call on an established behavior pattern and act automatically without contemplating every decision or action in great detail. Active thinking is not required, because the situation fits the mental prototype, which in turn triggers the script and the prescribed behaviors. According to Gioia, this is something like "cruising on automatic pilot." Many of us discover that we have been cruising on automatic pilot when we drive to a familiar destination, but we can't recall how we got there. We were following an established behavior pattern. The route was so familiar that we didn't have to think about it anymore. Somehow we were magically there. Similar things happen at work. Behaviors become routine or "scripted," and we do them pretty much without thinking. Many jobs have scripts associated with them. For example, insurance claims adjusters have a set of criteria they use to make decisions about claims, and emergency medical personnel have a script for deciding which medical problems require the most immediate attention. If a symptom is not a part of the accepted script, it is likely to be overlooked.

Given the huge information load expected of someone who was simultaneously managing hundreds of files on potential safety problems, scripts provided a great information processing advantage to the Ford recall coordinator. Rather than treating every potential problem situation as unique, Gioia could save time and mental energy by making quick and efficient decisions about problems as they arose. As early reports about the Pinto began to trickle in, they didn't raise any red flags because they fit the scripted criteria for a "normal" accident and didn't fit the scripted criteria for a recall. Among other criteria, Gioia was taught to look for a large number of cases, a pattern of component failure, and a traceable cause to a design or manufacturing problem before proposing a recall. Therefore, he filed the claims automatically and gave seemingly more important problems his active attention.

Besides contributing to information processing efficiency, however, script processing clearly has some disadvantages. Gioia admittedly "looked right past" potential problems because he had seen similar information patterns hundreds of times before. The scripted definition of a crisis case was not met by the information he received, so the Pinto wasn't singled out for attention. Consistent with research on script processing, he selectively perceived information that was consistent with the script and ignored information that didn't fit the pattern.

Muffled emotions can also become part of a script. Many jobs require the control of emotions, particularly negative emotions. The recall coordinator's job fit this category, as would the job of a health professional in the emergency room or an insurance claims handler who reads constantly about terrible accidents and the disabilities that result. For Gioia to function in his job every day, his emotions had to be squelched to some degree. Even when one event penetrated his script, it didn't lead to recall of the Pinto. He had received a photograph of a burned Pinto and subsequently saw in person the burned hulk of an actual automobile. These powerful visual images triggered an emotional response and moved him to bring the case before members of the field recall office. However, at the meeting, it became clear that the characteristics of the Pinto problem didn't meet the group's shared scripted criteria for a recall. For example, only a few field reports had come in about the Pinto, much fewer than the number that would generally support a recall decision. All members, including Gioia, voted not to recall.

Script processing can be particularly problematic for ethical decision making. First, ethical decision making requires active consideration of the moral dimensions of the situation and a "custom" decision, tailored to the complexities of that particular case. Yet, Gioia argues, in many situations organizational members are not even aware they are dealing with an ethical dilemma. In terms of our previous discussion, they are ethically unaware. They handle situations by following scripts that are likely to exclude ethical considerations. In other words, ethical dilemmas do not lend themselves to "automatic pilot" decisions. But the realities of our hectic work lives make this sort of default decision making very common.

Cost-Benefit Analysis

Frequently, in addition to the cognitive processing limitations of individual decision makers, institutionalized decision-making processes can powerfully influence the decisions made by individuals or groups. In the Pinto fires case, a controversial decision-making process was used to justify the decision not to change the gas tank design. The National Traffic Safety Association had approved the use of cost-benefit analyses to establish automotive safety design standards. This process involved the assignment of a dollar value for a human life—in 1970, the value was deemed to be approximately $200,000 (it's over $3 million today). As an internal memo revealed, Ford had tabulated the costs of altering the tank design (for all similarly designed vehicles) to be $137 million, or $11 per vehicle. The benefits were calculated to be $49,530,000. These included the savings to society that would be accrued by preventing 180 deaths at $200,000 each, plus 180 projected burn injuries at $67,000 per injury and 2,100 burned cars at $700 per car. Using the cost-benefit analysis made the decision seem straightforward. The costs of redesign outweighed the benefits and would therefore not be undertaken. Ethical considerations didn't figure into the equation.

Attempts to reduce complex decision making to quantitative terms aren't uncommon, especially in a highly competitive business environment. In this way, complex decisions can be simplified—apparently, an advantage. Today, insurance companies and many government agencies still assign a value to human life as they attempt to calculate the costs and benefits of new regulations. And those managing relief efforts after the World Trade Center terrorist attack had to decide how much money should be given to families who lost loved ones. What is a life worth? Are some people's lives "worth" more than others because they would have had more earning potential had they lived? Unfortunately, this kind of decision making is a part of our modern lives. Decisions like this are made in courtrooms and by insurance companies every day. But the potential disadvantages of reducing the value of human life to quantitative terms should be clear. Such simplification can remove moral criteria from the decision-making process and reduce ethical awareness.

The Pinto fires example also points to the importance of multiple ethical selves and role behavior that will be discussed further in Chapter 7. Gioia was an idealistic young student, but he admittedly dropped his idealism at the corporation door. In performing his job of recall coordinator, Gioia was heavily influenced by the role expectations and guiding scripts. As he says:

> The recall coordinator's job was serious business. The scripts associated
> with it influenced me more than I influenced [them]. Before I went to Ford
> I would have argued strongly that Ford had an ethical obligation to recall.
> After I left Ford, I now argue and teach that Ford had an ethical obligation
> to recall. But, while I was there, I perceived no obligation to recall and I
> remember no strong ethical overtones to the case whatsoever. It was a very
> straightforward decision, driven by dominant scripts for the time, place,
> and context.[73]

Clearly, these processes that individuals and organizations use to simplify complex decisions can have significant implications for the ethical decisions managers make. Although script processing and quantitative decision-making criteria clearly help us do our jobs more efficiently, they can also strip ethical considerations from the decision-making process.

One way to address this problem is to make ethical considerations part of the script. Gioia suggests that this may be possible, although he warns that "it will take substantial concentration on the ethical dimension of the corporate culture (see Chapter 5), as well as overt attempts to emphasize ethics in education, training, and decision making before typical organizational scripts are likely to be modified to include the crucial ethical component."[74] You can help your subordinates by working with them to make the scripts explicit and to analyze them for their ethical components.

You can also require decision-making groups to analyze the ethical aspects of their decisions and to include this analysis in their reports. Just as environmental impact statements are now a routine part of many business decisions, an ethical analysis could require that managers focus on the influence of a particular decision on stakeholders' rights and consequences for the community or communities affected by the decision. You can also require groups to justify their decision-making process (e.g., decision-making criteria and weighting) in moral as well as quantitative terms.

CONCLUSION

This chapter has introduced you to individual differences that can influence ethical decision making. It has also outlined the cognitive limitations and biases that can interfere with good ethical decision making. Hopefully, knowing about these and how they can be overcome will help you be a better individual decision maker. Chapter 4 provides some guidance regarding how you can find your moral voice and actually do what you think is right. Much of the remainder of the book moves beyond the individual focus to look at the group and organizational influences that can have a profound influence on your decisions and actions, sometimes making it difficult to do the right thing.

EXERCISE

Understanding Cognitive Moral Development

Molly has been a local newspaper reporter for over 10 years. She learned that Joe Thompson, a candidate for governor, had been arrested for shoplifting 20 years earlier. She also learned that early in his life, Thompson went through a confused period when he did things he later regretted. The shoplifting was treated as a minor offense and removed from his record. Since then, Thompson has had a distinguished career helping people and leading important community projects. Many people consider him to be the best candidate who will likely go on to other important leadership positions. Molly wonders whether she should write a story about Joe's earlier troubles that could ruin his chance to win.

Can you characterize Molly's thinking in terms of cognitive moral development levels? Which of the following questions represents preconventional, conventional, and principled thinking?

- Are there any laws against writing the story?
- Would getting "the scoop" help or hurt my career?
- If I don't publish the story, wouldn't another reporter write the story anyway?
- What action would best serve society in the long term?
- How would my boss react if I wrote, or didn't write, the story?

- Aren't reporters expected to report all the news regardless of the circumstances?
- Would Thompson pay me not to write the story?
- Would the election process be more just with or without reporting the story?

DISCUSSION QUESTIONS

Note that these questions apply to Gioia's "Reflections" as well as the rest of the chapter.

1. Steven F. Goldstone, chairman and CEO of RJR Nabisco (one of the four biggest U.S. cigarette manufacturers), said in a 1998 magazine interview, "I have no moral view of this business . . . I viewed it as a legal business. You shouldn't be drawing a moral judgment about a business our country says is perfectly legal and is taxed like crazy by it."[75] Think about Goldstone's statement in terms of ethical awareness. What might happen if he began thinking about his business in ethical, and not just legal, terms?

2. Evaluate yourself in terms of cognitive moral development, locus of control, ethical decision-making style, moral disengagement, and Machiavellianism. What does this evaluation tell you about your own ethical decision making? Do the same for someone you know well.

3. Can you think of times when you have used morally disengaged thinking?

4. Identify a situation in which you have used script processing in a work or other life situation.

5. Do you believe that scripts can override an individual's value system?

6. Answer the question posed in Gioia's "Reflections": Is a person behaving unethically if the situation was not even construed in ethical terms—if there was no ethical awareness?

7. Who should make the decision about taking risks with others' lives in designing products?

8. Should a person be permitted to place a value on a human life? Should a company? Should the government? If not, how would decisions be made about whether to market certain products (that might be risky for some, but helpful for others), how much those who have lost family members in disasters should be compensated, and so on?

9. How do you feel about the use of cost-benefit analysis where human life is part of the cost calculation? Might the infusion of moral language have changed the decision makers' thinking? For example, what if decision makers had talked about their responsibility for killing 180 human beings?

10. Given that all automobiles are unsafe to some degree, where do you draw the line on product safety? How safe is safe enough—and who decides?

SHORT CASE

Mary, the director of nursing at a regional blood bank, is concerned about the declining number of blood donors. It's May, and Mary knows that the approaching summer will mean increased demands for blood and decreased supplies, especially of rare blood types. She is excited, therefore, when a large corporation offers to host a series of blood drives at all of its locations, beginning at corporate headquarters. Soon after Mary and her staff arrive at the corporate site, Mary hears a disturbance. Apparently, a nurse named Peggy was drawing blood from a male donor with a very rare blood type when the donor fondled her breast. Peggy jumped back and began to cry. Joe, a male colleague, sprang to Peggy's defense and told the donor to leave the premises. To Mary's horror, the male donor was a senior manager with the corporation. What is the ethical dilemma in this case, and what values are in conflict? How should Mary deal with Peggy, Joe, the donor, and representatives of the corporation?

NOTES

1. D. Robertson, J. Snarey, O. Ousley, K. Harenski, F. D. Bowman, and R. Gilkey, "The Neural Processing of Moral Sensitivity to Issues of Justice and Care," *Neuropsychologia* 45 (2007): 755–66.
2. J. Moll, R. deOliveira-Souza, P. J. Eslinger, I. E. Bramati, J. Mourao-Miranda, P. A. Andreiuolo et al., "The Neural Correlates of Moral Sensitivity: A fMRI Investigation of Basic and Moral Emotions," *Journal of Neuroscience* 22 (2002): 2730–36; R. Salvador and R. G. Folger, "Business Ethics and the Brain," *Business Ethics Quarterly* 19, no. 1 (2009): 1–31.
3. K. Butterfield, L. K. Treviño, and G. R. Weaver, "Moral Awareness in Business Organizations: Influences of Issue-Related and Social Context Factors," *Human Relations* 53, no. 7 (2000): 981–1018.
4. S. T. Fiske, and S. E. Taylor, *Social Cognition*, 2nd ed. (New York: McGraw-Hill, 1991).
5. J. Darnton, "Revisiting Rwanda's Horrors with a Former National Security Advisor," *New York Times*, December 20, 2004, B1.
6. W. J. Clinton, *My Life* (New York: Knopf, 2004).
7. D. Darlin, "H.P., Red-Faced but Still Selling," *New York Times*, October 1, 2006.
8. T. M. Jones, "Ethical Decision Making by Individuals in Organizations: An Issue-Contingent Model," *Academy of Management Review* 16 (1991): 366–95.
9. S. E. Siwek, *The True Cost of Sound Recording Piracy to the U.S. Economy* (Lewiston, TX: Institute for Policy Innovation, 2007).
10. S. Rommel, and R. G. Folger, "Business Ethics and the Brain," *Business Ethics Quarterly* 19 (2009): 1.
11. D. R. Forsyth, "A Taxonomy of Ethical Ideologies," *Journal of Personality and Social Psychology* 39 (1980): 175–84.
12. D. R. Forsyth, "Judging the Morality of Business Practices: The Influences of Personal Moral Philosophies," *Journal of Business Ethics* 11, nos. 5, 6 (1992): 461–70.
13. T. Barnett, K. Bass, and G. Brown, "Ethical Ideology and Ethical Judgment Regarding Ethical Issues in Business," *Journal of Business Ethics* 13, no. 6 (1994): 469–80; D. R. Forsyth, "Individual Differences in Information Integration during Moral Judgment," *Journal of Personality and Social Psychology* 49 (1985): 264–72.
14. C. A. Henle, R. A. Giacalone, and C. L. Jurkiewicz, "The Role of Ethical Ideology in Workplace Deviance," *Journal of Business Ethics* 56 (2005): 219–30.
15. J. Kish-Gephart, D. Harrison, and L. K. Treviño, "Bad Apples, Bad Cases, and Bad Barrels: Meta-analytic Evidence about Sources of Unethical Decisions at Work," *Journal of Applied Psychology* 95 (2010): 1–31.

16. L. Kohlberg, "Stage and Sequence: The Cognitive-Developmental Approach to Socialization," in *Handbook of Socialization Theory and Research*, ed. D. A. Goslin (New York: Rand McNally, 1969), 347–80.

17. M. Rest, *Moral Development: Advances in Research and Theory* (New York: Praeger, 1986).

18. L. K. Treviño and S. A. Youngblood, "Bad Apples in Bad Barrels: A Causal Analysis of Ethical Decision-Making Behavior," *Journal of Applied Psychology* 75, no. 4 (1990): 378–85.

19. J. Weber, "The Relationship between Managerial Value Orientations and Stages of Moral Development: Theory Development and Empirical Investigation with Behavioral Implications" (Unpublished dissertation, University of Pittsburgh, 1998).

20. "Cartel Tells Smugglers to Live 'Clean' Life," Yahoo! News, April 20, 2009.

21. C. Gilligan, *In a Different Voice* (Cambridge, MA: Harvard University Press, 1982).

22. C. Gilligan and J. Attanuci, "Two Moral Orientations," in *Mapping the Moral Domain*, eds. C. Gilligan, J. V. Ward, and J. M. Taylor (Cambridge, MA: Harvard University Press, 1988), 73–86.

23. R. Derry, "Moral Reasoning in Work-Related Conflicts," *Research in Corporate Social Performance and Policy* 9 (1987): 25–50.

24. M. Rest, *Moral Development: Advances in Research and Theory* (New York: Praeger, 1986).

25. M. L. Ambrose and M. Schminke, "Sex Differences in Business Ethics: The Importance of Perceptions," *Journal of Managerial Issues* 11, no. 4 (1999): 454–74; Kish-Gephart et al., "Bad Apples, Bad Cases."

26. This phrase was used with different meaning by R. Jackall in Moral Mazes (New York: Oxford University Press, 1988).

27. L. K. Treviño, "Moral Reasoning and Business Ethics," *Journal of Business Ethics* 11 (1992): 445–59.

28. S. J. Thoma, and J. R. Rest, "The Relationship between Moral Decision Making and Patterns of Consolidation and Transition in Moral Judgment Development," *Developmental Psychology* 35 (1999): 323–34.

29. J. Dukerich, M. L. Nichols, D. R. Elm, and D. A. Vollrath, "Moral Reasoning in Groups: Leaders Make a Difference," *Human Relations* 43 (1990): 473–93.

30. M. Schminke, M. L. Ambrose, and D. O. Neubaum, "The Effect of Moral Development on Ethical Climate and Employee Attitudes," *Organizational Behavior and Human Decision Processes* 97 (2005): 135–51.

31. L. K. Treviño, "Moral Reasoning and Business Ethics," *Journal of Business Ethics* 11 (1992): 445–59.

32. J. B. Rotter, "Generalized Expectancies for Internal versus External Control of Reinforcement," *Psychological Monographs: General and Applied* 80 (1966): 1–28.

33. E. Midlarski, "Aiding under Stress: The Effects of Competence, Dependency, Visibility, and Fatalism," *Journal of Personality* 39 (1971): 132–49; E. Midlarski, and M. Midlarski, "Some Determinants of Aiding under Experimentally Induced Stress," *Journal of Personality* 41 (1973): 305–27; E. M. Ubbink, and S. W. Sadava, "Rotter's Generalized Expectancies as Predictors of Helping Behavior," *Psychological Reports* 35 (1974): 865–66.

34. R. C. Johnson, J. M. Ackerman, H. Frank, and A. J. Fionda, "Resistance to Temptation and Guilt Following Yielding and Psychotherapy," *Journal of Consulting and Clinical Psychology* 32 (1968): 169–75.

35. L. R. Propst, "Effects of Personality and Loss of Anonymity on Aggression: A Re-evaluation of Deindividuation. *Journal of Personality* 47 (1979): 531–45.

36. "Niccolo Machiavelli," Stanford Encyclopedia of Philosophy online (Metaphysics Research Lab, CSLI, Stanford University); at http://plato.stanford.edu/entries/machiavelli/.

37. Kish-Gephart et al., "Bad Apples, Bad Cases"; W. H. Hegarty and H. P. Sims, "Organizational Philosophy, Policies, and Objectives Related to Unethical Decision Behavior: A Laboratory Experiment," *Journal of Applied Psychology* 64 (1979): 331–38; S. Flynn, M. Reichard, and S. Slane, "Cheating as a Function of Task Outcome and Machiavellianism," *Journal of Psychology* 121 (1987): 423–27; G. E. Jones and M. J. Kavanagh, "An Experimental Examination of the Effects of Individual and Situational Factors on Unethical Intentions in the Workplace," *Journal of Business Ethics* 15 (1996): 511–23.

38. A. Bandura, *Social Foundations of Thought and Action: A Social Cognitive Theory* (Englewood Cliffs, NJ: Prentice Hall, 1986).
39. J. R. Detert, L. K. Treviño, and V. L. Sweitzer, "Moral Disengagement in Ethical Decision Making: A Study of Antecedents and Outcomes," *Journal of Applied Psychology* 93 (2008): 374–91.
40. M. H. Bazerman, *Judgment in Managerial Decision Making* (New York: Wiley & Sons, 1994).
41. D. M. Messick and M. Bazerman, "Ethical Leadership and the Psychology of Decision-Making," *Sloan Management Review* (Winter 1996): 9–22.
42. Ibid.
43. M. H. Bazerman, *Judgment in Managerial Decision Making* (New York: Wiley & Sons, 1994).
44. D. M. Messick and M. Bazerman, "Ethical Leadership and the Psychology of Decision-Making," *Sloan Management Review* (Winter 1996): 9–22.
45. Ibid.
46. G. Loewenstein, "Behavioral Decision Theory and Business Ethics: Skewed Trade-offs between Self and Other," in *Codes of Conduct: Behavioral Research into Business Ethics*, eds. D. M. Messick and A. E. Tenbrunsel (New York: Russell Sage, 1996).
47. D. M. Messick and M. Bazerman, "Ethical Leadership and the Psychology of Decision-Making," *Sloan Management Review* (Winter 1996): 9–22.
48. Ibid.
49. B. M. Staw and I. Ross, "Understanding Escalation Situations," in *Research in Organizational Behavior*, Vol. 9, eds. B. M. Staw and L. L. Cummings (Greenwich, CT: JAI Press, 1987).
50. D. M. Messick and M. Bazerman, "Ethical Leadership and the Psychology of Decision-Making," *Sloan Management Review* (Winter 1996): 9–22.
51. R. A. Prentice, "Ethical Decision Making: More Needed than Good Intentions," *Financial Analysts Journal* 63, no. 6 (2007): 17–30.
52. G. Loewenstein, "Behavioral Decision Theory and Business Ethics: Skewed Trade-offs between Self and Other," in *Codes of Conduct: Behavioral Research into Business Ethics*, eds. D. M. Messick and A. E. Tenbrunsel (New York: Russell Sage, 1996).
53. J. Haidt, "The Emotional Dog and Its Rational Tail: A Social Intuitionist Approach to Moral Judgment," *Psychological Review* 108, no. 4 (2001): 814–34.
54. S. Rommel, and R. G. Folger, "Business Ethics and the Brain," *Business Ethics Quarterly* 19 (2009): 1.
55. B. Bower, "The Bias Finders," *Science News*, April 22, 2006, 250–51, 253.
56. N. Eisenberg, "Emotion, Regulation, and Moral Development," *Annual Review of Psychology* 51 (2000): 665–97; A. Gaudine and L. Thorne, "Emotion and Ethical Decision Making in Organizations," *Journal of Business Ethics* 31, no. 2 (2001): 175–87.
57. S. Rommel, and R. G. Folger, "Business Ethics and the Brain," *Business Ethics Quarterly* 19 (2009): 1.
58. J. Lehrer, "Hearts and Minds," *Boston Globe*, April 29, 2007; available at www.boston.com; Rommel and Folger, "Business Ethics and the Brain."
59. J. D. Greene, R. B. Sommerville, L. E. Nystrom, J. M. Darley, and J. D. Cohen, "An fMRI Investigation of Emotional Engagement in Moral Judgment," *Science* 293 (2001): 2105–8.
60. R. L. Hotz, "Scientists Draw Link between Morality and Brain's Wiring" (May 11, 2007), Science Journal at WallStreetJournal.com; available at http://online.wsj.com/article/SB117884235401499300.html.
61. Eisenberg, "Emotion, Regulation, and Moral Development"; Gaudine and Thorne, "Emotion and Ethical Decision Making in Organizations."
62. R. Folger, R. Cropanzano, and B. Goldman, "What Is the Relationship between Justice and Morality?" in *Handbook of Organizational Justice*, eds. J. Greenberg and J. A. Colquitt (Mahwah, NJ: Erlbaum, 2005), 215–46.
63. J. Kish-Gephart, J. Detert, L. K. Treviño, and A. Edmondson, "Silenced by Fear: The Nature, Sources, and Consequences of Fear at Work," *Research in Organizational Behavior* 29 (2010), 163–193.
64. C. J. Turillo, R. Folger, J. J. Lavelle, E. E. Umphress, and J. O. Gee, "Is Virtue Its Own Reward? Self-Sacrificial Decisions for the Sake of Fairness," *Organizational Behavior and Human Decision Processes* 89 (2002): 839–65.

65. J. McGregor, "Sweet Revenge," *Businessweek*, January 22, 2007, 62–70.
66. Ibid.
67. P. Elkind, "Blood Feud," *Fortune*, April 14, 1997, 90–102.
68. Ibid.
69. Ibid.
70. Ibid.
71. D. Gioia, "Pinto Fires and Personal Ethics: A Script Analysis of Missed Opportunities," *Journal of Business Ethics* 11, nos. 5, 6 (1992): 379–89.
72. Ibid.
73. Ibid.
74. Ibid.
75. J. Goldberg, "Big Tobacco's Endgame," *New York Times Magazine*, June 21, 1998, 36–42, 58–60.

CHAPTER 4

ADDRESSING INDIVIDUALS' COMMON ETHICAL PROBLEMS

Here's the bad news about business ethics: your career can be irrevocably damaged if you mishandle an ethical issue. But there's also good news: many ethical issues in business are quite predictable. You can be fairly certain that during the course of your career, you'll run into myriad ethical problems such as a customer who asks for a special deal or terms in order to make the sale, or questions about the appropriate use of corporate resources, or discrimination of one sort or another. Since many ethical issues are somewhat predictable, you have a better chance of dealing appropriately with ethical problems if you think about what's likely to happen before it occurs. And you should now have tools to help you make better decisions.

Before we get into a discussion of ethical issues, however, it's important to look at the relationship that exists between you and your employer. Although most people don't sign a written contract on the day they join a company or organization, there is an implied contractual relationship of sorts between workers and employers. Both parties have expectations, and rights, and offer consideration to the other—all are characteristics of a contractual relationship. Your employer pays you in salary and benefits to perform a job, and your organization expects you to behave in a certain way; you have a responsibility to be "part of the family" and exhibit loyalty and other corporate "virtues" and to refrain from other, less desirable behaviors. On the other hand, you expect not only a salary for the work you perform but also a modicum of fairness. Most people expect employers to treat them decently and to provide an appropriate work environment. Whenever we discuss the employer-employee contract in this chapter, it's this complicated set of expectations that we're referring to.

So what are some typical ethical problems individuals face at work? We've compiled some of the more obvious ones and divided them into broad categories, including human resources issues, conflicts of interest, customer confidence issues, and the use of corporate resources. We address a number of specific topics under each broad category. To make it easy to follow, each topic contains the following information:

- What it is (a definition of the issue)
- Why it is an ethical problem
- How we can think about the issue

110

- Professional costs and possible penalties for ethical or legal transgressions
- Special notes and some topics that may include important information related to the topic

Identifying Your Values—and Voicing Them

Before we explore the various types of ethical problems covered in this chapter, we would like you to think again about what's important to you—in other words, what do you value? In Chapter 2, we discussed the various philosophical approaches to ethics, all of which can help you think through a dilemma. The principle-based approach encouraged you to think about your most cherished values. So, what happens if you think through a situation, figure out what to do based upon those values, and then hesitate to say or do what you believe to be ethical because of pressure that you feel from your organization's reward system or your boss or your peers? Once you've determined the right thing, how do you then do it? Well, according to some ethics experts at the Aspen Institute, it helps to practice.[1]

After World War II, researchers found that many of the people in Europe who had risked their own well-being to help others who were threatened by the Nazis did so because they had "practiced" making ethical decisions earlier in their lives by imagining themselves in hypothetical situations that challenged their values. They not only imagined these situations, but they also discussed their potential actions with others—what they might actually do if they encountered such a situation. Researchers theorize that this was a kind of "pre-scripting" that laid the groundwork for these people's later heroic actions. It was as if thinking about ethical issues long before they were actually confronted by the issues gave people a sort of head start in the moral courage department. The "Giving Voice to Values" program at the Aspen Institute is rooted in this interesting, worthwhile premise. Mary C. Gentile, the program developer, writes that the approach starts with "the assumption that we know what we want to do and then figuring out how we might make that happen—and then practicing our voice."

The program encourages students of all ages to first consider their values (as we encouraged you to do in Chapter 2). What do you care about? When you think deeply about your life, what are the values that attract you or stir deep feelings within you? Most people, for example, gravitate toward honesty, respect, responsibility, compassion, fairness, and other similar values.

In addition to values, we all have a personal narrative, a self-story that can help us when we face tough ethical issues. As you think about your life story, it can be helpful to look back on your life and search for experiences that might provide a source of passion or strength in difficult times. We often think of these as life situations that build character. Many of the best leaders say that difficult life experiences were transformative and provided new meaning and direction to their lives. For example, surviving a life-threatening illness can make other workplace threats seem much less dire. You might say to yourself, "Speaking up to my boss in a respectful way isn't going to kill me," so why not? Daniel Vasella, Chairman of the Board (and CEO for 14 years) of the pharmaceutical company Novartis, had his first hospital experience at age 4 as a result of food poisoning. He contracted tuberculosis and then meningitis at age 8 and spent a year in a sanatorium. At age 10, he lost his older sister. These are just a few of the challenges Vasella faced as a boy. He vividly recalls the loneliness and pain of these experiences, but he also remembers the powerful impact of a few special people who treated him with care and compassion and who fueled his desire to help other people, ultimately by becoming a physician. He later decided that by becoming a leader in a healthcare business, he could have even more impact and help more people than he could as a single practitioner.[2] So think about what your personal narrative is. What aspects of it might help give you the courage to do the right thing in tough situations?

Here's an abbreviated list of other self-assessment questions students are encouraged to consider as part of the Giving Voice to Values program:

1. Questions of purpose. What are your personal and professional goals? What do you hope to accomplish? What would make your professional life worthwhile?

2. Questions of risk. What is your risk profile? Are you a risk taker, or are you risk averse? What are the greatest risks you face in your line of work? What levels of risk can you live with, and which ones can't you live with?

3. Questions of personal communication style or preference. Do you deal well with conflict, or are you nonconfrontational? Do you prefer communicating in person or in writing? Do you think best from the gut and in the moment, or do you need time to reflect on and craft your communication?

4. Questions of loyalty. Do you tend to feel the greatest loyalty to family, work colleagues, your firm/employer, or other stakeholders, such as customers?

5. Questions of self-image. Do you identify yourself as being shrewd or naive? As idealistic or pragmatic? As a learner or as a teacher?

The point of this self-analysis is to first identify your own "self-story" or narrative—we all have one or are able to build one. Then, consider other personal characteristics that will help you find ways of behaving that align with your image of yourself. For example, if your own image of yourself is one of a bold, courageous character, you might be able to find a brave way of reacting to a situation—one that is aligned with the bold person you believe you are. And the converse is also true. If you are risk averse and timid, you may be able to find a way of reacting to a situation that is more "compliant" and that aligns with who you really are. The objective here, as you have probably already guessed, is to make it easier for you to voice your values and beliefs by creating a response and behavior that reflects your unique personality. Evaluating a dilemma through the lens of your own story makes it more likely that you will voice your values, and playing to your strengths makes it more likely that you'll stand up for what you believe.

The Giving Voice to Values program also encourages students to understand that values conflicts are absolutely normal. Far from being unusual or rare, ethical dilemmas happen all the time to everyone. The ethical dilemmas that we face every day test our ability to make good choices. If we anticipate the need to take risks—to make decisions that might turn out to be good ones or not—we will prepare ourselves. We'll internalize the idea that these situations are normal and survivable and that others are experiencing the same thing. These situations won't paralyze us.

Another important element of the program is to understand various communication techniques. *Voice* can mean dialogue or listening or other communication techniques such as researching and providing new data, questioning, negotiating, leading by example, identifying allies, and so forth. The point is that voice is not always about sounding off. In fact, it's more often about analyzing the situation, your audience, your own motivations and style, and then figuring out the best way to get your point across to others. In organizations, it can help greatly to find allies to support your viewpoint instead of being a lone voice, especially if you're bucking the system. Taking the time to convince allies to stand up with you for what you think is right can increase the chance that your viewpoint will prevail in the end.

The program also addresses the barriers we encounter in making decisions and voicing our beliefs—the reasons and rationalizations that can short-circuit our resolve. This part of the program asks us to identify the arguments that we're trying to counter, what's at stake for the various participants in the situation, how we might influence those we disagree with, and what is our most powerful argument. Some of these arguments are likely influenced by the barriers to good ethical judgment we discussed in Chapter 3.

Finally, the Giving Voice to Values program encourages students to consider choice: we all are capable of acting on our values, but sometimes we don't. The point of thinking about the issue of choice is to ensure that we understand that even the most ethical person may not always do the right thing. We make choices all the time that can reinforce our decision-making patterns or change them. If and when we make a mistake, we are capable of redefining ourselves the next time. The important point is to be self-aware, to acknowledge mistakes, and to be able to learn from them. To find out more about this impressive program, go to www.aspencbe.org/teaching/gvv/index.html.

Sometimes, voicing your values at work takes significant courage because of the risks involved. We'll talk later in this chapter about some of the potentially riskiest situations, where whistleblowing (on your boss or your organization) becomes a possibility.

PEOPLE ISSUES

We use the term *people issues* to describe the ethical problems that occur when people work together. The problems may concern privacy, discrimination, sexual and other types of harassment, or simply how people get along.

The word to remember when considering these issues is *fairness*. When most people think about fairness, they mean equity, reciprocity, and impartiality.[3] A situation is said to be equitable when something is divided between two people according to the worth and inputs of the two individuals. For example, in a situation where two people have shared responsibility for a project, one might ask: "Did we work equally hard? Did we receive equal shares? Most people think it's unfair when two people have performed the same duty but receive a different share of the reward. Another measure of fairness is reciprocity, or the fairness of exchanges: "You did this for me and I'll do that for you." Most people perceive a situation as being unfair if one person fails to hold up his or her part of a bargain. A third measure of fairness is impartiality: "Is the person who's going to listen to my story biased in some way, or has he or she prejudged the situation?" Most people think of fairness as being inconsistent with prejudice and bias.

Most protective legislation and corporate human resources policies also try to incorporate those elements. The goal is to hire, treat, promote, appraise, and lay off or fire employees based on their qualifications and not on factors like sex, race, or age. The goal is to level the playing field and create a fair environment where performance is the only factor that counts (equity), where employer-employee expectations are understood and met (reciprocity), and where prejudice and bias are not factors (impartiality).

It's important to remember that, to employees, fairness is not just about the outcomes they receive (pay, promotion, etc.). Employees care at least as much about the fairness of decision-making procedures and about the interpersonal treatment they receive when results are communicated. People are more likely to accept bad news if they believe the decision was made fairly and if the supervisor or organization explains the decision with sensitivity and care. An organization that uses fair procedures and treats employees with sensitivity sends a powerful message to all employees that it values them as important members of the community.[4]

Discrimination

> You and Lisa met five years ago when you were hired into the management training program of a large utility. Although you're now in different parts of the organization, you have managed to stay close over the years. Lisa recently had a baby and plans to take advantage of the full six months of maternity leave the company offers. She told you that she's definitely coming back to work after her leave and that her department has promised to hold her job for her. Meanwhile, you've seen a posting for her job on the company's website. You run into one of Lisa's colleagues in the hall and ask about the posting. He says, "Oh yeah, they're going to fill that job. But don't tell Lisa. She's got five more months to be a happy mom. Besides, they'll find something for her to do if she decides to come back."

Since discrimination by race, religion, national origin, sex, disability, and age is prohibited by federal law in the United States, many companies have defined policies prohibiting any kind of discrimination. Unfortunately, there can be quite a gulf between where corporate policy leaves off and reality begins. When people from various backgrounds get together to provide a service or manufacture a product, there surely will be people who have conscious or unconscious biases toward various groups, and there will be others who are simply ignorant of the effect their behavior has on others.

WHAT IS IT?   Discrimination occurs whenever something other than qualifications affects how an employee is treated. Unequal treatment, usually unfavorable, can take many forms. Older workers who suddenly find themselves reporting to younger ones can be resentful since they feel younger workers lack experience. Younger employees can be tempted to ignore advice from older workers, who they feel are out of touch. The attitudes toward age will most likely become increasingly important over the next decade as the general population grows older.

Racial, ethnic, religious, or sexual stereotypes can creep into the behavior of even the most sophisticated individuals, even without their conscious awareness. The importance of being able to manage different types of people can't be overstated. In the United States, ethnic and racial minorities are growing faster than the population as a whole, and the U.S. workforce is becoming increasingly diverse.

In the case involving Lisa, the new mother, her maternity leave could result in discrimination. Although pregnant employees are protected by law (see "Why Is It an Ethical Problem?" which follows), in this case her time away from her job is clearly being viewed as a liability. Of course, employers have the right to replace workers who are on extended leave because of illness, disability, or other reasons such as finishing an education. The problem in Lisa's case is that her department seems to be doing an end run around her by keeping her in the dark while her job is filled. If Lisa knew what the department's plans were, she might shorten her leave or arrange a part-time working situation for a few months. But unless you, her colleague, tell her what you have found out, the job she left won't be the one she comes back to. It seems unfair to keep Lisa in the dark.

Discrimination can be a subtle or not-so-subtle factor not only in working relationships but also in hiring, promotions, and layoff decisions. People who don't fit a "corporate profile" may be passed over for advancement because they're female, or a member of a minority group, or too old, or for other reasons that may or may not be covered in protectionist legislation. Surely there are many barriers in the workplace, not just the glass ceiling that refers to barriers to female advancement. There probably are also barriers for people who are over 50 years old, or who have medical problems, or who are short, disabled, overweight, bearded, balding, or homosexual—any quality that varies from the "norm." And some employers create job requirements that could automatically eliminate certain employees, not because of their qualifications, but because of personal circumstances.

HOW WE CAN THINK ABOUT THIS ISSUE   We can use the various theories described in Chapter 2 to analyze the situation. These theories can serve as various "lenses" that we can use in viewing a problem. None of these theories are likely to give us the perfect answer, but they'll help us think through the implications of an issue so that we can make a good decision.

Suppose we look though the consequentialist lens? Who are the stakeholders, and what are the harms and benefits to each? What could we do in this situation that would benefit the most people? If we think about it in that way, we might conclude that it's better to say nothing to Lisa. We might imagine that more people would benefit (at least in the short term) by Lisa's manager filling her old job right away. After all, Lisa's being away could cause problems for her coworkers. However, a longer-term perspective might cause us to ask how other women employees would respond to Lisa's seemingly unfair treatment. Their dissatisfaction could seriously harm the company. So, what is the best decision for society overall?

Looking through a deonotological lens would cause us to ask whether we have a duty or obligation to Lisa, our employer, or both. What values or principles are involved in this case? Using the Golden Rule, think of how you would want Lisa or your colleague to behave if the situation was reversed. Following Kant's categorical imperative, what kind of world would it be if employers routinely treated employees in this way? And, using Rawls's veil of ignorance, how would you make this decision if you had no idea if Lisa was a man or a woman?

Finally, if we think about virtue ethics and our own character, we would consider our intentions and motivations. We would also consider how professional human resources managers would think about this decision. We would ask ourselves how our decision would look to others if it were made public. What would our ethical role model or harshest moral critic think? If you consider your own character and what you value, what decision feels best? We might also consider some of the psychological issues described in Chapter 3. Are we considering all of the consequences of telling Lisa, or not? What could happen to her and to you if you tell, or if you don't tell?

This situation could test what you as an individual really care about, which is important if you're going to lead an ethical life. It's also a way to begin assessing your own values and asking how you can act more consistently with those values, as we suggested earlier in this chapter when discussing the Giving Voice to Values program.

If you decided that the right thing to do was to take action on Lisa's behalf, how might you go about it? Whom would you approach, and what would you say? Or, would you consider providing Lisa with information so that she could act on her own behalf?

WHY IS IT AN ETHICAL PROBLEM?   Discrimination is an ethical issue—beyond any legal protections—because it's at the core of fairness in the workplace. While concepts of fairness are incorporated in business law around the world, in the United States fairness is considered to be an inalienable right.[5] The U.S. government has attempted to ensure fairness and justice; the word *trust* is on every piece of currency, and the Pledge of Allegiance declares "with liberty and justice for all." In addition, the entire U.S. legal system has justice and the protection of individual rights as its cornerstone. Consequently, people expect fairness from organizations in general and specifically from their employers.

COSTS   While laws and regulations governing fairness differ around the world, in the United States victims of discrimination can file under Title VII of the Civil Rights Act of 1964 with the Equal Employment Opportunity Commission (EEOC) or bring suit under tort or contract law. This legislation specifically prohibits discrimination based on race, religion, sex, color, and national origin. Groups specifically protected by Title VII include women, African Americans, Hispanics, Native Americans, and Asian Pacific Islanders. (Some states and local communities have added more protections, like sexual orientation and marital status, to that list.) The Pregnancy Discrimination Act of 1978 prohibits discrimination against pregnant women. The 1967 Age Discrimination in Employment Act extends protection to people 40 years of age and older. The 1973 Rehabilitation Act was the first federal legislation to protect disabled Americans against discrimination by federal, state, and local governments, agencies, and contractors. The Americans with Disabilities Act (ADA) of 1990 extended protection to the private sector by requiring all companies with more than 15 employees to make reasonable accommodations to employ workers with disabilities. Although the law doesn't list conditions or diseases that are protected—since people react differently to disease, some may be disabled and some may not be—some conditions are specifically included or excluded. HIV infection, for example, is considered a disability; people who have it are protected by the ADA. Indications of how costly bias suits can be for corporations are evident in several recent judgments: in 2005, UBS (Europe's largest bank) was ordered to pay damages of $29 million to a single plaintiff—a woman who complained of unequal treatment.[6] In other cases, a judge awarded $70 million for gender discrimination to 2,800 female employees of Morgan Stanley who were registered financial advisors,[7] and an arbitration panel in New York ordered Merrill Lynch to pay more than $100 million to a group of women who were found to have been discriminated against.[8]

Discrimination lawsuits can be costly for employers not simply in terms of legal fees and damages and media coverage. The morale of victims certainly suffers as they endure discrimination lawsuits, but the morale of other employees can also suffer. It's embarrassing for employees when the company they work for is publicly accused of wrongdoing.

If you're an individual accused of discriminating against another employee, the least you'll endure is an investigation. If you're found guilty, you'll probably be penalized or even fired. If you're found innocent, you or your accuser will most likely be counseled about your behavior and its effects, and one or both of you may be transferred to another area. If you manage someone who has been accused of discrimination, expect a lot of questions concerning why you were unaware of it or tolerated it. If you were aware of it and didn't do anything about it, be prepared for disciplinary action, particularly if a lawsuit results.

SPECIAL NOTE   The many programs that train employees to "value diversity" can seem at odds with the efforts to assimilate various groups and especially with the laws and policies that prohibit discrimination. Learning to appreciate differences flies in the face of what many of us are taught from the time we're children—that we should "fit in." Many of us are taught not only to downplay our own uniqueness in an effort to blend in but also to ignore differences in other people. We usually are taught "not to notice" different colors, religions, accents, ways of dressing, and physical disabilities or abilities. Even sexual differences, which can be hard to ignore, have been played down in the not-too-distant past.

Valuing diversity means treating people equally while incorporating their diverse ideas. Discrimination means treating people unequally because they are, or appear to be, different. Valuing diversity is a positive action, while discrimination is a negative action. Valuing diversity tries to incorporate more fairness into the system, while discrimination incorporates unfairness into the system. The key to valuing diversity is understanding that different doesn't mean deficient, and it doesn't mean less. Different means different.

Harassment, Sexual and Otherwise

As women began to enter the workforce in great numbers in the 1970s and 1980s, and as social and business mores began to change, sexual harassment became an issue in the workplace. Forty years later, it is still an issue and many companies have paid huge fines in sexual harassment lawsuits. As a result, the EEOC now requires all organizations with more than 15 employees to have a sexual harassment policy and to train employees in these issues. Another result was a growing apprehension by employees, especially men, toward workers of the opposite sex. Sometimes the line between friendly and offensive is blurry.

> One of your coworkers is Joanne, a computer whiz with an offbeat style and a great sense of humor. Two of Joanne's favorite "targets" are you and Bill, another coworker who tends to be quite standoffish in his business relationships. Joanne is the department clown and is forever goading you and Bill; you, because you're a great audience and clearly think she's hilarious; Bill, because she likes to try to get him to be more approachable. Joanne frequently alludes to sexual subjects and has called both you and Bill "little alley cats" and "studs." While Joanne's behavior doesn't offend you at all, you're surprised when Bill approaches you in the men's room and bitterly complains about Joanne's constant teasing.

WHAT IS IT? Sexual harassment is defined as unwelcome sexually oriented behavior that makes someone feel uncomfortable at work. It usually involves behavior by someone of higher status toward someone of lower status or power. Sexual harassment claims are not initiated only by women; the EEOC (www.eeoc.gov) reported receiving 11,364 sexual harassment claims in 2012, and more than 16 percent were made by men.

Federal law has defined two types of sexual harassment: quid pro quo and hostile work environment. *Quid pro quo* harassment means that sexual favors are a requirement—or appear to be a requirement—for advancement in the workplace. *Hostile work environment* means that a worker has been made to feel uncomfortable because of unwelcome actions or comments relating to sexuality. This type of sexual harassment is especially murky because it is like beauty: it's in the eye of the beholder. What constitutes sexual harassment for one person may not be so for another. Putting an arm around a person's shoulder may feel like harassment to one individual, and someone else may be comfortable with such a gesture. This type of sexual harassment includes not only physical gestures but also remarks of a sexual nature—even compliments—and displays of sexually provocative material, like nude or revealing photographs, in an office.

In both types of sexual harassment, the decision about whether the behavior constitutes harassment is determined from the viewpoint of a "reasonable" person, and the harasser's intentions aren't considered. This is why sexual harassment issues can be confusing. Since sexual harassment is determined by the reaction of the victim, you have to consider not what you mean by your comments or actions, but how they might be interpreted by the other person.

Most people will readily agree that patting a coworker on the rear end is sexual harassment. But are you sexually harassing someone if you compliment her appearance, or touch his arm, or make jokes of a sexual nature? In Joanne's case, she hasn't done a very good job of considering exactly who her audience is and how each of her two coworkers might react to her jokes. While you might think it's funny to be called a little stud, Joanne probably should think more carefully about how someone like Bill might react to being called a name with sexual connotations. Is Joanne out of line? Is Bill overreacting? According to the law, it doesn't matter if you and Joanne think Bill is overreacting. The yardstick for determining whether sexual harassment occurred will be how uncomfortable a reasonable person would be with Joanne's comments, and not what Joanne intended with her remarks. How Bill *felt* will be considered more than what Joanne *intended*.

HOW WE CAN THINK ABOUT THIS ISSUE Consider how a consequentialist might think about this situation. Can you identify all of the stakeholders and the harms and benefits to each? What are your options? What action on your part would benefit the most people and harm the least, thus contributing the most to societal good? For example, have you thought about the potential effects on Joanne if she continues such behavior? Daniel Goleman, the well-known psychologist and author of numerous books on emotional and social intelligence, describes three qualities that differentiate great leaders from average ones: (1) self awareness—knowing your own strengths and limits and strengthening your inner ethical radar, (2) self-management—being able to manage your emotions in ways that allow you to effectively lead yourself, and, (3) empathy—understanding the emotional reactions of others in order to lead them effectively. If Joanne is unable to see how her remarks might upset a coworker, she is unlikely to be promoted to a supervisory or management position. If she can't self-regulate her behavior, it's unlikely that the organization will promote her to a leadership position where that unregulated behavior will affect other employees.[9] So, intervening in a thoughtful and sensitive way may help everyone involved, even Joanne.

Now use another lens: Do you have ethical duties or obligations here? What are those and to whom? What ethical principles apply to this situation, and what rules would help you decide what's right? For example, if the situation was reversed and you were in either Bill's or Joanne's shoes, how would you like them to help you?

You might think about the "reasonable person standard" as providing insight into the relevant ethical community. How would a reasonable person assess the situation and determine the right thing to do? How would you feel if Bill spoke to a reporter and this situation appeared in the local newspaper? If you do nothing in this case, would you be chagrined to read about it in the newspaper? Could you proudly describe your actions to your mother or your priest (or minister, rabbi, imam, etc.) without embarrassment?

Think about your organization's culture. What values does your organization hold dear? Most companies pride themselves on being places where all employees can feel respected. If you look at your company's values statement, you'll likely find verbiage about respect. Given that value of respect, what would your manager and others in positions of authority in your organization want you to do?

If you decide to act on your values, you have quite a few options. One option is to nip this issue in the bud by helping Bill address it with Joanne. Perhaps Joanne is unaware of the effect her comments are having on Bill. You could encourage Bill to talk with her, explain his reaction, and request that she stop. You could role-play Joanne to give Bill the opportunity to practice what he is going to say. What could Bill say to Joanne, and how could he say it in a way that will likely achieve his intended result and allow the parties to continue working together in the future? If Bill is unwilling to do this, what other options do you have? You could report the issue to the organization's ethics help line, but would it be appropriate to do that without Bill's permission? Under what circumstances would you report something that affected a coworker without that person's permission?

WHY IS IT AN ETHICAL PROBLEM?   Harassment (sexual or otherwise) is considered to be a form of discrimination. It is therefore an ethical issue because it unfairly focuses job satisfaction, advancement, or retention on a factor other than the employee's ability to do the job. Most instances of sexual harassment have nothing to do with romance and everything to do with power and fairness.

COSTS   Victims of sexual harassment can file under Title VII of the Civil Rights Act of 1964 with the EEOC, or they can bring suit under tort or contract law. An employer can be held liable for an employee's sexual harassment activities if the employer had knowledge of the conduct and did nothing to correct it. As a result, most companies take a sexual harassment charge very seriously.

Responsible companies will launch an immediate investigation if someone is accused of sexually harassing another employee. If this is a first-time event and the incident that prompted it is not determined to be lewd or violent—think of the scenario featuring Joanne, discussed earlier—the employee may be warned, disciplined, or transferred to another area. (However, in some major companies a first-time offense is enough to get someone fired.) If the behavior is judged to be lewd or forceful, or if there's evidence that the employee has demonstrated a pattern of behavior, the employee will most likely be fired—and often very quickly. (One corporation was able to conduct an investigation, find evidence of a pattern, and terminate the harasser in less than 48 hours.) If the accused is found innocent, or if it's determined that a misunderstanding exists between the two parties, the accused and the accuser will probably be counseled by human resources professionals. If necessary, one of the parties may be transferred to another area. The manager of a sexual harasser can expect a lot of questions. If the manager was aware of harassment and did nothing about it, he or she should be prepared for disciplinary action, particularly if a lawsuit results.

Nearly a third of the claims filed with the EEOC are sexual harassment claims. And sexual harassment lawsuits are very expensive for corporations. Awards to victims have been substantial, as is the toll such charges can take on coworker's morale and on the firm's ability to hire qualified candidates. For example, in June 1998, Mitsubishi Motors' North American division agreed to pay $34 million to settle its sexual harassment case. The settlement was based on charges brought by 350 female factory workers at an Illinois factory. The women alleged that coworkers and supervisors kissed and fondled them, called them "whores" and "bitches," posted sexual graffiti and pornography, demanded sex, and retaliated if they refused. They also complained that managers did nothing to stop the harassment. Besides paying the fine, Mitsubishi fired 20 workers and disciplined others. The company also agreed to provide mandatory sexual harassment training, revise its sexual harassment policy, and investigate future sexual harassment allegations within three weeks of a complaint.[10]

A NOTE ABOUT OFFICE ROMANCE Flirtations and office romance are a part of work life. After all, we spend most of our time at work, interacting with people who share our interests, and we have an opportunity to really get to know them. So why not engage in a consensual relationship with a coworker? Well, it's true that most office romances are benign, and quite a few of them either end quietly or may even lead to happy marriages. But such relationships can also be dangerous; in fact, these are the stories we end up hearing about. For example, if a relationship ends badly, one party may accuse the other of sexual harassment or retaliation, thus requiring the company to get involved after the fact.

From an ethics perspective, it's most important to avoid romance with anyone you supervise or who supervises you because of the conflict of interest involved and the potential for unfair treatment of other direct reports (and most companies have antinepotism policies). The supervisor's judgment is likely to be compromised by the relationship, and others in the work group are likely to lose respect for both parties and be concerned about preferential treatment. Honesty is another ethical issue that emerges. Because you don't know where the relationship is going, it's tempting to keep it to yourselves at first. Even if you're discreet, word travels fast in work groups, and others are likely to find out via the grapevine. It's best to be honest and keep your supervisor in the loop. If you work in the same department, the organization may want to move one of you to avoid any negative repercussions. And finally, remember—if you don't think your behavior would look good on the front page, it's best not to engage in it.[11]

CONFLICTS OF INTEREST

People and corporations are naturally involved in a tangle of relationships, both personal and professional. Your personal reputation and the reputation of your company are inextricably tied to how well you handle relationships with other employees, customers, consultants, vendors, family, and friends. Your ability to act impartially, and to look as if you are acting impartially, is key to your fulfilling your end of the employer-employee contract.

> Your daughter is applying to a prestigious university. Since admission to the school is difficult, your daughter has planned the process carefully. She has consistently achieved high marks, taken preparatory courses for entrance exams, and participated in various extracurricular activities. When you tell one of your best customers about her activities, he offers to write her a letter of recommendation. He's an alumnus of the school and is one of its most active fund-raisers. Although he's a customer, you also regularly play golf together, and your families have socialized together on occasion.

What Is It?

A conflict of interest occurs when your judgment or objectivity is compromised. The appearance of a conflict of interest—when a third party could think your judgment has been compromised—is generally considered just as damaging as an actual conflict.

A recent example of a conflict of interest likely contributed significantly to our financial crisis. Rating agencies such as Standard & Poor's rated the complex mortgage-backed securities we described in Chapter 1. A triple-A rating made investors feel secure about buying these securities. As Americans learned the hard way, however, many of these securities were not deserving of anything near such a high rating. Many factors contributed to the debacle (including the fact that rating agencies were using old methods to rate these newfangled products). A major contributor was a serious conflict of interest—the rating agencies are paid by the companies whose securities they rate, thus making it difficult or impossible to assign truly objective and unbiased ratings.

Another example might be of particular interest to college students. In 2007, the University of Texas fired its director of financial aid when it learned that he had financial ties to particular student loan companies that he then touted to students and peers. Students were not steered toward companies that provided the best loans or service, but toward those that provided gifts (including stock) to the director of financial aid.[12]

If a customer offers to do a favor for you—or your daughter or another family member—here are some of the questions you'll need to ask yourself: Would your customer's offer influence your business relationship? Would someone think your business judgment had been compromised by accepting your customer's offer? Is your relationship more than just a business one, so that accepting an offer could be interpreted as a simple act of friendship?

Some corporations have a policy that permits the acceptance of favors from customers or vendors if there's also a "friendship" present; and these companies usually define *friendship* as a long-standing relationship that's well known in the community. For example, in small towns where everyone knows everyone else, many of a business owner's customers are also his or her friends; it's unrealistic to expect anything else. Other organizations (including government agencies) would discourage accepting a favor like this one under any circumstances. Here are some things to consider when making your decision in this case: How long have you been friends with your customer? How well known is the relationship in your community? What is his knowledge of your daughter's qualifications? Does your customer expect anything in return for his recommendation, or is the letter simply a gesture of friendship with no strings attached? How would others perceive his recommendation?

Almost every business situation can involve conflicts of interest. A conflict can occur when a vendor lavishly entertains you or when you entertain a customer—if the object is influence. Both situations could prompt an observer to think that a special deal or advantageous terms are part of the relationship. Conflicts of interest can occur when people who report to you observe that you have an especially close friendship with one of their coworkers. (This is one reason why it is never a good idea to date someone who reports to you!) Conflicts can occur when you're asked to judge the creditworthiness of your neighbor or if you perform consulting work for your employer's competitor. They can involve accepting handtooled cowboy boots from an advertising agency, being sponsored for membership in an exclusive private club by a consulting company, or allowing a supplier to give you a discount on equipment for your home when you place an order for your office.

Common conflicts of interest include overt or covert bribes and the trading of influence or privileged information.

OVERT BRIBES OR KICKBACKS Anything that could be considered a bribe or kickback is a clear conflict of interest. It doesn't matter whether the bribe or kickback is in the form of money or something else of substantial value that is offered in exchange for access to specific products, services, or influence.

SUBTLE "BRIBES" Bribes can be interpreted to include gifts and entertainment. Some organizations have instituted policies that allow no gifts at all, even gifts of nominal value. For example, we know of one teaching hospital that does not allow its employees to accept even a notepad or pen from pharmaceutical company representatives. They asked themselves, how will patients feel when we write a prescription for a product with a pen from the manufacturer? Won't the patient wonder if we're writing that prescription because it's really needed or because we've accepted such gifts? Many organizations have a policy that allows gifts of small value and places a ceiling of $25 to $100 on the value of gifts employees can accept from, or give to, customers or vendors. Reciprocity is one yardstick often used for determining whether a gift or entertainment is acceptable. If you can't reciprocate with the same kind of gift or entertainment being offered to you, it's probably inappropriate to accept it. For example, if a supplier offers you tickets to the Super Bowl, or a weekend of golf, or dinner for four at a $200-per-person restaurant, it's probably inappropriate for you to accept under any circumstances. The emphasis on reciprocity is to maintain a fair, even playing field for all suppliers, so that you (as a purchaser) will be unbiased when making a decision about a supplier. As mentioned earlier, both reciprocity and impartiality are elements of fairness.

Accepting discounts on personal items from a vendor will also be interpreted as a conflict. The formula to use when determining whether to accept a discount is simple: if it's a formal arrangement between your company and a supplier and it's offered to all employees, it's probably acceptable; if the discount is being extended only to *you*, it's generally not considered acceptable.

INFLUENCE   Your relationship with someone in itself can constitute a conflict of interest. For example, if you're in charge of purchasing corporate advertising and your cousin or neighbor or college friend owns an advertising agency, it will be considered a conflict if you make the decision to hire that firm. That doesn't preclude the firm from bidding, but it does preclude you from making the decision. If a decision involves anyone you have a personal relationship with, you should recuse yourself from the decision making. Another way to avoid the appearance of a conflict in a situation like this one, which is charged with issues of partiality, is to arrange for a "blind" competition, where the identity of various bidders is known only by someone not involved in the decision-making process. However, since any decision made by you in such a case will be suspect—even in blind evaluations—you should include other employees in the decision-making process.

PRIVILEGED INFORMATION   As an employee, you're naturally privy to information that would be valuable to your employer's competitors. That's why it's generally considered a conflict of interest if you hold a full-time job for ABC Insurance Company and decide to do some consulting work for XYZ Insurance Company. There are certainly exceptions to this rule of thumb. If you're a computer programmer at Green's Restaurant, for example, it probably isn't a conflict to wait on tables at Red's Restaurant. Two factors could make such a situation acceptable: if the work you perform at your second job doesn't compromise the work you do at your first one, and if both employers are aware of your activities. Transparency is the best policy.

In addition, it can appear as if you're involved in a conflict if you and a close relative or friend work for competitors, or if one of you works for an organization—such as a media company—that might have a particular interest in your company's activities. For example, if you work as an investment banker for Goldman Sachs and your sister holds the same position at Morgan Stanley, you both should alert your managers to the situation. These are potential problems that can be defused when your manager knows about the relationship. Full disclosure removes substantial risk.

How We Can Think about This Issue

The prescriptive ethical decision-making lenses can be helpful when considering conflicts of interest. For example, using a consequentialist approach encourages us to think about what would benefit the most people. Suppose that your brother owns an advertising agency, and you have to place ads as part of your job at another firm. Will hiring your brother benefit anyone other than your brother? Might it not harm your organization's reputation if others learn about the relationship? Using the deontological approach raises other issues. It's probably most relevant to consider what's fair. What decision would place all bidders on a level playing field? What could you do that would make the bidding absolutely fair and unbiased? Isn't that the kind of world you would most like to live in?

In fact, the veil of ignorance would ask you to act as if you didn't know that the person leading the advertising agency was your brother. What if you were the CEO of a competing advertising firm? Wouldn't you want a shot at the business? Think about looking at this issue through the lens of virtue ethics. What could you do that you wouldn't mind reading about in your local newspaper? You probably would want to read about your impartiality as a purchaser and as a representative of your company. You would not want to read that the contracts you enter into are rigged to benefit your family and friends.

This is also a good place to think about how you might handle these issues and to discuss your ideas out loud and with others. You will absolutely experience some of these conflicts—everyone does—and just as "rehearsals" helped the World War II rescuers, thinking about these situations in advance could greatly help you when the time comes—as it surely will. Imagine that your brother's company is experiencing rough times, and he tells you that he expects you to help. Once you have decided that it is unethical to do so, what will you say to him to explain your decision? Do you think you can do it in a way that will preserve your relationship? Here is where company policy can actually help employees a great deal. If you work for a company with a clear policy regarding conflict of interest, you could point to that and explain to your brother that you're obligated to abide by the policy and remove yourself from the decision making.

Why Is It an Ethical Problem?

The basis of every personal and corporate relationship is trust, and it exists only when individuals and corporations feel they're being treated fairly, openly, and on the same terms as everyone else. Conflicts of interest erode trust by making it look as if special favors will be extended for special friends; that attitude can enhance one relationship, but at the expense of all others.

Costs

Depending on the offense, myriad federal and state laws cover conflicts of interest. Certain professions, such as banking, accounting, law, religion, and medicine, have special obligations—often spelled out in professional codes of ethics—commonly referred to as fiduciary responsibilities. These professions are widely known as the trust professions, meaning that these practitioners have been entrusted with sensitive, confidential information about their clients. Fiduciary responsibilities concern the obligations resulting from relationships that have their basis in faith, trust, and confidence. After the financial debacle of 2008, much attention is being paid to fiduciary responsibilities.

A recent survey of private banks and wealth management companies by the accounting firm PricewaterhouseCoopers (PwC) indicated that the "economic crisis has presented client relationship managers with challenges that they have neither the experience nor the skills to deal with." In the survey, only 7 percent of the relationship managers felt they had enough training to meet the highest standards expected of them. The PwC survey noted that the old model for managers, which focused on sales, was being replaced by a model that focuses on fiduciary responsibilities.[13]

If you're suspected of a conflict of interest, the least you can expect is an investigation by your company. If it determines that your behavior demonstrates a conflict or the appearance of a conflict, you may be warned, disciplined, or even fired depending on the nature of your behavior. If you've accepted a bribe or kickback, you could face termination and even arrest. Being involved in a conflict of interest means that your judgment has been compromised, and this can severely damage your professional reputation.

Consider that in 2006, the Jeffries Group was fined $5.5 million by the National Association of Securities Dealers (NASD) (now the Financial Industry Regulatory Association—FINRA) for conflicts of interest concerning Fidelity Investments. A Jeffries trader with a $1.5 million expense account lavished gifts and entertainment on Fidelity traders, including trips to Las Vegas and Palm Beach, cases of wine, and custom golf clubs. Throwing money at Fidelity apparently worked: Jeffries ranked 50th in 2002 in brokerage commissions received from Fidelity. By 2005, Jeffries had moved up to 15th place. As a result of this activity, the Jeffries broker was fired, the firm and the industry were investigated, the firm was fined, and the practice has received reams of negative press.[14]

CUSTOMER CONFIDENCE ISSUES

We've all heard the saying, "The customer is always right," and companies like L.L. Bean and Sears have benefited by weaving that slogan into the fabric of their corporate cultures. But excellent customer service is more than being able to return a defective refrigerator or having cheerful customer service representatives (although that helps). Excellent customer service also means providing a quality product or service at a fair price, honestly representing the product or service, and protecting the customer's privacy.

What Is It?

Customer confidence issues include a range of topics such as confidentiality, product safety and effectiveness, truth in advertising, and special fiduciary responsibilities.

> You work for a consulting company in Atlanta. Your team has recently completed an analysis of Big Co., including sales projections for the next five years. You're working late one night when you receive a call from an executive vice president at Big Co. in Los Angeles, who asks you to immediately fax to her a summary of your team's report. When you locate the report, you discover that your team leader has stamped "For internal use only" on the report cover. Your team leader is on a hiking vacation, and you know it would be impossible to locate him. Big Co. has a long-standing relationship with your company and has paid substantial fees for your company's services.

CONFIDENTIALITY Privacy is a basic customer right. Privacy and the obligation to keep customer information in confidence often go beyond protecting sales projections or financial information. It can also mean keeping in strict confidence information concerning acquisitions, mergers, relocations, layoffs, or an executive's health or marital problems. In some industries, confidentiality is so important an issue that companies prohibit their employees from publicly acknowledging a customer relationship. In the financial services industry, for example, it's common practice to refuse to divulge that XYZ Company is even a customer.

In the case involving Big Co., an executive is demanding access to a confidential report. First, are you absolutely certain that the caller is indeed a Big Co. executive? Competitive intelligence work often involves deceptively impersonating a client or someone else. If you have conclusively verified her identity, do you know whether she has clearance from Big Co. to examine your team's report? If she does have clearance, is your team's report in a format that your company wants to share with Big Co., or does it need revision? Think about what you read in Chapter 2—how would you feel if your actions in this case were reported on the front page of your local newspaper? Do you think readers would be critical of what you plan to do? What would they say? Whenever you see "For internal use only," that's what it means, and it can be enormously risky to release the report to anyone—including the customer—without permission from someone within your company who has responsibility for that client. In a case like this one, you should track down someone who's in a position of authority in your company—your manager's manager, perhaps—before you override the warning on the report and release any information.

On occasion, third parties may ask for customer information. For example, a reporter or a client may ask you about customer trends. It's never acceptable to discuss specific companies or individuals with a third party or provide any information that might enable a third party to identify a specific customer. If you want to provide information, you can offer aggregate data from a number of companies, as long as the data doesn't allow any one customer to be identified.

> You're the head of marketing for a small pharmaceutical company that has just discovered a very promising drug for the treatment of Alzheimer's disease. You have spent months designing a marketing campaign that contains printed materials and medication sample kits for distribution to almost every family physician and

gerontologist in the country. As the materials are being loaded into cartons for delivery to your company's representatives, your assistant tells you that she has noticed a typographical error in the literature that could mislead physicians and their patients. In the section that discusses side effects, diarrhea and gastrointestinal problems are listed as having a probability of 2 percent. It should have read 20 percent. This error appears on virtually every piece of the literature and kits, and ads containing the mistake are already in press in several consumer magazines.

PERSONAL RESPONSIBILITY   Another basic customer right involves our taking personal honesty and responsibility for the products and services that we offer. There's probably no issue that will more seriously affect our reputation than a failure of responsibility. Many ethical disasters have started out as small problems that mushroomed. Especially in service businesses, where the "products" are delivered by individuals to other individuals, personal responsibility is a critical issue.

In the case concerning the typographical error about a new drug's side effects, the head of marketing faces a nasty dilemma. If she reproduces all of the printed material, it could be at a very great cost to this small company, and it may result in a significant delay in getting the drug to physicians. However, since many elderly people are prone to gastrointestinal upsets and can become very ill and even die as a result, this typo is a significant one. The material cannot go out as-is. Certainly the ideal solution would be to redo all of the marketing materials. However, if time and financial considerations prohibit that, there are other solutions. One solution might be to quickly produce a "correction" to be inserted into every kit. Also, a letter could be distributed to every physician to explain the correction as well as emphasize your company's commitment to quality and full disclosure. This solution will still be costly, but not nearly as costly as doing nothing and letting the kits go out with an error. What do you suppose would be the cost of even one wrongful death lawsuit? How about a class action? How about the accompanying publicity?

TELLING THE TRUTH   Many salespeople simply exaggerate their product's (or service's) benefits to consumers. Do fast sports cars automatically turn every young man into a James Bond? Will investing in a certain bond ensure you a safe retirement? Hype is generally a part of most sales pitches, and most consumers expect a certain amount of hype. In other cases, however, fudging the truth about a product is more than just hype—it's unfair.

Imagine that your financial firm is offering a new issue—a corporate bond with an expected yield of 7 to 7.5 percent. In the past, offerings like this one have generally been good investments for clients, and you have sold the issue to dozens of large and small clients. You're leaving on a two-week vacation and have only a few hours left in the office when your firm announces that the yield for the bond has been reduced; the high end will now be no more than 7 percent. The last day of the issue will be next week, while you're away on vacation. What should you do?

The fact is that your customers have been misled (albeit unintentionally) about the yield on that particular bond, and now you are under an obligation to tell the truth about the instrument before the issue closes. Why? Because another basic consumer right is to be told the truth about the products and services purchased. Failure to tell the truth about a product can be devastating for an organization, and it also can cause big problems for the company employees who are involved in perpetuating the false information.

SPECIAL FIDUCIARY RESPONSIBILITIES As discussed earlier in this chapter, certain professions, such as banking, accounting, law, religion, and medicine have special obligations to customers. These obligations are commonly referred to as fiduciary responsibilities. The law and the judicial system have recognized these special obligations, and they are spelled out in the codes of ethics for those professions. Fiduciary responsibilities hold these professionals to a high standard, and when they violate those responsibilities, the punishment is often harsh. For example, some employees of Arthur Andersen's Houston office failed Enron shareholders when they allowed the high-risk accounting practices used by Enron to continue.

Although David Duncan, leader of the Andersen auditing team at Enron, warned the Enron board of directors in 1999 that the firm's accounting practices were "high risk, " he apparently did not take the extra steps that would have been required to get the board to take action (in fact, the board did nothing in response to his warning).[15] For example, Duncan could have threatened to withdraw Andersen's services or to turn the company in. At the time this would have looked risky because Enron might simply have fired the auditors, and Andersen would have lost a huge client. But in hindsight, exercising appropriate fiduciary responsibility could have saved two companies, thousands of jobs, and a huge amount of shareholder wealth. Al Bows, an accountant who helped open the Arthur Andersen office in Atlanta in 1941, said that the founder of his old company, the original Arthur Andersen, would be "disgusted with what these guys did to his company." Bows went on to tell a story about a big juice company in Atlanta. He discovered that "the CEO was starting another juice company on the side to profit for himself. I told him he'd better cut it out or I'd turn him in. He stopped. But he was mad."[16] Of course, Bows is describing the fiduciary responsibilities of accountants—one of which is to ensure the financial integrity of publicly traded companies. When Arthur Andersen employees breached their fiduciary responsibilities in 2001, they contributed to the collapse of a major company.

Here's another case:

> For 12 years, you've been the financial advisor for both an elderly man in his late 70s who is an active investor of his own portfolio, and for a trust that will benefit his two children. In the last few months, you've noticed a subtle yet marked change in his behavior. He has become increasingly forgetful, has become uncharacteristically argumentative, and seems to have difficulty understanding some very basic aspects of his transactions. He has asked you to invest a sizable portion of his portfolio and the trust in what you consider to be a very risky bond offering. You are frank about your misgivings. He blasts you and says that if you don't buy the bonds, he'll take his business elsewhere.

If you work for a large electronics chain, it's not your responsibility to assess the mental stability of a customer who's purchasing a new television. You're selling; he's buying. However, individuals in fiduciary professions have a responsibility to protect their customer's assets—and that entails "knowing" their customers; frequently, that can mean assessing behavior and saving customers from themselves. In this case, if a customer wants to make a risky investment against your advice, there's little you can do but wish him or her well. Who knows? You might be wrong, and the customer might make a fortune. However, if a financial professional sees clear signs of incompetence in a longtime customer who's suddenly interested in making a risky bet, he or she is under some obligation to seek help.

Cases involving the mental stability of a longtime customer are one of the most common dilemmas encountered by financial advisors. As this gentleman's advisor, you could try again to dissuade the client from making the investment, or you could involve the firm's senior management in negotiations with the client. You could contact a member of the client's family—one of the children perhaps—and explain your reservations. You could also possibly contact the client's lawyer or accountant, who also would be bound by confidentiality constraints because of the fiduciary nature of their professions. However, most financial executives will agree that something must be done to help this long-time customer.

How We Can Think about This Issue

It's hard to imagine that any of us would find encouragement to ignore product safety or fiduciary responsibilities in any of the ethical theories. Producing safe products clearly benefits the most and harms the fewest. Customer confidence is rooted in trust. Trust is very much built slowly, over time, experience by experience. We can't trust something that we don't know or that we lack confidence in. Again, this is an area where you will no doubt experience difficulties and conflicts as you go out into the business world. It's another great area to discuss out loud and ahead of time—to practice making your decisions now, and voicing your arguments aloud, as a way to prepare for challenges you may face in the future.

Why Is It an Ethical Problem?

We use the term *customer confidence issues* as an umbrella to address the wide range of topics that can affect your relationship with your customer. These are ethical issues because they revolve around fairness, honesty, responsibility, truth, and respect for others. Customer relationships can't survive without these basics of trust.

Costs

On the organizational level, there are severe penalties for being dishonest in advertising or for misleading the public about the effectiveness or safety of a product or service. While individual failures in the area of trust usually don't warrant a lot of publicity (although sometimes they do—think about Bernie Madoff), nothing can destroy an individual's reputation as much as dishonesty. When you're a student who hasn't entered the workforce yet, it's difficult to imagine that the world of work is small, but it is. In some industries—like banking and biotech—it's a very small world indeed, and your reputation will follow you around like your shadow. Anyone who has been in business for even a few years can regale you with stories of colleagues who are as "honest as the day is long" or, conversely, "can't be trusted as far as you can throw them." Your reputation is built slowly with countless gestures, actions, and conversations over time, but it can be destroyed in an instant by one foolish mistake. You need to safeguard your reputation carefully—it is without question the most valuable thing you have in business.

USE OF CORPORATE RESOURCES

As discussed in the introduction, you and your employer have a special relationship, and each owes the other a modicum of loyalty based on that relationship. In addition, since you're a corporate representative, you're considered an "agent" of your company. This means that your actions can be considered as the actions of the corporation. This section of the chapter presents the flip side of the above section on human resources issues—your employer's responsibilities to you are described in that section, and your responsibilities to your employer are described here.

What Is It?

The use of corporate resources involves your fulfilling your end of the employer-employee "contract." It means being truthful with your employer and management and being responsible in the use of corporate resources, including its finances and reputation.

> A young woman who works for you is moving with her husband to another city, where she'll be looking for a new job. She's an excellent worker and when she asks you for a reference, you're glad to do it for her. She specifically asks for a written recommendation on your corporate letterhead.

USE OF CORPORATE REPUTATION Whenever you identify yourself as an employee of your company, people can infer that you are speaking on behalf of it, which is why you have to be careful how you link yourself to your company. For example, if you use corporate letterhead to write a recommendation for someone or simply to complain to the telephone company, it can be construed as a "corporate" position. Consequently, corporate letterhead should be used only for corporate business. If, as in the case of the recommendation, you need to identify yourself as an employee, use your personal stationery and attach your business card. The objective is to differentiate between your personal opinions and any official stance of your organization.

Recommendations, in particular, present a challenge for employers and individuals. Many companies attempt to check with former employers when hiring someone.

This can present a problem since most companies prohibit their personnel from officially supplying this type of information because of lawsuits that have resulted from employer-supplied recommendations. Today, some social networking sites allow people to write posts about others in their professional network. But be careful, especially if writing about someone you supervise. What if your flattering post online differs from the more critical performance evaluation that's on file, and what if the employee is subsequently let go? The person's lawyer could use the post in an unjust termination lawsuit. (To protect themselves, many employers supply only the following information concerning former employees: name, date of employment, and job title. Most employers also require the former employee's written consent before they supply any salary information to a third party. That raises another ethical issue: If one can't get good, honest recommendation information about prospective employees from their former employers and supervisors, poor employees can just be passed off to other unsuspecting organizations. Is that right?)

Similarly, if you're asked to make a speech, write an article, serve on the board of a nonprofit organization, or participate in any activity that would identify you (and your personal opinions) with your company, be sure to get permission from your manager, the legal department, or human resources. You may unwittingly be supporting a position or organization with which your company may not wish to be associated. For example, while it might seem like a great idea for you to serve on the board of your local Society for the Prevention of Cruelty to Animals (SPCA), if you work for a pharmaceutical company that tests drugs on animals, you may be placing your employer in an embarrassing position. Of course, you can serve on the board as a private citizen, but not as an employee of XYZ Drug Company unless you've received corporate authorization. Social networking, blogging, and twittering are all adding complexity to such issues, and more and more organizations are developing policies to guide appropriate employee conduct in these new arenas.

> You joined one of the country's largest retail chains, and already you've been promoted to department manager in one of your employer's largest stores in an upscale shopping mall. Imagine your surprise when you log on to Facebook and see that one of your "friends"—a young woman who heads one of the other departments in your store—has posted confidential store sales on her wall and has also posted sexual comments about a young man who reports to her.

Social networking sites and other social media present new and thorny problems. What happens when an employee posts confidential company information on a pubic site? Is it okay to post sexual comments about a coworker or your boss on a public site? This kind of behavior can reflect poorly on an employer as well as make the author of such comments look like an idiot or worse. The scariest part of this scenario is that items posted on the Internet last forever. You can't just "erase" them and ensure that they're really obliterated forever. Organizations take this behavior very seriously. One recent college graduate hired into a plum job by a national retailer was fired for posting inappropriate content about his employer on his Facebook wall. In a similar situation, an employee posted vacation pictures on her Facebook wall—taken while she was on a company-paid medical leave—showing the employee horseback riding, playing tennis, and climbing a Hawaiian volcano. Everyone she worked with saw the photos and her boss immediately launched a fraud investigation to determine if the employee falsely used a medical leave to take a vacation. She ended up having to make a choice: pay back the company for the paid leave or resign from her job.

Another difficult issue involving social media is when an employee already has an online personality—perhaps he is a well-known blogger, or perhaps she has made a name for herself providing "color" or "background" or "observations" on an industry website. How do you handle something like that? It's one thing when his comments are not terribly visible or when her observations track with her employer's views and interests. But what happens when a visible employee begins advocating a position that is diametrically opposed to his or her employer's views? Can you ask him to reconsider his views? Can her reputation be separated from her employer's? Could you instruct the employee to specify somewhere on the site that his or her views are personal and do not represent the views of his/her employer? What if the employee is tweeting on the job? Can you or should you set limits on this kind of activity? How can you set clear expectations about what is acceptable? How can you handle potential coworker resentment? If you're the employee in this situation, it's a good idea to speak with your manager (and your coworkers) about all of this in advance and negotiate a plan that works for everyone.[17]

Here's another thorny case:

> You're an employment counselor at a large outplacement firm. Your company is currently negotiating with Black Company to provide outplacement services to 500 employees who are about to lose their jobs as the result of a layoff. Your neighbor and good friend is a reporter for the local newspaper, who mentions to you over coffee one Saturday that she's writing a story about Black Company. According to her sources, 1,500 employees are about to lose their jobs. You know her numbers are incorrect. Should you tell her?

Dealing with the press—even when the reporter is a friend or relative—is a tricky business that shouldn't be attempted by a novice. In a case like the one above, where you may think your friendly reporter might have incorrect numbers, silence is truly the best policy. Her numbers may in fact be correct, and your numbers may represent only the employees who are eligible for outplacement services, not the total number who are losing their jobs.

Another issue that can be confusing to businesspeople is what "off the record" means. For the most part, *off the record* means that a reporter won't quote you directly or attribute any remarks to you. You can't, however, tell a reporter that your remarks are off the record after the fact. The way to tell a reporter that remarks are off the record is to inform him or her before offering your information. But the very best way to make sure something is off the record is to keep your mouth shut in the first place. Reporters with the best of intentions can very innocently get their sources into trouble by providing information that only the source would know, thereby identifying the source.

If you are contacted by the press, immediately alert your company's public relations department. Unless you're trained to answer press inquiries and receive authorization to do it, you should not comment to the press. It's easy to innocently supply confidential information or cast a negative light on your company when you're untrained to deal with probing or ambiguous questions posed by a skilled journalist.

> You've been working very long hours on a special project for the chairman of your company. Your company policy states that employees who work more than 12 hours in one day may be driven home by a company car at company expense. Policy also states that employees who work longer than two hours past the regular end of their day can have a meal delivered to the office at company expense. You and your colleagues who are also working on the project are arriving at the office at 8:00 a.m. and order dinner at 7:00 p.m.; then you enjoy dinner and conversation for an hour and are driven home by company cars. Is this okay?

CORPORATE FINANCIAL RESOURCES   In a game entitled "Where Do You Draw the Line: An Ethics Game," produced by Simile II, players explore the differences between taking $10 worth of pencils from their company and distributing them to poor children, making $10 worth of personal long-distance calls at work, and taking $10 from their company's petty cash drawer. Do you think these scenarios are different, or pretty much the same thing? Most people eventually conclude that all of them, regardless of the employee's intentions, involve stealing $10 worth of corporate resources. The bottom line is that corporate equipment and services should be used only for company business. Whether it involves making personal phone calls, padding expense reports, appropriating office supplies, sending personal mail through the company mail room, or using copy equipment to print a flyer for your scout troop, personal or inappropriate use of corporate resources is unethical and violates most corporate policy.

In a case like the one above, where you and colleagues are working long hours to complete a special project for the company's chairman, you are following corporate policy to the letter, so your actions are probably acceptable to most organizations. However, if you and your coworkers are stretching out the last hour of dinner so that you can take a company car home, you're getting into ethical hot water. Are you also stretching out the work in order to have a free meal? If you would have no problem explaining your actions to the chairman, or if you wouldn't mind if he or she sat in on one of those dinner hours, then the meals and the cars are perfectly acceptable. The important thing is to treat your company's resources with as much care as you would your own.

> Your manager is being transferred to another division of the company in early January. He calls a meeting in early November and asks that every department head delay processing all invoices until after January 1. He wants to keep expenses low and revenues high so that his last quarter in your area shows maximum revenue.

PROVIDING HONEST INFORMATION   Another key issue concerns truth. We discussed truth with customers earlier in this chapter, but now we're talking about telling the truth within your organization and providing honest information to others within your company. Although everyone will agree that telling the truth is important, someday you may have a manager who says something like, "These numbers look too negative—let's readjust them so it looks better to senior management. We'll make up the difference in the next quarter." Many managers feel it necessary to put a positive spin on financial reports before submitting them up through the ranks. As a result, some companies have suffered serious financial penalties because their numbers have been positively spun on so many succeeding levels, they bear no resemblance to reality by the time they reach the top. "Fudging" numbers can have serious consequences since senior management may make crucial decisions based on flawed data. (Corporations are fined by regulators if inaccurate financial information is submitted to regulators or incorporated into formal financial statements.) If you're asked to skew any kind of corporate information, you should consult with someone outside your chain of command—such as the legal, human resources, or audit department—and then decide whether it's time to move on. Serious corporate scandals, sometimes leading to jail terms for those involved, often begin with these "one-time" requests. Once you're involved, it's almost impossible to extricate yourself from an almost inevitable downward spiral. Ask employees at HealthSouth and WorldCom; some of them spent years in prison for going along with such requests.

In the case about a manager wishing to delay paying expenses until after he leaves the area, think about it from a consequentialist perspective. Such creative bookkeeping harms not only the person who is taking his place in January, but also the suppliers who are relying on prompt payment of their invoices. It's grossly unfair to ask suppliers to wait almost 60 extra days before getting paid. One solution might be to approach the other department heads and gain their cooperation in refusing to follow your manager's request. Another course of action would be to relate the incident to the audit department, which would surely be interested in your manager's shenanigans.

How We Can Think about This Issue

Once again, using the various theoretical approaches can be extremely helpful. Thinking broadly about potential harms and benefits for all stakeholders will inevitably lead you to be honest in your dealings. From a deontological perspective, most of us put honesty and integrity at or near the top of our values lists. We would certainly want to be treated that way if the tables were reversed. And that's certainly the ethical standard we would want to guide our world.

Even more important, however, may be thinking about how to live your values in this particular area. If you seriously consider who you are and what you want to be known for, your decision making in this area will be much easier. For example, if you want to be known as a straight shooter who can be trusted at high levels and with delicate customer accounts, would you ever consider misusing corporate resources or fudging the numbers? What would that say about you, and how would it affect your reputation? It would undermine everything else you were trying to do in your professional life. In this arena, doing the right thing often requires standing up for your values—especially standing up to those at higher levels who might be requesting or even demanding that you go along. In such cases, you'll need to summon up courage to stand up for what you believe. You have a better chance of doing that if you practice what you're going to say. Find a coworker who agrees with you and practice. You may be surprised to find that once you get clear about your ethical stance and can express it in a clear and nonaccusatory way, you won't get such a request again. If you fear for your job because you won't go along, that's the time to polish your résumé and begin looking elsewhere.

Why Is It an Ethical Problem?

Your use of corporate resources is an ethical issue because it represents fulfilling your end of the employer-employee contract. Its roots are in fairness and honesty.

Costs

Obviously, if you've stolen corporate assets or filed an inflated expense report, you'll almost certainly be fired—and you may be arrested. If you have divulged confidential information to another corporation (as in supplying a recommendation for a former employee), your company may be placed at risk for a lawsuit. If you've posted derogatory remarks about your boss, coworkers, or company on a social networking site, you may short-circuit your career and cause people around you to mistrust you.

   If you fail to uphold your end of the employer-employee loyalty contract, your career at your company can be damaged. Ethical corporate cultures place tremendous importance on honesty, loyalty, and teamwork. Generally, successful corporations are communities where a sense of family has been encouraged. Just as family members try to protect one another and keep family information private, the company community tries to encourage the same behavior. Individuals who violate the corporate "family" trust by squandering resources, being dishonest, or misusing the family reputation are frequently isolated or fired.

WHEN ALL ELSE FAILS: BLOWING THE WHISTLE

A section on ethics and the individual wouldn't be complete without a discussion of what happens when you suspect serious wrongdoing within your organization. If your observations are serious and keeping you awake at night, you may have to report the problem—blow the whistle—and you need to proceed with great caution. This also is why understanding what you value and practicing living your values is so important. If you haven't practiced living your values by the time you get embroiled in a sticky dilemma at work, the situation will be much more difficult for you to handle. With practice (and a bit of luck), you may have been able to stop the problem from developing into a serious one. We hope so. But occasionally you may find yourself with knowledge about serious wrongdoing, and blowing the whistle (either internally or externally) may seem like your only option.

In these really tough situations, voicing your values at work takes significant courage because of the increased risks involved. Kathleen Reardon encourages us to think about courage at work as "calculated risk taking."[18] She recommends that you do the following:

1. Ask yourself how strongly you feel about the particular issue. When people are asked, "where do you draw the ethical line?" the most important issues are clearly over the line either because acting in a certain way or not acting at all is likely to cause great harm or breach our most cherished values. According to Reardon, these are "spear in the sand" issues that compel action. So, ask yourself which kind of issue you're facing. Is this a "spear in the sand" issue for you?

2. Ask yourself about your intentions. Are you just advancing a personal agenda, or do your goals serve the greater good? If you see a coworker being treated unfairly by an abusive supervisor, what should you do? For example, will rescuing your coworker by reporting the abusive supervisor serve the greater good?

3. Consider power and influence. As we noted above, unless you're the CEO, you're rarely in a position to make a decision for the organization. If you feel strongly about something, you're likely going to have to convince others. So think about how your social network might help convince your manager or organization to do the right thing. This usually isn't about following the organization chart. Rather, it's about knowing where the power rests and developing good, trusting relationships with those people. But you can't do this at the last minute. Trusting relationships are developed over time. If you have developed these, you should be able to address the issue before it becomes a whistleblowing possibility.

4. Weigh the risks and benefits of action. This isn't quite the same as the consequentialist analysis of harms and benefits to multiple stakeholders (discussed in Chapter 2). That analysis is more wide-ranging and focuses on societal good. Here, you're looking more pragmatically at the people involved, at whether reputations or standing in the organization (yours or others') will be tarnished by taking action. Perhaps you can reduce the risks and increase the potential benefits by finding a creative way to address the issue. For example, can you report an incident anonymously rather than confronting someone directly? Can you offer apologies for something you have done in the past, in hopes that the person at fault in this situation is inspired to do the same?

5. Think about timing. If the issue isn't urgent, and especially if it isn't a spear-in-the-sand issue, ask yourself whether you can put off action a bit to better prepare and to ensure that you've reflected on the risks and what you're

considering doing. Have you given yourself the opportunity to practice what you would say in a meeting with your boss, for example? Have you looked for allies who might join you in attempting to address the issue?

6. Develop alternatives. In dicey situations, it's extremely helpful to have alternatives in mind. What will you do if you don't get your desired outcome? Do you have an alternative in mind? For a spear-in-the-sand issue, are you willing to either lose your job or leave it, if it comes to that?

Once you decide to blow the whistle, you need to think carefully about how to go about it. How *not* to blow the whistle might be best illustrated by a case that involves a high-level investment banker who discovered that some of his colleagues were engaged in unethical dealings with several customers. The investment banker brought the situation to the attention of his manager, who told him to forget it. Determined to raise the issue, the banker wrote an irate memo to his company's CEO outlining the situation and naming names. The banker copied the memo to several other top managers. Even though there were only three levels of management between the banker and the CEO, and even though the banker was right about his colleagues and they were eventually fired, the banker was also fired.

In another large, multinational company, a young trainee in an Asian country felt he was being treated unfairly by his local management. In a fit of anger, he wrote a long message outlining his grievances on his company's e-mail system (today, he might have posted something on his blog or sent a Twitter message about his situation). Although he addressed his message to the company CEO, president, and head of human resources (all three senior managers were based in New York), he copied everyone else on the system—approximately 30,000 managers worldwide. The trainee was fired not because of the message, but because of how he communicated it. The head of human resources commented, "He was being groomed for management, and we couldn't have someone with such poor judgment in that role. If he had complained only to senior management, he would have been heard, he would have been protected, and we would have corrected the situation. After copying the world with his complaint, we felt he was a loose cannon and we had no choice but to get him out."

Unless you want to be branded as someone with poor judgment, you have to be very careful about how you raise ethical concerns. Usually, the CEO is one of your last resorts, to be approached only after you've exhausted every other internal resource. There are exceptions to this guideline. A notable exception occurred at PPG Industries, where former CEO Vince Sarni asked and encouraged employees to contact him directly with issues. A hotline for that purpose sat on his desk, and he personally answered that phone. Warren Buffett, the CEO of Berkshire Hathaway, also used the "call me" approach when he served as a director of Salomon Brothers back in 1991. As the company became embroiled in a bid-rigging scandal (see Chapter 10 for the details), Buffett stepped in as interim CEO. He wrote a letter to Salomon Brothers managers that said, "Here's my home phone number in Omaha. If you see anything unethical, give me a call." Managers did call him, and they were able to devise a plan to save Salomon Brothers from Andersen's fate.[19]

So how do you blow the whistle? First, let's talk about when.

> A long-time customer approaches you for financing for a new business venture. The customer offers as collateral a piece of property he has purchased in a rural location for the purpose of building a housing development. You send an appraiser to the property, and he accidentally discovers that this property holds toxic waste. You're sure this customer is unaware of the waste; in fact, the waste is migrating and in a few years will invade the water table under a nearby farmer's fields. You explain the situation to your manager, who naturally instructs you to refuse to accept the property as collateral, but he also forbids you to mention the toxic waste to the customer. "Let them find out about it themselves," he says. Do you alert the customer to the toxic waste? Do you alert government regulators?

When Do You Blow the Whistle?

Let's assume first that your concern involves a serious issue. Reporting toxic materials, for example, is a serious issue, because of the potential for serious harm. Recall that serious harm raises the moral intensity of an issue. So your ethical antennae are likely to be highly sensitized in this situation, and you're going to feel more compelled to do something. A colleague padding an expense report a bit on one occasion isn't quite as serious. Once you've informed your manager about a fudged expense report, your responsibility is probably fulfilled. However, one colleague fudging an expense report one time is a far cry from a group of employees systematically altering all of their expense reports with their manager's knowledge. If you suspect something of that magnitude, of course you should report it to someone outside your chain of command, such as the ethics office or your organization's internal auditor.

Many might disagree with this approach, but few people in business have the time to be "on patrol." Once a manager is alerted, it's his or her responsibility to deal with issues like expense reports, except in extraordinary circumstances. This could be termed "picking your battles" and responding appropriately to your gut feelings. Obviously, you should use the prescriptive frameworks to help you decide what to do. But let's also consider a number of simple triggers that can help you determine whether an issue is serious.

Some of the triggers to help you determine whether an issue is serious enough to be raised beyond your immediate manager include an issue that involves values such as truth, employee or customer (or other stakeholder) rights, trust, fairness, harm, your personal reputation or the reputation of your organization, and whether the law is being broken or compromised. In the toxic dump case, for example, serious harm could certainly result; customer (and other stakeholder) rights are involved; your organization's reputation is at risk; a public trust may be violated; and the law may very well be compromised or broken if you keep quiet about toxic waste under a proposed housing development, because the toxic waste could ultimately affect the food supply. A situation like this has all the earmarks of a serious ethical dilemma that requires action.

Suppose your manager asks you to supply inaccurate numbers in a financial report to another level of management. That situation involves not only a breach of truth but also potential fraud and harm; it could damage your reputation and ultimately your company's reputation. It's a serious issue that you'll probably want to report.

How to Blow the Whistle

Let's assume that you're dealing with a serious issue, you've assembled the facts, they're accurate to the best of your knowledge, you've asked your peers or your manager for advice, and there's a law or company policy about to be violated, or one of the other triggers discussed earlier indicates a serious problem. Now what?

1. **Approach Your Immediate Manager First If You Can (your manager isn't involved in the problem)**   If your manager tells you to ignore a situation or belittles your concern, approach him or her again. The second time you approach your manager, you may want to write a memo and spell out your concerns in black and white so it's more difficult for your manager to ignore or dismiss them. Writing a memo is frequently enough to convince your manager that this is serious, and so you'll get a more favorable response. You should also do some soul searching to make sure your decision to pursue this issue is an objective one, and not based in any feeling of revenge you might have for your manager, coworkers, or company. This is also a good time to rehearse out loud and to others (maybe a trusted coworker, your parents, or your spouse) what you want to say. It is helpful to state the problem in terms of your concerns for people and the company and why those are concerns for you (rather than pointing fingers). Also, you should find out exactly how your company wants issues raised and if there is a special process for doing it. If there is, follow the process to the letter.[20]

2. **Discuss the Issue with Your Family**   Since any whistleblowing activity can affect your family as well as yourself, it's imperative that they know what's going on. It's also the time to document your activities. Obtain copies of correspondence that relate to the issue and any memos you've written in an attempt to alert management. Keep a diary to track activities related to the issue and describe any conversations you've had concerning the issue.[21]

3. **Take It to the Next Level**   If you receive no satisfaction from your manager, it's time to go to the next level of management. The most diplomatic way of going around your manager is to say to your manager something like, "I feel so strongly about this that I'd like a meeting with you and your manager to discuss it." The positive aspect of asking your manager to go with you to the next level is that he or she will be less likely to feel betrayed, and you'll appear to be a team player. The negative aspect is that your manager may forbid you to approach his or her manager. If that happens, or if you're still not satisfied after meeting with the next level of management, you'll need to consider going outside your chain of command.

4. **Contact Your Company's Ethics Officer or Ombudsman** Find out if your state has any special legislation regarding whistleblowing. Your state may have legislative protection for whistleblowers, but it may require you to follow certain procedures to protect yourself.[22] You may choose to go to these officials first, especially if your manager is part of the problem. As a result of the U.S. Federal Sentencing Commission Guidelines (see Chapter 6) and Sarbanes-Oxley legislation, most large organizations now have reporting systems that allow you to report problems and to do so anonymously.

5. **Consider Going Outside Your Chain of Command** If your company has no formal department or process for handling such complaints, think about other areas that would be receptive to your concerns. If your issue is human resources related—if it involves relationships or activities within your company such as discrimination or sexual harassment—you may be able to approach your human resources officer or department. If the issue is business related—if it involves external relationships such as those with customers, suppliers, regulators—you can still approach human resources, but a better choice would probably be the legal department or your company's internal auditors. Obviously, if the issue involves the law or an actual or potential legal issue, you should contact the legal department. And if the issue concerns a financial matter, it's probably better to approach your organization's auditors. Most auditors have a system of internal checks they can trigger that will confirm or refute your suspicions and even protect you. Also, some auditors in some industries have an underground network of sorts; there are relationships that exist among auditors from various organizations. They can quietly investigate situations and keep them from blowing out of proportion if that's indicated and appropriate.

   Since the role of human resources, legal, and audit departments is to protect the corporation, they should be receptive to any concerns that could put the company at risk. If, however, the activity you're concerned about has been approved or condoned by the highest levels of management, these internal departments may be inclined to go along with "business as usual." And since their role is to protect the company, you're likely to find that their first allegiance is to the company, and not to you.

   It's usually safe to approach these departments, but it's not completely without risk. You can reduce the risk if you can persuade one or more of your colleagues to join you in the process. Having an ally can encourage lawyers and auditors to take you more seriously. It also may be wise to consult your personal lawyer or a law firm that specializes in representing whistleblowers at this point in the process. According to Hoffman and Moore, your attorney can "help you determine if the wrongdoing violates the law, aid you in documenting information about it, inform you of any laws you might be breaking in documenting it, assist you in deciding to whom to report it, make sure reports are filed on time, and help you protect yourself against retaliation."[23]

Once you've approached your management, the ethics or compliance office (if your company has one), and human resources, legal, or audit, you should have received some satisfaction. The vast majority of whistleblowing cases are resolved at one of those levels. However, if you're still concerned, the risks to you personally escalate significantly from this point on. Your last resort within your company is your organization's senior management, including the CEO, president, or board of directors. Obviously, you should contact whoever has a reputation for being most approachable. Understand that your immediate management will most likely be irate if you approach senior management. However, if you're right about your concerns, you may end up a hero if the issue you're raising is a localized problem and senior management is unaware of what's going on.

Before contacting your senior management, be sure to have your facts straight and documented. (This is where a diary and copies of correspondence are useful.) If you're wrong, few people are going to understand or forgive you. You may be harassed, reprimanded, or penalized, or some pretext may be found to fire you. However, there is evidence that you can contact the CEO and keep your job. For example, Sherron Watkins, vice president of corporate development at Enron, still had her job at Enron one year after CEO Ken Lay received her fearful letter about accounting irregularities and months after the executive team resigned. However, she wrote her letter to the CEO and not to the local newspapers.[24] Like many other whistleblowers, Sherron Watkins is now making her living as a public speaker and consultant.

6. **Go Outside of the Company**   If you've raised the concern all the way to the top of your company, still have a job, and are still unsatisfied, your only choice now is to go outside. If your company is part of a regulated industry, such as defense contracting and commercial banks, you can contact the regulators who are charged with overseeing your industry. Or you can contact the press. However, if you've already contacted numerous individuals in your company about the issue, it won't take a genius to figure out who is talking outside of the company. Even if you contact the press or the regulators anonymously, your coworkers and management probably will know it's you.

Recent legislation has made it easier and potentially more lucrative for employees to blow the whistle to regulators when companies are government contractors or when the federal government has somehow been defrauded. Under the False Claims Act, whistleblowers who report corporate wrongdoing against the government to prosecutors can be awarded 15 to 30 percent of whatever damages the federal government recovers, which are to be three times the damages the government has sustained. Because the government has recovered billions of dollars since the law's inception, this has become a powerful incentive for some employees to tell all to prosecutors. For example, Jim Alderson was fired from his accounting job at Quorum Health Group when he refused to go along with the company practice of keeping two sets of books for Medicare reimbursements, one for the government and one marked "confidential." He filed a wrongful termination lawsuit that developed into False Claims Act lawsuits against his employer and its parent company for overbilling the government. The government recovered almost $2 billion, and Alderson received $20 million. The number of such lawsuits has grown significantly in recent years. In one of the biggest suits ever, TAP Pharmaceuticals paid $875 million to the government for engaging in illegal pricing and marketing practices with a cancer drug (you'll read more about TAP Pharmaceuticals in the end-of-chapter case for Chapter 5).[25]

An even bigger case involves four whistleblowers from GlaxoSmith-Kline, which will pay $3 billion to settle a fraud case. According to the whistleblower advocacy group Taxpayers Against Fraud, the pharmaceutical industry will pay $10 billion to settle various fraud cases in the fiscal year ending in September 2012. That's a lot of money going to whistleblowers.[26]

In 2002 Congress passed the Sarbanes-Oxley Act (SOX), which, among other things, provides whistleblowers in publicly traded companies with revolutionary new protections if they "make a disclosure to a supervisor, law-enforcement agency, or congressional investigator that could have a 'material impact' on the value of a company's shares."[27] Under the law, board committees must set up procedures for hearing whistleblower concerns; executives who retaliate can be held criminally liable and can go to prison for up to 10 years; the Labor Department can force a company to rehire a whistleblower who has been fired; and workers who have been fired can request a jury trial after six months. Corporate attorneys are now required to report misconduct to top management and to the board if executives don't respond. But, unlike the False Claims Act, SOX did not provide for financial incentives. And it does not protect employees at private companies.

Under the Dodd-Frank Wall Street Reform and Consumer Protection Act (passed in the wake of the 2008–2009 financial crisis), the Securities and Exchange Commission (SEC) will pay 10 to 30 percent of the amount the government recovers from financial fraud if the whistleblower provides original information leading to a recovery of more than a million dollars. During fiscal 2012, the SEC received over 3,000 tips. That sounds like a lot but is actually only a very small percentage of potential calls, according to Ethics Resource Center data about observed misconduct of the type covered by the Act.[28]

In a survey of chief audit executives in 2012, the executives had confidence in their internal systems. Fewer than five percent expected internal whistleblowers to blow the whistle to regulators. Also, in the annual report submitted by the SEC to Congress that outlines whistleblowing activities, the total amount paid to whistleblowers in 2012 was a bit over $45,000 to just one person making a complaint. So, while the SEC Investor Protection Fund (to pay whistleblowers) contains $450 million, almost none of it has been paid out.[29] Perhaps corporate programs to encourage internal whistleblowing are working (we hope so).

You may be wondering whether people should be paid to blow the whistle, to essentially do the right thing. This is certainly a debatable issue and one you may want to discuss in class. However, we believe that most whistleblowers are not motivated primarily or initially by these financial rewards, and this is consistent with findings of the National Business Ethics Survey. When asked why they reported, 82 percent of the respondents said they would report if the crime were big enough.[30] Once they learn about the rewards, however, they may feel more emboldened to act. We do know that many whistleblowers have lost their livelihoods as a result of whistleblowing. So, perhaps we should think about these rewards as a means to tide whistleblowers over until they can find a new way of earning a living.

For additional guidance about whistleblowing, several websites can answer myriad questions; just type the keyword *whistleblower* in your Internet search engine. Probably the most comprehensive website for whistleblowers is the National Whistleblower's Center, a nonprofit, tax-exempt organization that is dedicated to providing educational and advocacy services to whistleblowers (www.whistleblowers.org).

7. **Leave the Company**   Some situations might be so disturbing to you that you have no alternative but to quit your job. The toxic dump situation described earlier might be one of those situations. Frankly, the stress involved in blowing the whistle is so intense that you might consider quitting your job after step 3 or 4, and you'll need all of the prescriptive ethical decision-making frameworks to help you decide whether you are ethically obligated to report the problem to someone or whether simply leaving is okay.

Whistleblowing is so stressful that in one study, one-third of the whistle-blowers surveyed would advise other people not to blow the whistle at all.[31] Senator Charles Grassley likened whistle-blowers to "a skunk at a picnic."[32] However, note that two-thirds of those whistleblowers would not provide such advice. Many people would find it extremely difficult—perhaps impossible—to live with certain situations on their conscience. The knowledge of a toxic dump about to poison private wells would probably be almost impossible for most people to live with without reporting. When knowledge becomes unbearable, blowing the whistle and ultimately quitting your job may be the only solution (or the other way around—find another job and then blow the whistle).

CONCLUSION

This chapter highlights some of the most common ethical problems you might encounter during your career and provides some advice on raising issues if you feel the need. Although ethical problems can be difficult to evaluate, it can be easier to decide what to do when you've spent some time thinking about them ahead of time—before they happen. We also strongly believe that identifying what you value, thinking about various ethical situations, and practicing your responses in advance are effective ways to prepare you to live an ethical professional life.

DISCUSSION QUESTIONS

1. What do you value? Can you make a list of the three or four values you would stand up for? How will you explain to others what your values are and why?

2. Have you ever practiced raising an ethical issue to a professor or to your manager? What did you do? What were the results?

3. Have antidiscrimination laws helped or hurt the fair treatment of workers?

4. Is diversity management an ethical issue?

5. Is sexual harassment as important an issue for men as it is for women?

6. What conditions would make accepting a gift from a vendor or a client acceptable?

7. Describe the conditions under which you could hire a college friend.

8. Why do certain professionals—bankers, accountants, lawyers, physicians, clergy—have fiduciary responsibilities?

9. What would you do if a former subordinate asked you to write him or her a letter of reference on corporate letterhead?

10. Do employers have a responsibility to alert other employers to an employee's wrongdoing by supplying an unfavorable reference? Why or why not? Discuss the conflict between community responsibility and self-protection.

11. What conditions would have to be present for you to blow the whistle about unethical conduct you observed at work? How would you go about it?

12. If Sherron Watkins had blown the whistle to the *Houston Chronicle* and not to Enron's CEO Ken Lay, do you think she would have kept her job at Enron?

13. Research a story of whistleblowing. Relate what "your" whistleblower did with the seven steps recommended in the chapter. What have you learned from the comparison?

14. Do you think that "paying" whistleblowers encourages people to look for ethical misdeeds or to "game up" ethical misdeeds?

SHORT CASES

Think about what you most value. For each of the ethical dilemmas below, describe at least two courses of action you might take and state the pros and cons of each course. Describe your actions out loud to someone else in class or to a friend. What can you say or do that would be consistent with your personal values?

VOICING YOUR VALUES

You're a trader who joined a large investment bank two years ago. Pat, one of your fellow traders, is well known on the Street for being a big risk taker and a big money maker for the firm. Consequently, he is popular among your firm's senior management. You see him at a party one night and notice that he surreptitiously used cocaine several times. Several weeks later in the office, you notice that he seems exceptionally high-spirited and that his pupils are extremely dilated—you know that both are signs of drug use. You're thinking of mentioning something about it to his managing director, Bob, when Pat makes a particularly impressive killing in the market for your firm's own account. Bob jokes that he doesn't know how Pat does it, but he doesn't care. "However he is pulling this off, it's great for the firm," Bob laughs. You feel strongly that this is a problem and that it places your firm at risk. You've already raised the issue to Pat's manager, Bob, who ignored the issue. Do you raise it further? How can you voice your values in this case?

PEOPLE ISSUE

Your division has formed a committee of employees to examine suggestions and create a strategy for how to reward good employee ideas. The committee has five members, but you are the only one who is a member of a minority group. You're pleased to be part of this effort since appointments to committees such as this one are viewed generally as a positive reflection on job performance. At the first meeting, tasks are assigned, and all the other committee members think you should survey minority members for their input. Over the next few weeks, you discover that several committee meetings have been held without your knowledge. When you ask why you weren't notified, two committee members tell you that survey information wasn't needed at the meetings and you'd be notified when a general meeting was scheduled. When you visit one committee member in his office, you spot a report on the suggestion program that you've never seen before. When you ask about it, he says it's just a draft he and two others have produced.

CONFLICT OF INTEREST ISSUE

You've just cemented a deal between a $100 million pension fund and Green Company, a large regional money manager. You and your staff put in long hours and a lot of effort to close the deal and are feeling very good about it. As you and three of your direct reports are having lunch in a fancy restaurant to celebrate a promotion, the waiter brings you a phone. A senior account executive from Green is calling and wants to buy you lunch in gratitude for all your efforts. "I'll leave my credit card number with the restaurant owner," he says. "You and your team have a great time on me."

CUSTOMER CONFIDENCE ISSUE

You're working the breakfast shift at a fast-food restaurant when a delivery of milk, eggs, and other dairy products arrives. There's a story in the local newspaper about contaminated milk distributed by the dairy that delivers to your restaurant. Upon reading the article more closely, you discover that only a small portion of the dairy's milk is contaminated, and the newspaper lists the serial numbers of the affected containers. When you point out the article to your manager, he tells you to forget it. "If you think we've got time to go through every carton of milk to check serial numbers, you're crazy," he says. "The article says right here that the chances are minuscule that anyone has a contaminated carton." He also explains that he doesn't have the workers to check the milk, and what's more, destroying the milk would require him to buy emergency milk supplies at the retail price. So he tells you to get back to work and forget about the milk. He says, "I don't have the time or the money to worry about such minor details."

USE OF CORPORATE RESOURCES ISSUE

You work for Red Company. You and a colleague, Pat Brown, are asked by your manager to attend a weeklong conference in Los Angeles. At least 25 other employees from Red Co. are attending, as well as many customers and competitors from other institutions. At the conference, you attend every session and see many of the Red Co. people, but you never run into Pat. Although you've left several phone messages for her, her schedule doesn't appear to allow room for a meeting. However, when you get back to the office, the department secretary, who is coordinating expense reports, mentions to you that your dinner in L.A. must have been quite the affair. When you ask, "What dinner?" she describes a dinner with 20 customers and Red Co. employees that Pat paid for at a posh L.A. restaurant. When you explain that you didn't attend, she shows you the expense report with your name listed as one of the attendees.

NOTES

1. Mary C. Gentile, "Giving Voice to Values," The Aspen Institute, www.aspencbe.org/teaching/gvv/index.html.
2. B. George, P. Sims, A. N. McLean, and D. Mayer, "Discovering Your Authentic Leadership," *Harvard Business Review* 85, no. 2 (2007): 1–8.
3. J. Q. Wilson, *The Moral Sense* (New York: Free Press, 1993), 55–78.
4. E. A. Lind and T. R. Tyler, *The Social Psychology of Procedural Justice* (New York: Plenum Press, 1988).
5. B. Sheppard, R. Lewicki, and J. W. Minton, *Organizational Justice: The Search for Fairness in the Workplace* (New York: Lexington Books, 1992).
6. Eduardo Porter, "UBS Ordered to Pay $29 Million in Sex Bias Lawsuit," *New York Times*, April 7, 2005, www.nytimes.com.
7. Insider Exclusive, "Wall Street Women Win $70 Million Against Morgan Stanley," 2013, http://www.insiderexclusive.com/justice-in-america/legal-wall-street-women-win-70-million-against-morgan-stanley.
8. Jenny Anderson, "After She Sued Merrill, It's Back on the Job," *New York Times*, July 22, 2005, www.nytimes.com.
9. D. Schawble, "Daniel Goleman on Leadership and the Power of Emotional Intelligence," *Forbes*, September 15, 2011, www.forbes.com
10. E. Warren and N. Millman, "Abuse on the Line for Years, Women at Mitsubishi Say They've Endured the Degrading Deeds and Words of Co-workers. Now They're Doing the Talking," February 15, 1998.
11. J. Lever, G. Zellman, and S. J. Hirschfeld, "Office Romance: Are the Rules Changing?" *Across the Board*, March–April 2006, 33–37.
12. J. D. Glater, "University of Texas Fires Director of Financial Aid," *New York Times*, May 14, 2007.

13. Paul Sullivan, "In Search of Competent (and Honest) Advisers," *New York Times*, August 1, 2009, www .nytimes.com.

14. J. Hechinger and S. Craig, "SEC Tells Fidelity Probe May Yield Civil Complaint," *Wall Street Journal*, July 26, 2005, A3.

15. J. A. Byrne, "No Excuses for Enron's Board," *Businessweek*, July 29, 2002, 50.

16. I. J. Dugan, "Auditing Old-Timers Recall when Prestige Was the Bottom Line," *Wall Street Journal*, July 15, 2002.

17. A. Samuel, "Meet your newest management headache: the co-branded employee," *Wall Street Journal* online. October 29, 2012.

18. K. Reardon, "Courage as a Skill," *Harvard Business Review*, January 2007, 2–7.

19. H. Wee, "Corporate Ethics: Right Makes Might," *Businessweek*, April 11, 2002.

20. R. Webber, "Whistle Blowing," *Executive Excellence*, July 1989, 9–10.

21. Ibid.

22. A. Dunkin, "Blowing the Whistle without Paying the Piper," *Businessweek*, June 3, 1991, 138–39.

23. W. M. Hoffman and J. M. Moore, *Business Ethics: Readings and Cases in Corporate Morality* (New York: McGraw-Hill, 1984), 257.

24. F. Pellegrini, "Person of the Week: 'Enron Whistleblower' Sherron Watkins," *Time*, January 18, 2002.

25. R. Rothracker, "Whistle-blower law reap big payoffs for U.S. Treasury." *Legi-Slate,* August 29, 1997, 1; S. McDonough, "Wanted: Snitch for good pay." *Centre Daily Times,* November 29, 2004, B9; D. B. Caruso, "Whistleblowers help feds to build cases." *Centre Daily Times,* August 25, 2004, B9.

26. K. Thomas and M. Schmidt, "Glaxo Agrees to Pay $3 Billion in Fraud Settlement," *New York Times*, July 2, 2012, www.nytimes.com

27. P. Dryer, and D. Carney, "Year of the Whistleblower," *Businessweek*, December 16, 2002, 107–10. T. Wilkinson, "After Eight Years, An Insider Gets His Reward Thanks to Whistleblower's Efforts, U.S. Government Reaps Largest Single Cash Award Under False Claims Act," *Todd Wilkinson Special to the Christian Science Monitor. The Christian Science Monitor*. Boston, Mass.: July 24, 2001, 4.

28. P. Harned. "Putting whistleblowing in perspective," *Huffington Post*, December 5, 2012.

29. Eric Krell, "Whistle-Blowers Not a Top Concern," *Business Finance Magazine*, December 13, 2012.

30. P. Harned. "Putting whistleblowing in perspective," *Huffington Post*, December 5, 2012.

31. K. L. Soeken and D. R. Soeken, "A Survey of Whistleblowers: Their Stressors and Coping Strategies," *Proceedings of the Hearing on H.R. 25* (Washington, D.C.: U.S. Government Printing Office, 1987), 156–66; M. Miceli and J. Near, *Blowing the Whistle* (New York: Lexington Books, 1992), 303.

32. P. Dryer, and D. Carney, "Year of the Whistleblower," *Businessweek*, December 16, 2002, 107–10.

MANAGING ETHICS
IN THE ORGANIZATION

CHAPTER 5

ETHICS AS ORGANIZATIONAL CULTURE

INTRODUCTION

Thus far, we have discussed business ethics primarily in terms of how individual employees think and respond. But anyone who has ever worked knows that employees are not "just" individuals. They become part of something larger; they're members of an organizational culture that affects how they think and behave. Here, we apply this culture concept to organizational ethics. You can think about the *ethical culture* of an organization as a "slice" of the larger organizational culture that represents the aspects of organizational culture that affect the way employees think and act in ethics-related situations.

In terms of how we've been thinking about ethical decision making, you can consider ethical culture to be a significant organizational influence on individuals' ethical awareness, judgment, and action, along with the individual differences and other influences already discussed in Chapter 3. Recall that most employees are at the conventional level of cognitive moral development, meaning that they are looking outside themselves for guidance about how to think and act. Ethical culture is a source of a good bit of that guidance and can influence employees to be aware of ethical issues (or not), to make good or bad judgments, and to do either the right thing or the wrong thing.

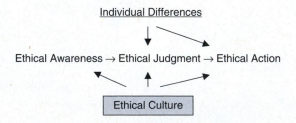

Individual Differences

Ethical Awareness → Ethical Judgment → Ethical Action

Ethical Culture

ORGANIZATIONAL ETHICS AS CULTURE

What Is Culture?

Anthropologists define *culture* as a body of learned beliefs, traditions, and guides for behavior shared among members of a group.[1] This idea of culture has been particularly useful for understanding and differentiating among work organizations and the behavior of people in them.[2] It's a way of differentiating one organization's "personality" from another. The organizational culture expresses shared assumptions, values, and beliefs[3] and is manifested in many ways, including formal rules and policies, norms of daily behavior, physical settings, modes of dress, special language, myths, rituals, heroes, and stories.[4] To assess and understand an organization's culture requires knowledge of the organization's history and values, along with a systematic analysis of multiple formal and informal organizational systems.

Organizational cultures can vary widely, even within the same industry (consider Wal-Mart, Target, and Costco—all big-box retailers that have very different cultures). In the computer industry, IBM was known for many years for its relative formality, exemplified by a dress code that mandated dark suits, white shirts, and polished shoes. Apple Computer, on the other hand, was known for its informality. Particularly in its early days, T-shirts, jeans, and tennis shoes were the expected Apple "costume." *Fortune* magazine described IBM as "the sensible, wingtip, Armonk, New York computer company, not part of that sneaker-wearing, tofu-eating Silicon Valley crowd."[5] Although that characterization was made a long time ago, it's still pretty applicable today.

Strong versus Weak Cultures

Organizational cultures can be strong or weak.[6] In a strong culture, standards and guidelines are widely shared within the organization, providing common direction for day-to-day behavior. This is likely because all cultural systems, formal and informal, are aligned to provide consistent direction and to point behavior in the same direction. In the 1980s, Citicorp's culture was so strong that when Katherine Nelson, a coauthor of this text and former vice president and head of human resources communications at Citicorp, traveled to the firm's offices in the Far East to deliver ethics training, she felt right at home (despite huge differences in national culture). "You could tell that you were in a Citicorp facility," she said, "whether you were in London, Tokyo, or New York." When Nelson facilitated an ethics training session for Japanese managers, she presented them with a common ethical dilemma—what do you do if you have raised an important ethical issue with your manager and nothing is done? Moreover, the manager discourages you from pursuing the issue. The potential answers included do nothing, go around the manager to the next level, raise the issue in writing to the manager, or take the issue to a staff department such as human resources.

The Japanese managers unanimously gave the "correct" answer according to Citicorp culture and policies at the time. They said they would go around their manager and take the issue to the next level. Nelson was surprised at their response, thinking that it conflicted with the wider Japanese culture's deference to authority and seniority. So she asked these managers, "Doesn't this conflict with Japanese culture?" To which they responded, "You forget—we are much more Citicorp than we are Japanese." Citicorp's culture proved to be so strong that standards and guidelines spanned continents and superseded national culture. (Citicorp merged with Travelers in 1998 to form Citigroup, and its culture changed significantly as a result.)

This type of experience has since been echoed by some of our international students who worked for U.S.-based multinationals before returning to school for their MBA degree. For example, one student worked for Baxter Healthcare in a country known for corruption and bribery. Baxter's strong ethical culture didn't allow such conduct, and employees were proud to be a part of such an organization and happy to comply (even or perhaps especially in the midst of a corrupt business culture).

In a weak organizational culture, strong subcultures exist and guide behavior that differs from one subculture to another. Many large public universities can be thought of as having weak cultures. For example, for faculty, departmental subcultures are often stronger than the overall college or university culture; the romance languages department differs from the accounting department. Among students at a large state university, the fraternity-sorority subculture coexists with the political activist subculture, the devout religious subculture, the jock subculture, and many other subcultures, and behavior is quite different within each. It's important to note that weak doesn't necessarily mean bad. In some situations, weak cultures are desirable. They allow for strong subcultures featuring diversity of thought and action. However, in a weak culture, behavioral consistency across the organization is tough to achieve. Look around your own school or work organization. Would you characterize its culture as strong or weak?

How Culture Influences Behavior: Socialization and Internalization

Employees are brought into the organization's culture through a process called enculturation, or *socialization*.[7] Through socialization, employees learn "the ropes." Socialization can occur through formal training or mentoring, or through more informal transmission of norms of daily behavior by peers and superiors. New members learn from observing how others behave or through informally transmitted messages. When effectively socialized into a strong culture, employees behave in ways that are consistent with expectations of the culture (or subculture). They know how to dress, what to say, and what to do.

With socialization, people behave in ways that are consistent with the culture because they feel they are expected to do so. Their behavior may have nothing to do with their personal beliefs, but they behave as they are expected to behave in order to fit into the context and to be approved by peers and superiors.[8] As an example, the president of a huge financial firm once took a young, high-potential manager out to lunch and walked him right over to Brooks Brothers for a new suit. "You can't get where you're going in a cheap suit," the president told the young man, who continued to buy his suits at Brooks Brothers.

But individuals may behave according to the culture for another reason—because they have internalized cultural expectations. With *internalization*, individuals have adopted the external cultural standards as their own. Their behavior, though consistent with the culture, also accords with their own beliefs. They may come into the organization sharing its values and expectations, thus making for a very smooth transition. Or, they may internalize cultural expectations over time. In the above example, the young manager may have initially bought the Brooks Brothers suit because he felt compelled to; but over time, he continued to buy those suits perhaps because he had internalized the expectation and wanted to do so.

The concepts of socialization and internalization apply to understanding why employees behave ethically or unethically in an organization. Most people prefer to behave ethically. When they join an organization with a strong ethical culture, the messages about honesty and respect resonate with their personal beliefs and are easily internalized. They act ethically because it's natural for them to do so and consistent with the cultural messages they're receiving. But unfortunately, most employees can be socialized into behaving unethically, especially if they have little work experience to contrast with the messages being sent by the current unethical culture. If everyone around them is lying to customers, they're likely to do the same as long as they remain a member of the organization.

ETHICAL CULTURE: A MULTISYSTEM FRAMEWORK

We said earlier that ethical culture can be conceptualized as representing a slice of the organization's broader culture. Ethical culture is created and maintained through a complex interplay of formal and informal organizational systems (Figure 5.1). Formally, executive leader communications, selection systems, orientation and

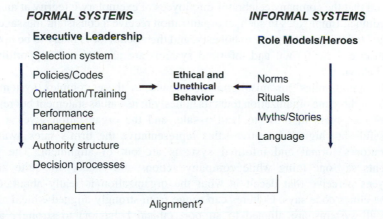

FIGURE 5.1 A Multisystem Ethical Culture Framework

training programs, rules, policies and codes, performance management systems, organizational structures, and formal decision-making processes all contribute to creating and maintaining ethical culture. Informally, heroes and role models, norms of daily behavior, rituals, myths, stories and language indicate whether the formal ethics-related systems represent reality or facade. The next section provides examples of each of these important ethical culture systems. Although we discuss these systems separately, keep in mind that they are all interconnected.

Alignment of Ethical Culture Systems

To create a consistent ethical culture message, the formal and informal systems must be *aligned* (work together) to support ethical behavior. To have a fully aligned ethical culture, the multiple formal and informal systems must all be sending employees consistent messages that point in the direction of ethical behavior. For example, imagine a company whose formal corporate values statement and ethics code tell employees that honesty is highly valued in the organization and that employees should always be truthful with customers and each other. Consistent with that values statement, the selection system does background checks on potential employees, incorporates ethics-related questions in interviews, and highlights the company's values to recruits. Once hired, new employees are further oriented into the ethical culture by learning about the values of the founder, how the history of the company supports those values, and how the current executive team is carrying on that tradition. They're also trained in the specific kinds of ethical issues they could face in their jobs and how to handle them ethically. They learn that the performance management system will assess them on values-related criteria, including honest and trustworthy interactions, and that these assessments will be important to decisions about compensation and promotion. They are also encouraged to take personal responsibility and speak up about any ethical concerns. On the informal side, they learn that high-level managers routinely tell customers the truth about the company's ability to meet their needs and that the company celebrates employees of exemplary integrity at an annual awards dinner. Employees in such an organization receive a consistent message about the organization's commitment to honesty, and their behavior is likely to be honest as well because these formal and informal systems are aligned and supporting their ethical behavior.

But opportunities for misalignment abound in these complex systems. For example, if the same organization touts its honesty in its values statement but regularly deceives customers in order to land a sale, and the organization gives a highly "successful" but highly deceptive sales representative the firm's sales award, the organization's formal and informal systems are out of alignment. The formal statements say one thing while company actions and rituals say quite another. Employees perceive that deceit is what the organization is really about, despite what the ethics code says. Cultures can range from strongly aligned ethical cultures (where all systems are aligned to support ethical behavior) to strongly aligned unethical cultures (where all systems are aligned to support unethical behavior) to those that are misaligned because employees get somewhat mixed messages due to conflicts between the formal and informal systems.

DOW CORNING: AN ETHICAL CULTURE OUT OF ALIGNMENT? Developing a strongly aligned ethical culture is easier said than done. Managers need to be careful because an organization may easily be lulled into thinking that its ethical house is soundly constructed, only to find that the roof has been leaking and it's about to cave in. This may be what happened to Dow Corning.

Dow Corning had been recognized as a corporate ethics pioneer. It was among the first, in 1976, to establish an elaborate formal ethics program and structure. Then-chairman John S. Ludington set up a Business Conduct Committee comprised of six company executives, each of whom devoted up to six weeks a year to the committee's work and reported directly to the board of directors. Two of these members were given responsibility for auditing every business operation every three years. In addition, three-hour reviews were held with up to 35 employees who were encouraged to raise ethical issues. The results of these audits were reported to the Audit and Social Responsibility Committee of the board of directors. John Swanson, manager of corporate internal and management communication at the time, headed this effort and was quoted as saying that the audit approach "makes it virtually impossible for employees to consciously make an unethical decision."[9]

This apparently impressive formal program failed to help the organization avoid its problem with breast-implant safety, however, despite documented warnings from a company engineer in 1976 that suggested that the implants could rupture and cause medical problems. It isn't entirely clear why this well-intentioned ethics program failed. It's likely that, although it was designed to cultivate an overall environment of ethical conduct, aspects of the ethical culture were out of alignment—sending employees different messages.[10] "Layering in a bureaucracy is no substitute for a true corporate culture.

Workers have a genius for discovering the real reason for a system and learn quickly how to satisfy its minimum requirements."[11] The system relied on managers to identify the key ethical issues covered by the auditors. Were these managers likely to alert the auditors to their most serious ethical problems? What would the consequences be? The system also relied on periodic planned audits. Did commitment to ethics peak during the planned audit sessions, only to disappear into the woodwork after the auditors left?[12] We don't know, but a comprehensive multisystem audit of the ethical culture might have provided the answer.

Leaders should be interested in creating a strongly aligned ethical culture because American employees strongly prefer working for such an organization. A 2006 study found that 82 percent of Americans would actually prefer to be paid less but work for an ethical company than be paid more but work for an unethical company. Importantly, more than a third of people say that they've left a job because they disagreed with the company's ethical standards. So having a strong ethical culture is an important way to retain the best employees.[13]

Another reason leaders need to create and maintain a strongly aligned ethical culture is that the U.S. Sentencing Commission revised its guidelines for sentencing organizational defendants in 2004 (see www.ussc.gov and Chapter 6 for more information about these guidelines). When the U.S. Sentencing Commission (www.ussc.gov) evaluated the effect of the original 1991 guidelines, it noted that many organizations seemed to be engaging in a kind of "check-off approach" to the guidelines. In responding to guideline requirements to qualify for reduced sentencing and fines, these organizations would establish formal ethics and/or legal compliance programs, including ethics offices, codes of conduct, training programs, and reporting systems. But the commission learned that many of these formal programs were perceived to be only "window dressing" by employees because they were inconsistent with the employees' day-to-day organizational experiences. The commission subsequently revised its guidelines to call for developing and maintaining a strong ethical culture. As a result, many companies are now assessing their ethical cultures to determine how they're doing in relation to ethics so if they do get into legal trouble, they can demonstrate that they have been making sincere efforts to guide their employees toward ethical conduct.

ETHICAL LEADERSHIP

Executive Leaders Create Culture

Executive leaders affect culture in both formal and informal ways. Senior leaders can create, maintain, or change formal and informal cultural systems by what they say, do, or support.[14] Formally, their communications send a powerful message about what's important in the organization. They influence a number of other formal culture dimensions by creating and supporting formal policies and programs with resources, and they influence informal culture by role modeling, the language they use, and the norms their messages and actions appear to support.

The founder of a new organization is thought to play a particularly important culture-creating role.[15] Often, the founder has a vision for what the new organization should be. He or she often personifies the culture's values, providing a role model for others to observe and follow, and guides decision making at all organizational levels. For example, Thomas Jefferson founded the University of Virginia. Although he's long gone, it's said even today that when the governing board of the university is faced with a difficult decision, they're still guided by "what Mr. Jefferson would do." Founders of small businesses frequently play this culture-creating role.

Herb Kelleher is the legendary founder of Southwest Airlines. The no-frills airline started in 1971 and has been growing and flying pretty high ever since, despite many difficulties in its industry. Southwest Airlines has never served a meal, and its planes are in and out of the gate in 20 minutes. During Kelleher's tenure as CEO and chairman, other airlines went bankrupt, suffered strikes, or disappeared. But Southwest continued to succeed even after the terrorist attacks of September 11, 2001, that sent the entire industry reeling. The secret is thought to be the company's culture and an esprit de corps inspired by Kelleher—he believed in serving the needs of employees, who would then take great care of customers and ultimately provide shareholder returns. The culture continues to combine efficiency, a family feeling, and an emphasis on fun. In support of efficiency, pilots have been known to load luggage or even clean planes if necessary.

During a fuel crisis, Kelleher asked employees to help by providing money-saving ideas. The response was immediate: within only six weeks after Kelleher's request, employees had saved the company more than $2 million. In the area of fun, Kelleher was known for his crazy antics, jokes, and pranks. He settled business disputes by arm wrestling; and when a fellow airline CEO criticized Southwest's promotion that featured Shamu, the killer whale, Kelleher sent him a huge bowl of chocolate pudding (meant to resemble whale poop) with a note reading, "With love, from Shamu."[16] Employees are encouraged to make flying fun, so that customers leave every Southwest flight with a smile, and they're encouraged to do that in a way that's spontaneous, emotional, and from the heart.[17] Southwest is seen as a leader in its industry and regularly shows up near the top of *Fortune* magazine's most admired companies. It continues to perform well even after Kelleher stepped down as CEO in 2001. In explaining how they have remained so successful, Colleen Barrett (who stepped down as president in 2008) referred to the culture, saying that Southwest does "everything with passion. We scream at each other and we hug each other . . . we celebrate everything."[18] The walls at Southwest's headquarters are covered with photos of employees dressed in crazy outfits or with their pets. But the company is also financially conservative and cost-conscious, and these cultural attributes contribute to their ongoing success.

Leaders Maintain or Change Organizational Culture

Current executive leaders can also influence culture in a number of ways.[19] They can help maintain the current culture, or they can change it by articulating a new vision and values; by paying attention to, measuring, and controlling certain things; by making critical policy decisions; by recruiting and hiring personnel who fit their vision of the organization; and by holding people accountable for their actions.

Sometimes new leaders significantly change long-standing corporate culture. Jack Welch, retired CEO of General Electric Company, radically changed the formerly staid bureaucratic culture of GE into a lean and highly competitive organization during his leadership tenure. Welch began the culture change effort by clearly articulating his vision that the new GE would be number one or number two in the world in each of its businesses. Businesses that could not measure up would be sold.

Traditional GE employees had been attracted to the job security of the old GE. But Welch wanted to encourage competitiveness, risk taking, creativity, self-confidence, and dynamism. He recruited managers who were interested in doing a great job and then moving on, if GE no longer needed them. Many of the old-line GE employees found themselves unhappy, out of sync—and, frequently, out of a job.

Welch also focused on identifying and eliminating unproductive work in the organization. He told managers to eliminate reports, reviews, and forecasts; to speed decision cycles; and to move information more quickly through the organization by eliminating unnecessary bureaucratic layers. All of this contributed to the "leaner and meaner" GE culture he created.

Welch's successor, Jeff Immelt (who became CEO in 2001), has changed the GE culture yet again. He announced in 2004 that four things would be required to keep the company on top: execution, growth, great people, and virtue. The first three were consistent with the GE everyone knew. However, most people don't expect the word *virtue* to be associated with a company that earns billions in revenue. But Immelt had learned that people perceived GE to be "a laggard" on the social responsibility front, and he vowed to change that. He has said that, in a world of business ethics scandals, people don't admire business as they used to and that the gulf between rich and poor is growing. As a result, he believes that companies are obligated to provide solutions to the world's problems—not to just make money for shareholders and obey the law. "Good leaders give back . . . It's up to us to use our platform to be a good citizen."[20]

In line with this new focus on virtue, Immelt appointed GE's first vice president for corporate citizenship and has been publishing corporate citizenship annual reports. The company is committing itself to becoming a leader in environmental cleanup and a catalyst for change. You may be familiar with its "Ecomagination" initiative that focuses on green initiatives and concern about climate change. This initiative even has its own devoted website (http://www.ecomagination.com/), as does the GE Citizenship initiative more generally (www.ge.com/citizenship). The company also now audits suppliers in developing countries to ensure compliance with labor, environmental, and health and safety standards. And the company has increased its focus on diversity, including granting domestic partner health benefits to employees, and has entered into dialogue with socially responsible mutual funds.

In response to a request from African American employees to do more in Africa, GE has worked with the public health service in Ghana, where it has provided equipment, water treatment, and leadership training. In a previous edition of this book, we noted that GE's foreign subsidiaries were still doing business with Iran.[21] But in 2008, the company decided it would not do business in any of the countries that the U.S. State Department designates as sponsors of terrorism (including Iran). This move suggests that the company is engaged in ongoing evaluations about where in the world it should and should not be doing business, based upon its values and concern about its reputation (a topic we will discuss more in Chapter 11).

ETHICAL LEADERSHIP AND ETHICAL CULTURE Clearly, employees take their cues from the messages sent by those in formal leadership roles. But most employees don't know the senior executives of their organization personally. They only know what they can make sense of from afar. Therefore senior executives must develop a "reputation" for ethical leadership by being visible on ethics issues and communicating a strong ethics message. Research[22] has found that such a reputation rests upon dual dimensions that work together: a moral person dimension and a moral manager dimension (see Figures 5.1 and 5.2). In this section, first we explain what each dimension represents and then we combine these dimensions into a matrix that shows

Executive Ethical Leadership Is about Reputation, Which Rests on These Two Pillars	
Moral Person	**Moral Manager** Tells followers how they should behave and holds them accountable
Tells followers how leader behaves	
Traits	**Role Modeling**
• Honesty	Takes visible ethical action
• Integrity	
• Trust	
Behaviors	**Rewards/Discipline**
• Openness	Holds people accountable for ethical conduct
• Concern for people	
• Personal morality	
Decision making	**Communicating**
• Values-based	Sends an "ethics and values" message
• Fair	

Executive Ethical Leadership Reputation Matrix

Moral Person

	Weak	Strong
Moral Manager Strong	Hypocritical leader	Ethical leader
Moral Manager Weak	Unethical leader	?

← Ethically neutral leader →

FIGURE 5.2 Executive Ethical Leadership

how leaders can develop a reputation for ethical leadership, unethical leadership, hypocritical leadership, or ethically neutral leadership.

The moral person dimension represents the "ethical" part of the term *ethical leadership* and is vital to developing a reputation for ethical leadership among employees. As a moral person, the executive is seen first as demonstrating certain individual traits (integrity, honesty, and trustworthiness). For example, one executive described ethical leaders as "squeaky clean." But probably more important are visible behaviors.

These include doing the right thing, showing concern for people and treating them with dignity and respect, being open and listening, and living a personally moral life. To some extent, senior executives live in glass houses. They are often public figures who are active in their communities. So they need to be particularly careful about their private behavior. Rumors can begin quickly and taint an otherwise solid reputation. Finally, an important contributor to being perceived as a moral person is to make decisions in a particular way—decisions that are explicitly based on values, fairness, concern for society, and other ethical decision rules.

But being a moral person is not in itself enough to be perceived as an ethical leader. Being a moral person tells employees how the leader is likely to behave, but it doesn't tell them how the leader expects them to behave. So to complete the ethical leadership picture, executives must also act as "moral managers"—they must focus on the "leadership" part of the term *ethical leadership* by making ethics and values an important part of their leadership message and by shaping the firm's ethical culture. They do that by conveying the importance of ethical conduct in a variety of ways.

Most of the messages employees receive in business are about bottom-line goals. Therefore, senior executives must make ethics a priority of their leadership if ethics is to get attention from employees. Moral managers do this by being visible role models of ethical conduct, by communicating openly and regularly with employees about ethics and values, and by using the reward system to hold everyone accountable to the standards. This "moral person/moral manager" approach is similar to what executive headhunters Thomas Neff and James Citrin list as their number one strategy (of six) of corporate stars: "Live with Integrity, Lead by Example." They say, "Integrity builds the trust in senior management that is critical for high-performing organizations."[23]

James Burke, former CEO of Johnson & Johnson, is probably the best-known example of a highly visible ethical leader. Soon after being appointed CEO in the late 1970s, he challenged his senior managers to revisit and update the company's age-old credo (discussed later in more detail). He wasn't willing to have it hanging on the wall unless his senior managers were committed to living it. After much disagreement, discussion, and input from J&J sites around the world, the credo was revised and its commitment to customers first and foremost was intact. Less than three years later, the Tylenol poisoning occurred (described in Chapter 10), and the credo guided corporate decision making successfully through the crisis. Following that crisis, Burke initiated a regular credo survey process in which employees were asked about the company's performance regarding the credo—and that process continues to this day.[24] It was clear to employees that Burke really cared about the credo and the values it represented.

When Paul O'Neill first became CEO at Alcoa, he brought with him a profound concern for worker safety. Although Alcoa already had an enviable safety record at the time based on industry standards, O'Neill created a goal of zero lost work days from accidents—a goal that flabbergasted even the safety director. When O'Neill visited plants, he told employees that the company was no longer going to budget for safety— if a hazard was fixable, they should do it and the company would pay for it, no questions asked. Then he gave the hourly workforce his telephone number at home and told them to call him directly about safety problems. He created an accident reporting system that required reporting within 24 hours of any accident, no matter how small, and he used the reports as an opportunity for learning so that future accidents could be avoided. He also got on an airplane and visited employees who had been seriously hurt, no matter where in the world they were. Safety messages were everywhere, including woven into the carpets at some Alcoa sites. And when employees in the Pittsburgh headquarters crossed the street, they were careful not to jaywalk because it was "unsafe." Years after O'Neill retired, Alcoa continued to improve until it became the safest company in the world. And Alcoa employees tell us that the emphasis on safety continues today.

In the completely different arena of diversity, O'Neill again stood out for his principled leadership. In his first week on the job, his secretary asked him to sign papers to join a country club. This had been standard procedure in the past because CEO membership was required in order for other Alcoa executives to join and use the club. Upon asking for certification that the club did not discriminate, he learned that the club did not have an open membership policy. O'Neill refused to sign the papers and developed a new policy saying that Alcoa would not reimburse any employee expenses at a place that did not allow admission to anyone who wanted it. O'Neill was encouraged not to rock the boat and to wait before making such a huge change. His response was, "What excuse am I going to use six or twelve months from now? I've just discovered my principles? They were on vacation . . . when I first came?" He explained that you have to have the courage of your convictions and insist on them all of the time, not just when it's convenient.[25]

Business executives are subject to immense pressure to win, and it can be tempting to put intense pressure on their people to bend or even break the rules. Ethical leaders maintain their principles through good times and bad. Bill George, retired CEO of Medtronic, a maker of medical devices, recounts a story about the time he had to tell analysts that, despite growing 15 percent for the quarter, the company's earnings would fall short of analysts' expectations. The analysts berated him and called him a liar. Such experiences drive some executives to fudge the numbers to meet Wall Street expectations. But true ethical leaders are not dominated by this pressure. They learn to ignore these outside voices and begin to listen more to their own inner voice and values. In George's case, he learned an important lesson when he visited a doctor who was performing an angioplasty with one of the company's balloon catheters that literally fell apart during the procedure. The doctor was so angry that he took the blood-covered catheter and threw it at George. What was the lesson for this ethical leader? Medtronic workers don't make pacemakers to please Wall Street. Their goal is to save lives. According to George, "the CEO can't have the shareholder centrally in mind when making decisions. . . . America's leading corporations became great not by getting their share prices up but by doing what they were set up to do incredibly well."[26]

UNETHICAL LEADERSHIP   Unfortunately, unethical leaders can just as strongly influence the development of an unethical culture. In terms of our matrix, unethical leaders have reputations as weak moral persons and weak moral managers. Al Dunlap was a senior executive with a reputation for unethical leadership. John Byrne of *Business Week* wrote a book about Dunlap (*Mean Business*, 1997) and published excerpts in the magazine. Dunlap became famous for turning struggling companies around. When hired at Sunbeam, he was considered such a celebrity CEO that the stock price spiked 49 percent in one day. But while at Sunbeam, he was also known for "emotional abuse" of employees—being "condescending, belligerent and disrespectful." "At his worst, he became viciously profane, even violent. Executives said he would throw papers or furniture, bang his hands on his desk, and shout so ferociously that a manager's hair would be blown back by the stream of air that rushed from Dunlap's mouth."

Dunlap also demanded that employees make the numbers at all costs, and he rewarded them handsomely for doing so. As a result, they felt pressure to use questionable accounting and sales techniques. Dunlap also lied to Wall Street, assuring them that the firm was making its projections and would continue to reach even higher. After just a couple of years, Dunlap couldn't cover up the real state of affairs, and Sunbeam's board fired him in 1998. But he left the company crippled.[27] In 2002, Dunlap settled a civil suit filed by the Securities and Exchange Commission (SEC). He paid a $500,000 fine and agreed that never again would he be an officer or a director of a public company. Investigators learned that allegations of accounting fraud on Dunlap's watch go back to the 1970s and follow him through a number of companies.

HYPOCRITICAL LEADERSHIP Perhaps nothing can make us more cynical than a leader who talks incessantly about integrity and ethical values but then engages in unethical conduct, encourages others to do so either explicitly or implicitly, rewards only bottom-line results, and fails to discipline misconduct. This leader is strong on the communication aspect of moral management but clearly isn't an ethical person— doesn't "walk the talk." It's a "do as I say, not as I do" approach. Al Dunlap made no pretense about ethics. All that mattered was the bottom line, and he didn't pretend to be a nice guy. But hypocritical leadership is all about ethical pretense. The problem is that by putting the spotlight on integrity, the leader raises expectations and awareness of ethical issues. At the same time, employees realize that they can't trust anything the leader says. That leads to cynicism, and employees are likely to disregard ethical standards themselves if they see the leader doing so.

Jim Bakker remains the best public example of hypocritical leadership. In the late 1970s and early 1980s, Bakker built his Praise the Lord (PTL) ministry into one of the world's biggest religious broadcasting empires. At its peak, Bakker's television ministry reached more than 10 million homes and had 2,000 employees. Bakker, along with his wife, Tammy Faye, claimed to be doing "the Lord's work" as he raked in millions of dollars, convincing the faithful to purchase a limited number of lifetime memberships in two hotels he claimed would be built at the PTL's Heritage USA Christian theme park. The problem was that the 25,000 lifetime memberships (promising a free annual family stay for four days and three nights) in the Heritage Grand Hotel morphed into 66,683 memberships. And, instead of the limited 30,000 memberships at the proposed Heritage Towers, PTL sold 68,755 memberships. You do the math. It would be impossible to provide promised services to this many people. On top of that, the second hotel was never completed.

The funds donated for these projects were being tapped to support PTL operating expenses, including huge salaries and bonuses for the Bakkers and other top PTL officials. When questioned at times about PTL's finances, Bakker referred to the organization's annual audits conducted by big auditing firms. Unfortunately, PTL filed for bankruptcy in 1987, three months after Bakker resigned in disgrace. The IRS revoked PTL's tax-exempt status, and in 1989 Bakker was convicted on fraud and conspiracy charges. He spent eight years in prison.[28]

A more recent example of hypocritical leadership is Lord John Browne, formerly the CEO of BP. Under Browne's leadership, the company launched a $200 million "Beyond Petroleum" campaign to promote its image as a highly socially responsible company that would deliver performance without trading off worker safety or environmental concerns. But when BP's Texas City plant exploded (killing 15 workers and injuring many more) and two big oil spills occurred in Alaska, regulators and employees cited cost cutting on safety and negligence in pipeline corrosion prevention as causes. It seemed that the Beyond Petroleum campaign was more about words than action. Greenpeace awarded Browne the "Best Impression of an Environmentalist" award in 2005, and the CEO was finally asked to resign in 2007 after a scandal in his personal life surfaced.[29] The lesson is pretty clear. If leaders are going to talk ethics and social responsibility (as they should), they had better "walk the talk" or risk cynicism or worse.

ETHICALLY NEUTRAL OR "SILENT" LEADERSHIP   The fact is that many top managers are not strong leaders either ethically or unethically. They fall into what employees perceive to be an ethically "neutral" or ethically "silent" leadership zone. They simply don't provide explicit leadership in the crucial area of ethics. They are perceived to be silent on this issue, and employees aren't sure what the leaders think about ethics, if anything. This may be because the leader doesn't realize how important executive ethical leadership is to the organization's ethical culture, isn't comfortable with talking about ethics issues, or just doesn't care that much. On the moral person dimension, the ethically neutral leader is not clearly unethical but is perceived to be more self-centered than people oriented. On the moral manager dimension, the ethically neutral leader is thought to focus on the bottom line without setting complementary ethical goals. Little or no ethics message is coming from the top. But it turns out that silence represents an important message. In the context of all the other bottom-line-oriented messages being sent in a highly competitive business environment, employees are likely to interpret silence to mean that the top executive really doesn't care how business goals are met (only that they are met), and they'll act on that message.[30]

Consider Sandy Weill, former charismatic CEO of Citigroup. Well before the current financial crisis, a *Fortune* magazine article described the firm as a "blockbuster money machine." But the article also recounted scandalous allegations about Citigroup and its Salomon Smith Barney unit (now sold off). "Citi helped Enron hide debt; Salomon peddled worthless WorldCom debt; Star analyst Jack Grubman recommended Winstar as it was heading for bankruptcy; Salomon rewarded telecom execs with hot IPOs," and more.[31] In 2004, Japan shut down Citigroup's private bank in Japan that had made $84 million for the company in 2003. Regulators listed a long series of transgressions including money laundering, sales of unsuitable products to customers, and generally sloppy business practices.[32] The company spent lots of time and money playing defense with the media, responding to ugly headlines on a regular basis. According to *Fortune*, Weill eventually became contrite and "got religion," if a bit late. Weill told his board that . . . his most important job . . . was "to be sure that Citigroup operates at the highest level of ethics and with the utmost integrity."[33] However, the article also cited widespread cynicism about that statement, noting that Weill was often "tone deaf" on these ethics issues.

At least from the perspective of outside observers, Weill exemplified "ethically neutral" leadership. Being tone deaf on ethics issues is exactly what ethically neutral leadership is about. Weill's public statement that the "company is too big to micromanage" applies to his approach to managing ethics. He said a CEO relies on "very competent people" and trusts them to do a good job. In the case of ethics management, that meant leaving it to the executives running Citi's various businesses. If the head of a division thought ethics was important, ethics got resources and attention. If the head didn't promote ethics, attention turned elsewhere, and most likely to financial performance goals. So, with a kind of benign neglect, Weill provided little explicit ethical leadership. And with corporate rewards focused on the bottom line, managers (and ultimately employees) had little motivation to attend to other issues.

This approach to ethics is in sharp contrast to prior CEO John Reed's leadership on ethics issues. Reed spent almost his entire career at Citicorp and was its CEO when the huge American financial powerhouse merged with Weill's Travelers organization to form Citigroup. Reed, who was a banker his entire life, understood in his gut how important reputation is to a financial institution. As a result, he encouraged and supported the development of a strong, centralized corporate ethics program with global reach. Interestingly, the people associated with that program were quickly gone, and much of the program itself was dismantled after Weill took over.

Weill stepped down in 2003 and handed the CEO reins to Chuck Prince, who was left to address the ongoing scandals—including $8 billion in scandal-related charges that had to be absorbed. Prince fired high-level people involved in scandals, including the chairman of Citigroup International who had been credited with a 30 percent increase in international earnings in 2003. In an interview with *Fortune* magazine, Prince said:

> John Reed [CEO before Weill] told me once that culture is a set of shared, unspoken assumptions. . . . I think the larger the company has become, the more we need to *speak* about those unspoken assumptions. We need to add to our celebration of financial performance a focus on long-term compliance activities, long-term franchise building, being in it for the long term. So one of the things we're going to put into place, starting in 2005, is a series of activities—training, communications, performance appraisals—that will lend a little more balance to the aggressive financial culture that we have always celebrated, and that I still do.

Short-term growth at the cost of long-term growth is a very bad trade. Some people make that bad trade when they only hear one instrument in the orchestra. If they hear the full orchestra, the full panoply of messages, then people have "no excuses"— that's the sign on my desk—no excuses.[34]

The more Prince scrutinized the organization, the more concerned he became about loose internal controls. He began to add resources to legal compliance. He even moved his office, from next to Weill's to the floor below, and began consulting more with John Reed.[35] But Prince seemed to feel powerless to really change the culture that

Weill had planted and that had taken root. Prince once confessed that he knew the bank's aggressive deal making could mean big trouble if the easy money stopped flowing. But, he also said, "As long as the music is playing, you've got to get up and dance," he told the *Financial Times* in summer 2007, even as credit markets began to shudder. "We're still dancing."[36]

The firm suffered severe performance problems under Prince's leadership, and he was replaced by Vikram Pandit in late 2007 (Pandit then resigned in 2012 under board pressure over perceived mismanagement). Citigroup, along with several other financial institutions considered "too large to fail," was rescued in the fall 2008 U.S. government bailout of financial institutions. The firm was in trouble because of losses related to risky mortgage-backed securities, which we speculate may have something to do with the laxity around ethical standards created under Weill. Many point to the repeal of the Glass-Steagall Act, which separated commercial banks from investment banks and insurance, as one of the root causes of the 2008–2009 financial crisis. Weill had championed this deregulation, and it made Citigroup possible. When John Reed expressed regret at his role in urging repeal of Glass-Steagall, Weill would have none of it at the time. "When asked about Reed's apology, Mr. Weill said, 'I don't agree at all.' Such differences, he said, were 'part of our problem.'"[37] Recently, however, Weill softened his stance and now advocates reinstatement of the Glass-Steagall law he fought so successfully to repeal.[38]

Research has found that executive ethical leadership is critical to employees. In firms that have an ethical culture characterized by top executives who are strong ethical leaders, unethical behavior is lower, and employees are more committed to their organization, more ethically aware, and more likely to engage in positive helping behaviors (including reporting problems to management).[39] Research has also revealed evidence that executive ethical leadership flows down through the organization, affecting supervisors' ethical leadership behavior and finally employee behavior.[40] But interestingly, senior executives are often not aware of how important their ethical leadership is. Many believe that being an ethical person who makes ethical decisions is enough. But it isn't enough. Executives must lead on this issue (be moral managers) if it is to register with employees. In a highly competitive environment of intense focus on the bottom line, employees need to know that the executive leaders in their organization care about ethics at least as much as financial performance. An ethical leader makes it clear that strong bottom-line results are expected, but only if they can be delivered in a highly ethical manner. Leaders may talk in terms of reputation or values, or use other language they find comfortable. But the message must be that the firm's long-term reputation is an asset that everyone must protect.

OTHER FORMAL CULTURAL SYSTEMS

Selection Systems

Selection systems are the formal systems that are in place for recruiting and hiring new employees. Selection systems are vital to hiring people who fit the culture of the firm. For example, all employees at Southwest Airlines (including pilots) are selected based on their personalities (traits that include cheerfulness, optimism, and team spirit) among other credentials. So it's not surprising to find flight attendants throwing gate parties on Halloween and telling jokes to passengers over the plane's loudspeakers.[41]

When considering the ethical culture, organizations can avoid ethical problems by recruiting the right people and by building a reputation that precedes the organization's representatives wherever they go. Companies can conduct background checks, check references, administer integrity tests, and survey applicants using some of the individual differences discussed in earlier chapters. For example, they should be wary of hiring someone high on Machiavellianism if they're trying to create a cooperative culture where people help and support each other. Interviewers can also ask ethics-related questions in interviews, for example, by asking candidates about ethical issues they've confronted in the past and how they've handled them.

In an article entitled, "Can You Interview for Integrity?" William Byham[42] offered a series of questions an interviewer concerned about ethics might ask a recruit. Here are adaptations of some of them:

1. We sometimes have to choose between what we think is right and what's best for the company. Can you give an example of such a time and tell how you handled it?

2. Can you describe your current employer's ethics? Are there things you feel good about? Bad about?

3. Please provide an example of an ethical decision you've made at work and tell how you handled it. What factors did you consider?

4. Can you provide an example of some past work behavior that you've regretted? How would you behave differently today?

5. Have you ever felt the need to exaggerate or bend the truth to make a sale?

6. Have you ever observed someone else stretching the rules at work? What did you do, if anything?

7. People are often tempted to make something seem better than it is. Have you ever been in such a situation?

8. Have you ever had to go against company policies in order to accomplish something?

9. Have you ever managed someone who misled a client? How did you handle it?

10. What's your philosophy of how to think about policies? Are they guidelines, to be followed to the letter?

Our students have been asked similar types of questions in interviews with the best companies. Are you prepared to answer questions like these?

Recruiters can also inform prospective employees about the importance of integrity in their organization and what happens to those who break the rules. Companies that are serious about integrity can include statements about their values and expectations in recruiting literature, in the scripts recruiters use when interviewing job candidates, in offer letters to candidates, and in new-hire orientation programs.

These days, companies also need to be very selective when recruiting leaders who are being considered for important decision-making roles in the firm. Many recent business scandals have zeroed in on company chief financial officers (CFOs) who played with the numbers to make it look as if profit goals expected by Wall Street had been achieved when, in reality, they had not. Such individuals must display the strongest moral character in order to withstand marketplace pressures to make the numbers look good. Questions about how they would respond to such pressures and how they have handled them in the past can be useful in selecting these key players.

Values and Mission Statements

Once employees are on board, many organizations aim to guide employees' behavior through formal organizational value statements, mission statements, credos, policies, and formal codes of ethical conduct. Value and mission statements and credos are general statements of guiding beliefs. Most companies have them, but it's important that the values and mission statement be closely aligned with other dimensions of the culture. According to James Collins, coauthor of *Built to Last: Successful Habits of Visionary Companies*, "the words matter far less than how they are brought to life. The mistake most companies make . . . is not setting up procedures to make sure the mission is carried out." If the policies and codes are followed in daily behavior and people are held accountable to them, this is another example of a strong ethical culture in alignment.

In the year 2000, Verizon's published core values were integrity, respect, imagination, passion, and service. But consider this. Customer service representatives were expected to finish each call with the following question (in precisely these words) to the customer: "Did I provide you with outstanding service today?" During a strike in the fall of 2000, workers cited this disconnect between values and operating procedures as a source of stress and cynicism. Asking customer service representatives to follow a specific "script" (that sometimes led to irate customers becoming even more irate) did not respect the individual customer service representative's ability to serve the customer in a more natural way, and it certainly didn't allow the employee to use imagination or passion in providing customer service. The script may have been well intentioned, but it conflicted with several of the core values professed by the company and appeared hypocritical to employees. Stated values that are inconsistent with management practice can quickly generate employee cynicism.[43] Wouldn't it be better and more consistent with the value of respect to simply ask service representatives to end their calls with a question about whether the customer was satisfied with the quality of service, but let the representatives choose their own words?

Probably the most famous example of a mission and values statement is the Johnson & Johnson credo, which outlines the pharmaceutical company's commitments. Probably most important is the statement that the company's "first responsibility is to the doctors, nurses and patients, to the mothers and fathers and all others who use our products and services." Other responsibilities follow, for example, to employees, suppliers, communities, and finally stockholders. Notably, stockholders are listed last under the assumption that if the other responsibilities are taken care of, stockholders will do well. On its website (www.jnj.com), the company includes information about the credo.

Most famously, the corporation drew on its credo for guidance during the Tylenol crises of the 1980s, when the company's product was adulterated with cyanide by someone who was never identified. Company managers and employees made countless decisions (including recalling all Tylenol at huge cost) that were inspired by and consistent with the credo's guidance. Today, company employees participate in a periodic survey and evaluation of how well the company performs its credo responsibilities. Survey results are then fed back to the senior management, and corrective action is taken to correct any shortcomings. As one recent example, in 2007, the company reported itself to the SEC and Justice Department when it discovered possible violations of the Foreign Corrupt Practices Act (the FCPA is discussed further in Chapter 11).

It takes little for a company to make a formal statement like the J&J Credo, but it takes quite an ongoing commitment to actually follow it.[44] Questions have arisen about whether J&J has sustained that commitment, because of some serious legal and ethical problems in recent years. We speculate that it is a monumental management challenge to integrate a credo (and the rest of a strong ethical culture) across such a large decentralized organization with many divisions and subunits even if the chief executive is strongly committed to doing so. But when we talk to current J&J employees, we find that most (if not all) still talk easily about the credo, its importance in the J&J culture, and how it guides ethical conduct in the organization.

When you are considering joining an organization, look for the organization's values statement and ask employees for examples of how the organization lives its values (or doesn't). Such a question can provide useful insight into cultural alignment and misalignment by making clear whether the values statement represents lofty formal statements with little basis in reality or "values in use" that represent how people really behave every day. It's important to ask yourself whether your own stated values (you should have assessed them in Chapter 2) match up with the organization's values. If they do, and you have evidence that this is an organization that lives its values, you're on your way to a job you'll find satisfying.

Policies and Codes

Formal ethics policies (often called codes of ethics or codes of conduct) are longer and more detailed than broad values and mission statements. They provide guidance about behavior in multiple specific areas. For example, most ethics codes address issues of respectful treatment of others, conflicts of interest, expense reporting, and the appropriateness of giving and receiving gifts. Policy manuals are even lengthier than codes and include more detailed lists of rules covering a multitude of job situations that are specific to the industry, organization, and type of job. An extended discussion of policies and codes follows in Chapter 6.

In a 2007 Ethics Resource Center study, 83 percent of respondents from a wide variety of private sector employers across the United States reported that the organizations they work for have formal ethics policy standards. That percentage was 98% for public sector employees.[45] So it's fair to say that most employers are making an effort to provide formal guidance to their employees regarding ethical and legal conduct. It's also important to note that these codes are living documents that are revised regularly in response to changing conditions. For example, early ethics codes said nothing about Internet privacy or social networking guidelines, but these topics are much more common in today's codes.

Most companies with codes now distribute them quite widely. A 1995 survey of *Fortune* 1000 firms found that 75 percent of responding companies reported distributing their code or policy to at least 80 percent of their employees.[46] This finding may be a by-product of the U.S. Sentencing Guidelines (discussed at length in Chapter 6), which specify communication of compliance standards to all employees as a guiding principle. Research has found that when employees are familiar with the code and refer to it for guidance, they are less likely to engage in unethical behavior, more likely to seek advice about ethical issues, and more likely to report ethical rule violations.[47] But, to have real influence on behavior, a code must be enforced and aligned with other culture components.[48] Otherwise, codes of conduct are more likely to be viewed as mere "window dressing" rather than guides for actual behavior.

Many firms post their codes on their websites. Some firms also distribute their codes beyond their own employees to vendors and suppliers who are explicitly asked to comply. For example, a supermarket company distributed its code to its suppliers along with a letter, signed by the president:

Dear Business Associate:

As the holidays draw near, we are mindful of the mutually satisfying and mutually profitable relationship which exists between our company and our suppliers. We look forward to many more years of successful growth together through our joint efforts to provide our customers with quality products, excellent service and low price.

In recent years, we have found many of our staff members embarrassed by well-intentioned gifts from those with whom we do business. Our Board of Directors approved the enclosed Code of Ethics which clearly states our policy prohibiting our Associates from accepting gifts from our suppliers and customers. We feel that this policy should apply during the holidays as well as throughout the year.

With so much attention being given to practices which bring the business community's ethics into question, we urge your support of our efforts to maintain the respect and confidence of the industry for the objectivity of our dealings with suppliers.

Since failure to comply with our policy will result in disqualification from further business dealings with us, we request that you distribute this letter to those in your company who have business dealings with our corporation and its subsidiaries.

The most significant means of expressing your appreciation to our staff continues to be your efforts to help us grow together by anticipating and meeting the changing consumers' needs and wants.

If you have any questions regarding this policy, please contact. . . .

With our best wishes for happy holidays and a healthy and prosperous New Year.

Companies are also taking more responsibility for the behavior of suppliers, even if those suppliers are in foreign countries. If Nike or Wal-Mart buys shoes or clothes from a factory in Asia, these firms are increasingly aware that the supplier's actions are their responsibility. As an example, Wal-Mart requires its suppliers to agree to comply with its code of ethical conduct and requires that suppliers post its free 1-800 reporting telephone number at work sites. We'll discuss this topic further in Chapter 11.

The idea of guiding behavior with codes of conduct extends to higher education institutions, where many colleges have honor codes that apply to academic (e.g., test cheating, plagiarism) and sometimes even nonacademic (job search) behavior. Research on honor codes in colleges and universities suggests that students cheat less in institutions that have honor codes.[49] However, students' perceptions of their peers' cheating has an even stronger influence on cheating behavior than the existence of a code. In addition, the certainty of being reported and the severity of penalties are important because they support the idea that the code alone is not the most important influence.[50]

Remember, cognitive moral development research tells us that most people are looking outside themselves for guidance, and stated organizational policy can be an important source of that guidance. To determine where policy is needed, the organization can ask or survey employees and managers about areas of ethical concern and their perception of the need for policy in each area. In one study, managers made it clear that policy was needed in such areas as expense claims, gifts and bribes, and treatment of competitor information.[51]

Orientation and Training Programs

Socialization into the ethical culture is often begun through formal orientation programs for new employees and is reinforced through ongoing training. The organization's cultural values and guiding principles can be communicated in orientation programs. Employees often receive an introduction to the values and mission statements as well as the company's history and current code of conduct. But new employees are so overwhelmed with information that it's important to follow up regularly with training programs that offer more specific guidance. An increasing number of firms have added ethics to their list of training programs. Some have done so as a result of the revision of the U.S. Sentencing Commission Guidelines and the Sarbanes-Oxley legislation that requires public companies to conduct compliance training at all levels, including senior executives and the board of directors. Most *Fortune* 1000 firms provide some ethics training,[52] and many of them do so annually. In the 2007 Ethics Resource Center study,[53] 75 percent of people surveyed said that their employers provide ethics training and that this training is generally mandatory. Some companies use online ethics training; others use classroom face-to-face training. In Chapter 6, we'll present more specifics about how different firms conduct ethics training.

It's important to note that the ethics training must be consistent with other ethical culture systems, because a training program that is out of alignment with other culture systems is thought of, at best, as a pleasant day away from the office. At its worst, the ethics training is seen as an obstacle to getting "real" work done—or even as a joke. For example, a young man who worked in mortgage lending in 2006 said that his company had provided a high-quality weeklong training program to prepare him for his job. Among other more technical aspects of his job, he was taught to advise clients to be sure that they could afford their payments and to avoid incurring additional credit card debt. He felt that this was smart and caring advice, and he felt good about his new role. But when he returned to the office, his "mentor" (who had been in the job only six months longer than he had) told him that all that mattered was closing the deal and making money for himself and the company, and that "advising" clients was a waste of time. If his "advisor" role had been reinforced by his mentor, the cultural message would have been entirely different. Perhaps the company's fate would have been different too—it no longer exists. And, to his credit, this young man left the job voluntarily after considering the harm that was being done to the firm's clients.

Performance Management Systems

Performance management systems involve the formal process of articulating employee goals, identifying performance metrics, and then providing a compensation structure that rewards individual—and frequently team—effort in relation to those goals. Performance management systems also include formal disciplinary systems that are designed to address performance problems when they arise. An effective performance management system is a key component of the ethical culture. The system plays an essential role in alignment or misalignment of the ethical culture because people pay attention to what is measured, rewarded, and disciplined. So if employees with integrity are the ones who get ahead, and unethical behavior is disciplined, that process goes a long way toward promoting an ethical culture.

DESIGNING A PERFORMANCE MANAGEMENT PROCESS THAT SUPPORTS ETHICAL CONDUCT Because people "do what's measured and rewarded," the best way for an organization to design a comprehensive performance management system is to spend time identifying which factors drive the results the organization strives to achieve. This type of corporate soul-searching generally results in a list of these factors, both financial and nonfinancial. Just as *Fortune* magazine considers reputation when designing its famed "lists" of admired companies, many sophisticated companies understand that reputation, in many cases, drives long-term financial results. However, many companies continue to design performance management programs that consider only short-term financial results. They ignore the nonfinancial drivers that can actually serve as the underpinning of the numbers. These companies focus on *what* business results are delivered, and they ignore *how* those results were achieved. That is probably the fastest way for an organization's ethical culture to get out of alignment.

Here's how performance management systems can be designed to get great results the right way. First, an organization needs to focus on the mechanics. For example, once an organization understands what is necessary to drive results, it needs to set goals to achieve those desired results and metrics to determine whether the goals are being met. Real success in this area comes when organizations effectively communicate those goals to every employee, helping employees identify how each person can create value for the organization and then rewarding employees fairly for their contribution to achieving those corporate goals.

Once the mechanics are in place, the next challenge is to marry the *what* with the *how*, and that's where an organization's articulated values come in. Those values—probably concerning the importance of people, integrity, diversity, customer service, and so forth—need to be translated into behavior metrics that every employee is held accountable for. When such a process is in place, high fliers who exceed all of their numbers can be held accountable for *how* they met those numbers because this step is built right into their performance expectations and rewards process.

A good example is an account executive with a leading consulting company who managed her firm's relationship with many of the largest companies in New York City. Her clients generated revenues in the millions for her firm, and that fact alone would ordinarily be enough to ensure that she was named a partner in the firm. However, the senior management team was so upset at how she trounced the firm's stated value of "treating people with respect"—she was extremely abusive to her coworkers—that they repeatedly denied her promotion. Of course, one could argue that she shouldn't have a job at all. But at least her behavior—the *how* involved in attaining her huge results—prevented her from being promoted and esteemed as a partner.

American Express has tied its performance appraisal system directly to its values and code of conduct. The values are associated with a culture that focuses on long-term results as well as the desire to be an "employer of choice." The company's ethics code states the expectation that leaders will be ethical role models who exhibit the highest standards of integrity, develop employees, communicate the company's ethical expectations and their own support for those expectations, and create an open environment so that employees feel free to express their concerns. The company's 360-degree performance management process for senior leaders then identifies a number of leadership competencies, including explicit examples of high performance such as the following:

- Treats others with respect at all times; is fair and objective
- Actively listens and incorporates input from others
- Acts with integrity
- Inspires the trust of the team, is reliable and consistent
- Talks openly and honestly—says it as it is

Examples of poor performance are also part of the system (e.g., "breaks promises, is inconsistent, fails to show respect for others").

The ratings of these competencies are weighted substantially in promotion and compensation decisions, thus making it difficult to get promoted if one is rated poorly on these ethical leadership competencies and important to be rated highly if an employee wants to advance. Finally, the company is investing resources in providing leaders with the necessary skills so that they can effectively fulfill the company's expectations consistent with its values.[54]

Alignment of the goals and rewards with the organization's values is essential because employees will generally do what's measured and rewarded, and they'll assume that the behaviors that are rewarded represent the "real" ethical culture. So, in the American Express example, behavior consistent with the company's stated values is measured and rewarded with promotions and compensation. This is a great example of ethical culture alignment.

But misalignment of rewards with other aspects of the ethical culture is quite common. For example, imagine an organization where everyone knows that the top sales representative's sales depend on lying to customers about delivery dates despite an ethics code that talks about customer satisfaction as a key value. Not only does the unethical conduct go undisciplined, but the sales representative receives large bonuses, expensive vacations, and recognition at annual sales meetings. Members of the sales force recognize that information about what is rewarded carries the "real" cultural message, and so the code becomes meaningless—or worse yet, an example of top management's hypocrisy.

For an ethical culture to be in alignment, poor performance against stated ethical goals must also be addressed quickly and fairly. For example, dishonest or disrespectful behavior (or any behavior inconsistent with ethical values) should be disciplined using a progressive disciplinary system that employees perceive to be fair. A first offense (unless it is particularly serious) is usually addressed in a constructive manner that gives the employee the opportunity to provide input and to change the behavior. Subsequent misconduct is addressed more severely, and dismissal is the ultimate outcome for repeat or serious offenses.

It's also important that employees be disciplined equally across organizational and performance levels. That means the successful star executive as well as the lower-level employee must be disciplined for knowingly breaking the rules. In fact, at that higher level, the discipline should probably be quicker and harsher because the higher in the organization one goes, the more responsibility one holds, and the more one is a role model for others. As a result of recent scandals and increased scrutiny by regulators, companies are taking discipline more seriously. Even the perception of unethical behavior can lead companies to dismiss high-level executives in the current environment.

The bottom line is that performance management systems are important in themselves because they provide guidance about expected behavior, but they're particularly important in the sense that people look to them to reflect the "real" message about what is valued in the organization. The essential question is whether consistency exists between what the organization says (e.g., values statements, codes) and what it actually measures, rewards, and punishes.

Organizational Authority Structure

Ethical cultures should guide individuals to take responsibility for their own behavior, question orders to behave unethically, and report misconduct or problems. A strong ethical culture incorporates a structure that emphasizes and supports individual responsibility and accountability at every level. Employees are encouraged to take responsibility for their own actions and to question authority figures if they have concerns. And individuals are held accountable for negative consequences when they occur and for reporting problems they observe. One manager we know created the idea of "Velcro" to convey the importance of responsibility. She tells her direct reports, if you know about a problem, it's yours until you address it. It's stuck to you like Velcro!

Most modern organizations are bureaucratic,[55] meaning that they have a hierarchy of authority, a division of labor or specialization, standardization of activities, and a stress on competence and efficiency. Bureaucracy provides many advantages, and large organizations require a certain amount of bureaucracy in order to function. The bureaucracy can also be used to create a structure that supports ethics, and you'll learn more about this in Chapter 6. For example, ethics and legal compliance offices in organizations signal to everyone that these are important issues worthy of resources, expertise, and staff. However, certain characteristics of bureaucracy—such as specialization, division of labor, and hierarchy of authority—can present problems for the organization's ethical culture.

AUTHORITY, RESPONSIBILITY, AND ETHICAL CULTURE   With bureaucracy comes the idea of legitimate authority. Look at any organizational chart. It will tell you who supervises whom—who has authority over whom. These authority figures serve important bureaucratic roles. They direct work, delegate responsibility, conduct performance appraisals, and make decisions about promotions and raises.[56]

But the idea of legitimate authority can present problems for the ethical culture. First, as you'll learn in Chapter 7, people tend to obey authority figures no matter what they are ordered to do.[57] This natural tendency toward unquestioning obedience can be a real threat to the organization's attempt to build individual responsibility into its ethical culture. In attempting to control employee behavior, many firms expect loyalty; some demand unquestioning obedience from their employees. You might think that's a good idea—that authority figures have more experience and should know what's right, and employees should follow their orders. But even the military with its authoritarian structure expects soldiers to question unethical orders. Loyalty is generally a good thing, but you shouldn't be expected to be loyal or obedient to an unethical boss or organization.

Unquestioning obedience to authority means that employees are not expected to think for themselves, to question bad orders, or to take responsibility for problems they observe. Therefore, a "do as you're told" and "don't ask any questions" culture that expects unquestioning obedience from employees can become involved in serious ethical problems. Research has found that the more a firm demands unquestioning obedience to authority, the higher the unethical conduct among employees, the lower their tendency to seek advice about ethical issues, and the lower the likelihood that employees would report ethical violations or deliver "bad news" to management.[58]

Some managers create a structure designed to help them avoid blame.[59] Their greatest fear is that when it comes time to blame someone, the finger will point their way, and their job will be at risk. By delegating responsibility to those at lower levels in the organization, the authority figure can often avoid personal blame for mistakes or ethical blunders. When it comes time to blame someone, the finger of blame frequently points down. Underlings, in particular, can become the scapegoat for mistakes made at higher levels. CYA (cover your a—) memos proliferate as managers look to blame someone in a relatively powerless position who is considered to be expendable.

The structure of an organization can also fragment jobs and roles.[60] It isn't necessarily that individuals don't want to take responsibility. But jobs and roles get so divided up that they simply can't see the big picture.[61] We'll see in Chapter 7 how military bureaucrats passed the buck for responsibility during an investigation of the My Lai massacre in Vietnam. Those involved saw themselves only as cogs in a machine. No one felt responsible for the larger outcomes of their actions.

NEW ORGANIZATIONAL STRUCTURES   Organizations today are developing structures designed to remove bureaucratic layers, push responsibility down, and empower individuals to make decisions at every organizational level. Take the example of office furniture manufacturer Herman Miller, Inc. (HMI), which is committed to the values of "open communication," "the dignity of each individual," and "quality relationships based on mutual trust and integrity." Kevin Knowles, a crew leader for six years, said, "What always surprises me is that everyone in the company . . . is free to talk with anyone in management about whatever they'd like to talk about." Managers at HMI cite workers' ability to go over their managers' heads as a major reason for the company's success. "There's no fear of retribution if you call someone three levels above." HMI touts a process its chairman calls "roving leadership" that allows anyone to be a leader on a particular issue.

Here is an example of how roving leadership was tested successfully. In the years when AIDS was still a highly feared disease with much misinformation flowing, an employee with AIDS decided that he should let others know about his illness. A coworker took the roving leader responsibility and informed the human resources manager. Quickly, the entire plant was informed, and a physician from headquarters flew in with a training videotape and a question-and-answer session. According to the roving leader, what's important is that HMI's value system "allows us to act on our instincts and know the company will support us. Because the value of each individual is important to us, we were able to stop the manufacture of furniture for one day to take care of Peter."[62] Such a culture likely contributes to the ongoing success of the company. These recent changes in organizational structure have powerful implications for taking responsibility and for ethical decision making, and they increase the importance of having a strongly aligned ethical culture. When individuals are independently making decisions, with less direct supervision, they need a strongly aligned ethical culture to guide them. An important part of this culture is a structure that supports taking individual responsibility for ethical action.

STRUCTURES TO SUPPORT REPORTING OF PROBLEMS In today's organizations, fewer employees are directly supervised and organizations rely increasingly on employees to alert them to problems or report misconduct. Yet employees are often reluctant to do so. Therefore, most large organizations have set up formal structures and systems for making suggestions and for reporting misconduct internally. These systems use intranets and phone systems to answer employees' concerns and take complaints and reports about observed wrongdoing.

As we all know, powerful norms exist against reporting on peers or superiors (internal whistleblowing). The words we use to describe this behavior—*tattling*, *squealing*, *snitching*, *informing*, and *ratting*—all have negative connotations. In fact, there isn't a nice or even a neutral word to describe it. Can you come up with one? As suggested in Chapter 4, whistleblowers frequently suffer retaliation, particularly when they report managerial or organizational misconduct.[63] They perceive (often rightly) that they are punished rather than rewarded for doing what they think is right. Therefore, employee fear of reporting misconduct is widespread and silence is the default.[64] If an organization claims that it's attempting to develop a strongly aligned ethical culture, retaliation against a whistleblower is a powerful example of misalignment. Again, the workers view this "punishment" of the whistleblower as an example of the organization's "real" ethical beliefs.

The ethical organization, however, should view an employee who takes responsibility for reporting a problem or misconduct as important to an effective control system and must find ways to make such activity safe and encouraged. Some organizations have even rewarded whistleblowing. For example, in 1996, *Fortune* magazine published memos from the chairman of a Wall Street financial services firm. The following memo was addressed to senior managing directors, managing directors, and associate directors.

> We need your help. Please help us get a message out to every associate. It is essential that once again we stress that we welcome every suspicion or feeling that our co-workers might have about something they see or hear that is going on . . . that might not measure up to our standards of honesty and integrity. . . .
>
> We want people . . . to cry wolf. If the doubt is justified, the reporter will be handsomely rewarded. If the suspicion proves unfounded, the person who brought it to our attention will be thanked for their vigilance and told to keep it up.
>
> Forget the chain of command! That is not the way [the company] was built. If you think somebody is doing something off the wall or his/her decision making stinks, go around the person, and that includes me. . . .
>
> *Get these messages out loud and clear.*

We have had some senior people who resented "end runs." They quickly became associated with more conventional firms—you can draw your own conclusions about whether their career change worked out for the best.[65]

This leader sent a clear message that whistleblowing was encouraged and rewarded. In the second memo, he shared information about a specific instance in which two administrative assistants detected that fictitious taxicab vouchers were being submitted by an employee. The employee was terminated, and the administrative assistants were provided a cash award.

Decision-Making Processes

The organization's formal decision-making processes are another important part of the ethical culture. In an aligned ethical culture, leaders make ethical concerns a formal and expected part of decision making. This emphasis on ethics in decision making can be reinforced by regularly addressing ethical concerns in meetings and by making them an expected part of managers' reports regarding new products or new business ventures. For example, managers may be asked to consider potential harm to multiple stakeholders when proposing a new product or process.

As one example, environmental impact is now an expected and routine part of corporate decision making in many firms. Some organizations such as hospitals are also creating special high-level "ethics" committees charged with reviewing major organizational level decisions from an ethical perspective.[66] For example, one can imagine a responsible pharmaceutical company making such assessments about whether to launch a new drug that has serious side effects even after the FDA has approved it. Some have advocated the implementation of moral quality circles, groups set up to assess the morality of business decisions.[67]

OVER-RELIANCE ON QUANTITATIVE ANALYSIS   Decision-making processes can contribute to unethical behavior by relying exclusively on quantitative analysis and focusing only on financial outcomes. For example, in Chapter 3 we discussed the decision-making process that kept the Ford Pinto from being recalled. In that situation, exclusive reliance on a quantitative cost-benefit analysis to the exclusion of ethical considerations had disastrous consequences. In another example, Johns Manville, the former corporate giant and producer of asbestos, was brought down by decision-making processes that focused on the bottom line to the exclusion of worker health. Decades ago, top management began to receive information implicating asbestos inhalation as a cause of severe lung disease in workers. Managers and medical staff suppressed the research and concealed the information from employees. During testimony, a lawyer reported on a confrontation with the corporate counsel about the failure to share X-ray results with employees. The lawyer reported asking, "You mean to tell me you would let them work until they dropped dead?" The Johns Manville lawyer replied, "Yes, we save a lot of money that way." It was apparently cheaper to pay workers' compensation claims than to develop safer working conditions.

A New Jersey court found that the company had made a "conscious, cold-blooded business decision to take no protective or remedial action."[68] Obviously, organizational decision makers must rely on quantitative analyses in making business decisions. But their reliance on numbers, to the exclusion of ethical considerations, is problematic and contributes to an unethical culture. Discussions about whether the decision is the "right" thing to do must accompany discussions about the effect of a particular decision on the bottom line. Important decisions should be subjected to a discussion of ethical concerns, especially potential impacts on stakeholders.

BURDEN OF PROOF   In 1986, Beech-Nut Nutrition Corporation, the second-largest U.S. baby food manufacturer, pleaded guilty to 215 felony counts and admitted to selling apple products that were a blend of synthetic ingredients. How did this happen? There were many causes, among them the company's financial difficulties, the belief that other companies were selling fake juice (industry norms), and the belief that the juice was perfectly safe.

A chief cause may also have been the decision-making processes that were used. When Jerome LiCari, director of research and development, recommended changing suppliers in 1981 (because he suspected adulteration), Operations Head John Lavery turned the traditional burden of proof around. Generally, baby food manufacturers would switch suppliers if the supplier couldn't demonstrate that the product was genuine. In this case, Lavery said that if LiCari wanted to go with a more expensive supplier, he would have to prove that the concentrate they were buying was adulterated (rather than genuine). Given the technology available at the time, this was difficult, and the supplier was retained.[69]

A similar decision-making criterion was used in the decision to launch the space shuttle *Challenger* despite engineers' concerns about O-ring failure in cold weather. In previous launches, engineers had been required to show evidence that the launch was safe (which would have been difficult, if not impossible). In the case of the *Challenger*, the burden of proof was changed. Engineers who balked at the impending launch decision were asked to prove that it was unsafe (rather than that it was safe).

These examples suggest that it's relatively easy to alter decision-making processes to support whatever decision managers have already made. That's why it's extremely important that organizations design formal decision-making processes in good financial times and before a crisis occurs. Then, when trouble strikes, they can rely on these effective decision-making processes to guide them. The space shuttle *Challenger* might never have been launched if engineers had been required to prove that the launch would be safe, rather than unsafe. Managers must be particularly alert to changes in traditional decision-making criteria, especially in times of crisis.

INFORMAL CULTURAL SYSTEMS

In addition to the formal systems described previously, ethical culture is kept alive informally and symbolically through informal norms, heroes, rituals, myths, and stories. Employees experience the "real" organization through these informal systems, and information about them is carried through informal communication systems such as the grapevine and water cooler gatherings. In this way, people come to know what behaviors are "really" rewarded, how decisions are "really" made, and what organizational leaders "really" care about and expect. If messages from the formal and informal cultural systems differ, the ethical culture is out of alignment. It's important to note that employees are more likely to believe the messages carried by the informal system. Research has found that employees' perceptions of informal cultural systems influence their ethics-related behavior more than the formal systems do.[70] Therefore the management of these informal systems is extremely important.

Role Models and Heroes

Much socialization about ethics is informally conducted by role models and mentors. Role models may be senior managers, immediate superiors, or just more experienced coworkers. Kent Druyvesteyn, former staff vice president of ethics, General Dynamics Corporation, made an important point about senior leaders as ethical role models. "People in leadership need to . . . set the tone by the example of their own conduct. We could have had all the workshops in the world. We could have even had Jesus and Moses and Mohammed and Buddha come and speak at our workshops. But, if after all of that, someone in a leadership position then behaved in a way which was contrary to the standards, that instance of misconduct by a person in a leadership position would teach more than all the experts in the world." By contrast, if senior leaders consistently model behavior of the highest integrity, employees learn that the formal messages about ethics are real.

Mentoring occurs at all levels in the organization and is an informal process of socialization whereby a more senior person takes a junior person under wing, providing information, career strategies, rules of the road, and so on. Individuals who are passing through organizational "boundaries," such as new hires, or those who are transferring from one part of the organization to another are most affected by these socialization influences.[71] In an ethical culture, the mentor emphasizes the importance of integrity and resistance to pressure to behave unethically. In an unethical culture, the mentor may indoctrinate the individual into accepted unethical practices, making it difficult for the individual not to go along.[72] The new accounting graduate who was told by his superior in a public accounting firm, "You're too honest to be an auditor," received a powerful message about ethics (or, actually, the lack thereof) in that organization. When looking for evidence of ethical culture alignment and misalignment, ask whether the organization's role models behave consistently with the organization's espoused values and codes.

In an ethical culture, heroes should personify the organization's values.[73] Heroes are symbolic figures who set standards of performance by modeling certain behaviors, and they can be the organization's formal leaders. The CEO can be seen as an organization's hero. But, heroes can also be founders who are no longer even present in the organization. As we noted earlier, Thomas Jefferson is still very much alive at the University of Virginia. Stories about the values of these heroes continue to influence decision making. Thus, a hero who champions integrity and stands up for what is right may influence the behavior of many in the organization.

An organization's hero can also be someone who is not a founder, the president or chief executive officer. For example, at universities or on professional sports team, coaches or star players often become organizational heroes. The important question is what values do these heroes represent? Savvy executives understand the role that heroes play in forming or changing a culture. One CEO of a financial services firm was very serious about identifying and rewarding people who lived his organization's values. He challenged his executives to bring him stories of employees who were doing the right things in the right way, who were models of the culture. He collected these stories and sent personal, handwritten thank-you notes to those model employees. While a phone call might have sufficed, employees were so thrilled with his written recognition and praise that they displayed his notes in their offices. Those framed notes sent a rather loud message to other employees about what kind of behavior was valued at high levels. Of course, they also helped spread word of the "heroes" and their deeds. In a similar example, Southwest Airlines publishes letters from customers in its monthly newsletter about employees who provided outstanding customer service (a key organizational value). They publish the employees' pictures in the newsletter and post them on the wall in the headquarters. By doing so, they are identifying these individuals as heroes and role models for others to emulate.

Norms: "The Way We Do Things around Here"

Norms are standards of daily behavior that are accepted as appropriate by members of a group. They exert a powerful influence on individual behavior in organizations, and they can serve to support an ethical or unethical culture. For example, imagine an individual entering a computer software sales job who is told immediately by peers in the sales force that customers should always be dealt with honestly because long-term customer relations are so important to the firm. Here, the norm of honesty with customers supports ethical conduct and an ethical culture. On the other hand, consider the individual who begins a new job and is told by his or her colleagues that making the sale is all that counts, even if you have to lie to the customer about the capabilities of the software or delivery dates. This norm supports unethical conduct and contributes to an unethical culture. Either kind of norm (ethical or unethical) can become "the way we do things around here" in the organization.

Formal rules are often inconsistent with the informal norms that develop. For example, the salesperson described previously may have attended a mandatory ethics training session that taught rules of honesty in customer relationships. But if the message being sent on the job is to make the sale no matter what, the formal rule is overridden. Similarly, at a fast-food restaurant, new employees may be told about a rule against eating food without paying for it. However, once on the job, they may see coworkers eating while the supervisor looks the other way. These coworkers may rationalize their behavior because of their low pay or poor working conditions, or because the supervisor doesn't seem to care or eats food himself or herself.

Encouraged to join in, the new employee is likely to do so, having learned the "real" rules. Thus, despite formal rules, regulations, codes, and credos, informal norms are frequently the most influential behavior guides and clues to the culture. When the formal messages are consistent with the informal norms, this contributes to an ethical culture in alignment. And when informal norms are inconsistent with formal rules and codes, the culture is clearly out of alignment.

Rituals

Rituals are an important part of an ethical culture. They tell people symbolically what the organization wants them to do and how it expects them to do it.[74] Rituals are a way of affirming and communicating culture in a very tangible way.[75] Organizations have meetings, parties, banquets, barbecues, and awards ceremonies that all convey messages about what's valued in the organization. Years ago, General Motors of Canada introduced a new vision and values by asking each manufacturing unit to create a small float representing one of the key values. These floats were part of a parade that kicked off a full day of culture-building ritual surrounding the theme "Customers for Life" and the motto "I Am GM." During the day, the CEO unveiled a large painting of the group vision and told a story about the company's future. To reinforce the "I Am GM" motto, employees were asked to see themselves as being responsible, at any moment, for the company, its products, and services. The day ended with the "GM Acceleration Song" performed by the 100-person Up With People singing and dancing group. The song had been revised to incorporate the new values created by the leadership team.[76]

Some companies have annual family picnics and "bring your child to work days" that encourage employees to value time with their families. Some have on-site child care so that having lunch with your preschool child in the company cafeteria becomes a valued daily ritual and symbol of the extent to which the organization values family. Others have awards ceremonies that convey the values of the organization, including awards for exemplary ethical conduct (see the discussion of Lockheed Martin's Chairman's Award in Chapter 6). It's important to ask what values are celebrated at these rituals and ceremonies because they can easily support unethical behavior, such as making the numbers no matter how. For example, sales meetings occur in most organizations. So is success with integrity being touted and celebrated at these meetings, or are only those who make their numbers celebrated at these events? Is the ritual of getting together after work to drink at a sports bar reinforcing an "old boys network" in an organization that touts its attempt to diversify its work force? Look for whether the rituals are consistent with the company's stated values, formal rules, and reward systems to help determine whether the culture is in alignment.

Myths and Stories

Another extremely important way organizational culture is communicated and kept alive is through the informal communication network. If you want to learn about an organization's culture, ask insiders to tell you stories that characterize the organization. People tell stories to give meaning to their world and life.[77] Organizational myths and stories explain and give meaning to the organizational culture. They may be anecdotes about a sequence of events drawn from the organization's history such as J&J's story of the Tylenol recall. The story's characters are employees, perhaps the founder or other company heroes, and the moral of the story expresses the organization's values.[78]

At IBM, a story that has been told and retold describes how a low-level employee denied Tom Watson, then IBM president, entry into a restricted area of the company because Watson was not wearing his IBM identification badge. Watson praised the employee, suggesting the importance of upholding company rules and applying them to everyone.

In other ethical organizations, stories that convey the importance of the ethical culture may refer to rule violators being disciplined harshly or fired for unethical or illegal behavior. Because discipline is so salient, people tend to remember and recount these stories, and they reinforce the value the organization places on doing the right thing.

To the extent that a story becomes a part of the organization's culture, it serves to reinforce the culture's emphasis on the organization's values and alignment between the informal and formal cultural systems. But note that stories can easily reinforce an unethical culture if they're about rule violators who succeed despite unethical behavior.

Organizations can also create stories to enhance the ethical culture. Medtronic, a medical technology firm, has embraced storytelling as a way to do just that. At their annual holiday party, the company invites patients and their doctors to share their stories of how the company's products helped them. For example, one patient with a long history of Parkinson's disease told a story about how his life had become uncontrollable until his doctor suggested trying a new Medtronic device for deep-brain stimulation that gave him his life and his smile back. The CEO noted how these stories help reinforce the company's mission of serving others.[79]

The best stories are simple ones based on real people and experiences that tap into the company's values and employees' pride. Leaders interested in creating an ethical culture should be on the lookout for examples of exemplary ethical behavior to celebrate and find ways to communicate those stories on corporate websites and in newsletters and award ceremonies. If you want to learn about an organization's culture, ask an employee to tell you a story that exemplifies the culture. Then just sit back and listen. Hopefully the story will be consistent with and help to carry the message of the organization's ethical values.

Language

Cultures develop and use language to communicate values to employees. The old joke that *business ethics* is an oxymoron suggests the conventional wisdom that the language of ethics is out of place in the business context. But in a strong ethical culture, ethics becomes a natural part of the daily conversation in the organization. Employees feel comfortable talking ethics with each other and with their managers. Organizational values are invoked in decision making. And managers routinely talk ethics with their direct reports. It could be as simple as asking whether the decision is the right one, in an ethical as well as a business sense. Is this the "proper" thing to do for customers, suppliers, the community? What is the potential harm to employees, customers, or the community?

The use of ethical language is likely related to decision-making behavior. In one study, individuals who discussed their decision-making using ethical language were more likely to have actually made an ethical decision.[80] These people talked about ethics, morals, honesty, integrity, values, and good character. Those who had made the unethical decision were more likely to recount the decision in the more traditional business language of costs and benefits.

But, without cultural support for the use of ethical language, business managers are reluctant to describe their actions in ethical terms even when they are acting for ethical reasons. This reluctance, referred to as "moral muteness," can be attributed to the value placed on "efficient" decision making such that ethics talk can be thought of as a distraction as well as to the desire to appear powerful and effective. Ethics talk can also appear overly idealistic and utopian and inconsistent with the expectation that effective business managers can solve their own problems.[81]

Interestingly, getting managers to talk with their employees about ethics has been likened to parents discussing sex with their children. Although parents agree that sex education is a good thing, they often find it difficult to broach the subject with their children. Similarly, managers may find it difficult to begin a conversation about ethics with other managers or with their subordinates. If these topics are typically not discussed, the manager who brings it up may feel like a goody-goody or a spoilsport.[82] But managers who become comfortable talking about ethics will be role models of important behaviors for their subordinates.

Kent Druyvesteyn, one of the first corporate ethics officers, told us an anecdote about the early development of ethics training at General Dynamics.

> Early on, at General Dynamics, we declared that our ethics training workshops were to be small and interactive, and that they were to be led by managers. And, we heard some complaints from managers who said, "We don't know anything about this." They thought we were going to have them teach Aristotle and Kant, but that's not what we were trying to do. We also had people in training say, "We can't have people in management do this. There won't be any quality control."
>
> At that point I said, "Let's consider what it is we're trying to do here. What we are trying to do is raise awareness, to increase knowledge of company standards and stimulate commitment to those standards. That's the most important thing." Here's an analogy I'd like you to consider. You have some small children and you decide that you want to teach them about sex. There are a number of ways that you could do this. You could

hire an expert—someone who knows all about sex, who knows the right words to use, who knows all the latest terminology, who is pedagogically very skilled. You could hire this person to come into your home, sit down in your living room with your children, and teach them about sex. I mean, isn't that good management technique—to delegate it to someone? On the other hand, you could do it yourself. You may have limitations. You don't know everything. You might be embarrassed or tongue-tied. In the end though, who do you think would be more effective? To have the expert do it or for you to do it yourself? I have never had a person say that the expert would be more effective.

Top managers can also make ethics an acceptable topic of conversation by sending a message that it's not only okay, but expected, to talk about one's ethical concerns. They can do this by leading discussions about ethics, discussing the ethics code and its application in a video that is shown to employees, and otherwise openly discussing ethical problems with managers and employees. Senior managers can also build "ethical talk" into the fabric of the organization by requiring routine discussion of ethical issues when important decisions are made.[83]

In unethical cultures, ethical language is mostly absent, or unethical language may be used (as when employees talk about "screwing" customers). And, as we noted in our discussion of euphemistic language in Chapter 3, organizational language can also be used to avoid the ethical implications of actions. This can happen either by design or inadvertently. For example, in Nazi Germany, the code names for killing and genocide were *final solution*, *evacuation*, and *special treatment*. This use of euphemisms allowed people to avoid confronting the true meaning of their behavior.[84] Similarly, companies use euphemisms to avoid the pain of decisions to lay off employees. *Downsizing*, *rightsizing*, *restructuring*, and *targeted outplacement* are just a few terms we've encountered. It may be easier to impose a targeted outplacement than a layoff, but are the ethical considerations as obvious for targeted outplacement as they are for layoffs? Recall from Chapter 3 that using ethical language increases individuals' ethical awareness. So, it's essential that ethical language become a part of the organization's ethical culture.

ORGANIZATIONAL CLIMATES: FAIRNESS, BENEVOLENCE, SELF-INTEREST, PRINCIPLES

Beyond these specific systems, we have learned that employees' perceptions of broad climates within the organization are influential. These climates tend to cross cultural systems. For example, when employees think about ethical culture, they tend to think first about the *climate for fairness* in the organization. This refers to whether they believe employees are treated fairly every day, in terms of outcomes (pay, promotions, termination), processes (are processes for making these important decisions about employees fair, nonarbitrary, and unbiased?) and interactions (are employees treated every day with dignity and respect?). It makes sense that it would be hard to talk seriously with employees about their ethical behavior if they believe that the organization isn't behaving fairly toward them and their peers. Research has demonstrated that these very general perceptions of fair treatment can be as powerful an influence on employees' ethical conduct as just about any of the formal or informal cultural systems just described. Employees appear to reciprocate the organization's fair treatment with their own ethical behavior.[85]

Consistent with these findings about the fairness climate, employees' behavior is also influenced by their general perceptions related to whether the organization is characterized by a *benevolence climate*—meaning the organization is one that "cares" about multiple stakeholders, including employees, customers, and the broader community and public. So employees are much more likely to demonstrate ethical behavior in an organization they see as one that cares.

By contrast, employees in some organizations see their firm as promoting a very instrumental *self-interest climate*, in which people protect their own interests above all and everyone is essentially out for him or herself. Little attention is given to the social consequences of one's actions. You can imagine that an organization that focuses exclusively on financial outcomes would create such a climate; and, logically, employee unethical behavior is higher in such organizations.

Finally, in a *rule-based climate*, employees perceive that the organization is one where employees follow both laws and the organization's rules when making decisions. One can imagine that organizations in highly regulated industries that take their codes, rules, and policies quite seriously would be rated highly on this climate dimension, which has the largest impact on reducing unethical behavior. This may be because this climate taps into perceptions of ethical culture alignment. An organization in which employees follow the rules is more likely to be one whose formal (codes, policies) and informal systems (norms of daily behavior) are aligned.[86]

DEVELOPING AND CHANGING THE ETHICAL CULTURE

We can conclude from this cultural perspective that ethics at work is greatly influenced by the organization's ethical culture. Both formal and informal systems and processes channel and reinforce certain kinds of behavior. Each of the systems on its own can support either ethical or unethical conduct. In addition, these multiple systems can work together or at cross purposes, thus leading to an organization that is aligned to support ethical (or unethical) conduct or one that is misaligned and creating mixed messages. Imagine an organization with an ethics code that forbids employees from accepting gifts of any kind, but a senior executive is known to have accepted box seats at the ball game from a client. This "we say one thing, but do another" approach leads to widespread cynicism. The code loses all credibility as workers pay more attention to the behavior around them than to what's said. On the other hand, when the organization disciplines that executive, this action visibly reinforces the code and supports the firm's ethical stance with all workers.

How an Ethical Culture Can Become an Unethical Culture

The story of Arthur Andersen, the now defunct auditing company, provides a sad example. It demonstrates how a solidly ethical culture can be transformed into an unethical culture rather quickly and lead to the demise of an 88-year-old firm.

Founder Arthur Andersen created the company when he was in his twenties. As chief executive, the messages he conveyed about ethical conduct were strong, consistent, and clear. Andersen's mantra, "Think straight—talk straight," guided employee behavior in an organization where "integrity mattered more than fees." Stories about the founder's ethics quickly became part of the firm's mythology and lore. For example, at the age of 28, Andersen confronted a railway executive who insisted that the accounting firm approve his company's books. Andersen said, "There's not enough money in the city of Chicago to induce me to change that report."[87] Andersen lost the railway company's business, but when that company later went bankrupt, Arthur Andersen became known as an organization people could trust to be honest and to stand up for what was right.

In the 1930s, Arthur Andersen emphasized accountants' special responsibility to the public. The founder died in 1974, but because his values were internalized by so many others, he was followed by leaders with similar beliefs, and the strong ethical culture continued for decades. The management style Andersen initiated was a centralized, top-down approach that produced employees who were systematically trained in the "Andersen Way." Customers around the world knew they could expect quality work and integrity from Andersen employees, who were all carefully social-ized to speak the same language and to share "Android" values. Through the 1980s, people were proud to say they worked for Arthur Andersen, which would provide a good career with a respected company.

In the mid-1990s, Arthur Andersen still provided formal ethical standards and ethics training. In 1995 it even established a consulting group, led by Barbara Toffler, to help other businesses manage their ethics. But Toffler quickly became concerned about the ethics of her own employer, which she chronicled in her book *Final Accounting: Ambition, Greed, and the Fall of Arthur Andersen.*[88] Toffler attributed much of the change from ethical culture to unethical culture to the fact that the firm's profits increasingly came from management consulting rather than auditing. Auditing and consulting are very different undertakings, and the cultural standards that worked so well in auditing were inconsistent with the needs of the consulting business. Under the new business realities, rather than standing for principles of honesty and integrity, consultants were encouraged to keep clients happy and to concentrate on getting return business because only revenues mattered. They were even expected to pad prices or create work to increase profits.

Even the training that had always been so important to Andersen's culture wasn't immune from change. Traditionally, new employees (recent college graduates) had been required to attend a three-day enculturation session, but now new consultants (often hired with experience outside the firm) were told not to forgo lucrative client work to attend the training. So Toffler and lots of other consultants never received the cultural training.

By the time Toffler arrived at Andersen, no one referred to the ethical standards, although they still existed in a big maroon binder. Toffler says, "When I brought up the subject of internal ethics, I was looked at as if I had teleported in from another world." So Andersen still had ethics policies, and they still talked about ethics in formal documents, but the business had changed dramatically and the approach to ethics management had not kept pace.[89]

Andersen was convicted of obstruction of justice for shredding documents associated with its role as Enron's auditing firm and quickly went out of business. The Supreme Court reversed the decision in 2005, ruling that the jury had not been advised that conviction in a white-collar crime case requires evidence of criminal intent. However, the Supreme Court reversal did not clear Andersen of wrongdoing. In fact, prosecutors provided evidence of criminal intent.[90] In the end, even if someone had wanted to, there was no firm left to resurrect.

Was Andersen's transformation from ethical culture to unethical culture a conscious process? Did anyone ever say, "Now we're going to create an unethical culture at Arthur Andersen"? That's doubtful. But leaders' lack of attention to the ethical culture as the organization was undergoing a significant business transformation practically guaranteed that the messages sent by the informal culture (revenues, revenues, revenues) would begin to overpower those sent by the formal culture (ethics standards) and lead to a culture that was seriously out of alignment as well as one that increasingly sent messages suggesting that only the bottom line mattered.

Becoming a More Ethical Culture

What should an organization do if it wants to transform itself into a more ethical culture? Given our multisystem perspective on ethical culture, changing organizational ethics in a positive direction involves simultaneously developing or changing multiple aspects of the organization's ethical culture. If the effort is to be successful, this ethical culture development or change should involve the alignment of all relevant formal and informal organizational systems to focus on ethics. Obviously, this requires a major commitment from the most senior levels in the organization. Culture change attempted at lower levels is likely to be ineffective unless it is fully supported and modeled by senior management. Unfortunately, some companies (e.g., Arthur Andersen) go out of business before they have this opportunity.

Changing organizational culture is more difficult than developing it. In a new organization, workers are quite open to learning and accepting the culture of their new organizational home, especially if it fits with their own values. However, anthropologists and organizational scientists agree that changing an existing culture is an extremely difficult process.[91] This view is consistent with an idea basic to all organizational change and development efforts—that changing individual and group behavior is both difficult and time-consuming. The human tendency to want to conserve the existing culture is referred to as cultural persistence, or inertia. Culture has an addictive quality, perhaps because culture members are aware that culture components cannot be altered without affecting other cherished values and institutions.[92] Also, an unethical culture tends to feed on itself. Why would successful (but unethical) managers want to change? They wouldn't. They would tend to hire people like themselves and perpetuate the culture that exists.

Most often, pressure for culture change comes from outside—from stockholders, the government, regulators, and other outside stakeholders. The public's general mistrust of business executives[93] and the threat of increased government regulation may encourage leaders to look more closely at their ethical cultures. In addition, organizations whose members have been "caught" engaging in unethical behavior, or those faced with costly lawsuits, are prime candidates for such ethical culture change attempts. Finally, the government's sentencing guidelines for corporate crime turned the attention of many organizations to an evaluation of their ethical cultures during the 1990s.

The influence of bad publicity and costly lawsuits extends beyond the targeted organization. Organizations scan the environment for information that is relevant to their concerns. When one organization in an industry is called on the carpet for a legal or ethical violation, other organizations in the industry take notice and act. Arthur Andersen's indictment for document shredding in the Enron case, as well as its mishandling of multiple audits over a number of years, sullied the reputation of the entire auditing industry. Thus any organization that senses increased vulnerability to external pressure is also more likely to consider the need for attention to the management of its ethical culture.

The pressure to change organizational ethics can also come from within, but it is not likely to occur unless the CEO decides that change is required. Often a new CEO is brought in to lead the charge when serious culture change is needed, because only the CEO has the clout and resources to make such significant changes. John A. Swainson was brought in after a nearly 30-year career at staid and solid IBM to lead Computer Associates (CA) in 2004. CA provides IT management software to large users and generates billions in annual revenue. According to Swainson, the "tipping point" for the company occurred when its board instituted a new stock option plan for senior executives in the 1990s. Executives had to hit stock price numbers and keep them up over a period of time if they were to get payouts of more than $1 billion (you read that right—it's a *b*). These senior managers started breaching accounting rules in order to adjust revenues, and they started down a slippery slope of accounting malfeasance. Over time, they became desperate to cover themselves and engaged in ever more illegal acts. To make matters even worse, when the government started investigating, the senior managers engaged in a cover-up. The government's investigation resulted in a huge fine and the firing of more than 15 executives including the CEO, who went to prison.

Swainson was brought in under a deferred prosecution agreement (DPA) with the government. With a DPA, the government sets aside prosecution because prosecuting the company would likely put it out of business and its employees (most of them innocent) out of a job. The company accepts a full-time government overseer on the premises and agrees to all sorts of actions aimed at righting the ship. Perhaps the most important requirement was to institute a new ethical "tone at the top." As part of that effort, Swainson held hundreds of town hall meetings and began an internal blog where he communicated with employees about what he was thinking or what they were thinking. He also answered "ask John" questions in a question-and-answer forum where employees wrote him directly and he answered. He hired a highly experienced senior-level legal compliance officer with access to the senior executive team, set up an ethics training program and a hotline, and improved investigation capabilities.

In regard to the basic business, Swainson visited major customers and learned that the sales force needed to be reorganized and their performance management system changed to support building relationships rather than just making transactions. Also, employees had to be brought into "a single, cohesive, ethics-based culture." Because CA had grown so rapidly through acquisition, employees identified more with their previous companies than with CA. (Note that the need to combine "ethical cultures" is often overlooked in mergers and acquisitions and can cause problems for years. A merger should be thought of as a "marriage" where shared values help to insure success. If those are missing and are not a focus of attention, the marriage is likely to suffer).

Employees at CA are now surveyed annually. Morale and trust in management are improving, and just about everyone says they understand the importance of the CA's core values and ethical behavior. At the end of his talk to students, Swainson said, "Today we are back on track. Employees are proud of where they work. Customers want to do business with us . . . Regaining our reputation and our credibility has been a long and arduous process. We can't and won't go back."[94] Swainson retired in 2009, leaving it up to a new CEO to sustain the ethical culture Swainson created.

A CULTURAL APPROACH TO CHANGING ORGANIZATIONAL ETHICS

Hopefully, we have made it very clear that changing the ethical culture requires simultaneous and systematic attention to all cultural systems, with the goal of making changes that align all of these systems to support ethical conduct.

This is a huge job, so many companies employ consultants to help them design their ethics initiatives. That may be appropriate, especially if the firm doesn't have the expertise in-house. But for these initiatives to go beyond superficial cookie-cutter prescriptions, they need to be based on an in-depth analysis of the company and its current ethical culture. Many consultants provide this kind of service. Unfortunately, what firms sometimes receive is an off-the-shelf report with standard prescriptions that could apply to any firm in what has sometimes been referred to as "spray and pray." "Consultants sprayed some ethics over [big companies] and prayed that something happened."[95] These spray-and-pray programs can breed cynicism because they raise employees' awareness of ethics problems while simultaneously suggesting, in many cases, how little the organization is doing about them. Employees are likely to say, "We had our ethics-for-a-day training program. Now we're back to doing things the way we've always done them."

Companies that are looking for advice from consultants need a unique plan, one designed to fit their firm's needs and culture. Obviously, a unique plan takes more resources to develop than the off-the-shelf variety. It requires that consultants get to know the firm, its leaders, and its operations. They must interview and survey employees, managers, and executives to learn about the current state of affairs. Such knowledge will allow the consultants to propose a culture shift that addresses the firm's unique needs.

Audit of the Ethical Culture

The only way to determine if the culture is aligned to support ethical behavior is to conduct regular, comprehensive audits of all relevant cultural systems, both formal and informal. If the ethical culture audit determines that aspects of the current culture are not aligned to support ethical behavior, and the goal is to produce consistent ethical conduct, then the culture must change.

Any attempt to develop or change organizational ethics can benefit from an organizational change approach that includes a system-wide, long-term view. In addition, the approach should be based on the assumption that human beings are essentially good and capable of development and change.

A Cultural Systems View

The cultural approach relies on the idea that to be successful, any attempt to develop or change the organization's ethics must take the entire cultural system into account.[96] The change effort must target multiple formal and informal organizational subsystems. All of these subsystems must work together to create clear, consistent messages about what is and is not appropriate behavior in the organization. If subsystems conflict, confusion and mixed messages will result. Thus, the entire range of formal and informal subsystems must be analyzed and targeted for development and change.

This complex, multisystem approach to managing organizational ethics argues against any short-term, quick-fix solutions that target only one system. The idea that an organization could solve its ethics problem simply by establishing a code of ethics or by hiring a consultant to deliver a one-hour ethics training program becomes ludicrous when the complexity of the ethics culture is understood. The management of ethical conduct must be complex because it is influenced by multiple systems, each of them complex in itself. Thus the complexity of the solution must match the complexity of the problem. A solution that isn't sufficiently complex will miss important information, make incomplete diagnoses, and produce overly simple and short-sighted solutions.

The organization that creates a code of ethics in response to external pressure and files it away without making changes in other systems such as the reward system and decision-making processes is more likely making a negative statement about organizational ethics rather than a positive one. The informal message is that management is hypocritical and that the code of ethics serves no useful purpose beyond creating a facade. The same can be said of lofty values statements. For example, many of these statements talk about valuing diversity. But what happens when people look around the organization and see few minority managers? Executives need to understand that when they put a values statement in writing, employees expect a commitment to follow through. The bottom line about systems thinking is understanding that if an organization decides to get into the "ethics business" with a values statement, code, or training program, employees expect follow-through in other parts of the organization. A failure to follow through will be interpreted as hypocrisy.

A Long-Term View

The development of organizational culture takes place over a number of years; effective culture change may take even longer, as much as 6 to 15 years.[97] It requires alterations in both formal and informal organizational systems that take time to implement and take hold. Resistances must be overcome. New rules and values must be reinforced via training programs, rites and rituals, and reward systems. Although not all organizational change efforts take this long, deep interventions in the organizational culture should be considered long-term projects.

Assumptions about People

Mainstream economics rests on the assumption that human beings are driven by self-interest and opportunism and are likely to shirk responsibility.[98] Acceptance of this assumption logically leads to change efforts focused almost exclusively on behavioral control.

We believe, however, that human beings are essentially good and open to growth and change. Most employees prefer being associated with a fair organization that supports ethical behavior and disciplines unethical behavior. Given this type of environment, most individuals can be expected to choose ethical behavior. Individuals who engage in unethical behavior should not simply be labeled "bad" people. They are often responding to external pressures or behaving according to organizationally sanctioned definitions of what's appropriate. Although unethical behaviors must be disciplined, the organization should also treat unethical behavior as a signal to investigate itself and the cultural context in which the behavior occurred. Through culture, the organization can change definitions of what is appropriate and inappropriate and can relieve pressures to behave unethically.

Diagnosis: The Ethical Culture Audit

Formal attempts to develop or change organizational ethics should begin with diagnosis. Diagnosing culture calls for time-consuming techniques, such as auditing the content of decision making, coding the content of organizational stories and anecdotes, and holding open-ended interviews with employees at all levels.[99] It also requires systematic analyses of formal organizational systems, such as the structure and criteria for rewards and promotion.

Table 5.1 Selected Questions for Auditing the Formal System

1. Do organizational leaders send a clear ethics message? Is ethics part of their "leadership" agenda? Are managers trained to be ethical leaders?
2. Does the organization incorporate ethics into its selection procedures? Is integrity emphasized in orienting new employees and training existing ones?
3. Does a formal code of ethics and/or values exist? Is it distributed? How widely? Is it reinforced in other formal systems, such as performance management and decision-making systems?
4. Does the performance management system support ethical conduct? Are only people of integrity promoted? Are ethical means as well as ends important in performance management systems?
5. Is misconduct disciplined swiftly and justly in the organization, no matter what the organizational level?
6. Are workers at all levels encouraged to take responsibility for the consequences of their behavior? To question authority when they are asked to do something that they consider to be wrong? How?
7. Are employees encouraged to report problems, and are formal channels available for them to make their concerns known confidentially?
8. Are ethical concerns incorporated into formal decision-making processes? How? Or, are only financial concerns taken into account?
9. Are employees and managers oriented to the values of the organization in orientation programs? Are they trained in ethical decision making?
10. Are ethical considerations a routine part of planning and policy meetings and new venture reports? Does a formal committee exist high in the organization for considering ethical issues?

The framework presented in this chapter can provide guidance for an audit of the organization's ethical culture.[100] The audit should include probes into the formal and informal organizational systems that are maintaining the ethics culture in its current state. First, formal organizational systems can be analyzed in a number of ways. Through surveys, interviews, observation at meetings, orientation and training sessions, and analysis of organizational documents, perceptions of how formal organizational systems either encourage or discourage ethical behavior can be identified. The kinds of questions that can be asked are listed in Table 5.1.

Auditing informal systems is equally important. In small organizations that don't have formal policies and decision processes, the informal systems are often more important than the formal ones. The culture can be analyzed to identify the organization's heroes as well as the daily behaviors that are reinforced through stories, rituals, and language. This can be accomplished through open-ended interviews, observation of organizational rituals, and analysis of the organization's stories. Some questions that might be asked in an audit of the informal system are offered in Table 5.2. The questions in Tables 5.1 and 5.2 are designed to suggest the general direction of an ethical culture audit. Specific questions that arise out of the particular system being analyzed must be developed to tap that system's unique problems and needs. Canned approaches to discovering culture that assume they can identify the

Table 5.2 Selected Questions for Auditing the Informal System

1. Identify the organization's role models and heroes. What values do they represent? What advice do mentors give?
2. What informal socialization processes exist, and what norms for ethical/unethical behavior do they promote? Are these different for different organizational subgroups?
3. What are some important organizational rituals? How do they encourage or discourage ethical behavior? Who gets the awards—people of integrity who are successful, or individuals who use unethical methods to attain success?
4. What are the messages sent by organizational stories and myths? Do they reveal individuals who stand up for what's right despite pressure, or is conformity the valued characteristic? Do people get fired or promoted in these stories?
5. Does acceptable language exist for discussing ethical concerns? Is "ethics talk" part of the daily conversation?

relevant dimensions in advance are bound to fail.[101] In addition, the multisystem nature of organizational culture suggests that responses must be compared within and across systems to answer the key question of whether formal and informal systems are aligned within themselves and with each other.

As you may have determined by now, a full-fledged ethical culture audit is a complex process that the average manager is probably not prepared to conduct. Many large organizations will have human resources staff with the required expertise, and conducting such an audit within the firm can send a powerful message that the firm cares about ethics (assuming that the audit is followed up with action). But other organizations that do not have the expertise in-house will need assistance with these diagnoses and intervention efforts. And in some firms, employees may be more willing to discuss sensitive ethical issues with a trusted outsider.

Understanding the cultural issues addressed in this chapter can help any manager become more sensitive to the complex nature of organizational ethics and the importance of cultural alignment. In fact, with a few changes, the questions in Tables 5.1 and 5.2 could be used to assess the ethics of an organization you're considering joining. You can ask your prospective manager or peers relevant questions and see how they respond. If they welcome such questions, and respond to them easily, that's a good sign that people in the organization are comfortable talking about ethical issues.

Ethical Culture Change Intervention

Once the audit is complete, the data should be discussed with employees, who can then be enlisted in developing a culture change intervention plan. The plan will be guided by the diagnosis and the cultural, multisystem framework shown earlier in Figure 5.1. Complementary changes in both the formal and informal organizational systems should be a part of any recommended change effort.

Though difficult, changing formal systems is a more straightforward process than changing informal systems. Gaps and problems identified in the diagnosis can be addressed in a number of ways. Structure can be altered to encourage individuals to take responsibility for their behavior and to discourage unquestioning deference to authority. Codes of ethics can be designed participatively, distributed, and enforced. Performance management systems can be designed with an emphasis on *what* people do as well as on *how* they do it. Reporting misconduct can be encouraged by providing formal communication channels and confidentiality.[102] Orientation programs can be designed to incorporate the organization's values, and training programs can be set up to prepare individuals to handle the ethical dilemmas they are most likely to face in their work. Integrity can be emphasized in selection and promotion decisions. Decision-making processes can incorporate attention to ethical issues by devoting time at meetings and space in reports.

It's more difficult to change the informal systems, particularly those that have been found to maintain unethical behavior in the organization. However, these changes must be undertaken if the total change effort is to be effective. These changes require attention to the "art" rather than the science of management and are consistent with ideas about the importance of "symbolic management." With symbolic management, organizational leaders and managers are encouraged to create rituals, symbols, and stories that will influence those they manage.[103]

The organization may have to be "remythologized" by reviving myths and stories of its founding and resurrecting related tales that can guide organizational behavior in the desired direction.[104] For example, Alexander Graham Bell's comment, "Come here, Watson, I need your help," set up Bell's concept of service that was so important to AT&T's success for many years. However, myths must also be frequently evaluated for their continuing usefulness. New ones may have to be found or developed to fit the organization's current needs and goals. Remythologizing should be done carefully and infrequently. Employees generally know what's "really going on" in the organization. If the revived myth doesn't fit with organizational reality, it will only increase their cynicism. Also, myths can't be changed frequently. Their strength and value in the culture come from their stability across time.

ETHICAL CULTURE CHANGE EVALUATION As with any organizational change and development effort, results should be evaluated over an extended period of time. Evaluation, like diagnosis and intervention, should be guided by the multisystem framework. Surveys and interviews can be repeated regularly to determine whether norms have changed and to pinpoint potential problem areas. Documents can be analyzed to determine if ethical issues are being consistently considered. Other outcomes, such as the number of lawsuits or reports of unethical behavior, can also be tracked. However, interpretation may need to go beyond simply analyzing the numbers. Increased reporting to a hotline, for example, may mean only that ethical sensitivity has been raised and can be viewed as a positive outcome rather than a negative one. This part of culture building is probably the most neglected. Most organizations are unwilling to make the investment in evaluation, and therefore they really can't calculate the effectiveness of their efforts.

THE ETHICS OF MANAGING ORGANIZATIONAL ETHICS

An effort aimed at changing organizational ethics requires us to face a particularly knotty ethical dilemma: whose values or ethics are to prevail? We believe that a change effort that involves employees is not manipulative or coercive and is most consistent with a concern for the ethics of the change effort itself. Employees should participate in the problem diagnosis and planning process. They should be aware of what's happening and should take part in identifying problems and recommending solutions.

CONCLUSION

This chapter has proposed a cultural framework for thinking about ethical and unethical behavior in the organizational context. Although individual character traits may predispose a person to ethical or unethical behavior (as we learned in Chapter 3), the cultural context in the organization also has a powerful influence on the behavior of most employees. An organization that wishes to develop or change its ethical culture must attend to the complex interplay of formal and informal systems that can support either ethical or unethical behavior. Quick-fix solutions are not likely to succeed. A broad, multisystem approach to developing and changing organizational ethics was outlined to guide organizations in diagnosing and, if necessary, changing their ethical culture.

Although most managers are not prepared to conduct a broad culture change effort themselves, we hope this chapter has helped them understand that organizational ethics is a complex cultural phenomenon. With this knowledge, the manager can begin to assess the ethical culture of his or her organization and will know what questions to ask the consultant who is brought in to help with a culture change effort. Individuals can also use these questions to help them assess their own organization and their fit within it.

DISCUSSION QUESTIONS

For the following questions, focus on an organization you are familiar with. If you do not have significant organizational experience, discuss the questions with someone who is currently in a managerial role.

1. Does your organization address ethical issues in a formal, systematic way? How has the organization customized an ethical culture to match its unique needs?
2. To the best of your ability, use Figure 5.1 and the questions in Tables 5.1 and 5.2 to conduct an ethics audit of the formal and informal systems in your organization.
3. Having conducted the ethics audit, identify the formal and informal systems that are in need of attention. Where is the culture out of alignment (if it is)? Design a change program to address weaknesses and to align formal and informal systems into a strong ethical culture.
4. How would you change the culture audit questions if you were planning to use them to conduct an ethics culture audit of a firm you were considering joining?

CASE

CULTURE CHANGE AT TEXACO

In 1999, Texaco settled a lawsuit that charged the firm with discriminating against African American employees. Texaco paid $175 million, the largest settlement of this kind ever. The stock had fallen $3 per share after damning audiotapes became available to the public. Peter Bijur, then CEO, decided to stop fighting the lawsuit and settle. Minority employees received $140 million in damages and back pay, and $35 million was used to establish an independent task force to evaluate the firm's diversity efforts for the next five years.

Apparently, there had been very real problems throughout the Texaco organization. These included blatant racist language and behavior on the part of Texaco employees and managers, documented lower pay for minority employees (in some cases lower than the minimum for the job category), and comments such as the following overheard from a white manager: "I never thought I'd live to see the day when a black woman had an office at Texaco." Unfortunately for Texaco, and fortunately for minority employees, a Texaco official taped meetings about the lawsuit in which executives used racial epithets and discussed disposing of incriminating documents. The tapes were made available to the *New York Times* and, through it, to the public. To make matters worse for Texaco, a former senior financial analyst, Bari-Ellen Roberts, wrote a book detailing the humiliating experiences faced by many minority employees, including herself. One time, a white official referred to Roberts publicly as a "little colored girl." She also detailed how the organization regularly ignored grievance claims from minorities.

Bijur's unusual solution to the problem was to launch a complete culture change effort. During 1998 and early 1999, the company was in difficult financial straits due to low crude oil and natural gas prices. Revenues and earnings dropped precipitously, and the number of employees was reduced from 27,000 to 18,500. At a time like that, another CEO might have put diversity issues aside in favor of a focus on the bottom line. But Bijur took advantage of the opportunity to "make us a better company." First, as leader, he made it clear that he would simply not tolerate disrespect and that those who didn't go along with the culture change would be dismissed. He even went outside the company, speaking to groups such as the Urban League, saying that "a real commitment must be more than a diversity checklist. It must be integrated into a company's business plan. It must guide our strategies for hiring, developing, promoting and retaining a diverse workforce. And it must extend beyond our corporate boundaries—not only to our customers and suppliers, but also to the communities in which we work and live."[105] Bijur hired African Americans in key positions such as director of global business development, general counsel, and head of diversity for the company. All of these individuals said that they agreed to join the company because they were convinced of Bijur's personal commitment to real culture change. New recruiting systems were set up to increase the pool of minority candidates for every position. Women and minorities were included on all human resources committees.

Search firms with success in minority hiring were brought in to help in the effort. For a longer-term solution, the company set up scholarship and internship programs to interest minorities in areas of study of importance to the firm.

Next, Bijur set specific diversity goals and timetables and linked managers' career success and bonus compensation to their implementation of the initiatives. For all supervisors, he instituted 360-degree feedback that included performance on diversity issues in evaluation criteria. He also established formal mentoring and leadership development programs to ensure that the company was preparing minorities for leadership positions. All employees were required to attend diversity training, and such training is now being incorporated into more general management training. And multiple methods were set up for filing grievances. These included hotlines, an alternative dispute resolution process with independent arbitration and mediation, and a confidential outside ombudsman. Finally, the company set up a Minority and Women Business Development Program to increase the number of minority wholesalers it works with. This entire change effort is overseen by the independent task force set up as part of the settlement. The task force meets frequently with employee groups and monitors the firm's progress.

How is Texaco doing? Angela Vallot, director of corporate diversity initiatives, says, "You're not going to change the way people think, but you can change the way people behave." Evidence suggests that changes in behavior are real. The new general counsel has few discrimination lawsuits to work on. In 1999, a total of 44 percent of new hires and 22 percent of promotions went to minorities. The company spent over $1 billion with minority and women-owned vendors in 1997 and 1998 and exceeded a goal set in 1996. Texaco even applied for inclusion in *Fortune* magazine's 1999 list of America's 50 Best Companies for minorities. It didn't make the list, but the application suggests that company officials were feeling pretty good about their progress. Weldon Latham, diversity expert at a Washington, D.C., law firm, says, "They are absolutely a model for how to approach one of the biggest problems facing this country."[106] Reports of the monitoring task force were posted on Texaco's website. In a report, released in July 2000, the task force acknowledged the commitment of Texaco's leadership. "Through the values espoused by its leadership and its efforts to improve its employment practices, the Company continues to communicate effectively the message that it will not tolerate discrimination, harassment, or retaliation in its workplace and that equality and fairness for all employees are central to its mission as a highly competitive business enterprise." The report also cited the ombudsman program as employees' preferred way to resolve grievances that might otherwise have become serious problems.[107]

The task force's subsequent report cited more mixed results. Although the overall percentage of women and minority employees increased slightly, the percentage of new hires and promotions in both categories declined, and the representation of women and minorities in executive positions fell slightly as well. Nevertheless, the percentage of promotions in these groups exceeded the percentage represented in the overall Texaco workforce, and this was viewed as a sign of continuing progress.[108] These reports noted that there was much more work to be done, particularly after the firm became part of Chevron in 2001. On its website, Chevron says that it values diversity and runs the business "in a way that respects our employees and the world community." The company has recently received awards for its treatment of women and of gay, lesbian, and transgender employees and was named a 2008 Best Diversity Company by *Diversity/Careers in Engineering & Information Technology* magazine.

Case Questions

1. Identify the ethical culture problem at Texaco in the mid-1990s.
2. Based on the facts in the case and what you have learned in this chapter, evaluate the culture change effort that is under way. What cultural systems have been targeted in the culture change effort? What systems are missing, if any? Does the culture appear to be in alignment? Misalignment? What else might management do that it hasn't already done to make the culture change successful?
3. How long might such a culture change take?

CASE

AN UNETHICAL CULTURE IN NEED OF CHANGE: TAP PHARMACEUTICALS

In 1995, Douglas Durand was offered the position of vice president for sales at TAP Pharmaceuticals. TAP had been formed 25 years before by Takeda Chemical Industries of Japan and Abbott Laboratories. Durand, 50 years old at the time, had married his high school sweetheart and worked for Merck & Co. for 20 years, during which he moved up in the sales organization to senior regional director. TAP offered him the opportunity to earn 40 percent more per year (in addition to a $50,000 signing bonus) and help the company move from niche player to mass-market purveyor of ulcer and prostate cancer medicine. He took advantage of the opportunity and looked forward to the challenge.

But only a few months after arriving at TAP, he was shocked to find a very different culture from the one he had become accustomed to at Merck. Merck has long had a reputation for ethics and social responsibility, and these qualities had been borne out in Durand's two decades of experience. For example, at Merck, every new marketing campaign was evaluated by a legal and regulatory team before being launched, and drugs were pulled back if necessary. But TAP turned out to be very different. It quickly became clear that this was a culture where only numbers mattered. On his very first day on the job, Durand learned that TAP had no in-house legal counsel. The legal counsel was considered a "sales prevention department." At one point, Durand found himself listening in on a conference call where sales representatives were openly discussing bribing urologists with an up-front "administration fee" to doctors who prescribed Lupron, the company's new drug for prostate cancer. TAP sales representatives also gave doctors Lupron samples at a discount or for free; then they encouraged the doctors to charge Medicare full price and keep the difference. Durand overheard doctors boasting about their Lupron purchases of boats and second homes. TAP offered a big-screen TV to every urologist in the country ($\sim$10,000!), along with offers of office equipment and golf vacations. And reps weren't accounting for the free samples they gave away—as required by law. Durand knew that failure to account for a single dose can lead to a fine of as much as $1 million. Finally, rather than selling drugs based on good science, TAP held parties for doctors. One such party for a new ulcer drug featured "Tummy," a giant fire-belching stomach.

Durand soon became frantic and worried about his own guilt by association. Initially, he tried to change the culture. After all, he had been hired as a vice president. But everything he tried was resisted. He was told that he just didn't understand the culture at TAP. When he talked about the importance of earning physicians' trust, the sales reps just rolled their eyes. He then tried to influence change "the TAP way" by offering a bonus to reps who kept accurate records of their samples. The program actually worked, but then senior management discontinued the bonus—and, of course, the reps stopped keeping track. Over time, Durand began finding himself excluded from meetings, and he felt trapped. What would happen to him if he left this new job in less than a year? He wouldn't collect his bonus, and he wondered if anyone else would hire him. What would happen to his family? But he also worried about becoming the corporate scapegoat.

In desperation, Durand turned to an old friend he knew from Merck—Glenna Crooks, now president of Strategic Health Policy International. Appalled by what she heard, Crooks encouraged him to document the abuses he had observed and share the information with Elizabeth Ainslie, a Philadelphia attorney. Given the documented fraud against the U.S. government, Ainslie encouraged Durand to sue TAP under the federal whistleblower program. Armed with documents, he filed the suit and federal prosecutors ran with it. Durand left TAP for Astra Merck in 1996. But under the whistleblower program, investigations are conducted in secret. Neither TAP nor Astra Merck was supposed to know about it. The investigation took years, and, when called to testify, Durand had to make excuses to take time off from his new job. He was uncomfortable living as a "double agent." In the end, TAP pleaded guilty to conspiracy to cheat the federal government and agreed to pay a record $875 million fine. In October 2001, Durand collected $77 million ($28 million went to taxes), his 14 percent share of the fine paid under the federal whistleblower statute. He retired to Florida to be closer to his parents, but he had yet to face the unpleasant task of testifying against six TAP executives, some of whom had worked for him.

Case Questions

1. Analyze the ethical culture at TAP. Does the culture appear to be in alignment? Misalignment?

2. Based on the facts in the case and what you have learned in this chapter, evaluate the culture change effort that Douglas Durand undertook. What cultural

systems did he target in the culture change effort? What systems were missing, if any?

3.   Why did his culture change effort fail? What would it take for it to succeed?

Source: C. Haddad and A. Barrett, "A Whistle-Blower Rocks an Industry," *Businessweek*, June 24, 2002, 126–30.

CASE

"BAD TO THE BONE"

In 2012, after a significant amount of research, *Fortune* magazine published an expose entitled "Bad to the Bone,"[109] about a Pennsylvania company named Synthes. The company had its roots in Switzerland where Swiss surgeons developed products aimed at fixing broken bones with implants. One of these surgeons met Hansjorg Wyss, a Harvard Business school graduate who went on to lead Synthes in the U.S. and then to become the company's CEO. Wyss is known for his philanthropy to Harvard and other causes and for being an outdoorsman who loves to hike. As a corporate leader, Wyss was described as intimidating and a micromanager who wanted to decide everything from the toilet paper the company purchased to the shape of the plates in the company cafeteria (square). The company was described as "highly regimented—the kind of place where employees do what they're told" (p. 146), and Wyss was known for being an "800-pound gorilla" who did not tolerate dissent.

In the late 1990s Wyss became interested in a California startup called Norian that had developed a special kind of cement that could fill cracks in bone but also transform itself into bone. The FDA approved its use in the arm and the skull where it was being used successfully. Synthes was hoping that the cement could also be useful in filling spinal fractures called vertebral compression fractures (VCFs) that often accompany osteoporosis. However, the FDA had not yet given its permission to use the product for that purpose. The product would have to be proven safe and effective in expensive clinical trials. In the meantime, the FDA prohibited marketing products for unapproved uses or even mentioning such uses to surgeons.

Nevertheless, Synthes conducted market research and learned that the potential market for the product was huge—almost 500,000 VCFs a year. When one regulatory staffer, Michael Sharp, learned by chance of the talk about marketing the product to spine surgeons, he warned senior executives via email that Synthes employees were prohibited from discussing Norian with these surgeons. He was assured that this wouldn't happen and thought the issue had been resolved. Then, in 2001, a California surgeon used Norian in two VCF surgeries. Both patients experienced serious drops in blood pressure and nearly died. Sharp learned of this and again contacted executives and the head of the North American Division, Michael Higgins, who sent the sales force an email about the dangers of off-label marketing (marketing a drug or medical device for uses that have not been formally approved by the FDA). Yet, mixed signals continued to come from management and the project continued. In fact, Higgins himself organized a focus group with interested surgeons. The group recommended research on animals before using Norian in humans, and the company agreed to provide funding for a small study. A meeting of top executives rejected the idea of conducting a human clinical trial when they learned that it would cost about $1 million over three years. Instead the company applied for a different type of FDA approval for the modification of existing medical devices. And, in late 2001, the FDA gave its approval but said that Norian must not be mixed with any other substance before being injected into the spine (which is what the use of Norian in VCFs required).

In the meantime, bad news came from the animal study. The researchers found that, in pigs, Norian caused dangerous blood clotting problems that led to death. A test in the lab also found that mixing Norian with blood causes significant clots in test tubes. Then, one of the company's medical consultants happened to learn, by accident, that the company was shipping Norian to a spine surgeon with directions on how to mix it, creating a mixture called SRS-R. He warned executives that they were treading on thin ice and learned, a bit later, that his contract was not renewed. Others in the company tried to raise concerns with their bosses but were assured that all was fine.

Despite all of this, executives decided to move ahead with an earlier decision to recruit a few doctors to do the VCF procedure and report their clinical experiences. Doctors are allowed to prescribe off-label uses and orthopedic surgeons are prone to do so. A young business school graduate and product manager was teaching surgeons how to mix their product with barium sulfate for VCFs (something that was prohibited by the FDA). Many surgeries went well and the FDA approved the mixture (now called Norian XR) but continued to warn that it was not to be used for VCFs.

Within a month, a Texas surgeon lost a patient whose blood pressure dropped precipitously on the operating table. The company did not report the death as required by the FDA because no autopsy had been done and the cause of death wasn't certain. Moving on, the sales team predicted multi-millions in revenue and 50 percent profit margins after taxes. The company sponsored a surgeon forum in California where surgeons practiced injecting the Norian XR mixture into cadavers. But soon thereafter, a California surgeon lost a patient in a similar way and blamed Norian XR for the death. That surgeon's partner, who had used Norian successfully 20–30 times, then had a similar experience and another patient died on the operating table. At that point, the company sent a letter stating that "deaths had been reported" and that Norian should not be used for VCFs. But, there was no recall and Norian continued to be sold.

In May 2004, an FDA investigator who had received a tip about the off-label marketing of Norian by Synthes showed up to conduct an investigation and determined that the company was in violation of FDA rules. It took a while, but in 2009, the company and four individuals were indicted. In 2010, Synthes pleaded guilty and agreed to pay $23 million in fines and to divest Norian. Four executives were sentenced to prison terms of between four and nine months. The prison sentences were unusual and sent a chill through the industry. But the government wanted to send a message that prison time for executives was a real possibility in these off-label marketing cases. Civil suits brought by the families of those who died continue to be litigated.

In 2012, Johnson & Johnson acquired Synthes for about $20 billion and Synthes appears to be doing fine. It sold the bone cement unit to a small manufacturer nearby for $22 million (just a million dollars less than the fine) and J&J's DePuy Synthes unit distributes the product exclusively.

Case Questions

1.   What information did you glean about the culture at Synthes? How do you think the culture might be related to the behavior of the company's employees?

2.   Johnson & Johnson, a company with a reputation for ethics and social responsibility, acquired Synthes. From an ethical culture perspective, what would you recommend if you were going to try to combine these companies, especially if you wanted to change the ethical culture at Synthes?

3.   Do you think jail time for the executives was appropriate in this case?

Source: M. Kimes, "Bad to the Bone," *Fortune*, October 8, 2012, 140–154.

NOTES

1.   R. A. Barrett, *Culture and Conduct: An Excursion in Anthropology* (Belmont, CA: Wadsworth, 1984).
2.   T. E. Deal and A. A. Kennedy, *Corporate Cultures* (Reading, MA: Addison-Wesley, 1982); M. R. Louis, "A Cultural Perspective on Organizations: The Need for and Consequences of Viewing Organizations as Culture-Bearing Milieux," *Human Systems Management* 2" (1981): 246–58; J. Martin and C. Siehl, "Organizational Culture and Counterculture: An Uneasy Symbiosis," *Organizational Dynamics* (Autumn 1983): 52–64; A. M. Pettigrew, "On Studying Organizational Cultures," *Administrative Science Quarterly* 24 (1979): 570–80; E. H. Schein, *Organizational Culture and Leadership* (San Francisco: Jossey-Bass, 1985); L. Smircich, "Concepts of Culture and Organizational Analysis," *Administrative Science Quarterly* 28 (1983): 339–58.
3.   L. Smircich, "Concepts of Culture and Organizational Analysis," *Administrative Science Quarterly* 28 (1983): 339–58.
4.   T. E. Deal and A. A. Kennedy, *Corporate Cultures* (Reading, MA: Addison-Wesley, 1982).
5.   B. Morris, "He's Smart. He's Not Nice. He's Saving Big Blue," *Fortune*, April 14, 1997, 68–81.
6.   T. E. Deal and A. A. Kennedy, *Corporate Cultures* (Reading, MA: Addison-Wesley, 1982).
7.   J. Van Maanen and E. H. Schein, "Toward a Theory of Organizational Socialization," in *Research in Organizational Behavior* (vol. 1), eds. L. Cummings and B. Staw (New York: JAI Press, 1979); C. D. Fisher, "Organizational Socialization: an Integrative Review," in *Research in Personnel and Human Resources Management* (vol. 4), eds. K. Rowland and G. Ferris (Greenwich, CT: JAI Press, 1986), 101–45.
8.   R. A. Barrett, *Culture and Conduct: An Excursion in Anthropology* (Belmont, CA: Wadsworth, 1984).
9.   P. Murphy, "Creating Ethical Corporate Structures," *Sloan Management Review* 30, no. 2 (1989): 221–27.

10. P. Murphy, "Creating Ethical Corporate Structures," *Sloan Management Review* 30, no. 2 (1989): 221–27.

11. P. Wesslund, "Ethics Are No Substitute for the Real Thing," *Businessweek*, April 27, 1992, 10.

12. P. Murphy, "Creating Ethical Corporate Structures," *Sloan Management Review* 30, no. 2 (1989): 221–27.

13. "The Business Effect of Ethics on Employee Engagement," LRN Ethics Study, 2006, www.lrn.com.

14. E. H. Schein, *Organizational Culture and Leadership* (San Francisco: Jossey-Bass, 1985).

15. Pettigrew, "On Studying Organizational Cultures"; E. H. Schein, "How Culture Forms, Develops, and Changes," in *Gaining Control of the Corporate Culture*, eds. R. H. Kilmann, M. J. Saxtion, and R. Serpa (San Francisco: Jossey-Bass, 1985), 17–43; P. Selznick, *Leadership in Administration* (New York: Harper & Row, 1957).

16. K. Brooker, "Can Anyone Replace Herb?" *Fortune*, April 17, 2000, 186–92.

17. J. Guinto, "Wheels Up," *Southwest Airlines Spirit*, June 2006, 109–17.

18. A. Sewer, "Southwest Airlines: The Hottest Thing in the Sky," *Fortune*, March 8, 2004, 88–89.

19. E. Schein, "How Culture Forms, Develops, and Changes"; Selznick, *Leadership in Administration*.

20. M. Gunther, "Money and Morals at GE," *Fortune*, November 15, 2004, 177–78.

21. Ibid.

22. L. K. Treviño, M. Brown, and L. Pincus-Hartman, "A Qualitative Investigation of Perceived Executive Ethical Leadership: Perceptions from Inside and Outside the Executive Suite," *Human Relations* 56, no. 1 (2003): 5–37; L. K. Treviño, L. P. Hartman, and M. Brown, "Moral Person and Moral Manager: How Executives Develop a Reputation for Ethical Leadership," *California Management Review* 42, no. 4 (2000): 128–42.

23. T. J. Neff and J. M. Citrin, *Lessons from the Top: The Search for America's Best Leaders* (New York: Doubleday, 1999).

24. K. Treviño, L. P. Hartman, and M. Brown, "Moral Person and Moral Manager: How Executives Develop a Reputation for Ethical Leadership," *California Management Review* 42, no. 4 (2000): 128–42.

25. P. O'Neill, "O'Neill on Ethics and Leadership," Speech at the Berg Center for Ethics and Leadership, Katz Graduate School of Business, University of Pittsburgh, 2002.

26. B. George, "Why It's Hard to Do What's Right," *Fortune*, September 29, 2003, 98.

27. J. A. Byrne, "Chainsaw," *Businessweek*, October 18, 1999, 128–49.

28. G. Tidwell, "Accounting for the PTL Scandal," *Today's CPA*, July–August 1993, 29–32.

29. J. Sonnenfeld, "The Real Scandal at BP," *Businessweek*, May 14, 2007, 98.

30. L. K. Treviño, G. R. Weaver, D. G. Gibson, and B. L. Toffler, "Managing Ethics and Legal Compliance: What Works and What Hurts," *California Management Review* 41, no. 2 (1999): 131–51.

31. C. Loomis, "Whatever It Takes," *Fortune*, November 25, 2002, 74–75.

32. C. Loomis, "Tough Questions for Citigroup's CEO," *Fortune*, November 29, 2004, 115–22.

33. C. Loomis, "Whatever It Takes," *Fortune*, November 25, 2002, 74–75.

34. C. Loomis, "Tough Questions for Citigroup's CEO," *Fortune*, November 29, 2004, 115–22.

35. M. Vickers, "The Unlikely Revolutionary," *Fortune*, March 6, 2006, 132–44.

36. Peter S. Goodman, "Sluggers and Bankers in the Strikeout Era," *New York Times*, January 16, 2010, www.nyt.com.

37. Katrina Brooker, "Citi's Creator, Alone with His Regrets," *New York Times*, January 3, 2010, www.nyt.com.

38. S. Denning, "Rethinking Capitalism: Sandy Weill Says Bring Back Glass-Steagall," *Forbes*, July 25, 2012, www.forbes.com.

39. L. K. Treviño, G. R. Weaver, D. G. Gibson, and B. L. Toffler, "Managing Ethics and Legal Compliance: What Works and What Hurts," *California Management Review* 41, no. 2 (1999): 131–51.

40. D. Mayer, M. Kuenzi, R. Greenbaum, M. Bardes, and R. Salvador, "How Does Ethical Leadership Flow? Test of a Trickle-Down Model," *Organizational Behavior and Human Decision Processes* 108 (2008): 1–13.

41. K. Brooker, "Can Anyone Replace Herb?" *Fortune*, April 17, 2000, 186–92.

42. W. C. Byham, "Can You Interview for Integrity?" *Across the Board*, March–April 2004, 34–38.
43. J. L. Seglin, "The Values Statement vs. Corporate Reality," *New York Times*, September 17, 2000, www.nytimes.com.
44. G. Colvin and J. Shambora, "J&J: Secrets of Success," *Fortune*, May 4, 2009, 117–21.
45. *2007 National Business Ethics Survey* (Washington, D. C.: Ethics Resource Center, 2007).
46. G. R. Weaver, L. K. Treviño, and P. L. Cochran, "Corporate Ethics Practices in the Mid-1990s: An Empirical Study of the *Fortune* 1000," *Journal of Business Ethics* 18, no. 3 (1999): 283–94.
47. L. K. Treviño, G. R. Weaver, D. G. Gibson, and B. L. Toffler, "Managing Ethics and Legal Compliance: What Works and What Hurts," *California Management Review* 41, no. 2 (1999): 131–51.
48. J. Kish-Gephart, D. Harrison, and L. K. Treviño, "Bad Apples, Bad Cases, and Bad Barrels: Meta-analytic Evidence about Sources of Unethical Decisions at Work: Understanding Calculated and Impulsive Pathways," *Journal of Applied Psychology* 95 (2010):1–31.
49. W. J. Bowers, *Student Dishonesty and Its Control in College* (New York: Bureau of Applied Social Research, Columbia University, 1964); W. G. Campbell, *A Comparative Investigation of Students under an Honor System and a Proctor System in the Same University* (Los Angeles: University of Southern California Press, 1935); R. Canning, "Does an Honor System Reduce Classroom Cheating? An Experimental Answer," *Journal of Experimental Education* 24 (1956): 291–96.
50. D. L. McCabe and L. K. Treviño, "Academic Dishonesty: Honor Codes and Other Situational Influences," *Journal of Higher Education* 64, no. 5 (1993): 522–28.
51. D. Nel, L. Pitt, and R. Watson, "Business Ethics: Defining the Twilight Zone," *Journal of Business Ethics* 8 (1989): 781–91.
52. G. R. Weaver, L. K. Treviño, and P. L. Cochran, "Corporate Ethics Practices in the Mid-1990s: An Empirical Study of the *Fortune* 1000," *Journal of Business Ethics* 18, no. 3 (1999): 283–94.
53. *2007 National Business Ethics Survey* (Washington, D. C.: Ethics Resource Center, 2007).
54. G. Weaver, L. K. Treviño, and B. Agle, "Somebody I Look Up To: Ethical Role Models in Organizations," *Organizational Dynamics* 34, no. 4 (2005): 313–30.
55. M. Weber, *The Theory of Social and Economic Organizations*, trans. A. M. Henderson and T. Parsons (New York: Free Press, 1947).
56. G. Sjoberg, T. R. Vaughan, and N. Williams, "Bureaucracy as a Moral Issue," *Journal of Applied Behavioral Science* 20, no. 4 (1984): 441–53.
57. S. Milgram, *Obedience to Authority: An Experimental View* (New York: Harper & Row, 1974).
58. L. K. Treviño, G. R. Weaver, D. G. Gibson, and B. L. Toffler, "Managing Ethics and Legal Compliance: What Works and What Hurts," *California Management Review* 41, no. 2 (1999): 131–51.
59. R. Jackall, *Moral Mazes: The World of Corporate Managers* (New York: Oxford University Press, 1988).
60. R. M. Kanter, *The Changemasters* (New York: Simon & Schuster, 1983).
61. H. C. Kelman and V. L. Hamilton, *Crimes of Obedience: Toward a Social Psychology of Authority and Responsibility* (New Haven, CT: Yale University, 1989).
62. Joani Nelson-Horchler, "The Magic of Herman Miller," *Industry Week*, February 18, 1991, 11–12, 14, 17.
63. M. P. Glazer and P. M. Glazer, "Whistleblowing," *Psychology Today*, August 1986, 36.
64. Ibid.
65. A. C. Greenberg, "Memos from the Chairman," *Fortune*, April 29, 1996, 173–75.
66. H. Schwartz and S. M. Davis, "Matching Corporate Culture and Business Strategy," *Organizational Dynamics*, Summer 1981, 30–48.
67. L. Tiger, "Stone Age Provides Model for Instilling Business Ethics," *Wall Street Journal*, January 11, 1988, 18.
68. S. Gellerman, "Why 'Good' Managers Make Bad Ethical Choices," *Harvard Business Review* 64, no. 4 (1986): 85–97.
69. C. Welles, "What Led Beech-Nut Down the Road to Disgrace?" *Businessweek*, February 22, 1988, 124–37.

70. L. K. Treviño, G. R. Weaver, D. G. Gibson, and B. L. Toffler, "Managing Ethics and Legal Compliance: What Works and What Hurts," *California Management Review* 41, no. 2 (1999): 131–51.

71. B. Morris, "He's Smart. He's Not Nice. He's Saving Big Blue," *Fortune*, April 14, 1997, 68–81.

72. J. A. Waters, "Catch 20.5: Corporate Morality as an Organizational Phenomenon," *Organizational Dynamics*, Spring 1978, 319.

73. T. E. Deal and A. A. Kennedy, *Corporate Cultures* (Reading, MA: Addison-Wesley, 1982).

74. Ibid.

75. J. M. Beyer and H. M. Trice, "How an Organization's Rites Reveal Its Culture," *Organizational Dynamics* 15, no. 4 (1987): 524.

76. J. Channon, "Creating Esprit de Corps," in *New Traditions in Business: Spirit and Leadership in the 21st Century* (San Francisco: Berrett-Koehler, 1992) 53–66.

77. I. Mitroff and R. H. Kilmann, "On Organizational Stories: An Approach to the Design and Analysis of Organization through Myths and Stories," in *The Management of Organization Design: Strategies and Implications*, eds. R. Kilmann, L. Pondy, and D. P. Slevin (New York: North-Holland, 1976).

78. J. Martin and C. Siehl, "Organizational Culture and Counterculture: An Uneasy Symbiosis," *Organizational Dynamics*, Autumn 1983, 52–64.

79. S. Fisher, "Telling Tales: The Art of Corporate Storytelling," *Costco Connection*, October 2007, 22–23.

80. K. Butterfield, L. K. Treviño, and G. R. Weaver. "Moral awareness in business organizations: Influences of issue-related and social context factors." *Human Relations* 53, no. 7 (2000): 981–1018.

81. F. B. Bird and J. A. Waters, "The Moral Muteness of Managers," *California Management Review*, Fall 1989, 73–88.

82. K. Berney, "Finding the Ethical Edge," *Nation's Business*, August 1987, 18–24.

83. F. B. Bird and J. A. Waters, "The Moral Muteness of Managers," *California Management Review*, Fall 1989, 73–88.

84. H. C. Kelman and V. L. Hamilton, *Crimes of Obedience: Toward a Social Psychology of Authority and Responsibility* (New Haven, CT: Yale University, 1989).

85. L. K. Treviño, G. R. Weaver, D. G. Gibson, and B. L. Toffler, "Managing Ethics and Legal Compliance: What Works and What Hurts," *California Management Review* 41, no. 2 (1999): 131–51.

86. K. D. Martin and J. B. Cullen, "Continuities and Extensions of Ethical Climate Theory: A Meta-analytic Review," *Journal of Business Ethics* 69 (2006): 175–94.

87. B. Toffler, *Final Accounting: Ambition, Greed, and the Fall of Arthur Andersen* (New York: Broadway Books, 2003).

88. Ibid.

89. B. Toffler, *Final Accounting*; L. K. Treviño and M. E. Brown, "Managing to Be Ethical: Debunking Five Business Ethics Myths," *Academy of Management Executive* 18, no. 2 (2004): 69–81.

90. K. Eichenwald, "Reversal of Andersen Conviction Not a Declaration of Innocence," *New York Times*, 1 June 2005, C6.

91. R. A. Barrett, *Culture and Conduct: An Excursion in Anthropology* (Belmont, CA: Wadsworth, 1984); B. Uttal, "The Corporate Culture Vultures," *Fortune*, October 17, 1983, 66–71.

92. Ibid.

93. R. Ricklees, "Ethics in America Series," *Wall Street Journal*, October 31–November 3, 1983, 33.

94. J. A. Swainson, "Back from the Brink: Rebuilding a Company after a Near-Fatal Ethics Breakdown," Raytheon lectureship in Business Ethics at Bentley University, Waltham, MA, 2008.

95. J. Byrne, "The Best-Laid Ethics Programs," *Businessweek*, March 9, 1992, 67–69.

96. N. Tichy, *Managing Strategic Change* (New York: Wiley & Sons, 1983).

97. R. A. Barrett, *Culture and Conduct: An Excursion in Anthropology* (Belmont, CA: Wadsworth, 1984); B. Uttal, "The Corporate Culture Vultures," *Fortune*, October 17, 1983, 66–71.

98. W. R. Nord, "OD's Unfulfilled Visions: Some Lessons from Economics," in *Research in Organizational Change and Development*, eds. R. W. Woodman and W. A. Pasmore (Greenwich, CT: JAI Press, 1989), 39–60.

99. R. A. Barrett, *Culture and Conduct: An Excursion in Anthropology* (Belmont, CA: Wadsworth, 1984); B. Uttal, "The Corporate Culture Vultures," *Fortune*, October 17, 1983, 66–71.

100. A. L. Wilkins, "The Culture Audit: A Tool for Understanding Organizations," *Organizational Dynamics* 12 (1983): 24–38.

101. F. Luthans, "Conversation with Edgar H. Schein," *Organizational Dynamics* 17, no. 4 (1989): 60–76.

102. J. P. Near and M. P. Miceli, "Whistleblowers in Organizations: Dissidents or Reformers?" in *Research in Organizational Behavior*, eds. Cummings and Staw, 321–68.

103. T. Peters, "Symbols, Patterns, and Settings: An Optimistic Case of Getting Things Done," *Organizational Dynamics* 7 (1978): 3–23.

104. W. McWhinney and J. Batista, "How Remythologizing Can Revitalize Organizations," *Organizational Dynamics* 17, no. 2 (1988): 46–79.

105. "Texaco Chairman and CEO Tells National Urban League that Diversity Commitment Must Be Worked on Daily," Press Release (August 4, 1998), Chevron Texaco Corporation.

106. K. Labich, "No More Crude at Texaco," *Fortune*, September 16, 1999, 205–12.

107. "Fourth Annual Report of the Equality and Fairness Task Force for the Year ending June 30, 2001," Chevron Texaco Corporation, 2001.

108. Ibid.

109. M. Kimes, "Bad to the Bone," *Fortune*, October 8, 2012, 140–154.

CHAPTER 6

MANAGING ETHICS AND LEGAL COMPLIANCE

INTRODUCTION

Chapter 5 presented ethics as organizational culture, but it may have raised as many questions as it answered, such as "What are real organizations doing to create and communicate an ethical organizational culture?" This chapter is designed to help answer that question by focusing more narrowly on ethics and legal compliance programs in several large American corporations. These programs are designed to manage and communicate ethics in a variety of ways.

Whatever your organizational level, you should find the information in this chapter helpful. If you're at a high level, it should give you ideas about how to manage ethics and legal compliance in your firm. If you're at a lower or middle management level, it should help you understand your own organization's approach to ethics management and how it compares to what other organizations are currently doing. If you're a student, it will help you think about what to look for during the job search.

In preparing this chapter, we spoke with executives from four companies in a variety of industries: Lockheed Martin Corporation (global security); United Technologies Corporation (UTC—Otis elevators, Carrier air conditioners, Pratt & Whitney jet engines, Sikorsky helicopters); Merck (medicines, vaccines, and consumer care and animal health products); and Adelphia (telecommunications/cable). We are grateful to these executives for their time and contributions to this book. These companies vary in size. UTC has over 220,000 employees (more than half outside the United States) and a presence in more than 180 countries. Merck has 80,000 employees in 140 countries. Adelphia had 14,000 employees across the United States when its assets were purchased in 2005 by Comcast and Time Warner. Lockheed Martin has 118,000 employees and operates in 572 locations across 46 states in the U.S. and internationally in 75 nations and territories.

Think about the challenge of managing ethics and legal compliance in these firms, many with employees at locations around the globe. All of the companies are engaged in a variety of efforts, but their approaches differ somewhat due to differences in industries and organizational cultures. For example, some industries (e.g., defense and chemicals) are more highly regulated than others, so compliance with laws and regulations is an important goal, and it must be managed. For many of these companies, ethics and legal compliance are closely tied to maintenance of the firm's reputation and brand value. In such an environment, integrity becomes a key driver of corporate action.

STRUCTURING ETHICS MANAGEMENT

Many businesses are allocating significant resources to formal ethics and legal compliance programs. The increasing attention to formal ethics management programs has come about partially because of media attention to scandals in American business and management's awareness of the U.S. Sentencing Guidelines (see more about the guidelines at the end of this chapter); because for a number of years, organizations such as the Conference Board have held business ethics conferences at which formal ethics management systems are encouraged; and because some corporate leaders are simply committed to the importance of ethics in their organizations.[1]

Perhaps nothing, however, has influenced corporate ethics programs in the United States more than the U.S. Sentencing Guidelines, which took effect in the early 1990s. Until the mid-1980s, criminal law focused on the individual defendant rather than the corporation, and fines on corporations were relatively modest. In 1984, Congress created the U.S. Sentencing Commission in response to criticism of judicial discretion in sentencing and perceived disparities between sentences for "white-collar" and other types of crimes. In 1987, the Commission imposed federal sentencing guidelines for individual offenders, and as a result the trend has been toward increasing fines for both individuals and organizations convicted of felony crimes. The guidelines limited judicial sentencing discretion and mandated some incarceration for virtually every felony offender.

In 1991, the Commission issued new sentencing guidelines for organizations convicted of federal crimes. The organization can be convicted even if only one employee is caught breaking the law. The guidelines cover most federal crimes, including fraud, antitrust, securities, tax, bribery, and money-laundering offenses, and they impose a schedule of mandatory fines. "Virtually without exception, the Guidelines require a convicted organization to make restitution and to pay a substantial fine (which is not tax deductible)."[2] The guidelines even include a provision calling for a "corporate death penalty." The provision was used by federal prosecutors in the case of American Precision Components Inc., a Farmingdale, New York, company that sold ordinary nuts and bolts to government contractors as highly tested space components.[3] The company agreed to divest all of its assets. Arthur Andersen, the former auditing firm that once "stood for integrity," put its stamp of approval on a long list of dirty books (e.g., Sunbeam, Waste Management, Enron, Global Crossing, Qwest, and WorldCom) and has now become the biggest case ever of corporate capital punishment.[4]

The sentencing guidelines were designed to use a "carrot and stick" approach to managing corporate crime. The carrot provides incentives to organizations to develop a strong internal control system to detect and manage illegal behavior. The guidelines list seven requirements (outlined in detail in Table 6.1) for due diligence and an effective compliance program. For example, the guidelines propose that organizations establish and communicate compliance standards and set up communication, monitoring, reporting, and accountability systems. In this approach, the stick provides for severe punishment for organizations that are convicted of crimes and were not proactively managing legal compliance within the organization. Fines and other sanctions vary widely depending on prior violations, whether management reports itself and cooperates with investigative authorities, and whether the company has an effective program in place to prevent and detect illegal behavior. The 1991 guidelines listed the following seven specific requirements for an effective legal compliance program.

Therefore, the same crime can be subject to a wide range of penalties. The minimum fine under the guidelines is $250, and the maximum is $290 million or even more if the crime meets certain criteria. (For more specific information about how fines are determined, see the appendix, "How Fines Are Determined under the U.S. Sentencing Guidelines" at the end of this chapter.) The guidelines also recommend that a defendant organization that does not have an effective legal compliance program should be put on corporate probation. Some of the recommended conditions of probation include requiring that the organization publicize (at its own expense and as directed by the court) the fact of its conviction and the nature of the punishment; periodically report to the court regarding its financial condition and operating results; submit to periodic, unannounced reviews of books and records, and interrogation of employees by court-appointed experts (paid by the organization); and inform the court of any material adverse change in business conditions or prospects.

Table 6.1 Seven Requirements for Due Diligence and an Effective Compliance Program*

1. Establishing compliance standards reasonably capable of preventing criminal conduct
2. Assigning specific high-level individuals with responsibility to oversee those compliance standards
3. Exercising due care to ensure that discretionary authority is not delegated to individuals with a propensity to engage in illegality
4. Taking necessary steps to communicate compliance standards and procedures to all employees, with a special emphasis on training and the dissemination of manuals
5. Taking reasonable steps to achieve compliance with written standards through monitoring, auditing, and other systems designed to detect criminal conduct, including a reporting system free of retribution to employees who report criminal conduct
6. Consistently enforcing the organization's written standards through appropriate disciplinary mechanisms, including, as appropriate, discipline of individuals responsible for failure to detect an offense
7. After an offense is detected, taking all reasonable steps to respond and to prevent future similar conduct

*These requirements are from the U.S. Sentencing Guidelines of 1991 (see www.ussc.gov for more information).

According to the U.S. Sentencing Commission's reports (found at www.ussc. gov), more and more firms are being sentenced under the guidelines. Because the guidelines were not applied retroactively, they remained under the radar for a number of years. However, their impact has steadily increased and companies are paying attention. For example, in 1995, Con Edison was convicted of an environmental offense and was subject to probation that included onerous compliance requirements. In 1996, in what has come to be known as the *Caremark* decision, corporate boards of directors were put on notice to take the guidelines into account as part of their corporate governance responsibilities or face personal liability. In 1999, Hoffman-LaRoche was convicted of antitrust conspiracy charges and was fined $500 million, the largest criminal fine imposed to that point in the United States, and Rhone Poulenc was granted amnesty because it reported the offense. In 2001, TAP Pharmaceuticals received the third largest fine ever imposed to that date under the guidelines— $290 million.[5] (See Chapter 5 for a case study about TAP Pharmaceuticals.) In recent years, fines have climbed astronomically. AT&T paid almost $1 billion in fines in 2011 for improperly charging taxes to customers who use AT&T lines to access the Internet. Intel paid $1.25 billion in 2010 for redesigning its chips to retaliate against computer makers who used a rival's chips. In 2009, Pfizer was fined $2.3 billion for illegally marketing a painkiller, and finally, the big banks (Bank of America, Wells Fargo, JPMorgan Chase, Citigroup, Ally) paid $25 billion in fines in 2012 over faulty foreclosures and mishandling customer requests for mortgage modifications.[6]

In 2004, the U.S. Sentencing Commission released revisions to the guidelines, including the expectation that the board of directors will oversee the compliance and ethics program, that senior management will ensure its effectiveness, and that the compliance officer will have adequate authority and access to senior management. In addition, organizations must train employees and conduct risk assessments to identify potential areas of concern. The revision also ensures that organizations cannot just "check off" the list of guidelines (for example, with a code of conduct that just sits on the shelf). Rather, the program in place must be seen as an integral part of the organization's culture (see Chapter 5 for more on ethical culture). With the Supreme Court's 2005 *United States v. Booker* decision, judges are no longer required to follow the guidelines strictly. The guidelines remain advisory, and federal prosecutors have been told they are expected to take steps to ensure adherence to them. Therefore, most observers now expect that the guidelines will continue to be followed in most cases.[7]

In recent years, the U.S. Sentencing Guidelines continued to evolve with refinements being announced on an almost annual basis, and that is a good thing. Instead of being a dead document, the guidelines are very much alive and the commission regularly revises them to try to reward good corporate citizenship. As you'll see in the material that follows, most of the elements of the Sentencing Guidelines have become integral parts of organizational ethics programs throughout the United States. While most companies make a real effort to meet the "letter" of the guidelines, others go much further to incorporate the "spirit" of the guidelines. We discuss some of those efforts in this chapter.

Making Ethics Comprehensive and Holistic

The U.S. Sentencing Guidelines very clearly aim to encourage organizations to create ethics programs that drive integrity and ethical behavior in their business operations. As the guidelines have become more refined and sophisticated over time, responsible organizations have found numerous ways of making ethics and values central to how they do business. As we read in the last chapter, values such as ethics and integrity become part of an organization's culture by aligning various elements throughout the organization. Integrating any corporate value into the organizational culture starts with strong executive commitment. Once executives are clearly behind the effort, then the effort must be communicated to every employee and compliance must be measured and rewarded for the value to become part of the culture.

Managing Ethics: The Corporate Ethics Office

Some organizations delegate ethics management responsibilities widely, finding that a strong statement of values and a strong ethical culture can keep the ethics management effort together. This approach may be particularly effective in smaller firms. However, most large firms find that ethics initiatives need to be coordinated from a single office to ensure that all of the program's pieces fit together and that all of the U.S. Sentencing Guidelines' requirements are being met.

   The corporate ethics office concept can be traced to 1985 and General Dynamics, then the second-largest U.S. defense contractor. The secretary of the Navy, out of concern about the appropriateness of certain indirect expenses that had been billed to the government, directed General Dynamics to establish and enforce a rigorous code of ethics for all employees that included sanctions for violators. The company turned to a nonprofit consulting firm in Washington, D.C., the Ethics Resource Center, for help in developing the code. As part of this process, an ethics office was also set up and an ethics officer was hired.[8] In 1986, General Dynamics joined with other defense industry companies in the Defense Industry Initiative (see www.dii.org) to "embrace and promote ethical business conduct." The companies shared best practices, and these best practices provided much of the foundation for the U.S. Sentencing Commission requirements.

   The 1991 U.S. Federal Sentencing Guidelines gave impetus to the move toward establishing formal ethics programs in firms outside the defense industry. The guidelines also called for the assignment of specific high-level individuals with responsibility to oversee legal compliance standards. This requirement led to the development of a brand new role—that of the corporate ethics officer.

Ethics and Compliance Officers

Until the mid-1980s, the title "ethics and compliance officer" didn't exist in American business. Today, with a growing number of ethics and compliance practitioners worldwide, these high-level executives have their own professional organization, the Ethics and Compliance Officer Association (ECOA—see www.theecoa.org). The association's stated mission is "to promote ethical business practices, serving as a forum for the exchange of information and strategies." The organization began in 1991 when over 40 ethics and compliance officers met at the Center for Business Ethics at Bentley University in Waltham, Massachusetts. The organization was officially launched later that year and began holding annual meetings in 1993. As of 2009, the ECOA has more than 1,300 members representing more than half of the *Fortune* 100 companies, nonprofits, municipalities, and international members from over 30 countries. The organization holds regular conferences, workshops, and webcasts and provides a variety of classroom and distance learning opportunities for ethics and compliance officers and their staff.

The demand for qualified and knowledgeable compliance and ethics professionals is so high that more organizations are being created to help them share information and design more effective ethics and compliance programs. One of these is the Society for Corporate Compliance and Ethics (SCCE), a nonprofit started in 2002 and head-quartered in Minneapolis. The SCCE boasts more than 3,000 members and has a robust web presence (www.corporatecompliance.org).

Many firms designate their legal counsel as the ethics officer. Others create a title such as vice president or director of ethics, compliance, or business practices, director of internal audit, ethics program coordinator, or just plain ethics officer. Most firms locate the ethics officer at the corporate level, and these high-level executives generally report to a senior executive, the CEO, the board of directors, the audit committee of the board, or some combination. These individuals are expected to provide leadership and strategies for ensuring that the firm's standards of business conduct are communicated and upheld throughout the organization.

INSIDERS VERSUS OUTSIDERS   An ethics or compliance officer may be an insider or someone brought in from the outside. We talked to past and present ethics officers who represent both categories. It can sometimes be more difficult for an outsider to achieve credibility in the ethics or compliance role, but someone brought in from outside the company has the advantage of being able to evaluate the situation with a fresh eye. If change is needed, that person may be better able to guide the organization through the change process. Most of the ethics officers we interviewed believe that, if available, a respected and trusted insider who knows the company's culture and people is usually the best choice. Results of a 1995 survey support the insider preference; 82 percent of the firms responding to the question hired their ethics officer from inside the firm.[9] The very best situation may be when the ethics officer is also a part of the senior management team or being groomed for an executive position. However, outsiders are often brought in if the organization is responding to an ethical crisis of some kind.

At Lockheed Martin, ethics is taken so seriously that an assignment managing an ethics office is part of the grooming process for executive positions that high-potential employees receive. Lockheed Martin has a vice president of ethics and sustainability for the entire corporation and five ethics directors—one for each of Lockheed Martin's five huge business areas. These positions report to the executive vice presidents in the business areas and are largely rotational. High-potential executives are recruited into these jobs as a development experience; they serve for two to three years and then go back to the businesses. Other high-potential employees replace them as ethics directors, and the process continues. This is a novel approach to enhancing an ethics program and grooming executives, and it should go a long way toward truly integrating ethics and integrity into the business rhythm.

Lockheed Martin will soon have a full cadre of executive-level employees who have served the company as ethics professionals. One employee involved in this process is Craig Cash, who is currently (2013) the director of ethics and business conduct for Lockheed Martin Mission Systems and Training (MST) in Washington, DC. Cash holds an undergraduate degree in engineering and a Masters in Leadership and Business Ethics from Duquesne University. Cash was working in engineering when he was tapped for the ethics officer job in Syracuse in 2003. Now he is the Director for MST and is managing investigations, overseeing ethics and compliance training, tracking metrics through surveys and other studies, and looking for trends in this area. He is also talking to leaders, working with them to integrate ethics and compliance into the business by creating a "culture of trust" throughout the organization. With his unique background and advanced education in the field, Cash is the sole exception among business area ethics directors and is nonrotational. According to Cash, working in the Ethics Office at Lockheed Martin is a joy since the business takes the topic so seriously and supports its employees 100 percent in doing the right thing.

ETHICS OFFICER BACKGROUND   The job of ethics officer has been called "the newest profession in American business."[10] Individuals holding this position come from many backgrounds. With insiders, the job is often assigned to someone in a staff function (e.g., someone in the corporate secretary's office, office of the legal counsel, audit, or human resources). According to past ethics officer surveys, law was the most common background. That is true of most of our interviewees as well. Interestingly, some people believe that lawyers shouldn't be considered for the job, because corporate lawyers are hired to defend the corporation and can't objectively handle an ethical issue that calls the corporation's own behavior into question. But the ethics officers we interviewed agreed that the most important thing is earning other employees' respect as being fair, trustworthy, credible, and discreet.

The Ethics Infrastructure

Ethics offices can be centralized, decentralized, or some combination of both. The decision to centralize or decentralize may depend on the overall structure of the firm. For example, if the firm's other staff functions are highly decentralized, it may be difficult to centralize the ethics function. The structuring decision may also depend on whether different business units have very different ethics management needs. For example, if one division of a firm deals in government contracts and others do not, that division may need a different approach that emphasizes compliance with government contracting regulations. Thus, local ethics offices might better meet the needs of different units that are in different businesses. However, decentralized ethics offices can be difficult to manage effectively because they must communicate with each other constantly to ensure consistency and commitment to the organization's key values.

Even where different units have different requirements, it's usually helpful to have a central office that coordinates ethics and compliance activities and ensures management support for those activities. Most large organizations, such as the ones we talked with, have a headquarters ethics office that functions as the central point of communications for ethics and compliance activities. For example, the corporate ethics office at Lockheed Martin has a staff of around ten people, led by Leo Mackay, the vice president of ethics and sustainability. In addition, each of the five large business areas, corporate enterprise operations, and international operations has a full-time ethics director who has responsibility for overseeing ethics and business conduct in his or her business areas. These ethics directors, following a matrix reporting structure, report to Mackay as well as to an executive vice president for their business area. Mackay reports directly to the president and chief executive officer. In addition, Mackay reports (in written and oral form) to the Ethics and Sustainability Committee of the corporation's board of directors.

Ethics officers seem to agree that, whatever other reporting relationships exist, the ethics officer should have a direct reporting relationship to the CEO. They were particularly concerned about the ethics function being "stuck" under law, human resources, audit, or finance, where it would be just another part of the "silo mentality" that still exists in many organizations. Ethics would then be perceived as audit's job or HR's job rather than as part of the total culture. For example, it was common at one time (and still is in some companies) to have the ethics office report to the general counsel (legal department). In a recent survey conducted among compliance professionals, 88 percent said that this was not a good arrangement.[11] The person who leads the ethics office is in a much better position to "press the envelope" if he or she reports directly to the CEO. (If the CEO *is* the ethics problem, then a reporting line to the audit committee of the board is essential).

The Corporate Ethics Committee

In some organizations, ethics is managed by a corporate committee staffed by senior-level managers from a variety of functional areas. This committee is set up to provide ethical oversight and policy guidance for CEO and management decisions.[12] It also represents an affirmation that top management really cares about ethics.

At Lockheed Martin, the Corporate Sustainability Council meets at least twice a year and has done so since 1995 when the company was formed. The Council provides the organization with strategic direction and oversight on matters of ethics and business conduct along with other sustainability matters. Each business area and international region has also established an Ethics and Business Conduct Steering Committee to oversee its ethics and business conduct operations. In some of the larger business areas, subordinate-level steering committees have been set up as well. Members of the corporate committee include the general counsel, executives of large operating entities, and vice presidents from functional areas such as human resources, finance, audit, and communications. The corporate committee is chaired by Mackay, and the business area committees are chaired by their executive vice presidents. The two-way communication between the ethics office and these senior executives is essential. It gives the ethics office information about what concerns senior-level management, and it gives the firm's leadership information about the types of issues that are coming into the ethics office from employees. The group's role is viewed as strategic. The steering committees at all levels of the corporation review the ethics awareness training and business conduct compliance training programs, metrics on investigations and requests for guidance, trends, employee survey results, and matters referred by the business areas and business units.

COMMUNICATING ETHICS

Within the ethics infrastructure, good communication—downward, upward, and two-way—is essential if an organization is to have a strong, aligned ethics culture. The organization must evaluate the current state of ethics communication and initiatives. It must communicate its values, standards, and policies in a variety of formal and informal ways that meet its employees' needs. These communication efforts should be synergistic, clear, consistent, and credible. They also need to be executed in a variety of media, because people learn things in different ways. In general, the old advice to speechwriters still holds. "Tell 'em what you're going to tell 'em, then tell 'em, then tell 'em what you told 'em." In addition to receiving downward communication from management, employees must also have opportunities to communicate their ethical concerns upward. Finally, an open communication environment must be created that says it's okay to ask questions, and it's okay to talk about ethics. In the following section, we begin with some corporate communications basics—principles that should guide all ethics communication initiatives.

A number of the ethics officers we interviewed were sensitive to the negativity sometimes attached to the word *ethics*. Employees can get defensive when they hear this word. They think to themselves, "Why are you here talking to me about ethics? Mine are fine." Kent Druyvesteyn, former ethics officer at General Dynamics, put it this way. "Using the word 'ethics' unfortunately implies that somebody has a deficiency. So, I would urge you not to use that word at least until you can make clear what you mean by it." This negative reaction to the word *ethics* may be more of a problem at some organizations than at others. Again, it depends on the culture of the firm. Companies have used the term *values* or *business conduct* or *business practices* successfully. The key is to know your own company and use terminology that sounds authentic within your organization's culture.

Basic Communications Principles

ALIGN THE FORMAL AND INFORMAL COMMUNICATION SYSTEMS   When most people think of a corporate communication system, they think of the obvious—the company newspaper, website, and annual report. However, like culture, a corporate

communication system consists of formal and informal components. Formal communications include all formal written and electronic communication—newspapers, magazines, memos, recruiting literature, policy manuals, annual reports, websites, and advertising—as well as formalized oral communication such as meetings and speeches. But perhaps the most powerful component in a corporation's communication system is an informal one known as the grapevine.

The grapevine—a continual stream of information among employees about "what's really going on"—exists in every organization. It contains news, rumors, impressions, and perceptions. Surprisingly, research has shown that from 70 to 90 percent of the information that passes through the grapevine is accurate.[13] In survey after survey of employees in numerous and varied businesses, the grapevine is where they said they received most of their information about their employer. (In those same surveys, most people said they would rather receive information from their managers.) The grapevine can be examined to shed light on a corporation's credibility since most employees are plugged into it, it provides information fast and continually, and it contains the "inside" scoop on corporate events.

One way to determine corporate credibility on various issues—especially ethics—is to compare the messages on the formal and informal communications systems. For example, suppose that Big Company has a policy prohibiting employees from entertaining customers excessively. The policy is spelled out in a manual, and the president of Big has reinforced the policy in speeches to employees. Now imagine that Big's head of marketing repeatedly wines and dines clients. The costs of the lavish entertainment are detailed in expense reports that are approved by management and processed by clerical and financial control employees. In addition, other employees are invited along when the clients are entertained, and still more employees observe the head of marketing entertaining guests in expensive restaurants. Regardless of how strongly Big's formal communication system states the official policy, the informal communication system—the grapevine—will communicate what's really going on: Big is saying one thing and doing another. The company says it prohibits lavish entertainment, yet it condones that forbidden behavior in at least one high-level employee. As a result, Big's ethics culture is out of alignment and employees might well conclude that the company has no corporate credibility on the subject of customer entertainment. Furthermore, its credibility on other ethical issues is probably suspect.

Now imagine another situation. Little Company has a strongly worded policy regarding sexual harassment. Moreover, Little's senior executives have frequently stated that sexual harassment will not be tolerated. Suppose a manager, Pat, is accused of sexual harassment. The charge is investigated, found to be accurate, and Pat is fired. The exact details of the incident may not be on the grapevine, but in most cases, just the bare bones of that story will send a strong message. The messages on the grapevine will match what's said by Little's formal communication system. Employees will get the word very quickly that Little means business on the issue of sexual harassment, and the corporation will have increased its credibility by "walking the ethics talk."

The importance of informal communications can't be overstated. Since truth and honesty are at the core of any ethics effort, if a company is saying one thing and doing another—if the messages on its formal communication system and its grapevine don't match—it has little or no credibility and probably shouldn't attempt a formal ethics communication effort until it has regained its credibility. How can you compare the formal and informal messages? Ask employees. Employee surveys and focus groups can provide feedback that will serve as the beginning of an effective comparison. One particularly effective way of measuring this is to ask employees to compare what the company "says" with what the company "does." How does an organization establish or regain credibility? Designing consistent policies and enforcing those policies are the only route an organization can take to gain credibility on ethics issues. If policies are enforced for only part of the employee population, or if there are different rules and treatment for different employees, there's little an organization can do to gain credibility until consistency is established.

ANALYZE THE AUDIENCE The first thing to do when designing a communication program is to analyze the needs of your audience. Consider what employees already know, what they need to know, what biases and abilities they have, what the desired and required behaviors look like, when they should be asking questions, and where they can go to report their concerns and to ask for help.

When designing ethics communication for a typical employee population, organizations need to consider three kinds of people. (Because the terms are easy to visualize and remember, we use military jargon to describe the three types.)

Good Soldiers Group I includes the "good soldiers." These people understand and follow the rules and policies of the organization, and they have good ethical compasses. They have the judgment or experience required to discern the difference between right and wrong, and they have the moral grounding to do the right thing. Be careful to note that these aren't just soldiers who follow orders, right or wrong. They know that good soldiers are expected to question an order they believe to be illegal or morally wrong, and they would do so.

Loose Cannons In Group II are the "loose cannons"—these people may have good ethical compasses, but they don't know their corporation's policies. They may not even be familiar with general ethical standards in business. Loose cannons may be inexperienced, or they may have transferred from another, unrelated industry with very different norms; they may never have read a policy manual. Whatever the reason, loose cannons may be well meaning, but they're naive. Without guidance, loose cannons may not even consider ethics in the business environment.

Grenades People in Group III are "grenades," and they're neither ignorant nor benign. These employees may or may not know the rules, but they don't care either way. They have their own agenda, and they lack any company or professional loyalty.

We call them grenades because their activities can blow up suddenly and severely damage the organization.

Although the communication needs of the three groups overlap, the emphasis for each specific group is clear. Good soldiers need support because good people often feel pressured to compromise in order to "fit in." Good soldiers need to know that their instincts are right and their behavior is not the exception; in fact, it represents the organizational model. Loose cannons need to be educated; they need to know and understand basic norms of ethical conduct and specific company policy and standards. Grenades need to know unequivocally that ethical lapses will not be tolerated. They need to see good behavior rewarded and ethical lapses dealt with swiftly, consistently, and firmly.

There are probably only a few grenades in any organization. But they surely exist everywhere, and the system must be prepared to deal with them. Good soldiers may account for a substantial portion of employees, but perhaps not the majority. Since very few employees ever read a policy manual cover to cover, most people learn policy on a need-to-know basis. It's safest to assume that most employees fit into the loose cannon category. The challenge in designing effective ethics communication programs is meeting the needs of all types of employees.

This focus on the ethics audience assumes that most employees don't come to the organization perfectly principled and completely prepared to make the right decision in every situation. Recall from earlier chapters that most employees are highly susceptible to influence from outside themselves, so the organization has to provide guidance—and, despite advances, the perfect integrity test hasn't been invented. Since polygraphs were outlawed for most types of employee screening in the United States, more organizations have turned to paper-and-pencil honesty or integrity tests to screen prospective employees. Most of these tests attempt to predict the prospective employee's inclination to steal from the organization, although others have a more general focus on workplace deviance. Integrity tests have been evaluated by the American Psychological Association. Their report concludes that research on integrity tests is improving and that evidence supporting the tests' ability to predict dishonest behavior has increased.[14] Nevertheless, many problems remain, and organizations will continue to have imperfect employees who need guidance on ethical issues.

Evaluating the Current State of Ethics Communications

Before beginning the actual design of an ethics communication program, it's essential to conduct an evaluation that asks the following questions.

WHAT KINDS OF ETHICAL DILEMMAS ARE EMPLOYEES LIKELY TO ENCOUNTER? In addition to common ethical dilemmas faced by employees everywhere, organizations need to identify the kinds of issues and dilemmas that might be unique to their particular industry. For example, a chemical company needs to pay special attention to environmental and safety dilemmas. A financial firm should pay extremely close attention to fiduciary, confidentiality, and conflict-of-interest issues. A manufacturing company may have to look at the ethical issues involved in worker safety, product quality, product liability, and labor relations. Along with identifying issues specific to their industry, companies need to examine the various jobs within their organization to uncover what specific professional dilemmas their communication program will have to address. For example, an internal auditor faces one set of dilemmas, whereas a manufacturing supervisor faces an entirely different set. Once these dilemmas are identified, an organization can develop a program that's useful for employees—one that shows them how to deal with their own most common dilemmas.

WHAT DON'T EMPLOYEES KNOW? Is the company hiring numerous midcareer hires who may come from other industries with different standards of conduct? Does the company regularly hire large numbers of recent college or business school graduates who may have little knowledge of business standards, much less specific corporate policy or industry standards? The communication program needs to target the specific needs of these different groups.

HOW ARE POLICIES CURRENTLY COMMUNICATED? How is policy communicated now? Does the policy manual weigh in at 40 pounds, or is it online and easy to search? When a manager has a policy question, what does he or she do—look it up in the manual, ask human resources, ask a colleague, search online resources, or guess? Is corporate policy ever discussed in orientation or training programs? No one is ever going to memorize a policy manual. Therefore, an ethics communication program needs to take a "snapshot" of key policies and concentrate on communicating them. Organizations also need to send a clear message that employees need to know when to ask questions and that the organization encourages employees to inquire. Companies generally do a very good job of telling new hires how to succeed; what they usually don't do nearly as well is telling new hires how they're going to fail or get fired or worse. It's vital for new employees to understand their employer's standards. What does the company expect from them?

Policy communication also needs to be in plain language—not legalese. It is very tempting for company lawyers to try to protect an organization by using legal language to communicate complex policy issues. However, it is not helpful at all to the non-lawyers (most employees) who need to understand what a particular policy means. Every effort should be made to simplify language, explain "why" your organization has a particular policy, and then give examples of how the policy might be applied in everyday business situations.

WHAT COMMUNICATION CHANNELS EXIST? How do employees receive messages from management? How does management receive messages from employees? Is "management by walking around" a common practice, or is senior management isolated from most employees? Is there a suggestion program? If so, do suggestions get responses? Are employees generally comfortable approaching their managers with problems, concerns, and questions? Is there a grievance process or a whistleblowing procedure? Do most employees know where to go for help if their managers are unavailable or if their manager is part of the problem? Are human resources, legal, and audit professionals accessible to most employees? Analyzing the answers to these questions will give an organization a good idea of where effective communication channels exist, where they don't, and where to build new ones.

Multiple Communication Channels for Formal Ethics Communication

The company's ethics message can and should be communicated in a variety of ways. The most obvious ethics communication channels include a mission or values statement, a code of conduct, policy statements, a formal process for reporting concerns or observed misconduct, and communications from leaders. In addition to these channels, the ethics message needs to be reinforced in all formal communication materials, including recruiting and orientation materials, newsletters, magazines, annual reports, and websites. The following are some types of communication materials that can be used to send an ethics message.

WEBSITES   The company's website is an important source of information about the company and its values and policies. Many companies are hesitant to include ethics information on their external website and instead use their firm's intranet to convey the information. But stakeholders such as investors, potential employees, customers, and suppliers are likely to use the company's website to gather information about the company. So, if ethics is important to these relationships, it should be included on the external site. For example, Lockheed Martin provides a large amount of information about ethics on its external website (www.lockheedmartin.com): its ethical principles, code of conduct, annual ethics awareness training, information about compliance training, information about how the ethics process works, and information for suppliers and other business partners who are asked to be guided by high ethical standards and to respect the restrictions the firm places on its employees with regard to such issues as giving and receiving gifts. The code, "Setting the Standard," is translated into 16 languages. United Technologies Corporation (www.utc.com) also provides information about ethics on its website, including the code and other brochures in portable document format (PDF). The information is also available in multiple languages.

SOCIAL MEDIA   New technology provides organizations with new ways of communicating the ethics message and encouraging employee involvement. As with any other subject, the introduction of social media into the communication equation can be a double-edged sword. There are many social media factors that can benefit and harm organizations—global reach, instantaneous distribution, anonymity, and a lack of security—all can play a positive or a negative role in an organization's ethics communication strategy.

One company communicator described an ethics communication effort he designed and implemented for his employer, a large national health insurance company. This company's strategy involved an employee blog, managed by the communication department, where executives and employees could discuss all kinds of issues affecting employees (including ethics) online. The company executives were very reluctant to adopt this approach and it took months of lobbying by the communication director to convince the executives to approve the blog. Finally, they did approve it and it went live. After only a few days, they were horrified when a disgruntled employee launched a diatribe against the company on the blog. The executives were tempted to end it right there, but again the communication director persuaded them to stay with it. Within a few hours, several other employees, completely of their own volition, answered the disgruntled employee's charges and redirected the conversation. Over the next few weeks, that pattern happened repeatedly, and eventually the executives calmed down. As this book goes to press, the blog has been in place for almost three years and the executives feel that it has had a positive influence on the ethical culture of the organization and has helped executives communicate some difficult messages to employees. Plus, internal research shows that employees trust it as a source of information and guidance.

Another even more successful story involves Best Buy and its chief ethics officer, Kathleen Edmond, who won the Ethics Resource Center's Carol R. Marshall Award for Innovation in Corporate Ethics in 2013.[15] Edmond employs a variety of tools to communicate the ethics message among Best Buy's 170,000 employees, and one tool that has been very effective is a personal blog (www.kathleenedmond.com). The blog has been popular with employees and has explored a wide range of topics from vendor contracts to employees posting confidential details of a new video game release date.[16] Each entry describes an ethical issue and often a real case, Edmond's thoughts on the issue/case, and finally, questions to get readers thinking about the issue and how they might respond in a similar situation. For example, one entry in February 2013 posed an interesting situation for any retail employee.

The case involved the spouse of a corporate employee who came into a store, behaved badly, and said that he was entitled to special treatment because his wife was a corporate employee. Edmond asked a number of questions about the situation, including this one: *"Whether at Best Buy or any other company, should employees receive special treatment that ordinary customers do not?"* Of course, any of us who have worked in retail can empathize with this very uncomfortable and infuriating situation. Not only did Edmond raise a fascinating issue that surely happens repeatedly throughout any company, but employees got the opportunity to respond, and the website contains numerous comments from employees who deal with this type of thing every day.[17] This kind of openness, where employees can discuss approaches and ideas to deal effectively with ethics issues, can only benefit a company and is a powerful new communication tool.

RECRUITING BROCHURES These can include the mission or values statement, a discussion of corporate values, and a description of how people in the organization succeed and fail. Ethical conduct can be highlighted. Many organizations also have a website for those interested in finding out about careers within the firm and applying for jobs.

CAMPUS RECRUITING At Lockheed Martin, the ethics office participates with university relations for on-campus recruiting. Ethics officers travel to college and university campuses across the country to assist in recruiting and to speak about the Lockheed Martin ethics program.

ORIENTATION MEETINGS AND MATERIALS   Orientation materials can include the mission or values statement, descriptions of common ethical dilemmas and advice for handling them, explanations of resources to help employees make ethical decisions, and instructions on how to raise an ethical issue or report an ethical concern. Organizations should pay particular attention to how their orientation meetings communicate values and expectations. New employees are eager to learn about their new employer, and orientations are a wonderful venue for communicating what an organization stands for and what it expects of employees. How *not* to introduce values and ethics during an orientation might best be illustrated by a manufacturing company's general counsel we heard about who, when asked to address new hires on the company's ethics and compliance program, simply read the code of conduct aloud to a group of new employees. (Yawn.)

NEWSLETTERS AND MAGAZINES   These materials can be print-based or web-based. They may include the mission statement, stories about corporate "heroes"—employees who illustrate the corporate values—and features that describe ethical dilemmas and include comments from employees and managers about how they would deal with the problems. Some companies regularly publish lists of the types of ethical or legal violations they have addressed and how they addressed them. For example, the communication may say that, in the last six months, the company dealt with a particular number of reports of Internet pornography, bribery, time reporting, travel charge reporting, lying to customers, or abusive supervision. They may say how many of these resulted in a variety of actions ranging from warnings to terminations. Such communication helps keep the ethical culture alive and lets employees know that the company means what it says about the importance of ethics. These kinds of regular communications can also be targeted to specific groups of employees with specific needs.

BOOKLETS   These materials can vary given employees' need for information in particular areas of the business. Booklets can be in print or electronic forms and can also be easily updated or added to, thus making the program adaptable to the dynamic business environment.

Interactive Approaches to Ethics Communication

One novel approach to ethics communication is based on a "mini-case study" approach. It gives employees an opportunity to learn about "real" ethics cases in an ongoing manner, and it sustains the focus on ethics in the organization.

An approach like this was introduced in the early 1990s at Texas Instruments (TI), and in TI's system, employees were encouraged to send in questions. This internal corporate communication tool, called "Instant Experience," allowed employees to raise timely issues quickly and without a lot of bureaucracy, and it provided the ethics office with a constant line to the ethical pulse of the organization. The idea was the brainchild of Glen Coleman, a retired Air Force helicopter pilot and an aerospace engineer who worked for TI's ethics office at the time. Coleman admitted that while in Vietnam, he and his fellow helicopter pilots sometimes made potentially life-threatening mistakes. On their return, they freely entered their "stupid mistakes" into a book they called "Instant Experience," so that their buddies wouldn't make the same mistakes and lives could be saved.

In a variation of the idea that not everyone should have to get burned to find out that the stove is hot, Coleman reasoned that the ethics office could be a clearinghouse for ethical experiences that members of the organization were willing to share with others. As a result, these "instant experiences" were regularly transmitted to all employees via an e-mail communication system. The experiences were retained on the system so that new employees could get up to speed and ongoing employees could check the system whenever they wished.

Here's an example of an anonymous question posed by a TI employee and then posted on the communication system.

> Suppose I'm in a restaurant and I happen to overhear a conversation from behind me. It's two TI competitors discussing sensitive, competitive information that would be very valuable to TI. What do I do? Continue to listen? Put my fingers in my ears? Tell them to stop? And what should I do with the information that I've already heard? Forget it and pretend it never happened? Mark it TI STRICTLY PRIVATE and distribute it?
>
> I didn't go out looking for the information and I couldn't change my table location to get away from the conversation. It seems a little ridiculous to just throw away an opportunity to use valuable information that I've acquired but didn't solicit in any way. What's the right course of action?

And, here's how Carl Skooglund, TI's ethics director at the time, responded:

> There is nothing illegal or unethical about accidentally being in the right place at the right time and overhearing a competitor's conversation. They must accept the responsibility for irresponsibly discussing sensitive information in a public place. If you have overheard the conversation, your best course of action is to document to your best ability what you heard and notify TI Legal, telling them how you acquired it. The TI employee who raised this question is correct. It would be ridiculous to pretend that you never heard the information. Under these circumstances you can share the information with TI. The competitor must accept responsibility for his carelessness. Our ethical principles do not exclude common sense.

Skooglund's response then took the issue a step further, inviting dialogue by asking TI employees if the response should be different if the TI employee had intentionally sat at a table adjacent to known competitors. Many employees responded, and over 95 percent of the responses agreed that intentional eavesdropping was clearly unethical. Here are some of their responses:

> "We are not in the spy business. It's totally unethical."
>
> "I was disappointed that you would even ask us this."
>
> "Spying is spying."
>
> "What happened to the golden rule?"
>
> "My grandmother told me that if something makes you feel guilty, don't do it."
>
> "If our customers knew about this, would their opinion of us suffer?"
>
> "I would be ashamed."
>
> "It's unmitigatedly unethical."
>
> "Would I be proud to have my TI badge on?"
>
> "Let's leave trickery to magicians."
>
> "Stay far enough away from legal limits so that TI's character is never questioned."

Skooglund agreed with the large majority of responses and assured the respondents that their ethical compasses were pointing in the right direction. This Instant Experience system allowed employees to openly share their ethics-related questions and experiences, and everyone in the organization learned from the open exchange. In an organization without such a system, this individual may have struggled silently with the issue or may have asked a few peers or a manager for advice. But with the system, the entire organization can learn from one employee's experience.

In addition to the weekly transmissions and interactions, a collection of the weekly articles was retained on the Instant Experience system as an archive with a chronological index and a subject index. A survey of TI employees found that 30 to 40 percent were reading it every week, and 70 to 80 percent read it at least monthly. Supervisors were also encouraged to print the messages and post them on a bulletin board.

This system was particularly effective because it fit TI's culture and was based on sound communication principles. First, electronic communication was an essential part of the high-tech TI culture, so e-mail ethics discussions were a natural extension of that culture. Second, e-mail is appropriate for "ethics" discussions because it allows for interaction with reflection. Ethical issues generally require some introspection, perhaps even a trip to the file cabinet to check the code of conduct. The Instant Experience system allowed employees to think about the issue and then participate in relatively informal discussions with other employees. Finally, research suggests that people are less inhibited when communicating electronically. They may be more willing to discuss sensitive ethical issues electronically than they would be face-to-face, thus contributing to the "it's okay to talk about ethics" atmosphere.

Mission or Values Statements

In recent years, many corporations have developed mission or values statements. A mission statement, values statement, or credo is a succinct description of "how we do business"—the corporate principles and values that guide how business is to be conducted in an organization. A mission statement is a short description of the organization's reason for existence—a sort of "here's what we do." Values statements are the next step in the process of explaining an organization to the world—"and here's how we do it"—a codification of essential corporate behavior. It's a sort of "Ten Commandments" for an organization. If it's to be effective, it should be short, memorable, and in plain language so that everyone can be clear about its message. It's also essential that the organization's own employees have input because a mission statement and values statement must accurately reflect the organizational culture. Something scribed by outsiders just won't ring true and is likely to end up as the subject of a *Dilbert* cartoon. But statements that develop out of the firm's true values and history can be mainstays of the corporate culture. Merck posts its values statement prominently on its website (www.merck.com):

Our Values

Our core values are driven by a desire to improve life, achieve scientific excellence, operate with the highest standards of integrity, expand access to our products and employ a diverse workforce that values collaboration.

Improving Life

We embrace our quest to tackle health challenges because we are inspired by the differences we can make in the lives of people around the world.

Ethics and Integrity

We are committed to the highest standards of ethics and integrity.

We are responsible to our customers, to Merck employees, to the environments we inhabit, and to the societies we serve worldwide.

Innovation

We are dedicated to the highest level of scientific excellence.

We strive to identify the most critical needs of consumers and customers, and through continuous innovation we challenge ourselves to meet those needs.

Access to Health

We aspire to improve the health and wellness of people around the world by expanding access to our medicines and vaccines.

Diversity and Teamwork

Our ability to excel depends on the integrity, knowledge, imagination, skill, diversity and teamwork of our employees.

Obviously, it's possible to have meaningless values statements when the words are posted on websites and bulletin boards but aren't really a part of the organizational culture. To be meaningful, corporate values must guide corporate and individual decision making on a regular basis. Ethics and integrity are part of the "DNA" at Merck, where employees know that "how" they achieve results counts as much – or more – than their results alone. The role of the "customer first" value that guided Johnson & Johnson's decision making in the Tylenol crisis (see Chapter 10) is perhaps the most famous single example of a corporate value being meaningfully applied.

What happens when a company ignores the importance of having in place a mission and vision and values? That was the situation at Adelphia, the telecommunications/cable company that imploded in 2002. The Rigas family, who founded and managed the organization, ran the company like a mom-and-pop corner store, even after the company—mainly through a series of acquisitions—grew to 15,000 employees. In 2002, the founder and CEO, John Rigas, and his sons were indicted for looting hundreds of millions of dollars from the company's coffers and concealing the true debt load from investors.[18] When the new management team took over, they were surprised to find that Adelphia had no guiding principles, no mission, no vision, no ethics, no code—nothing! Ray Dravesky was soon hired to head communication at Adelphia, and his first project was to get the company back on track by helping the executive team create and communicate a new mission, vision, and code of conduct. Because the company had filed for bankruptcy, the ethics project had to be created on a shoestring. Within weeks, however, the company launched its new vision and code of conduct and installed an employee ethics hotline. Employee satisfaction scores later indicated that employees—after living in an ethics vacuum for years—were pleased to receive this kind of direction from the top of the company. Although the company was purchased shortly thereafter, employees throughout the company were pleased with the new direction these formal statements had established.

Organizational Policy

Policy—the "rules of the organization"—is critical to any company, and most organizations create a policy manual or an intranet site to house all relevant company rules. Generally, policy manuals and websites describe not only laws and regulations pertaining to the company and its industry but also all company policy, including human resources policy. Although it's critical for a corporation to define its policies and communicate them—it's a stipulation of the U.S. Sentencing Guidelines—most employees don't read every page of a manual or website. Employees consider policy manuals and websites to be for reference purposes only. As a result, employees consult policy manuals in the same way they use a dictionary—periodically and on a need-to-know basis. Many managers never consult a policy manual, however—it's much easier to ask someone than to look up the rules in a voluminous book or website—and, depending on whom they ask, they may or may not get the right answer.

The very nature of policy—it's usually voluminous and written in legalese—makes it a poor way to communicate important rules. Also, since all policy is detailed, all policy may be viewed as having the same importance. Obviously, some policies are much more important than others and should receive special emphasis.

When you're designing policy communication, first analyze the audience. Who needs to know all the policy? Does some corporate policy apply only to certain employees? What do employees really need to know, and what's nice for them to know? Here are some guidelines to follow.

COMMUNICATE RELEVANT RULES TO THE PEOPLE WHO NEED THEM Although much of a firm's policy applies to everyone, surely some policy applies only to specific employee groups. For example, if accountants in the organization need a specific policy, either separate it from the main manual or site under a specific heading, or leave it out and distribute accounting policy only to accountants. If some policy applies to all employees, it can be incorporated into the code of conduct.

PRIORITIZE POLICY The material describing confidentiality is more important than a description of how to code a time sheet for sick time. Policy should be presented in a way that lets employees see, at a glance, what the most important rules are.

MAKE IT UNDERSTANDABLE First, eliminate the legalese—only lawyers like legalese; the rest of us like simple English. Second, tell employees what the policy means. Most policies prohibit conflicts of interest, yet few employees can define what a conflict of interest is. Give examples of conflicts of interest, and tell employees what a conflict of interest looks like. If people can't tell you what a conflict of interest is, it will be difficult for them to avoid one. If you provide employees with examples of when a particular ethical issue is likely to happen, they will be more likely to recognize the issue when it arises and know how to handle it.

MAKE POLICY COME ALIVE Effective communication occurs not when you send the message, but when people receive it and understand it. Important policy needs to be communicated in creative ways that highlight important rules. Policy also needs to be communicated in a variety of venues: in person, in staff meetings, in orientation programs, in training sessions—wherever there's an opportunity.

Codes of Conduct

A code of conduct is not a substitute for an ethics program; a code is only the start of an ethics effort. Codes come up frequently because most ethics programs, good or bad, have them. Codes vary substantially in length, content, and readability, but they're generally designed to be the main road map, the ground rules for ethical conduct within the organization.

It's probably fair to say that the longer the code, the less likely it is that employees will read it. On the other hand, the shorter the code, the broader and more abstract the guidelines will be. Reducing the number of pages represents acknowledgment that the company can't have rules to cover the hundreds of choices employees make every day.

Rather, a focus on the values that should guide decision making can help employees make the best decisions in a wide variety of situations.

Many organizations deal with a longer code by dividing it into parts. The first part provides the broad guiding principles. These are followed by a more detailed section that includes more specific application to cases, answers to commonly asked questions, and reference to more detailed policy manuals. Some organizations create separate booklets, as supplements to a more general code, for workers in particular functions such as purchasing or human resources management. These booklets can provide details and answers to the questions likely to arise in that particular type of job, and the individuals in that job are more likely to read those details.

Code content may vary depending on the industry and the degree to which the firm has entered the global marketplace. Specific issues are addressed depending on the industry. Firms in the defense industry carefully outline the guidelines for charging one's time to particular government projects. If the firm is global, the code almost certainly deals with issues such as bribery. We'll talk more about this in the next chapter.

If the code is to be taken seriously, it should be updated regularly and redistributed throughout the organization, and many companies circulate such a code every year or two. Also, many organizations ask employees to sign a statement acknowledging that they have read the company code and abided by it during the previous year. The real test is whether it is regularly used. For example, in decision-making meetings, if managers regularly refer to the code's guidelines, employees will learn that the code is vital to how important decisions are made.

ETHICS AND THE SUPPLY CHAIN   More and more companies are realizing that the ethics programs of their vendors have a significant impact on their own operations. If a significant vendor suffers an operational loss resulting from an ethical misstep, it could harm the customer company's ability to produce and/or distribute their product. As a result, numerous companies are now routinely expressing interest in the robustness of the ethics program(s) of their vendors. Some industry groups, such as Defense Industry Initiative on Business Ethics and Conduct (DII), are developing subcontractor codes of conduct that can be sent down through the supply chain in order to ensure a level of uniformity in their ethics expectations. In fact, in government contracting, such a posture has become law. For example, Federal Acquisition Regulation (FAR) clause 52.203-13 requires that firms entering into a contract with the U.S. Government for more than $5 million and with a performance period of more than 120 days must have a robust ethics program that is designed to "promote an organizational culture that encourages ethical conduct and a commitment to compliance with the law." Further, this FAR clause must flow down to subcontractors who meet those criteria and will be participating in the performance of the prime contract.

On this front, Lockheed Martin has developed an ethics mentoring program to more directly and personally assist the growth and development of subcontractor ethics programs. Under this program, experienced Lockheed Martin ethics officers are paired with key vendors to work with them on their ethics programs. In this relationship, both sides learn as the Lockheed Martin ethics officer and the vendor's counterpart spend time working through the key elements of a robust ethics program. The early returns from this program are strongly positive, with the vendors expressing appreciation for being able to tap into the expertise housed in a mature ethics program such as Lockheed Martin's.

Communicating Senior Management Commitment to Ethics

In *Corporate Culture and Performance*, Kotter and Heskett[19] pointed to one factor that could turn around a company that was heading in the wrong direction—a strong leader who can communicate the culture. They explained how the top managers of great companies lead.

> Visions and strategies were communicated with words—spoken simply, directly, and often—and with deeds . . . they encouraged people to engage in a dialogue with them, not allowing the communication to flow in one direction only. In almost all cases, the leaders became living embodiments of the cultures they desired. The values and practices they wanted infused into their firms were on display in their daily behavior; in the questions they asked at meetings, in how they spent their time, in the decisions they made. These actions gave credibility to their words. The behavior made it clear to others that their speeches were serious. And successes, which seemed to result from that behavior, made it clear that the practices were sensible.

Without the buy-in and active support of senior management, ethics initiatives are doomed. But senior managers don't have a great track record in communicating a vision, ethical or otherwise. In a survey of professional and management employees, respondents revealed a lack of trust in their senior executives.[20] Most said that their company's leaders failed to communicate a "clear understanding of a corporate vision, mission, and goals." They also said that they trust their top management only about 55 percent of the time.[21] A more recent survey of employees indicates that trust levels have fallen precipitously and that only one in ten Americans believe that the leaders of their company are ethical and honest. The survey also indicates that only one in ten Americans trust that their company's leaders will make the right decision in times of uncertainty. The percentage of employees trusting leaders rises to 16% among younger employees (18–24 years old) who entered the workforce recently and did not experience many of the scandals associated with the financial crisis of 2008–2009.[22]

Nevertheless, most employees want to hear from senior executives. Another study of 14,250 employees in 17 companies in the United States and Canada found that "62 percent of employees list top executives as their preferred source of information, but only 15 percent say they actually get their company news from this source."[23]

What can senior managers do to establish better communication and more trust with employees? How can they begin to build an organization in which ethics are valued?

They can take a look at the advice that Peters and Waterman offered in their classic book, *In Search of Excellence*.[24] "An effective leader must be the master of two ends of the spectrum: ideas at the highest level of abstraction and actions at the most mundane level of detail. The value-shaping leader is concerned, on the one hand, with soaring, lofty visions that will generate excitement and enthusiasm. . . . On the other hand, it seems the only way to instill enthusiasm is through scores of daily events." With this advice in mind, here are some concrete steps senior managers can take:

- Set high standards and communicate them loudly and repeatedly in public and in private. Be known for the consistency of your standards. Never let your standards be a mystery.

- Act swiftly and firmly when someone violates the standards. Be consistent— don't have special rules for special people.

- Insist on complete candor from your direct reports. Tell them that you don't want to be protected from bad news.

- Never, never shoot the messenger of "bad news," or it will be the last one who reports problems to you. And if you don't know about problems, you can't fix them.

- Talk to a wide variety of employees on different levels and in different locations. Get out there and find out what's really going on. Don't be satisfied with others' interpretations.

- In a crisis, take responsibility, be accessible, and be honest. Take the high road. If you do, the company will probably pull through the crisis with a minimum of damage. This is one reason why Johnson & Johnson received such high marks for its handling of the Tylenol crisis and why Exxon received bad marks for its handling of the *Valdez* oil spill (CEO Lawrence Rawls didn't visit Alaska until three weeks after the incident). You'll read more about these two crises in Chapter 10.

- Finally, put your money where your mouth is—fund and support ethics initiatives. Without supporting systems, most corporate value statements are collections of empty platitudes that only increase organizational cynicism.[25] To develop ethics initiatives, get help from your communications and training professionals. Don't leave your ethics strategy just to the lawyers.

At many firms, the code of conduct is introduced with a message from the senior executive. At UTC, Louis Chênevert, president and chief executive officer, introduces the company code with the following message:

> Dear UTC Colleague: The UTC Code of Ethics does not merely require compliance with laws. It embodies a commitment to positive behaviors that build *trust*, promote *respect*, and demonstrate *integrity* . . . Working together, we can assure that ethics are at the foundation of our performance culture.

The message goes on to introduce the code and the business practices/compliance infrastructure.

At Lockheed Martin, the corporation has instituted the annual NOVA Award for Ethics. This award—part of Lockheed Martin's prestigious NOVA award series—recognizes a single employee or a group of Lockheed Martin employees for extraordinary actions or behavior that exemplify the corporation's commitment to ethical business conduct and integrity. The award is presented at a gala awards ceremony along with other NOVA Awards. Nominations come from the corporation's leaders, who are encouraged to designate someone from their organization each year. The first winner in 2002 was Ron Covais, a vice president in business development. He was recognized for demonstrating the highest standards for integrity and ethical business conduct during the bidding phase of a significant new business opportunity with a foreign customer. Covais demonstrated the corporation's values and set the standards with an international customer and the U.S. government by his willingness to walk away from an important contract. Covais had received an inappropriate "request for payment" by a foreign official. Lockheed Martin employees are expected to reject such bribes, and Covais did. By itself, rejecting the bribe was considered routine and would not have merited the award. But Covais halted the bidding process (placing at risk an important contract), reported the problem to senior officials, and worked with both U.S. government officials and the foreign government to have the foreign official removed from the decision-making process. The customer subsequently agreed to conduct a new bidding process on ethical terms. Covais's action and his award were publicized, color photos and all, in *Lockheed Martin Today*, the company newspaper that went to every employee. The other nominees, one from each business area and from corporate organizations, were also named in the story. And every top corporate executive witnessed the chairman giving the award. The tradition of honoring commitment to the highest level of integrity has continued since that time.

Think about the impact of such an event on the ethical culture. Every senior leader must expend effort each year to find employees who demonstrate exemplary ethical conduct. The award ceremony itself is exactly the kind of "ritual" that helps create an ethical culture. As the stories become part of the organization's cultural lore, its impact grows as the stories accumulate over time. This impact is particularly important to a company like Lockheed Martin, which has scandal in its past. Misconduct by one of Lockheed Martin's predecessor companies contributed to the passage of the anti-bribery Foreign Corrupt Practices Act (discussed in Chapter 11). It has become very important to the senior leadership of the firm to counteract any perception that the organization is unethical.

ETHICS TRAINING PROGRAMS Values statements, policy manuals, and conduct codes aren't enough. Organizations that are serious about ethics distribute these materials widely and then provide training in their meaning and application. Effective training programs are ongoing efforts to teach everyone from new recruits to high-level managers. In Chapter 1 we discussed whether ethics can be taught; we hope that by now, you're quite convinced that it can. Ethics in organizations is about awareness of ethical issues and knowledge of appropriate conduct, and these ideas can and must be taught to employees at all levels.

Training should be designed to suit the group of individuals being trained. A new employee needs different training than a manager who has been with the firm for 10 years. An assembly-line worker might require only an hour of training, with regular refresher sessions, whereas a manager might require several days of training that address a variety of issues. Furthermore, training needs to be based on program goals. Is the training supposed to increase awareness of ethical issues, convey knowledge of laws and policies, change attitudes or behaviors? Finally, ethics training need not—and probably should not—be solely the province of the ethics office. Ethics training should be incorporated into leadership development and other programs so that it becomes integrated more fully into the culture of the organization.

TRAINING NEW RECRUITS   Many firms provide ethics training through new employee orientation. For example, to set the stage properly, every new Lockheed Martin employee gets a briefing on ethical and legal issues as part of the first day on the job. This training is complemented throughout each year of employment, with the intent of setting the stage properly from the first day.

TRAINING EXISTING EMPLOYEES   Training is also provided to existing employees and takes a variety of forms. Some companies provide a basic ethics training module to all employees. For example, at Lockheed Martin, every employee participates in annual ethics awareness training. This training focuses on the firm's ethics, diversity, and leadership values and how employees can and should apply these values to their work. Each year, the ethics office staff is challenged to make the training different and memorable—something that employees will discuss with each other after leaving the training session.

The 2013 training, entitled "Voicing Our Values 2013," focuses on the corporation's values, commitment to diversity, and leadership imperatives. This is the third year of the "voicing values" theme, which was developed in collaboration with Dr. Mary Gentile of Babson College, and is described in her book, *Giving Voice to Values: How to Speak Your Mind When You Know What's Right* (we described Dr. Gentile's work in Chapter 4.) The session begins with an introductory video in which the president and chief executive officer emphasize the Lockheed Martin vision and how ethics and business conduct are integral to the company's success. The training is video-based and contains nine case scenarios, each one highlighting different ethical dilemmas including records falsification, time-card fraud, and intercompany relationships. Not all of the scenarios have clear-cut answers, because the intent is to stimulate conversation during and after the session.

Each training session contains from 5 to 25 people and is led by the group's manager or an ethics officer. The annual training kicks off in early May when the Board of Directors receives their training, and then president and chief executive officer Marillyn A. Hewson trains her staff. Each member of the executive staff then trains her or his employees, and the process continues until October, by which time all

118,000 employees will have been trained. This annual ethics awareness training has become integral to the Lockheed Martin culture. People expect it and look forward to what the ethics staff will create each year. One limitation of this training is that, depending on the length of the dialogue regarding the cases, teams can get through only three or four of the case scenarios in a single training session.

To complement its annual ethics awareness training, Lockheed Martin launched an initiative called "The Integrity Minute," a series of short (about one-minute) video messages sent to employees via e-mail. Each series contains three or four episodes on a central ethics theme. The episodes, which are sent in consecutive weeks, contain a cliff-hanger to maintain employee interest in the series.

Other engagement initiatives that Lockheed Martin has used include the Ethics Arts and Film Festival and the "Ethics Be a Star" contest. The Ethics Arts and Film Festival invites employees to participate in a celebration of the creative arts to promote ethics, diversity, and good leadership. The entries come from across all business areas, both domestically and internationally. Participants use a variety of creative media to produce posters, videos, photographs, poems, and other works of art with a focus on ethics, diversity, and leadership. Employees use their own resources, on their own time and away from the office, to prepare their submissions. Most of the submissions are team entries that provide work groups with a team-building opportunity. An independent panel of judges selects the top entries, and the winners are invited to a recognition event. The 'Ethics Be A Star' contest invited employees to submit 'audition tapes' to the Ethics Office. The winners of the contest were filmed and featured in Integrity Minute episodes. Such activities are designed to engage employees with the ethics processes and the Ethics Office at Lockheed Martin.

TOP MANAGEMENT INVOLVEMENT IN TRAINING   When organizations conduct ethics training for the first time, many of them begin the training at the top of the organization. *Cascading* is a term frequently used to describe ethics initiatives that begin at the top of the organization and work their way down, level by level. This technique is often used because of the importance of leadership to the credibility of ethics training. Each leader trains his or her direct reports, modeling the expected training behavior and the necessary commitment to integrity.

LOCAL MANAGEMENT INVOLVEMENT IN TRAINING   Many organizations recommend having local management conduct the ethics training, using common everyday ethical dilemmas as the basis for discussion. Training sessions are thought to be more useful and effective if they address real ethical issues that people face every day in their own work setting. Examples of calls that have come in to the ethics office can be used as the basis for training. Employees make ethical decisions every day. Anybody who reports the time that they work—or decides how to divide their time across different government contracts, or decides whether they are going to engage in some kind of an outside business activity that might be in conflict with their job, or has to decide what to tell a customer about a delayed order—is making an ethical decision. Using common everyday issues in training gives employees a feeling of comfort that the issue they've faced has been a problem for others and that they're not some screwball who is worrying about something that doesn't matter.

A TRAINING MODEL: THE ETHICS GAME   A powerful method of communicating a corporate ethics message is through an ethics game. Katherine Nelson, coauthor of this book, created the first corporate ethics game, "The Work Ethic: An Exercise in Integrity," when she was head of human resources communication at Citicorp in the late 1980s.

The game worked like this: A group of employees were divided into teams, and a facilitator then positioned the exercise with the following messages:

"We're playing a game about ethics because we want to make sure we get your attention. Integrity is critical here."

"This is an opportunity for you to practice making ethical decisions in a risk-free environment."

"We're doing this to give you an overview of corporate policy and how things are done here. We're also going to outline all of the resources available to you if you think you'd like some help or advice if you're faced with an ethical dilemma."

A facilitator presented the teams with a series of ethical dilemmas related to such topics as sexual harassment, reporting ethical concerns, responsibilities of customers, the need for confidentiality, and conflicts of interest. The ethical dilemmas were written so that there was no clearly right answer.

For each issue, the teams took a few minutes to discuss what they considered to be appropriate action. Then, based on a consensus among team members, they chose one of four possible courses of action. Once the teams decided, the facilitator played devil's advocate and questioned the entire group about why they voted the way they did. The discussions could get very heated, as participants and teams loudly defended their positions. The facilitator then revealed the scores for each course of action (scores are predetermined, preferably by the management of the organization where the game is being played). If the participants disagreed with the scores, they could take them to an appeals board of senior managers. Again, the discussions could get quite impassioned and lively, and the competition for the best scores kept interest high.

The senior management appeals board was one of the most important aspects of the ethics game. The very presence of senior managers for 90 minutes or so sent a strong message that integrity and ethics must be important in this company, or all these executives wouldn't be spending so much time talking about it. In addition, when discussing an appeal, the appeals board often communicated the ethics message about company standards and expectations more powerfully than any other element of the ethics program. Along the way, employees could see how senior managers worked through an ethical dilemma and what factors they considered important in making decisions.

Groups could disagree with the scoring of a question and appeal to the senior managers, who had the power to change scores if they heard a good argument for doing so.

This process somehow "stamped" participating managers as approachable. Managers who participated in appeals boards frequently reported a marked increase in the number of employees seeking them out and asking for advice. One manager described how he had been stopped in hallways, restrooms, cafeterias, and even on the street to be asked advice by employees who had seen him as a judge on an ethics game appeals board. Most companies would do just about anything to have their employees seek advice from managers on ethical issues.

Senior managers also learned a lot by participating in the game, which gave employees an opportunity to raise issues directly to management. In one session, several male managers were made aware of how offensive young female trainees found any kind of sexual stereotyping. The young women were so determined to let management know how strongly they felt on this issue that the women continued the discussion face-to-face with the executives at a reception after the game had officially ended.

Since the game usually raised more questions than it answered, it was crucial to debrief the group. At the end of the game, the facilitator gave advice on how to solve ethical dilemmas and outlined the resources available to help employees if they found themselves in need of advice.

The ethics game met many communication and training goals, but it was especially effective in raising awareness, creating a dialogue, and describing expected dilemmas and how employees might handle them. However, for an ethics program to be effective over the long term, training and communications should continue over time. A game is an excellent beginning and can be used repeatedly with different dilemmas. However, it can't exist in a vacuum or be all things to all people. It needs to be part of an integrated ethics program with other media and complementary messages.

Although some may view an ethics game as heresy, those who have seen this type of training program in action are quickly convinced of its effectiveness. Other companies have developed their own versions of the game and have used them successfully. For example, years ago, Lockheed Martin developed an ethics game modeled after the Citicorp game, but with a twist. At the time, the company received permission from Scott Adams, author of the *Dilbert* cartoons (popular with employees), to use the Dilbert character in their game. Then Chairman of the Board Norm Augustine appeared with Dilbert in an introductory video, and the game included a humorous "Dogbert answer" to each ethical question. With the introduction several years ago of online ethics training, the Citicorp format featuring a series of scenarios with scored answers has become increasingly popular with a wide range of companies.

Formal and Informal Systems to Resolve Questions and Report Ethical Concerns

An organization with a strong ethical culture is one where employees feel free to speak openly about ethical issues, question authority figures, and report concerns, and where managers are approachable and listen to their people. This may be the most important thing an organization can do to open up the communication lines and set up an environment of candor: make sure people feel they can discuss their opinions, their ideas, and their thoughts openly. Most important, set up an environment where people feel they can sincerely bring up and resolve problems without being embarrassed or fearing retribution. The first time you shoot the messenger who brings you bad news, you've taken the first step toward squelching ethics in the organization. News of the "dead messenger" will spread like wildfire on your organization's grapevine.

Although most organizations encourage employees to bring their concerns to their immediate supervisor first, employees sometimes want to ask a question anonymously, or they may have a concern about their supervisor's behavior. Also, the U.S. Sentencing Guidelines require that organizations "take reasonable steps to achieve compliance with written standards through monitoring, auditing, and other systems designed to detect criminal conduct, including a reporting system free of retribution to employees who report criminal conduct." As a result, many firms have established a more formal system for raising concerns. This generally takes the form of a telephone line employees can call to ask for help in resolving an ethical dilemma or to report an ethical problem or behavior they've observed in the organization. A number of names have emerged for these reporting systems—"Communication Lines," "Guideline," "Open Line," "Helpline," "Hotline," and "Ethics Action Line." These phone lines generally ring in the ethics office, if there is one.

For example, at Lockheed Martin, the Corporate Ethics helpline is available during regular working hours, and employees can leave a voice message 24 hours a day. In addition to the helpline, Lockheed Martin provides an e-mail option, a web-based "Ask-Us" channel, a fax number, and a postal address that employees may use to submit ethical concerns. Each business unit advertises the local ethics program on posters that include a prominent photo of the site ethics officer and the phone number for the ethics helpline. Some large organizations provide separate reporting lines for each business unit. In a few firms, the line actually rings on the chairman's desk. Other firms have hired an outside consulting firm or law firm to take the calls at a toll-free number and then transfer the information to the company.[26] That system is especially prevalent in many global firms, where a call can come at any time of the day or night because of time zone differences.

We believe that, where possible, it's best for ethics office staff to talk with callers directly. As ethics office staff, they need to be in touch with what's going on in the organization. If they delegate the task, they lose the tone and perspective of the callers. For example, the nonverbal clues that come through on the phone can easily get lost in a paper report. One way to handle this is to answer calls during business hours and then contract with an outside firm for after-hours capability. Around-the-clock answering capability is essential for a global business. The ethics office can explain the decision to hire an outside contractor to employees as its solution to handling calls from around the globe.

Organizations that have experience with telephone reporting lines find that most of the calls represent requests for clarification. The individual says, "Here's what I want to do. Is it okay? Does it follow procedure?" Most of the calls in many organizations represent HR-related issues, such as fairness concerns. Some are relatively routine. But occasionally calls come in that represent serious breaches of the code of conduct or even illegal conduct. Managing these lines is no small feat. It's not unusual for a company hotline to receive thousands of calls per year. One ethics officer reported that 90 percent of the calls to his company's hotline were to report HR-related issues. "But many of the other 10 percent were issues of great interest to us, and it's well worth dealing with all of the HR issues to get to the others," he said. This situation points to how necessary it is for ethics officers and ethics departments to have a good working relationship with HR. If employees trust their HR department, ethics messaging can help manage employees' HR concerns and direct them to HR. Of course, that only works if employees view HR as being trustworthy.

One concern often raised about these reporting lines is that individuals will make invalid reports—"tattling" on people they don't like. But that's not the experience of the ethics officers we interviewed. Most people call about valid issues. Although their motives may not always be noble, the content is usually correct. Most of the people who use the communication line are using it because they sincerely have a question or concern about something they think is wrong. It's one reason that confidentiality is so important within the entire reporting and investigative system. The identity of both the reporter and the alleged violator must be protected throughout the process. The alleged violator must be protected because allegations can result from simple misunderstandings. The reporter must be protected from any retaliation from the accused.

Another relevant question concerns how to interpret the meaning of the number of calls and letters. Obviously, if an organization institutes and promotes an easy way to ask questions, express concerns, and report violations, the number of calls should increase dramatically. Does this mean that there are more ethical problems? Probably not. The executives who run these programs generally interpret such increases as evidence that their programs are working. However, in an ideal world, the ethics office should aim to put itself out of business. In other words, ethical conduct should become so institutionalized that there would be no reason for people to call. They would handle issues locally, with their managers. Like the old ad about a Maytag repairman, the ethics officer would have a very boring job. On the other hand, a quiet telephone may also signal a number of other positive or negative conditions:

- Lack of concern or recognition of ethical problems (negative)
- An intimidating environment where people fear retribution (negative)
- Good problem solving at the local level (positive)
- No one knowing the ethics office exists (negative)

Ultimately, it's up to the ethics office to devise ways to determine what the numbers and changes in the numbers mean.

Most ethics officers prefer to see a relatively low and stable level of allegations of misconduct and a higher level of advisory questions. That means that people are calling for advice—which is a good thing. The question remaining is whether employees are aware of and willing to use the resources that are made available to them.

Confidentiality and the protection of reporters remain important issues. Some firms use outside individuals, often called ombudspersons, who may answer the reporting line, provide information, investigate complaints, serve in an alternative dispute resolution role, and report problems to a corporate compliance or audit committee while maintaining the confidentiality of the reporter.[27]

Whether a telephone line, an ombudsperson, or some other formal procedure is most appropriate for a particular corporate culture, the important thing is to have some way for employees to raise issues without fear of retribution. If there's no way for employees to raise issues without such fear, the first time an executive hears about a problem may be from a district attorney, a regulator, or a newspaper reporter.

Finally, each of the firms we talked with has a system for investigating reports of misconduct. These are multistage processes that can be quite complex, depending on the seriousness of the allegation. Obviously, facts must be gathered to determine whether the allegation can be verified. Confidentiality must be maintained throughout these investigations, and they must be coordinated with other parts of the organization such as the legal, audit, security, or human resources department, depending on the problem. Then, based on a thorough analysis of the findings, recommendations must be made and actions taken to discipline employees and/or correct systemic problems in the organization.

USING THE REWARD SYSTEM TO REINFORCE THE ETHICS MESSAGE

Recall from Chapter 5 that the reward system is vital to alignment in an ethical culture. At Lockheed Martin, the performance management process, called LMCommit, rates employees not just on results of the job such as increased sales or profits. Employees are also rated on *how you got there* through attributes that include ethics, excellence, integrity, and people and teamwork. Leaders, in particular, are evaluated against the company's model of leadership called Full Spectrum Leadership. The Full Spectrum Leadership model consists of five tenets: Shape the Future, Build Effective Relationships, Energize the Team, Deliver Results, and Model Personal Excellence, Integrity & Accountability. Along with operating and financial results, every leader is evaluated against this model to ensure that he or she is demonstrating the values that the company embraces. For example, under the category Model Personal Excellence, Integrity & Accountability, LMCommit looks for a leader to "demonstrate a commitment to personal excellence, ethical behavior, and integrity," to "exhibit managerial courage to overcome obstacles," and, of course, to "lead with integrity." Specific examples of these behaviors are required, and all compensation decisions are directly tied to every employee's and leader's LMCommit results.

In some organizations, as much as half of every employee's performance appraisal is devoted to *how* an employee did his or her job. Measuring the *how* and not just the *what* (results achieved) is an excellent and proven way to drive desired behavior and discourage unethical behavior.

At Otis Elevator Company (a subsidiary of United Technologies Corporation), Stephen Page, then president and now retired as UTC's vice chairman, wrote a letter to employees making it clear that Otis seriously disciplines breaches of integrity. In his words:

> Our company is making substantial changes in the way we do business. I am writing today to highlight what has not changed, and never will change: our commitment to the highest ethical standards and business practices.
>
> We know that Otis employees are honest, mature, independent, and scrupulous in their conduct at work. We know that Otis employees care about ethics and our company's reputation. And we know that employees support sanctions for any colleague whose behavior shows he or she does not hold these fundamental Otis values.
>
> Our ethics program grows out of this knowledge. We provide training and communications programs to all employees in our Code of Ethics, which offers guidance in how to behave in specific business situations. Through our worldwide network of business practices officers (BPOs), we also provide expert advice to employees who have questions or who face ethical dilemmas.
>
> But for those few who do not care about ethics; who think they can cut corners; who violate the law, our policies or our standards, there is no place in Otis. To our regret, we have had to terminate the employment of nearly a dozen colleagues this year alone for violations of our Code of Ethics—a record that is simply unacceptable. Unlawful or unethical conduct can only harm our company and we will take whatever actions are necessary to prevent that from happening.
>
> Our actions reflect our fundamental belief: Otis would rather lose business than compromise our standards of conduct.
>
> Please take this opportunity to refresh your knowledge of our Code of Ethics, and to recommit yourself to its guidelines and principles. We have so much to be proud of at Otis, and our reputation as an ethical company stands in the first rank of our accomplishments. We are determined to protect this priceless asset. Thank you for your continued support.

This letter confirms the company's willingness to take firm action to uphold standards through discipline when necessary, and it was likely welcomed by the company's many ethical employees (see Chapters 7 and 8 for information about the appropriate use of discipline).

EVALUATING THE ETHICS PROGRAM

Many organizations have committed significant resources to their ethics efforts— hiring high-level executives, developing values statements and codes, designing and implementing training programs, and more. But few organizations have systematically evaluated these efforts, because doing so presents many challenges. For example, as suggested earlier, more calls to the telephone line can mean different things and can be interpreted in a variety of ways. And asking employees at an ethics training program whether they "liked" it or not doesn't tell you much about the quality of the ethics program. Many employees will respond affirmatively just because they liked the idea of a few hours or a day away from the office. Whether or not they liked it should be secondary. The most important question should be whether the program is accomplishing its goals.

Otis has gone the extra mile in the area of evaluation. It has over a million elevators in operation in more than 200 countries around the world! You may not have thought much about it, but all of us depend on the integrity of a company that provides many of the elevators we ride daily. As part of a toolkit provided to each of its companies, Otis requires a self-assessment process that involves regular evaluations of program effectiveness including training, communication, work practices reviews, instances of misconduct, corrective actions, reports, and records. Companies are also asked to identify the strengths and weaknesses of their programs and to implement changes to overcome weaknesses. Finally, they are asked to share their successes, program strengths, and lessons learned with the rest of Otis.

Organizations that are members of the Defense Industry Initiative (DII) are often at the forefront on evaluation because the DII asks each of its member organizations each year to certify that the firm is complying with the six DII principles. These self-certifications are available to all members, and a report is published and sent to the U.S. Congress annually.

Surveys

Surveys are probably the most common approach to evaluation. Many organizations already conduct regular employee attitude surveys; some have added ethics to the list of survey topics, and some conduct separate ethics surveys. Surveys can target knowledge, attitudes, skills, and behaviors. For example, if ethics training has been recently required of all employees, surveys can evaluate the extent to which employees understand the company's expectations and standards. Baseline data can be collected before ethics training is begun, and then again several months after it's completed, to analyze whether positive change has occurred. Surveys can help evaluate employees' skill at recognizing and resolving ethical issues, and they can measure the extent to which employees observe unethical conduct in the organization. Finally, attitudes toward ethics management programs and processes can be evaluated. It's important to survey regularly so that changes and progress can be evaluated. A final suggestion about surveys—don't ask questions if you're not willing to accept the answer. Employees will expect action based on survey results. If you've asked them to take the time to complete a survey, you should communicate the results and planned action.

The most famous ethics-related survey is likely Johnson & Johnson's Credo survey. Then Chairman James Burke had been on the board of IBM Corporation in the 1980s and became impressed with IBM's employee survey program. He decided that one way to keep the Johnson & Johnson Credo alive would be to survey employees about how the company was doing relative to the Credo. The survey went through a number of iterations after being tested on employees at a variety of locations. The first survey was conducted in the United States in 1986–87. The first international survey was conducted the following year. The first part of the survey contains 118 items and takes about 25 minutes to complete. It asks employees to rate things such as the company's "customer orientation" on five-point scales. The second section is open-ended for written comments. One of the findings has been the impact of top leadership and corporate culture on the survey's results. For example, former Chairman Burke had emphasized the customer above all. President David Clare emphasized safety first. In an analysis of the survey results, ratings on these two survey dimensions were highest. Most of all, the survey is viewed as a way to keep the Credo alive, a way of "closing the loop on this thing called the Credo."[28]

Lockheed Martin conducts a complete employee survey every two years, so that the firm can gauge whether ethical principles are being applied and whether employees have observed wrongdoing—and, if so, whether they have reported it. The major surveys are augmented with interim "pulse" surveys and have been combined with the company's employee perspectives and diversity survey. The survey allows the firm to assess its culture, determine the impact of ethics programs, and point out areas in need of attention. All 118,000 employees are asked to participate in the voluntary survey, for which the participation rate has increased over the years. Results of the survey are shared with employees, and are used to gauge the health of departments down to the first-line managers.

In 2007, Lockheed Martin's ethics and employee perspectives surveys were combined for the first time, and results were benchmarked with data from the DII and the Mayflower Group, a consortium of blue-chip companies. More than 80 percent of the Mayflower Group's member companies are included in the *Fortune* magazine list of the most admired companies in America. The ethics survey measurements include pressure to compromise standards, observed/reported misconduct, and commitment to ethics. Most survey results were positive and consistent with favorable results from the 2005 survey. For example, a high percentage of employees reported that they know what constitutes ethical business conduct, how to obtain guidance on ethical issues, and how to report misconduct.

The 2012 results demonstrated that Lockheed Martin continued to progress on key metrics. For example, over the years Lockheed Martin has seen a steady decline in the percentage of people who believe they observed misconduct and in the perceived pressure to commit misconduct. In general, employees indicated that management will act on reports, and managers are held accountable for their conduct. Where areas of concern were noted, action plans were developed by the business unit leadership; where particular business units showed strong positive results, they were studied for best practices that contributed to the results.

VALUES OR COMPLIANCE APPROACHES

Formal corporate ethics initiatives can be categorized as emphasizing either a values or a compliance approach to managing ethics. The values approach is proactive and aspirational. It emphasizes expected behavior and an effort to achieve high standards represented by the spirit of the law and organizational values. It relies on such techniques as leader communication and role modeling to affirm the organization's commitment to its stated ethical values and goals. Employees learn that these are not empty words, but words that organizational leaders believe and live by. Ethics becomes a point of pride in the organization: "We're so good we don't have to cheat!" The response to a values-oriented program is generally good until violations occur. Then, employees expect that commitment to be backed up with sanctions against the violators.

With a compliance emphasis, the focus is more on required behavior—obeying the letter of the law rather than aspiring to lofty ethical principles. Disciplinary procedures for violators are also important to compliance efforts. Many organizations that are motivated by the U.S. Sentencing Guidelines and Sarbanes-Oxley legislation mandate a compliance approach. Employees are told that compliance with the law is essential and that employees who break the law will be punished. The danger with a compliance-only focus is the possibility that employees will believe anything goes as long as there isn't a rule against it, or that the company is interested only in protecting itself, not in helping them.

An effective program should have both values and compliance components. By themselves, abstract values statements can appear hypocritical to employees. "Management makes these lofty statements, but they don't tell us what we should do." Values must be translated into rules for behavior; and to give the rules meaning, violators must be disciplined. Employees welcome information that reduces ambiguity about what they can and can't do. And if enforcement is applied consistently across all organizational levels, they are likely to perceive the system as fair and just.

On the other hand, employees often view a strictly compliance-oriented program with cynicism. Without a strong values base, compliance programs seem to focus on catching employees doing something wrong rather than on aspiring to do things right. Employees translate this emphasis into mistrust and a "protect yourself" approach. Either "the organization doesn't trust its employees," or "the organization is just out to protect its own behind." The best programs aim to focus on aspiring to a set of values first and foremost, supported by just and fair enforcement of the rules.

At Merck, development of a formal ethics program was driven by its long-standing values-based culture. Interestingly, Merck did not have a formal ethics code until 1999. In rolling out the code initiative, the firm was careful to position it as simply a continuation of the good things the company was already doing. It also worked hard to get participation and buy-in through focus groups and surveys. This is typical of values-based programs, where employee buy-in and support are essential.

GLOBALIZING AN ETHICS PROGRAM

In Chapter 11, we'll talk about business ethics in a global environment. What sets UTC apart is the truly global extent of its ethics and compliance efforts. Recall that UTC has over 220,000 employees, more than half outside the United States, and a presence in more than 180 countries. Imagine how difficult it must be to design systems and programs to effectively reach such a wide audience across multiple cultures. UTC's program rests on three coordinated efforts: management engagement, the Ombudsman/DIALOG program, and a worldwide Business Practices Organization.

Management engagement is the keystone, because no "program" succeeds without direct management support. At UTC, managers are evaluated on an "ethics competency" that is based on behaviors identified by the research of the Ethics Resource Center as well as on a complementary set of ethics and compliance objectives. The ethics and compliance objectives are developed annually and cascaded through management from the CEO and require ongoing communications to employees, customers, and UTC's business partners; training of employees and key business partners; continuous implementation, evaluation, and improvements in compliance risk management systems; and efforts to improve the ethics scores on the biennial employee survey. UTC policy states specifically that the business leaders are responsible for fostering a culture of ethical conduct, encouraging open communications, and instilling a commitment to the Code of Ethics. Both the competency and the objectives are evaluated through the company's "Performance Feedback Tool," which was developed by the human resources department.

The Ombudsman/DIALOG program at UTC is an alternative communications channel for raising issues to management. Created in 1986, it fields questions or concerns on essentially any subject. Ombudsman/DIALOG is a confidential channel that does not reveal the user's identity; it serves as a neutral intermediary between employees and management by advocating only for clear communication, it works independently of management, and it performs under the standards of the International Ombudsman Association. Inquiries come via phone contacts through toll-free calling, or via written contacts, through either postage-paid mailers or an encrypted, web-based system. UTC has three ombudsmen who handle more complex issues, including those with legal implications. Less complex issues are managed by DIALOG coordinators who work directly under the supervision of the ombudsmen.

Users of Ombudsman/DIALOG can choose to remain completely anonymous to the organization, and the company goes to great lengths to keep this commitment. For example, an assistant to a senior business-unit executive called with concerns about expense report behavior. If investigated openly, the source of the information would have been identifiable. Instead, the company audited all expense reports of people at the same level, as a routine review. In that way, they protected the reporter's identity. They found the problem, fired the executive, and no one was the wiser. However, the ombudsmen do not conduct investigations. If the issue requires investigation or intervention, it is turned over to people in other areas (e.g., human resources, business practices, legal) for further action. Ultimately, the ombudsman or DIALOG coordinator reviews the answer from the company. If it doesn't completely and fairly address all of the issues raised by the employee, it goes back to management with the suggestion that it be fixed. Ombudsman/DIALOG receives more than 2,800 inquiries per year, from around the world, and makes translators readily available. Over the past five years, with respect to those Ombudsman/DIALOG inquiries requesting change, about half resulted in change. Moreover, in recent years, more than half of all Ombudsman/DIALOG inquiries came from outside the United States.

UTC's Business Practices Organization is led by Kevin J. O'Connor, UTC's Vice President, Global Compliance, a former United States Attorney and Associate Attorney General of the United States. O'Connor is one of the company's top executives. He reports to the senior vice president and general counsel as well as to the audit committee of the board of directors, with whom he meets at least four times per year. His staff consists of experienced ethics and compliance professionals (including a former federal prosecutor, FBI agent and head of the Connecticut State Police) at UTC's headquarters. His team also includes five international lawyers/ Directors of Business Practices who work alongside UTC's businesses overseas, including Russia, the Middle East, China, India, and Europe. Additionally, he supervises a network of almost 600 business practices officers (BPOs) who are embedded in UTC businesses around the globe. Overall, about 48 BPOs are full-time, five of those serving as the business practices leaders at UTC's major businesses.

O'Connor participates in selecting and appointing the BPOs as well as in evaluating their performance, and he can veto appointments. Most have at least several years of experience in the company and are familiar with internal controls and the company culture. They are considered high-potential people who generally come from staff functions such as finance or safety. Good communication skills are considered a must for business practices staff, along with the ability to take the ball and run with it when a problem arises. UTC has a BPO Handbook, an investigations handbook, standard work for case management, an online case management system, toolkits for communications and risk management, and an online knowledge management system. In addition, UTC has a standard curriculum for training BPOs, which includes written materials, online modules, WebEx meetings, and regional conferences. BPOs generally serve for about two or three years, a turnover rate that is considered to be both a boon and a bane. It's a boon because these individuals bring fresh ideas and energy to the function, and they take their business practices experience with them to their future roles, becoming continuing champions for the business practices organization. It's a bane because training new people is a constant challenge.

The business practices unit manages UTC's code of ethics (in place since 1990), a companion policy statement on doing business with the U.S. government, and the corporate policy manual. The code applies to UTC employees worldwide and includes sections that specifically address ethical issues relating to doing business abroad. But the code is not ethnocentric, so it allows for some adaptation to the cultural mores of different cultures. It is made clear, however, that this flexibility does not permit violations of U.S. or local laws, and the code states that UTC will not facilitate illegal conduct or fraud by others, regardless of local norms. In 2012, a total of 379 employees were discharged for violations of the code of ethics.

CONCLUSION

This chapter has offered specifics about how ethics is managed in large business organizations. Large businesses that are committed to ethics are likely to have formal ethics management systems such as an ethics office, ethics officer, explicit ethics training, a telephone counseling/reporting line, and a system for investigating and following up on reports of misconduct. However, the specifics of these systems vary with the context and culture of the firm. Some companies in highly regulated industries may focus more on legal compliance. Others that have a long-standing values-based culture will want to make sure that the ethics management system is designed with a heavy emphasis on values and aspirations. Research has found that the best of these formal ethics management programs have an overarching values-based approach that incorporates legal compliance within the framework of a broader set of company values. Smaller firms with a strong commitment to ethics are less likely to have separate formal ethics management structures and systems. Whether an organization is large or small, the keys to effective ethics management are commitment to ethics from the very top, the involvement of leaders and employees at every level, and the recognition that ethics management is an ongoing effort requiring continuous reinforcement and integration into the larger corporate culture.

DISCUSSION QUESTIONS

1. Think about the impact of the U.S. Sentencing Guidelines. Would organizations have tried to drive ethical behavior among employees without government encouragement?

2. After reading about how a number of large companies try to encourage ethical behavior, what stands out? What approach is most unique? Which one do you think is most effective? Which one would make the biggest impression on you if you were an employee?

3. Imagine that it's your responsibility to select an ethics officer for your organization. What qualities, background, and experience would you look for? Would you ever be interested in such a position? Why or why not?

4. What are the advantages of having an ethics office or officer report to a company's chief executive officer, the legal department, human resources, or audit? What are the disadvantages?

5. Think about an organization where you've worked. What kinds of ethical dilemmas are unique to that organization? To that industry? What might be the best way to prepare employees to deal with those dilemmas?

6. Think about all of the communication opportunities provided by social media. How could an organization use social media such as Facebook, Twitter, and the like to promote ethical behavior and communicate the organization's values? What are the advantages and dangers of those media? Think about Best Buy and

its ethics blog for employees. Would you read an ethics blog? If you saw an interesting case, would you comment? Why or why not?

7. Which of the following exist in an organization where you've worked: mission or values statement, policy manual, code of conduct, ethics training (who conducts it), a hotline? Were they consistent and credible?

8. Is senior management committed to ethics? How do you know? What could they do differently or better?

9. Are leaders at all levels held accountable for their ethical conduct? If so, how? If not, why not? What would you recommend?

10. What recommendations would you make for handling frivolous calls to the hotline?

11. Does the organization evaluate its ethics initiatives? How? If not, why not?

12. Would you characterize the ethics efforts in this organization as taking a values, compliance, or combination approach? Is it effective? How could it be improved?

13. How would you raise an ethical concern in this organization? List all of the resources available to you. Which ones would you be likely to use? Why or why not?

14. Imagine that you're the CEO of a small manufacturing company. An employee has dumped toxic waste in a nearby stream. Who would you call into your office, and what would you want to know? Develop a short-term and long-term action plan for dealing with the crisis. Who would you communicate with and why?

15. Evaluate the ethics program at your organization from the perspective of "fit." Has the ethics program been designed to fit the organization's overall culture? If so, how? If not, what could be done to make the program a better fit?

16. Think about your own positive, memorable, "peak experiences" when it comes to ethics. Be prepared to discuss them with others in your class and to think about the conditions that would make it possible for such experiences to happen more regularly at work. Or, if you don't have much work experience yourself, interview someone who has, and ask these questions. Be prepared to report on what you learned from the interview.

SHORT CASE

WHAT'S WRONG WITH THIS PICTURE?

You're a management consultant who has been asked by Green Company to help design an ethics communication and training program for all Green Company employees. Your meetings to date have been with the head of human resources, and your contract with the company has been negotiated with him. Once the papers have been signed, you begin your research and are quickly stymied by Green's corporate counsel. He says you will not be allowed to ask employees about ethical dilemmas that have occurred at Green. He specifically asks you to get your information from other sources such as press accounts of problems in the industry, or from other organizations you've worked with. In addition, the head of human resources has told you that you'll be unable to meet the three most senior executives because they're busy negotiating a large acquisition. You will have access to other high-level managers who can tell you what they think the seniors want. You're instructed to write a code of conduct for the company and a mission statement, and to prepare presentations for the senior managers to give to employees sometime next month on corporate expectations and values.

CASE QUESTIONS

1. Based on what you know about developing ethical cultures and programs, identify the problems presented by this case.

2. Why do you think the corporate counsel has responded in this way? What will be your response to him, if any?

3. As a consultant, what are your ethical obligations, if any?

4. How will you proceed?

APPENDIX

How Fines Are Determined under the U.S. Sentencing Guidelines

For more details, see www.ussc.gov.

Part 8C1.1 of the guidelines states that "If, upon consideration of the nature and circumstances of the offense and the history and characteristics of the organization, the court determines that the organization operated primarily for a criminal purpose or primarily by criminal means, the fine shall be set at an amount (subject to the statutory maximum) sufficient to divest the organization of all its net assets."

If that is not the case, penalties are based on a base fine and the "culpability score" assigned by the court. The base fine is the greatest of the following: the pretax gain from the crime, the amount of intentional loss inflicted on the victims, and an amount based on the Sentencing Commission's ranking of the seriousness of the crime (ranging from $5,000 to $72.5 million). This amount is then multiplied by a number that depends on the culpability score. The culpability score ranges from 0 to 10, and the multipliers range from 0.05 to 4.

Every defendant starts at a culpability score of 5 and can move up or down depending on aggravating or mitigating factors (see Table 6.A.1). The presence of aggravating factors can cause the culpability score to increase. These aggravating factors include (1) organizational size, combined with the degree of participation, tolerance, or disregard for the criminal conduct by high-level personnel or substantial authority personnel in the firm; (2) prior history of similar criminal conduct; and (3) role in obstructing or impeding an investigation.

The presence of mitigating factors, however, can cause the culpability score to drop. To decrease the culpability score, the organization must have in place an "effective program to prevent and detect violations of the law." If the court determines that the organization has such a program, 3 points can be removed from the base culpability score

Table 6.A.1 Method for Determining Minimum and Maximum Fines

Culpability Score	Minimum Multiplier	Maximum Multiplier
10 or more	2.00	4.00
9	1.80	3.60
8	1.60	3.20
7	1.40	2.80
6	1.20	2.40
5	1.00	2.00
4	0.80	1.60
3	0.60	1.20
2	0.40	0.80
1	0.20	0.40
0 or less	0.05	0.20

Factors That Can Increase or Decrease Culpability Scores

Aggravating Factors: Result in an increase to the base level of 5

- The size of the organization coupled with the degree of participation, tolerance, or disregard for the criminal conduct by "high level personnel" or "substantial authority personnel." In a firm with greater than 5,000 employees, this factor can result in an increase of as much as 5 points.

- Prior history: Organizations that have been either civilly or criminally adjudicated to have committed similar conduct within the past five years can have up to 2 points added.

- Obstructing, impeding, (or attempting to obstruct or impede) during the investigation, prosecution, or something can result in 3 points added.

Mitigating Factors: Result in decreases from the base level of 5

- Having an effective program to prevent and detect violations of the law can result in a downward departure of 3 points.

- Self-reporting, cooperating, and accepting responsibility for the criminal conduct can result in a downward departure of 5 points.

of 5. Besides having an effective compliance program in place, the culpability score can be substantially reduced if the organization reports the criminal conduct promptly after becoming aware of the offense and before government investigation. According to the guidelines, an organization that reports its own misconduct, cooperates with authorities, and accepts responsibility can have as many as 5 points subtracted from the base culpability level of 5.

The mitigating factors that reduce the culpability score have important implications for the way companies manage ethical conduct. For example, many believe that overseeing an "effective" program for preventing and detecting legal violations is a full-time job for at least one person. It would likely involve the development of a conduct code, training programs, scrutiny of performance management systems, the development of communication systems, detection systems, and so on. Many of these elements have been described in this chapter.

NOTES

1. G. Weaver, L. K. Treviño, and P. Cochran, "Corporate Ethics Programs as Control Systems: Managerial and Institutional Influences," Unpublished working paper, 1998.
2. S. A. Reiss, Speech given at the Conference Board meeting on business ethics, 1992.
3. *United States of America v. David D'Lorenzo*, 96-CV-1203, U.S. Dist. Ct., 1996.
4. J. A. Byrne, "Fall from Grace," *Businessweek*, August 12, 2002, 50–56.
5. J. M. Kaplan, "The Sentencing Guidelines: The First Ten Years," *Ethikos and Corporate Conduct Quarterly* 15, no. 3 (2001): 1–4.
6. U.S. Public Interest Research Group, "Rogues Gallery of Major Corporate Legal Settlements," April 17, 2012, uspirg.org
7. *Governance, Ethics, and the Sentencing Guidelines: A Call for Self-Governing Cultures* (Los Angeles: LRN, 2004).
8. Personal communication, Kent Druyvesteyn, 1994.
9. G. Weaver, L. K. Treviño, and P. Cochran, "Corporate Ethics Practices in the Mid-1990s: An Empirical Study of the *Fortune* 1000," *Journal of Business Ethics* 18, no. 3 (1999): 283–94.
10. Society for Corporate Compliance and Ethics, "Should Compliance Report to General Counsel?" March 2013, www.corporatecompliance.org
11. Ibid.
12. N. K. Austin, "The New Corporate Watchdogs," *Working Woman*, January 1994, 19–20.
13. D. G. Simmons, "The Nature of the Organizational Grapevine," *Supervisory Management*, November 1985, 39–42.
14. T. DeAngelis, "Honesty Tests Weigh in with Improved Ratings," *APA Monitor* 7 (1991); D. S. Ones, C. Ziswesvaran, and F. Schmidt, "Comprehensive Meta-analysis of Integrity Test Validities: Findings and Implications for Personal Selection and Theories of Job Performance," *Journal of Applied Psychology* 78 (1993): 679–703; P. R. Sackett, L. R. Burris, and C. Callahan, "Integrity Testing for Personal Selection: An Update," *Personal Psychology* 42 (1989): 491–529.
15. Ethics Resource Center, *Kathleen Edmond of Best Buy Receives ERC's Carol R. Marshall Award for Innovation in Corporate Ethics,* March 27, 2013, www.ethics.org
16. J. Davis, *Best Practice at Best Buy: A Pioneering Ethics Blog for Employees,* January 29, 2013, http://www.convercent.com/company-ethicist/best-practice-at-best-buy-a-pioneering-ethics-blog-for-employees/
17. K. Edmond, *Are Corporate Employees More Important Than Other Employees?"* February 14, 2013, www.kathleenedmund.com
18. R. Farzad, "Jail Terms for 2 at Top of Adelphia," *New York Times*, June 21, 2005, C1.
19. J. P. Kotter and J. L. Heskett, *Corporate Culture and Performance* (New York: Free Press, 1992).
20. A. L. Smith, *Innovative Employee Communication: A New Approach to Improving Trust, Teamwork and Performance* (Englewood Cliffs, NJ: Prentice-Hall, 1991).
21. Ibid.
22. Maritz Research, *2011 Employee Engagement Poll Executive Summary,* June 2011, http://www.maritzresearch.com/~/media/Files/MaritzDotCom/White%20Papers/ExcecutiveSummary_Research.pdf
23. A. L. Smith, *Innovative Employee Communication: A New Approach to Improving Trust, Teamwork and Performance* (Englewood Cliffs, NJ: Prentice-Hall, 1991).

24. T. J. Peters and R. H. Waterman Jr., *In Search of Excellence: Lessons from America's Best-Run Companies* (New York: Harper & Row, 1982).
25. M. Hammer and J. Champy, *Reengineering the Corporation: A Manifesto for Corporate Revolution* (New York: HarperCollins, 1993).
26. J. M. Powell, "Pinkerton Responds to the Federal Sentencing Guidelines," *Corporate Conduct Quarterly* 3, no. 1 (1994): 10.
27. S. S. Miller, "The Ombudsperson," in *Corporate Ethics: Developing New Standards of Accountability*, Conference Board Report No. 980 (New York: The Conference Board, 1991), 29–30.
28. "Johnson & Johnson's Credo Survey: Genesis and Evolution," *Ethikos* 7, no. 2 (1993): 2.

CHAPTER 7

MANAGING FOR ETHICAL CONDUCT

INTRODUCTION

We talked (in Chapter 3) about how most employees look outside themselves (to leaders and others) for guidance about how to behave. We have also discussed ethical culture and how organizations, especially large ones, manage ethics and legal compliance. Within this broad organizational context, managers oversee employee behavior every day, and they can have enormous influence. Therefore managers need simple and practical tools for managing the ethical conduct of their direct reports in the context of the broader organizational culture—to be ethical leaders at their own organizational level. This chapter introduces some basic management concepts that provide a foundation for understanding how to lead in a way that increases the probability that employees will behave ethically. Consistent with the focus of the book, each section concludes with practical implications for managers. Underlying our recommendations to managers are three key assumptions:

1. Managers want to be ethical.
2. Managers want their subordinates to be ethical.
3. Based on their experience, managers will have insight into the unique ethical requirements of the job.

IN BUSINESS, ETHICS IS ABOUT BEHAVIOR

In business, when people talk about ethics, they're talking about behavior. In this context, ethics isn't mysterious or unusual, nor does it depend on the individual's innate goodness, religious conviction, or philosophical understanding (or lack of these qualities). In work situations every day, people face ethical dilemmas—questions of right and wrong where values are in conflict. Should I hire, fire, promote, or demote this individual? Should I offer or accept a gift in this or that situation? How should I respond when my supervisor asks me to act against my own beliefs?[1]

The study of ethical behavior in business involves understanding the factors that influence how people behave in these situations. Although we've seen (in Chapter 3) that internal factors such as individual moral development are important, we know that for most people ethical conduct depends largely on external factors such as the rules of the work context, rewards and punishments, what peers are doing, what authority figures expect, the roles people are asked to play, and the broad ethical culture discussed in Chapter 5. In this chapter, we're focusing on the factors managers can influence the most. Once leaders understand how management principles apply to ethical conduct, they can manage the ethical behavior of their direct reports more proactively and effectively. On the other hand, if managers fool themselves into thinking that ethical conduct is determined exclusively by some mysterious character trait, they'll throw up their hands and walk away from situations they could proactively manage. Or they'll think that simply getting rid of a "bad apple" will make unethical conduct stop. However, unethical behavior is rarely as simple as a bad apple. It's often something about the work environment that allows the bad apple to behave badly. Plus, the work environment is the manager's responsibility. Top executives are responsible for the broad organizational culture (as we saw in Chapter 5). In most cases, though, lower-level leaders can do a lot to influence the subordinates in their own departments—and ethical leadership at the department level is what this chapter is about.

Practical Advice for Managers: Ethical Behavior

What are the practical implications for managers? First, think of ethics in concrete behavioral terms. Specifically, what kind of behavior are you looking for in your subordinates, and how can you lead in a way that creates a departmental work context that will support that behavior? Specifying concrete expectations for ethical behavior means going beyond abstract statements, such as "integrity is important here" to more concrete statements, such as "I expect sales representatives to be absolutely honest with our customers about such things as the characteristics of our products and our ability to deliver by a certain date." Providing a reason for these expectations is also important. "We're interested in building long-term relationships with our customers. We want them to think of us as their most trusted supplier." Finally, it's the manager's responsibility to create a work environment that supports ethical behavior and discourages unethical behavior just as much as it's his or her responsibility to manage for productivity or quality. Don't just set ethical behavior goals. Follow up to make sure that they're achievable and that they're being met, and model ethical conduct yourself. Your people will pay more attention to what you do than to what you say. Take advantage of opportunities to demonstrate the ethical conduct you expect.

OUR MULTIPLE ETHICAL SELVES

To understand ethics at work, we must understand that people are socialized to accept different behavior depending on the context. Cultural anthropologists have known for years that we have multiple selves and that we behave differently depending on the situation we confront.[2] Children in our society are taught very early that it's all right to be loud and boisterous on the playground, but they must be reverent at the church, synagogue, temple, or mosque. Table manners are important when visiting, but eating some things with one's fingers may be acceptable at home. As adults, we play highly differentiated roles, and we assume that each social context presents different behavioral expectations. Football players are expected to tackle each other deliberately and aggressively on the playing field, but they would be arrested for such behavior on the street. Businesspeople are expected to be aggressive against competitors but gentle with their spouses and children. Game jargon is often applied to business dealings—like the term *playing field*, which makes the business dealings seem like a game and therefore less subject to moral scrutiny. One may bluff and conceal information in business negotiations the same way one bluffs in a poker game. "Bluffing" sounds a lot better than lying (the word *lying* would raise ethical awareness, as discussed in Chapter 3), and the game analogy helps distinguish business behavior from morality in other situations. Although we might prefer to think that we take a single ethical self from situation to situation, reality suggests that most people behave differently in different contexts. This means that we can and often do have multiple ethical selves.

The Kenneth Lay Example

Kenneth Lay, former chairman of Enron Corporation (until he was forced out by the firm's creditors in 2002), exemplifies the concept of multiple ethical selves. A *Newsweek* article written after Enron's bankruptcy described the paradox that was Ken Lay.[3] First, we see the affable leader who was loved and admired by Enron employees. Even Sherron Watkins, the Enron whistleblower who brought Lay her concerns about the accounting problems (and was rebuffed) described Lay as a man of integrity. He grew up a poor preacher's son who pulled himself up by his bootstraps and eventually won the Horatio Alger Award (designed to foster entrepreneurship and honor the American dream of success through hard work). At the University of Missouri, he was president of a dry fraternity and went on to earn a Ph.D. in economics. He created Enron, and by 2000 it was the seventh largest company in the United States in terms of revenue.

Despite becoming quite rich, Lay never flaunted his wealth. He drove an old Cadillac and used rental cars rather than limos when traveling. He was highly philanthropic in the Houston community. He talked about making Houston a world-class city and worked to make that happen, spreading his largesse to the ballet, symphony, museums, the United Way, the NAACP—you name it. He was even discussed as a possible mayoral candidate.

But Lay had another side. He has been described as an arrogant gambler who valued risk taking and boosting the firm's stock price above all. He transformed Enron from the 1980s merger of two old-fashioned pipeline companies into a huge energy trader. Enron "became a giant casino, taking positions, hedging, betting on winners and losers."[4] Interestingly, the merger deal was financed by Michael Milliken, 1980s junk-bond trader and one of Lay's heroes (even though Milliken had done jail time for financial fraud). Lay fired Enron's conservative accounting firm, Deloitte Haskins Sells, early on because they were "not as creative and imaginative" as he wished, and he replaced them with Arthur Andersen. He created a corporate culture that was described by insiders as "cutthroat" and "vicious," and hired Ivy League "hot shot risk takers" like Jeff Skilling (CEO) and Andrew Fastow (CFO) to run it. People who didn't make their numbers were quickly fired, and a large internal security force came to be feared by employees.

Lay was also a political pro. He gave generously to political candidates and received favors in return, including exemptions from a variety of local and state regulations; his reach extended all the way to the White House. As the largest single contributor to George W. Bush's presidential campaign, Lay and other Enron officials met at least six times with Vice President Richard Cheney and his aides while the vice president headed the National Energy Policy Development Group and formulated the Bush administration's energy policy.[5]

After CEO Jeff Skilling resigned in August 2001, Lay told employees that the company's upcoming financials looked fine and encouraged them to "talk up the stock and talk positively about Enron to your family and friends." In an online discussion, he told employees that he had been buying stock himself. In fact, he had bought about $4 million worth, but what he failed to mention was that he had sold $24 million worth in the previous few months. Those who heeded his suggestion to buy or hold saw their retirement plans wiped out and were furious when they learned that Lay had been unloading his own stock for years. According to *Newsweek*, although he claimed that he was deceived by unscrupulous subordinates,[6] Lay had to know about Enron's "elaborate schemes to hide losses and debts"—the off-the-books partnerships that no one, including stock analysts, really understood.

> The difference between "lie" and "lay"
> Has fallen into deep decay.
> But now we know from Enron's shame
> That Lay and "lie" are just the same[7]

So was Kenneth Lay ethical or unethical? Had he lived (in 2006 he died of a heart attack at age 64—after being found guilty, but before being sentenced), perhaps he would have written a book that would have helped us understand his motivations and behaviors. But we'll never know. We suspect the answer is that, like many people, he had multiple ethical selves. In some areas of his life he did good, ethical things, including his many philanthropic efforts. But philanthropy shouldn't be equated with ethical conduct in daily business dealings. In fact, if he felt responsibility for what happened, wouldn't he have turned over at least some of his estimated $20 million net worth to help those who lost so much?

A prominent victim of the Enron bankruptcy was Cliff Baxter, Enron's 43-year-old former vice chairman, who committed suicide following Enron's collapse. We can only speculate about the reason, but a clash of his multiple ethical selves may have played a role. Those who knew him described Baxter as a family man who balanced his home and work lives. He was certainly instrumental in creating the massive Enron fortune in the 1990s. Over time, however, he clashed with Andrew Fastow and openly criticized the firm's involvement in financial deals he considered to be questionable and inappropriate. Upon realizing he couldn't influence what was happening, Baxter left the company in May 2001 (citing a desire to spend more time with his family). We will likely never know for sure why he committed suicide. Friends said he was "devastated by the company's demise." He may have felt responsible for the many employees who lost their life savings in the collapse that could have been prevented. It's possible that the ethical self who cared about those employees could no longer live with the self who contributed to their pain.[8]

The Dennis Levine Example

Now for another example. Dennis Levine was a mergers and acquisitions specialist at a prominent investment banking firm in the 1980's. His personal account of his insider trading activities, which resulted in his arrest and imprisonment also suggests multiple ethical selves. He described himself as a good son, husband, and father, and a man who had been encouraged by his parents to "play straight." "I come from a strong, old-fashioned family . . . [my father] taught me to work hard, believe in myself, and persevere . . . as a kid I always worked."[9] Levine's wife, Laurie, had no idea that he had been secretly and illegally trading in stocks for years. In fact, the family lived in a cramped one-bedroom apartment for nearly three years after their son was born despite Levine's huge insider trading profits. That someone is "from a good family" or is "a family man or woman" is no guarantee of ethical behavior in the office. At the office, the manager is dealing with the "office self," who may be very different from the "family self" or the "religious self."

Levine was a good son, husband, and father, but he separated his family self from his insider trading self. Why was his insider trading self allowed to exist? We can only speculate that this office self fit into an environment where peers were crossing the ethical line and not getting caught. Most important, his continuing huge profits led Levine into a downward spiral of unethical behavior that he found difficult to stop despite his recognition that it was illegal.

Practical Advice for Managers: Multiple Ethical Selves

So what should managers do? First, recognize that many people find it quite possible to divide themselves into multiple ethical selves and to behave differently in different life contexts. That means you too. So, begin by analyzing yourself. Is your office self consistent with your personal ethical self? If not, what will be required to bring the two together? You're an important role model for your subordinates. If you're clearly a "whole" person of integrity, they're more likely to aspire to "wholeness" themselves.

Next, think about those who report to you. Make no assumptions about ethics at work based on a person's background, religious affiliation, family life, or good deeds in the community. Instead, find out what norms and expectations guide their work selves, and make sure that these influences support ethical behavior. You can learn a great deal simply by keeping your eyes and ears wide open. Of course, the best way to find out how your people think about these issues is to ask them, either in person or in survey form. You may be surprised what they'll tell you. And you're sending an important symbolic message about what concerns you just by asking. Do employees feel, as many surveys have suggested, that they must compromise their personal ethics to get ahead in your organization? If so, what do they think can be done about it?

Find out what influences their thoughts and behavior in ethical dilemma situations. Find out what inhibits them from being the best they can be, from doing the right thing. You can base your questions on real or hypothetical situations. Most supervisors have never bothered to ask such questions. Is it any wonder then that most subordinates end up believing that their leaders don't really care about ethics? Once you've had this type of discussion, it's essential for you to follow up in ways that support ethical conduct. A number of practical ideas for how to do that follow.

Finally, it's important to evaluate the broader organizational environment to be sure that it supports the best in you and your people. As a lower- or middle-level manager, you can do little to influence the broad ethical culture. If senior executives are creating a cutthroat, Darwinian culture where only bottom-line results count, it's probably time to look elsewhere for a job because you won't be able to protect yourself or your people from the effects of such a culture. Chapter 5 provides information about how to conduct an "ethical culture audit" that can help you make that tough decision. But let's assume that senior management is supportive. It is then up to you to contribute to the larger organizational culture by creating a local work environment that supports ethical conduct and integrity for the people you manage. *Integrity* is defined as "that quality or state of being complete, whole, or undivided." Individuals of high integrity are thought to be consistent and ethical across contexts. So, the ultimate goal is to help those who work for you to be as ethical at the office as they are at home.

REWARDS AND DISCIPLINE

People Do What Is Rewarded and Avoid Doing What Is Punished

In Chapter 5 and our discussion of ethical culture, we described the importance of performance management systems and the signals they send about what the organization cares about (because it signals what the organization measures, rewards, and disciplines). Managers implement those systems through their application of rewards and discipline every day. Rewards and discipline are probably the most important influences on people's behavior at work. Most managers can probably recite a few basics recalled from a college psychology or management class. For example, most of us remember something about reinforcement theory—people are more likely to behave in ways that are rewarded, and they're less likely to do what is punished. In fact, people in work organizations are constantly on the lookout for information about rewards and punishments—especially if this information isn't explicit. In fact, the more ambiguous the situation, the more people search for clues. They know that to be successful at work, they'll have to determine what's rewarded and do those things while avoiding behaviors that are punished. *Remember this simple adage: what gets rewarded gets done!* Financial industry employees were rewarded handsomely for creating and selling risky mortgages and mortgage-backed securities. They did this without much attention to the risks to customers or the financial system as a whole.

People Will Go the Extra Mile to Achieve Goals Set by Managers

In combination with rewards, goal setting is one of the most powerful motivational tools. That's why managers use goals so much. Rewards are often tied to explicit goals (e.g., Sandy will win a trip to the Caribbean by hitting a particular sales target within a particular period of time). Goals focus attention on the desired outcome (the sales target and vacation), and they lead individuals to strategize about how to achieve the goals that have been set. That is generally considered to be a good thing. Meeting the goal makes Sandy feel good (providing psychological benefits), *and* it results in a significant valued reward.

Researchers are beginning to understand more about how people think about goals, what they will do to achieve goals, and what happens when they fall short of achieving a goal.

For example, intense focus on attaining a task goal can distract people from other goals, such as ethical goals. Consider the goals that Lee Iacocca set for design and production of the Ford Pinto—recall from the Pinto fires case (Chapter 2) that goals were set—the car had to weigh less than 2,000 pounds and cost less than $2,000. An intense organizational focus on striving for those goals may have contributed to shortcuts and safety problems. Apparently, Iacocca had not set explicit safety goals to accompany these challenging production goals. Thus the employees involved likely focused on achieving the stated weight and price goals without giving equivalent attention to safety. Researchers have found that employees may be less likely to report problems to management if they are intently focused on achieving a task.[10] In addition, attempting to achieve a task goal increases risky behavior, whereas falling short of the goal can lead to increased lying about performance.[11]

Imagine that a claims handler at an insurance company is assigned an explicit goal to close a certain number of claims within a particular period of time and is offered a financial reward for doing so. He's likely to find ways to reach that goal even if it means denying some legitimate claims, and he'll be less likely to report concerns about legitimate claims being denied. On the other hand, setting goals for ethical performance can make a difference. For example, one study found that participants who were given a goal to revise a paragraph from their boss were more likely to correct misinformation if they were given an explicit goal to ensure the accuracy and truth of the information.[12]

Incentives and goals are popular with managers because they work well to motivate behavior. But managers often fail to recognize the potential of goals and incentives to motivate unethical behavior if not used thoughtfully. Let's look at a more specific example.

How Goals Combined With Rewards Can Encourage Unethical Behavior

THE ELECTRONICS APPLIANCE SALES EXAMPLE   Suppose an electronic appliance store has a sales force that is paid on the basis of a modest salary plus commission. In other words, the salespeople are paid a percentage of the items they sell. The company frequently advertises specials on certain television models in the local newspaper—and, of course, people come into the store asking about those models. But because of the lower profit margin on these sale items, the company also lowers its salespeople's commission on these models. The higher rewards (i.e., higher commissions) come with sales of models that aren't on special. The company prefers to sell the higher-priced models but advertises the lower-priced ones to get customers into the store. The company has set sales goals for each salesperson, and the goals are higher for the higher-priced models. The company offers little sales training. New salespeople spend a day or so working with the store manager and then are pretty much on their own. The manager doesn't seem to care how sales are made—just that they are made. The manager's own commissions are based on store sales.

If the salespeople value money (and their jobs), and let's assume that they do, they'll be motivated to sell more of the higher-priced models. They can do this in a variety of ways. For example, they might point out that some of these models have features that the sale models don't have. Some customers will probably listen to the advice and buy the more expensive models. As buyers listen and go through with the purchase, the connection between selling higher-priced items and positive outcomes (commissions, praise from the manager) becomes stronger for salespeople, and their motivation to sell more of these items grows.

Still, lots of folks will probably insist on buying the sale models. To sell more of the higher-priced models, a salesperson might try stressing the advantages of the high-priced model's features even when the customer doesn't need them. The salesperson may find that a good number of people go along with this sales tactic. The salesperson then receives more rewards—higher commissions, more praise from the manager— and no obvious negative outcomes. This behavior can even be justified, or at least rationalized. These customers are getting features they wouldn't otherwise get, right? And the salesperson doesn't know much about their finances or personal life, so there would be no way to know (without asking) if spending more money really had negative consequences for the customer.

Things are going so well that the salesperson might now be tempted to go a bit further—perhaps playing with the controls to make it look as if the picture on the sale TV is a bit fuzzier than the picture on the more expensive models. That makes it even easier to sell the more expensive models.

Explained this way, the connection between goals, rewards, and unethical behavior seems pretty clear. Although no one was explicitly telling salespeople to be unethical, the motivating factors were there: management set higher sales goals for higher-priced models and rewarded the sale of these models with higher commissions. The store manager didn't seem to care how the sales got made and may not have objected to the salesperson playing with the controls to deceive customers.

Management wanted to sell higher-priced models and set higher sales goals for those models. But the exclusive focus on goals frequently obscures the method of reaching a goal. If managers are concerned about ethical conduct, it's essential that they focus at least as much on how the goal is being achieved. They must let their workers know that they're interested in ethical means as well as ends and that they plan to evaluate both. If individuals are rewarded for meeting goals no matter what methods are used, they're much more likely to try methods that cross the line between ethical and unethical behavior.

Many people have told us of their experience with managers who say something like this: "I don't care how you do it, just do it." Or "I don't want to know how you meet the goal, just meet it." These statements are clearly giving permission to use any means necessary (ethical or unethical) to meet the goal. Managers who have uttered these words shouldn't be surprised to find that unethical behavior is often the result. Goal setting and incentives combine to create the most effective motivational method available to managers. Set challenging and achievable goals, reward people for meeting them, and people will go to great lengths to achieve the goals that have been set. That's why responsible managers need to be clear about the importance of using only ethical means to achieve the goals they have set for their employees. The statement, "I don't care how you do it, just get it done," should send up a huge red flag that triggers ethical awareness. Managers shouldn't say it, and workers should beware of ethical land mines if they hear it.

Practical Advice for Managers: Goals, Rewards, and Discipline

First, remember that people do what's rewarded. And these rewards don't have to be explicit. The electronics store in our example would probably never have dreamed of saying that it was rewarding salespersons for being unethical. In fact, they weren't doing this explicitly. But if the designers of the motivational plan had thought carefully about the plan's potential effects (and it's their responsibility to do so), they might very well have identified its fatal flaw—it focuses on ends only and leaves it to the salespeople to figure out the means (how to accomplish the goals). Managers are more likely to identify these flaws in advance if they put themselves in their employees' shoes. Think about what the average individual would be likely to do given the rewards. What kinds of attitudes and behaviors are being rewarded explicitly or implicitly? How can you find out? Ask your staff. If you have good, open communication with them, they'll tell you.

Second, think carefully about the goals you've set for your employees. Combining specific, challenging, and achievable goals with rewards for achieving them is a powerful motivational tool. People set their sights on those goals and work hard to reach them. It's up to the manager to think about the likely behavioral outcomes and potential unintended consequences. Again, put yourself in employees' shoes and ask yourself what those consequences might be. Also ask yourself whether you have set goals for ethical conduct (e.g., safety, honesty with customers) as well as for bottom-line performance (e.g., number of TVs sold) that focus on the means (building trusting customer relationships) as well as the ends. Are you measuring and rewarding both? We believe in an ethical "Pygmalion effect." In tests of the more general Pygmalion effect, researchers have found that people in school and work settings generally live up to the expectations that are set for them, whether they're high or low.[13] Students and workers perform better in response to a teacher's or supervisor's high expectations, but they fall behind if they're expected to fail. With the ethical Pygmalion effect, expectations for ethical behavior (as well as performance) are set high, and people are expected to fulfill them. This ethical Pygmalion effect appeals to people's desire to do what's right. It is also likely to get people to think about how they achieve their goals, not just whether they've achieved them.

Recognize the Power of Indirect Rewards and Punishments

It's important to recognize that workers don't have to be personally rewarded (or punished) for the message to have an impact. A powerful extension of reinforcement theory is social learning theory.[14] According to social learning theory, people learn from observing the rewards and punishments of others. Imagine if we had to touch a hot stove to learn that we'll get burned if we do so! Luckily, we can observe others to learn most of what we need to know about what works and what doesn't in life and at work. So, workers' behavior is influenced even when they don't experience a reward or punishment themselves. If they see that others get away with lying, cheating, or stealing—or worse yet, if they see those individuals getting promotions or big bonuses—they're much more likely to try such behaviors themselves. On the other hand, if they see that someone is quickly dismissed for lying to a customer, they learn that such behavior is unacceptable.

THE TAILHOOK EXAMPLE   As an example of how people learn about rewards and punishments by observing others, consider the 1991 Tailhook scandal. The Tailhook Association is a nonprofit organization of naval aviators that, in 1991, had formal ties with the U.S. Navy. According to many insiders, the type of sexual harassment (of some 90 women) that occurred at the annual Tailhook Association meeting held in the Las Vegas Hilton in 1991 had been implicitly rewarded (or at least not punished) in the Navy for some time. These sexual harassment rituals were regular events that the male participants experienced as fun (rewarding). The Navy brass was known to turn a blind eye to reports, responding with a "boys will be boys" attitude. Investigations were torturously slow and resulted in little, if any, punishment. The reward system became well known, and therefore the men continued to engage in these "rewarding" behaviors that weren't punished.

Many people (especially women) looked to the Navy's reaction to the Tailhook scandal as an opportunity to change the messages being sent about the acceptability or unacceptability of such conduct. Some early signs were encouraging, but the longer-term results disappointed many women. The secretary of the Navy resigned his post at the outset of the scandal, and the Navy severed ties with the Tailhook Association in late

1991. Investigations of potential criminal misconduct were also launched. However, the Navy's discussions with 1,500 men resulted in only two suspects. When the Pentagon took over, 140 aviators were accused of indecent exposure, assault, or lying under oath. However, only 80 of these individuals were ever fined or even moderately disciplined. None of those involved in the assault of the 90 women was court-martialed or seriously disciplined. Perhaps most significant, in early 1994 the young woman who filed the first complaint, Lieutenant Paula Coughlin, resigned from the Navy, explaining that Tailhook "and the covert attacks on me that followed have stripped me of my ability to serve."[15] Lieutenant Coughlin left amid "rumor mongering by officers trying to impugn her credibility" and with a "stack of hate mail." However, also in 1994, a federal jury awarded Lieutenant Coughlin $1.7 million in compensatory damages and $5 million in punitive damages and held the Hilton Hotel responsible.[16] The Tailhook Association continues to hold an annual convention, but it is now a much tamer affair. In 1999, after an investigation of the Tailhook Association and its 1999 convention in Reno, the Navy restored its ties with the organization. Secretary of the Navy Richard Danzig said, "The shameful events of the Tailhook Convention in 1991 led to a withdrawal of our support for the Association. Over the past eight years, however, the Association took a number of constructive steps that warranted a review of its status . . . [and] we've concluded that the time is right to restore ties." The association has committed itself to prevent the type of misconduct that occurred in 1991. (See www.tailhook.org for more information on the association.)

The message to Navy men (and women) has clearly been mixed. Yes, the event caused a lot of turmoil, probably enough to suggest to Navy men that assaulting their female colleagues was not going to be as "rewarding" as it used to be. In fact, membership in the Tailhook Association dropped dramatically after the incident, especially among younger members.[17] Moreover, several admirals have been discharged for inappropriate sexual behavior committed since Tailhook. Sexual harassment sensitivity training is now required in the Navy. But in 1996 *Newsweek* reported that in the four years after Tailhook, the Navy received more than 1,000 harassment complaints and more than 3,500 charges of indecent assault. Women still complained that they faced reprisals for filing complaints.[18] To sum up, organizations send a powerful message to all personnel every time a decision is made to respond to a sexual harassment complaint. Everyone watches and learns from what happens to the perpetrators and to the victims.

The problem with sexual harassment and sexual assault continues today and goes well beyond the Navy. For example, the most recent Defense Department annual survey (2012) showed that sexual harassment and sexual assault remain serious problems in the military, with reports increasing dramatically. Anonymous surveys put the estimate of sexual assault in the military at over 26,000 in 2012. In Spring 2013, the U.S. Secretary of Defense called sexual assault in the military a "scourge that must be stamped out" and a "profound betrayal of sacred oaths and sacred trusts." Clearly, much more work will be required to create a culture across the military where such behavior is not tolerated.[19]

Managers, take note of the messages you're implicitly sending to all of your workers by what you reward and punish (or fail to punish). Employees are constantly on the lookout for these cues. They want to know what's okay and not okay in your work environment. If they observe that people advance by stepping on others, lying to customers, and falsifying reports, they'll be more inclined to do so because they will have learned that such behavior is rewarded. If they see sexual harassment go undisciplined, they may feel free to engage in it themselves. If they see those who report misconduct suffering reprisal, they won't risk reporting problem behavior. So if you become aware of unethical behavior in your group, chances are that it's being rewarded somehow. Ask yourself how the system might be intentionally or unintentionally rewarding the undesired behavior, and take responsibility for changing it. On the other hand, if unethical individuals are dismissed, and persons of integrity advance, the ethical lesson is also clear: integrity is valued and unethical behavior won't be tolerated.

Can Managers Really Reward Ethical Behavior?

For years, management writers have preached that whenever possible, managers should use rewards instead of punishment—that punishment is inherently a bad management practice. This idea, good as it sounds, is impractical when the goal is to encourage ethical behavior and discourage unethical behavior. Relying on rewards means rewarding ethical behavior. So let's think about how a manager might regularly reward routine ethical behavior. Perhaps he or she could give awards or bonuses to those whose expense reports were honest and accurate or to those managers who didn't harass their secretaries. Does this seem ridiculous to you? Of course it does. Workers don't expect to be rewarded for behaviors that are expected of everyone—for simply doing the right thing every day. So in the short term, it's quite difficult to reward routine ethical behavior. However, as we noted in Chapter 6, some organizations do reward extraordinary ethical behavior that goes above and beyond the routine. Doing so sends a powerful message to everyone that such extraordinary behavior is highly valued in the organization.

If we switch to longer-term thinking, there should be rewards for doing the right thing. For example, most people know how to get ahead in their own organization. As we noted in our discussion of ethical culture, large organizations have performance management systems that provide regular feedback to employees about their performance. This information is used to make important decisions about pay and promotion. Is information about integrity incorporated into those systems? Is it weighted heavily enough to make the point that integrity matters at least as much as bottom-line performance if an employee wants to advance in the organization? Or do people get highly compensated and promoted despite ethical lapses? If so, the message is clear. If you want to get ahead around here, you have to do whatever it takes. People who advance are likely the ones who have decided to go along to get along or, worse yet, the ones who stepped on others along the way. On the other hand, are those who have advanced to the highest levels known for their integrity? If so, the organization is sending a message about the importance of integrity. Rewards may be a limited tool for influencing specific ethical behaviors today or tomorrow, but they should be used to set the tone for what's expected and rewarded in the long term.

What About the Role of Discipline?

As for discipline, we all know that managers sometimes have to discipline errant subordinates, just as responsible parents are expected to discipline unruly children. It's an essential part of the manager's job to step in when an employee is headed down the wrong path. In fact, it can be a real gift to give an employee a heads-up and the opportunity to correct bad behavior and avoid severe negative consequences later. We also know that discipline works. If people expect their misconduct to be detected and punished, they're less likely to engage in it. So if it works, why not use it? Well, it turns out that managers are often told to avoid punishment and to rely on rewards as much as possible because of a belief that employees will automatically react badly to punishment. They'll dislike the supervisor or engage in sabotage to retaliate. But we now know that discipline can produce good results when it's carried out in a particular way—when workers perceive it as fair.

If we examine the idea that punishment should be avoided, we find that it's based on old psychological research that was conducted on rats and small children. It has little to do with adults in work settings who can distinguish discipline that's fair (i.e., punishment that is deserved and fairly administered) from discipline that's unfair. Have you ever heard an adult say, "I had it coming; I deserved it"? As Dennis Levine said of his arrest and imprisonment for insider trading, "I've gained an abiding respect for the fairness of our system of justice . . . When I broke the law, I was punished. The system works." He also said, "My former life was destroyed because I figured the odds were a thousand to one against my getting caught."[20] If he had thought he would be caught and punished, the odds would have been reversed, and he may never have cut an insider trading deal. Once caught and punished, he acknowledged that the punishment was just.

Discipline should be administered fairly. Research evidence suggests that punishment results in more positive outcomes (e.g., the behavior improves and the employee becomes a better corporate citizen) if the recipient perceives it to be fair.[21] These positive outcomes are linked primarily to the appropriate severity of the punishment and employee input. The punishment should "fit the crime," and it should be consistent with what others have received for similar infractions. It's also important that you give the employee an opportunity for input—to explain his or her side of the story. In addition, the disciplined worker is more likely to respond positively to the punishment if you approach it in a constructive fashion and carefully explain the reasons for the punishment. Finally, if you discipline someone, do it in private. Punishment can be a humiliating experience, and public punishment adds insult to injury.

Recognize the indirect effects of punishment. The punished employee should not be the manager's only concern. Social learning theory suggests that other workers will be affected as well. Remember, we learn a great deal from observing the rewards and punishments of others. But if the punishment occurs in private, how will others know about it? Anyone who has worked in a real organization knows about the grapevine, the communication network that flashes organizational news throughout a department or company. Good managers are aware of the power of the grapevine and rely on it to transmit important information. Research has discovered that when people are aware that unethical behavior has taken place, they want the violators to be punished.[22]

People want to believe that their workplace is "just"—that the organization rewards good guys and punishes bad guys. They also want to feel that they aren't suckers who, in a sense, are being punished for following the rules when others get away with breaking them. This is an important reason that managers must discipline unethical behavior when it occurs. There must be no exceptions. High-level rule violators must be held to the same standards (or higher ones). By clearly disciplining all rule violators, managers send an unequivocal message to the violator and all observers that this behavior won't be tolerated. They also support the notion that the company is a just place to work, where the rules are enforced fairly and consistently.

Imagine how the honest employees at Enron must have felt—long before the public implosion of the company in 2001—when two Enron energy traders in New York made massive fraudulent energy trades and siphoned off company money into their own personal accounts in the mid-1980s. In short, the traders had kept two sets of books and had routinely destroyed records to obliterate any paper trail. When Enron's board heard of these shenanigans, CEO Ken Lay said openly at a board meeting that the two traders "made too much money to let them go." So the trading crooks were allowed to stay on, until an internal investigator discovered the magnitude of the fraud and the company took an $85 million charge to after-tax earnings to cover losses. Lay complained at an all-employee meeting that he never knew about these activities. Later, a lawyer involved in a lawsuit against the company said, "Any honest, competent management, confronted with the conduct of Borget and Mastroeni, as revealed to Enron's senior management in January 1987, would have fired these gentlemen without delay."[23] It makes us wonder if Enron's later difficulties could have been avoided if only the executive team had regularly disciplined the company's rogue employees.

In his book *Father, Son & Co.; My Life at IBM and Beyond* (1990), Thomas Watson Jr., the son of IBM's founder, described his experiences in running the company for almost 20 years at a time when IBM dominated the computer industry. He discussed the importance of imposing swift, severe punishment for breaches of integrity, as well as the indirect effects of punishing or not punishing. He said, "If a manager does something unethical, he should be fired just as surely as a factory worker. This is the wholesome use of the boss's power." But, as he explains in the following excerpt, his managers didn't always follow his advice.

> On one occasion some managers in one of our plants started a chain letter involving U.S. savings bonds. The idea was that one manager would write to five other managers, and each of those would write to five more, who would each send some bonds back to the first guy and write to five more, and so on. Pretty soon they ran out of managers and got down to employees. It ended up that the employees felt pressure to join the chain letter and pay off the managers. I got a complaint about this and brought it to the attention of the head of the division. I expected him to say, at a minimum, "We've got to fire a couple of guys, I'll handle it." Instead, he

simply said, "Well, it was a mistake." I couldn't convince him to fire anybody. Now, you could admire him for defending the team, but I think there is a time when integrity should take the rudder from team loyalty. All the same, I didn't pursue the matter any further, and my failure to act came back to haunt me.

A couple of years later in that same division, a manager fired a low-level employee who had been stealing engineering diagrams and selling them to a competitor. Firing him would have been fine, except that the manager handled it in a brutal way. The employee in question had one thing in his life that he was proud of—his commission in the U.S. Army Reserve, where he held the rank of major. Instead of simply going to the man's house and telling him, "You swiped the drawings and we're going to fire you," the manager picked a week when the fellow was in military camp to lower the boom. Somehow the military authorities got involved as well, and the man was stripped of his commission. The humiliation caused him to become insanely angry, and for the next few years he devoted himself to making me uncomfortable. He sent pictures of Tom Watson Jr. behind bars to his senators and his congressman and to every justice of the Supreme Court. And he kept harking back to that chain letter, because he knew we had tolerated the men responsible for it. Eventually he simmered down, but the incident really taught me a lesson. After that I simply fired managers when they broke rules of integrity. I did it in perhaps a dozen cases, including a couple involving senior executives. I had to overrule a lot of people each time, who would argue that we should merely demote the man, or transfer him, or that the business would fall apart without him. But the company was invariably better off for the decision and the example.[24]

Sometimes employees are punished for trying to do the right thing. For example, Owen Cheevers was an experienced researcher at the Bank of Montreal who wrote an honest report expressing his concerns about the radio industry. Investment bankers at the firm asked him to make his report more positive. When he refused to write a more glowing report, Cheevers was fired. Obviously, such punishment sends a powerful message to all other employees who are aware of it—go along or be fired.[25]

Practical Advice for Managers: Discipline

Tom Watson learned the hard way what can happen when breaches of integrity aren't disciplined swiftly and severely. Workers have long memories about incidents such as the chain letter and how management handles them. They tuck that sort of information away for later use. When the IBM employee who stole the engineering drawings was fired in a particularly humiliating way, he was outraged. His severe and public punishment seemed particularly unfair when compared with the way others had been treated. And he reacted in ways that managers are told to expect from punished employees. He was angry at the punisher and the organization.

The important point about discipline is that adults differentiate between fair and unfair punishment. If you use punishment consistently to enforce the rules, employees will expect to be punished when they break them. However, they expect punishment that fits the crime and that is consistent with how others have been treated. In most cases, if you impose discipline fairly, the problem behavior improves and the subordinate goes on to be a productive organizational citizen.

Remember that you should be concerned about observers who pay a great deal of attention to how rule violations are handled. When the chain letter offenders weren't severely disciplined, an implicit message was sent to all who were aware of the scheme, and expectations were set up for how management would respond to future breaches of integrity. A just organization is one that disciplines rule violations fairly and consistently and doesn't punish people who try to do the right thing. Workers expect managers to discipline fairly, and they're morally outraged when management doesn't do its job.

PEOPLE FOLLOW GROUP NORMS

"Everyone's Doing It"

"Everyone's doing it" is the refrain so frequently used to rationalize—or justify or even encourage—unethical behavior. We've all heard it. From fraternity brothers who are expected to advise their peers about the content of exams to college football players who accept booster money, to waiters and waitresses who don't claim all of their tip income for tax purposes, to auditors who sign off on financial statements that haven't been thoroughly checked and to insider traders who share secrets about upcoming financial deals, individuals are much more likely to engage in unethical behavior if they're convinced that others are doing it too. It lets them off the hook by providing an acceptable justification and rationale for the behavior. Also, recall what you learned about ethical awareness in Chapter 3. People are more likely to recognize issues as being ethical ones if there is social consensus in the group that the issue raises ethical concerns. But if, instead, everyone agrees that a particular behavior is not a problem because "everyone is doing it," it's more likely that ethical concerns just won't come up.

Rationalizing Unethical Behavior

For some behaviors, the refrain "everyone is doing it" is used primarily to rationalize behavior that's guided by unethical group norms. The employee who inflates his or her expense reports believes that it's justified first because everyone else is doing it (and getting away with it, too). Within the group, inflating expenses may also be explained as a way of compensating for the extra hours spent away from home, to pay for the drink at the bar or a movie, or to cover other expenses that aren't deductible under the organization's formal travel cost reimbursement policy. These rationalizations are often explicitly or implicitly supported by the boss, who suggests the behavior or engages in it himself or herself. Either way, the manager sends a powerful message that it's okay to bend the rules, and that message can easily be generalized to other rules in the organization.

A better way to manage the process is to state the rules clearly and then enforce them. In other words, if it seems reasonable to reimburse a traveling employee for a drink at the bar, a movie, or a telephone call home, then change the rules so that these expenses can be legally reimbursed under the organization's formal travel policy. Then abuses of the system can be disciplined.

Pressure to Go Along

For other behaviors, the "everyone is doing it" refrain represents not just a rationalization but actual pressure to go along with the group norms. The argument is used to encourage those who are reluctant. "Aw, c'mon, everybody does it!" Not going along puts the individual in the uncomfortable spot of being perceived as some sort of goody-goody who is highly ethical but also unlikable, and certainly not someone who can be trusted. The result can be ostracism from the group, and most of us would rather go along than be ostracized.[26] Many individuals will go along with unethical behavior because of their strong need to be accepted. If left to their own devices, they might very well follow the rules. But in the group situation, they feel that they have no choice but to comply, or at least to remain silent about what others are doing.

Practical Advice for Managers: Group Norms

So what does the notion of group norms mean for the manager? Above all, you must be acutely aware of the power of group norms (informal standards of behavior), which aren't always consistent with the formal, written rules.

Group norms represent what's really happening in the group, and you must be in touch with this reality. Any new employee will be quickly schooled in "the way we do things in this group" and will be expected to go along. Loyalty to the group may be the most powerful norm and one that's extremely difficult to counteract. If the group norms support ethical behavior, you have no problem; but if they don't, you face a particularly tough situation. If the group is strong and cohesive, one approach you can use is to identify the informal group leader and attempt to influence that individual, hoping she or he will influence the others. It's also important to consider the reward system. Norms often arise to support behaviors that are implicitly rewarded. If people are doing something, it's usually because they find it rewarding and the system somehow encourages it. Changes in the reward system can lead to changes in group norms.

A PROBLEMATIC GROUP NORM EXAMPLE   A classic organizational behavior case explains how a highly productive manufacturing work group with a strong informal leader created a problematic group norm for punching in and out at the time clock. After the foreman leaves, all but one of the group members goes home. The one person remaining behind punches out all of the other group members. The result is that group members are paid for more hours than they actually work. On occasion, when a group member is delayed in the morning, the group punches him in. But this practice is carefully controlled, and the group has developed norms so that it is not abused.

Although the punch-out system seems to be clearly wrong, the case is complicated because management admits that even though the group's pay is low, their productivity is high. What's more, the group is highly cohesive and very willing to work hard when necessary to fulfill last-minute orders or solve unusual production problems. The workers also value the ability to have some control over the workday. Finally, management has known about the practice for some time and has ignored it.

The solution to the case isn't clear-cut. The case writers suggested that management might be better off leaving well enough alone. "If it ain't broke, don't fix it." However, this is impossible if the ethical dimensions of the case are brought into focus. Leaving it alone implies tacit acceptance and approval of rule breaking and sends that message not only to this work group but to all of the others as well. Other groups that, for some reason, can't manage to do the same (perhaps because of less cohesion or because their supervisor stays later) will no doubt resent the injustice. Management must also accept some responsibility for tacitly approving this practice over a long period of time.

Remembering that people do what's rewarded, we believe that the norm is most likely to change via adjustments in the reward system. For example, moving to a five-day salary (somewhat higher than their current average take-home pay) rather than hourly pay would reward people for getting the job done rather than staying a certain number of hours on weekdays. Group members could still be paid extra for weekend overtime work when it's available. If the late-arrival norm isn't being abused, it could be institutionalized: if someone must be late, a new rule could state that he or she must inform someone in the work group by a certain time. As with absences, a certain number of late arrivals would be allowed within a specified period. The informal group leader should be involved in devising the solution through an appeal to his or her concern for fairness to other workers in the organization.

PEOPLE FULFILL ASSIGNED ROLES

Roles are strong forces for guiding behavior, and workers are assigned roles that can powerfully influence their behavior in ethical dilemma situations. Roles can reduce a person's sense of his or her individuality by focusing attention on the role and the expectations that accompany it. It doesn't really matter who fills the role. It's the role requirements that are important. This focus on the role reduces the individual's awareness of the self as an independent individual who is personally responsible for an outcome. This psychological process is called *deindividuation.*[27]

So the individual acts "in role" and does what's expected. This is fine when behaving in role means doing the right thing. But what happens when in-role behavior involves behaving illegally or unethically? For example, aggression is a necessary part of the police officer role, although police officers are expected to use aggression only under very specific circumstances. Sometimes, though, police officers step over the ethical line; they become overly aggressive at inappropriate times and assault suspects without cause. Several such incidents have been videotaped by bystanders in recent years. Another important part of a police officer's role is loyalty to other police officers and protection of his or her peers. Police officers often travel in pairs and must rely on each other in difficult, life-threatening situations. Loyalty, protection, and trust within the ranks thus serve an important, positive purpose. But loyalty can also end up supporting unethical behavior when, for example, a fellow police officer is overly aggressive and a peer who observes the conduct doesn't report it.

Consider this example from an old television series. Two female police detectives were part of a stakeout intended to catch one of their fellow police officers stealing heroin. The detectives realized they were facing a complex moral dilemma when the officer told them he was stealing the heroin for his mother, who was dying of cancer and in severe pain. He had clearly broken the law, and the rules clearly said that they must turn him in. But loyalty and protection were important parts of their police role. Their colleague had good intentions—to help his dying mother. After much discussion and individual soul searching, they decided to protect their colleague and keep silent about what they knew. Although we may disagree about whether they made the right decision, the point here is that the peer protection and loyalty aspects of the police officer role were an important part of that decision.

The Zimbardo Prison Experiment

A powerful and widely cited social psychology study illustrates the power of roles to influence behavior.[28] The researchers created a prison environment in the basement of the psychology building at Stanford University. Twenty-four psychologically healthy subjects (people like us) were recruited and randomly assigned to play the roles of prisoners or guards. General rules were provided regarding how to fulfill the role, but subjects were left free to interact within those general guidelines. With the cooperation of the local police, the guards were actually sent out to arrest the prisoners, book them, and transport them to their simulated cells. The prisoners were given uniforms and were referred to by identification numbers. The guards were given comfortable quarters and a recreation area. The guards wore uniforms and mirrored sunglasses, and they worked standard eight-hour shifts during which they were given a great deal of control over the prisoners (physical abuse was not allowed). With rare exceptions, the guards enjoyed the social power and status of the guard role. Some "guards" were exhilarated by the experience and reinforced their guard role with aggression, threats, and insults. The "prisoners" quickly began to show dramatic signs of emotional change, including acute anxiety, helplessness, and passivity verging on complete servility. Some became severely distressed and physically ill.

Although the experiment was originally scheduled to last two weeks, it was halted after only six days due to concern about the prisoners' well-being. "At the end of only six days . . . it was no longer apparent to most of the subjects (or to us) where reality ended and their roles began. The majority had indeed become prisoners or guards, no longer able to clearly differentiate between role playing and the real self. There were dramatic changes in virtually every aspect of their behavior, thinking, and feeling."[29]

After the experiment ended, the guards expressed a combination of excitement and dismay at the darker side of themselves that had emerged. The simulated situation had become real very quickly, and both sides had readily assumed the roles expected of them as members of their respective groups (prisoner or guard). This occurred despite the other roles these individuals may have played in their "normal" lives just days before. Finally, when individuals attempted to deviate from the role behavior, the deviation was quickly suppressed by pressure to conform as expressed by other group members. The experimental results were used to support the "situational" explanation for prison behavior. In other words, perfectly normal people behaved cruelly and aggressively when placed in a role where these behaviors were either expected or allowed.

The Zimbardo experiment can help us better understand the 2004 Abu Ghraib prison scandal in Iraq. At Abu Ghraib, beginning in 2003, poorly trained American military police officers (MPs) and civilian contractors tortured Iraqi captives in what had ironically been one of Saddam Hussein's most infamous prisons. The brutal torture ranged from physical violence to verbal, psychological, and sexual abuse. The American public became incensed when photographs of the abuse showed up on the Internet thanks to one young military policeman, Joseph Darby. The most famous photos include one of a supervisor giving a thumbs-up sign while standing next to a pyramid of hooded, naked Iraqis. Another shows female Private Lyndie England leading a naked Iraqi around on a leash. According to the Red Cross, most of the prisoners at Abu Ghraib had committed no crime. They had just managed to be in the wrong place at the wrong time.

So what drove these Americans, men and women, to engage in such horrific behavior and to laugh at the humiliation of other human beings? What happened at Abu Ghraib was complex and likely caused by many factors. But at least some of them seem hauntingly reminiscent of the Zimbardo experiment. The Abu Ghraib guards quickly donned the role of prison police, and they relished the power over prisoners that accompanied the role. This in-role behavior was likely enhanced further by intelligence officers' encouragement to use more aggressive techniques to soften up the prisoners for interrogation and by praise when such techniques "worked."[30]

Roles at Work

But prisons aren't your average work setting. How do the results of this experiment apply to work organizations? People enter work organizations in a state of "role readiness."[31] In this state, they're likely to engage in behaviors that are consistent with their organizationally prescribed role, even if those behaviors violate other values they hold (another example of multiple ethical selves). A particularly interesting example is provided by corporate professionals such as lawyers, physicians, and accountants. Professionals are thought to adhere most closely to their professional roles. In fact, this is part of the definition of a professional.

Although there's little research evidence, much anecdotal evidence suggests that many corporate physicians, lawyers, and accountants identify more closely with their organizational role than with their professional role. For example, when asbestos was still being used in building insulation, Johns Manville medical personnel conformed to corporate policy and remained silent about asbestos exposure that was adversely affecting employees' health, despite the known medical dangers.[32] In their dual roles of physician and organizational member, the latter took precedence. The same can be said of auditors who are supposed to adhere to the ethical guidelines of their professional organization, the American Institute of Certified Public Accountants (AICPA). They are supposed to protect the public interest and report any financial irregularities they find. As we have learned from auditing scandals, however, the corporate organizational role seems to take over for many.

Conflicting Roles Can Lead to Unethical Behavior

In their jobs, people are sometimes expected to play different roles that may make competing demands on them, causing internal conflict and stress that may be resolved via unethical behavior such as lying. For example, professional nurses are taught that patient education and patient advocacy are important aspects of the nursing role. Yet these nursing role expectations may conflict with physicians' orders, or they may be difficult to implement because of time pressures and paperwork that take nurses away from patients. In a research study, nurses responded to various scenarios, some of which placed them in role-conflict situations.[33] The nurses who were in role-conflict situations said they would be more likely to lie by misreporting their behavior on the patient's chart.

Managers must be aware that conflicting role demands can pressure workers to be dishonest. The best way to avoid this type of dishonesty is to minimize conflicting role demands. Ask your staff to analyze their jobs and to identify sources of conflict that could cause them to feel they have to lie to you or someone else in order to successfully accomplish some aspect of their job. Then, see if the job can be redesigned to minimize these conflicts.

Roles Can Also Support Ethical Behavior

Roles can also work to support ethical behavior. For example, whistleblowing (reporting the misconduct of others) is sometimes prescribed for individuals in certain jobs. This makes a difficult behavior easier to carry out. A survey of internal auditors found that whistleblowing was more likely when the auditors saw reporting as a prescribed job requirement.[34] Managers should consider the extent to which organizational roles encourage either ethical or unethical behavior. Obviously, those that support and encourage unethical behavior should be changed. Those that encourage ethical behavior (e.g., whistleblowing) should be bolstered. For example, research has found that although reporting a peer's misconduct is a distasteful and difficult act, people are more likely to report a peer if doing so is explicitly made a part of their role via an honor code or code of conduct.[35] In other words, if their role requires them to report misconduct when they see it, they're more likely to do so. Many colleges and universities have honor codes that require students to report any cheating they observe. The requirement makes it easier for the reporter because the behavior becomes a duty, a role responsibility rather than a voluntary ethical act.

Practical Advice for Managers: Roles

The key concept for managers to understand is that roles influence behavior. Think about the roles people play in your department or organization. What are the implications of their role expectations for ethical and unethical behavior? Do some individuals experience conflicts between their roles? For example, are professionals torn between their organizational and professional roles? Or do employees experience conflicts within a role—for example, nurses, who are often required to fulfill the conflicting roles of patient advocate and subordinate to the physician? Again, the individuals who hold the jobs are probably the best source of information about their role expectations and potential conflicts. Once you've analyzed roles and role conflicts, determine whether jobs need to be altered to reduce conflict. If change isn't possible, at least you can anticipate the problems that are likely to arise for people in these jobs.

OBEDIENCE TO AUTHORITY: PEOPLE DO WHAT THEY'RE TOLD

In a *60 Minutes* segment, Americans working for a Japanese company in the United States reported that their supervisor told them to unpack machine tools manufactured in and shipped from Japan, remove the "Manufactured in Japan" label, change a few things, replace the label with a "Manufactured in the U.S." label, and repack the machine tools for shipping. These products were then shipped as if they had been manufactured in the United States to, of all places, the American military (where the U.S. manufacture of machine tools was a requirement). An American accountant at the firm finally blew the whistle, but when the workers who had been doing the unpacking and repacking were asked why they did it, they replied that they were doing what their supervisor had told them to do. One of the men who had attempted to protest was told that he could find another job if he didn't like it, so he continued doing what he was told to do.

This is just one of many examples we could cite of workers at all levels doing what they're told by managers. Participants in the famous 1972 Watergate break-in referred to their unquestioning obedience to superior orders in testimony before the Senate investigating committee, as did Nazi SS officers in war crimes trials and participants in the Iran-Contra affair.[36] Organizations (corporate, political, or military) are authority structures whose members accept the idea that, to be members in good standing, they must give up a certain amount of independence and autonomy. They expect that managers will tell them what to do. That's the managerial role. They also assume that they should do what's expected of them. That's the subordinate role. These assumptions and expectations allow organizations to avoid chaos and function in an orderly way. In addition, individuals often feel that they owe the organization and their manager their loyalty, thus further reinforcing the pressure to comply.

The Milgram Experiments

Probably the most famous social psychological studies of all time were conducted by Stanley Milgram in the 1960s. They provide uncomfortable insights into how normal adults behave in authority situations.[37] Most adults will carry out the authority figure's orders even if these orders are contrary to their personal beliefs about what's right and will lead to harming other human beings.

In a number of laboratory experiments, Milgram paid subjects recruited from the New Haven, Connecticut area to participate in a one-hour study on the effects of punishment on learning. The subject was asked to play "teacher" in a learning experiment; the "learner," unbeknownst to the teacher/subject, was a member of the research team (known in research parlance as a "confederate"). The learner was strapped into a chair with an electrode attached to his or her wrist. The teacher/subject was seated at a shock generator and was told to pose questions to the learner. Each time the learner provided an incorrect response to a question, the teacher/subject was told to turn a dial to administer an increasingly severe shock—though in fact no shocks were actually given. As the apparent "shocks" intensified, the learner verbally expressed scripted responses representing increasing discomfort, finally screaming and then going silent. During the experiments, many teacher/subjects would question the experimenter and express the desire to stop. The experimenter, dressed in a white lab coat, would provide the following scripted response, "Although the shocks may be painful, there is no permanent tissue damage, so please go on." If the teacher/subject continued to resist, the experimenter would respond with three successive prods: "The experiment requires that you continue"; "It is absolutely essential that you continue"; "You have no choice, you must go on." If the teacher continued to resist, the experiment was finally terminated.

To the surprise of Milgram and other observers, about 60 percent of the teacher/subjects in these experiments continued to the end, obeying the authority figure's instructions despite the conflict they felt and expressed. It's not that they felt okay about what they were doing. In fact, their emotional appeals to the experimenter suggested that they very much wanted to stop. But most of them didn't. They may have felt that refusing to continue would challenge the experimenter's authority, affect the legitimacy of the experiment, and cause embarrassment for themselves.[38] They acted as if they were constrained to do as they were told by the authority figure, rather than as independent adults who could end the experiment at any time. We should also note that teacher/subjects who were at the principled level of cognitive moral development (see Chapter 3) were more likely to challenge the experimenter's authority as well as more likely to stop giving the electric shocks. So, although some participants did resist the authority figure's commands to continue, most of them did not.

Do you think that people today are different somehow—that they would be less susceptible to authority figure dictates? Jerry Burger, a psychology professor at Santa Clara University carried out a partial replication of the original Milgram experiment and published the results in 2009.[39] Much like Milgram had done, he recruited people from the community. The recruitment process screened out individuals who might have been familiar with the original Milgram experiments or whose screening suggested that they might have a negative reaction to participating. In its design, the study closely followed the original. The main difference was that, in keeping with modern-day ethics rules about protecting human subjects in research, the experiment was stopped when the teacher/subject thought she or he had administered a 150-volt shock (rather than continuing all the way to 450 volts, as in the original version). In the original experiment, 150 volts appeared to be a turning point. Most subjects who passed that point continued all the way up the shock generator. In the replication, subjects were also told multiple times that they could leave at any time and keep the $50 they were being paid. Once the experiment was completed, the learner immediately entered the room and told the teacher/subject that he or she was fine. In addition, the experimenter was a trained clinical psychologist who stopped the experiment immediately at any sign of serious stress. Even with all of these changes, the results were quite similar to those Milgram found more than 40 years ago. About two-thirds of the teacher/subjects continued to deliver shocks up to 150 volts.

No matter what the results, this is still an experiment that took place in a behavioral laboratory. Do the findings apply in the real world? Apparently, yes. A few years ago, ABC TV showcased a horrifying "real-world" version of the Milgram experiment. A person posing as a police officer telephoned a McDonald's in 2004 and told the assistant manager (named Donna Summers) that a young woman employee (whom he described) had stolen a purse and should be brought into the office. He also claimed that he had Summers's boss on another phone line. Once the employee was in the office, the caller instructed the manager to take the employee's cell phone and car keys and have her remove her clothes and do jumping jacks in the nude. Having done so, the manager said that she needed to get back to the busy restaurant so the caller suggested that she tap her middle-aged fiancé, Walter Nix, to watch the employee. Nix followed further phone instructions from the alleged police officer and eventually sexually abused the young woman employee. The entire event was recorded on the restaurant's surveillance camera, and much of it was broadcast in the ABC special report. Nix was sentenced to several years in prison for sexual assault. The caller was caught when police discovered that he had used a telephone card bought at a Wal-Mart. They identified the man using Wal-Mart's surveillance cameras (he was a corrections officer and the married father of five!) and he was arrested—but surprisingly, not convicted. Summers was fired and received probation. The victim also brought a civil suit against McDonald's, which she won in late 2008 (the case was appealed and settled). We share this story with you because it provides a too real (some might say surreal) example of obedience to authority at two levels. First, the young woman employee obeyed her boss's instruction to hand over her keys, cell phone, and clothes. It didn't occur to her to resist these extraordinary requests, because they were coming from an adult authority figure, her boss. Even more outrageous is the willingness of Summers and Nix to harm another person simply because someone posing as a police officer told them to do so. In the broadcast interview, Summers claimed that she believed he was a police officer and that she was doing the right thing.

Obedience to Authority at Work

The obedient behavior seen in the Milgram experiments and their modern counterparts is similar to behavior observed again and again in work organizations. The notion of legitimate authority is an accepted tenet of organizational life. In 1968, American military men massacred hundreds of innocent civilians at My Lai, Vietnam. They didn't ask questions. They did what they were told to do despite the military's efforts in training soldiers to believe that it is their duty to disobey unjust authority.

More recently, Lyndie England, who was found guilty of prisoner abuse at Abu Ghraib prison in Iraq, claimed that she and others were following orders of authorities above her. In addition, such behavior is not limited to organizations we think of as authoritarian such as the military. Individuals who testified to the U.S. Congress about price-fixing practices in the electrical industry were asked why they didn't report these practices to higher authorities. They responded that they felt they couldn't because they reported to a prescribed superior only.[40] Roger Boisjoly, who questioned the safety of the O-rings and attempted to convince managers to cancel the launch of the space shuttle *Challenger*, never went outside the chain of command at his company to protest.[41] So, as current or future work organization members, we encourage you to stop and think hard when an authority figure asks you to do something that could harm another person or seems wrong in some other way. Think for yourself—and as difficult as it might seem at the time, say no.

Practical Advice for Managers: Obedience to Authority

Managers must also realize the power they hold as authority figures in work organizations. Old concepts die hard. And even today in team-oriented organizations, most people will do as they're told. Authority figures therefore must exhibit ethical behavior, and they must send powerful signals that high ethical standards are expected of everyone and that employees are expected to question authority figures if they believe they are being asked to do something that is wrong. This message should begin at the top of the organization and work its way down through every level. Moreover, when unethical behavior is uncovered, the investigation must consider the explicit or implicit messages being sent by authority figures. Don't assume that the individual acted alone and without influence. Our tendency is to try to isolate the problem, find the one "culprit" (bad apple), and get on with our lives. But the culprit may have been explicitly or implicitly encouraged by a superior, and this possibility should be investigated and taken into account.

RESPONSIBILITY IS DIFFUSED IN ORGANIZATIONS

For a relationship to exist between what people think is right and what they do, they must feel responsible for the consequences of their actions.[42] Therefore the sense of personal responsibility is a prerequisite for moral action. If you yourself decided to market a certain product that might hurt small children or the environment, you would be much more likely to seriously consider the moral implications of the decision. But in organizations, the individual often becomes disconnected from the consequences of his or her actions and doesn't feel personally responsible for them. Responsibility becomes diffused. No individual feels the need to take responsibility, so in the end, no one does; unethical behavior is then more likely.

For at least four reasons, individuals may not feel personally responsible for their organizational actions. Responsibility is diffused because it is taken away, shared with others in decision-making groups, obscured by the organizational hierarchy, or diluted by psychological distance to potential victims.

"Don't Worry—We're Taking Care of Everything"

At work, individuals are often encouraged to turn responsibility over to those at higher levels. This behavior is related to our earlier discussion of obedience to authority. But in this case, the individual is simply told not to worry—that the problem or decision is someone else's responsibility. For example, an individual who expresses concern about a safety or environmental problem may be told, "We appreciate your concern, but you don't need to worry about it. We're taking care of everything." This type of response absolves the subordinate of feelings of responsibility for the consequences of the organization's action. Someone, particularly someone at a higher level, has taken the responsibility.

Even if the superiors are highly responsible and highly ethical, however, the act of absolving subordinates of responsibility may have significant implications for their subsequent ethical behavior. Because of the feeling that they must do as they're told by authority figures, most people feel they have no choice but to follow superiors' orders. In this case, the orders are to hand over responsibility for decision making, and the individual feels that she or he has no choice but to give it up. If this sort of response becomes routine, individuals will come to believe that it isn't their responsibility to be on the lookout for ethical violations, and they may stop bringing potential problems to the attention of superiors.

Diffusing Responsibility in Groups

Because important organizational decisions are often made in groups, responsibility for the decision becomes diffused among all group members. No single individual feels responsible. Diffusion of responsibility in groups is used to explain the results of classic research on the likelihood that bystanders will help a seizure victim.[43] This research suggests that when others are present, responsibility is diffused among all of the bystanders and individuals are less likely to help.

Diffusion of responsibility also operates in group decision making through a process known as groupthink,[44] which has been used to explain a number of historical group decision-making disasters such as the Bay of Pigs fiasco in John F. Kennedy's presidential administration. Groupthink can occur in cohesive groups whose members are committed to the group and have a strong desire to remain group members. A major characteristic of groupthink is individual group members' tendency to conform to the decision they think most of the group's members prefer. Individual group members may find it difficult to express disagreement and tend to censor themselves even if they disagree with the group decision.

One important symptom of groupthink is the group's "illusion of morality," the sense that the group simply wouldn't do anything wrong. In a classic instructional film on groupthink, a group of managers makes a decision to market a new drug despite disturbing evidence that it may cause dangerous side effects. The illusion of morality is expressed by a group member who states that the company has a well-earned good reputation and would never do anything to hurt its customers.

Clearly, decisions with ethical overtones that are made in a group setting require special attention. The manager must make sure that the ethical implications are identified and carefully analyzed. The group leader should be careful not to state his or her preference up front, because group members will tend to censor their own beliefs to conform to those of the leader. Other techniques can be used to make sure that alternative viewpoints are aired. For example, group members can be asked to provide anonymous criticism of the decision being considered. Computer-based group decision support systems often provide such a feature. An individual can be appointed to the role of devil's advocate, or multiple individuals can be appointed to voice multiple alternative perspectives. It's easier for these individuals to take an alternative stance when it's their role to do so. Another alternative is to open the group to outside stakeholders who would come in to present their concerns and perspectives.

Diffusing Responsibility by Dividing Responsibility

Responsibility in organizations is often so divided that individuals see themselves as only a small cog in a large machine. Or they simply don't have vital information that would be required to make a good decision. Division of responsibility is essential for the kind of specialization required in modern jobs. But this means that organizational members often do their jobs with blinders on; they see only what's directly ahead of them, and no one sees (or takes responsibility for) the whole picture.

Scott Peck is a psychiatrist and author of the best-selling book, *The Road Less Traveled* (1978).[45] He was part of a group dispatched to study the 1968 My Lai massacre in South Vietnam. At My Lai, American troops slaughtered a village of unarmed women, children, and elderly men. The killing took all morning, and only one person, an observant helicopter pilot, tried to stop it. Peck's interviews with military people revealed a bureaucratic organizational structure that allowed individuals to see only their own narrow part of the problem, thereby allowing them to avoid feelings of responsibility. When Peck wandered the halls of the Pentagon, questioning those involved in directing the manufacture of napalm and its transportation to Vietnam as bombs, the replies he received were something like the following: "We appreciate your problem and your concerns, but we are not the department you want. We are in ordnance. We supply the weapons, but we don't determine how they're used." Down the hall, another group suggested that the broad issues were also beyond their purview. "We simply determine how the war will be conducted—not whether it will be conducted."[46] Peck termed this process "the fragmentation of conscience." "Any group will remain inevitably potentially conscienceless and evil until such time as each and every individual holds himself or herself directly responsible for the behavior of the whole group—the organism of which he or she is a part. We have not yet begun to arrive at that point."[47]

Research has documented the process of diffusing responsibility. In a variation on the Milgram obedience-to-authority experiments discussed earlier, diffusion of responsibility was simulated by dividing the original teacher's role between two people, a "transmitter" and an "executant." The transmitter would inform the executant when a shock had to be administered and at what level. The experiment found that transmitters were significantly more likely to obey than executants.[48] One can imagine that it was easier for the transmitter to rationalize his or her actions. "I didn't actually do the harm—someone else did." This rationalization should become easier and easier, the greater the distance between the individual decision maker and the actual outcome.

Diffusion of responsibility also occurs at a broader system level. Think about September 11, 2001, and the discussions about whether the government should have been able to "connect the dots" and anticipate the terrorist attacks. Different people in different government agencies had extremely relevant information (about specific terrorists, their activities in the United States such as flight training, and plans to fly planes into other key structures such as the Eiffel Tower). But these agencies were not set up to communicate with each other on a regular basis. In fact, some of them (the CIA and FBI) were explicitly designed to operate independently because of concerns about the power of an integrated agency. So the design of an organization (and decisions about who communicates with whom) influences the nature of information individuals receive in organizations and whether they can be held responsible.

Similarly, many individuals at multiple financial industry organizations contributed to the recent financial crisis. Realtors sold houses to people who couldn't afford them. Mortgage lenders created risky loans for these buyers. Investment bankers securitized those loans. Ratings agencies scored the securities highly based upon past performance. No one stepped back to consider that the system of continuously increasing real estate prices was unsustainable and would eventually self-correct, if not crash. The responsibility was widely diffused. The actions of single individuals did not create the crisis, but the combined actions of many did. Therefore it is important to consider how we can get individuals to think more broadly about the potential consequences of their individual actions when combined with the actions of others.

Diffusing Responsibility by Creating Psychological Distance

Responsibility can also be diffused because of the psychological distance between the decision maker and potential victims.[49] When potential victims are psychologically distant or out of sight, it's more difficult to see oneself as responsible for any negative outcomes. This principle was exemplified in further variations on the studies of obedience to authority; in those studies, Milgram varied the closeness of the learner "victim" to the teacher.[50] For example, when the learner was placed in the same room with the teacher, the level of obedience dropped more than 20 percent (to 40 percent). In another variation, when the teacher was asked to physically force the learner's hand onto the shock plate, the obedience level dropped another 10 percent. In these situations, as psychological distance decreased, the teacher felt personal responsibility more strongly and was less likely to comply with the authority figure's demands to harm the learner.

In yet another variation on the obedience experiments, Milgram posed as an ordinary man—not as a scientist in a white lab coat. When Milgram, dressed like an ordinary man, conducted the experiments, obedience by the subjects dropped from 60 percent to 20 percent. The influence of a uniform (like a lab coat) on obedience is startling.

This research suggests that personal responsibility for the outcomes of our organizational decisions will be less clear in situations where the potential harm is far removed. For example, when the plant is not in our community, but in Mexico or somewhere in Asia, potential negative consequences are more distant; we may feel less personal responsibility, and we may be more willing to make decisions that would harm other people. Similarly, when we see a decision as someone else's responsibility (not my job), we are more likely to go along with decisions that harm others.

Practical Advice for Managers: Personal Responsibility

People are much more likely to act ethically if they perceive themselves as personally responsible for the outcomes of their decisions and actions. That means they also need to have the relevant information. As a manager, you should make individual responsibility a highly salient issue for yourself and others. Spell out the responsibilities associated with specific positions, and hold individuals to those expectations. When a worker brings up an ethical concern, don't take it completely off his or her hands. And don't say that it's someone else's responsibility. If it becomes necessary to do so, be sure to keep the concerned individual informed of the progress and outcome of the decision.

When it comes to groups, make it clear that every group member will be held personally responsible for the outcome of group decisions. Ask groups to present minority reports or recommendations so that a communication mechanism exists for those who don't agree with the group. Appoint a devil's advocate or multiple advocates to question the assumptions of the group and the group's decision.

Don't forget to think about the design of your organization. How is the work divided? Does the division of labor contribute to a diffusion of responsibility by keeping people in the dark about relevant facts? Does the organizational structure make people feel like they're just cogs in a bigger wheel? Encourage information and responsibility sharing across bureaucratic divides.

The current movement to decrease levels in the organizational hierarchy may have a positive side benefit. People find that they have to communicate more laterally—across the organization. Also, with fewer levels, it should become more difficult for organizational members to rationalize that higher-ups were responsible. Finally, personal visits to geographically distant work sites and personal contact with customers should decrease psychological distance and increase the manager's feeling of responsibility for the outcomes of any decisions or actions that impact people in these locations.

CONCLUSION

You now have some important management concepts in your toolbox that can be applied to the management of ethical and unethical conduct at whatever organizational level you find yourself. The remaining challenge is to ask yourself questions that will help you determine whether you are an ethical leader who creates a work environment that supports doing the right thing and discourages unethical conduct.

Am I Walking My Ethical Talk?

A common phrase used by today's managers is "walking the talk." If your intention is to be an ethical leader, here are some questions to ask yourself to see if you're walking your ethical talk.

1. Do I talk about the ethical implications of decisions with the people who report to me as well as with the job candidates I'm interested in hiring? With my peers? With my manager?

2. Have I made it clear to the people who report to me that I don't want to be protected from bad news? Do they understand that they can tell me anything without fear of retribution? Do my reports come to me with ethical concerns?

3. Do I provide guidance on ethical decision making, and have I participated in the ethics training of those who report to me?

4. When evaluating the performance of my staff, do I value ethical goals at least as highly as performance and quality goals? Do I focus on the means as well as the ends in decision making and performance appraisals?

5. Do I reward ethical conduct and discipline unethical conduct?

6. Do I require my people to take responsibility for their decisions?

7. Do I support employees who challenge unjust authority?

8. What are the informal norms in my department? If my employees were asked to list the "rules" of working for me, what would they say? Are any of these problematic if ethical conduct is the goal?

9. Do my direct reports know I care about them and will be there for them in good times and bad?

10. If I were to die tomorrow, would the people who report to me say that I had integrity? How would my peers describe me? And what would my manager say?

The answers to these questions should form a sound beginning for understanding and managing ethical behavior in your work group and within the broader ethical culture.

DISCUSSION QUESTIONS

For the following questions, if you don't have work experience, interview someone who does and ask them these questions. Otherwise, ask them of yourself.

1. Have you ever been in a situation—especially a work situation—where the norms supported a particular behavior, ethical or unethical, that you felt pressured to go along with? Explain.

2. Have you ever been in a situation where the rewards explicitly or implicitly supported unethical conduct? Explain.

3. Can you think of situations in which unethical behavior was dealt with appropriately (punished justly) or inappropriately? What were the reactions of others in the organization?

4. What do you think would be appropriate punishment for those found guilty of assault or indecent exposure in the Tailhook situation? Why?

5. Have you ever felt obligated to do something you felt was wrong because a person in a position of authority told you to do it?

6. Think about how you might design work to maximize workers' taking responsibility for the consequences of their actions.

7. Evaluate yourself or a manager you know using the "do you walk your talk?" questions above.

CASE

SEARS, ROEBUCK, AND CO.: THE AUTO CENTER SCANDAL

Sears, Roebuck, and Co. began in the late 1800s as a mail-order company that sold farm supplies and other consumer items. Its first retail store opened in the mid-1920s. Responding to changes in American society, such as the move from farms to factories and the presence of the automobile in many homes, hundreds of retail stores opened over the years. The company expanded rapidly, and eventually it diversified to include other businesses: insurance (Allstate Insurance), real estate (Coldwell Banker), securities (Dean Witter Reynolds), and credit cards (Discover). Each of these other businesses became its own division, in addition to the merchandising group that included retail stores, appliances, and auto service centers. By the early 1990s, the company was reporting revenues and earnings in the billions of dollars.[51]

Despite its long history of high earnings and its penetration into the U.S. market, the Sears retail business began to experience serious financial difficulties in the 1980s.

Discount retailers such as Wal-Mart were pulling ahead in market share, leaving Sears lagging. Sears responded by adding non-Sears name brands and an "everyday low price" policy. But despite these efforts, in 1990 Sears reported a 40 percent decline in earnings, and its merchandising group dropped a whopping 60 percent! Cost-cutting measures were planned, including the elimination of jobs and a focus on profits at every level.[52]

In 1991, Sears unveiled a productivity incentive plan to increase profits in its auto centers nationwide. Auto mechanics had traditionally been paid an hourly wage and were expected to meet production quotas. In 1991, the compensation plan was changed to include a commission component. Mechanics were paid a base salary plus a fixed dollar amount for meeting hourly production quotas. Auto service advisors (the counter people who take orders, consult with mechanics, and advise customers) had traditionally been paid a salary. To increase sales, however, commissions and product-specific sales quotas were introduced for them as well. For example, a service advisor might be given the goal of selling a certain number of front-end alignments or brake repairs during each shift.[53]

In June 1992, the California Department of Consumer Affairs accused Sears, Roebuck, and Co. of violating the state's Auto Repair Act and sought to revoke the licenses of all Sears auto centers in California. The allegation resulted from an increasing number of consumer complaints and an undercover investigation of brake repairs. Other states quickly followed suit. Essentially, the charges alleged that Sears Auto Centers had been systematically misleading customers and charging them for unnecessary repairs. The California investigation attributed the problems to Sears Auto Centers' compensation system.[54]

In response to the charges, Sears CEO and Chairman Edward A. Brennan called a news conference to deny that any fraud had occurred, and he defended Sears' focus on preventive maintenance for older cars. He admitted to isolated errors, accepted personal responsibility for creating an environment where "mistakes" had occurred, and outlined the actions the company planned to take to resolve the issue. These included

- Eliminating the incentive compensation program for service advisors
- Substituting commissions based on customer satisfaction
- Eliminating sales quotas for specific parts and repairs
- Substituting sales volume quotas

According to Brennan, "We have to have some way to measure performance."[55] Sears also introduced "shopping audits" of its auto centers, during which employees would pose as customers, and Brennan published a letter of explanation to the company's customers in the *Wall Street Journal* and *USA Today* on June 25, 1992.

Note that the compensation system for mechanics, based on the number of tasks performed and parts replaced, was maintained. In the summer of 1992, Chuck Fabbri, a Sears mechanic from California, sent a letter about Sears's wage policy for mechanics to U.S. Senator Richard Bryan. Fabbri said:

> It is my understanding that Sears is attempting to convince your committee that all inspections in their auto centers are now performed by employees who are paid hourly and not on commission. This is not the case. The truth is that the majority of employees performing inspections are still on commission . . .
>
> The Service Advisors . . . sell the repair work to the customer . . . The repairs that they sell are not only based on their inspections, but to a larger degree based on the recommendations of mechanics who are on commission . . .
>
> On January 1, 1991, the mechanics, installers and tire changers had their hourly wages cut to what Sears termed a fixed dollar amount, or FDA per hour which varied depending on the classification. At present the mechanic's FDA amount is $3.25 which, based on current Sears minimum production quotas, is 17% of my earnings. What this means is that for every hour of work, as defined by Sears, that I complete, I receive $3.25 plus my hourly base pay. If I do two hours worth of work in one hour I receive an additional $3.25 therefore increasing my earnings.
>
> Sears calls this type of compensation incentive pay or piecework; however, a rose by any other name is still a rose. This is commission plain and simple. The faster I get the work done the more money I make, and as intended, Sears' profits increase. It is therefore obvious to increase his earnings, a mechanic might cut corners on, or eliminate altogether, procedures required to complete the repair correction. In addition to this, since the mechanic often inspects or performs the diagnosis, he has the ideal opportunity to oversell or recommend more repair work than is needed. This would be especially tempting if it has been a slow day or week. In part greed may create this less than ethical situation, but high pressure to meet quotas by Sears' management also presents a significant contribution. I have recently been threatened with termination if my production didn't at least equal Sears' minimum quotas. I might add that prior to this new wage policy, management had only positive responses to my production, and my record proves this. . . .
>
> There is no doubt in my mind that before their auto center employees were put on commission Sears enjoyed the trust of its customers. Today presents a different story. The solution is obvious not only for Sears, but for the industry.[56]

Sears agreed to a multimillion-dollar settlement with the state of California and the 41 other states that had filed similar charges. The company was placed on three-year probation in California. It also settled a number of consumer class-action suits. In July 1992, the U.S. Congress held hearings on fraud in the auto repair industry.

The long-term impact of the scandal is unclear. Sears has now sold off its securities firm, the Discover card, most of its real estate and mortgage business, and 20 percent of Allstate Insurance. At the end of 1992, auto center sales lagged behind prior levels.[57] Also in 1992, *Business Week* reported that employees in other areas of Sears's business, such as insurance and appliance sales, were feeling the same kinds of pressures from sales quotas.[58]

Case Questions

1. Identify the ethical issues involved in the case from a consequentialist and deontological perspective (refer to Chapter 2).

2. Identify the management issues involved in the case. For example, think about the case in terms of multiple ethical selves, norms, reward systems, diffusion of responsibility, obedience to authority. What factors contributed the most to the alleged unethical conduct on the part of service advisors and mechanics?

3. How would you evaluate Sears's response to the allegations and the changes the company made? Has Sears resolved its problem? Why or why not?

4. What do you think is the impact of the scandal on Sears's reputation for quality and service?

5. Respond to Brennan's comment, "We have to have some way to measure performance." What can management do to prevent employees from overselling? Propose a management plan (including a compensation system) that allows management to measure performance and encourages auto center employees to behave ethically. Be specific.

6. Should anyone be disciplined? If so, who, and when? What should the discipline be?

7. Think more generally about Sears management's response to the firm's financial problems. How else could they have increased auto center sales without providing incentives to employees to sell specific products?

SHORT CASE

You've recently been promoted into the position of marketing manager in the communications division of your company. Your new job involves managing a staff and creating the publications and marketing materials for insurance sales professionals in three regions.

You have met the directors of the three regional sales forces before, and now you ask each one for a meeting to discuss in depth how your team can best meet their needs. Two of the sales directors were very cordial, and each explained what the technical demands of their areas are and how your department can best meet their needs.

However, during your meeting with Bill—the sales director of the third region and one of your firm's biggest moneymakers—he lays down the law. He says that his area is the largest of the three regions, and it produces significantly more revenue for your company than the other two regions combined. "You and your people need to know that when I say, 'Jump,'" he says, "they need to ask, 'How high?'"

In return, he says, he'll recommend you and your people for every award the company has to offer. In addition, he says he'll personally give you a monetary bonus, based on your team's performance, at the end of the year. Although you have never heard of a manager giving someone a bonus out of his own pocket, you suspect that your company would frown on such a practice.

Case Questions

1. What are the ethical issues in this case?

2. What are some reasons the decision maker in this case might be inclined to go along? Not go along?

3. If you were the decision maker, how would you handle the situation?

4. Would you report the conversation to your manager? Why or why not?

NOTES

1. B. Toffler, *Tough Choices* (New York: Wiley & Sons, 1986).
2. R. A. Barrett, *Culture and Conduct: An Excursion in Anthropology* (Belmont, CA: Wadsworth, 1986).
3. E. Thomas and A. Murr, "The Gambler Who Blew It All," *Newsweek*, February 4, 2002, 18–24.
4. Ibid.
5. J. Nichols, "Enron: What Dick Cheney Knew," *The Nation*, April 15, 2002, 14–16, at http://www .thenation.com/article/enron-what-dick-cheney-knew.
6. A. Sloan, "Lay's a Victim? Not a Chance," *Newsweek*, July 19, 2004, 50.
7. R. Lederer, "Take the Money Enron," *Across the Board*, November–December 2003, 9.
8. A. B. Gesalman, "Cliff Was Climbing the Walls," *Newsweek*, February 4, 2002, 24.
9. D. B. Levine, "The Inside Story of an Inside Trader," *Fortune*, May 21, 1990, 80–89.
10. E. E. Umphress, A. Barsky, and K. See, "Be Careful What You Wish For: Goal Setting, Procedural Justice, and Ethical Behavior at Work," Paper presented at the Academy of Management meeting, Honolulu, Hawaii, 2005.
11. D. Knight, C. C. Durham, and E. A. Locke, "The Relationship of Team Goals, Incentives, and Efficacy to Strategic Risk, Tactical Implementation, and Performance," *Academy of Management Journal* 44 (2001): 326–38; M. W. Schweitzer, L. Ordoñez, and B. Douma, "Goal Setting as a Motivator of Unethical Behavior," *Academy of Management Journal* 47 (2004): 422–32.
12. E. Umphress, K. See, A. Barsky, C. Gogus, L. Ren, and A. Coleman, "Be Careful What You Wish For: Goals Influencing Ethical Behavior in Organizations," Symposium presented at the 65th annual conference of the Academy of Management, Honolulu, Hawaii, 2005.
13. D. Eden, "Self-fulfilling Prophecy as a Management Tool: Harnessing Pygmalion," *Academy of Management Review* 9 (1984): 64–73.
14. A. Bandura, *Social Foundations of Thought and Action: A Social-Cognitive Theory* (Englewood Cliffs, NJ: Prentice-Hall, 1986).
15. E. Goodman, "Nobody Deemed Accountable for Tailhook," (State College, PA) *Centre Daily Times*, February 15, 1994, 6A.

16. D. C. Waller, "Tailhook's Lightning Rod," *Newsweek*, February 28, 1994, 31.

17. A. Marshall, "Knowing What's Ahead Can Prevent Looking Back with Regret," *Hotel and Motel Management*, March 6, 2000, 10.

18. G. L. Vistica, "Anchors Aweigh," *Newsweek*, February 5, 1996, 69–71.

19. P. Stewart. "Sexual assault is a 'scourge' on U.S. military: Hagel." *Reuters online*, May 25, 2013 and R. Lardner. "Sexual assaults in military rose to over 26,000 in 2012: Pentagon Survey." *Huffingtonpost. com*, May 5, 2013.

20. D. B. Levine, "The Inside Story of an Inside Trader," *Fortune*, May 21, 1990, 80–89.

21. G. Ball, L. K. Treviño, and H. P. Sims Jr., "Just and Unjust Punishment Incidents," *Academy of Management Journal* 37 (1994): 299–322.

22. L. K. Treviño and G. A. Ball, "The Social Implications of Punishing Unethical Behavior: Observers' Cognitive and Affective Reactions," *Journal of Management* 18 (1992): 751–68.

23. B. McLean and P. Elkind, *The Smartest Guys in the Room* (New York: Portfolio, 2003), 21–24.

24. Thomas J. Watson Jr., *Father, Son & Co.: My Life at IBM and Beyond* (New York: Bantam, 1990).

25. G. Morgenson, "The Enforcers of Wall St.? Then Again, Maybe Not," *New York Times*, June 20, 2002, C1–C2.

26. L. K. Treviño and B. Victor, "Peer Reporting of Unethical Behavior: A Social Context Perspective," *Academy of Management Journal* 353 (1992): 38–64.

27. P. G. Zimbardo, "The Human Choice: Individuation, Reason, and Order versus Deindividuation, Impulse, and Chaos," In *Nebraska Symposium on Motivation*, eds. W. J. Arnold and D. Levine (Lincoln: University of Nebraska Press, 1969), 237–307.

28. C. Haney, C. Banks, and P. Zimbardo, "Interpersonal Dynamics in a Simulated Prison," *International Journal of Criminology and Penology* 1 (1973): 69–97.

29. P. Zimbardo, "Pathology of Imprisonment," in *Readings in Social Psychology: Contemporary Perspectives* (2nd ed.), ed. D. Krebs (New York: Harper & Row, 1982).

30. J. Barry, M. Hosenball, and B. Dehghanpisheh, "Abu Ghraib and Beyond," *Newsweek*, May 17, 2004, 32–38; D. Jehl and E. Schmitt, "Dogs and Other Harsh Tactics Linked to Military Intelligence," *New York Times*, May 22, 2004, A1; S. Sontag, "Regarding the Torture of Others," *New York Times Magazine*, May 23, 2004, 24–41; P. V. Zelbauer and J. Dao, "Guard Left Troubled Life for Duty in Iraq," *New York Times*, May 14, 2004, A11.

31. D. Katz and R. Kahn, *The Social Psychology of Organizations*, 2nd ed. (New York: Wiley & Sons, 1978).

32. F. N. Brady and J. M. Logsdon, "Zimbardo's 'Stanford prison experiment' and the Relevance of Social Psychology for Teaching Business Ethics," *Journal of Business Ethics* 7 (1988): 703–10; P. Brodeur, *Outrageous Misconduct: The Asbestos Industry on Trial* (New York: Pantheon, 1985).

33. S. Grover, "Why Professionals Lie: The Impact of Professional Role Conflict on Reporting Accuracy," *Organizational Behavior and Human Decision Processes* 55 (1993): 251–72.

34. M. P. Miceli and J. P. Near, "The Relationships among Beliefs, Organizational Position, and Whistle-Blowing Status: A Discriminant Analysis," *Academy of Management Journal* 27 (1984): 687–705.

35. L. K. Treviño and B. Victor, "Peer Reporting of Unethical Behavior: A Social Context Perspective," *Academy of Management Journal* 353 (1992): 38–64.

36. H. C. Kelman and V. L. Hamilton, *Crimes of Obedience* (New Haven, CT: Yale University Press, 1989).

37. S. Milgram, *Obedience to Authority: An Experimental View* (New York: Harper & Row, 1974).

38. H. C. Kelman and V. L. Hamilton, *Crimes of Obedience* (New Haven, CT: Yale University Press, 1989).

39. J. M. Burger, "Replicating Milgram: Would People Still Obey Today?" *American Psychologist* 64, no. 1 (2009): 1–11.

40. J. A. Waters, "Catch 20.5: Corporate Morality as an Organizational Phenomenon," *Organizational Dynamics* (Spring 1978): 319.

41. H. C. Kelman and V. L. Hamilton, *Crimes of Obedience* (New Haven, CT: Yale University Press, 1989).

42. S. H. Schwartz, "Words, Deeds, and the Perception of Consequences and Responsibility in Action Situations," *Journal of Personality and Social Psychology* 10 (1968): 232–42; S. H. Schwartz, "Awareness of Consequences and the Influence of Moral Norms on Interpersonal Behavior," *Sociometry* 31 (1968): 355–69.

43. J. M. Darley and B. Latane, "Bystanders' Intervention in Emergencies: Diffusion of Responsibility," *Journal of Personality and Social Psychology* 8 (1968): 373–83.
44. I. Janis, *Groupthink*, 2nd ed. (Boston: Houghton Mifflin, 1982).
45. M. S. Peck, M. D., *People of the Lie: The Hope for Healing Human Evil* (New York: Simon & Schuster, 1983).
46. Ibid.
47. Ibid.
48. W. Kilham and L. Mann, "Level of Destructive Obedience as a Function of Transmitter and Executant Roles in the Milgram Obedience Paradigm," *Journal of Personality and Social Psychology* 29 (1974): 696–702.
49. H. C. Kelman and V. L. Hamilton, *Crimes of Obedience* (New Haven, CT: Yale University Press, 1989).
50. S. Milgram, *Obedience to Authority: An Experimental View* (New York: Harper & Row, 1974).
51. M. A. Santoro, *Sears Auto Centers* (Boston: Harvard Business School, 1993).
52. K. Kelly, "How Did Sears Blow This Gasket?" *Businessweek*, June 29, 1992, 38.
53. M. A. Santoro, *Sears Auto Centers* (Boston: Harvard Business School, 1993).
54. K. Kelly, "How Did Sears Blow This Gasket?" *Businessweek*, June 29, 1992, 38.
55. D. Gellene, "New State Probe of Sears Could Lead to Suit," *Los Angeles Times*, June 12, 1992, part D: 1.
56. Hearing before Subcommittee on Consumer of the Senate Committee on Commerce, Science, and Transportation, 102nd Congress, 2nd Sess., July 21, 1992 (Sen. Hearing 102972), 83.
57. M. A. Santoro, *Sears Auto Centers* (Boston: Harvard Business School, 1993).
58. J. Flynn, "Did Sears Take Other Customers for a Ride?" *Businessweek*, August 3, 1992, 24–25.

CHAPTER *8*

ETHICAL PROBLEMS OF MANAGERS

INTRODUCTION

Good managers do four things really well: hire good people, define clear expectations (including ethical expectations), recognize excellence and praise it, and finally, show their people that they care.[1] We're going to focus on those managerial "basics" in this chapter, since managers are responsible for the entire range of human resources activities such as hiring, firing, disciplining, and evaluating performance. Consequently, some of the ethical responsibilities of managers and employees are different and require special thought and preparation. Also, since managers are responsible for employee supervision, the courts can hold them accountable for the activities and behavior of the people who report to them. Finally, because managers are role models for the workers in their department, it's critical that managers be able to discuss the ethical implications of decision making and provide advice to employees who find themselves in an ethical quandary. These facts of corporate life have frustrated many managers. "How can I possibly manage the ethics or morality of the people I manage? Is it even possible to manage ethics? Where are the special pitfalls for me as a manager?" In this chapter, we examine what responsibilities managers have and how you as a manager can encourage employee engagement and influence your direct reports to make ethical decisions. We also explore how organizational culture influences manager decisions and how managers can help reinforce the ethical culture of their organization.

Managers and Employee Engagement

An extremely important element in any corporate endeavor—whether it's an ethics program, productivity effort, employee engagement initiative, or anything else—is the quality of an organization's managers. To employees, managers *are* the company, and if managers are not able to manage the basics well, it will be extremely difficult to inspire people to meet business goals or live organizational values.

As more companies study how people work and what makes employees most productive, a clearer picture is emerging of exactly what motivates employees *and* encourages ethical behavior at the same time. We believe that those seemingly unconnected activities—encouraging employee engagement and ethical behavior—

are actually intertwined. Research indicates that perhaps the best way to encourage ethical behavior is to create an organizational culture that is built to enhance employee engagement and that uses as its linchpin the quality of managers.

What do we mean by "employee engagement"? In short, it is discretionary effort, or how committed employees are to their work. Are they willing to provide excellent customer service? Are they willing to work overtime if needed to meet a deadline? Are they willing to go the extra mile in providing solutions? We can divide employees into three groups along an engagement continuum. For our purposes, let's just call them actively engaged, not engaged, and actively disengaged. Here's how we might describe the characteristics of each of the three groups:

Actively Engaged Employees ←	Not Engaged Employees ←	Actively Disengaged Employees
• Passionate and enthusiastic • Feel profoundly connected to the company • Drive innovation • Move the company forward • Eagerly go the "extra mile"	• "Checked out" • Sleepwalking • Put time—but not passion or energy—into their work • May or may not go the extra mile	• "It's not my job." • Negative drag on the culture • Little or no company loyalty • Undermine what engaged coworkers accomplish • May well sabotage company initiatives and employee goodwill

It's hard to overstate the importance of increasing an organization's levels of employee engagement. Gallup, one of the first companies to put employee engagement research on the map, claims that actively disengaged employees cost world economies billions of dollars each year.[2] On the positive side, however, actively engaged employees help an organization through such benefits as lower turnover and absenteeism, higher customer loyalty, higher profits per employee, and fewer accidents.[3]

Although the connection between employee engagement and productivity is easy to see, the connection between engagement and ethical behavior may be less obvious. Take just a moment and think about the characteristics that describe each group along the engagement continuum. Which group do you suppose is most likely to engage in unethical behavior? Which group is more likely to misuse corporate resources? Which group is more likely to serve as role models for ethical behavior? Which group is more likely to include mavericks who have their own (not a corporate) agenda? Which group is more likely to raise an issue about suspected wrongdoing? Which group might tend to go to a regulator or newspaper reporter or some other external source if they perceive wrongdoing?

We think it's evident that improving levels of employee engagement can also improve an organization's ethical culture (see Chapter 5). But how does a company begin to do that? First, it needs to focus on the four drivers of engagement; second, it needs to identify and develop great managers. According to James Shaffer, an expert in communication and employee engagement, the four drivers of engagement are as follows:[4]

1. **Line of sight.** Employees understand the company's strategic direction, how the company makes money, and how their individual efforts play a role in that revenue-generating enterprise. *Note:* Business goals and ethical values are important elements in an organization's strategic direction.

2. **Involvement.** Employees are involved in the enterprise; they actively participate, and their ideas are heard. *Note:* This kind of employee involvement encourages the two-way communication that is critical for ethical issues to be identified and resolved.

3. **Information sharing.** People get the information they need to be effective, when they need it, and information goes in all directions—up, down, and across the organization as needed. *Note:* Cultures that encourage information sharing are more likely to be open organizations that identify and resolve ethical issues rather than sweeping them under the rug.

4. **Rewards and recognition.** Business goals and values are clearly spelled out, and employees know what they need to do and how they need to behave to get rewarded. *Note*: It is critical for companies to pay close attention to the incentives that goals and values will provide for ethical (or unethical) behavior.

While there are a number of employee engagement models, we think this one makes a lot of sense and that the four drivers of employee engagement are critical building blocks of an ethical culture.

In addition to focusing on the four drivers of engagement, organizations need to recognize on a fundamental level the critical role that managers play in increasing engagement and building an ethical culture. According to Towers Watson, the international human resources consulting firm, the following key senior manager behaviors influence employee engagement (and we believe these behaviors, when modeled and endorsed by senior managers, trickle down to lower-level managers and supervisors and can greatly influence employees' ethical behavior).[5]

■ Senior management is sincerely interested in employee well-being.

■ Senior management communicates openly and honestly.

■ Senior management is visible and accessible.

■ Senior management effectively communicates the reasons for key business decisions.

■ Senior management's actions are consistent with stated values.

Think about these manager behaviors. Which do you think play a direct or an indirect role in building an ethical culture? Which might build engagement but not influence ethical culture? Which do both?

MANAGING THE "BASICS"

A manager's most important responsibility is to bring good people into the organization and then manage in a way that makes those good people want to stay. The new people may be permanent employees, or they may be part-time employees, temporary workers, or consultants. Effective managers need to be proficient at hiring the best people who fit the organizational culture, evaluating their performance, recognizing and praising excellence, and disciplining or even terminating poor performers.

Hiring and Work Assignments

HIRING CASE

You're planning to hire a new sales manager, and the most promising candidate is really homely. You are concerned about how your customers—and even his colleagues—would react to him. The specific job he's applying for requires extensive customer contact, and his appearance is frankly disconcerting. On the other hand, his credentials are excellent, and he's certainly qualified for the job.

Federal law prohibits discrimination based on race, religion, sex, color, ethnic background, and age, and it protects those who are pregnant or disabled.

In this case of a homely candidate, the solution is ambiguous. He is certainly qualified for the job, and unattractive looks are not included in protectionist handicapped legislation, so the law isn't helpful. But the larger issues are what qualities should determine whether or not an individual should be hired, and is it ethical to consider a prospective employee's attractiveness?

All protectionist legislation points to the answer, as does the concept of fairness. Hiring, promotions, and terminations should be based on qualifications, period. However, it's one thing to ignore someone because of your own prejudice and quite another to hesitate to put someone in a situation where he or she might suffer discrimination from an external audience, such as your customers, that's out of your control. It's difficult to say whether you're doing someone a favor by setting him or her up for possible failure in an environment that's hostile.

Prejudice is difficult to overcome. As we've noted in earlier chapters, everyone has biases. Some people don't like very tall people, or very short people, or fat ones, or skinny ones, or old ones, or young ones. Others have biases against brown eyes, or blue eyes, or eyes with wrinkles, or big noses, or aquiline noses, or balding heads, or hair that looks too long. Some people favor individuals from certain schools or from particular parts of the country. What if someone interviews for a job and, as in this case, he is just plain unattractive; or she's deaf; or he had cancer three years ago; or she speaks English with an accent? Do those qualities have anything to do with an ability to do the job or with talent? What kind of response would the Golden Rule prescribe? Kant's categorical imperative? How about Rawls's veil of ignorance?

Some employers have a "corporate profile" in mind when they hire, especially when they're trying to fill positions with "extensive public contact." Some large *Fortune* 100 companies are well known for their penchant for hiring certain types of employees. They look for healthy young people with regular features, moderate height, a medium build, and no discernible accent. Do employers with a conscious or subconscious "corporate profile" think that the public or their customers are somehow homogeneous? If history had used a corporate profile as a yardstick, Abraham Lincoln, Benjamin Franklin, Marian Anderson, Albert Einstein, Sammy Davis Jr., and Franklin Roosevelt may have been relegated to positions with "no public contact."

Talent and ability come in a variety of packages. When managers use anything other than those two factors to evaluate qualifications for hiring, promotions, or work assignments, they shortchange not only the individual but also their employer and their customers (who surely come in a variety of packages). They also help perpetuate stereotypes, instead of trying to build a workforce that reflects real life. One way to hire is to deeply understand your own organizational culture and to hire based on how well a candidate will "fit" into the existing culture. Both the organization and the employee are likely to be more satisfied when a good fit is achieved. For example, think about a family-oriented organization, like Starbucks, that tries to demonstrate great care for its employees. What would happen if a manager hired an edgy, highly competitive person who doesn't care about relationships? How would that type of person fare in a "warm and fuzzy" company? It would be far smarter for a manager to look for candidates who demonstrate the same qualities that the company values, because those are the people who will succeed in the company culture. On the other hand, companies that stick too closely to a corporate profile can risk being accused of discrimination (as happened to Abercrombie & Fitch when the "look" the company was attempting to achieve seemed to exclude qualified individuals from certain minority groups). Or, they risk becoming too homogeneous and therefore resistant to needed change. So, managers must strike a delicate balance. They need to hire people who fit the current culture, but also they need to be open to people who fit, but may be different. To be successful, organizations need to nurture strong cultures that have enough differences to encourage innovation and balance and that counter the tendency to hire to a "profile."

Performance Evaluation

> You were recently promoted to manager of a department with five professionals and two clerical staff. One of the professionals, Joe, is a nice guy, but he simply hasn't been able to match the performance of the others in the department. When he tells you he has been interviewing for another job in a different part of your company, you pull his personnel file and see that your predecessor had rated Joe's performance as "good to excellent." You frankly

disagree. Joe has asked you for a recommendation. Based on the written appraisals, you could give him a good one—but your personal observation is at odds with the written evaluations. Joe's prospective manager—your peer in another department—asks for your opinion. What do you say?

When we talk about performance evaluation, we're really talking about two things. First, there's a written assessment of an employee's performance. Most large companies have a formal performance management system, with forms to standardize the process, and a mandate to complete a written evaluation on every employee (usually once each year). These written appraisals usually have some influence on any salary adjustments, and they usually become part of the employee's permanent personnel file. Second, there's the informal process of performance evaluation that ideally is an ongoing process throughout the year. When a manager gives continuous feedback—when objectives are stated and then performance against those objectives is measured—employees generally aren't surprised by the annual written performance appraisal.

Why is continuous evaluation important? First, rewards and recognition are one of the four drivers of employee engagement. Excellent managers recognize and reward excellence as well as manage and improve the performance of workers who are at a lower rung on the performance ladder. A training manager in New York City tells a story about the importance of accurately and continuously appraising performance. "Imagine you're bowling," he says. "A bed sheet is stretched across the lane and you can't see what you're doing. Your manager is the only person who can tell you how you're doing. What would happen if your manager told you how you were doing only occasionally or once a year? How would your performance be affected if he or she told you about your performance only when you got gutter balls? What would happen if he or she commented just when you did well?" It's only when your manager gives you consistent feedback—reflecting the complete range of your behavior—that you can improve your performance.

As we noted in Chapter 5, performance management systems do more than almost anything else to signal what the organization cares about (including whether ethics-related behaviors really matter) and to bake desired behaviors into the organizational culture. If managers don't do a good job at coaching employees and influencing their performance, this valuable tool to drive culture and performance is undermined. And if managers don't communicate clearly that ethics-related performance matters, employees will focus on what does.

The practical problem with performance evaluation is that most managers hate to do it. They especially hate to deliver negative feedback. It's certainly easier to recognize an employee's achievements than his or her shortcomings. In any case, many managers are so busy that they fail to recognize either. Pointing out an employee's deficient performance is extremely difficult for most managers. It's such a thorny issue that in a survey of 4,000 *Fortune* 500 executives, five out of seven executives said that they would rather lie to employees about performance than confront them about performance problems.[6] We even know of managers who have attempted to conduct performance appraisals via e-mail in order to avoid their discomfort. But performance evaluation is one of the most important activities managers do, and it should be conducted regularly and in person. Most employees can and will accept honest feedback if it is delivered in a clear, honest, and sensitive manner and if expectations were clear in the first place. It is especially important to provide the employee with the specifics of any problem behavior, explicit goals for improvement including a timeline, and follow-up.

Regular evaluations are important even if an employee is working on a temporary basis. A college student worked as a summer intern at a well-known company and received no feedback for more than two months, until her last day on the job. Her manager took her aside and said, "You would never work out here. We basically couldn't stand the way you worked." The student was devastated and the experience took a terrible toll on her self-confidence. But was this failure *her* fault? We think not. Most students don't magically know how to work in a corporate environment or what a company expects from them in terms of behavior. Managers are responsible for instructing new employees, especially interns, on work and behavioral norms. The student would likely have had a very different result if her manager had coached her from Day One. The important lesson here is this: you should never interpret no feedback as being positive. If you have received no feedback from your manager, ask for it. "How am I doing? Should I change anything? How can I improve?"

In the example featuring Joe, you as the manager suspect that he has been inaccurately (and perhaps even dishonestly) evaluated in the past. Since most employers require a rating of "good" or "satisfactory" before an employee can transfer to another job, you will probably feel pressure to supply such a recommendation so Joe can qualify for the transfer. This is a common problem. Many organizations have employees like Joe, who are less than stellar performers but who are never confronted with their poor performance and given guidance to improve. In Joe's company, no manager has been brave enough to bite the bullet and either try to get Joe to improve his performance or initiate the termination process. It's easier to pass Joe along to someone else—to turn him into a Ping-Pong ball, bouncing from department to department, never really improving his performance because no one will confront him with the truth. (In some organizations, passing poor performers around the organization is called "turkey farming.")

Because his previous written appraisals have been less than honest, prospective managers get buffaloed into thinking Joe's performance is adequate. It's a vicious cycle and a real disservice to the employee, his or her coworkers, and the organization. Coworkers who are doing a good job will perceive the system to be unfair if someone like Joe is getting a rating similar to theirs for his inferior work. They may even find themselves picking up the slack for Joe. Perhaps the party most disadvantaged by this kind of problem is the organization and its culture. Joe's manager has sent the message that "not very good" or "just OK" is good enough. It's a dishonest message that erodes organizational efforts regarding quality, integrity, and ethics.

One good way to ensure continuous performance evaluations is to establish a formal system with the employees who report to you—whether or not your company requires it—and certainly use it more than once each year. Meet regularly with every employee and jointly agree to job objectives and how to measure success for each objective. Make sure that your department goals are directly linked to corporate goals and that the individual goals of the people who report to you are directly linked to your department goals. Also ensure that ethics-related performance expectations are included in goals and evaluation discussions. For example, have you talked about your expectations for respectful interactions with coworkers, trusting relationships with customers, fair treatment of subordinates, honesty and integrity in all business dealings?

Remember the importance of driving employee engagement: establish a clear line of sight between the goals of individuals and the organization and between the results of the organization and the individual. Then meet weekly or monthly with each employee and discuss how the employee is meeting his or her objectives. When objectives and measurement standards are established in advance and progress is tracked, it's much easier for employees to perform. They know what the target looks like, how to get there, and how they'll know when they've met it. They will understand and internalize what it means to create value. An ongoing process eliminates the need to blast a nonperformer once a year and can greatly reduce misunderstanding, resentment, and charges of discrimination or bias.

Probably the best way to handle the situation with Joe is to meet with him and be completely honest. "I can't write you the kind of letter you want for the following reasons. [Spell out the performance problems.] We can either wait until you get your performance on track, or I can write you a letter that reflects my honest evaluation of your work at this time. It's your decision." This approach will obviously be much easier if you've been providing Joe with honest appraisal of his performance all along.

Discipline

> Steven is a salesman who reports to you, the regional director of sales for an office supply company. He has a great track record and has consistently surpassed his sales targets, but he has one terrible flaw: He's not on time for anything. He's late both for meetings with you and for lunches with clients, and the problem extends to his paperwork. His expense reports, sales reports—everything is handed in a week late. As his manager, you've counseled him about his tardiness, and he has improved. Now instead of being 15 minutes late for a meeting, he's only 5 minutes late. And instead of submitting his expenses a week late, they're only two days late. His lateness seems minor in view of his achievements, but it's driving you and his coworkers crazy.

Most managers view disciplining employees as something to be postponed for as long as possible. Many people in a work environment simply ignore a worker's shortcomings and hope the situation will improve. Discipline, however, is important not only to ensure worker productivity but also to set the standard that certain behaviors are expected from all employees, and to meet the requirements of the U.S. Sentencing Guidelines. As we discussed in Chapter 6, the Sentencing Guidelines specify that all employees in an organization must receive consistent discipline for similar infractions. For example, in the case of employee theft, a secretary and a senior vice president must be treated in the same way. The guidelines are violated if people in different job classifications are treated differently—if one receives a slap on the wrist and the other is suspended or fired.

In the case of Steven, the salesman who is always late, you as a manager could be tempted to view disciplining his lateness as nitpicking. He's a star after all, right? However, it's unrealistic and unfair to expect promptness from all of your other employees and not from Steven.

As we noted in Chapter 7, research has given us clues about the most effective ways to discipline employees. First, the discipline must be constructive and done in a professional manner. For example, although you might be tempted to scream at Steven and call him an inconsiderate jerk, that's not going to change his behavior. It's much more effective to meet with him, explain the consequences of his lateness, and focus the discussion on his behavior, not on him personally.

Second, the discipline should be done privately. Employees should never be criticized in front of other employees. It's just as embarrassing as being criticized in public by your parent or your spouse, and it encourages nothing but hard feelings. Those discussions should always be held behind closed doors.

Third, employees should have input into the process and be encouraged to explain their side of the story. The entire idea of "team" management revolves around individuals being encouraged to share their view of a situation. The real problem may not be with the particular employee you want to discipline. Steven, for example, may be late with reports because people are late in submitting data to him. To solve problems at the simplest point, it's wise to ask for an employee's explanation.

Finally, discipline should be appropriately harsh and consistent with what other employees have received for similar offenses. This aspect of discipline is perhaps the most important in ensuring good performance in the future.[7]

For example, a highly respected financial professional (let's call her Beth) was fired from her position at a large financial services company for providing an inaccurate calculation in a report to senior management. The director of human resources had given Beth an almost impossible assignment: use a new formula to calculate the company's pension obligations to all current employees. The assignment was given at 6:00 p.m. on a Tuesday, and the report needed to be written, typed, and copied for a senior management meeting the next morning at 9:00 a.m. Beth and her secretary stayed at the office all night long, doing calculations, writing the report, and finally preparing it for the meeting the next morning. When one of the senior managers discovered an error in one of the complex calculations, Beth was summarily fired by the human resources director. It sent a huge message not only to Beth, but to the entire human resources department. Other mistakes had been made—even by the director—and if those errors had been punished, it had been with a reprimand, certainly not a firing. And, of course, the impossible deadline constituted an extenuating circumstance in everyone's opinion except the director.

The effects of unreasonable discipline (and unreasonable assignments) are far reaching, and that's why discipline needs to be appropriate to the offense and consistent with what others have received. In the case of Steven, the chronically late salesman, unless you're willing to be consistent and accept tardiness in all other employees, his behavior needs to be addressed. Just don't follow the example of the human resources director who fired Beth. She had been placed in the role as part of her company's grooming process of high-potential executives and if she had succeeded, she surely would have moved on to bigger and better things. However, the executive team viewed her behavior with Beth and others as erratic and ill advised. She left human resources after a few years and ended up in a senior marketing role somewhere in one of the company's subsidiaries—not in the enterprise-wide role she had been on track for before the debacle.

How companies manage "star" employees is one of the most telling characteristics of their ethical cultures. If an organization treats stars in a way that is consistent with their organizational values, the culture of the organization will be strengthened. On the other hand, if an organization states one thing in its values statement and permits star behavior to deviate from the organization's stated values, the entire culture can be undermined. For example, if a star employee is allowed to be abusive to coworkers in an organization that has stated that people management and respect are core values, those values will be suspect. Employees will instead look to the very visible star and perceive that his or her attributes are the ones that are really valued by the organization (regardless of what appears on its values statement). Perhaps the biggest cultural question is who gets to be considered a star in the first place. Does only quantitative performance matter, or does performance based upon ethical values also figure in (as we recommend)? In a strong ethical culture, a star would be someone who not only performs well in terms of the bottom line but also achieves that bottom-line performance in a way that is consistent with other values such as respect for people and integrity.

Terminations

> You're a manager in a large commercial bank. You discover that Patricia, a loan officer who reports to you, has forged an approval signature on a customer loan that requires signatures from two loan officers. When you confront Pat with the forgery, she apologizes profusely and says that her husband has been very ill. The day she forged the signature, he was going into surgery and she just didn't have time to find another loan officer to sign the authorization for the loan. Pat has been with your bank for 15 years and has a spotless record.

Terminations come in many varieties, none of them pleasant. There are terminations for cause—meaning that an individual has committed an offense that can result in instant dismissal. "Cause" can represent different things to different companies, but generally theft, assault, cheating on expense reports, forgery, fraud, and gross insubordination (including lying about a business matter) are considered as cause in most organizations. Many companies define *cause* in their employee handbooks.

In the case above, Patricia will most likely be fired for cause. In banking, few things are as sacred as a signature, and a professional with 15 years of banking experience would certainly be expected to know this. Forgery of any kind cannot be tolerated in a financial institution. It's a sad case, and any manager would feel compassion for Patricia. However, some offenses are unpardonable in a financial institution, and this is probably one of them.

There are also terminations for poor performance. This type of firing is most often based on written documentation such as performance appraisals and attendance records. Many employers have a formal system of warnings that will occur before someone is actually terminated for poor performance. A verbal warning is usually the first step in the process, followed by a written warning and then termination. The process can differ from company to company.

Then there are downsizings or layoffs. Layoffs can result from many kinds of reorganizations, such as mergers, acquisitions, and relocations, or they can be the result of economic reasons or changes in business strategy. A layoff can result from a decision to trim staff in one department or from a decision to reduce head count across the company. Whatever the reason, layoffs are painful not only for the person losing his or her job but also for the coworkers who'll be left behind. Coworkers tend to display several reactions: they exhibit low morale; they become less productive; they distrust management; and they become extremely cautious.[8]

In addition, layoff survivors are generally very concerned about the fairness of the layoff. They need to feel that the downsizing was necessary for legitimate business reasons; that it was conducted in a way that was consistent with the corporate culture; that layoff victims received ample notice; and that the victims were treated with dignity and respect. If management provided "a clear and adequate explanation of the reasons for the layoffs," survivors are more likely to view the layoffs as being fair.[9] Once again, if a company espouses respect and concern for employees in its values statements or executive speeches and then lays off employees in a particularly brutal way, it undermines employee confidence in the organization. Layoffs and other terminations speak volumes about what a culture truly values. Smart companies make sure that their actions are aligned with their values. These are just a few reasons that layoffs have to be handled well.

Whatever the reason for a termination, you can take certain steps as a manager to make it easier for the employee being terminated and for yourself.[10] Again, the main goals are to be fair, to deliver the news in a way that is aligned with your organization's values, and to allow the employee to maintain personal dignity.

1. Do your homework before you meet with the employee. Prepare a brief explanation of why this termination is necessary, and have ready an explanation of the severance package being offered to this employee, including financial and benefits arrangements. It's also helpful to check the calendar and consult with your company's public relations department to ensure you're not firing someone on his birthday or on the day she receives recognition from an industry group or professional association.

2. If at all possible, you should arrange to have an outplacement counselor or human resources professional on hand to meet with the employee after you

have spoken to him or her. Most outplacement counselors advise managers to give the bad news to terminated employees early in the day and early in the week, if possible. This gives the employee time to meet with a counselor if necessary. (Obviously, this advice doesn't apply to employees who are fired for cause.)

3. It's generally a good idea to terminate someone on neutral ground—in a conference room, for example, rather than in your office. In that way, you can leave if the situation becomes confrontational. If possible, try to assess what the employee's reaction might be. If you're about to fire a violent person for cause (like assaulting a coworker), you might want to have security nearby or a human resources professional present when you deliver the news.

4. Speak privately with each individual and deliver the news face-to-face, not by e-mail, telephone, or in a meeting or other kind of public forum. When you deliver the news, be objective, don't be abusive in any way, be compassionate, do it quickly (if possible), and never, never get personal. This is a business decision and should be delivered in the most professional manner possible.

5. Finally, keep all information about the termination private. Never discuss the reasons for a firing with anyone who doesn't have a need to know. The exception to this advice is when numerous layoffs occur. Survivors—coworkers who are left behind—will require some explanation of why layoffs were needed. In this case, you will want to speak about the business reasons that made the layoff necessary. Never explain why particular individuals were involved and others weren't. (For more information on downsizing, see Chapter 10.)

Terminations for cause don't go unnoticed, and the employee grapevine will assuredly carry the news of a termination around your organization. That's a good thing because it's important for employees to understand that bad acts get punished. However, it's generally improper to publicly explain why an individual has been punished; the primary objective is to protect the dignity and privacy of the person who has been punished.

Why Are These Ethical Problems?

Hiring, performance evaluation, discipline, and terminations can be ethical issues because they all involve honesty, fairness, and the dignity of the individual. Rice and Dreilinger[11] say that the desire for justice is a "fundamental human characteristic. People want to believe that the world operates on the principles of fairness; they react strongly when that belief is violated." In fact, most calls to corporate ethics hotlines (discussed more fully in Chapter 6) relate to precisely these types of human resources issues.

Costs

Much federal legislation exists to protect the rights of individuals in situations that involve hiring, performance evaluation, discipline, and terminations. There are myriad legal remedies for employees who feel they have suffered discrimination (see discrimination costs in Chapter 4 for more details). In response to increased litigation, employment practice liability insurance is a hot product among corporations. This insurance covers organizations that are sued by employees over charges such as harassment, discrimination, or wrongful discharge. The insurance, which was virtually unheard of 15 years ago, has been purchased by many *Fortune* 500 companies. This is surely the result of the huge increase in litigation and in settlements. The Equal Employment Opportunity Commission received almost 10,000 workplace discrimination complaints in 2011, and monetary relief for victims totaled more than $364 million.[12]

Besides perhaps paying legal costs and fines, organizations that are charged with discrimination can expect to pay a price in terms of employee morale and organizational reputation. Research evidence indicates that employees who perceive that they have been unfairly treated are less satisfied, less likely to go the extra mile, and more likely to steal from the organization.[13]

Smart organizations look beyond monetary costs when it comes to training managers to manage the "basics" of the employer-employee relationship. Savvy companies understand that managing the basics is the aspect of organizational culture that's probably most visible to employees. Those day-to-day activities—hiring, firing, discipline, rewards, praise, and so on—are concrete signals to employees about how an organization really values its workers. If an organization pays no attention to those basics and does not identify and train managers to perform those basics well, it will be an uphill struggle to inspire workers to produce excellent results and to convince them that the culture values employees and their efforts.

MANAGING A DIVERSE WORKFORCE

Experts predict that the workforce is becoming more diverse and that the key to many managers' success will be how well they can persuade diverse groups to sing together as a well-tuned chorus. Companies that best address the needs of a diverse population will probably be in a better position to succeed than companies that ignore this new reality. Managers must be able to deal with individuals of both genders and all ages, races, religions, ethnic groups, and sexual orientations. Managers need to have this ability themselves, and they need to encourage this ability in team members. Managers must become "conductors" who orchestrate team performance—sometimes teaching, sometimes coaching, and always communicating with employees and empowering them to learn and make good decisions.

The second skill set required of the new manager involves positively influencing the relationships among other team members and creating an ethical work environment that enhances individual productivity. Everyone we work with has a range of issues that could affect their ability to perform well. Many people are responsible for children, parents, or other relatives. Many workers have chronic illnesses or medical conditions or allergies, and those workers who are lucky not to have a chronic condition can suddenly become ill or injured. Other employees have chemical dependencies, such as an addiction to drugs or alcohol. Managers must be able to accomplish tasks and the mission of a department or team despite the often painful events and conditions that can distract team members.

Since a bias-free person hasn't been born yet, managers also must be able to counsel team members in their relationships with one another. Because every team will include a wide range of personalities, a manager frequently needs to be a referee who mediates and resolves disputes, assigns tasks to the workers who can best accomplish them, and ensures that fairness is built into the working relationships of team members.

The examples that follow are similar to those in Chapter 4 but are presented from the perspective of the manager rather than the individual. And, as we said earlier in this chapter, managers have a different level of responsibility.

Diversity

> One of your best customers is a very conservative organization—a real "white-shirt" company. Reporting to you is David, a very talented African American who could benefit greatly from working with this customer account—and the customer account would benefit greatly from David's expertise and creativity. The issue is that David dresses in vibrant colors and wears a *kufi*, an African skullcap. Your company long ago recognized David's brilliance, and his dress within the company isn't an issue. But you know your customer would react to David's attire with raised eyebrows.

A diverse workforce consists of individuals of both genders and myriad races, ethnic groups, religions, and sexual orientations. The role of a manager is to create an environment that maximizes the contribution of each individual. Since the population of the United States is remarkably diverse, it makes perfect sense to believe that products and services offered to this population should be developed, produced, and marketed by a diverse workforce.

The danger of ignoring this diversity was illustrated during an interview with a chemical company executive. One of the company's products is wallpaper. Even though the wallpaper was of a very high quality and priced competitively, sales were down. This was even more of a mystery since home repairs and renovations, especially by do-it-yourself decorators, were at record numbers.

Baffled by the problem, several senior marketing managers conducted customer surveys and found that the company's wallpaper patterns were the problem. Consumers viewed the patterns and styles as being outdated and old-fashioned. The managers then investigated the process the company used to select patterns and styles. What kind of market research was performed before selecting patterns for the next season?

They discovered that even though female consumers made more than 90 percent of all wallpaper purchases, no women were on the team of chemical company employees who selected patterns for production. Male employees were making all style decisions. The marketing managers and other executives insisted that women and other diverse voices be included on the selection committee. The results were immediate. As soon as the new styles of wallpaper appeared in stores, sales increased substantially.

In the example at the beginning of this section, David's attire could be viewed as problematic by some managers. In this case, and others like it, honesty is the best policy. You may want to tell David frankly that you want him to work on this account because his ability would benefit the customer. You may perhaps say that the customer is conservative and that his attire may distract the customer from his ability. Let David decide how he wants to dress when meeting with the customer.

You may also be frank with your customer: Tell him or her that David is extraordinarily talented and is the best person to add value to your relationship. To lessen the surprise of the initial meeting, mention in advance that David often wears ethnic garb. This approach lets David know how the client might interpret his clothing, but it doesn't force him into some narrow corporate box. It also prepares the client to deal with diversity. The point is to balance your interpretation of what a customer might appreciate with David's individuality and diverse voice.

Dress codes tend to raise some people's hackles. The intention of most dress codes is not to restrict individuality, but to ensure a professional appearance in the workplace. Ethnic garb shouldn't really be an issue, as long as it's modest. The aim of most dress codes is to eliminate clothing that could be viewed as immodest or too casual to a customer. Dress codes are also a very visible manifestation of your organization's culture, and how employees are advised to dress should be aligned with other elements of culture. For example, if a company is casual and egalitarian, informal dress is part of that. Managers may encourage formal dress in certain situations (such as when employees meet with conservative clients), but the reason should be explained. This issue is all about having words match actions.

Harassment

> Your profession has been traditionally a male-dominated one, and Marcia is the only woman in your department. Whenever Sam, your senior engineer, holds staff meetings, he and the other males in the department compliment Marcia profusely. They say things like, "It's hard for us to concentrate with a gorgeous woman like you in the room," or "You've got to stop batting your eyelashes at us or the temperature in this room will trigger the air conditioning." They compliment her apparel, her figure, her legs, and her manner of speaking. Although flattering, their remarks make her feel uncomfortable. She has mentioned her discomfort to you on several occasions, and you've told Sam and the others to cut it out. They just laughed and told you that Marcia was too sensitive. You think that while Marcia was being sensitive, she did have justification for being upset about her coworkers' remarks. (For a review of the legal definitions of sexual harassment, see Chapter 4.)

Do compliments constitute harassment? They do when they embarrass someone and serve to undermine an individual's professional standing in front of coworkers. If

Marcia is disturbed by the remarks of her coworkers, it's your responsibility as her manager to do something about it. In cases like these, it's sometimes helpful to reverse the situation. Imagine that your department was predominantly female and that the women continually said to the lone male, "You're just a hunk." "We all get aroused when you bat your eyelashes at us." "That's a great suit you're wearing; those slacks really show off your gorgeous thighs." How ridiculous does that banter sound?

In this case, Marcia's discomfort is the issue, and it's irrelevant whether you or others think she's being a "little too sensitive." She has already taken the appropriate steps, first by telling her coworkers to stop and then by approaching you when they didn't. You should meet immediately with the members of your department, either individually or as a group. To show the men how ridiculous their comments would sound if women were saying such things to men, you could reverse the situation. Explain to them that inappropriate compliments are not acceptable and that anyone who behaves inappropriately in the future will be disciplined. Make it clear that every member of the team has the right to feel comfortable on the team and to be treated with respect. If you don't act swiftly and firmly, and then back up future offenses with disciplinary action, you may be inviting a lawsuit.

Here's another kind of harassment:

> One of your direct reports, Robert, belongs to an activist church. Although you have no problems with anyone's religious beliefs, Robert is so vocal about his religion that it's becoming a problem with other employees in your department. He not only preaches to his fellow employees, but criticizes the attire of some of his female coworkers and continually quotes religious verse in staff meetings. You've received complaints about his behavior from several employees. A few weeks ago, you suggested to Robert that he tone down his preaching, and he reacted as if you were a heathen about to persecute him for his beliefs. His behavior has since escalated.

It's the manager's job to maintain a balance between the rights of the individual and the rights of the group—in this case, the attempt by one individual to impose his or her opinions or behavior on other team members. The objectives are fairness and respect for each individual.

It appears that Robert has crossed the line from expressing diverse views to harassment. Although it's important to recognize the value of diverse backgrounds, it's just as important to have an environment where one individual can't constantly attempt to impose his beliefs on other team members. Robert has ignored your requests and those of his coworkers, and he continues to preach. This kind of behavior will no doubt disrupt the team's performance and the relationships among team members. In this case, it's probably reasonable to begin documenting Robert's performance since you've already verbally warned him. His hostility and his refusal to respect the opinions of his coworkers and his manager can be viewed as insubordination. In organizations that have a due process approach to discipline, the next step might be a written warning to curb his attempts to influence the religion of his coworkers, or termination will result. Then, if Robert's harassment of his coworkers doesn't stop, he could be fired.

Family and Personal Issues

> One of your direct reports is Ellen, who just returned from maternity leave. She now has two children; her infant is four months old, and her older child is three years old. Ellen is not only a talented worker but also a wonderful person. Before the birth of her second child, she had no problem handling the workload and the demands on her time; she had a live-in nanny who could care for her child regardless of when she returned home. Recently, however, her nanny left, and Ellen is now sending her children to a day-care facility with strict opening and closing times. Although Ellen is very productive when she's in the office, her schedule is no longer flexible—she must leave the office no later than 5:00 p.m. This has caused a hardship for all of her peers, who must complete team assignments whether or not she's present. Although you don't want to cause problems for her, the situation doesn't seem fair to her coworkers.

Family and personal issues are those situations and conditions that, though not directly related to work, can affect someone's ability to perform. People simply can't leave their personal and family problems at home. The difficulty in situations like these is achieving a balance between maintaining a worker's right to privacy and ensuring fairness to coworkers. The yardstick is that if someone is performing well, and his or her attendance is satisfactory, there's probably no cause for action by the manager, beyond offering assistance if the worker wants it.

In Ellen's case, she has a temporary inability to match her coworkers' schedules. Sooner or later, every worker must deal with situations that place limitations on the ability to maintain certain working hours. Similar situations could result from a variety of other causes, including illness, family responsibilities, home construction, and commuting schedules. The issue here is fairness in attendance, not in performance or productivity. Since many people have children and therefore have responsibilities that require them to either leave work at a specific time or stay home with a sick child, often the burden of "always being there" falls on single, childless employees, and that is not fair to them. We all want to be generous with our coworkers, but as managers, we have to ensure that we aren't helping people with children at the expense of people who are childless.

The ideal solution may be to build more flexibility into the working hours, not just for Ellen but for the entire team. The ideal solution would involve confronting the problem head-on by asking the people in your area to collaborate and find a solution. For example, you could make an attempt to hold all team meetings in the middle of the day, when everyone can attend. Individual activities could be relegated to the afternoon, so that it would not be essential for Ellen—or anyone else—to stay late and work as a group. If your organization has flexible work hours, you could talk to your manager about the possibility of your area incorporating flexible work schedules that allow people to arrive and leave at varying times, but ensure that the office and department are always covered. The objective is to make life easier for individual employees and fair for the entire group, and as a result enhance the team's overall productivity.

Personal illnesses and chemical dependencies of employees present a different set of issues. These situations can affect work schedules as well as an individual's ability to perform. Most corporations have explicit policies for managing employee illness. Generally, employees are guaranteed a specific number of sick days and then must go on some sort of disability program. If, however, an employee hasn't received a formal diagnosis and is simply taking sick days, acting erratically, or showing a change in his or her performance, you might suspect a physical or mental illness. Encourage the employee to see a doctor, and consult with the company medical department (if you have one) if you continue to be concerned about an employee's health. It's important to remember that illnesses of any kind—depression, cancer, AIDS—are private and should be kept confidential. These conditions cause no danger to coworkers, and many people who suffer from them can resume normal or modified work schedules. Managers can help these employees by protecting their privacy and by being fair and compassionate.

Drug or alcohol abuse is a different matter. Most corporations have policies that prohibit any kind of drug or alcohol use on company premises, and many companies have severe penalties for employees who are caught working under the influence of alcohol or drugs. Both alcoholism and drug addiction are costly in terms of the abuser's health, and they can both cause extreme danger in the workplace. A corporate bond trader who's high on cocaine can wreak havoc on himself, his employer, and his customers. A pilot who's drunk poses obvious risks to an airline and its passengers. Would you like to ride with a railroad engineer who just smoked a few joints, or have the sale of your home negotiated by a real estate broker who's inebriated, or have your child's broken leg set by a doctor who's high on amphetamines?

If you suspect that one of your employees is abusing drugs on or off the job, keep track of any changes in behavior and performance, in writing. (Even if an employee uses drugs or alcohol only off company premises, the residual effects of the substance may affect job performance. Also, the expense of some recreational drugs may present a risk to your organization.) This is an important step because some medications smell like alcohol on the breath, so it's important to be sure that you're dealing with abuse and not a medical condition. Once you're fairly certain that abuse is the problem, contact your human resources department. Substance abuse is considered an illness (and generally not an offense that will get the employee fired—at least in many large corporations), and the employee usually will be counseled by human resources. If abuse is present, most large employers offer substance abuse programs for employees and will probably insist that your employee participate in such a program. In most large companies, employees are given one or two chances to get clean. If the problem recurs, substance abusers can be terminated. For example, in one money management firm, an employee was sent to company-paid rehabilitation when it was discovered he was regularly using cocaine and was high on the trading floor. After 90 days at a rehab facility, the trader came back to work, was off drugs and highly productive. His career was not ended by his addiction, although he regularly has company-administered drug tests to ensure he does not relapse. The important issue here is to get fast help for the employee—for the sake of the employee, the company, and your customers.

Why Are These Ethical Problems?

These are all ethical issues because they concern fairness and respect for the individual. A large percentage of the ethical issues that arise in business are related to human resources, and they can usually be addressed by local managers who act quickly, fairly, and compassionately.

Costs

The personal, professional, and corporate costs of discrimination and sexual harassment are described earlier in this chapter and in Chapter 4. The costs for mishandling most issues connected to diversity are not clear-cut, and they're often difficult to quantify.

To glimpse how costly the publicity associated with such cases can be, we have to look no further than the now infamous Texaco case, which is described in detail at the end of Chapter 5. Texaco executives were heard on tape complaining about Hanukkah and Kwanzaa interfering with the celebration of Christmas, and recounting the destruction of documents connected to a pending discrimination case.[14] In the wake of a firestorm of bad publicity, Texaco was forced to settle the case for $176 million. Obviously, the costs to Texaco—both financially and in damaged reputation—were significant. Yet those costs are just the tip of a giant iceberg.

If we could combine all of the fairness issues—performance evaluation systems, harassment, subtle and not-so-subtle discrimination, and how managers handle family, substance, and illness issues—and figure out how much it costs businesses when employees are treated unfairly, the result would probably be astronomical, and not just in terms of financial costs and damaged reputations. How many people leave a job because of unresolved problems with a coworker? How many people choose not to go the extra mile because the organization doesn't treat its employees fairly? How many of the best performers choose to work for a company that allows them flexible hours to care for a child or an aging parent? How many people are depressed and frustrated because they're picking up the slack for a coworker who's a chronic alcoholic? The toll in human suffering, morale, loyalty, productivity, and lost opportunity is inestimable.

THE MANAGER AS A LENS

Managers perform a crucial role in organizations because they interpret company policy, execute corporate directives, fulfill all of the people-management needs in their particular area of responsibility, cascade senior management messages down the chain of command, and communicate employee feedback up the chain. More than almost anything else, managers communicate the culture of the organization up close and on the ground to everyone who reports to them. Managers are probably the most important ingredient in an organization's success, and they are frequently the most overlooked.

But make no mistake—managers are the lens through which employees view the company as well as the filter through which senior executives view employees. As we noted earlier in this chapter, managers are the critical ingredient in growing employee engagement: to many employees, managers *are* the company. Managers can be the inspiration for someone to stay with an organization or the impetus for someone to leave. As a result, managers have more influence and need more senior management attention, more training, and more communication skills than any other employee group.

The Buck Stops with Managers

If we could take a peek at the innermost thoughts of managers, we might very well encounter this sentiment: "I hope we do good work and get recognized for it. But most of all, I hope there's nothing going on that I don't know about that could hit the fan."

As a manager, you'll soon discover that your employees can bring you glory as well as get you into big trouble. But the good news is that you can make investments over time to help ensure that nothing hits the fan; or if it does, that you find out about it before it mushrooms out of control. As a manager, you can design your own little insurance policy to help protect you and your organization from employees who might cause problems.

You can begin to protect yourself by understanding and internalizing the idea that the people who report to you are looking to you for guidance and approval. That means that you need to actively manage ethics. Your employees want to know what your rules are, so you need to think carefully about your standards and consciously try to communicate and enforce them. Most important, you need to understand that you are a role model and your employees will follow your example. (Read more about the importance of ethical leadership in Chapter 5.)

Boris Yavitz, former dean of Columbia University's Graduate School of Business and a member of several large corporate boards, had sage advice for managers. First, communicate your expectations and standards publicly and privately. Employees are more likely to respond to a direct verbal challenge from you—"Are we doing it right?"—than they are to an expectation that's expressed only in a policy manual. Second, managers should prove their commitment through personal example. They need to "walk the talk," or no one will take their expectations seriously. Finally, since employees are naturally inclined to protect managers from bad news, managers need to explicitly tell employees that they don't want that kind of protection. "Tell me everything." The best policy is to communicate loudly and clearly that you don't want protection. Of course, that also means that you can't shoot the messenger who brings you bad news, or it will be the last time you ever hear from a messenger.

BEGIN WITH CLEAR STANDARDS   All organizations have standards, and many organizations even have written standards. Written standards—usually in the form of a mission statement or guiding principles—can be a double-edged sword. It's great if an organization has written standards that actually guide how it does business. It's a huge problem if those written standards are just window dressing, and the real standards have nothing to do with the ones that are printed up and hanging on the wall. The disconnect between written standards and reality (referred to as cultural misalignment in Chapter 5) destroys credibility, and a company can't be effective over the long term without credibility.

The same is true for managers. Any employee can tell you what the rules are for working for a particular manager. "You must tell the truth here or you'll be fired," might be a rule, or "Don't rock the boat," or "Don't tell me how you do it, just do it." The very best way for managers to gain credibility and respect among employees is to set clear standards, live by those standards, very deliberately communicate them, and insist that everyone adhere to them. And, don't be afraid to set ethical standards that say "how" you want your people to behave. Remember, ethical standards are needed in order to balance the financial goals that can narrow employees' attention to just focusing on bottom line outcomes rather than how those outcomes are achieved.

The truth is that employees are always trying to figure out if managers mean what they say and if they support the values that the company has communicated so well. Think about this case: The manager of a food processing plant consistently talks about the importance of quality. "The consumer should always come first," he says. Then one day, a shipment of food is delivered for processing. The factory equipment is ready to go, the employees have been waiting for this huge delivery—and the food is just on the wrong side of spoiled. "It's good enough," the manager says. "The processing will kill any contaminants and the consumer will never know the difference because this will be flash-frozen after the processing. We'll lose a lot of money if we don't process something now." What message has he just sent to his employees? Suppose that a month later, an employee finds a few rodent droppings in a food processing unit. It'll cost a lot of money to stop the machinery and clean it, plus the food already in the hopper would have to be destroyed. What do you think the employee would do? Would he or she believe that the consumer comes first? Or would the employee decide that it's okay to cut a corner to save money?

It's important to understand that, as a manager, you are setting standards and communicating organizational culture all the time. In fact, failing to deliberately set ethical standards is a standard in itself, since your employees may very well interpret it as meaning you have *no* standards. In this era of teams and empowered employees, managers need to be very deliberate in spelling out what they stand for and "how things are going to be done around here." Those ethical standards have to be demonstrated by the manager and enforced, or people won't believe them. It's what "walking the talk" really means. Plus, employees figure out what really matters to an organization by observing manager behavior. This is how culture gets baked into an organization (and once employee perceptions are baked in, they are very difficult to change).

DESIGN A PLAN TO CONTINUALLY COMMUNICATE YOUR STANDARDS Good communication skills are at the very heart of effective ethics management. Without them, it's virtually impossible to encourage ethical behavior. Regardless of where you are in the management hierarchy, if you haven't made effective communication your top priority, you had better get ready for some big surprises. Here's a Big Truth: If you don't communicate with your employees, they won't communicate with you. You won't know what's going on; you'll be out of the loop; you'll be ignorant; you'll be inviting ethical transgressions. And in business, ignorance is definitely not bliss.

Communicating with one group of employees is not enough, because you'll know what's going on only with them. You'll see information about other employee groups only through the filter of that one group. That's why "management by walking around" always gets such high marks from management experts. Managers can be knowledgeable only when they regularly interact with and listen to many different people on many different levels. (You may think this is simplistic, but think about how many top executives think they are communicating when they do it just with the executives who report to them.)

Consider this example. A young, newly named CEO decided to create an executive floor and bring all of his most senior people together to improve communication within the group and make it easy to work together. It happens all the time in companies around the world. Is it a good idea? Maybe not, since he effectively isolated not only himself but also the rest of the executive team. He also created an atmosphere of elitism within the organization.

You can improve the communication within your department by holding regular staff meetings where you discuss the company mission, business results, and the way you want things done. Talk about what you stand for and what you want your department to stand for. Use ethical language—for example, when employees are designing a new program or product, ask them in a staff meeting if they have considered everyone who could be affected by their plans. Ask them if they think they're doing the right thing. Framing business decisions in ethical terms goes a long way toward increasing moral awareness, communicating your standards, and emphasizing the importance of ethical behavior. It also helps reinforce ethical culture.

Once you have deliberately articulated and communicated your standards both privately to individuals and publicly in front of your team, you need to think about how approachable you are. You need to think long and hard about how you react when people raise issues or ask questions or deliver criticism. If you kill the messenger or react with hostility if someone asks a question, or if you seem too busy to clarify directions, you are asking for trouble. Your people may well consider you unapproachable, and managers who aren't approachable lay the groundwork for being blindsided. The first time they hear about a problem may not be from an employee, but from a lawyer, a newspaper reporter, or a regulator. So, if you are a manager, work hard at being approachable. Drop in on people who work in your area and shoot the breeze. Ask them what they're doing in and out of the office. Take your people out to lunch, and stay interested in what they are thinking and feeling. Get to know one another. Build a relationship. Learn to trust one another. Those relationships will be invaluable when problems occur, as they surely will.

Managers Are Role Models

A number of years ago, the famous professional basketball player Charles Barkley made sports headlines when he proclaimed, "I'm not paid to be a role model."[15] A colleague on the courts, Karl Malone, responded in an issue of *Sports Illustrated*,

"Charles, you can deny being a role model all you want, but I don't think it's your decision to make. We don't *choose* to be role models; we're *chosen*. Our only choice is whether to be a good role model or a bad one." Like Barkley, some managers may not want to be role models. But Barkley and managers are indeed role models—not because they want to be, but because of the positions they hold. Being a manager and a good role model means more than just doing the right thing; it means helping your employees do the right thing. A manager who is a good role model inspires employees, helps them define gray areas, and respects their concerns.

Managers can provide guidance to employees who encounter ethical dilemmas by encouraging them to gather all of the facts and then evaluate the situation using some of the advice detailed in Chapter 2. And after that, managers need to go further. What happens if one of your employees raises an issue with you, and you don't see where there's a problem? The employee goes away, satisfied for the moment with your response that nothing's wrong. But soon she is back because she still doesn't feel right about the situation. What do you do now? Probably the most responsible thing you can do at that point is to offer to pursue it with her to make sure there is no problem. This sends a huge message to the employee and to her colleagues. First, you're saying that you're glad she brought this to your attention. Second, you're taking her seriously even if you don't particularly agree with her. Third, you're saying that you trust her instincts and that she should, too. Fourth, you're declaring that ethics are important to you and to your organization—so important that you're willing to pursue this issue, even though you don't agree, in an effort to make her feel more comfortable. These are all critical messages to send to employees. (You also may find that she is right in her suspicions.)

The most important thing for managers to remember about their job as role model is that what they do is infinitely more important than what they say. They can preach ethics all they want; but unless they live that message, their people won't. As a manager, all eyes are upon you and what you're doing. Your actions will speak much louder than your words, and if there is a disconnect between the two, you will have no credibility—and employees may even question the credibility of your organization.

MANAGING UP AND ACROSS

Gone are the days when a person could advance in an organization by impressing only the next level of management. The new team structures mandate that workers treat everyone well. An example of how some corporations are institutionalizing this approach is an increasingly popular method of performance appraisal that some companies call 360-degree feedback. This means that when reviewing an employee's performance, a manager asks for input from the employee's coworkers and subordinates. Feedback of this sort, which comes from all directions, is probably a much more effective barometer of performance than old methods that measure only how well people manage up. Of course, it means that workers need to carefully consider all of their work relationships: up, down, and across. It's also an indicator of what astute workers have always known: since you never know who you might end up reporting to, or who is going to be crucial to your success in the future, it's critical to effectively manage all of your work relationships.

In team situations, managers can still profoundly affect your future. They sign off on or approve performance appraisals, pay raises, transfers, and generally are a primary influence on your career mobility and trajectory. It can be difficult to overcome a poor relationship with a manager unless you have solid relationships with individuals on or above your manager's level. That's why it's important for you to cultivate your manager's respect.

Although it may appear that your peers don't have as direct an impact on your career as your manager does, they nevertheless can significantly affect your future success. Since you generally "get as good as you give, " if you don't cooperate with your peers, they'll probably refuse to cooperate with you—perhaps even sabotage you behind the scenes—and that lack of cooperation could cripple you. In addition, peers can be promoted to management positions; this outcome can be truly unfortunate if you haven't developed good relationships with them.

Honesty Is Rule One

> Michael is a lawyer who reports to Paula, the corporate counsel for a chemical company. During one particularly busy period, Paula asks Michael to prepare a summary of all pending lawsuits and other legal activity for the company's senior management. Michael has several court appearances and depositions cluttering his schedule, so he assigns the report to one of his paralegals, who completes the report in several days. Since he's so busy, Michael simply submits the report to Paula without reviewing it. When Paula asks him what he thinks of the report, he assures her that it's fine. The next day, Paula asks Michael into her office and says that she has found a major omission in the report. Michael has no choice but to admit that he didn't have time to review it.

Probably nothing trips up more people than the temptation to lie or stretch the truth. And probably nothing will trip up your career faster than a lie or an exaggeration. In business, your reputation is everything, and lying or exaggerating can quickly undermine it.

Michael has basically lied to his manager. Even if he can weasel his way out of the hot seat by saying he didn't have time to thoroughly review the report, he has created an indelible impression with Paula. She may question not only his future reports but also his activities in general. Michael could have told Paula up front that he didn't have time to prepare a report. He could have suggested that one of the paralegals prepare it. He could have asked for more time so that he could carefully review it. Paula may not have been thrilled with his analysis of the situation, but she probably would have understood and helped him look for another solution. However, by implying that he had completed and reviewed the report when in fact he hadn't looked at it, Michael has severely damaged his reputation with his manager. A worker's responsibility includes identifying a problem and then proposing a solution. If you provide a solution when you report a concern, you stand a good chance of having your idea implemented. If you just report an issue with no solution, you'll probably have a solution imposed on you.

Managers and peers rely on the information they receive from the people who report to them and who work with them. Obviously, that information must be truthful and accurate, or someone else's work will be skewed. Once someone has reason to doubt your veracity, it may be impossible for you to recover. As one executive said, "Lying will end someone's relationship with me, period." The message: Be completely honest about all aspects of your work, including your ability, the information you provide, and your ability to meet deadlines. Keep your promises.

Standards Go Both Ways

It began when Bruce asked Andy to lie to his wife about his whereabouts. "If Marcia calls, tell her I'm in Phoenix on a business trip," he told Andy. Of course, he had also confided to Andy that in case of an office emergency, he could be reached at a local golf tournament or at a nearby hotel where he was staying with another woman. Since Bruce was senior to Andy and was a powerful contributor in the department, Andy went along with his request. When Marcia called, Andy told the lie about Bruce being in Phoenix. Bruce asked several more "favors" of Andy, and Andy complied. Then Bruce asked for a big favor: he instructed Andy to inflate monthly sales figures for a report going to senior management. When Andy objected, Bruce said, "Oh, come on, Andy, we all know how high your standards are."

Just as it's important for managers to set standards within their departments, it's equally important for workers to set ethical standards with their managers and peers and stick to them. The best way to ensure that you're not going to be asked to compromise your values is to clearly communicate what people can expect from you.

In Andy's case, he made his first mistake by going along with Bruce's lie to his wife. Although it's tempting to help out a colleague—especially one who's powerful and senior to you—you're sliding down a slippery slope when it involves a lie. The chances are excellent that Bruce would not have asked Andy to lie about the monthly sales figures if he hadn't already known that he could manipulate Andy. If Andy had refused to lie for Bruce on that first occasion, Bruce would probably have vastly different expectations of him. When Bruce asked Andy to lie to his wife, Andy could have replied, "Hey, Bruce, don't drag me into that one! I'll tell her you're not in the office, but I'm not going to outright lie to her." Andy could have said it in an unthreatening way and Bruce probably would have understood. Bruce might even have been embarrassed. But once Andy got caught up in Bruce's conspiracy, Bruce felt he would probably go along with other untruths. The message: Say it politely, but say it firmly and unequivocally. If a coworker or manager asks you to betray your standards—even in the tiniest of ways—refuse to compromise your standards, or you'll end up being confronted with increasingly thorny dilemmas.

CONCLUSION

Employees are strongly influenced by the conduct of management, and managers build and reinforce organizational culture with everything they say and do. That's why it's so critical that individual managers understand how they are viewed by employees. It's also critical that managers understand that if they set high standards, foster good communications, and act as ethical role models, they will have the power to create an environment that encourages employees to behave ethically. Good managers also understand their pivotal role in influencing subordinates, building ethical culture, growing employee engagement, and inspiring people to do their best work. It's equally important that workers appreciate the importance of managing their relationships with the manager and their peers and know how to alert the company's senior executives to wrongdoing in the safest way possible.

DISCUSSION QUESTIONS

1. Why is employee engagement important, and what is its relationship to ethics?

2. How does employee engagement relate to organizational culture? How do managers contribute to the ethical culture?

3. In addition to identifying and training good managers, what else could an organization do to increase levels of employee engagement?

4. What specific action could a manager take to help move employees up the employee engagement continuum—for example, from not engaged to actively engaged?

5. Why should performance be measured as an ongoing process, and not just as a once-a-year event?

6. Should high performers be allowed to work by rules that are different from those that apply to other workers? Why or why not?

7. Imagine that you're the manager of a facility where 200 layoffs are scheduled. Design an action plan for how the layoffs would occur. How would you handle both those being laid off and the survivors?

8. Are there ways in which managers can avoid harassment issues among employees who report to them? What would your strategy be?

9. Imagine that someone who reports to you is on a prescription medication that makes his breath smell like alcohol. How would you handle this situation?

10. Imagine that one of your employees complained about being harassed by a coworker. Also imagine that you suspect the motives of the person who is complaining to you. How would you handle this situation? Is there a way you could discern motivation, or does it matter? When would you involve your company's human resources department?

11. As a manager, how would you respond when a worker's performance has declined and you suspect a problem at home is the cause? How might you

respond if you think an alcohol or drug problem is the cause? What language could you use to confront the employee? Are there others you might want to bring into the discussion?

12. List some ways you can communicate your ethical standards to your employees and to your peers. As an employee, how can you communicate your ethical standards to your manager?

SHORT CASES

EMPLOYMENT BASICS

You've recently been promoted to a supervisory position and are now responsible for coordinating the work of four other employees. Two of these workers are more than 20 years older than you are, and both have been with the company much longer than you have. Although you've tried to be supportive of them and have gone out of your way to praise their work, whenever there is some kind of disagreement, they go to your boss with the problem. You've asked them repeatedly to come to you with whatever issues they have; they just ignore you and complain to other workers about reporting to someone your age. Design a strategy for dealing with these workers and your manager.

MANAGING A DIVERSE WORKFORCE

After two years of sales calls and persuasion, a large, multinational petroleum company—Big Oil Ltd.—decides to sign with your employer, Secure Bank. Since Big Oil is headquartered in Saudi Arabia and most of the meetings with the client have been in the Middle East, Secure Bank's senior executive in charge of oil and oil products companies, Julie, has not attended. Although the Secure Bank employees who have met with the company have told the Big Oil executives that the lead on their account will be a woman, the news must not have registered, perhaps because of language difficulties. Today, the Big Oil reps are in Chicago to sign on the dotted line and meet with Secure Bank's senior managers, and of course, they've met with Julie. A member of your sales team calls you to say that Big Oil's senior team member has told him he does not want Julie to work on their account, period. Because of cultural issues, Big Oil execs are uncomfortable dealing with women from any country. As Julie's manager, what do you do? Can you think of ways to respect Julie's expectations and those of the Big Oil executives?

MANAGING UP AND ACROSS

As an operations professional, you need to be able to interact effectively with many internal customers—from corporate managers to field representatives. One of your peers is Jessica, who is a talented operations professional but who is downright rude to her internal customers. Her attitude is so bad that people around your company ask specifically to deal with you instead of Jessica. You've heard many tales about her sarcasm and her unwillingness to deliver anything other than the absolute minimum to other employees. You've thought about talking to Bruce, the manager to whom both you and Jessica report, but you and everyone else knows that they're dating. In the meantime, your workload is increasing because of Jessica's reputation. How do you handle Jessica and Bruce?

NOTES

1. M. Buckingham, *The One Thing You Need to Know* (New York: Free Press, 2005), 73–85.
2. A. Gopal, "Disengaged Employees Cost Singapore $4.9 Billion," *Gallup Management Journal*, October 9, 2003, www.gallup.com.
3. J. Shaffer, "Communicating for Business Results: How to Choose and Execute Communication Projects That Dramatically Help the Company," *Journal of Employee Communication Management*, March–April, 2003, www.ragan.com
4. Ibid.
5. Towers Perrin, "Global Workforce Report" (2008), http://www.towerswatson.com/.
6. J. Halper, *Quiet Desperation: The Truth about Successful Men* (New York: Warner Books, 1988).
7. G. Ball, L. Treo, and H. P. Sims Jr., "Just and Unjust Punishment Incidents: Influence on Subordinate Performance and Citizenship," *Academy of Management Journal* 37 (1994): 299–332.
8. D. Rice and C. Dreilinger, "After Downsizing," *Training and Development Journal* (May 1991): 41–44.
9. J. Brockner, "Managing the Effects of Layoffs on Survivors," *California Management Review*, Winter 1992: 928.
10. Kenneth Labich, "How to Fire People and Still Sleep at Night," *Fortune*, June 10, 1996, 65–71.
11. D. Rice and C. Dreilinger, "After Downsizing," *Training and Development Journal* (May 1991): 41–44.
12. Equal Employment Opportunity Commission website (2010), http://www.eeoc.gov.
13. J. Greenberg, "Employee Theft as a Reaction to Underpayment Inequity: The Hidden Cost of Pay Cuts," *Journal of Applied Psychology* 75 (1990): 56–64.
14. J. Leo, "Jellybean: The Sequel," *U.S. News & World Report*, February 10, 1997, 20.
15. D. Gelman, "I'm Not a Role Model," *Newsweek*, June 28, 1993, 56.

ORGANIZATIONAL ETHICS AND SOCIAL RESPONSIBILITY

CHAPTER 9

CORPORATE SOCIAL RESPONSIBILITY

INTRODUCTION

Thus far, we have emphasized ethical behavior "inside" the organization. We have discussed why ethical behavior is important at work and how individuals who aim to be ethical can make good ethical decisions. We have also discussed the psychology of ethical decision making, including why individuals with the best of intentions can find it difficult to do what's right. We have outlined what organizations can and should do to create strong ethical cultures that support employee ethics and what managers can and should do, within those cultures, to lead their employees in an ethical direction.

In this chapter's discussion of corporate social responsibility (CSR), we extend beyond the organization to focus on the relationship between the organization and its external stakeholders. In today's highly interconnected, global and transparent world, corporations are finding that social responsibility is essential to fundamental business strategy. They are also discovering that it is difficult to separate "internal" organizational ethics from "external" social responsibility. Although most large companies have separate people and structures to deal with "internal" ethics and "external" social responsibility issues, these efforts are overlapping more and more because both depend on a solid set of ethical values and an organizational culture that supports doing the right thing. For example, making business decisions today to invest in environmentally sustainable business practices is a strategy that is consistent with the organization's value of respect for the community and the natural environment while also signaling to employees that the organization cares about people, the community, and its longer-term legacy. Because many corporate social responsibility issues stem from the global nature of business today, we will focus more extensively on global CSR issues in Chapter 11.

WHY CORPORATE SOCIAL RESPONSIBILITY?

A rich literature on corporate social performance suggests three reasons that corporations should care about social responsibility:[1] a pragmatic reason, an ethical reason, and a strategic reason. These reasons are not mutually exclusive and can and do overlap.

The *pragmatic* reason is based upon the recognition that business must use its power responsibly in society or risk losing it. Corporations exist as legal entities with certain advantages (such as limited liability) because society allows them to do so, and these corporate rights and advantages can be removed from firms that are perceived to be irresponsible. That's exactly what happened to Arthur Andersen, formerly one of the "Big Five" auditing firms, when it lost its license to operate after being involved in the Enron scandal.

The perception of the corporation as a responsible societal actor is dependent on a stakeholder view of the firm. Recall that we defined a *stakeholder* in Chapter 1 as "any party (e.g., customers, employees, suppliers, the government, stockholders, the community) who is affected by the business and its actions and who has a stake in what the organization does and how it performs."[2] In Chapter 2, we used the concept of stakeholders a bit differently to refer to the people or groups affected by a particular ethical decision. There, we said that a good ethical decision considers harms and benefits to multiple stakeholders, and the best ethical decision is one that creates the greatest societal good.

Here, at the level of the corporation, the stakeholder view provides a particular lens on the firm that is broader than the view offered in many other courses you may have taken (e.g., marketing highlights customers, finance highlights shareholders, management highlights employees, etc.). With the stakeholder perspective, the assumption is that a responsible executive will take multiple stakeholders into account in decision making and will find ways to balance their needs and concerns. The stakeholder perspective places the corporation at the center of a web of constituents (or stakeholders; Figure 9.1) who are affected by the actions of the business, but who can also affect the business in dramatic ways that can interfere with a firm's autonomy, economic success, and license to operate. Maltreated employees can strike, dissatisfied customers can boycott products, interest groups can create harmful publicity, owners can bring shareholder resolutions, and the government can pass laws and regulations that limit a firm's activities or even put the firm out of business. Therefore a pragmatic reason for being responsible is that corporations must anticipate multiple

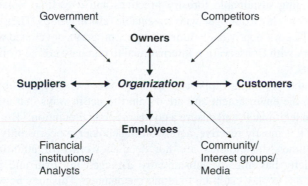

FIGURE 9.1 Stakeholder Perspective on the Firm

stakeholder concerns simultaneously and act defensively to protect their reputation and viability.

It can be costly not to anticipate stakeholder concerns. With the power of instantaneous electronic communication, social networking, cell phone cameras, Twitter, and YouTube videos, even relatively small stakeholder groups can get the word out quickly about their concerns and have a huge, usually negative, impact on very large companies. For example, when the organization People for the Ethical Treatment of Animals released a hidden camera videotape from a West Virginia chicken slaughterhouse showing workers stomping on chickens, squeezing them to death, and flinging them against the wall, the company acted quickly, sent in inspectors, and told the contractor that owned the plant to fix the problems or lose its contract. The contractor fired 11 employees and made every remaining employee at its 25 plants pledge to treat animals humanely.[3]

Although a frequent corporate response to such a charge is denial or resistance, KFC and its parent Yum Brands responded quickly to the challenge from an important stakeholder group.[4] Taco Bell, a fast-food restaurant selling Mexican food, is also a Yum Brands company. After Mexican tomato pickers led a boycott, hunger strike, and protest against the chain, the company agreed to pay a penny more per pound of Florida tomatoes, to monitor suppliers, and to adopt a code of conduct that would allow the company to drop suppliers who abuse farmworkers.[5]

Another case in point is the environmental organization Rainforest Action Network (RAN; www.RAN.org), which has influenced well-known companies such as Citigroup, Home Depot, Lowe's, Staples, Office Depot, and Chevron. In the short term, it may be hard to make the business case for the "green" practices that RAN promotes. But when companies believe that their reputations as good corporate citizens are at risk, the calculation quickly changes. And once they seriously consider the organization's environmental concerns, executives often adopt them as their own. For example, RAN targeted Home Depot for sourcing wood from endangered forests. In fact, the company realized that it didn't even know where its wood came from at the time.[6] Now, the company knows the source of all of its wood; on its website (www.corporatehomedepot.com), it claims to be integrating environmental planning into its business, including sustainable forestry practices and recycling. Smart CEOs have benefited from opening a dialogue with reasonable reform groups. They cite as success stories, Home Depot's eco-friendly lumber supply program, developed with RAN, and Starbucks' work with Conservation International to purchase coffee from farmers who preserve forests.[7]

So, with the pragmatic approach to corporate social responsibility, a firm's managers scan the environment and are on alert to act in ways that avoid economic harm, maintain legitimacy, and ensure a good corporate reputation.[8] But this approach can be risky if it is mostly reactive, acting on stakeholder concerns only after they are voiced. Sometimes stakeholders are not deemed worthy of attention until after negative publicity has already substantially damaged the firm and its reputation. Then, the firm has to play catch-up to repair the damage. This may be what happened with Apple and its Foxconn supplier in China, where iPhones and iPads are assembled.

When an explosion and fire at a Foxconn facility in May 2011 killed two and injured others, Apple was harshly criticized for the working and living conditions at the facility, including excessive overtime, crowded living conditions, underage workers, and use of harmful chemicals.[9] As a result, stakeholders began to watch the company and its suppliers more intently. Apple does have a code of conduct for suppliers and publishes an annual report of their compliance.[10] If violations are not corrected, the supplier is terminated. But, as other firms have learned, it takes more than codes of conduct and audits to avoid the kind of bad publicity that faced Apple in this situation.

Constructive engagement with stakeholders, including a company's critics, offers a new and increasingly popular approach. Executives are learning that the plea to "just trust us" rarely works in a world plagued by regular corporate scandals. Rather, a better approach is proactively analyzing the stakeholder landscape and working with selected stakeholders who are willing to engage in constructive dialogue. Goldman Sachs actually brought Rainforest Action Network into the company to help draft its plan to become more environmentally responsible, and Dell included environmentalists on a task force to craft a recycling strategy.

These efforts are in line with a more proactive, *ethical* reason for corporate social responsibility, which argues that businesses, as part of society, have a responsibility to behave ethically. In this view, responsible executives have an ethical duty to care about multiple stakeholders because it is simply the right thing to do. It might also be pragmatic to do so, but the focus here is on the ethical intention to "do the right thing." Social responsibility becomes as integral to the business as is economic performance. With this perspective, deciding which issues and stakeholders a firm should prioritize is an ongoing process of executive ethical decision making. Consistent with our earlier discussions about how ethical decisions should be made, executives weigh the harms and benefits to multiple stakeholders (including shareholders) of the firm's activities, and they aim to make decisions that benefit the societal greater good. They prioritize their organization's ethical values and apply moral rules. And they consider their intentions, how the broader society would react to a contemplated behavior, and what a "virtuous firm" would do.

This ethical perspective is more likely to support proactive corporate policies and practices that extend beyond current legal or regulatory requirements, such as the development of quality products that contribute to societal welfare (whether or not these are the most profitable), human resources practices that treat all employees fairly and respect human rights everywhere, business processes that protect the environment beyond current government regulations, and philanthropic contributions that help the community. It also supports constructive engagement with stakeholders. As we'll discuss later, these proactive policies and practices may "pay" in the long term. For example, the very best employees may be attracted and committed to firms that treat people well. In addition, organizations that act in values-based ways often avoid legal costs and other negative outcomes. But those who argue for the duty-based perspective contend that the positive ethical duty exists whether or not an economic payoff is likely to result.[11]

In an interview in 2009, John Allison, former Chairman of Branch Banking and Trust Corporation (BB&T) talked of how ethical values affect his business.[12] Along with others, BB&T's values include honesty, integrity, and justice. Allison said that the company decided not to be in the business of negative amortization mortgages. These mortgages (where the payment is less than the interest and the mortgage balance actually increases) became popular for a while (before the financial crisis), and they were highly profitable. But BB&T avoided the business because they didn't think it would be right for customers. According to Allison, "we got beat up in the market. We also lost a number of mortgage producers who could make more money working for Countrywide. . . . We believe that doing our best to help our clients make the right financial decisions is good for BB&T. I believe that while there may be short-term trade-offs by sticking to your values, you are never making a sacrifice in the long run."[13] By sticking to its values, the company not only protected its clients, it avoided contributing to the broader financial crisis as well.

Honda provides another excellent example of a company with strong ethical values that drive its business. The company is guided by its founder's visionary principles, called "the Power of Dreams." On the company website (http://corporate.honda.com), "The Honda Philosophy" says: "We see things from a global perspective, always striving to create and produce products of the highest quality at a reasonable price for worldwide customer satisfaction. . . . We see it as our responsibility to serve humanity through our global commitments to helping protect the environment and enhancing safety. . . . In every endeavor we pursue, we strive to be a company that people all over the world want to exist." In an interview in 2005, Honda's chief engineer said, "everybody at Honda is fired by the dream of creating great products that are the most fuel efficient in their class."[14] So, even when SUV sales were booming, the company was committed to fuel economy. That meant that Honda was late getting into the truck market; and when they eventually did, they aimed to do it with better fuel economy. Certainly, the company lost out on potential profit. But, according to the chief engineer, "The point is not that customers demand it [fuel economy] or don't demand it, because that's absolutely not the viewpoint of Honda. When you are a philosophy-driven company, you don't ask the customer if they agree with your philosophy. . . . [At Honda] you are never going to get anything approved by the board . . . without proving you have the best fuel economy in class. That's it." So, at Honda, protecting the natural environment is a core principle guiding business decisions—one that has proven to be costly in the short run but is likely to pay off in the longer term.

A third reason to be socially responsible is a *strategic* one. Because Michael Porter is a world-renowned business strategy scholar, writer, and consultant, many observers were surprised to find him writing a major *Harvard Business Review* article about corporate social responsibility in 2006.[15] But, with coauthor Mark Kramer, he outlined a strategic approach to CSR that begins by emphasizing the interdependence of business and society. The authors rely on the premise that business needs a healthy society because only a healthy society can produce a productive workforce and the rules of the road that make business transactions possible. A healthy society also needs business to innovate, create jobs, goods, and services, and pay the taxes that support societal activities. Therefore the best CSR initiatives will be simultaneously good for the business and for society.

Importantly, the strategic approach to CSR offers managers a strong basis for making decisions about which stakeholders and social responsibility issues should garner their attention and resources given the multitude of options available. Porter and Kramer proposed that each firm should carefully analyze its own business in search of two things: those places where the firm is doing harm and those initiatives where the firm can do good by providing unique opportunities to create shared value— value for the business *and* for society simultaneously. Companies should begin the harm reduction part of this analysis by scrutinizing the social impacts of the company's value chain. The value chain, a concept Porter introduced earlier to strategic management, describes all the normal business activities of a firm that add value as a product or service passes from one part of the business to another.

For example, in a manufacturing operation, one would consider inbound logistics (e.g., raw material acquisition and transportation), manufacturing operations, outbound logistics, marketing and sales activities, and post-sales support. Support functions such as human resources management and firm infrastructure undergird the entire value chain and should also be considered. Managers involved in the firm's daily operations are asked to look carefully at the value chain and consider where in the chain the firm creates harm or has the potential to do so, with an eye toward reducing such harm. Therefore a natural resources company would need to focus more on environmental issues while a company that sells toys might need to focus more on child safety issues or labor conditions in its overseas plants.

Value chain activities should be considered prime candidates for a firm's corporate social responsibility initiatives because they benefit society by reducing harm (or doing social good) and can also help the company by reducing costs or by improving its reputation. According to Porter and Kramer, the firm should study best practices for addressing these issues, create clear goals and evaluation criteria, and implement the initiatives. The authors call this approach "responsive CSR."[16]

The second part of the strategic CSR analysis attempts to identify where the company has the potential to do social good because of its unique knowledge and expertise. For example, one could say that FedEx is in the dependability business. Packages need to arrive at their destination no matter what the weather or other contingency, so the company prepares itself to handle these contingencies. Such preparation made the company invaluable after Hurricane Katrina. It had prepared by positioning ice, water, generators, and facility repair kits in key locations. The company was also ready with 60 tons of Red Cross provisions, something it does routinely in advance of such disasters. The company was able to repair a FedEx radio antenna in New Orleans, thus providing rescuers with reliable radio communications that had been lacking for days.[17]

To further this approach toward creating social good, Porter and Kramer argue that firms should also consider how they can leverage potential CSR initiatives in a way that also helps the company succeed in its competitive environment. Such initiatives contribute to societal good while strengthening the company's competitive position. The most strategic CSR initiatives are those that go beyond reducing harm. They add a social dimension to the firm's overall competitive strategy. For example,

Porter and Kramer note that Toyota did this quite successfully by devoting significant resources to developing its Prius hybrid car. Given societal need for more fuel-efficient cars and reduced carbon emissions, it made a lot of sense for a car company to focus resources on developing a more environmentally sustainable automobile and to do so in a way that enhanced its reputation with customers as an innovator. Not only did Toyota have the expertise to do this work, but being among the first to offer affordable hybrid cars helped the company's competitive position and its bottom line. Toyota's CSR situation was complicated by a number of safety problems with its vehicles that received much attention from multiple stakeholders including the government, media, and of course customers (case to be discussed more in Chapter 10). However, the company seems to have remedied the problems and the Prius remains a good example of strategic CSR.

The strategic approach is more proactive and affirmative than the pragmatic approach because it asks companies to identify and acknowledge company activities that can do harm (or that can be particularly helpful) and encourages firms to scrutinize their practices and address potential harms by focusing on their own value-chain activities. In this way, companies need not wait for stakeholders to identify issues for them and then react. They are proactively out in front of the issues, dealing with them before they become reputational problems. This approach also provides guidance for how an organization can make the tough choices about where to focus resources, thus targeting social responsibility issues that they can and should do something about given their expertise rather than just following the crowd. Companies that follow this strategic approach will also not limit their CSR efforts to only those that will enhance their bottom line, because focusing on the value chain requires firms to address the harms they cause. This approach challenges businesses to be innovative, to think about how they can be socially responsible in ways that leverage their unique competencies and help the business and society simultaneously, and it encourages business to actually measure the social impacts of their efforts.

But we would like to offer a caveat: This approach can give the false impression that social responsibility always has the potential to be profitable. In a book about managing "ethics," it's important to acknowledge that socially responsible business practices are sometimes costly; but for ethical reasons, companies should do them anyway. Students are often surprised to learn that many companies make decisions that they know, at least in the short term, will reduce their financial bottom line—and they do it simply because it is consistent with their values and because they have decided that it's the right thing to do. BB&T's decision to forgo the negative amortization mortgage business is one example. Many more such examples come from the overseas business environment. For example, a company may decide not to venture into a potentially profitable overseas market (say Russia or Nigeria) because it would have to engage in corruption in order to do so, and such behavior goes against its corporate values of honesty and transparency. Or, a company that has committed itself to sustainable business practices will adhere to its more expensive U.S. guidelines when disposing of toxic wastes in developing countries despite little in the way of local regulation or oversight. They do this because respect for human health is a fundamental value that has no national boundaries. Therefore we believe that, in addition to assessing the company's value chain and the competitive environment, companies need to identify the core values that will help them make tough ethical decisions about what they will and will not do, and where to focus social responsibility resources.

We'll offer one final caveat about the strategic approach. Social responsibility efforts can backfire if the public perceives that the company engages in CSR programs only if and when it can profit from doing so. We routinely find that students are cynical in reaction to efforts that are perceived in this way. An interesting question to ask yourself (and to discuss in class) is how you perceive such corporate efforts and what influences your perceptions and those of your classmates. How do you feel about companies such as Ben & Jerry's or Patagonia that integrate corporate social responsibility and sustainability into their DNA and then market themselves accordingly? Do you feel differently about these firms compared to those that seem to treat corporate social responsibility as something "nice to do" that may garner goodwill with customers? Understanding your own and others' perceptions can yield important insights that can help you later when you're in a position to make these kinds of management decisions.

TYPES OF CORPORATE SOCIAL RESPONSIBILITY

Another way to think about corporate social responsibility is to think of it in terms of multiple *types* of responsibility. CSR has been conceptualized as a pyramid constituting four types of responsibility that must be considered simultaneously: economic, legal, ethical, and philanthropic (Figure 9.2).[18]

Economic Responsibilities

The economic responsibilities of a business involve its primary function of producing goods or services that consumers need and want, while making an acceptable profit. This responsibility is considered to be primary and the bedrock of corporate social

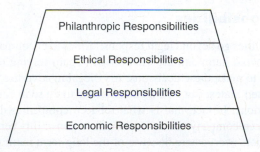

FIGURE 9.2 Corporate Social Responsibility Pyramid
Source: Reprinted from Archie B. Carroll, The Pyramid of Corporate Social Responsibility: Toward the Moral Management of Organizational Stakeholders, *Business Horizons,* July-August 1991, pp. 39–48, with permission from Elsevier.

responsibility because without financial viability, the other responsibilities become moot issues. Fulfilling this responsibility effectively is considered to represent an important ethical purpose of business because it provides good jobs, important products and services, and contributes to a vibrant economy.

The late economist Milton Friedman is the best-known proponent of the 40-year-old argument that management's *sole* responsibility is to maximize profits for shareholders. Yet people often forget what Friedman actually said—that management should "make as much money as possible while conforming to the basic rules of society, both those embodied in the law and those embodied in ethical custom."[19] So, maximizing profits is not the sole responsibility after all, even for a staunch free-market economist like Friedman. Interestingly, the statement above tacitly embraces two of the three other components of the CSR pyramid: legal responsibility and ethical responsibility. This statement also means that some businesses simply should not exist, because society has deemed them to be harmful no matter what their potential for profit. An example might be child pornography, which is illegal in the United States and many other countries. Most of us agree that no matter how many people it might employ, or how much potential profit exists, child pornography is not a socially responsible activity and organizations that engage in it should not be allowed to exist.

Legal Responsibilities

Beyond its economic responsibilities, the pyramid shows that business is expected to carry out its work in accordance with the current law and government regulations. The law guiding business practice can be viewed as a fundamental precept of the free enterprise system and as coexisting with economic responsibilities. As we said in Chapter 1, the law can also be viewed as representing the minimum norms and standards of business conduct agreed upon within a society. But not every societal expectation has been codified into law, and laws vary from state to state in the United States and even more from country to country.

Ethical Responsibilities

Ethical responsibilities go beyond legal responsibilities to encompass the more general responsibility to avoid harm and do what's right, again relying on ethical decision-making processes to make these decisions. It's illegal to advertise or sell cigarettes to minors in the United States. But a firm can continue to do so in countries that have no such legal restrictions. In fact, that is what tobacco companies do in many parts of Asia. Still, a tobacco company taking its ethical responsibility seriously would cease advertising to minors everywhere because of the long-term harm to health caused by tobacco addiction.

There are many good examples of companies going beyond legal requirements to fulfill what they perceive to be their ethical responsibilities. Johns Manville, a manufacturer of specialty building products, goes beyond its legal responsibilities regarding product safety—perhaps not surprisingly, given its problematic history (more than 150,000 lawsuits alleging health problems from exposure to asbestos). In addition to complying with U.S. law by placing warning labels on all of its fiberglass products, the company also places warning labels on fiberglass products being shipped to Japan. Such warnings are not required by local law, and the company was even advised against it by the Japanese government because the warnings might result in cancer fears. Tom Stephens, former chairman, president, and chief executive officer, said, "But a human being in Japan is no different from a human being in the U.S. We told them we had a policy. We had to have a label." Although the company lost 40 percent of its sales to Japan in one year, it was later able to rebuild its Japanese business.[20] Thus the ethical responsibility category frequently intersects with the legal category, pushing the expansion of legal responsibilities and placing expectations on businesspersons to function at a level above the law.

Levi Strauss invokes its values when it says on its website (www.levistrauss.com) that "Our values are fundamental to our success. They are the foundation of our company, define who we are and set us apart from the competition. They underlie our vision of the future, our business strategies and our decisions, actions and behaviors. We live by them. They endure." Its four core values are empathy, originality, integrity, and courage. In keeping with the values of empathy and integrity, Levi Strauss was the "first multinational company to develop a comprehensive code of conduct" designed to ensure that the company's workers "anywhere in the world are safe, and treated with dignity and respect." Further, the company's commitment to diversity began in the 1940s, well before the U.S. Civil Rights Act of 1964. As an example of courage (a value not commonly found on corporate lists), the company notes that it became the first *Fortune* 500 company to extend full medical benefits to employees' domestic partners, in 1992. That benefit was controversial at the time, but the company believed it was the right thing to do.

Philanthropic Responsibilities

Philanthropic responsibilities center on the corporation's participation in activities that promote human welfare or goodwill generally through donations of time and money or products and services. Because many people consider philanthropy to be a completely voluntary or discretionary aspect of corporate social responsibility, failure to be philanthropic is generally not considered as unethical; some may question whether it is a corporate "responsibility" at all. But, at least in the United States, those with wealth (including wealthy businesses) are expected to share their good fortune and are offered tax incentives for doing so. Andrew Carnegie, the nineteenth-century steel baron who gave millions to charity (it would be over $7 billion today), said, "He who dies rich dies thus disgraced." He believed that the rich were morally obligated to give their riches to the community and should do so during their lifetime.[21]

In a more recent version of the same belief, Bill Gates (the cofounder of Microsoft) and his wife, Melinda, created the world's largest (multibillion-dollar) endowment. Gates stepped away from playing a day-to-day management role at Microsoft in 2008 to focus full-time on philanthropy. The Gateses have decided to give away 95 percent of their wealth. They are particularly interested in health (AIDS, malaria, tuberculosis), agricultural development, and education. The foundation has been credited with much of the progress in research on malaria, one of the world's worst killers. The Gates endowment is now supplemented by many more billions pledged to the foundation by Warren Buffett, who decided to speed up his own philanthropy when he learned that Gates was going to focus on the foundation full-time[22] (see www.gatesfoundation.org). These modern-day philanthropists are actively involved in tackling huge global ills, and they demand accountability and results.[23]

These previous examples are of philanthropic individuals from business. Many companies also engage in philanthropy routinely, often through foundations that they create. It is difficult to know how much companies actually give, because public disclosure is not required. But, many firms now voluntarily disclose this information in their CSR reports, and *Business Week* and *Fortune* both publish annual lists of corporate giving. Some companies, such as Target and Whole Foods, regularly donate a set portion of their profits to charity. Whole Foods stated in its mission statement that it would donate 5 percent of its net profits, something it has done annually since 1985. Target has been doing the same since 1962 and, interestingly, it surveys customers to find out where it should give. Many companies will also match employee giving or give employees time off to contribute in their communities. These companies may think of philanthropy from a stakeholder perspective. They see philanthropy as allowing them to improve relations with employees, communities, customers, or other stakeholders by giving to particular causes.

However, philanthropy can also be aimed at causes that are strategically tied to a company's competencies and business. As an example of a philanthropic effort tied to its business, Boston's Bain & Company provides heavily discounted management consulting to charities through a nonprofit it created, something it is particularly competent to do. Similarly, many pharmaceutical companies either give drugs away to those who can't afford them or slash prices to make them more affordable.[24]

When the tsunami of 2004 hit Southeast Asia, FedEx jumped in to help. The firm quickly chartered a plane at company expense to send 344,000 pounds of Pedialyte to rehydrate children in need. Over 100 companies (mostly in the United States) sent an estimated $178 million in cash and medicine. Companies also used their distinctive competencies to help. For example, Coca-Cola offered the use of bottling facilities and pledged to deliver 500,000 bottles of water in Thailand. Colin Powell said that the aid gave the Muslim world the "opportunity to see American generosity, American values in action." Many of these companies helped quietly, not announcing or commenting on their contributions.[25]

In September 2005, corporations responded similarly to Hurricane Katrina victims in Louisiana, Mississippi, and Alabama. In fact, Wal-Mart responded so quickly, efficiently, and generously to hurricane victims that many observers felt the company should play an official role in U.S. federal emergency management response efforts because of its logistics expertise. Wal-Mart donated over $20 million in cash to Hurricane Katrina relief and donated 1,500 truckloads of free merchandise, food for 100,000 meals, and the promise of a job for all of its displaced workers. The company's response was so unparalleled that one observer said, "Wal-Mart has raised the ante for every company in the country. This is going to change the face of corporate giving."[26]

An interesting question to discuss in class is whether corporations that engage in philanthropy should publicize their philanthropic efforts. For example, Berkeley business school students advised Birkenstock to stop giving quietly to a pediatric AIDS foundation as the company had done for years, and instead to sponsor walks for causes that could be publicized to advance the shoe company's image. But the CEO at the time rejected this advice, suggesting that the meaning of the word *responsibility* is lost if social responsibility is just about making money.[27] Similarly, we heard the CEO of Lens Crafters speak about the company's efforts to collect customers' old eyeglasses and fit them on needy individuals in the United States and overseas. He showed a heartwarming video about the work and its meaning to employees, the company, and most of all to the recipients (many of whom could see well for the first time). When asked if the company would be willing to share the video for use in business ethics classes, he was obviously uncomfortable, saying that he would prefer not to do so because the company doesn't engage in this work for publicity purposes. On the other hand, the philanthropy is an important part of the organization's culture and, in his view, creates an important sense of unity and employee commitment.

In our teaching, we often encounter student cynicism in response to corporate philanthropy efforts, especially when students perceive that companies are engaging in philanthropy in an attempt to compensate for other clearly harmful activities. For example, people know that Enron was very philanthropic in the Houston community and that Philip Morris touts its philanthropic activities while avoiding the fact that its product, cigarettes, causes lung cancer and kills millions. If observers perceive that a company is simply attempting to polish its image, cynicism is likely to result. Therefore the decision to engage in corporate philanthropy should be separate from management decisions about whether and how to publicize such giving. What do you think? Should companies publicize their philanthropic efforts externally? Or, should they treat philanthropy as a more internal matter?

If one believes that philanthropy is a responsibility for corporations, many other questions remain about what types of initiatives make most sense (how closely they should be tied to the company's business, for example), how much to invest in them, how to monitor and evaluate them, and whether to pay for philanthropic initiatives through a firm's operating budget or a foundation. Unfortunately, little research exists to help us answer these questions.[28] *Fortune* magazine reports corporate gifts as a percentage of revenue. Others suggest that a better measure would be donations as a percentage of pretax or after-tax income or net earnings. Whatever the best measure, it is clear that most U.S. businesses are serious about their responsibility to give back to the community through philanthropy.

TRIPLE BOTTOM LINE AND ENVIRONMENTAL SUSTAINABILITY

An increasingly popular way to think about corporate social responsibility is in terms of what has been referred to as the *triple bottom line*—a firm's economic, social, and environmental impacts. We have already discussed the economic bottom line, which refers to the economic impacts of a firm. The social dimension refers to a firm's impacts on multiple stakeholders such as employees, customers, suppliers, and the broader community. The third dimension of the triple bottom line is the environmental dimension. It recognizes the impact of business on the natural environment. The term *sustainability* has sometimes been used to represent harmony among these three dimensions. At other times, sustainability has come to be associated with environmental impact—"long-term growth that doesn't deplete natural resources and lowers emissions of greenhouse gases."[29] *Sustainable development* has been defined as "meeting the needs of the present without compromising the ability of future generations to meet their needs."[30]

Some companies are using *sustainability* as an umbrella term to encompass all CSR efforts that make business more sustainable in the long term, including environmental efforts. Others use *corporate social responsibility* as the umbrella term (as we do) and sustainability to represent their social responsibility efforts aimed at preserving the natural environment. Whatever the terminology, it's clear that more and more attention is being paid to this type of corporate effort. In 2008, *Fast Company* published a list of 50 ways companies are greening their businesses—everything from Ford's process for applying three coats of paint at one time to Enterprise Rent-A-Car's increasing the miles per gallon of its fleet to Staples' modifying thousands of its private label products to be more eco-friendly.[31]

In 2011, Forbes magazine created a list of the top 10 "greenest" companies in the US, companies that have conserved energy and increased their commitment to green power. They noted that Intel almost doubled its commitment to green power even during the economic downturn, a remarkable accomplishment. And Intel ties every employee's annual bonus to the company's sustainability performance. As we noted in our discussion of culture in Chapter 5, this is a sure-fire way to get employees to focus on particular ethics-related goals.[32] Whole Foods was in the Forbes top 10, as was Starbucks, Cisco Systems, and Kohl's Department Stores, all companies that say they want to be part of the effort to "drive a new U.S. green economy."

In 2012, *Newsweek* partnered with *The Daily Beast* and two research organizations to publish a list entitled "Greenest Global," that ranked the 500 largest publicly traded companies worldwide based on environmental footprint, management, and transparency.[33] The top companies represent a wide variety of industries, including information technology, telecommunications, retail, pharmaceuticals, and financial services. Well-known names such as IBM, Microsoft, Accenture, Toshiba, Staples, and Novartis are all in the top 50.

Despite being criticized in many CSR arenas (e.g., employee relations, overseas bribery), Wal-Mart has had a huge impact on the sustainability initiatives of its suppliers by announcing in 2009 that it was working to create a "Sustainability Index" that would help its customers evaluate products based on their sustainability. In 2011, as a pilot program, the company developed an index for six different product categories and accompanying category scorecards. Wal-Mart buyers then used these scorecards to evaluate products and worked with suppliers on improving their products in accordance with the scorecards. The stated goal was to develop scorecards to cover 100 product categories by the end of 2012.[34]

Early environmental efforts date back to concerns about air and water pollution reduction that began in the 1960s and then to concerns in the 1970s about chemicals called chlorofluorocarbons (CFCs) that, when released into the environment, were eating away the earth's ozone layer. Although ongoing concerns remain, efforts to reduce pollution have been quite successful, particularly in Western countries. More recent attention has focused on global climate change. A growing consensus exists among the most respected scientists around the world (including those at the first author's institution, Penn State University) that global climate change is real and is influenced by human-generated emissions of greenhouse gases. In early 2007 the UN Intergovernmental Panel on Climate Change, including the world's leading scientists on the subject, issued a report documenting that climate change exists, that human activity is a key driver, and that the many resulting likely threats to humans include water shortages, dropping crop yields, rising sea levels, and harsher storms. The report resulted from a review of hundreds of peer-reviewed scientific studies. Insurers are certainly taking notice, especially after the increasing number and intensity of recent storms. According to a report by German reinsurance company Munich Re, North America has seen a rising number of extreme weather events that have caused losses of over one trillion dollars from 1980 through 2011.[35] Although climate scientists acknowledge that no single storm can be attributed to climate change, Jonathan Foley, director of the University of Minnesota's Institute on the Environment put it this way in a tweet following Superstorm Sandy that hit the U.S. northeast in 2012: "Would this kind of storm happen without climate change? Yes . . . Is [the] storm stronger because of climate change? Yes."[36]

Many American companies, including General Electric, Wal-Mart, and DuPont Chemical, are making sustainability an essential part of their business strategy. This is largely because executives of these companies agree with the scientific consensus. But it is also a response to stakeholder expectations that companies will use resources responsibly, recycle and reuse when possible, eliminate harmful toxins, and reduce greenhouse gas emission.[37] In addition, executives are rightly concerned because energy costs are likely to continue increasing in this environment. Further, many companies also operate in multiple markets, many of which (e.g., the European Union) are increasing government regulation of carbon emissions. Therefore it makes sense for a global business to operate according to the most stringent requirements. Savvy business executives also see the call for change as a grand opportunity for business to innovate and create the businesses and jobs of the future that provide solutions to climate change problems. Following Porter and Kramer's advice,[38] some firms are making environmental sustainability a cornerstone of their broader strategy and an opportunity to achieve competitive advantage.

This attention to the natural environment represents quite a change from earlier days when General Electric dumped toxic chemicals into New York's Hudson River and fought efforts to clean it up, DuPont was considered the country's worst polluter, and Wal-Mart was known for bulldozing its way across the country. In 2007, *Fortune* magazine highlighted a number of companies that are seen as leaders in environmental sustainability efforts.[32] One somewhat surprising entry on the list was DuPont, which has gone from being known as a corporate polluter to a sustainability leader. DuPont learned a great deal from its earlier experience with CFCs. Initially, it resisted efforts to reduce them and suffered a battering of its reputation as a result. Once it was forced to replace CFCs, the firm developed a highly profitable and environmentally friendly substitute. Beginning in the 1990s, the company's efforts really intensified when a new CEO focused attention on these issues. Since then, DuPont has substantially cut greenhouse gases, carcinogens, and hazardous wastes of all kinds. It tries to do this by fundamentally changing (rather than tweaking) its processes. Now, when managers are considering new products, they are required to address the product's environmental footprint as part of the business evaluation. In addition, employees are challenged to develop new products that can help solve the world's problems while contributing to the bottom line. Another of the leading companies identified by *Fortune* is Hewlett-Packard, which outlines its sustainability efforts in a detailed Global Citizenship Report. Although high-tech companies tend to be particularly sensitive to these issues, Hewlett- Packard is seen as one of the best. For example, the company's own machines are now completely recyclable, and HP makes huge efforts to mitigate the deleterious impacts of "e-waste."[39]

Yet another way companies are "going green" is through their buildings. Adobe, the software maker, became the first company to receive the U.S. Green Building Council's platinum award for its headquarters in San Jose, California, in 2006. This achievement is especially impressive because the company did it not by building a new structure, but by overhauling an existing one. An investment of over $1 million is yielding nearly $1 million in annual savings, including substantial reductions in electricity and gas usage.[40]

William McDonough and Michael Braungart's book, *Cradle to Cradle: Remaking the Way We Make Things* (2002), is causing many organizations to adopt a new way of thinking about how to make their business more sustainable. The authors offer a manifesto for transforming industry through what they call intelligent design and a concept called "waste equals food," in which no material is actually wasted but is either used by another organism or returned to the earth through biodegradation. The entire process is patterned after natural ecosystems. You can learn more about it at the authors' website (www.mcdonough.com).

A particularly stellar example of sustainability in action is Interface Carpets, founded by Ray Andersen in 1973 to produce carpet tiles. Although you may not have heard of this company, you have likely walked on its ubiquitous carpet tiles. Interface Carpets is a billion-dollar global firm with sales in over 100 countries. Andersen had a personal epiphany after reading Paul Hawken's book, *The Ecology of Commerce* (1994). He set the company on a new course to become a restorative enterprise with a long-term commitment to sustainability and the goal of demonstrating to others that the company could operate in such as way as to "take nothing from the earth that is not naturally and rapidly renewable, and to do no harm to the biosphere."[41] This goal is summed up in the company's Mission Zero promise and its pledge to climb "Mount Sustainability." The company aims to be restorative not just through its own efforts but by helping others do the same. The company's website (www.interfaceglobal.com) lists the seven fronts of Mount Sustainability: eliminating waste, ensuring benign emissions, using renewable energy, closing the loop, achieving resource-efficient transportation, sensitizing stakeholders (including suppliers and investors), and redesigning commerce. It lists milestone markers and what it considers to be its greatest achievements. Here are just a few. The waste sent to landfills is down 77 percent. Over a third of the raw materials the company now uses are bio-based or recycled materials. Since 1996, water use in manufacturing is down 80 percent and energy intensity is down 43 percent. Eight of nine company facilities operate completely on renewable electricity. The company refers to its efforts as a long-term journey that continues. We encourage you to visit the company's website to learn more about its admirable accomplishments.

We'll say more later about how corporate executives often have a knee-jerk reaction to any additional government regulation. Interestingly, though, many executives are actually supporting increased government regulation in the environmental arena as a way to reduce uncertainty about the future and level the playing field. For example, influential CEOs from America's carmakers and utilities have stated publicly that the climate change threat requires national legislative action to reduce greenhouse gas emissions. In January 2009, executives from more than a dozen companies (including General Electric, Xerox, ConocoPhillips, Caterpillar, and Duke Energy) joined together to encourage the U.S. Congress to pass climate legislation and offered their own policy recommendations. In another surprising turn of events, in 2009, a number of companies (including Apple Computer and public utilities PG&E, Exelon, and PNM Resources) resigned from the U.S. Chamber of Commerce because of disagreements over the Chamber's fierce resistance to climate change legislation.

As with other social responsibility efforts, firms' environmental initiatives often trigger cynical reactions. Terms like *greenwashing* have been used to describe corporate efforts that are seen as disingenuous attempts at public relations rather than sincere efforts to reduce environmental harm or to do good. Greenpeace even launched a website (stopgreenwash.org) devoted to helping people distinguish the pretenders from firms that deliver legitimate environmental benefits. So, once again, firms need to think hard about how to represent their efforts publicly. Interested stakeholders are quick to target insincere attempts to use the public's interest in the environment to simply advance corporate interests.

On a more positive note, we've also found a great deal of interest in sustainability initiatives among our students. In fact, many are beginning to see the sustainability movement as a career opportunity that aligns with their own values. Students with such an interest are finding more colleges and universities developing sustainability training programs, including MBA programs that prepare students to operate sustainable businesses or to help traditional business become more environmentally responsible. At Boston College's Carroll School of Management, teams of students are competing to give companies ideas that do good while creating unique business opportunities. The winners of a 2009 competition created a program called "Green with Envy" that offered green products and services including a recyclable telephone and a program customers can use to reduce their carbon footprint and stay aware of environmental issues.[42] We expect to see more of such programs in coming years.

IS SOCIALLY RESPONSIBLE BUSINESS GOOD BUSINESS?

This is an age-old question to which we don't have a perfect answer, although we know a lot more about it than we used to. Anecdotes abound. We can probably all name companies that appear to have "gotten ahead" in irresponsible ways, at least in the short term. The financial companies that helped precipitate the 2008 financial crisis come to mind. On the other hand, we can also identify companies that have paid dearly for their irresponsible behavior; and finally, we can point to many successful companies that are based on a foundation of social responsibility. Let's see if we can get beyond the anecdotes and look to the evidence.

The Benefit of a Good Reputation

One argument that social responsibility does "pay" focuses on the value of a company's reputation with key stakeholders. Norman Augustine, retired chairman of Lockheed Martin, one of the largest defense contractors, recounted a situation when the company's ethics and social responsibility were on the line. When competing on a government contract, the company received a brown paper bag containing their competitor's bid. They immediately turned it over to the U.S. government and told the competitor about it. Lockheed lost the contract, employees lost jobs, and shareholders lost money—huge short-term losses. But Augustine is convinced that the loss was only short term. "We helped establish a reputation that, in the long run, will draw us business . . . it always pays off in the long term."

But does reputation really matter? According to *Business Week*, "business has a huge stake in the way the rest of society perceives its ethical standards." On the negative side, scandals give business "a black eye"[43] and cost money. For example, Exxon faced years of negative media scrutiny after the *Exxon Valdez* oil spill. On a more positive note, a favorable corporate reputation "may enable firms to charge premium prices, attract better applicants, enhance their access to capital markets, and attract investors."[44] In general, research has supported the idea that having a good reputation pays off in lower costs, higher sales, and the ability to charge higher prices than firms with poor reputations can.[45] Studies have also found that workers are more attracted to firms with a reputation for social responsibility.[46] In a Stanford University study of 800 MBA graduates from 11 leading European and North American business schools, 94 percent of the students said they would be willing to forgo financial benefits to work for an organization with a better reputation for ethics and corporate social responsibility.[47] Once employed, people are also more committed to organizations that have a "benevolent climate"—one that focuses on the welfare of employees and the community, while organizational commitment is lower in "egoistic" climates (based on self-interest and people being out for themselves).[48]

Socially Responsible Investors Reward Social Responsibility

Another way to think about this question is to focus on shareholders as a particularly important stakeholder group and ask whether shareholders reward social responsibility. We focus here on a particular group of shareholders who do; they're socially responsible investors. It's important to note that shareholders are not a unified group. *Socially responsible investors* are those shareholders who clearly care about the financial and the social bottom line of a business. Socially responsible investors insist that their investments meet ethical as well as financial criteria. They "put their cash where their conscience is." Although the social criteria vary, many of these investors shun certain types of industries, such as tobacco, while supporting companies that use energy wisely, protect the environment, practice good governance, and market safe products and services. They may also consider the firm's human resource practices, such as female and minority advancement, day care, profit sharing, and executive pay policies. Several socially responsible stock indexes have emerged (e.g., KLD, FTSE4Good, Dow Jones Sustainability Group Index, Domini Social Index 400), and being listed on one of those has value in terms of corporate reputation. A number of brokers, financial planners, and mutual funds also serve these investors' needs in the United States and internationally where socially responsible investing is also growing. A nonprofit trade association, the Social Investment Forum (www.socialinvest.org), reported that socially responsible investing grew from $40 billion in 1984 to nearly $4 trillion in 2012. The association provides a long list of 140 socially responsible mutual funds, and these funds have generally managed to keep investors better than other funds have.[49] Growth in socially responsible investing is attributed to demand for such products from both institutional and individual investors and growing concern about the natural environment, among other forces. Institutional investors' concern about social responsibility has also grown. For example, CalPERS (the huge California Public Employees' Retirement System) pressures the companies it invests in to engage in good corporate governance and socially responsible practices in areas such as human rights and environmental responsibility (see www.calpers.ca.gov). What does this mean for ethics and social responsibility? At least for this group of investors, shareholders' interests are not distinct from employee, customer, and community interests; they're all interconnected.[50]

The Cost of Illegal Conduct

We said earlier that fulfilling legal responsibilities is one type of corporate social responsibility. Failing to fulfill those responsibilities results in criminal conduct that is extremely costly to the individuals and firms convicted.[51] Since the passage of Sarbanes-Oxley, hundreds of corporate fraud cases have been brought to trial. Senior executives have been sentenced to lengthy prison terms, such as Bernie Ebbers' 25-year prison sentence for his involvement in cooking the books at MCI and Walter Forbes' 2007 sentence to 12 years and 7 months in prison and $3.275 billion in restitution for accounting fraud at Cendant. Despite the myth that white-collar criminals go to a summer-camp-like "Club Fed," that is far from true. Some who commit financial crimes serve their time in higher-level prisons along with rapists, pedophiles, and drug dealers.

For example, Dennis Kozlowski, the former CEO of Tyco, and Mark Swartz, the former Tyco CFO, were sentenced in September 2005 in a New York State court (not a federal court) to 8 to 25 years and will have to serve their terms in a maximum-security state prison such as Attica—not a Club Fed by any means.[52] Even the minimum-security federal prisons are not pleasant places. Although there is no razor wire, inmates have no privacy, are subject to body cavity strip searches, and eat prison food.[53] Just ask Charles Gile, a former energy derivatives trader for Citigroup who left behind his degrees from Vanderbilt and Wharton, medals from Desert Storm, a home on the Connecticut coast, and a lovely wife and three children to become inmate No. 59449-054 at a federal prison camp in Jesup, Georgia. He was charged with overstating the value of energy-based derivatives and understating their risk as a way to boost bonuses. He said, "This notion of Club Fed is terribly inaccurate...That place doesn't exist. No nice meals—unless you consider the bologna soup we had a couple of weeks ago a nice meal. I live in an open-air cinderblock building. Sleep in a triple-decker bunk bed. There are six toilets. Seven showers for 75 men." He was allowed two possessions, eyeglasses and his wedding ring.[54] Most inmates say that even worse than serving time in prison is the shame that a criminal investigation and conviction bring to one's family. Criminals often lose their families as a result. Finally, many of these executives, even if not convicted of a criminal offense, will likely lose their personal fortunes as a result of other lawsuits. As one former CEO inmate put it, "Life as you know it is over."[55]

From the firm's perspective, stock prices also drop in the short term in response to announcements of allegations of corporate crime and in response to announced penalties.[56] Financial performance also suffers significantly over the five years following a conviction.[57] Companies often settle with prosecutors to avoid lengthy litigation. For example, in late 2002, the top 10 U.S. brokerage firms agreed to pay $1.44 billion in fines, completely separate their stock research from their investment banking operations, and pay for independent stock research. Merrill Lynch agreed to pay a $100 million fine earlier in 2002. The conventional wisdom says that firms don't suffer enough for illegal behavior. But one academic study examined the penalties imposed on nearly 600 firms for financial misrepresentation over more than two decades. Beyond the monetary penalties, which averaged $23.5 million, the researchers found a much larger reputational penalty imposed by the market that was felt only after the legal penalty was revealed. Firms lost 41 percent of market value on news of the misconduct, and most of that decrease can be attributed to lost reputation.[58]

Interestingly, punishment comes from business partners as well. When illegal or unethical conduct is revealed via the media, firms lose legitimacy with business partners such that, after the illegal conduct is revealed, their executives are more likely to serve on the boards of firms with lower reputations and profitability than before, and the company's own board members are more likely to come from firms with lower reputations and profitability. More serious illegal or unethical conduct is associated with even stronger effects. So, firms that engage in illegal or unethical conduct find that high-quality network connections are severed as those associated with more profitable and reputable firms distance themselves.[59]

The Cost of Government Regulation

Another huge cost of irresponsible business behavior is increased government regulation. Government is responsible for preventing serious risks to our system (for example, by regulating industries such as financial services and electricity) and for holding companies accountable for the "externalities" they create. *Externalities are costs to society, such as environmental damage, that are produced by companies but not reflected in the company's cost structure.*[60] As consumers, we rely on the government to hold companies accountable for their actions. We want to be sure that our air, food, and water are safe; that airlines don't skimp on maintenance, security, or pilot training; that physicians who work for managed care companies put patient care ahead of profits; and that large financial institutions don't take huge risks that can bring down the entire economy.

After so many business scandals, business has experienced a regulatory backlash. You may have noticed that deregulated businesses (e.g., energy, telecommunications, and financial services) have been at the forefront of recent business scandals. The lack of regulation of the mortgage-backed securities business contributed to the recent financial crisis and led to new financial industry regulations. In earlier scandals, Enron clearly took advantage of the lack of regulation of its energy trading business to influence government officials and play games with the numbers.[61] And companies like WorldCom took advantage of deregulation in the telecommunications industry. As a result of these scandals, people lose trust in the ability or will of business to self-regulate and demand more government regulation.

The 1990s financial reporting scandals led the New York Stock Exchange to call for reform. The reforms, passed in August 2002, enforce corporate board and audit independence and require members to have codes of conduct. Congress passed the Sarbanes-Oxley Act (commonly referred to as SOX) legislating corporate governance and accounting reform in July 2002. Among other things, the law sets up a new oversight board for the accounting industry, requires that companies change their lead auditor or coordinating partner every five years, reduces the range of services auditors can offer, and bars senior executives from selling stock during certain periods.[62] In addition, CEOs and CFOs of public companies are required to certify the accuracy of their financial statements, which they did for the first time in August 2002. A false certification can get the executive a $5 million fine and up to 20 years in prison.

Securities fraud is punishable with up to 25 years in jail, and shredding or destroying documents in federal investigations can get the perpetrator up to 20 years.[63]

Section 404 of the Sarbanes-Oxley Act is considered the most burdensome for companies. It requires firms to be able to show that their internal financial control systems are sound and can prevent fraud. This requirement is difficult at best and, according to the *Wall Street Journal*, has enriched the firms that conduct audits while taking attention away from innovation and day-to-day business.[64] So, although some executives have acknowledged that the law has resulted in worthwhile improvements in their internal control systems (e.g., GE, United Technologies), other business leaders have complained that the regulation is too costly—especially for smaller businesses—and has driven companies away from U.S. stock exchanges. But *Business Week* writes that the reforms have been successful because they have increased the credibility of the markets and have caught a lot of real problems before they became serious.[65] Further, costs have decreased over time as companies have streamlined their processes and become more efficient, and other countries (e.g., France, Japan, China, Canada) have adopted similar rules. Finally, according to *Business Week*, non-U.S. companies continue to flock to U.S. stock exchanges. Some analysts say that the more stringent regulatory environment actually helps companies by increasing shareholder confidence in financial reporting.[66]

The Securities and Exchange Commission is still in the process of making and implementing the rules called for by the Dodd-Frank Wall Street Reform and Consumer Protection Act, which was passed in response to the 2008 financial crisis. The overarching idea is to increase transparency in a wide variety of markets such as securities-based swaps and hedge funds. In addition, investors now have more of a say in executive compensation and the SEC has implemented a new whistleblower program that incentivizes individuals to come forward with information about securities law violations (see www.sec.gov for more information).

Boards of directors of public companies are taking their oversight responsibilities more seriously because of the new regulations as well, largely out of concern for their own personal liability. Boards have fired a number of CEOs as a result (Harry Stonecipher at Boeing, Hank Greenberg at the insurance company AIG, and many more). At MCI (formerly WorldCom, of scandal fame), the board has taken a broad stakeholder perspective on its duties. Its governance guidelines say that the board should "maximize the long-term value of the company for its shareholders" by "responsibly addressing the concerns of other interested parties including employees, customers, suppliers, government and regulatory officials, communities and the public at large." Those guidelines came into play when MCI's board rejected a higher takeover bid from Qwest in 2005 in favor of one from Verizon—leaving over $1 billion on the table and angering short-term investors. The board looked ahead and concluded that, in the long term, the Verizon bid would be worth more.[67] As this story points out, those who argue that a public company owes responsibility first to its shareholders must answer a very important question—which shareholders? Day traders have very different interests than do those who plan to hold a stock long term.

In some cases, probably in attempts to stave off further government regulation, companies in specific industries come together to self-regulate. In July 2002 the

Pharmaceutical Research and Manufacturers of America (PhRMA) embraced new voluntary guidelines for how pharmaceutical sales representatives can market to physicians. For decades this has been fertile territory for conflicts of interest, and PhRMA's guidelines are the beginning of a cleanup. The code, an updated version of which took effect in 2009, is posted on the organization's website and specifically prohibits pharmaceutical sales reps from paying for a range of perks they had employed in the past to get access to physicians who make the decisions about which drugs to prescribe. The perks ranged from dinners to ski vacations, sporting events, and cruises, and even to paying for a physician to fill up his car at a service station—all in an attempt to get air time with the doctors. Although PhRMA has no enforcement provisions, many of the pharmaceutical companies are expected to take the new guidelines seriously. Executives from Merck, GlaxoSmithKlein, Wyeth Ayerst, and others have spoken publicly in support of the guidelines,[68] and a long list of companies have now stated publicly that they intend to abide by the code.

However, the government was not content to leave the companies to regulate themselves on this issue. In September 2002, the Department of Health and Human Services issued similar guidelines prohibiting pharmaceutical companies from offering incentive payments or any other "tangible benefits" to reward the prescribing or purchasing of their drugs. Companies that flout the new standards can be investigated and prosecuted under federal fraud and kickback statutes.[69] In 2005, PhRMA also released a voluntary conduct code for print and television advertising of prescription drugs. Among other principles, the companies pledge to educate doctors before beginning consumer advertising campaigns (see www.phrma.org).

Responsible Care, a voluntary initiative of the chemical industry, was launched in the United States in 1988 in response to major accidents such as the 1984 disaster at a Union Carbide plant in Bhopal, India. The aim of this program is to secure the public's trust in the chemical industry by demonstrating responsible corporate citizenship. Members subscribe to a voluntary code of conduct that is monitored and enforced by the Chemical Manufacturers Association. The codes cover the following areas: community awareness and emergency response, pollution prevention, safe distribution of chemicals in transit, employee health and safety, and safe handling of chemicals from manufacture through disposal. The codes and policies extend beyond legal compliance and focus on continuous improvement, communication with external stakeholders, and training of suppliers on the standards.[70]

What the Research Says about Social Responsibility and Firm Performance

In academic circles, arguments are made on both sides about whether corporate social responsibility is related to financial performance. Some argue that CSR should contribute positively to the bottom line by making multiple important stakeholders more positively disposed toward the firm. Others argue that social responsibility is a cost that robs resources from profits. Although difficult to research, studies on this question have become more sophisticated over the years and they're providing answers.

In an early and simple attempt to demonstrate a positive link between good ethics and firm financial performance, James Burke, former CEO of Johnson & Johnson, compiled a list of major companies with a reputation for ethics and social responsibility. The group, including such recognized names as Johnson & Johnson, Coca-Cola, Gerber, IBM, Deere, 3M, Xerox, J.C. Penney, and Pitney Bowes, grew at a rate of 11.3 percent annually from 1950 to 1990, while the growth rate for Dow Jones industrials as a whole was only 6.2 percent for the same period.[71]

In a similar study, researchers compared the 2001 "100 Best Corporate Citizens"—as measured by a synthesis of the rankings by Kinder, Lydenberg, Domini (KLD), an independent service that assesses corporate social performance of companies in the S&P 500, based on firms' responses to key stakeholder interests—with *Business Week*'s financial rankings. The average financial performance of the 100 best corporate citizen firms was significantly better (more than 10 percentage points higher) than the average financial performance of the rest of the S&P 500.[72] These firms also had higher rankings in *Fortune* magazine's 2001 reputation survey. Corporate citizenship was measured by rating companies' service to seven different stakeholder groups: stockholders, community, minorities and women, employees, environment, non-U.S. stakeholders, and customers.[73]

Over the last 30 years or so, a growing number of academic studies have attempted to document the relationship between social responsibility and financial performance more rigorously.[74] A recent statistical review (a meta-analysis) of 52 such studies found a positive relationship between CSR and financial performance, especially when reputation-based measures of corporate social performance and accounting-based measures of financial performance were used. In addition, researchers have found that a reputation for higher corporate social performance is associated with decreased firm financial risk.[75] Finally, research has demonstrated that companies with good corporate governance structures and policies (such as strong shareholder rights provisions) have higher profitability, sales growth, and market values as well as higher stock prices than do companies without such structures and policies. Gavin Anderson at GovernanceMetrics International (a firm that evaluates corporate governance practices) suggests that, before investing in a company, wary investors should search for a pattern of previous litigation and regulatory problems (available through the Securities and Exchange Commission and other public data sources). Such a pattern suggests that the firm has a culture that tolerates unethical and illegal behavior and should be avoided.[76]

Research also suggests a reciprocal relationship, meaning that social responsibility leads to increased financial performance *and* financial performance provides firms with more slack resources that they can then devote to future social responsibility efforts.[77] The study used an index of eight attributes of CSR as rated by KLD. Firms with strong financial performance were rated higher on corporate social performance, suggesting that companies that do well financially also allocate more resources to social concerns—they "do good by doing well." Those that are not in good financial health may not have the funds to engage in philanthropy or other discretionary social performance activities. The study also found that financial performance depends on good social performance, suggesting that firms also "do well by doing good." The authors termed this the "good management theory," arguing that good social performance is related to other good managerial practices.

It's likely that these relationships are linked in what the authors termed a "virtuous circle" in which good corporate social performance feeds financial performance and good financial performance makes it possible to continue good corporate social performance. Clearly, being socially responsible doesn't harm the firm's bottom line as some economists have suggested in the past. In fact, the study's findings suggest that a firm's relationships with key stakeholders (e.g., employees, community, natural environment) are important to its financial performance.[78]

One difficulty of understanding the relationship between CSR and financial performance is that most studies combine all types of social responsibility into one composite. But different types of initiatives may have different effects. For example, firms that made *Working Mother* magazine's list of "Most Family Friendly Companies" for the first time experienced significant, positive, abnormal stock market returns following the announcement that they were on the list.[79]

Further, many corporate executives believe that philanthropy contributes to the bottom line, helping to attract and retain the best employees and helping to create a brand that consumers will associate with caring and generosity. But previous research had found mixed results. In one study the authors argued that these mixed results may occur because the relationship is not a simple linear one.[80] Interestingly, this study found an inverted U-shaped relationship between corporate philanthropy and financial performance. The authors found that firms can benefit from philanthropy up to a point, arguably because key stakeholders will be more cooperative and supportive of the firm as theory suggests. The authors used the term *excessive philanthropy* to explain that, beyond some optimal point, philanthropy becomes more of a cost and may raise concerns among wary stakeholders who worry that too many resources are being expended. The study also found that firms operating in more dynamic business environments, where corporate reputation and image are likely most important, benefit the most from corporate philanthropy.[81] Therefore, although it's clear that philanthropy can be beneficial, research suggests that executives must work hard to find the optimal point beyond which additional philanthropy is likely to be counterproductive.

In yet another attempt to look at specific types of initiatives, a 2008 study investigated the relationship between "green" initiatives (in particular, strategic investments to reduce emissions and pollution) and financial performance.[82] Previous research had generally found a positive relationship between environmental performance and financial performance and had credited that relationship to more efficient utilization of resources. In this study of 267 firms, the authors argued that such investments reduce the risk of litigation, allowing the firm to direct resources more strategically and ultimately improving investors' perceptions of the company's risk profile. As a result, the authors argued, the firm's cost of debt and equity capital should be reduced, and they found support for these relationships. Therefore, in addition to improving internal efficiencies, external stakeholders respond positively to environmental initiatives by reducing the firm's cost of capital.[83]

Research has also found that failure to be socially responsible is costly. One study synthesized the results of 27 studies that covered over 2,000 incidents of socially irresponsible or illegal behavior. Across these studies, stock prices decreased significantly in response to socially irresponsible or illegal acts, thereby decreasing shareholder wealth.[84] These results suggest that there are definitely costs to being socially irresponsible.

It is important to remember, however, that stellar social responsibility cannot compensate for a poor business strategy. Levi Strauss has long been known for its values and CSR initiatives (see www.levistrauss.com). The company is proud of its commitment to diversity, philanthropy, and its early establishment of an ethical code for overseas manufacturers. But in the late 1990s, the company experienced a slide in revenue that took quite some time to turn around. A new CEO was hired in 1999. He initiated a turnaround strategy aimed at product innovation, the system of styles and sizes, and information technology initiatives. Over the long term, it is clear that, to be successful, companies must have *both* excellent business strategies and socially responsible business practices.

Being Socially Responsible Because It's the Right Thing to Do

Finally, we propose that businesspeople may have another reason (besides the financial bottom line) to practice "good ethics" and social responsibility—because they're people first, who value their good reputations and the opinion of their friends, family, and community. They're guided by a moral compass that points them in an ethical direction as well as a financial compass that points them toward considering the costs and benefits of a decision.

Consider Malden Mills, the Massachusetts manufacturer of Polarfleece and Polartec fabrics. On December 11, 1995, while the CEO was celebrating his seventieth birthday, the company experienced a catastrophic industrial fire that wiped out three of four factories in Lawrence, Massachusetts. The fourth building was saved through the heroic efforts of 27 union employees who fought the fire all night. No one was killed in the fire, thanks to the efforts of employees who checked attendance sheets, made a human chain, and dragged their fellow employees to safety. After the fire, CEO Aaron Feuerstein carried the welfare of his employees, customers, and the Lawrence community on his shoulders. "There is no way I would throw 3,000 workers into the street—no way I would take Lawrence, Massachusetts, and condemn them to economic oblivion."[85] He quickly announced that he would keep his 3,000 jobless employees on the payroll for a month, which he extended to two months, and then three months, while the factory was being rebuilt. Feuerstein paid out a total of more than $15 million in wages and benefits to jobless employees after the fire. Employees jumped to the challenge. Just a few weeks after the fire, productivity was higher than it had been before the fire because of employees' creativity and willingness to work "25 hours a day."[86] By summer, almost all of the employees had returned to work, and the 400 unemployed got extended health benefits, help finding work, and a promise of a job when the new plant opened. Feuerstein received accolades from the workforce and the media, and President Bill Clinton invited him to attend the State of the Union Address in 1996.

Many in the business community thought Feuerstein should have pocketed the insurance money and moved the company somewhere with lower labor costs, perhaps overseas. But *Fortune* magazine later praised Feuerstein as an astute businessman in his handling of the disaster. He treated his employees as an asset rather than an expense, cultivated their loyalty, and bet on the company's future. The decision to rebuild the factory was also a rational one because insurance covers the replacement cost of a factory only if it is rebuilt. If he hadn't replaced the factory, Feuerstein might have had to settle for the depreciated value of the burned building and its contents. And moving the factory overseas would have risked losing the quality advantage. Finally, Feuerstein took advantage of a mountain of free media attention from *People* and *Parade* magazines, TV newsmagazines such as *Dateline*, and more.[87]

According to *Fortune*, "Any idiot with a strong enough stomach can make quick money, sometimes a lot of it, by slashing costs and milking customers, employees, or a company's reputation. But clearly that's not the way to make a lot of money for a long time. The way to do that is to create so much value that your customers wouldn't dream of looking for another supplier. Indeed, the idea is to build a value creation system of superior products, service, teamwork, productivity, and cooperation with the buyer."[88] This view jibes with Feuerstein's philosophy. In a 1997 talk to management professors at their annual Academy of Management meeting, Feuerstein said his business objective is to win by creating a better-performing, higher-quality product that is different from what competitors are making. To do that, you have to have the right people, trust, and understanding. You have to extend to your people the loyalty you want them to extend to you. Clearly, Feuerstein is an accomplished businessman. But he is also driven by deeply held moral beliefs. In that talk to business professors, he quoted the Bible (in Hebrew!) on the responsibility of a rich man not to praise himself for his riches, and to do kindness, justice, and charity in the community. Given his moral beliefs, he believed that he had no choice but to rebuild his factories.

In an unfortunate turn of events, Malden Mills was forced to file for bankruptcy when it ran short of cash in late 2001 due to the cost of rebuilding after the devastating 1995 fire. However, Feuerstein remained optimistic because key customers remained loyal (L.L. Bean, Patagonia, The North Face, the U.S. Military), union employees volunteered major concessions, and members of the general public (including local townspeople) sent notes of encouragement and sometimes checks! *60 Minutes* aired a laudatory segment about Feuerstein and the company on March 24, 2002, and the company worked hard to develop new specialty products for growing markets including the American military.

The company emerged from bankruptcy protection in 2003. Michael Spillane, a Tommy Hilfiger executive, was named CEO in August 2004 about the same time the company announced that the U.S. Congress had approved $21 million to purchase Polartec garments for the military and to support continued research and development of electronic textiles that can remotely monitor the physiology of soldiers in combat. But, in 2007, the company filed for bankruptcy again. The new company that emerged is named Polartec LLC and is owned by Versa Capital Management. It offers a wide variety of Polartec products, which it sells to the military and other familiar names such as Patagonia, The North Face, Lands End, and L.L. Bean.

Feuerstein lost control of his former company in June 2004.[89] But he has said that he didn't expect anything in return for his magnanimous behavior in 1995. He did it because it was right, not because there would be a financial payoff.[90] "There are times in business when you don't think of the financial consequences but of the human consequences."[91] So to Feuerstein, the question, "Is socially responsible business good business?" is the wrong question. Good business doesn't refer to just the financial bottom line. Good business is business that does well financially by producing products that meet customers' needs *and* by being responsible to employees and the broader community.[92]

CONCLUSION

This chapter was designed to introduce the concept of corporate social responsibility (CSR). Hopefully, we have convinced you that it's good for business and that it's worth bothering about. The next chapter provides both classic and more recent examples of corporate social responsibility and irresponsibility, and the final chapter provides examples from the global business environment.

DISCUSSION QUESTIONS

1. Do you think corporate social responsibility is important? Why or why not?

2. Choose a company and analyze its CSR report. In doing so, think about what seem to be its reasons for being socially responsible. Is it pragmatic, ethical, strategic, or some combination? Can you identify its key stakeholders?

3. Using the same company as an example, think about the four types of corporate social responsibility. What is your assessment of how the company is doing?

4. With reference to the CSR pyramid, what are the implications of stopping at a particular pyramid level? For example, would it be all right if a company took its sole responsibility to be financial responsibility to its shareholders? Financial responsibility and legal responsibility? Do you agree that CSR is best represented by a pyramid? Why or why not? Can you think of a better way to graphically represent a company's social responsibility?

5. Think about the television programs and films you've seen recently in which business' social responsibility (or lack thereof) was portrayed in some way. How were business and businesspeople portrayed? Is there anything the business could or should do to improve its media image? Some businesses try to stay out of the limelight. Why might that be? What do you think of that strategy?

6. Do you believe that employees are more attracted and committed to socially responsible companies? Why or why not? Are you? Why or why not?

7. If you were running your own company, how would you communicate your CSR strategy with employees, with external stakeholders, and why?

CASE

MERCK AND RIVER BLINDNESS

Headquartered in New Jersey, Merck & Co. is one of the largest pharmaceutical companies in the world. In 1978, Merck was about to lose patent protection on its two best-selling prescription drugs. These medications had provided a significant part of Merck's $2 billion in annual sales. Because of imminent loss, Merck decided to pour millions into research to develop new medications. During just three years in the 1970s, the company invested over $1 billion in research and was rewarded with the discovery of four powerful medications. Profits, however, were never all that Merck cared about. In 1950, George W. Merck, then chairman of the company his father founded, said, "We try never to forget that medicine is for people. It is not for the profits. The profits follow, and if we have remembered that, they have never failed to appear. The better we have remembered that, the larger they have been." This philosophy was at the core of Merck & Co.'s value system.

RIVER BLINDNESS

The disease onchocerciasis, known as river blindness, is caused by parasitic worms that live in the small black flies that breed in and about fast-moving rivers in developing countries in the Middle East, Africa, and Latin America. When a person is bitten by a fly (and some people are bitten thousands of times a day), the larvae of the worm can enter the person's body. The worms can grow to almost two feet long and can cause grotesque growths on an infected person. The real trouble comes, however, when the worms begin to reproduce and release millions of microscopic baby worms into a person's system. The itching is so intense that some infected persons have committed suicide. As time passes, the larvae continue to cause severe problems, including blindness.

In 1978, the World Health Organization estimated that more than 300,000 people were blind because of the disease, and another 18 million were infected. In 1978, the disease had no safe cure. Only two drugs could kill the parasite, but both had serious, even fatal, side effects. The only measure being taken to combat river blindness was the spraying of infected rivers with insecticides in the hope of killing the flies. However, even this wasn't effective since the flies had built up immunity to the chemicals.

MERCK'S ETHICAL QUANDARY

Since it takes ~$200 million in research and ~12 years to bring the average drug to market, the decision to pursue research is a complex one. Resources are finite, so dollars and time have to go to projects that hold the most promise in terms of making money to ensure the company continues to exist as well as of alleviating human suffering. This is an especially delicate issue when it comes to rare diseases, when a drug company's investment could probably never be recouped because the number of people who would buy the drug is so small. The problem with developing a drug to combat river blindness was the flip side of the "orphan" drug dilemma. There were certainly enough people suffering from the disease to justify the research, but since it was a disease afflicting people in some of the poorest parts of the world, those suffering from the disease could not pay for the medication.

In 1978, Merck was testing ivermectin, a drug for animals, to see if it could effectively kill parasites and worms. During this clinical testing, Merck discovered that the drug killed a parasite in horses that was very similar to the worm that caused river blindness in humans. This, therefore, was Merck's dilemma: company scientists were encouraging the firm to invest in further research to determine whether the drug could be adapted for safe use with humans, but Merck knew it would likely never be a profitable product.

Source: D. Bollier, *Merck & Company* (Stanford, CA: The Business Enterprise Trust, 1991).

Case Questions

1. Think about the definition of *stakeholders*—any parties with a stake in the organization's actions or performance. Who are the stakeholders in this situation? How many can you list? On what basis would you rank them in importance?

2. What are the potential costs and benefits of such an investment?

3. If a safe and effective drug could be developed, the prospect of Merck's recouping its investment was almost zero. Could Merck justify such an investment to shareholders and the financial community? What criteria would be needed to help them make such a decision?

4. If Merck decided not to conduct further research, how would it justify such a decision to its scientists? How might the decision to develop the drug, or not to develop the drug, affect employee loyalty?

5. How would the media treat a decision to develop the drug? Not to develop the drug? How might either decision affect Merck's reputation?

6. Think about the decision in terms of the CSR pyramid. Did Merck have an ethical obligation to proceed with development of the drug? Would it matter if the drug had only a small chance to cure river blindness? Does it depend on how close the company was to achieving a cure, or how sure they were that they could achieve it? Or does this decision become a question of philanthropy only?

7. How does Merck's value system fit into this decision?

8. If you were the senior executive of Merck, what would you do?

SHORT CASE

You have a long-standing consulting relationship with a large consumer products company. This company represents 50 percent of your consulting revenues and is clearly your most important client. The CEO has called to ask you to commit a significant amount of time over the next couple of months to assist with a large merger project. The company is merging with a large conglomerate whose primary business is the sale and distribution of tobacco products. The CEO is relying on you to assist in facilitating a smooth integration of the two companies. You promised yourself that because your father died of lung cancer, you would never work for a tobacco company. Is there a way that you can accept the consulting assignment and still keep your promise to yourself? How will you handle this dilemma if you decide that you cannot work for the tobacco company?

NOTES

1. D. Swanson, "Addressing a Theoretical Problem by Reorienting the Corporate Social Performance Model," *Academy of Management Review* 20 (1995): 43–64.
2. E. Freeman, *Strategic Management: A Stakeholder Approach* (Boston: Pitman/Ballinger, 1984).
3. D. G. McNeil, "At Last, a Company Takes PETA Seriously," *New York Times*, July 25, 2004, 4.
4. Ibid.
5. "First, They Took on Taco Bell. Now, the Fast Food World," *New York Times*, May 22, 2005, 30.
6. M. Gunther, "The Mosquito in the Tent," *Fortune*, May 31, 2004, 158–63.
7. "Confronting Anti-globalism," *Businessweek*, August 6, 2001, 92.
8. K. Davis, "The Case For and Against Business Assumption of Social Responsibilities," *Academy of Management Journal* 16 (1973): 312–22; D. J. Wood, "Corporate Social Performance Revisited," *Academy of Management Review* 16 (1991): 691–718.
9. C. Duhigg and D. Barboza, "In China, Human Costs Are Built Into an iPad," *The New York Times*, January 25, 2012, http://www.nytimes.com/2012/01/26/business/ieconomy-apples-ipad-and-the-human-costs-for-workers-in-china.html
10. "Compliance by the Numbers," *The New York Times*, http://www.nytimes.com/interactive/2012/01/26/business/apple-suppliers-compliance-by-the-numbers.html?ref = business
11. D. Swanson, "Addressing a Theoretical Problem by Reorienting the Corporate Social Performance Model," *Academy of Management Review* 20 (1995): 43–64.
12. J. A. Parnell and E. B. Dent, "Philosophy, Ethics, and Capitalism: An Interview with BB&T Chairman John Allison," *Academy of Management Learning and Education* 8 (2009): 587–96.
13. Ibid.
14. "Counting the Miles," *Newsweek*, June 27, 2005, 40–42.
15. Michael E. Porter, Mark R. Kramer, "Strategy and Society: The Link Between Competitive Advantage and Corporate Social Responsibility," December 1, 2006.
16. Ibid.
17. E. F. Kratz, "For FedEx It Was Time to Deliver," *Fortune*, October 3, 2005, 83–84.
18. A. B. Carroll, "The Pyramid of Corporate Social Responsibility: Toward the Moral Management of Organizational Stakeholders," *Business Horizons* 34, no. 4 (1991): 39–48.
19. M. Friedman, "The Social Responsibility of Business Is to Increase Its Profits," *New York Times*, September 13, 1970, 122–26.
20. C. Hess and K. Hey, "'Good' Doesn't Always Mean 'Right'." *Across the Board* 38, no. 4 (2001): 61–65.
21. J. A. Byrne, "The New Face of Philanthropy," *Business Week,* December 2, 2002, 82–86.
22. P. Sellers, "Melinda Gates Goes Public," *Fortune*, January 21, 2008, 44–56.
23. J. A. Byrne, "The New Face of Philanthropy," *Business Week*, December 2, 2002, 82–86.
24. H. Bruch and F. Walter, "The keys to rethinking corporate philanthropy," *MIT Sloan Management Review*, Fall, 2005, 49–55.
25. C. Chandler, "A Wave of Corporate Charity," *Fortune*, January 24, 2005, 21–22.
26. M. Barbaro and J. Gillis, "Wal-Mart at Forefront of Hurricane Relief," *Washington Post*, September 6, 2005.
27. M. Lewis, "The Irresponsible Investor," *New York Times Magazine*, June 6, 2004, 68–71.

28. J. D. Margolis and J. P. Walsh, "Misery Loves Companies: Rethinking Social Initiatives by Business?" *Administrative Science Quarterly* 48, no. 2 (2003): 268.

29. Z. Karabell, "Green Really Means Business," *Newsweek*, September 22, 2008, E6.

30. Brundtland Commission, *Our Common Future: Report by the World Commission on Environment and Development* (Oxford: Oxford University Press, 1987).

31. M. Borden, J. Chu, C. Fishman, M. A. Prospero, and D. Sacks, "50 Ways to Green Your Business," *Fast Company*, November 2007, 90–99.

32. D. McGinn, "The Greenest Big Companies in America," *Newsweek*, September 28, 2009, 35–56.

33. http://www.forbes.com/2011/04/18/americas-greenest-companies.html, and http://www.thedailybeast.com/newsweek/galleries/2012/10/22/newsweek-green-rankings-2012-world-s-greenest-companies-photos.html.

34. "Sustainability Index," http://corporate.walmart.com/global-responsibility/environment-sustainability/sustainability-index.

35. P.M. Barrett, "It's global warming stupid," *Bloomberg Businessweek*, November 5–11, 2012, 6–8.

36. Ibid.

37. A. A. Marcus and A. R. Fremeth, "Green Management Matters Regardless," *Academy of Management Perspectives* 23 (2009): 17–26.

38. Michael E. Porter, Mark R. Kramer, "Strategy and Society: The Link Between Competitive Advantage and Corporate Social Responsibility," December 1, 2006.

39. "Green Is Good," *Fortune*, April 2, 2007, 43.

40. "It's Easy and Cheap Being Green," *Fortune*, October 16, 2006, 53.

41. R. C. Anderson, "Doing Everything Right the First Time, Every Time," *American Way*, October 1, 2007, 53–56.

42. "Boston College MBA Students Compete to Propose Socially Responsible Business for Verizon," *The Corporate Social Responsibility Newswire* (January 6, 2010), at www.csrwire.com.

43. "Yes, Business and Ethics Do Go Together," *Business Week*, February 15, 1988, 118.

44. C. Fombrun and M. Shanley, "What's in a Name? Reputation Building and Corporate Strategy," *Academy of Management Journal* 333 (1990): 233–56.

45. M. Rhee and P. R. Haunschild, "The Liability of Good Reputation: A Study of Product Recalls," *Organization Science* 17 (2006): 101–20.

46. D. W. Greening and D. B. Turban, "Corporate Social Performance as a Competitive Advantage in Attracting a Quality Workforce," *Business & Society* 39, no. 3 (2000): 254–80.

47. D. B. Montgomery and C. A. Ramus, "MBA Graduates Want to Work for Caring and Ethical Employers" (January 2004), at www.gsb.stanford.edu/news/research/hr_mbajobchoice.shtml.

48. L.K. Treviño, K. Butterfield, and D. McCabe, "The ethical context in organizations: Influences on employee attitudes and behaviors," *Business Ethics Quarterly*, 1998, 8 (3): 447–476.

49. S. Scherreik, "Following Your Conscience Is Just a Few Clicks Away," *Businessweek*, May 13, 2002, 116–18.

50. J. Melton, "Responsible Investing: $639 Billion and Counting," *Co-Op America Quarterly*, Spring 1996, 13.

51. Adapted from a speech given by attorney Steven Alan Reiss at the Conference Board meeting on business ethics, New York, 1992.

52. A. R. Sorkin, "Ex-Tyco Executives Get 8 to 25 Years in Prison," *New York Times*, September 20, 2005, www.nytimes.com/2005/09/20/business/20tyco.html.

53. G. Colvin, "White-Collar Crooks Have No Idea What They're in For," *Fortune*, July 26, 2004, 60.

54. "Trader, Father, Veteran, Convict," *Fortune*, June 9, 2008, 92–102.

55. G. Burns, "White Collars, Prison Blues," (State College, PA) *Centre Daily Times*, January 18, 2004, E1, E6.

56. J. L. Strachan, D. G. Smith, and W. L. Beedles, "The Price Reaction to (Alleged) Corporate Crime," *Financial Review* 18, no. 2 (1983): 121–32.

57. M. S. Baucus and D. Baucus, "Paying the Piper: An Empirical Examination of Longer-Term Financial Consequences of Illegal Corporate Behavior," *Academy of Management Journal* 40 (1997): 129–51.

58. J. M. Karpoff, D. S. Lee, and G. S. Martin, "The Cost to Firms of Cooking the Books," *Journal of Financial and Quantitative Analysis* 43, no. 3 (2008): 581–611.

59. B. N. Sullivan, P. Haunschild, and K. Page, "Organizations Non Gratae? The Impact of Unethical Corporate Acts on Interorganizational Networks," *Organization Science* 18 (2007): 55–70.

60. R. Kuttner, "Everything for Sale," *Fortune*, March 17, 1997, 92–94.

61. B. Nussbaum, "Can You Trust Anybody Anymore?" *Business Week*, January 28, 2002, 31–32.

62. C. Murphy, "D.C. Gets It Right," *Fortune*, September 2, 2002, 38.

63. H. Fineman and M. Isikoff, "Laying Down the Law," *Newsweek*, August 5, 2002, 20–25.

64. "Sox and Stocks," *Wall Street Journal*, April 19, 2005, A20.

65. D. Henry and A. Borrus, "Governance: Death, Taxes & Sarbanes-Oxley?" *Businessweek*, January 17, 2005, 28–31.

66. J. Weber, "SarbOx Isn't Really Driving Stocks Away," *Businessweek*, July 2, 2007, 87.

67. K. Belson, "Why MCI Is Turning Up Its Nose at $1.3 Billion," *New York Times*, April 10, 2005, 3.

68. J. George, "Big Pharma Kills Doc Giveaways," *Philadelphia Business Journal* 21, no. 19 (2002), 1.

69. R. Pear, "Drug Industry Is Told to Stop Gifts to Doctors," *New York Times*, October 1, 2002, A1.

70. A. Prakash, "Responsible Care: An Assessment," *Business & Society* 39, no. 2 (2000): 183–209.

71. K. Labich, "The New Crisis in Business Ethics," *Fortune*, April 20, 1992, 167–76.

72. C. Verschoor and E. Murphy, "Best Corporate Citizens Have Better Financial Performance," *Strategic Finance* 83, no. 7 (2002): 20.

73. S. J. Graves, S. Waddock, and M. Kelly, "Getting There: The Methodology Behind the Corporate Citizenship Rankings," *Business Ethics* 16, no. 2 (2000): 13.

74. K. E. Aupperle, A. B. Carroll, and J. D. Hatfield, "An Empirical Examination of the Relationship between Corporate Social Responsibility and Profitability," *Academy of Management Journal* 28 (1985): 449–59; J. B. McGuire, A. Sundgren, and T. Scheeweis, "Corporate Social Responsibility and Firm Financial Performance," *Academy of Management Journal* 31 (1988): 854–87; A. H. Ullman, "Data in Search of a Theory: A Critical Examination of the Relationships among Social Performance, Social Disclosure, and Economic Performance of U.S. Firms," *Academy of Management Review* 10 (1985): 3, 540–47; J. D. Margolis and J. P. Walsh, *People and Profits? The Search for a Link between a Company's Social and Financial Performance* (Mahwah, NJ: Erlbaum, 2001); Margolis and Walsh, "Misery Loves Companies."

75. M. Orlitzky and J. D. Benjamin, "Corporate Social Performance and Firm Risk: A Meta-analytic Review," *Business & Society* 40, no. 4 (2001): 369–96.

76. P. J. Lim, "Gauging That Other Company Asset: Its Reputation," *New York Times*, April 10, 2005, 6.

77. J. D. Margolis and J.P. Walsh, "People and Profits?"; Margolis and Walsh, "Misery Loves Companies"; M. Orlitzky, F. L. Schmidt, and S. L. Rynes, "Corporate Social and Financial Performance: A Meta-analysis," *Organization Studies* 24, no. 3 (2003): 403.

78. S. A. Waddock and S. B. Graves, "The Corporate Social Performance—Financial Performance Link," *Strategic Management Journal* 18 (1997): 303–19.

79. R. Jones and A. J. Murrell, "Signaling Positive Corporate Social Performance: An Event Study of Family-Friendly Firms," *Business & Society* 40, no. 1 (2001): 59–78.

80. H. Wang, J. Choi, and J. Li, "Too Little or Too Much? Untangling the Relationship between Corporate Philanthropy and Firm Financial Performance," *Organization Science* 19 (2008): 143–59.

81. Ibid.

82. M. P. Sharfman and C. S. Fernando, "Environmental Risk Management and the Cost of Capital," *Strategic Management Journal* 29 (2008): 569–92.

83. Ibid.

84. J. Frooman, "Socially Irresponsible and Illegal Behavior and Shareholder Wealth," *Business & Society* 36, no. 3 (1997): 221–49.

85. A. Feuerstein, Presentation at the Academy of Management annual meeting, Boston, 1997.

86. M. Ryan, "They Call Their Boss a Hero," *Parade*, September 8, 1996, 4–5.

87. T. Teal, "Not a Fool, Not a Saint," *Fortune*, November 11, 1996, 201–4.

88. Ibid.

89. S. Malone, "Spillane: Malden's Next Chapter," *New York Magazine*, April 18, 2005, 24.

90. J. Seglin, "The Right Thing: A Boss Saved Them. Should They Save Him?" *New York Times*, January 20, 2002, Section 3, p. 4.

91. L. Browning, "Fire Could Not Stop a Mill, but Debts May," *New York Times*, November 28, 2001, C1, C5.

92. M. Porter and J. Rivkin, "What business should do to restore U.S. competitiveness," *Fortune*, October 29, 2012, 168–169.

CHAPTER 10

ETHICAL PROBLEMS OF ORGANIZATIONS

INTRODUCTION

In August 2009, the International Monetary Fund estimated that the global financial crisis of 2008–09 would cost the world an estimated $11.9 trillion—enough to provide a gift of $2,880 to every man, woman, and child on the planet.[1] It is, in a word, staggering. (See the chart detailing the squandered wealth in Chapter 1.)

Long before this recent financial crisis or the collapse of Enron in 2001, a number of business ethicists and business professionals watched with concern as Wall Street analysts demanded increasingly strong corporate financial performance to support rising corporate stock prices. At the same time, the gargantuan compensation packages (including stock options) of the top executives running these companies became inextricably linked to their companies' stock prices. In 1973, average CEO pay at major corporations was 27 times the pay of the average worker.[2] By 2012, the average CEO was earning 380 times what the average worker earned.[3] Experts warned of a bubble—even Alan Greenspan, head of the Federal Reserve, cautioned against "irrational exuberance" in the markets.[4] But few predicted how bad things would get.

In a June 2002 interview on PBS's *Frontline*, Arthur Levitt, former head of the Securities and Exchange Commission (SEC), explained how stock prices influence executives and their ethical decision making (or lack thereof): "There is an obsession with short-term earnings and short-term results, and our stock markets reflect that obsession. . . . We've developed a short-term culture in American business, where executives have become obsessed with the selling price of their stock. They drive earnings in whatever way they possibly can to meet the expectations of analysts, rather than presenting a picture that is totally accurate."[5]

In the second decade of the new century, with news of unfathomable greed and misdeeds and just plain stupidity at the banks and other companies such as Enron, Arthur Andersen, WorldCom, Adelphia, Citigroup, and Tyco, it's easy to wonder if any organization is doing the right thing. Well, wonder no more. As we've noted in other chapters, thousands of organizations are working every day to uphold ethical standards and train employees in what those standards mean. If you try to imagine the hundreds of thousands of transactions that occur every day and then think about how many you hear about as being illegal or unethical—even with all of the bad news in the years since the turn of the new century—the real proportion of wrongdoers is probably quite small. However, as small as the actual number of wrongdoers might be, they can have an outsized effect on the economy—as we've seen with the financial crisis. As these crises have made clear, the need for ethical behavior and managing for the long term could not be more necessary.

In this chapter, we'll look at a series of business ethics and social responsibility cases within the framework of stakeholders—those individuals or groups who have a stake in what the organization does or how it performs. Many of the cases you'll read about here are well known as major business disasters. You might wonder why we're focusing on disasters instead of typical ethical issues within corporations. Here's why: if you read these cases carefully, you'll discover that many of them started as small issues until mismanagement, denial, or other more malevolent motives caused these seemingly minor situations to mushroom into huge legal, ethical, and public relations nightmares. We also believe that there is much to be learned from studying others' mistakes.

Some of the issues we look at in this chapter are similar to the issues we explored in Chapters 4 and 8. But now we're focused on the organizational level, where the stakes are much higher and events can escalate into disaster much faster. In addition to the business ethics nightmares, we'll look at a few positive examples and at some hypothetical cases that we hope will get you thinking.

MANAGING STAKEHOLDERS

Business wasn't always as complex as it is today. At the end of the nineteenth century, many of the country's largest corporations were privately held; consequently, their owners had very few constituencies to answer to. The magnates and robber barons of a century ago ruled their companies with an iron hand. There were no unions or laws to protect workers, and the sporadic media attention of the era left the public largely unaware of most corporate abuses. Also, most average, middle-class citizens did not invest in stocks and bonds. Investing in those days was largely a rich person's game. Of course, all of that has changed.

As we've explained in earlier chapters (especially Chapter 9), modern corporations have multiple stakeholders with myriad and often conflicting interests and expectations. Few corporations today are run unilaterally by one individual, as they well might have been 100 years ago. Even in the handful of companies where an individual founder or owner has had a looming presence—like Bill Gates at Microsoft, Steve Jobs at Apple, or Mark Zuckerberg at Facebook—there are boards of directors, regulatory agencies, and consumer groups that dramatically influence how an organization is managed. Public corporations are traded on the various stock exchanges and have numerous taskmasters—institutional and individual—in the investor community. In addition, because individuals have invested in the stock market in numbers unprecedented even a decade ago, the press is vigilant in its coverage of corporate misdeeds or any other factor that could influence corporate earnings.

What do businesses owe their stakeholders? Once we have determined who the stakeholders in a situation are, how do we determine our organization's obligations to them? And if those obligations conflict, how does an organization resolve those conflicts? There is no simple answer to these questions, but it's the task of senior executives to resolve them. To a large extent, thinking through these obligations requires use of the ethical decision-making frameworks studied in Chapter 2. It also requires careful thinking about how one might balance multiple and often competing stakeholder interests.

Perhaps the easiest way to think about multiple stakeholders is to divide them into primary and secondary groups.[6] Primary stakeholders are those groups or individuals with whom the organization has a formal, contractual relationship. In most cases this means customers, employees, shareholders or owners, suppliers, and perhaps even the government. Secondary stakeholders are other individuals or groups to whom the organization has obligations, but who are not formal, contractual partners. Obviously, organizations should strive to satisfy their obligations to their primary stakeholders while also trying to keep their secondary stakeholders satisfied. It's a difficult balancing act, but a helpful exercise if companies are to take into account and be fair to the people and groups they can affect.

This approach is so useful that David Abrahams, a managing consultant with Marsh Ltd. in London, designed a similar stakeholder model to help his corporate clients identify and quantify risk to their brand. As one of the largest insurers in the world, Marsh has great interest in developing tools to help companies mitigate reputational and other types of risk. Abrahams' model identifies three primary stakeholders—business partners, customers, and employees—and three secondary stakeholders—opinion formers, community, and authorities. He maintains that by analyzing a company and its business using those six groups as a guide, one can begin to identify how a variety of calamities might affect a company's reputation and the value of its brand, and how much those calamities might ultimately cost.[7]

The cases that follow are divided into categories representing four of the major stakeholder groups in many business decisions: consumers or customers, employees, shareholders, and the community. In all the cases, more than one stakeholder group is affected; we have categorized the cases under headings that represent the stakeholder group that we feel is most affected. However, as you read through the cases, we urge you to identify all of the stakeholders in each case and try to discern each organization's obligations to all of its various stakeholders.

ETHICS AND CONSUMERS

It might surprise many people to learn that there were few laws protecting consumers before the 1960s. At the turn of the last century, consumers didn't even have the right to sue a manufacturer for a defective product. The first real consumer law took effect early in the twentieth century when, in *McPherson v. General Motors*, a consumer was given the right to sue the auto manufacturer for a defective vehicle. Until then, the only recourse for the owner of an auto was to go after the dealer who sold the vehicle. Another landmark law was the Pure Food and Drug Act, which was passed in 1906 to prohibit adulteration in food and drugs.[8]

Although more consumer laws were passed in the first half of this century, consumers had to wait until the early 1960s for any real protectionist legislation that positioned consumers as a major stakeholder group. The framework of consumer protection as we know it today was constructed during the Kennedy administration. In his speech to Congress on consumers in 1962, President John F. Kennedy outlined four consumer rights: the right to safety, the right to be heard, the right to choose, and the right to be informed.[9] This message and the legislation that resulted laid the groundwork for today's consumer movement.

Exactly what do companies and organizations owe their customers? According to some observers, products and services should be produced and delivered according to the "due care" theory.[10] This theory stipulates that due care involves these elements:

■ *Design.* Products and services should meet all government regulations and specifications and be safe under all foreseeable conditions, including misuse by the consumer.

■ *Materials.* Materials should meet government regulations and be durable enough to withstand reasonable use.

■ *Production.* Products should be made without defects.

■ *Quality control.* Products should be inspected regularly for quality.

■ *Packaging, labeling, and warnings.* Products should be safely packaged, should include clear, easily understood directions for use, and should clearly describe any hazards.

■ *Notification.* Manufacturers should have a system in place to recall products that prove to be dangerous at some time after manufacture and distribution.

Although we've certainly alluded to some organizational responsibilities in earlier chapters, we're going to concentrate on three duties in this chapter: to respect the customer and not engage in activities that conflict with the interests of an established customer base, to produce a safe product that is free from any known defects, and to honestly advertise a product or service.

Conflicts of Interest

Although we usually think of conflicts of interest as situations involving individuals, they can also involve organizations. As we've seen over the last few years, conflicts involving organizations are even more damaging than those that involve individuals. Many people think the poster child for corporate conflicts is Arthur Andersen and other large accounting firms that at one time offered both auditing and consulting services to clients. It's hard to believe that the company executives didn't see how gargantuan consulting fees might color the judgment of auditors. However damaging those accounting firm conflicts were, they are dwarfed by what happened at Enron. (Please note that although this case appears under "Ethics and Consumers," it could just as easily appear under "Ethics and Employees" or "Ethics and Shareholders" because its effects were so far reaching. Evidence also clearly suggests that Enron's manipulation of the energy markets harmed energy consumers in California, so the company could appear under "Ethics and the Community" as well. It seems that when an ethical debacle is big enough, a range of stakeholders are affected.)

COMPANY: ENRON

INDUSTRY: ENERGY

SITUATION

In 2002, *Fortune* magazine still ranked Enron as the fifth-largest company in the United States, although by the time the magazine was published, Enron had already filed for Chapter 11 bankruptcy protection.[11] It was quite a ride: from a regional gas pipeline trader to the largest energy trader in the world, and then back down the hill into bankruptcy and disgrace. With the help of its investment bankers, accountants, and others, Enron constructed a series of off-the-books partnerships that were used to hide the company's massive debt and inflate its stock price. These partnerships were managed by Enron executives—a clear conflict of interest—who stood to benefit financially from the deals. Enron also used very aggressive accounting practices to bolster the bottom line. A particularly sad aspect of this debacle was how much Enron employees lost in their 401(k) plans as the stock price plummeted. In the fall of 2000, Enron changed administrators for its 401(k) plan and, as is typical, the plan was "closed" while that transfer took place. When a plan is closed, no one can buy, sell, or trade in his or her 401(k) until the moratorium is over. Sadly, this moratorium began just as the company's stock really began to tank, and by the time Enron employees could once again make changes in their 401(k) elections, the stock price had dramatically decreased and the retirement savings of many average employees were wiped out.

HOW THE COMPANY HANDLED IT

Executives denied there was trouble for as long as they could, but the fall from grace was swift and dramatic. Top executives resigned in disgrace, and one committed suicide. The company filed for Chapter 11 bankruptcy in December 2001 and later sold its primary energy-trading unit.[12]

RESULTS

Andrew Fastow, Enron's former CFO, settled civil and criminal lawsuits in 2004. The complaint by the SEC charged that he "defrauded Enron's shareholders and enriched himself and others by, among other things, entering into undisclosed side deals, manufacturing earnings for Enron through sham transactions, and inflating the value of Enron's investments." Fastow agreed to serve a six-year prison sentence, pay a fine of more than $23 million, cooperate with the government's ongoing investigation into Enron, and be permanently barred from acting as a director or officer in a public company.[13] In addition, Lea Fastow, Andrew Fastow's wife and a former assistant treasurer of Enron, was sentenced to serve a year in prison after pleading guilty to charges relating to the Enron mess.[14] In May 2006, former CEO Kenneth Lay and former president Jeffrey Skilling were convicted of multiple counts of fraud and conspiracy and were sentenced to 24 years in prison. Ken Lay died of a massive heart attack in July 2006, before he began to serve his sentence. Jeff Skilling is currently in jail, and has just won an appeal to reduce his sentence to 14 years.[15] He was also ordered to pay restitution of $45 million.[16] Matthew Kopper, a former managing director, pleaded guilty to money laundering and conspiracy to commit wire fraud, and he forfeited $8 million to settle an SEC civil fraud case. The accounting firm, Arthur Andersen, was convicted in a federal court of obstruction of justice and relinquished its license to practice public accountancy.[17]

The fines paid by various other players in the Enron collapse are startling. Enron itself paid over $2 billion in fines, including $1.5 billion for manipulating energy markets in California. Financial services corporations also paid huge sums to settle investor lawsuits connected to Enron: Citigroup paid $2.4 billion; JPMorgan Chase paid $2.2 billion; and other banks paid fines in the hundreds of millions to settle similar suits.[18]

COMMENTS

Former SEC chairman Arthur Levitt aptly described the scope of the problems at Enron:

> I think the Enron story was a story, not just of the failure of the firm but also the traditional gatekeepers: the board, the audit committee, the lawyers, the investment bankers, the rating agencies. All of them had a part in this.
>
> Take the rating agencies, for instance. They deferred downgrading Enron, pending a merger which they knew very well might never have taken place.
>
> Take the investment bankers, who developed the elaborate scheme that Enron used to hide the obligations of the parent company in subsidiaries. That didn't come out of the blue; that was a scheme concocted between the investment bankers and the chief financial officer of Enron.
>
> Take the accounting firm. . . . Enron was the most important audit client that they had, and Enron was also the largest consulting client that they had—a client that paid them over a million dollars a week in fees. In my judgment, that accounting firm was compromised. Their audit was compromised. Putting aside any

fraudulent activity that may have been part of this, they were clearly compromised by the nexus of consulting with auditing.

Take the lawyers that were paid vast fees. I think here you have a very interesting case where the American Bar Association prevents lawyers from revealing financial fraud of clients to regulators. And here we had a case in point where a major client of the law firm was obviously involved in practices that may well prove to have been fraudulent, and they didn't blow the whistle.

And [take] the analysts, who were claiming that Enron was a buy even after this story had broken and Enron had declared bankruptcy. These are analysts that were being paid by investment bankers that were receiving large fees from Enron for performing a variety of services. How independent could their research have been? And what could an investor have expected from an analyst who was recommending the purchase of Enron, while at the same time his employer was receiving millions of dollars in fees from that company? How likely was it that the analysts would tell it as it was? Very unlikely, in my judgment.[19]

It appears that Enron had plenty of help in constructing its massive fraud from professionals (such as auditors) who were supposed to be protecting the public interest. Its true financial performance was shrouded in partnerships that hid debt from its books and, as a result, from investors and from rank-and-file employees.

Enron was not alone, however, in its involvement in corporate conflicts of interest. The investment banking community has also been embroiled in myriad conflicts in recent years. In fact, investment banking firms—by their very nature— face a huge potential conflict of interest. They are in the business of helping corporations raise money in the markets and are consequently focused on keeping a client company's stock price as high as possible. Yet these same investment banks also serve investors, who are interested in buying stocks at as low a price as they can.[20] Talk about tension! And that tension spilled over for several big firms in the late 1990s and early 2000s. Merrill Lynch was fined $100 million when its analysts—in e-mails to one another— privately trashed the stocks of the companies they were publicly touting to investors.[21] That case and others like it were later parodied in a television commercial by investment firm Charles Schwab & Co. In the commercial, a Wall Street manager is seen urging his brokers to push an unfavorable stock. He tells them, "Let's put some lipstick on this pig." (Schwab does not underwrite stocks and consequently does not face the same conflict that other brokerage firms do.) James P. Gorman, a Merrill Lynch executive, called Schwab's commercial a "cheap shot" for "kicking someone when they're down."[22] We wonder whether investors thought Schwab's commercial was a cheap shot or a pretty accurate portrayal of some Wall Street bankers.

Investment bankers were investigated for another major conflict—how much they knew about the alleged frauds committed at Enron, WorldCom, Adelphia, and other companies. At Enron, for example, banks such as Credit Suisse First Boston, Citigroup, and JPMorgan Chase helped Enron structure the secret partnerships that hid Enron's debt and kept Enron's stock price high. Then these investment banks not only received fees for helping to structure debt but also made money from their investments in Enron stock.[23] And as we've seen, those firms paid enormous fines for assisting Enron with its shenanigans.

But perhaps no conflict in investment banking is as egregious as what happened during the housing bubble of the last decade. Investment banks were furiously creating and selling bundled mortgage products, many of which represented subprime mortgages—in other words, the mortgages faced a higher risk of default and were riskier than other mortgages. Firms like Goldman Sachs eagerly sold these funds to their clients, all the while buying insurance on those same funds (in the form of credit default swaps (CDSs). In other words, the investment banks felt that the mortgage products they were selling to clients were so risky that they bet against the products at the same time they were advising clients to buy the products. Also, while pushing these products to their clients, the investment banks encouraged rating agencies to give the products high ratings that would signal to investors that the mortgage products were safe. And, of course, they were anything but safe investments and the banks knew that. It's a colossal conflict of interest and hopefully one of the things that new government regulation will address.[24]

Here's another very public conflict of interest involving Marsh & McLennan, the insurance conglomerate that ran afoul of New York State's former attorney general, Eliot Spitzer.

COMPANY: MARSH & MCLENNAN (MARSH, INC., PUTNAM FUNDS, AND MERCER CONSULTING)

INDUSTRY: INSURANCE (MARSH, INC.), MUTUAL FUNDS (PUTNAM FUNDS), AND CONSULTING (MERCER)

SITUATION

Starting in late 2003, Marsh & McLennan (MMC), with a reputation as one of the most staid and well-managed companies in the United States, became embroiled in a series of ethical scandals. The first involved Putnam Funds, a mutual fund company in Boston and traditionally the cash cow of MMC. Putnam first lost huge bets on technology and growth stocks when the stock market imploded in 2000. Then it was the first mutual fund company named in the market-timing scandal that involved mutual fund companies across the industry. (Market timing is shifting money in and out of mutual funds based on the performance of one or more market indicators. In the recent scandal, large investors were allowed to "time the market" by trading late—after the markets had closed—which provided a clear advantage for the big guys and a clear disadvantage for the little guys.) There is no doubt that of all the mutual fund companies, Putnam took the biggest hit for the scandal, and it continues to struggle to make its way back. Its assets under management—the major measure of stability and heft in the industry—fell from $370 billion in late 2000 to $194 billion during the first quarter of 2005.[25] But Putnam was only the beginning of trouble at MMC.

In October 2004, New York State Attorney General Eliot Spitzer filed a civil complaint against MMC, the parent company of Marsh, Inc., the world's largest insurance broker. In the suit, Spitzer charged that Marsh betrayed clients by steering business to underwriters with whom it had cozy relationships in exchange for millions in backdoor payoffs. As one Marsh executive said, "We need to place our business in 2004 with those that have superior financials, broad coverage, and pay us the most." Spitzer's complaint uncovered a broad mosaic of industry-wide bid rigging for which Marsh served as the chief architect. Other companies such as AIG, Hartford, and ACE were involved, but Marsh was the big player in the arrangement.[26] (At the time of Spitzer's suit, Jeffrey Greenberg was CEO of MMC; his brother, Evan Greenberg, was CEO of ACE; and the legendary Maurice "Hank" Greenberg, father of Jeffrey and Evan, was CEO of AIG and would later face enormous troubles of his own.)

HOW THE COMPANY HANDLED IT

To stanch the bleeding at Putnam, MMC forced out Putnam's CEO, the imperious Lawrence Lasser, who took a $78 million severance payout and left the company that he had captained for years.[27] MMC quickly hired squeaky-clean Charles "Ed" Haldeman as the new CEO to lead Putnam out of the swamp. In April 2004, Putnam settled with the SEC and agreed to accept new employee trading restrictions and to conduct and provide regular compliance reviews. The company also paid $110 million in various fines. (There were additional charges, settlements, and fines from a variety of sources, including the Commonwealth of Massachusetts.)[28] Haldeman brought in a new management team and made other changes, but the company continues to struggle to regain its former position as a leader in the industry.

Its parent, MMC, had a more difficult time with its woes. In a highly unusual move, Spitzer refused to negotiate with the company as long as its executive team was in place. Soon after, CEO Jeffrey Greenberg and the top company lawyer resigned and Michael Cherkasky took the helm. Cherkasky was Spitzer's former boss in Manhattan's district attorney's office and the CEO of Kroll, Inc., a leading risk consulting company acquired by MMC shortly before its legal woes began. Cherkasky's relationship with Spitzer proved very helpful for MMC—the company quickly agreed to a settlement of

$850 million and also agreed to lead the insurance industry in reforming industry practices.[29]

A note: Mercer HR Consulting, the other third of the MMC business, also had its own troubles. It disgorged more than $440,000 in fees from the New York Stock Exchange (NYSE) after admitting that it misled the NYSE board of directors regarding the $140 million pay package of Richard Grasso, then CEO of the NYSE.[30]

RESULTS

In 2004, MMC's stock price fell from a 52-week high of $47.35 to a low of $22.75—an incredible fall from grace for a company that had performed so well and so predictably for decades.[31] In a mere four days of trading, the company lost $11.5 billion in market value.[32] That plunge hurt MMC employees more than most investors because, until shortly before these problems, MMC employees could invest their MMC retirement savings only in MMC stock. The thinking among MMC senior executives was that people would be more motivated to produce excellent results if their entire retirement savings were tied up in MMC stock. In a real ethical lapse, senior executives had other investment options—it was only rank-and-file employees who were restricted to MMC stock. MMC's strategy was particularly unfathomable when you consider that MMC's Mercer HR Consulting employed numerous retirement experts who routinely advised their clients about the importance of providing employees with diversified options for retirement investments. After years of listening to employees plead to be allowed to diversify and after watching Enron's employees lose their shirts when their company's stock plunged, MMC executives finally allowed for limited diversification. Beginning in 2003, MMC employees could diversify part of their retirement investments into a few Putnam funds—nowhere near the number or range of options provided by other large corporations to their employees. Many MMC employees who did not move quickly enough to diversify lost much of their retirement investments after MMC stock plummeted. Note to students—diversify your investments, and never put all your investments in company stock! (Also, in the interest of full disclosure, please note that one of this book's authors, Katherine Nelson, was employed as a principal at Mercer HR Consulting from 1998 to 2001 and was an "employee investor" of MMC.)

In addition to the substantial settlements, the financial losses, the pessimism of financial analysts, and the enormous hit taken by MMC investors and employees, 5,000 jobs were lost and the company's reputation remained damaged for a number of years.[33]

COMMENTS

One of the wisest comments about the crisis at MMC comes from the former CEO of Putnam Funds, Charles Haldeman, who said, "What our parents told us about protecting our reputation is true. If you lose it, it's hard to win it back again." Haldeman also talked about the isolation that existed in Putnam before his arrival. Apparently, Putnam had a history of not cultivating relationships with the press or the government, and when the scandal broke, it had no friends to turn to. Haldeman also vowed to change that. "At the time of our problems," he said, "We didn't have those relationships and it was difficult for us. At a time of need we didn't have too many friends or supporters. We don't want to be in that position again."[34] Haldeman served as CEO of Putnam from the time the crisis broke in 2004 until 2008, when MMC sold Putnam to Power Corporation and replaced Haldeman.[35]

The scandal that rocked MMC was an example of how former New York State Attorney General Eliot Spitzer liked to turn an industry upside down. Writer Peter Elkind wrote of Spitzer's strategy in *Fortune* magazine: "The strategy has been remarkably consistent. Step one: Wade broadly into a gray area of odorous but long-accepted industry practices. Step two: Seize on evidence of black-and-white outrageous conduct—typically in email form— and use it to marshal public outrage. Step three: In the resulting tsunami of scandal, swiftly exact reform of the whole industry, including gray-area behavior." Within two weeks of filing charges, Marsh and its largest competitors had agreed to stop bid rigging. Similarly, industry-wide mutual fund abuses stopped within weeks of Spitzer filing charges against Putnam.[36] Please note that Eliot Spitzer has had his own ethical lapses. A little over a year after being elected governor of New York State, he was caught up in a federal wiretap of a prostitution ring (he was found to be a client) and resigned in disgrace in early 2008.[37]

The results of these very public conflicts of interest will be felt for years. Various regulators and attorneys general from a number of states are still investigating the banks and their business practices. As a result of the various debacles in the banking industry, Citigroup has been fined more than $5.5 billion since 2003, and JPMorgan Chase has been fined more than $4 billion.[38] Other financial institutions have also been fined sums totaling in the billions, and numerous corporate brands have been muddied. However, all of that "justice" has not yet restored the faith of the public in the markets, nor will it help the hundreds of thousands of individual investors who have lost their shirts because of these shenanigans. In a 2002 *Business Week* poll of its readers, 93 percent said they had "only some" or "hardly any" trust in the executives who run big companies, and 95 percent felt that way about big auditing companies.[39] More recently, a 2010 survey indicated that 70 percent of the public believes that businesses and financial companies will go back to "business as usual" after the 2008–09 recession.[40] In the same survey, only 29 percent of respondents in the United States thought that they could trust banks "to do the right thing." That's down from 68 percent in 2007.[41] In a 2012 survey, Wall Street and Congress were in a dead heat as the least trusted institutions in the U.S., and public confidence in them could be measured in single digits.[42] It is a sad commentary.

In Chapter 4, we defined a conflict of interest as occurring when someone could think that your judgment might be clouded because of a relationship you have. The definition is the same for organizations: if an organization's customers or other stakeholder group think that an organization's judgment is biased because of a relationship it has with another company or firm, a conflict could exist. Corporate or organizational conflicts are just as risky as those that exist between individuals, and they should be avoided at all costs.

Product Safety

Obviously, a major ethical obligation of any organization is to produce a quality product or service. Just as obviously, nothing will put a company out of business faster than offering a product that is dangerous, poorly produced, or of inferior quality. Competition in the marketplace generally helps ensure that goods and services will be of a quality that is acceptable to consumers. However, sometimes a company becomes the victim of external sabotage (like Johnson & Johnson), and sometimes a company makes a foolhardy decision, and the result is a product that is not safe. Let's look at these classic cases.

COMPANY: JOHNSON & JOHNSON

INDUSTRY: PHARMACEUTICALS

SITUATION

In September 1982, seven people in the Chicago area were killed when they ingested Tylenol, a painkiller produced by McNeil Labs, a division of Johnson & Johnson. The Tylenol in question was found to have been laced with cyanide, and it was not known for several weeks whether the contamination was the result of internal or external sabotage. A thorough investigation later proved that the poisonings were the result of external sabotage, and the culprit has never been found.

HOW THE COMPANY HANDLED IT

First, the company pulled all Tylenol from the shelves in the Chicago area. That was quickly followed by a nationwide recall of all Tylenol—31 million bottles with a retail value of over $100 million. Johnson & Johnson sent Mailgram messages explaining the situation and the recall to over 500,000 doctors, hospitals, and distributors of Tylenol. It also established a toll-free crisis phone line so that consumers could ask questions about the product. In addition, its CEO, James Burke, and other executives were accessible to the press and were interviewed by a variety of media.

Before the poisoning, Tylenol had captured over a third of the painkiller market, so Johnson & Johnson decided to rebuild the brand and its franchise. That wasn't going to be easy, since consumer fear ran high immediately after the poisoning. In one survey conducted a month after the incident, 87 percent of the respondents understood that Johnson & Johnson was not to blame for the Tylenol deaths, yet 61 percent declared they would be unlikely to buy Tylenol in the future. So even though most consumers knew the poisonings were not the fault of Johnson & Johnson, most of them wouldn't buy the product again. Johnson & Johnson tackled this problem head-on by offering coupons to entice consumers back to Tylenol and, ultimately, by redesigning Tylenol's packaging to be tamper-resistant.

RESULTS

Johnson & Johnson's reaction to the Tylenol poisoning has been hailed as the benchmark for how organizations should react to a crisis. As we've mentioned in other chapters, the firm's reaction to the Tylenol crisis proved that its famous Credo, in which it outlines its responsibilities to its consumers, employees, community, and stockholders, wasn't hollow. It was that concern for the customer—its primary stakeholder—that drove its response to the crisis. By being accessible to the press, which is yet another important stakeholder in a crisis, Johnson & Johnson's executives displayed concern for the consumer by refusing to dodge responsibility or blame any other party for their difficulties.

The results of the crisis were far reaching. The tamper-resistant packaging pioneered by Johnson & Johnson after the crisis has become commonplace in a wide variety of products, from food to pharmaceuticals. Two decades after the crisis, Johnson & Johnson's reputation as a quality producer of pharmaceuticals and as a company that cares about its customers is still strong. Its former CEO, James Burke, is renowned for his concern about ethical issues and became a sought-after speaker on a wide variety of topics related to ethics. Also, by the mid-1980s, Tylenol had regained almost all of its market share.

COMMENTS

The background of former Johnson & Johnson CEO James Burke was probably critical to the company's behavior during the Tylenol crisis. Burke was a marketing man who knew and understood the importance of public perception and the value of timely, accurate communication. Not many executives are comfortable with open communication, and their natural reticence can be enormously harmful to their organizations when a crisis strikes.[43] Burke was open with the public, but he was also extremely open with the press and created a relationship of trust with them. It came in handy when, several weeks into the investigation, a small amount of cyanide was found in a company plant. It was also learned that it could in no way have been involved in the Tylenol contamination. The press was told and asked not to reveal the information, and they didn't! We know about this only because the story was relayed by Lawrence Foster, then head of company communications, in a talk with our students. Burke also took the long-term view, believing that a recall would be costly in the short term but would help rebuild brand loyalty and trust in the long term.

UPDATE

While Johnson & Johnson has long been admired for its handling of the Tylenol crisis, in recent years it has stumbled. For example, J&J's LifeScan division pleaded guilty to criminal charges in 2000 and paid $60 million in fines for selling defective glucose-monitoring devices to diabetics and for later submitting false information about the problem to federal regulators. Lawyers who filed the class-action suit against LifeScan estimated that at least three diabetics had died because of the faulty readings they obtained from Life-Scan's SureStep monitoring device. LifeScan, in court documents, admitted that it had not adequately described the product's defects to the Food and Drug Administration (FDA), failed to disclose the problem to patients, and then failed to notify the FDA once problems began to occur. It's difficult to reconcile this image of Johnson & Johnson with the Tylenol one. The chairman of Johnson & Johnson, Ralph S. Larsen, wrote in a statement, "Mistakes and misjudgments were made. We fully acknowledge those errors and sincerely apologize for them. We are committed to learning from this experience."[44] More recently, the company has experienced a series of problems with the manufacture of its over-the-counter products. In 2008 and 2009, a recall of Tylenol products was prompted by consumer complaints of nausea. In 2010, metal and wood particles where found in chewable Rolaids. In 2011, J&J recalled 47 million units of cold medicine because of safety issues concerning the cleaning of production equipment. This "drip, drip, drip" of bad news and multiple recalls, while not posing serious illness or death among consumers, has nonetheless eroded trust in the iconic brand.[45] In Barron's annual "most respected companies" survey of money managers, J&J fell from second place in 2010 to number 25 in 2011.[46]

COMPANY: TOYOTA

INDUSTRY: AUTOMOBILES AND TRUCKS

SITUATION

When Toyota first entered the U.S. market in 1957, the automotive landscape was dominated by the Big Three American automakers—Chrysler, Ford, and General Motors. In 1961, the Big Three sold 85 percent of the cars purchased in the United States, and the remaining 15 percent were sold by a number of smaller foreign (mostly European) companies such as Volkswagen, BMW, and Mercedes Benz.[47] Toyota, one of Japan's leading auto companies, didn't gain a significant U.S. market share until the price of oil became an issue for Americans in the 1970s. Toyota made small, fuel-efficient cars, and Americans began to turn from large Detroit gas guzzlers to cars that got higher gas mileage. Then, for several years in the late 1970s to mid-1980s, the Big Three suffered severe quality issues. Consumers were frustrated and turned even more attention to those fuel-efficient Toyota models with a reputation for high quality. This shift revolutionized the nation's car buying; by 2008, Toyota had become the largest automaker in the United States.[48] However, a problem loomed on the horizon. Beginning in 2002, consumer complaints began pouring in to Toyota and to the National Highway Traffic Safety Administration (NHTSA), the U.S. regulatory body overseeing auto safety. More than 2,000 consumers reported that the accelerators in their Toyotas were sticking. Suddenly and without warning, the cars would accelerate, and drivers found it almost impossible to stop their cars.[49]

HOW THE COMPANY HANDLED IT

Although the complaints began in 2002, the company was slow to respond. Toyota was so confident of its product quality that the firm repeatedly underestimated the severity of the problem and reacted by either discounting early problems altogether or announcing diagnoses and solutions that proved to be insufficient. When the company did start to recognize the problem, its engineers blamed floor mats. They believed that floor mats were bunching up and creating a wedge under the accelerator, thus causing the car to speed up inadvertently. In the fall of 2009, Toyota sent an advisory to millions of Toyota owners to remove the floor mats on the driver's side and stated that, "there is no evidence to support" any other cause of the sudden acceleration. The company added that the NHTSA agreed with this conclusion. The NHTSA, in fact, did not agree and responded with a sharp rebuke to Toyota. The event that truly altered the debate was a crash of a Toyota Lexus on a California highway in August 2009. An off-duty California highway patrol officer (who should know how to stop a speeding car) called 911 in a total panic. His Lexus was hurtling down the highway with its accelerator stuck and with no brakes. The 911 system recorded the call and the subsequent crash, which killed the driver and three passengers. Another crash—this one involving a Toyota Avalon outside of Dallas, Texas—again resulted in four deaths. After that accident, investigators found the floor mats in the trunk of the car.[50] In January 2010, Toyota ordered a massive recall of more than 7.7 million vehicles.[51] The company also suspended sales of eight of its most popular models (including the Camry, the best-selling passenger car in the United States for the last 10 out of 11 years.) and even stopped making those models until the problem was solved. It's important to note that Toyota halted production because the NHSTA ordered it to stop.[52]

RESULTS

According to some analysts, the accelerator problem is the result of Toyota trying to grow too fast—so fast that its quality slipped, which is a particularly thorny problem for the company.[53] Toyota has made huge gains globally based on its quality pledge. The entire Toyota brand is tied to quality; for example, its corporate slogan is "The Relentless Pursuit of Perfection," and its manufacturing methods have long been the envy of other automakers.[54] As this book goes to press, the Toyota story is still evolving. In 2010, Toyota settled the case of the crash involving the off-duty California highway patrol officer for $10 million, and more cases are being settled.[55] In late 2012, the company was fined a record $17.4 million for failing to quickly report the acceleration problems to regulators in the U.S. and for delaying a recall.[56] The company also reached a $1 billion settlement in a class action lawsuit brought by Toyota car owners who claimed the value of their automobiles decreased after the millions of recalls for sudden acceleration.[57] Toyota's new CEO in the U.S., Jim Lentz, has focused on regaining market share by emphasizing manufacturing basics – always Toyota's core strength – and in 2012, the company took its title as the world's top-selling automaker back from General Motors.[58]

COMMENTS

At the time, a number of media stories called this "Toyota's Tylenol Moment," comparing the crisis directly to the famous Johnson & Johnson crisis described earlier in this chapter.[59] A number of analysts pointed to Toyota's cost cutting over the last few years as the likely culprit behind the crisis, and some lawsuits claimed that this issue was larger than a faulty accelerator and involved the electronics of the car, which would have been a much bigger issue.[60] It appears even now that the company has not completely identified the problem or an adequate solution. One dealer called the current accelerator fix "a Rube Goldberg solution that is hardly representative of the kind of work usually done by Japanese engineers."[61] Erich Merkle, president of Autoconomy.com (an industry analysis company), predicted that Toyota would be hard hit by this crisis because so much of its sales strength was rooted in an untarnished reputation for quality and reliability. He speculated, "They'll get through this, but I don't think it's anything they'll recover from quickly."[62] Frankly, Toyota's decades-long reputation for quality has served as a powerful counterweight to the negative publicity generated at the time over the sudden acceleration issue. This is one more example of how a good reputation and a trusted company brand can help an organization survive scandal. Toyota's "fix" for the problem may not have been perfect or complete, but if sales are an indication, consumers appear to have regained trust in the company to do the right thing.

As we saw in Chapters 2 and 3, one of the most common faults in ethical decision making is to ignore the long-term consequences of a decision. Although most organizations try hard to produce a product or service of high quality (to stay in business, if for no other reason), many don't take the time to identify all stakeholders and think long term about the consequences of their decisions. In issues that involve product safety and possible harm to consumers, thinking long term is critical. Is this product going to harm someone? How serious is the potential harm? Even if it might harm only one person, is there a way that can be avoided? Is there a way we can warn against possible harm? What can we do to ensure this product's safety? Other cognitive barriers to good ethical decision making may also have affected the thinking of Toyota's managers. For example, consider the possible effects of confirmation bias, the consideration of too few consequences, or an illusion of superiority,

How quickly do you think companies need to initiate a recall? If the product is sabotaged by angry insiders or outsiders, or if problems with this product or service are discovered at a later date, how can a company protect the public, consumers, and itself? Does the company have a crisis management plan? How closely do you think the companies involved in the classic cases adhered to the due care theory described earlier?

Advertising

The subject of ethics in advertising is a murky one, simply because there are varying opinions of exactly what *truth* is, and furthermore, what *responsible* is. Does a certain moisturizer really make skin look younger, or is it the 20-year-old model who has a young, dewy complexion? How would that moisturizer work for a 50-year-old? Do automakers and beer makers really need young women in skimpy bathing suits to sell their products? Do companies have a responsibility to respect all consumers? Are certain segments of the population fair game when it comes to the art of selling? Should we protect children from sugary cereal ads or teenagers from ads for expensive athletic shoes? How truthful or responsible does advertising have to be to qualify as ethical? Let's take a look at a few cases that point out some ethical issues in the marketing of pharmaceuticals to consumers.

INDUSTRY: PHARMACEUTICALS

SITUATION 1

Novartis, the large Swiss drug company, paid actress Lauren Bacall to mention one of its products, Visudyne, during an interview with Matt Lauer on NBC's *Today* show. Visudyne is a drug used to treat macular degeneration, an eye condition that strikes many people beginning in middle age. Bacall described how macular degeneration had caused a friend to go blind, urged viewers to get tested for the condition, and then plugged Visudyne.[63] What's the problem? Remember, this was not a commercial but an interview. The viewing public had no idea that Bacall was a paid Novartis spokesperson. Bacall is not alone, nor is Novartis. Actors Kathleen Turner and Rob Lowe have also pitched drugs, and other drugs have been mentioned by name on shows such as *Law and Order, The West Wing, ER*, and on the other morning shows such as *Good Morning America* by drug firms such as Amgen, Schering Plough, and Pfizer. Is marketing drugs the same as marketing breakfast cereal or deodorant? Should there be a higher standard for healthcare products in general? Should television viewers be informed when a celebrity or a sitcom is being paid by a drug company to talk about or display its products?

SITUATION 2

A few years ago, investigators for the U.S. government's General Accounting Office (GAO) claimed that several drug companies had repeatedly made misleading claims about prescription drugs in their advertising on TV and in print, even after being cited for violations. The reason is not surprising: advertising results in significant increases in the use of prescription drugs and in higher drug spending. The GAO study estimates that 8.5 million Americans each year ask their doctors for specific drugs that they have seen advertised, and their doctors prescribe the desired drugs.[64] The numbers continue to increase. In 2012, a study in the British Medical Journal described how pharmaceutical companies spend 19 times more on self-promotion and advertising than they do on research and development. In other words, for every dollar they spend on R&D, they spend $19 on advertising.[65] The cost and use of prescription drugs is one of the engines that has driven the astronomical increases in healthcare costs in recent years. Why have pharmaceutical companies spent so much money marketing to patients as well as to physicians? What are the advantages of direct marketing to consumers? What are the disadvantages? Do pharmaceutical companies have any ethical obligation to create a better balance between advertising and research and development?

SITUATION 3

In 2002, the drugstore chain Walgreens and the pharmaceutical company Eli Lilly were sued after a Florida consumer received an unsolicited free sample of the antidepressant drug Prozac Weekly in the mail. The recipient had kept her depression secret for many years—from her family, friends, and employers —fearing that she would suffer repercussions if her mental condition was known. Imagine her surprise when she received Prozac Weekly in the mail, along with a letter from Walgreens and her doctors. The sample itself was supplied free by the manufacturer, Eli Lilly. She filed a class action suit alleging invasion of privacy, unfair trade practices, and commercial exploitation of confidential medical information by all parties.[66] Is it acceptable for drug makers to market products directly to drugstore customers, using past patient records as indicators of the drugs they might need? Are patients helped by this practice? Are they harmed? What about their rights to privacy? What are the dangers of drug companies being closely aligned with drugstore chains?

SITUATION 4

Beginning in 2002, prescription Prilosec (a drug approved to combat acid reflux disease) lost patent protection and was marketed over the counter as Prilosec OTC to consumers. This was great news to consumers because a monthly supply of Prilosec OTC cost only 7 cents per pill versus several dollars a pill for similar prescription medications. Imagine consumers' surprise, however, when they couldn't find Prilosec OTC on their pharmacy shelves for more than a year in 2004. Procter & Gamble (the maker of Prilosec OTC) and its partner, the huge drug company AstraZeneca, claimed that they underestimated demand for the drug and were working hard to ramp up production. The shortage was so acute that an executive for a large drug distributor in the Northeast contacted Procter & Gamble every day to ask for more Prilosec OTC, but rarely received any. The dearth of Prilosec OTC was a good thing for AstraZeneca, however, because the shortage vastly increased sales of Nexium, its prescription medication for acid reflux. While AstraZeneca and Procter & Gamble maintained that they did not manufacture the shortage, Wall Street analysts, academic researchers, and consumer advocates all argued that the companies could meet demand for the cheaper over-the-counter medication if they wanted to.[67] Do companies have an obligation to keep supplies of less-expensive medications available to consumers? Do you think it is reasonable to imagine that huge companies would create a shortage of a particular product in an effort to steer consumers toward a more costly alternative?

SITUATION 5

The off-label marketing of drugs is an area where a number of pharmaceutical companies have run afoul of the regulators and have been fined hundreds of millions and, in at least one case, billions of dollars. British drugmaker GlaxoSmithKline was fined $3 billion for aggressively promoting its family of antidepressant medications (such as Avandia, Wellbutrin, and Paxil) to treat conditions other than depression or to consumers for whom the drugs had not been tested (such as children). The problem with this seemingly widespread practice of off-labeling is that drugs are approved for sale only after they have been tested for particular conditions or with a particular segment of the population. Using drugs for something for which they have not been tested can be dangerous and even life-threatening. For example, Glaxo salespeople pushed the use of Paxil among children, although it had been approved only for adult use. To encourage doctors to prescribe it for children, Glaxo paid doctors for trips to Bermuda and Jamaica, and paid for spa treatments and hunting excursions—practices that most feel are highly unethical. After the widespread, off-label use of Paxil among adolescents to treat depression, the drug was found to increase the likelihood of suicidal thoughts and actual suicide among young people. A warning was later added to the label.[68]

In another recent case, Amgen, the giant biotech company, paid $762 million in criminal and civil penalties for off-label use of the anemia drug, Aranesp. Not only did Amgen continue to market the drug for unapproved uses after the FDA explicitly forbade it, a subsequent study by Amgen found that off-label use of the drug increased the risk of death among patients using it.[69] Another even more egregious case of off-label marketing is described at the end of Chapter 5. In that case, medical device company Synthes marketed Norvin for unapproved conditions and people died as a result.[70] Why do drug makers think they can flout the regulations? How do doctors rationalize being wined and dined by drug company representatives? Describe the conflicts of interest in these situations.

HOW THE COMPANIES HANDLED IT

The pharmaceutical companies argue persuasively that their marketing tactics do nothing but help educate the consumer. No doubt many consumers now are much more aware of prescription medications than they were before the advertising of such medications became common. But we also have to wonder how the cost of these drugs have driven up the cost of healthcare as a whole and how the relationships among doctors, patients, and the pharmaceutical companies have changed as a result of the pharmaceutical industry's advertising and marketing tactics.

RESULTS

If you look at the lawsuits that have been filed against drug companies over the last 20 years, many deal with advertising and marketing issues. It's clear that the system for advertising drugs and bringing them to market poses huge ethical issues for the drug companies, many of which have been admired for their ethical reputations. Lawsuits centering on the marketing tactics of the drug companies continue to pile up, and they have tarnished some of the most sterling corporate reputations in the world. How big is the problem? Between 2009 and 2012, fines against six drugmakers (Eli Lilly, Pfizer, Merck, GlaxoSmithKline, Abbott, and Astra Zeneca) in six different cases of inappropriate or illegal marketing of prescription drugs totaled almost $10 billion.[71] The Op-Ed page of the *Wall Street Journal*—not exactly a bastion of company-bashing—featured an article a few years ago profiling the pharmaceutical industry and entitled, "The Companies Everyone Loves to Hate." The writer described how a movie (*The Constant Gardener*) portrayed the drug industry as rigging drug trials and as being no better than the illegal arms trade. The writer also described how in a recent poll, only the oil and gas industry ranked lower than the pharmaceutical companies. According to the poll, the percentage of adults who say they can trust what drug companies say in advertising dropped by almost half in the last seven years.[72] It is also interesting to note that this drop of consumer confidence in the pharmaceutical industry corresponds exactly with the deregulation that allowed the industry to advertise directly to consumers in 1997. It seems as if direct advertising has harmed the companies' reputations. Of course, none of this is good news for the industry.

However, some drug companies are beginning to rethink how they advertise to consumers. For example, Johnson & Johnson began a new advertising approach in 2005 that devoted as much space to describing drug risks as drug benefits. They also challenged their competitors to follow its lead in being more forthright and direct about the risks of prescription drugs.[73] Pfizer, in its 2004 annual report to shareholders, included a 36-page booklet, "Ten Questions: An Open Dialogue," that answered consumer questions head-on. Here are some of the questions Pfizer tackled: "Why does a little pill cost me so much?" "If Pfizer medicines are cheaper overseas, why not have them shipped in from outside the U.S.? And just why are they cheaper overseas?" And "I can't write my own prescriptions. Why spend any money advertising to me?"[74] These recent moves by Pfizer and Johnson & Johnson are important signals that the pharmaceutical may be indeed pursuing a new marketing direction. In addition, the pharmaceutical industry group Pharmaceutical Research and Manufacturers of America (PhRMA, discussed in Chapter 9) has established guidelines that if followed should eliminate many of the industry's questionable practices in the future. Companies are joining forces because they recognize that bad press about practices in the industry can harm all of them.

Yet, despite all the attempts to clean up the practice of off-label marketing, drug companies keep doing it because the fines are tiny compared to the potential profits from a successful drug. For example, Eliot Spitzer, former attorney general of New York, sued Glaxo over Paxil in 2004, which didn't get the company to stop the practice. After Glaxo's $3 billion fine in 2012, Spitzer said, "What we're learning is that money doesn't deter corporate malfeasance. The only thing that will work in my view is CEOs and officials being forced to resign and individual culpability being enforced."[75] Executives going to jail might be the most powerful tactic for persuading these companies to obey the regulations.

In advertising, there's a thin line between enthusiasm for a product and high-pressure sales tactics, between optimism and truth, and between focusing on a target market and perhaps tempting that market into unfortunate activities. A classic example of a company tempting consumers into unhealthy activities is, of course, the tobacco industry. Although the hazards of smoking have been well documented for many decades, tobacco companies spent most of that time denying the health risks of smoking and used "benign" advertising devices, such as Joe Camel, to market their very dangerous products. Another example is gambling casinos, where consumers are urged to have a good time playing roulette, blackjack, or slot machines. Are there ethical obligations for casinos, which know that they may be tempting compulsive gamblers into a binge? Who are the stakeholders for the tobacco industry and the casino industry? And what are the companies' ethical responsibilities? Does the fact that tobacco is physically addictive and the knowledge that most people begin smoking as children change our expectations of the tobacco industry and make our assessment of its obligations different?

Another case involves various brands of bottled water, which most consumers believe come from freshwater springs in Maine, Minnesota, or some other location with a reputation for a clean environment. In fact, despite the picture of the mountain on the label, some bottlers package filtered water from the municipal water supplies of several American cities. Is it up to consumers to read labels closely, or are companies obligated to represent their products honestly on all labels and in advertisements?

Can you think of any products for which outrageous claims have been made? Is it fair to appeal to the emotions of a particular market segment? Why not? Can you think of particular advertising devices or symbols that are used to appeal to a specific group of consumers? How far is "too far" in advertising?

ETHICS AND EMPLOYEES

Certainly, one of the key stakeholder groups in any corporate situation should be the employees of the organizations involved in the case. Organizations have myriad ethical obligations to their employees. Some of these could include the right to privacy, the right not to be fired without just cause, the right to a safe workplace, the right to due process and fair treatment, the right to freedom of speech (e.g., whistleblowing), and the right to work in an environment that is free of bias.[76] We've addressed a number of these rights in other chapters. In this section, we focus on two specific rights: a safe workplace and the right to keep a job unless just cause can be found for a firing.

Employee Safety

The most basic of employee rights is the right to work without being maimed or even killed on the job. In 1970, the Occupational Safety and Health Administration (OSHA) was created in an attempt to protect workers from hazards in the workplace. OSHA's mission is not only to protect workers against possible harm but also to ensure that employees are informed of the hazards of their particular industry and job. Let's look at a classic employee safety case.

COMPANY: JOHNS MANVILLE[77]
INDUSTRY: ASBESTOS

SITUATION

For decades, asbestos was the favored insulator in myriad construction products. Some estimate that over 3,000 products contained one or more asbestos components. Millions of homes, schools, workplaces and other buildings contained asbestos insulation; thousands of ship workers in World War II installed asbestos in battleships and other watercraft; and thousands of auto mechanics had fixed innumerable automobile brakes lined with asbestos. The danger of inhaling even minute amounts of asbestos was not publicly known until the 1970s, mainly because the incubation period for many of the asbestos-related lung diseases and cancers is anywhere from 10 to 40 years. However, by the mid-1970s tens of thousands of people who worked with asbestos were beginning to suffer from the fatal diseases we now know are characteristic of asbestos exposure.

HOW THE COMPANY HANDLED IT

Johns Manville was the largest manufacturer of products containing asbestos in the US for much of the twentieth century. According to company documents, the management tier of Johns Manville became aware of the adverse health effects of asbestos exposure as early as the mid-1930s. (In fact, Prudential Insurance stopped insuring asbestos workers' lives in 1928.) Although some executives were disturbed by the connection between their products and workers' illnesses, the sentiments of the stonewallers prevailed. Warning labels were not placed on asbestos packaging until 1964. In addition, company doctors lied to asbestos workers at Manville facilities and told them they had no health problems. Johns Manville executives hid scientific data; lied to the public, the government, and their employees; and kept quiet about the danger to which tens of thousands of workers were being exposed. The only stakeholder groups considered by Johns Manville during this period seem to have been the senior executives and the shareholders. The company appeared to totally ignore the obligations it had to other stakeholder groups.

RESULTS

By 1982, more than 17,000 lawsuits had been filed against Johns Manville. That was the tip of the iceberg. Many more thousands are expected to be filed as more workers develop fatal diseases that were the result of exposure during World War II. Many of these deaths are lingering ones in which the quality of life diminishes greatly over many years. As a result of the massive litigation, Johns Manville established a fund containing hundreds of millions of dollars to settle claims. The company filed for Chapter 11 bankruptcy protection in

1982, has been reorganized, and has been renamed the Manville Corporation. The new corporation has a strong commitment to funding the costs of the claims filed against its former self, and Manville executives have voiced what appears to be a real commitment to ethics within the corporation in an effort to prevent what happened from happening again.[78]

COMMENTS

One of the real mysteries surrounding this case is how so many senior executives over so many years could manage to live with themselves while keeping the awful secret of asbestos-related illness. It's one thing to hide something for a few years. But to keep this devastating secret for more than 40 years, throughout many changes in management, is a staggering notion to contemplate. Bill Sells, a manager with Johns Manville and the Manville Corporation for more than 30 years, wrote a *Harvard Business Review* article in which he analyzed what happened.[79] He contends that management was in denial. "Manville managers at every level were unwilling or unable to believe in the long-term consequences of these known hazards . . . Had the company responded to the dangers of asbestosis and lung cancer with extensive medical research, assiduous communication, insistent warnings, and a rigorous dust-reduction program, it could have saved lives and would probably have saved the stockholders, the industry, and, for that matter, the product . . . But Manville and the rest of the asbestos industry did almost nothing of significance—some medical studies but no follow-through, safety bulletins and dust-abatement policies but no enforcement, acknowledgment of hazards but no direct warnings to downstream customers—and their collective inaction was ruinous."[80]

According to Sells, the denial was fed by the conviction that asbestos was an essential product that the world couldn't get along without. Managers also believed they were doing enough because Manville's air quality standards were higher than the allowable limit set by the American Conference of Governmental Industrial Hygienists. But how did the company know whether the standard was really safe? They did little to find out. And what about the need for standards to protect those working with asbestos products, such as brake shoe installers? Nothing was being done to protect them. Another factor feeding the denial was the fact that asbestos workers who were also smokers were much more likely to get sick. Managers could blame the tobacco industry and avoid self-blame. In addition, short-term financial consequences took precedence in managerial decision making. And, finally, managers sent a "don't tell me what I don't want to hear" message. Top managers actually may have been unaware of some of the problems. As Sells points out, however, juries convict companies based on what they "should have known,"[81] not necessarily what they did know.

Let's look at another particularly egregious case that was profiled in the *New York Times* and on public television in January 2003.

COMPANY: MCWANE, INC.

INDUSTRY: MANUFACTURER OF WATER AND SEWER PIPES

SITUATION

McWane, Inc., in Birmingham, Alabama, is a privately held pipe manufacturer that has expanded aggressively over the last 30 years—mainly by purchasing antiquated plants and increasing profitability through what the company calls "disciplined management practices." Although the industry—melting metal and casting pipe—is inherently dangerous, McWane's drive for profits was so relentless that worker safety was sacrificed in the name of profits for the McWane family, who own the company and answer to no shareholders. For a number of years after 1995, McWane accumulated four times more safety violations than its six major competitors combined! From 1995 to 2002, nine McWane workers were killed on the job and more than 4,600 workers were injured (out of a total of 5,000), many in particularly gruesome, maiming accidents. At one acquisition— Tyler Pipe Company in Tyler, Texas—McWane reduced the workforce by almost two-thirds and demanded increased productivity from the remaining workforce. An inspector from OSHA, the federal regulator charged with guarding worker safety, described what was found at Tyler Pipe: "Many workers have scars or disfigurations which are noticeable from several feet away. Burns and amputations are frequent. Throughout the plant, in supervisors' offices and on bulletin boards, next to production charts and union memos, is posted in big orange letters: "REDUCE MAN HOURS PER TON."[82]

HOW THE COMPANY HANDLED IT

After the *New York Times* and *Frontline* (a production of PBS) investigated and produced a shocking series—in the newspaper and on PBS stations—that exposed the horrific conditions at McWane, the company responded with a written statement denying allegations about its safety record. "We do not put production concerns ahead of safety and environmental compliance," said company officials in a written statement to the *New York Times* and *Frontline*. That publicity prompted a series of federal investigations, which led to myriad indictments in several states (including Alabama, New York, New Jersey, Texas, and Utah). Among them was a 25-count indictment charging the company with illegal dumping and other environmental crimes; other counts charged the company with conspiring to violate workplace safety and environmental laws and obstructing government investigations by lying, intimidating workers, and altering accident sites.[83]

RESULTS

In March 2005, McWane pleaded guilty to environmental crimes committed at its Tyler Pipe operation in Texas and was fined $4.5 million. In June 2005, McWane was found guilty of 20 environmental crimes at one of its factories in Alabama. In August 2005, the company pleaded guilty to federal safety and environmental crimes in one of its Alabama plants. In that incident, McWane admitted that it willfully violated federal safety rules by failing to install a required safety guard on a conveyor belt and that a young worker was crushed to death. A McWane employee in Texas had been killed two months earlier by another unguarded conveyor belt.[84] The *New York Times* and PBS won the 2004 Goldsmith Prize for Investigative Reporting for their series of articles and programs on McWane.[85]

COMMENTS

Few investigations have yielded more gruesome or tragic stories than the *New York Times/PBS* series on McWane. If the company was concerned with safety and the environment before this series, its concern certainly was not evident. Would this company have been more responsible if there had been shareholders to report to? As this book went to press, the McWane website (www.mcwane.com) contained various statements regarding safety and the environment. "Do It Safely or Not At All" is the slogan displayed in a section devoted to health and safety. And in a section devoted to the environment, McWane states that its goal is "Protecting the Environment for Generations to Come." Press releases on the site describe various awards for safety that the company has received from organizations in various states. So it appears that McWane is cleaning up its act—literally and figuratively. That said, on the PBS Frontline website (www.pbs.org/wgbh/pages/frontline/shows/workplace/mcwane) for "The McWane Story," there is a section entitled "Two Companies, Two Visions." It describes the McWane vision of driving profitability regardless of safety or environmental concerns and contrasts it with the vision of another pipe company in Birmingham called American Cast Iron Pipe Company (ACIPCO). At the time of the series, McWane had employee turnover rates of almost 100 percent. ACIPCO had turnover rates of less than 1 percent, and its rate of injuries at the time was a fraction of McWane's. While McWane rationed ice cubes to its employees, ACIPCO provided individual air conditioners to its workers. At the time of the series, ACIPCO ranked sixth on *Fortune* magazine's "100 Best Companies to Work For." The interesting irony of the story is that when John Eagan founded ACIPCO in 1905, he promised to run the business based on the Golden Rule. Only one employee dissented—the president of ACIPCO, who would soon leave and cross town to start his own pipe business, J. R. McWane.[86]

Can you think of examples in other industries where employee safety and health are major issues? Are there health and safety issues in service (nonmanufacturing) industries? Are employers responsible for conditions such as carpal tunnel syndrome, in which the wrist is injured as a result of repeated movements such as entering data into a computer? What recourse do employers have in situations where the performance of a job, in itself, can cause injury? If a company discovers that its employees are at risk for injury, is it under any obligation to inform the public?

Employee Downsizings

Employee downsizings or layoffs can result from many business conditions, including economic depressions, the desire to consolidate operations and decrease labor costs, and increased competition and unmet corporate objectives, to list just a few. However justifiable the reason may be, the result always involves human misery. Organizations may not have an ethical obligation to keep labor forces at a specific number. They do, however, have an obligation to hire and fire responsibly.

One of the most contentious downsizing cases in recent years involved a major employer in the Northeast.

COMPANY: SCOTT PAPER COMPANY

INDUSTRY: CONSUMER PAPER PRODUCTS

SITUATION

In late 1993, Scott Paper had tired product lines, some extraneous business ventures, and a lagging revenue stream and stock price. Scott's board of directors wanted to breathe some life into the slumbering giant. In April 1994, Albert J. Dunlap, a self-proclaimed "Rambo in pinstripes," was named CEO of Scott Paper. Dunlap immediately created his very own crisis to get the company moving. It was as if he'd lobbed a fire bomb through the doors of corporate headquarters.

HOW THE COMPANY HANDLED IT

Dunlap began by quickly selling off $2 billion worth of nonessential businesses.[87] He also quickly terminated one-third of the total workforce of Scott—over 11,000 workers lost their jobs. But perhaps the most painful blow to the Philadelphia area was Dunlap's decision to move Scott's corporate headquarters out of the city where it had been founded 116 years earlier to Boca Raton, Florida, where Dunlap had a home. According to some sources, the move was prompted by Philadelphia's climate, which Dunlap didn't like.

RESULTS

Scott's stock price increased 146 percent in 14 months, and its profits doubled after one year of Dunlap's management. The company was sold in mid-1995 to Kimberly-Clark Corporation for $6.8 billion in stock.[88] Some stakeholders were delirious. Scott shareholders made out like bandits. Wall Street financial types did a jig. But no one was more gleeful than Dunlap, who pocketed $100 million in salary, stock profits, and other perks. Not bad for 15 months of his time.

COMMENTS

Many people thought of Dunlap as a hero, including Dunlap himself. Many others, however, considered him to be the worst kind of villain—"Chainsaw Al," as some of his detractors called him. Though downsizing and restructuring measures are painful, many people can understand why they might be necessary to turn around a company that can no longer compete. What infuriated everyone in the Philadelphia area, however, was Dunlap's moving Scott's corporate headquarters because he didn't like the weather in Philadelphia. Certainly, it is a capricious reason to move an organization that was an institution in the area for over a century. Scott was not just some company. Rather, it had been an exemplary corporate citizen, providing talent and financing for local cultural and civic organizations. In addition, Dunlap's manner was arrogant, and he showed little or no sympathy toward the long-term employees who had been axed and to the area he gutted.

UPDATE

After selling Scott Paper Company, Al Dunlap went on to become CEO of Sunbeam (maker of electric blankets and outdoor grills) in 1996. In typical Al Dunlap fashion, he quickly announced the closing or sale of two-thirds of the company's factories and the firing of half of its 12,000 employees. The stock rose and Wall Street applauded. In March of 1997, Sunbeam bought three companies: Coleman (camping equipment), First Alert (smoke alarms), and Signature Brands (Mr. Coffee). A year later, it became clear to Sunbeam's board that the acquisitions had not been well managed and that the company was in financial trouble. The board also discovered that the company was using highly aggressive sales tactics and accounting practices that inflated revenues and profits.[89] In June 1998, Chainsaw Al got the ax himself. In 2002, Dunlap settled charges with the SEC, paid a fine of $500,000, neither admitting nor denying that he presided over accounting practices that resulted in Sunbeam overstating its profits in 1997 and 1998. And his legal woes did not end there. The Justice Department began an investigation of Sunbeam for the period it was managed by Dunlap.[90] Even more interesting was the disclosure that, early in his career, Dunlap was fired twice—once when the company's board accused him of overseeing a huge accounting fraud. Dunlap erased these two firings from his official employment history, and news of them surfaced only recently. Another interesting tidbit: in one of those companies that fired him, his relationships with his colleagues were so fractured that the entire senior team below Dunlap threatened to resign as a group unless he was canned.[91]

Contrast what happened to Scott Paper with the philosophy of Lincoln Electric Company in Cleveland, Ohio.

COMPANY: LINCOLN ELECTRIC COMPANY
INDUSTRY: ELECTRICAL COMPONENTS

SITUATION

Lincoln Electric has had an unusual relationship with its employees since it was founded by John C. Lincoln in 1895.[92] The company has been on the cutting edge of worker-friendly efforts. In 1923, it was among the first firms to offer company-paid vacation; in 1925, it was among the first to offer employee stock ownership plans; the first employee suggestion program was implemented in 1929, and Lincoln employees received incentive bonuses beginning in 1934. Perhaps the most controversial of its programs, however, is its guaranteed employment plan: after three years of continuous employment with Lincoln Electric, workers are guaranteed their jobs. In the early 1980s, however, the company experienced tremendous hardship. As a result of inflation, higher energy costs, and a recession in the United States, Lincoln's sales plummeted 40 percent. Company managers didn't know if they would be able to keep their promise of guaranteed employment.

HOW THE COMPANY HANDLED IT

The company was severely tested. However, not one Lincoln employee was laid off for lack of work. The company's loyalty to its employees was returned in 1993, when Lincoln urged its employees to attain record levels of sales and production. Employees voluntarily postponed 614 weeks of vacation in order to meet customer demands. Even after the financial crisis in 2008 and 2009, Lincoln seemed to be able to spread the pain across all ranks in an effort to survive the horrible economic conditions. Although austerity measures were needed, Lincoln still did not lay off anyone, and hasn't since 1948. In fact, here are some impressive facts from author Frank Koller, who wrote a book about Lincoln called *Spark: How Old-Fashioned Values Drive a Twenty-First Century Corporation*:

- 2011 is the 78th straight year that Lincoln has made a profit.
- The total bonus pool distributed to employees in 2011 equaled 32 percent of pre-tax profit of $84 million.
- The average employee bonus was more than $30,000.
- The average total compensation of a Lincoln Electric employee was $79,000.[93]

RESULTS

Incentive management is a cornerstone of Lincoln's culture. Having developed one of the first pay-for-performance systems in the country, this company

> is frequently a subject of research by academics and other companies. Lincoln
> also has an elected employee advisory board for direct and open communica-
> tions between employees and senior managers. The board was established
> in 1914 and has met every two weeks ever since. So, loyalty at Lincoln is
> nothing new. Lincoln's website (www.lincolnelectric.com) clearly describes
> the company's commitment to integrity: "More than 100 years ago, the
> founders of Lincoln Electric adopted a policy of absolute integrity—doing
> the right thing rather than what was expedient, popular or in vogue at the time.
> Today, that solid ethical heritage remains the foundation of Lincoln Electric's
> corporate governance practices."

As we mentioned in Chapter 8, employees have the right to be treated fairly,
without bias, and on the basis of their ability to perform a specific job. If a layoff or
downsizing is necessary—if it involves one person or many—the layoff should be
done with respect, dignity, and compassion. In the two cases we just outlined, what do
you imagine are the key differences in philosophy? How could companies become
more like Lincoln Electric? What are the pitfalls of Lincoln's approach? What are the
pitfalls of Dunlap's? If you had to lay off employees, what factors would you consider
in structuring a plan that would be as fair as possible to all involved?

Suppose the country experiences a recession. Should companies begin to lay
off employees in order to maintain expected growth rates? To satisfy Wall Street's
profit and growth expectations? What other stakeholder groups are affected? Are
companies in business only to make a profit for shareholders? Are employee
stakeholder groups more expendable than customer stakeholders? How can a
company reconcile long-term obligations to all stakeholders with short-term
financial crises?

ETHICS AND SHAREHOLDERS

Organizations also have a clear ethical obligation to shareholders and other "owners."
This ethical obligation includes serving the interests of owners and trying to perform
well in the short term as well as the long term. It also means not engaging in activities
that could put the organization out of business and not making short-term decisions
that might jeopardize the company's health in the future. As Kotter and Heskett say in
their book, *Corporate Culture and Performance* (1992), "only when managers care
about the legitimate interests of stockholders do they strive to perform well economi-
cally over time, and in a competitive industry that is only possible when they take care
of their customers, and in a competitive labor market, that is only possible when they
take care of those who serve customers—employees."[94] Thus taking care of shareholders also means ultimately taking care of other key stakeholder groups. Let's
examine how the ethics of the investment banking giant Salomon Brothers affected its
shareholders.

COMPANY: SALOMON BROTHERS

INDUSTRY: INVESTMENT BANKING

SITUATION

In December 1990, the head of Salomon's government bond trading desk, Paul Mozer, decided to test the regulatory resolve of the U.S. Treasury. Annoyed by the federal limits on the percentage of Treasury bonds any one firm could bid for in Treasury auctions—the ceiling was 35 percent—Mozer devised a plan to evade the regulation. He submitted a bid for Salomon Brothers, and he submitted an unauthorized bid in the name of one of his customers. The two bids combined represented 46 percent of the auction—a clear violation of the rules. Mozer got his bonds and repeated this maneuver in February, April, and May 1991.

HOW THE COMPANY HANDLED IT

In April 1991, Mozer described the tactic to four Salomon executives: Chairman John Gutfreund, President Thomas W. Strauss, Vice Chairman John W. Meriwether, and General Counsel Donald M. Feuerstein. These executives told Mozer to stop his scheme but did not report Mozer's activities to the Securities and Exchange Commission at that time. (In May, Mozer rigged the bidding again.) In June, the SEC subpoenaed Salomon for its auction records. In August, Salomon finally alerted the SEC to Mozer's activities. Immediately following the disclosure to the SEC, Mozer was suspended from his job; shortly afterward, the board of directors asked the four Salomon executives to resign from the firm and fired Salomon's outside law firm. The board named one of its own members, Warren Buffett, as interim chairman.[95]

RESULTS

The publicity generated by the Salomon scandal was devastating to the firm and its shareholders. Its market value dropped by over one-third—$1.5 billion—in the week following the disclosure. Its debt was downgraded by various rating agencies, and major banks reevaluated Salomon's loan terms. Because of the firm's decreased liquidity, its ability to trade was dramatically reduced. In addition to the immediate financial debacle, teams of Salomon Brothers personnel left the firm. For a year after the crisis, the financial press was awash in reports of high-level Salomon employees joining other firms. The defections no doubt damaged the firm for many years. In addition, at a time when the profits of other investment banks were soaring by as much as 50 percent over previous years, Salomon's underwriting revenues were down 26 percent—a huge and humbling disparity. Their profits were off substantially, customers left, and they were barred from some types of transactions or were rendered ineffective because of their weakened financial position. It took years for the firm to recover.[96]

COMMENTS

In the investment banking industry, reputation is everything. It's the yardstick customers use to evaluate quality and a firm's ability to do business. Nothing is more devastating for a financial services firm than the loss of reputation. Salomon is lucky it survived. It very well could have gone the way of E. F. Hutton and Drexel Burnham Lambert. E. F. Hutton was acquired by another financial firm after it could not survive pleading guilty to 2,000 felony counts of fraud in a check-kiting case. (Check kiting is a type of fraud that involves moving money in and out of accounts with insufficient funds to cover the withdrawals. This usually involves multiple accounts.) Drexel closed its doors after charges of wrongdoing in the high-yield market effectively crippled its ability to do business. In all cases, the firms put their own interests ahead of the interests of their primary stakeholders: their customers.

UPDATE

Salomon Brothers remained independent until 1998, when it was acquired by the Travelers Group, and eventually became part of Citigroup. For more than a decade it was known as Salomon Smith Barney, which was the investment banking arm of Citigroup. Former New York State Attorney General Eliot Spitzer investigated the company and its former star telecom analyst, Jack Grubman, who were named in approximately 62 class action lawsuits.[97] The plaintiffs accused Salomon and Grubman of issuing unreasonable research reports and of failing to disclose conflicts of interest with companies profiled in those research reports, including WorldCom, AT&T, Global Crossing, Winstar, and others.[98]

It turns out that this was an industry-wide practice. In late 2002, the Spitzer probe was resolved when Wall Street investment banks agreed to change their research practices to eliminate conflicts of interests like the ones exhibited by Grubman. Conflicts of interest were so rampant at the time that in a truly outrageous move, Sanford Weill (then CEO of Citigroup) asked Grubman to review his rating of AT&T in order to help win favor with Michael Armstrong, who at the time was CEO of AT&T and a board member of Citigroup. The point was to persuade Armstrong to side with Weill in a boardroom struggle. Weill later denied the charge. However, Weill, Citigroup, and other investment firms agreed to settle the conflict-of-interest suits and pay $1.44 billion in fines as well as to reform their practices. Citigroup paid $300 million of the fine, and the rest of it was divided among nine other banks, including Credit Suisse First Boston, Morgan Stanley, and Merrill Lynch.[99] Salomon Smith Barney also admitted to failing to manage conflicts of interest, publishing fraudulent and misleading research, ignoring internal warnings, and engaging in improper spinning and public offering stock distribution practices. In addition to the fines imposed, Salomon Smith Barney was ordered to report regularly on its compliance activities to Citigroup's board of directors; Citigroup was ordered to make a public statement of contrition for failing to address conflicts of interest, and it was ordered to prohibit the senior executives who function as investment bankers from communicating directly with the analysts who cover those companies. In addition, Grubman was fined $15 million and received a lifetime ban on functioning as a broker, dealer, investment advisor, or an employee of an investment company or municipal securities dealer.[100] The good news for Citigroup is that after an incredible spate of ethical lapses, high-profile investigations, horrendous publicity, almost $6 billion in fines, and truly mortifying behavior by a host of employees (including some at the very highest levels), the "take-no-prisoners" CEO Sandy Weill finally handed over the reins of the day-to-day management of the company to Charles Prince, former corporate counsel, in July 2003. (In March 2006, Prince became chairman and CEO of Citigroup.)[101] It appears, however, that the seeds of unethical behavior had been sown and even though Prince, a lawyer, headed the firm from 2006 to 2008, he could do little to change the culture of the giant company. The risk-taking culture that had been encouraged by Weill continued unabated. After Prince left, the new CEO, Vikram Pandit, struggled to right the huge ship[102] by shrinking Citigroup into a global bank modeled after the original Citicorp. He told the Congressional Oversight Panel in early 2010 that he was trying to "break it up" in order to return the organization to profitability, and Salomon Smith Barney was among the many businesses sold.[103] It is now Morgan Stanley Smith Barney. Citigroup, along with Bank of America, received more government assistance during the 2008 financial crisis than any other institution—$45 billion.[104]

While the money has been paid back, Citigroup remains fragile. Pandit was forced out by the board in late 2012 and Michael Corbat was named CEO—the first time in almost ten years that the bank will be led by a banker (not a lawyer like Prince or a hedge fund executive like Pandit).[105]

COMPANY: AIG (AMERICAN INTERNATIONAL GROUP)

INDUSTRY: INSURANCE AND FINANCIAL SERVICES

SITUATION

For many years, AIG was the picture of financial stability. Before the financial crisis of 2008–09, AIG held 81 million life insurance policies worth almost $2 trillion. It insured approximately 180,000 businesses around the world, which employed around 106 million people. It owned fleets of jet planes that it leased to airlines and other businesses, provided insurance to U.S. cities and municipalities and pension funds, and guaranteed investment contracts and products that protected 401(k) participants. Before the crisis, AIG was the largest health and life insurer in the U.S. and the second-largest property and casualty insurer. However, it was a classic "too-big-to-fail" company because its operations touched so many individuals, companies, and governments worldwide.[106] Letting AIG fail would be like pulling the rug out from under the global economy; its effects would reverberate throughout the world. AIG unwittingly began a downward spiral by getting deeply into the business of selling credit default swaps (CDSs) and collaterized debt obligations (CDOs). Nearly all of the company's losses stem from one very small business unit—a 400-employee business with offices in London and Greenwich (Connecticut) called AIG Financial Products (AIGFP). The current chairman of the Federal Reserve, Ben Bernanke, said that AIGFP was in essence a hedge fund, completely unregulated, that was attached to a very large and stable insurance company. AIGFP exploited a huge gap in the regulatory system and built up a $2.7 trillion portfolio of derivatives.[107] (Famed investor Warren Buffett once called derivatives "weapons of mass destruction." Long before the crisis, Buffett claimed that derivatives posed a "mega-catastrophic risk" for the economy and stated that the products were designed by "madmen.")[108] AIG got into trouble when financial companies bought increasingly risky investments (subprime mortgages) and went to AIG to insure that risk. When those securities were downgraded in value during the financial crisis in 2008, the firms that purchased the insurance demanded payment from AIG on their policies. Suddenly AIG needed collateral that it didn't have. It faced bankruptcy—a catastrophe for the company and the economy.

HOW THE COMPANY HANDLED IT

Actually, the company didn't handle it—*it couldn't handle it*. The problem was so enormous that the U.S. government had to step in and bail out AIG, to the tune of $180 billion.[109] U.S. taxpayer money kept the company in business, although it is currently a shadow of its former self and the bleeding is by no means over. It may need more bailouts in the future.

RESULTS

To stay afloat, AIG has desperately tried to raise capital and cut expenses. Layoffs occurred in some of its businesses, and other businesses were sold to raise capital. The financial mastermind of AIGFP, Joe Cassano, was paid $280 million in the eight-year run-up of his hedge fund. He is now retired and living in a London townhouse, trying to avoid the press who stalk him. A subsequent scandal that has dogged the company involves the AIGFP traders who had contractual bonus payments worth $165 million owed to them to clean up the mess they created. Their bonuses—in some cases paid to the very people who created the crisis for AIG—were the subject of endless press speculation and resulted in public fury over the unfairness of paying people millions to correct their mistakes.[110]

COMMENTS

At the time of the crisis, many experts questioned whether AIG would be able to survive. The company received $182 billion in U.S. government loans and commitments to prevent it from collapsing.[111] As this book goes to press, AIG has repaid every cent to the U.S. government and is working hard to recover its precrisis reputation. Its former CEO, Hank Greenberg, almost derailed AIG's recovery effort when he asked AIG's board to join him in suing the U.S. government for bailing out the company and supposedly harming shareholders. When the lawsuit became public, the media and the public went berserk with stories about the irony of a company essentially suing the taxpayers who saved it from catastrophe. The AIG board met and quickly decided not to join Greenberg in his suit. New AIG CEO Bob Benmosche said, "It is not acceptable socially for AIG to have taken this money and to think we can go back and sue the government."[112]

Shareholders—in particular, individual investors—have been abused in recent years as numerous ethical lapses have driven a collapse in the stock market. Several of the cases described earlier in "Ethics and Consumers" are also relevant here.

ETHICS AND THE COMMUNITY

As many people have discovered, companies don't exist in a vacuum. Companies are citizens in their communities, just as individuals are, and because of their size, companies can have an outsized impact on their communities. Therefore a major stakeholder in business must be the communities of which corporations and other organizations are a part. Perhaps the most obvious way a company can affect its community is through its approach to the environment.

The public's concern with the effect of business on the environment began in earnest with the publication of Rachel Carson's *Silent Spring* (1962).[113] In her book, Carson outlined the hazards of pesticides, and DDT in particular, to the environment. The resulting public outcry resulted in the Environmental Protection Act in 1969 and the creation of the Environmental Protection Agency (EPA) in 1970. The goal of both the act and the agency is to protect the environment—air, water, earth—from the activities of businesses and individuals. Of course, we all need to think long term about the health of the planet and its environs for ourselves, our children, and other generations to follow. Let's look at a classic environmental case.

COMPANY: EXXON

INDUSTRY: PETROLEUM

SITUATION

In 1989, the Exxon *Valdez*, an oil tanker bound for Long Beach, California from the Port of Valdez in Alaska, ran aground in Prince William Sound. The *Valdez* contained 52 million gallons of crude oil, 10 million gallons of which quickly began to leak into the pristine Alaskan waters. The captain of the tanker, Joseph Hazelwood, was later tested for alcohol consumption and showed an increased blood alcohol level. Although it was never proven that Hazelwood was drunk at the time of the accident, he did violate company regulations by not being on the bridge of the tanker when navigating in those waters.

In addition, Alyeska, the consortium of seven oil companies that originally established Alaska as an oil capital with the construction of the Trans Alaska pipeline, was charged with safeguarding Alaska from just such an accident and with providing immediate help should such a catastrophe occur.

HOW THE COMPANY HANDLED IT

Although Exxon immediately began efforts to clean up the oil spill—the largest spill ever at the time—critical equipment was either damaged and in the process of being repaired, or not on the scene. CEO Lawrence Rawls did place full-page apology ads in various newspapers one week after the accident, but he did not visit Alaska and was roundly criticized for that seeming insensitivity. In addition, Exxon appeared to blame everyone but itself for its problem. And Alyeska was not much help. Like Exxon, it was unprepared for a crisis of the magnitude of the Exxon *Valdez* spill. As a result, Exxon seemingly dropped the ball with this oil spill. It looked as if the firm denied responsibility.

RESULTS

Although over 800 miles of Alaskan beaches were initially covered with oil, 85 percent had been cleaned by 1990. Wildlife in the area was not so lucky—more than 30,000 birds and at least 2,000 sea otters died, and the fish population was contaminated. Exxon spent more than $2 billion on the cleanup and paid additional hundreds of millions to the city of Valdez and Alaskan fishermen. Captain Joseph Hazelwood was fired for not following the regulation about being on the bridge of the tanker.[114]

What really took a beating, however, was Exxon's image. Environmentalists publicly hammered the company, and some 40,000 consumers destroyed their Exxon credit cards in protest.

COMMENTS

The difference between the personalities of Exxon CEO Lawrence Rawls and Johnson & Johnson CEO James Burke could be why Exxon received such poor marks on its handling of the *Valdez* crisis. Rawls was an engineer and uncomfortable with the media. His reaction appeared slow and seemingly dispassionate, and the lemon he was handed remained a lemon. Burke, on the other hand, knew how to make lemonade.

The Exxon Valdez spill pales beside the 2010 BP oil spill in the Gulf of Mexico, when the explosion of the Deepwater Horizon rig killed 11 workers, injured many more, and spilled two hundred million gallons of oil into the Gulf. In early 2013, the company, which has already paid more than $24 billion in penalties and cleanup efforts, pleaded guilty to 14 criminal charges and paid $4 billion more in penalties. In addition, it faces significantly higher civil penalties for the explosion and significant fines for the pollution that resulted from the blowout. Plus, three BP employees have been charged with multiple crimes, including manslaughter and obstruction of justice. The magnitude of the environmental disaster for the Gulf and the financial bath for BP is unprecedented.[115] Interestingly, this accident served to point out how far Exxon has come since the Valdez incident. Exxon used the Valdez accident as a wake-up call to transform how it does business. As a result of a company-wide, comprehensive effort, it has not had a serious accident in the more than two decades since the Valdez. On the other hand, BP experienced a series of deadly and dangerous incidents leading up to the Deepwater Horizon disaster and apparently did not take the steps necessary to prevent accidents and ensure the safety of its workers and the public. In 2005, a BP refinery exploded in Texas City, Texas, killing 15 workers and injuring hundreds more. In 2006, a BP pipeline began leaking thousands of gallons of crude oil into the pristine Alaskan wilderness in Prudhoe Bay. Unlike Exxon, which learned from its mistakes, BP did not. The company talked a lot about safety, but its executives never made safety a priority and cut costs wherever possible, seemingly putting safety concerns dead last.[116] It appears now that the company has a renewed focus on safety. Time will tell.

UPDATE

In 2004, after years of civil litigation, the U.S. District Court of Alaska ordered Exxon to pay $4.5 billion in punitive damages to those affected by the 1989 oil spill.[117] In 2006, Representative Dave Reichert asked Congress to pressure Exxon to pay the $4.5 billion in punitive damages that it owed Alaskan citizens. After further legal wrangling and countless appeals, in 2008 the U.S. Supreme Court reduced Exxon's fine of $5 billion to $500 million.[118]

In addition to environmental concerns, another issue that affects all of us as a society is relatively new: Internet privacy. For example, many people around the world are concerned about Google's privacy policies and practices. With the advent of Google Street View, anyone around the world with access to a computer can check out where you live. But Google's Street View cars have been collecting a lot more than photographs of private homes. They have also been collecting snippets of emails, passwords, chat messages, photographs, and postings on social networks and websites. German regulators forced the company to admit that it engaged in such practices, but when the FCC tried to investigate Google, the company stonewalled and basically said "Trust us." The FCC fined them for obstructing the investigation.[119] In another case, Google agreed to pay $22.5 million to settle charges that it surreptitiously tricked Apple iPhone software into letting Google track users who had specifically blocked that kind of monitoring. It was a particularly brazen invasion of privacy, but once again, Google claimed it was inadvertent and did no harm.[120] Meanwhile, Facebook is facing a class action lawsuit by subscribers in 10 states who accuse the technology giant of secretly tracking users' Internet activity after they have logged off of Facebook. Like Google, Facebook has asked for the lawsuit to be dismissed because plaintiffs cannot prove how they were harmed.[121] The reality is that many people never think much about what they share online and how companies, marketers, hackers, etc., can access information about what they buy, write, think, share, and post, for example. Many people don't realize that much of what they think they are privately posting online or purchasing online is actually public. There is tremendous money to be made by capturing personal information about users and selling it to third parties—some of whom just want to target users for marketing purposes. But others may have far from benevolent purposes. It's an issue that is fraught with ethical concerns, and it is only going to get bigger as the world continues to embrace technology.

WHY ARE THESE ETHICAL ISSUES?

The situations described above are all ethical issues because they involve obligations to primary or key stakeholder groups. Consumers, shareholders, employees, and the community are probably the major constituencies of any organization that is not operating in a vacuum. What groups are more important to a company than the people who pay for their goods or services, the people who make or provide them, the people who buy them, and the place where the goods and services are made or performed? These ethical obligations all involve fairness, safety, and honesty to the four main stakeholders of most organizations.

COSTS

As we've seen in the classic cases described in this chapter, the costs of bungling an ethical obligation to any of the four primary stakeholder groups can be not only crippling, but fatal. Just as individuals who cross the line can short-circuit their careers or end up fired or prosecuted, organizations pay the same kind of price: Their ability to function can be severely limited, and they can even be forced out of business. At the very least, if a company's misdeeds are discovered, they will most certainly be excoriated by the press and the public. Their reputation can suffer long-term damage that may be difficult to repair. The organizational costs are horrific, but the personal tragedies are particularly sad because they were so preventable. Just think of the individuals who've received lengthy jail sentences and of how they and their families have suffered because of ethical misjudgments (or worse).

It's impossible to list here all of the regulatory bodies that watch over the rights of these four stakeholder groups. Certainly, as you enter a particular industry or company, you will need to learn what laws and which bodies govern compliance. In the United States, there are federal, state, and local government agencies that are charged with protecting the rights of stakeholder groups. Regulatory bodies such as the Securities and Exchange Commission, the Comptroller of the Currency, and the Federal Reserve

Board guard the rights of shareholders. The Food and Drug Administration, the Federal Trade Commission, and the Federal Communications Commission are federal watchdog agencies for consumer rights. Employee rights are protected by a wide range of agencies including the Equal Employment and Opportunity Commission, the Labor Board, and the Occupational Safety and Health Administration. The Environmental Protection Agency is the primary protector of the environment.

CONCLUSION

In this chapter we've described a few of the more memorable business ethics cases. No industry, and really no company, has been immune from ethical problems and unethical employees. Even Johnson & Johnson has taken its licks in recent years because of the LifeScan lawsuits as well as other alleged wrongdoing. The point of examining these cases is that truly smart managers should learn from the mistakes of others.

We hope it's obvious that all stakeholders are connected and that their interests frequently overlap. In a recent study, 52 percent of respondents believed that all stakeholders—investors, employees, customers, the government, and society at large—are equally important.[122] For example, the Enron and AIG debacles harmed not only consumers but also employees, shareholders, and the communities where those companies had facilities. It's also obvious that some senior executives need a hefty injection of morality. The lack of trust has become so acute that only 26 percent of respondents in a recent study believed that CEOs were credible.[123] A shocking reminder of that is contained in the book *What Went Wrong at Enron* (2002) by Peter Fusaro and Ross Miller. These authors claim that while at Harvard Business School, Jeff Skilling, later president of Enron, was asked how he would handle a situation where his company was producing a product that might harm or even kill the consumers who used it. He allegedly replied, "I'd keep making and selling the product. My job as a businessman is to be a profit center and to maximize return to the shareholders. It's the government's job to step in if a product is dangerous."[124]

It's also clear that at the turn of the twenty-first century, businesspeople are at a crossroads. We need to decide what kind of professionals we are going to be. Are we going to be honest and fair and deserving of the public's trust? Or are we going to push our own agendas and expect the government to make us behave à la Jeff Skilling, or bail us out like Citigroup and AIG or clean up after us like BP? A recent study identified the top three factors in corporate reputation with the public as being (1) transparent and honest practices, (2) a company I can trust, and (3) high-quality products and services.[125] If businesspeople are going to regain the public's trust, they will need to focus on integrity, openness, and quality. They also have to understand that this trust effort will take a very long time.

One company that understands the importance of trust and has taken bold steps to incorporate trust into its business model is salesforce.com, a leader in enterprise cloud computing. Several years ago, it was growing rapidly and experiencing growing pains as a result. Customers were experiencing service interruptions and salesforce.com was desperately trying to grow fast enough to provide seamless service. To monitor the outages and other system glitches, the company had an internal tracking system that showed where problems were and what caused them. When a company team advised Chairman and CEO Marc Benioff to post this system on the company website so customers could see what was happening in real time, he hesitated. No one else was being this transparent. Would customers or the press use this to sabotage the company?

It took a weekend for Benioff to agree with his team's idea to post the monitoring system on its website. It was an instant hit. Not only did the press do positive stories about the effort to be open with customers, other technology companies such as Amazon and Google noticed and started their own efforts to be more transparent. Benioff is now a complete convert to the transparency movement and urges business everywhere to incorporate openness and transparency into their business models because of the trust it engenders and the tremendous reputational benefits that follow as a result.[126]

The last decade has been painful to endure for businesspeople, and you've read about many of the most embarrassing episodes in this chapter—bad news always gets lots of publicity. The good news is that the vast majority of companies are committed to doing business in an honorable way, and most of them have long histories of doing just that. More and more companies are finding more and better ways to weave their values throughout their cultures, inspiring managers and employees alike to innovation, excellent service, and integrity.

SHORT CASES

CONFLICT OF INTEREST

Big Company is a large manufacturer of healthcare products, and it is under fire from the government to lower costs. Big Company has an excellent reputation and is widely acknowledged as one of the best-managed companies in the country. Despite the firm's reputation, however, Wall Street has reacted negatively to government efforts to reform the healthcare industry as a whole, and Big Company's stock price has lost 30 percent of its value in the last year. To counter the effect of possible government intervention, Big Company has just purchased Little Company, a discount healthcare supplier. Wall Street has greeted the acquisition with enthusiasm, and Big Company's stock price has rebounded by more than 10 percent since news of the acquisition was made public.

While this acquisition could give Big Company a foothold in a growing part of the healthcare industry, a real problem lies in the mission of Little Company. Little has made its reputation by providing objective healthcare advice to its customers. Now that it's owned by Big Company, Little Company's customers have expressed doubts about how objective it can be in recommending healthcare products if it's owned by a healthcare giant. Will Little Company be pressured to recommend the products offered by Big Company, its parent? Or will Little Company's advice remain objective?

As the senior executive charged with bringing Little Company into the corporate fold, how do you proceed? What are your obligations to Big Company, Little Company, and the customers of both? What do you owe to shareholders and the financial community? Are there other stakeholders, and what do you owe to them? What provisions would you include in an ethics code for Little Company?

PRODUCT SAFETY

As a brand manager at a large food manufacturer, you're positioning a new product for entry into the highly competitive snack food market. This product is low in fat and calories, and it should be unusually successful, especially against the rapidly growing pretzel market. You know that one of your leading competitors is preparing to launch a similar product at about the same time. Since market research suggests that the two products will be perceived as identical, the first product to be released should gain significant market share.

A research report from a small, independent lab—Green Lab—indicates that your product causes dizziness in a small group of individuals. Green has an impressive reputation, and its research has always been reliable in the past. However, the research reports from two other independent labs don't support Green's conclusion. Your director of research assures you that any claims of adverse effects are unfounded and that the indication of dizziness is either extremely rare or the result of faulty research by Green Lab. Since your division has been losing revenue because of its emphasis on potato chips and other high-fat snack foods, it desperately needs a low-fat money-maker. You were brought in to turn the division around, so your career at the company could depend on the success of this product.

What are your alternatives? What is your obligation to consumers? Who are your other stakeholders, and what do you owe them? What is your obligation to your employer and to other employees at your company? What should your course of action be? How can you apply the due care theory to this case?

ADVERTISING

At your company, a bottler of natural spring water, the advertising department has recently launched a campaign that emphasizes the purity of your product. The industry is highly competitive, and your organization has been badly hurt by a lengthy strike of unionized employees. The strike seriously disrupted production and distribution, and it caused your company to lose significant revenues and market share. Now that the strike is over, your company will have to struggle to recoup lost customers and will have to pay for the increased wages and benefits called for in the new union contract. The company's financial situation is precarious to say the least.

You and the entire senior management team have high hopes for the new ad campaign, and initial consumer response has been positive. You are shocked, then, when your head of operations reports to you that an angry worker has sabotaged one of your bottling plants. The worker introduced a chemical into one of the machines, which in turn contaminated 120,000 bottles of the spring water. Fortunately, the chemical is present in extremely minute amounts—no consumer could possibly suffer harm unless he or she drank in excess of 10 gallons of the water per day over a long period of time. Since the machine has already been sterilized, any risk of long-term exposure has been virtually eliminated. But, of course, the claims made by your new ad campaign could not be more false.

List all of the stakeholders involved in this situation. Do any stakeholder groups have more to gain or lose than others? Develop a strategy for dealing with the contamination. How much does a company's financial situation determine how ethical dilemmas are handled?

PRODUCT SAFETY AND ADVERTISING

For years, arthritis sufferers have risked intestinal bleeding from the long-term consumption of nonsteroidal anti-inflammatory drugs (NSAIDs) such as Advil, which are used to ease chronic joint pain. Your company, Big Pharma, introduced a new type of painkiller, a COX-2 inhibitor that addresses the pain without the intestinal effects. To get the word out to consumers, Big Pharma decided to market the new painkiller directly to consumers so that they could ask their doctors about it. The marketing was extraordinarily successful, ultimately creating a multibillion-dollar market. Over 100 million prescriptions were written in just five years, and the drug was a big contributor to your company's bottom line. Patients and doctors seemed grateful for the alternative, and doctors began using it to treat all kinds of pain. Then, complaints began coming in about cardiovascular events (heart attacks) associated with taking the new drug. Early scientific studies suggested that there might be a problem, but the science remained inconclusive. It appeared that many of these patients had other health problems that may have caused their heart attacks. So your company undertook a more definitive double-blind placebo-controlled study (the only kind that can truly demonstrate cause and effect), which eventually showed a link between your drug and an increased risk of cardiovascular events if the drug is taken consistently for more than 18 months. The Food and Drug Administration suggested a stronger black-box warning on the drug packaging to warn of potential cardiovascular side effects from prolonged use. Your senior management team met to discuss what to do. Should you follow the FDA's suggestion or do something else? The discussion included reference to your company's values and strong commitment to integrity and human welfare. You also referred to the famous Johnson & Johnson Tylenol incident and the success of that recall effort. After much discussion, you decided to recall the drug and cease manufacturing it.

The negative reactions were instantaneous. In stinging press reports and congressional hearings at which your CEO had to appear, your company was criticized for not recalling sooner based on the earlier evidence. And then the lawsuits began. It seemed that anyone who had ever taken your company's drug and then had a heart attack was bringing suit. Ironically, on the other side, patients and doctors who had been using the drug successfully also complained. They thought you should return the drug to the market with a stronger warning, so that they could do their own risk assessment. Nothing else worked for some patients, and they were suffering. But, after careful deliberation, you decided to stick to the recall decision and fight (rather than settle) the lawsuits. Early in the fight, your company won some lawsuits and lost some, but vowed to continue fighting them all because you were convinced that you had done nothing wrong. The fight was costly in dollars and reputation. Eventually, after several years and winning more lawsuits than you lost, you decided to settle all remaining lawsuits and move on, a decision that was considered to be wise in the business community. Your company's financial performance took a big hit, but it is now rebounding and the future looks more hopeful as some promising new treatments appear on the horizon.

Who are the stakeholders in this situation? Experts claim there's always a risk when people take prescription drugs. How much risk is too much? How widely do drug companies need to publicize the risks of prescription medications? Or, is that the doctor's responsibility? Do consumers really understand these risks? Do drug companies have an obligation to ensure that doctors don't overprescribe their drugs? Is that a reasonable expectation? Was direct-to-consumer marketing appropriate for this type of drug? When is it appropriate, and when is it not? Do drug companies have a bigger obligation to explain the risks of the drugs that they heavily market directly to consumers because such consumers are more likely to ask their doctors for these drugs? Why do you think the reaction to the decision to recall in this case was so different compared to the Tylenol situation? Should senior management have expected the reactions they got? Was there anything they could have done to change the reactions?

SHAREHOLDERS

You work for an investment bank that provides advice to corporate clients. The deal team you work with includes Pat, a marketing manager, Joe, the credit manager for the team, and several other professionals. Just before your team is scheduled to present the details of a new deal to senior management, Pat suggests to Joe that the deal would have a better chance of being approved if he withheld certain financials. "If you can't leave out this information," Pat says, "at least put a positive spin on it so they don't trash the whole deal."

The other team members agree that the deal has tremendous potential, not only for the two clients but also for your company. The financial information Pat objects to— though disturbing at first glance—would most likely not seriously jeopardize the interest of any party involved. Joe objects and says that full disclosure is the right way to proceed, but he adds that if all team members agree to the "positive spin," he'll go along with the decision. Team members vote and all agree to go along with Pat's suggestion—you have the last vote. What do you do?

In this hypothetical case, what is your obligation to the shareholders of your organization and to the shareholders of the two organizations that are considering a deal? Are shareholders a consideration in this case? Are customers? Are employees? Could the survival of any of the three companies be at stake in this case? In a situation like this one, how could you best protect the interests of key stakeholder groups?

COMMUNITY

You have just been named CEO of a small chemical refinery in the Northeast. Shortly after assuming your new position, you discover that your three predecessors have kept a horrifying secret. Your headquarters location sits atop thirty 5,000-gallon tanks that have held a variety of chemicals—from simple oil to highly toxic chemicals. Although the tanks were drained over 20 years ago, there's ample evidence that the tanks themselves have begun to rust and leach sludge from the various chemicals into the ground. Because your company is located in an area that supplies water to a large city over 100 miles away, the leaching sludge could already be causing major problems. The costs involved in a cleanup are estimated to be astronomical. Because the tanks are under the four-story headquarters building, the structure will have to be demolished before cleanup can begin. Then, all 30 tanks will have to be dug up and disposed of, and all of the soil around the area cleaned.

You're frankly appalled that the last three CEOs didn't try to correct this situation when they were in charge. If the problem had been corrected 15 years ago before the building had been erected, the costs would be substantially less than they will be now. However, as frustrated as you are, you're also committed to rectifying the situation.

After lengthy discussions with your technical and financial people, you decide that a cleanup can begin in two years. Obviously, the longer you wait to begin a cleanup, the riskier it becomes to the water supply. Before you begin the cleanup, it's imperative that you raise capital, and a stock offering seems to be the best way to do it. However, if you disclose news of the dump problem now, the offering will likely be jeopardized. But the prospect of holding a news conference and explaining your role in keeping the dump a secret keeps you up at night.

Who are the stakeholders in this situation? What strategy would you develop for dealing with the dump and its disclosure? Are you morally obligated to disclose the dump right away? How will Wall Street react to this news? Does your desire to correct the situation justify keeping it a secret for another two years?

Think about the due care theory presented earlier in this chapter. Can we draw parallels between due care for the consumer and due care for the environment? What if the dump for abandoned oil tanks mentioned in the hypothetical case was located in a foreign subsidiary of a U.S. company, and the country where it was located had no laws against such a dump? Would the CEO be under any obligation to clean it up? Should American companies uphold U.S. laws concerning the environment in non-U.S. locations? How much protection is enough?

DISCUSSION QUESTIONS

1. What factors contributed to Johns Manville's long silence on the dangers of asbestos?

2. What role do you think the personality and other characteristics of a CEO play in the handling of an ethical problem?

3. When other firms in your industry are behaving unethically, how can you buck the trend and position your company to value ethical behavior? Why is that important? Will it damage your company's competitiveness?

4. Imagine that you're the CEO of a large firm like any of the ones described in this chapter. What concrete steps would you take to restore your company's reputation if it's been sullied?

5. How much testing is enough when launching a new product?

6. How can the interests of multiple stakeholders be balanced?

7. Do you think long prison sentences will help deter corporate criminals?

8. Do you trust technology giants such as Google and Facebook to safeguard your personal data? Is posting online any safer than posting your personal information on a billboard along a busy highway? What kind of personal information would be OK to share with the world? What are the potential pitfalls for you personally of sharing sensitive information online?

9. How does a company's reputation play a role in your purchasing decisions?

NOTES

1. E. Conway, "IMF Puts Total Cost of Crisis at £7.1 Trillion," *Telegraph*, August 8, 2009, at www .telegraph.co.uk.

2. L. Mishel, *The State of Working America 2008/2009*, Economic Policy Institute (2009), at www .stateofworkingamerica.org.

3. J. Liberto, *CEO Pay is 380 Times Average Worker's – AFL-CIO*, CNN Money, April 19, 2012, at www .money.cnn.com

4. A. Greenspan, "Remarks by Chairman Alan Greenspan at the Annual Dinner and Francis Boyer Lecture of the American Enterprise Institute for Public Policy," Washington, D.C. (December 5, 1996), at www.federalreserve.gov.

5. A. Levitt, "Bigger than Enron," PBS *Frontline*, June 20, 2002, at www.pbs.org.

6. R. E. Freeman, *Strategic Management: A Stakeholder Approach* (Boston: Pitman, 1984).

7. *Investing in Social Responsibility, Risks and Opportunities* (London: Association of British Insurers, 2001), 41.

8. O. C. Ferrell and J. Fraedrich, *Business Ethics: Ethical Decision Making and Cases* (New York: Houghton Mifflin, 1994), 76.

9. R. D. Hay, E. R. Gary, and P. H. Smith, *Business and Society: Perspectives on Ethics and Social Responsibility* (Cincinnati, OH: South-Western Publishing, 1989), 288.

10. J. R. Boatright, *Ethics and the Conduct of Business* (Englewood Cliffs, NJ: Prentice-Hall, 1993), 332–35.

11. *"Fortune* 500 List," *Fortune* online (2002), at www.fortune.com.

12. "Enron Corporate Profile" (2002), at www.hoovers.com.

13. "Andrew S. Fastow, Former Enron Chief Financial Officer, Pleads Guilty, Settles Fraud Charges and Agrees to Cooperate with Ongoing Investigation," U.S. Securities and Exchange Commission (2004), at www.sec.gov.

14. "Lea Fastow Arrives Early for Prison," *USA Today*, July 12, 2004, at www.usatoday.com/money/industries/energy/2004-07-12-lea-fastow_x.htm.

15. J. Carney, "The Truth About Why Jeff Skilling's Jail Sentence Got Downsized," *CNBC*, June 21, 2013, at www.cnbc.com.

16. A. Barrionuevo, "Judge Sentences Former Enron Chief to 24 Years in Prison," *New York Times*, October 23, 2006, at www.nytimes.com.

17. "Called to Account: The Enron Saga. Scandal Scorecard," *Wall Street Journal* (2002), at www.wsj.com.

18. G. Draffan, "Multimillion Dollar Fines & Settlements Paid by Corporations" (2005), at www.endgame.org.

19. A. Levitt, "Bigger than Enron," PBS *Frontline*, June 20, 2002, at www.pbs.org.

20. "Who Dropped the Ball?" PBS *Frontline*, June 20, 2002, at www.pbs.org.

21. G. Morgenson, "Settlement Is a Good Deal for Merrill. How about Investors?" *New York Times*, May 22, 2002, at www.nytimes.com.

22. P. McGeehan, "Washington Insider, but Wall Street Pariah," *New York Times*, November 24, 2002, at www.nytimes.com.

23. A. R. Sorkin, "What the Financial Crisis Commission Should Ask," *New York Times*, January 10, 2010, at www.nytimes.com.

24. Ibid.

25. E. Mason, "Putnam Chief Holds Out Hope for Solid, If Slow, Recovery," *Boston Business Journal*, June 17, 2005, at www.bizjournals.com/boston.

26. P. Elkind, "Spitzer's Crusade: Inside the Muckraker-in-Chief's Campaign against Insurance Companies and Why—Surprise, Surprise—This Investigation Is Just Getting Started," *Fortune*, November 1, 2004, at www.fortune.com.

27. M. Goldstein, "Putnam's Lasser Gets $78 million Good-Bye Kiss," June 10, 2004, at www.thestreet.com.

28. Marsh & McLennan, *2004 Annual Report*, 62.

29. P. Elkind, "Spitzer's Crusade: Inside the Muckraker-in-Chief's Campaign against Insurance Companies and Why—Surprise, Surprise—This Investigation Is Just Getting Started," *Fortune*, November 1, 2004, at www.fortune.com.

30. Ibid.

31. *Argus Analyst Report* (Marsh & McLennan Companies, Inc., Argus Research Company, 2005).

32. P. Elkind, "Spitzer's Crusade: Inside the Muckraker-in-Chief's Campaign against Insurance Companies and Why—Surprise, Surprise—This Investigation Is Just Getting Started," *Fortune*, November 1, 2004, at www.fortune.com.

33. "Sentencing in Spitzer Insurance Probe Delayed," September 29, 2005, at www.reuters.com.

34. E. Mason, "Putnam Chief Holds Out Hope for Solid, If Slow, Recovery," *Boston Business Journal*, June 17, 2005, at www.bizjournals.com/boston.

35. "Ex-Fidelity Head Reynolds Becomes New Putnam CEO," *Boston Business Journal*, June 12, 2008, http://boston.bizjournals.com.

36. P. Elkind, "Spitzer's Crusade: Inside the Muckraker-in-Chief's Campaign against Insurance Companies and Why—Surprise, Surprise—This Investigation Is Just Getting Started," *Fortune*, November 1, 2004, at www.fortune.com.

37. D. Hakim and W. Rashbaum, "Spitzer Is Linked to Prostitution Ring," *New York Times*, March 8, 2008, at www.nytimes.com.

38. G. Draffan, "Multimillion Dollar Fines & Settlements Paid by Corporations" (2005), at www.endgame.org.

39. "Do You Trust Corporate America?" *Businessweek* online, June 21, 2002, at www.businessweek.com.

40. *2010 Edelman Trust Barometer*, Edelman Public Relations (2010), at www.edelman.com/trust.
41. Ibid.
42. Harris Interactive, "Current Confidence in Leaders of Institutions (2012), May 21, 2012, www.harrisinteractive.com
43. T. Donaldson and P. H. Werhane, *Ethical Issues in Business: A Philosophical Approach* (Englewood Cliffs, NJ: Prentice-Hall, 1988), 89–100, 414–24; R. R. Hartley, *Business Ethics: Violations of the Public Trust* (New York: Wiley & Sons, 1993), 295–305.
44. M. Petersen, "Guilty Plea by Division of Drug Giant," *New York Times*, December 12, 2000, C1.
45. N. Singer and R Abelson, "Can Johnson & Johnson Get Its Act Together?" New York Times, January 15, 2011, at www.nyt.com
46. M. Santoli, "*The World's Most Respected Companies*," *Barron's*, June 25, 2012, at www.online.barrons.com
47. "U.S. Vehicle Sales Market Share by Company, 1961–2009," *Ward's Auto Data* (2010), at http://wardsauto.com/keydata.
48. "World Ranking of Motor Vehicles 2008 by Manufacturers, " OICA (July 2009), www.oica.net.
49. B. Vlasic, "Toyota's Slow Awakening to a Deadly Problem," *New York Times*, February 1, 2010, at www.nytimes.com.
50. Ibid.
51. M. Chrysler, "Toyota Down but Not Out, Japan Analysts Say," *Ward's Auto Data*, January 29, 2010, at www.wardsauto.com.
52. B. Vlasic, "Toyota's Slow Awakening to a Deadly Problem," *New York Times*, February 1, 2010, at www.nytimes.com.
53. P. Ingrassia, "Toyota: Too Big, Too Fast," *Wall Street Journal*, January 28, 2010, at www.wsj.com.
54. "Toyota History," Official Toyota website (2010), at www.toyota.com.
55. Associated Press, *Toyota Settles Bellwether Wrongful Death Lawsuit*, National Public Radio, January 18, 2013, at www.npr.org
56. G. Risling, *Toyota Settlement May Signal Future Legal Strategy*, ABC News, January 18, 2013, at abcnews.go.com
57. Ibid.
58. A. Ohnsman, "Toyota as No. 1 Again Means Style Overhaul to Help Shares," *The Washington Post*, January 14, 2013, at http://www.bloomberg.com/news/2013-01-13/toyota-as-no-1-again-means-style-overhaul-to-help-shares.html
59. B. Vlasic, "Toyota's Slow Awakening to a Deadly Problem," *New York Times*, February 1, 2010, at www.nytimes.com.
60. A. Taylor, "Toyota's Tylenol Moment," *CNN Money*, January 28, 2010, at www.cnnmoney.com.
61. B. Vlasic, "Toyota's Slow Awakening to a Deadly Problem," *New York Times*, February 1, 2010, at www.nytimes.com.
62. C. Isidore, "Toyota's Reputation Takes a Huge Hit," *CNN Money*, January 27, 2010, at www.cnnmoney.com.
63. M. Petersen, "Heartfelt Advice, Hefty Fees," *New York Times*, August 11, 2002, at www.nytimes.com.
64. R. Pear, "Investigators Find Repeated Deception in Ads for Drugs," *New York Times*, December 4, 2002, at www.nytimes.com.
65. A. Eichler, "Pharmaceutical Companies Spent 19 Times More on Self-Promotion Than Basic Research: Report," *Huffington Post*, August 9, 2012, at www.huffingtonpost.com
66. V. S. Elliott, "Patient-Focused Drug Campaigns May Exploit Data, Invade Privacy," *Amednews* (American Medical News), July 29, 2002, at www.amednews.com.
67. A. Berenson, "Where Has All the Prilosec Gone?" *New York Times*, March 2, 2005, at www.nytimes.com.
68. K. Thomas and M. Schmidt, "Glaxo Agrees to $3 Billion Fraud Settlement," *New York Times,* July 2, 2012, at www.nytimes.com
69. A. Pollack and M. Secret, "Amgen Agrees to Pay $762 Million for Marketing Anemia Drug for Off-Label Use," *New York Times,* December 18, 2012, at www.nytimes.com

70. M. Kimes. "Bad to the Bone," Fortune, October 8, 2012, at www.fortune.cnn.com

71. L. Groeger, "Big Pharma's Big Fines, Pro Publica, July 3, 2012, at www.propublica.org

72. R. Bate, "The Companies Everyone Loves to Hate," *Wall Street Journal*, September 16, 2005, at http://online.wsj.com.

73. S. Hensley, "In Switch, J&J Gives Straight Talk on Drug Risks in New Ads," *Wall Street Journal*, March 21, 2005, B1.

74. "Ten Questions: An Open Dialogue," *Pfizer 2004 Annual Review*, 2005: 4, 8, 28.

75. K. Thomas and M. Schmidt, "Glaxo Agrees to $3 Billion Fraud Settlement," *New York Times,* July 2, 2012, at www.nytimes.com.

76. Carroll, *Business and Society.*

77. Donaldson and Werhane, "Ethical Issues in Business."

78. B. Sells, "What Asbestos Taught Me about Risk," *Harvard Business Review* (March–April 1994): 76–90.

79. Ibid.

80. Ibid., 76.

81. Ibid., 84.

82. "A Dangerous Business: Two Companies, Two Visions," PBS *Frontline* (2003), at www.pbs.org.

83. D. Barstow, "U.S. Brings New Set of Charges against Pipe Manufacturer," May 26, 2004, at www.nytimes.com.

84. D. Barstow, "Pipe Maker Will Admit to Violations of Safety Law," *New York Times*, August 30, 2005, at www.nytimes.com.

85. *"Times* and PBS Win a Reporting Prize," *New York Times*, March 19, 2004, at www.nytimes.com.

86. "A Dangerous Business: Two Companies, Two Visions," PBS *Frontline* (2003), at www.pbs.org.

87. A. Knox, "What Will Albert Dunlap Do Next at Scott?" *Philadelphia Inquirer*, May 16, 1995, E4.

88. N. Gorenstein and C. Mayer, "Scott, Kimberly-Clark to Merge," *Philadelphia Inquirer*, July 18, 1995, C1.

89. J. A. Byrne, "How Al Dunlap Self-Destructed," *Businessweek*, July 6, 1998, 58–65.

90. F. Norris, "Justice Department Starts Inquiry at Sunbeam," *New York Times*, September 9, 2002, at www.nytimes.com.

91. F. Norris, "An Executive's Missing Years: Papering over Past Problems," *New York Times*, July 16, 2001, at www.nytimes.com.

92. Lincoln Electric Company, at www.lincolnelectric.com.

93. B. Richards (from The Motley Fool), "For the 63rd Straight Year (at Least), This Remarkable Company Says 'No' to Layoffs," *Daily Finance*, December 13, 2011, at www.dailyfinance.com

94. J. P. Kotter and J. L. Heskett, *Corporate Culture and Performance* (New York: Free Press, 1992), 46.

95. R. Charan and M Useem, "Why Companies Fail: Company CEOs Offer Every Excuse But the Right One—Their Own Errors," *Fortune,* May 27, 2002, at www.money.cnn.com/magazines/fortune

96. C. W. Smith, *Ethics and Markets: Restructuring Japan's Financial Markets* (Homewood, IL: Business One Irwin, 1993), 335–45.

97. M. Gimein, "The Enforcer," *Fortune*, September 2, 2002, 77–78.

98. "Citigroup: Salomon, Grubman Face 62 Suits over Research," Dow Jones Newswire, *Wall Street Journal*, November 13, 2002, at www.wsj.com.

99. A. Geller, "Wall Street Firms Agree to Pay $1.44 Billion to Settle Conflicts of Interest," *Detroit News Business*, December 21, 2002, at www.detnews.com.

100. "Conflict Probes Resolved at Citigroup and Morgan Stanley," New York State Office of the Attorney General, April 28, 2003, at www.oag.state.ny.us.

101. M. Der Hovanesian, P. Dwyer, and S. Reed, "Can Chuck Prince Clean Up Citi?" *Businessweek*, October 4, 2004, 35.

102. K. Booker, "Citi's Creator—Alone with His Regrets," *New York Times*, January 2, 2010, at www.nytimes.com.

103. E. Dash, "Citigroup's Chief Shrinks Company, Eyeing Growth," *New York Times*, April 5, 2010, at www.nytimes.com.

104. P. Kiel, "The Bailout: By the Actual Numbers," ProPublica, September 6, 2012, at www.propublica.org

105. G. Morgenson, "Citi's Torch Has Passed. Now Find a Knife.," *New York Times*, October 20, 2012, at www.nytimes.com

106. B. Saporito, "How AIG Became Too Big to Fail," *Time*, March 19, 2009, at www.time.com.

107. Ibid.

108. "Buffett Warns on Investment 'Time Bomb, '" *BBC Business News*, March 4, 2003, at http://news.bbc.co.uk.

109. L. Laughlin and R. Beales, "AIG's Big Debt to U.S. Taxpayers," *New York Times*, January 27, 2010, at www.nytimes.com.

110. B. Saporito, "How AIG Became Too Big to Fail," *Time*, March 19, 2009, at www.time.com.

111. T.G. Massad. "Overall $182 Billion Committed to Stabilize AIG During the Financial Crisis Is Now Fully Recovered." *U.S. Department of the Treasury*, September 11, 2012, at www.treasury.gov.

112. B. Berkowitz, "As Public Fumes, AIG Says Will Not Sue U.S. Over Bailout," *Reuters*, January 9, 2013. At www.reuters.com.

113. D.J. Wood, *Business and Society* (New York; HarperCollins), 664.

114. R. F. Hartley, *Business Ethics: Violations of the Public Trust* (New York: Wiley & Sons, 1993), 220–29.

115. C. Krauss "Judge Accepts BP's $4 Billion Criminal Settlement Over Gulf Oil Spill," *New York Times*, January 29, 2013, at www.nytimes.com.

116. J. Nocera, "BP Ignored the Omens of Disaster," *New York Times*, June 18, 2010, at www.nytimes.com.

117. "Re: the Exxon *Valdez*,"#A89-0095CV, U.S. District Court for the District of Alaska, January 28, 2004, at www.seattleclassaction.com.

118. A. Liptak, "Damages Cut Against Exxon in *Valdez* Case," *New York Times*, June 26, 2008, at www.nytimes.com.

119. D. Streietfeld and K. O'Brien, "Google Privacy Inquiries Get Little Cooperation," *New York Times*, May 22, 2012, at www.nytimes.com.

120. J. Angwin, "Google, FTC Near Settlement on Privacy," *Wall Street Journal*, July 9, 2012, at www.wsj.com.

121. J. Rosenblatt, "Facebook Seeks Dismissal of $15 Billion Privacy Suit," *Bloomberg News*, October 5, 2012, at www.bloomberg.com.

122. *2010 Edelman Trust Barometer*, Edelman Public Relations (2010), at www.edelman.com/trust.

123. Ibid.

124. J. Plender, "Inside Track: Morals Pay Dividends, " *Financial Times*, September 18, 2002, at www.ft.com.

125. *2010 Edelman Trust Barometer*, Edelman Public Relations (2010), at www.edelman.com/trust.

126. M. Benioff, "ATrust: A New Era of Business Values," *Ethisphere*, October 17, 2011, at www.ethisphere.com.

CHAPTER 11

MANAGING FOR ETHICS AND SOCIAL RESPONSIBILITY IN A GLOBAL ENVIRONMENT

INTRODUCTION

With the increasing globalization of business, more managers are finding themselves in an international environment full of ethical challenges. If managing for ethics and social responsibility is a challenge in one's own culture, the difficulties only multiply when the culture and language are foreign, the manager is under increased stress, and the number of stakeholders grows enormously. The major stakeholders include multiple governments with their differing laws, regulations, and policies; business partners that may be incorporated in the United States or elsewhere; employees and customers from different cultures; and civil society, a large umbrella term that includes the media, academic institutions, not-for-profit organizations, and religious, political, and other groups with an interest in global business ethics. The simple fact that managers have to deal with so many different stakeholders makes decision making extremely complex. And the issues global managers face may be completely new to them. These include corruption and money laundering, human rights under totalitarian regimes, workplace conditions, environmental issues, respect for local customs and cultures, and more.

Particularly in developing nations, businesspeople face conditions, cultures, customs, and norms that may conflict with their own ethical standards and challenge them to consider which values they'll uphold no matter what the locale. In this chapter, we address the difficulties of foreign assignments in general terms. We also focus on the specific challenges of dealing with key ethical issues that arise in the context of international business. These issues include individual decision making about the conduct of business in different cultures, and organizational decision making about ethical and social responsibility issues such as whether and how to conduct business in foreign nations and how to guide employees working in a global business environment.

FOCUS ON THE INDIVIDUAL EXPATRIATE MANAGER

We begin by focusing on the individual expatriate manager, the difficulties inherent in foreign business assignments, and the importance of cultural understanding, sensitivity, and openness.

The Difficulties of Foreign Business Assignments

The globalization of business has contributed to a huge increase in interactions between people from different cultural backgrounds. These interactions may occur during brief business trips or in lengthy overseas assignments that last for years. Unfortunately, many overseas assignments end early and unsuccessfully because of the expatriate manager's (and his or her family's) inability to adjust to the foreign work environment. Recent research has demonstrated that the expatriate manager's adjustment impacts satisfaction, willingness to stay in the assignment, and job performance.[1]

The Need for Structure, Training, and Guidance

Studies show that American businesses often don't provide adequate support and cross-cultural training to their managers who are assigned to work overseas. Research has found that expatriates need clear guidance about goals and the expectations associated with their jobs[2] as well as a realistic preview of the living conditions in the new location.[3] Guidance and support should extend to the ethical issues that are likely to arise, because these contribute to ambiguity and confusion about appropriate behavior. Studies have also found that cross-cultural training can be highly effective. For example, training contributes to:

- Greater feelings of well-being and self-confidence for the American manager
- Improvement in relationships with host nationals
- The development of correct perceptions of host culture members
- Better adjustment to the new culture
- Higher performance[4]

In addition to training for the expatriate manager, recent studies have suggested the critical importance of providing training and support for the manager's spouse because families generally accompany the expatriate. The well-being of the spouse and family seriously affects the expatriate's adjustment and willingness to stick with an overseas assignment.[5] Also, the higher the level of the manager, the more likely it is that the spouse will serve in a corporate "ambassador" role.[6] So, the spouse's successful adaptation to the new environment is critical.

Research suggests that some people adapt to other cultures more successfully than others. The term *cultural intelligence* (CQ) has been used to describe an individual's ability to be effective in cross-cultural situations.[7] CQ involves a knowledge component (what the person knows about the new culture and his or her approach to learning), a motivational component (the person's confidence and motivation to adapt to the new culture), and an action component (the ability to translate knowledge and motivation into action). The rare individuals who are high on all three components are referred to as "cultural chameleons" because of their unique ability to adapt easily to new cultural environments.[8] Certainly, companies can help with the first part by providing information about the new culture. Research has found that employees who are higher on the motivational aspect of CQ, who are more motivated to explore different cultures and more confident in their ability to adapt to new environments, adjust better to the demands of foreign assignments.[9] So, before sending them overseas, companies should assess employees for their CQ level.

Foreign Language Proficiency

One kind of training that can improve one's international business experience is foreign language training. Language is an essential part of cultural learning that can contribute to productive international business relationships. Interestingly, this is particularly important for non-English speakers doing business in English-speaking countries. Other countries seem to be more accommodating of native English speakers who do not learn their language than the reverse. Nevertheless, the expatriate manager's effort to learn the language is generally taken as a symbol of his or her interest and commitment to understanding. Yet Americans speak fewer foreign languages than their trading partners do,[10] and some have argued that Americans pay a high price for this "monolingual arrogance."[11]

Language fluency isn't a matter of just knowing the words, but knowing how they are used within the particular cultural context. For example, an old story goes that a Scottish visitor to Japan had worked hard to develop a good relationship with his Japanese host. After several weeks, the Japanese host asked (in Japanese), "Can I sleep with you?" Luckily, the Scot was sophisticated in cross-cultural communication and didn't react negatively or dismiss the question while his mind raced to attempt to understand its meaning. Despite his confusion, he agreed to the apparently odd request. The Japanese host had a second mattress brought to the visitor's room, and the two slept through the night, comfortably and without incident. He later discovered that his Japanese host had paid him the highest compliment. The Japanese believe that an individual can easily be killed in his sleep. Therefore the request indicated a relationship of total trust.[12] A note of caution—you might not want to try this one today. Our students tell us that "Can I sleep with you?" now carries the same meaning in Japan as it does in the United States.

Learning about the Culture

Earlier in the book, we talked about organizational culture. Here, we focus on national culture—defined as "collective mental programming."[13] This definition of culture suggests that patterns of believing differ across national cultures and that individuals use these patterns to interpret the world and to guide action. If an individual operating in a foreign culture doesn't understand its particular patterns of believing and behaving, the individual will interpret experience purely in terms of his or her own culture and will thus inevitably misinterpret and misunderstand.

To understand how this collective mental programming can lead to misunderstanding, we'll focus on two cultural dimensions, developed by Geert Hofstede,[14] that are relevant for understanding international business ethics.[15] Readers who are heading overseas are encouraged to learn about the additional cultural dimensions that are more relevant for other aspects of the overseas business experience.

INDIVIDUALISM/COLLECTIVISM Individualism represents the extent to which people in a society think of themselves as autonomous individuals who are responsible primarily to themselves and their immediate families. This contrasts with collectivism, which emphasizes collective purposes over personal goals and group harmony over individual achievement. Americans, Canadians, Australians, and most Northern Europeans are individualists. They define themselves in terms of personal characteristics and achievements, and they generally value personal welfare over group harmony. For example, Americans are quick to praise individual accomplishment and individuals' ability to make good decisions independently. They aim to hire people with the highest educational and professional achievements.

Most Asian and Latin American countries represent collectivist societies. They value conformity to the group and define themselves in terms of their group memberships and their contributions to the success of those groups. A common Japanese saying reflects this collectivist orientation—the nail that sticks out will be pounded down. Hiring in collectivist cultures is certainly based on qualifications, but a person's ability to work well with coworkers and to make collaborative decisions is as important as individual technical proficiency. Knowing an applicant or his or her family is considered an important "qualification," and the hiring of family members is common and expected. An American without cultural knowledge would probably consider this approach to hiring to be wrong—biased and discriminatory. Indeed, many American firms have rules against nepotism. But a collectivist would consider the Americans' individualistic approach to hiring to be wrong—disloyal to friends and family as well as ineffective. To a collectivist, knowing someone is the best way to ensure that the person is trustworthy and will work well with others in the group. Furthermore, in a collectivist culture such as Japan, giving gifts is considered to be an important part of relationship building. Giving a gift can also be an important step toward acceptance and becoming a member of the group.[16] In individualistic cultures, gift giving is more likely to be considered to be a bribe—an attempt to influence an individual's business decisions.

Consider how the differences between individualism and collectivism might influence ethics management. In their attempts to manage ethics and legal compliance, many companies have formal reporting systems (hotlines or help lines) that encourage employees to report misconduct they observe. Such a system is likely to be distasteful to collectivists, who may see it as too impersonal and too focused on singling out and blaming a single individual who would be shamed as a result. A more informal system that aims to help the rule breaker mend his or her ways and return as a productive member of the group may work better in a collectivist culture.[17]

POWER DISTANCE Power distance represents the extent to which people in the society accept a hierarchical or unequal distribution of power in their organizations and in society. High power distance in a culture reflects acceptance of inequality and respect for social status or class boundaries. In these cultures, employees are more likely to accept the idea that the boss has power simply because she or he is the boss, and bypassing the boss is considered insubordination. Titles, status, and formality are important in these societies, and those with high status are given much leeway in their behavior. For example, when U.S. President Richard Nixon was forced to resign, members of cultures with high power distance found it hard to understand. They focused on the fact that he was president—which, after all, is a high-status position.[18] Americans, on the other hand, were more likely to focus on Nixon's misconduct associated with Watergate, regardless of his position or title. Some countries having the highest power distance are India, the Philippines, Mexico, and Venezuela.

Cultures with low power distance are more likely to deemphasize status and class distinctions. The United States, Israel, and most Northern European countries (with the exception of France and Belgium) are lower on power distance. In these cultures, employees accept a boss's power because he or she has knowledge, not just because he or she is the boss. Therefore workers in a culture of low power distance may be more willing to question the boss's authority or even blow the whistle on an unethical manager.

Recognizing the Power of Selective Perception

Human beings are constantly bombarded with information. They must therefore perceive selectively, or they would be totally overwhelmed. This selective perception process is influenced by culture. For example, in collectivist cultures, people pay more attention to social relationships than to behavior. And in Confucian philosophy, putting family first is praised above all. So what should one do if a close relative commits a crime? A federal prison camp inmate spoke with Penn State students about the reason for his imprisonment. The man, who was well-educated and well-spoken, had been a successful New York executive. He and his wife had helped the wife's nephew by providing a place for him to stay when he was having difficulties in his life, including drug use. But it turned out that the nephew was using their telephone to sell drugs right out of their home! The couple was accused of knowing about and supporting the drug dealing, and they were charged with conspiracy. Both were convicted and sentenced to many years in prison. Asian students in the audience were horrified that this man landed in prison for helping his nephew. To them, the familial relationship was more important than the crime, and that influenced how they perceived his story. So, it is essential to recognize that the visitor to another culture will notice things that are important at home but may not be important in the target culture. The visitor is also likely to overlook important behaviors, roles, and values because of selective perception. These aren't important at home, so they aren't even noticed. Furthermore, members of the target culture are equally selective, perhaps not noticing things that seem crucial to the visitor.[19]

With effective cross-cultural training, managers can be prepared to be on the lookout for things that would otherwise be ignored, and they will be more able to interpret their international business experiences in light of the belief patterns of the particular culture. These interpretations are extremely important because actions are likely to vary depending on the interpretation.[20]

Assumption of Behavioral Consistency

Understanding culture doesn't guarantee success, however. Much of the theory and research on international business conduct is grounded in an inaccurate key assumption—that if we understand cultural behavior (how people think and behave in their native environment), we'll understand how members of a particular group will behave in relation to cultural outsiders. In other words, if I understand the Japanese culture better, I can predict how my Japanese counterparts will behave toward me, what their expectations will be, and so on. And if I understand all of that, I'll know how to behave with them.

But people are amazingly adaptable, and just when you think you have them figured out, they change their behavior. Individuals from a different culture are likely trying to figure out how to behave with you as much as you're trying to figure out how to behave with them, and they may change their behavior as a result. A colleague related a story about a meeting between business and philosophy professors on his campus. Recognizing the cultural differences between the two departments, the philosophy professors decided to leave their khakis at home and dress up for the occasion—sporting crisp shirts and ties. The business professors all showed up in jeans. The moral of this story is that behavior is difficult to predict because people adapt their behaviors to what they believe others expect of them.

What can we glean from these studies? Don't assume that simply learning about another culture is enough. The foreign nationals you deal with in business interactions may behave differently with you than they would with individuals from their own culture, so understanding their cultural norms and behaviors is only a starting point. The foreign individuals you deal with may adapt their behavior based on what they expect you to do. Therefore you must be flexible and open to learning from the situation at hand. Perhaps one of the most important things to learn in preparation for a cross-cultural experience is that you can't be fully prepared—there will be surprises and daily opportunities for further learning and understanding.[21] The successful international businessperson will be open, flexible, and tolerant of ambiguity.

Assumption of Cultural Homogeneity

We should also not assume homogeneity within a culture—that individuals within a culture are all the same. Imagine if someone assumed that all Americans were like the characters in American films. Obviously, this kind of simplistic thinking and stereo-typing leads to grossly inaccurate expectations. Individual personalities and experiences vary widely within any culture, leading to behavioral differences. For example, a Japanese businessperson with an American MBA may behave quite differently from a Japanese businessperson who has never left the country.[22] Be open to learning as much as possible about the individuals you are going to be dealing with. The most effective international managers are those who modify stereotypes or discard them completely in the light of contradictory evidence.

Assumption of Similarity

Another problematic assumption is the assumption of cultural similarity. Many companies begin the internationalization process in countries that they believe to be more similar to their own because they believe that success will come easier in a more familiar culture. But research suggests that this perceived similarity can cause performance failures because managers are less likely to prepare for the cultural differences that do exist.[23] Researchers call this the psychic distance paradox. It may actually be quite difficult to do business in a country that is "psychically close." A study of Canadian retailers entering the American retail market found that familiarity often led to carelessness. Decision makers at Canadian retail companies had preconceived notions that the U.S. market was quite similar to the Canadian market and that what had worked for them in Canada would work in the United States. Therefore they didn't work as hard at understanding the American retail culture, and they tended to misinterpret information. So, if you're being sent to a country that you perceive to be similar to your own, don't assume similarity. Find out as much as you can about doing business in that country, just as you would for countries that you perceive to be more different.

ETHICS-RELATED TRAINING AND GUIDANCE   International business assignments require training that is more specifically related to ethics. Training should cover such topics as how to recognize the ethical issues likely to arise in a particular environment, how to negotiate in a particular culture, how to handle requests for payoffs and bribes, and anything else relevant to doing business ethically in that culture.

RECOGNIZING AND DEALING WITH ETHICAL ISSUES   Beyond general training in the culture, training with respect to business ethics beliefs and practices is essential. First, the expatriate manager must be prepared to recognize the ethical issues likely to arise in a particular business and cultural setting. Just as ethical issues at home vary somewhat from industry to industry (e.g., manufacturing vs. banking vs. defense) and profession to profession (e.g., marketing vs. accounting vs. procurement), the ethical issues that are likely to arise vary from culture to culture. The treatment of employees (e.g., child labor, worker safety) may be more of a problem in one culture, whereas the disposal of toxic wastes may be more likely to arise in another, and bribes may be more problematic in yet another culture.

Second, the expatriate manager needs help making ethical decisions in the more ambiguous international business context. At home, where we are familiar with community standards, it's easier to rely on simple guidelines such as the *New York Times* test (remember the disclosure rule from Chapter 2?). But simple guidelines often fall short when norms of the home culture conflict with those of the host country.[24] Individual expatriate managers shouldn't be left to fend for themselves in these unfamiliar circumstances. The organization owes it to them to provide guidance and help them navigate these unknown ethical waters.

NEGOTIATING ACROSS CULTURES The frequency of business negotiations is increasing with growth in foreign trade, joint ventures, and other interorganizational agreements. When working within one's own language and culture, being an effective negotiator requires the utmost in sensitivity, understanding, and communications skills. These requirements multiply when negotiating in an international business environment.

Cultural differences can influence the perceived purpose of the negotiation, negotiating styles, and preferences for conflict resolution approaches. For example, in collectivist cultures, people may see the purpose of the negotiation as the creation of a relationship. And in collectivist cultures, negotiators may avoid direct manifestations of conflict. So to avoid even the appearance of conflict, a negotiator in Japan who finds a request unacceptable might say, "I'll give your request careful consideration." Another collectivist is likely to recognize such a statement as meaning "no," while an American might interpret it to mean that we should return to discussing the issue later. When the American brings it up later and finds out that the negotiation partner really meant "no," the American is likely to perceive the negotiation tactic to be unfair. Similarly, when conflicts arise, preferences differ regarding how those conflicts should be resolved. For example, collectivists tend to prefer methods such as mediation, which involves compromise, because these approaches are more likely to result in harmonious relationships. Individualists like Americans prefer adjudication because they perceive it to be more fair.[25]

A number of research studies detail differences in negotiation styles and tactics across cultures.[26] Most relevant, given our focus on ethics, is an understanding of the use of "dirty tricks" and "psychological warfare" negotiation "tactics designed to pressure opponents into undesirable concessions and agreements."[27]

The use of dirty tricks is possible in any negotiation, but it becomes more complex in an international negotiation because of possible misinterpretation. For example, Brazilians generally expect deception among negotiators who are not well acquainted, so they may be more likely to use deception during early negotiation stages than are Americans.[28] Consequently, it may be wise for an American negotiator to expect deception to be a part of the initial negotiation stage with a Brazilian counterpart.

It's also important to recognize that what seems like deliberate deception may not be. Eastern Europeans are generally expected to check with their superiors about any changes. However, Americans often have wide authority to make important decisions at the negotiation table. Without this cultural knowledge, an American might interpret an Eastern European's claims about limited authority to be an attempt at deception when it isn't.

Psychological warfare—"tactics designed to make the other person feel uncomfortable"[29] and want to conclude the negotiation quickly—also has different meanings in different cultures. For example, too much touching or too much eye contact may make Americans extremely uncomfortable. Again, it's important to be able to distinguish real attempts at psychological warfare from the expression of typical cultural behavior. For example, Latins tend to touch more than Americans or Canadians, who touch more than Scandinavians. Arabs maintain greater eye contact than Americans, who use eye contact more than the Japanese. An understanding of the culture one is dealing with can help prepare the negotiator to correctly interpret these types of behaviors. The more knowledge each side has of the other's culture, the more options are available in terms of negotiation styles and strategies. But if negotiators are totally unfamiliar with each other's cultures, it is likely best to hire agents to represent each side.[30]

DEALING WITH PAYOFFS AND BRIBES Probably the most frequent source of anxiety for American businesspersons operating abroad is the expectation of payoffs and bribes. A bribe is a payment to someone to secure a sale or to obtain approval or assistance from an individual or organization (often a government bureaucrat). Although bribing is routine during commercial transactions in many Asian, African, Latin American, and Middle Eastern cultures, it's important to note that this practice is usually against the law in these very same countries.

On arrival in a foreign airport, many a businessperson has faced a government official's extended hand and the suggestion that payment was needed to facilitate the delivery of product samples to the hotel—no payment, no product. Without previous preparation, the expatriate is at a loss to know what to do. What is the meaning of this request in the context of the culture? Is making the payoff against U.S. or local law? What exactly is local custom? How much is expected? What's likely to happen if I do pay? And what if I don't pay? Will payment really expedite matters? Will it mean that I'm just contributing to a bigger request the next time? Is it legal to hire an intermediary to handle this (the answer is generally no)? What are my options? How will my company respond if my work is delayed?

In the 1970s, the practice of bribing foreign officials with huge payoffs was found to be rampant among U.S. multinational corporations. For example, in the mid-1960s, a major Korean political party asked Gulf Oil for a $10 million donation. The CEO personally negotiated it down to $4 million—still a huge sum.[31] As a response to the scandals, the U.S. Congress passed the Foreign Corrupt Practices Act (FCPA) in 1977.[32] The act prohibits representatives of U.S. corporations from offering or providing "corrupt payments" to foreign political parties, candidates, or government officials for the purpose of inducing the recipient(s) to misuse their powerful positions to assist the company to obtain, maintain, or retain business.[33]

The law does allow for small payments to lower-level figures. These so-called facilitating payments might be needed to persuade officials to perform their normal clerical or ministerial duties faster or better. Americans might think of these facilitating payments as tips, a little extra for the individual involved, to assure courteous or efficient service. To be classified as a facilitating payment, the offer must not significantly change the final decision or result. But, it is also important to know whether such payments are illegal in the country where you are doing business because that is often the case. It is against the FCPA and considered subversion of the free-market system if the money is paid to sway high-level people to make decisions they would not otherwise make. Companies are required to keep records of all such transactions, and these transactions are not tax deductible. Note that the law also applies to any intermediary who might make a payment for you. So you can't just hire an agent to make these payments. An exception is made for extortion payments, which are not prohibited under the law. For example, if a company official is abducted by Somali pirates and held for ransom, a company can legally pay the ransom.[34]

Enforcement of the FCPA has increased in recent years. Most corporations work hard to avoid even the appearance of impropriety, because Justice Department investigations are costly and time-consuming. A guilty verdict is usually devastating. For example, in 1995 Lockheed Corporation pleaded guilty to conspiring to pay a $1 million bribe to a member of the Egyptian parliament. Fines and penalties to the company totaled $24.8 million. In addition, a former Lockheed executive was sentenced to 18 months in prison.[35]

In a recent example, Wal-Mart's name has been in the news because of an alleged widespread bribery scheme in its Mexican operation where bribes are alleged to have been used for years to gain access to store building sites that would otherwise have been legally off limits. According to a searing *New York Times* report, "Wal-Mart de Mexico was an aggressive and creative corrupter, offering large payoffs to get what the law otherwise prohibited." (Perhaps if the manager involved had used the *New York Times* test, he wouldn't have engaged in these practices!) The *New York Times* reports that Wal-Mart "used bribes to subvert democratic governance—public votes, open debates, transparent procedures. It used bribes to circumvent regulatory safeguards that protect Mexican citizens from unsafe construction. It used bribes to outflank rivals." The newspaper also alleges that Wal-Mart executives attempted to cover up the bribery scandal when they learned about it rather than report it to authorities as they are expected to do. The Securities and Exchange Commission and the U.S. Justice Department are investigating. Wal-Mart has acknowledged the problem and is conducting its own extensive investigation, which it says may unearth bribery in other locations.[36] The company is also cooperating with government investigators and is beefing up its training, auditing, and internal controls including hiring staff devoted to insuring that the company is abiding by the FCPA.[37]

Companies with generally good corporate reputations are not immune to the bribery problem. In an attempt to avoid prosecution, more of them are self-reporting to the authorities when they learn of a problem. For example, in 2007 Johnson & Johnson voluntarily notified the U.S. Department of Justice of payments made to foreign officials in its medical device business, and a senior executive was forced to step down.[38]

American businesspeople generally prefer to conduct business in a way that's consistent with U.S. and local law and not to make illegal payments to anyone. But despite local laws, the centuries-old custom of bribes and payoffs continues in many cultures.[39] American businesspeople thus often feel that they are at a competitive disadvantage if they don't make such payments, especially if competitors make them. Some have argued that U.S. firms cannot compete effectively when they are constrained by the FCPA while companies in other countries are not.[40] For example, one study found that U.S. direct investment and exports declined in so-called corrupt countries after the FCPA was passed, whereas investments and exports in these same countries increased for non-U.S. competitor companies.[41] After lobbying by U.S. multinational companies, the FCPA was amended in 1988 to include a provision requiring U.S. presidents to seek international cooperation in reducing corruption. As a result, a number of international efforts have been undertaken to level the playing field (these will be discussed below).

In November 2012, the Justice Department and the SEC released a 130-page report on the FCPA to provide guidance to companies about FCPA enforcement practices (see http://www.justice.gov/criminal/fraud/fcpa/guide.pdf for a copy of the report). The report includes many examples that illustrate what is and is not allowable under the current act. Anyone doing business abroad would be wise to read it carefully.

Other countries, especially in Europe, are passing anticorruption laws. For example, Great Britain has made it a crime to pay incentives to win overseas contracts. The Anti-Terrorism, Crime, and Security Act makes it unlawful to bribe foreign officials, including government officials. The more expansive UK Bribery Act, enacted in 2010, has gained the attention of corporate lawyers around the world because it is even more restrictive than the FCPA. It's a complex law but here are a few highlights. It applies to anyone doing business in any part of the United Kingdom (that's most companies), and it prohibits bribery, not just of government officials, but in commercial transactions as well. It also does not allow facilitating payments as the FCPA does. Finally, receiving or accepting a bribe is also outlawed.[42]

In 1999, Germany joined the international convention banning bribery. In addition, both France and Germany now prohibit tax deductions for "commissions" paid to foreign officials or executives to win business, a formerly legal and common practice. Despite changes to these laws, some companies didn't change their ways. In 2008, Germany's Siemens paid $1.6 billion, the largest fine ever for corporate bribery. A high-level executive testified that he oversaw an annual bribery budget of $40 to $50 million from 2002 to 2006. The case was pursued by both German prosecutors and American authorities because the company trades on the New York Stock Exchange. The total cost to Siemens is estimated at $2.6 billion to account for the costs of internal investigations and reforms in addition to the fine.[43]

Where governments have been slow to respond, multinational companies often take matters into their own hands, creating strong codes of conduct, compliance programs to guide their employees, and strong internal financial controls. The companies do this largely because they recognize the potential damage bribery scandals can bring to their company's brand image and reputation in today's highly transparent world.[44]

The Conference Board (a NY-based member organization of business leaders that conducts independent research) released a report that recommends that companies wishing to successfully avoid problems with corruption adopt a strategy to do the following: clearly prohibit bribery, assign senior executives responsibility for oversight, train employees in legal requirements, establish a safe reporting system for suspected violations, discipline violators, conduct due diligence to ensure that joint venture partners, consultants, or any other agents employed by the company are following the rules, include such rules in contracts with partners, and make it clear that business partners are not to employ subcontractors without the company's permission.[45]

Some American companies have actually contended that the FCPA helps them because if they come under pressure for kickbacks or bribes, they can cite the law. And more companies have been working to convince locals of the benefits of playing by the rules. One clear benefit is that business flows to places that have controlled corruption. For example, a study by the International Monetary Fund found that the higher the level of corruption, the lower the level of direct foreign investment.[46] Hong Kong became a leading international financial center largely because of its reputation for rules and integrity. Corruption has been kept in check by a powerful local law enforcement agency called the Independent Commission Against Corruption (ICAC) that was given broad powers to control corruption and white-collar crime. The ICAC established the nonprofit Hong Kong Ethics Development Center in 1995. The center provides a number of services to businesses, including consultation on developing codes of conduct, training for staff, and seminars on ethics (see http://www.icac.org .hk/en/home/index.html for more information).[47]

The World Bank reported in 2004 that more than $1 trillion dollars is actually paid in bribes annually, worldwide. But they noted that countries that reduce corruption (Botswana, Chile, Costa Rica, and Slovenia are recent examples) significantly increase per capita income (see www.worldbank.org). Corruption can add huge costs to an international project. In a survey conducted by a London international business risk consultancy, almost 10 percent of respondents said that corruption could account for between 25 and 50 percent of the total cost of a project, and some said that figure could be even higher![48]

Increasing attention has been focused on corruption by Transparency International (TI), a nongovernmental international organization founded in 1993 (see www .transparency.org). TI aims to "support global integrity systems both nationally and on the international level." Since 1995, the organization has published an annual Corruption Perception Index (CPI), based on multiple international surveys of business-people, political analysts, and the general public, that measures perceptions of corruption in the public sector.[49] The 2012 index includes 176 countries for which data were available. Countries are ranked from 0 to 100 with those closest to 100 being the least corrupt and those closest to 0 being the most corrupt (Table 11.1 is a selected list of the least and most corrupt countries in the 2012 survey). Before considering doing business in any country, it would be wise to check its status on the corruption index.

Publication of the CPI has often had a profound political impact in countries listed as highly corrupt, because government leaders react strongly to the results. These leaders are aware of the relationship between perceived corruption and direct foreign investment. They know that investors are less likely to invest in countries with poor governance and high corruption. Imagine trying to do business in a country where bribery is required to get goods off the dock, contracts are not honored, and intellectual

Table 11.1 Transparency International Corruption Index, 2012. The least and most corrupt countries (see www.transparency.org for complete list)

Least Corrupt		Most Corrupt	
Country	2012 Score	Country	2012 Score
Denmark	90	Somalia	8
Finland	90	Korea (North)	8
New Zealand	90	Afghanistan	8
Sweden	88	Sudan	13
Singapore	87	Myanmar	15
Switzerland	86	Uzbekistan	17
Australia	85	Turkmenistan	17
Norway	85	Iraq	18
Canada	84	Venezuela	19
Netherlands	84	Haiti	19
Iceland	82	Chad	19
Luxembourg	80	Burundi	19
Germany	79	Zimbabwe	20
Hong Kong	77	Equatorial Guinea	20
Barbados	76	Libya	21
Belgium	75	Laos	21

property is routinely stolen. Some of these leaders are taking action, working with national chapters of Transparency International to reduce corruption levels.[50]

Some really interesting initiatives have emerged in some of the most corrupt countries. Indonesia has traditionally not fared well on the CPI, and it has undertaken a number of anticorruption initiatives. For example, it has opened thousands of cashier-free "honesty cafes" in schools and government offices, and more are planned for the private sector. These cafes work on the honor system with the goal of motivating honesty in participants. Customers take drinks and foods from the shelves and deposit money into a clear box. The cafes are reportedly working quite well in most locations. Teachers are even reporting less cheating in classes at the schools involved.[51]

In response to the CPI, observers noted that "it takes two parties for bribes to occur," suggesting that those who pay bribes should be considered corrupt as well. As a result, Transparency International began to publish the Bribe Payers Index (BPI) that ranks 28 leading exporting countries by the perception that their firms engage in bribery when doing business overseas. In its BPI 2011, TI cited particularly high levels of perceived bribery by companies from Russia, China, Mexico, and Indonesia. The United States was tenth among those least likely to bribe (www.transparency.org). Importantly, bribe paying was seen as most problematic in certain industries such as public works contracts and construction.

Transparency International also now publishes a report called the Global Corruption Barometer (also on its website), which is a public opinion survey of respondents across

100 countries and their perceptions about whether the private sector uses bribes to influence public sector decision making. Over half of the more than 100,000 respondents in 2011 perceived that private sector corruption was increasing. In addition, many see government efforts to reduce corruption as ineffective.

How Different Are Ethical Standards in Different Cultures—Really?

As we've just seen from our discussion of bribery, business "practices" certainly differ from culture to culture. There's no denying that bribery is more rampant in some places than others. But that doesn't mean ethical values and standards differ. Even in the most corrupt environments, if you ask people what they value, they'll say that they value honesty and would prefer to live in a less corrupt environment. The honesty cafes discussed earlier are a good example of that. Our international MBA students have also told us about strong ethical cultures that exist in the midst of corrupt surroundings. These individuals talk with pride about having worked in a corporate environment that supported honest business dealings. So we think it's important to distinguish between common practices and values because if you, as a manager, understand that most people share such values as honesty, respect, and fairness, you can appeal to those values and aspirations in managing business ethics overseas.

Certain ethical standards and values are accepted in all human societies. For example, the prescriptions "thou shalt not kill" and "thou shalt not steal" are universal. Furthermore, the Golden Rule, "do unto others as you would have them do unto you," appears in the teachings of every major religion from Judaism to Buddhism.

Buddhism: "Hurt not others in ways that you yourself would find hurtful."

Christianity: "Whatsoever you wish that men would do to you, do so to them, for this is the law of the prophets."

Confucianism: Tsze-Kung asked, saying, "Is there one word which may serve as a rule of practice for all one's life?" The Master said: "Is not reciprocity such a word? What you do not want done to yourself, do not do to others."

Hinduism: "This is the sum of duty: Do naught to others which would cause pain if done to you."

Islam: "No one of you is a believer until he desires for his brother that which he desires for himself."

Judaism: "What is hateful to you, do not to your fellow man. This is the entire Law: all the rest is commentary."[52]

These commonalities suggest a basis for common understanding across cultures. But it's important to recognize that values may also be interpreted differently in different cultures. For example, most cultures value honesty, but its meaning may differ from culture to culture. The notion of *caveat emptor* ("buyer beware") is considered dishonest and therefore wrong in the United States, but it may simply be considered good business in other cultures. Justice and fairness are also universal human values. But specific beliefs and preferences about what is fair vary widely. For example, people in some cultures follow an equity rule (outcomes should depend on performance inputs), while others prefer an equality rule (equal shares should be distributed). Still others believe resources should be distributed based on need. So it is essential to understand the meaning of values and how they are interpreted within the culture.[53]

In 1992, David Vogel argued that a substantial "ethics gap" existed and that U.S. companies were more interested in ethics than firms from the rest of the developed world.[54] Recent developments, however, suggest increasing interest in business ethics in many other countries and increasing similarities across countries in terms of enacting anti-bribery, environmental, and sexual harassment legislation and prosecuting illegal conduct. For example, in Great Britain, reports on British business practice identify business ethics as important, and a number of organizations and interest groups are raising and investigating business ethics issues.[55] In Europe and Scandinavia, many companies are regularly reporting on their environmental and sustainability practices.[56] In addition, the European Business Ethics Network (EBEN, www.eben-net.org), established in 1987, now has multiple chapters in different areas of Europe and members representing 44 countries. EBEN members focus on promoting ethical awareness and business ethics education and training as well as improving business practice. In 1999, the Business Ethics Network of Africa (BEN-Africa, www.benafrica.org) was launched and now has a number of national chapters and members in different African countries. The organization is committed to sharing information and expertise on business ethics among its members.

European firms also tend to take social responsibility, and especially sustainability, very seriously. But concern for the environment has increased in Asia as well. Because of its huge environmental problems and their increasingly negative impact, China has become particularly interested in environmental issues in recent years. It is investing in solar energy, wind turbines, and fuel cell technology and has adopted stringent fuel economy standards for automobiles. Companies selling cars there are figuring out how to profit from producing and selling fuel-efficient vehicles. Other companies are counting on China as a huge new customer for technologies such as clean coal technology and energy-saving building materials.[57] As interest in business ethics and social responsibility increases internationally, the message seems to be that those involved in international business need to stay informed about the rapidly changing sociopolitical, legal, and ethical landscapes in the countries where they work and do business.

Development of Corporate Guidelines and Policies for Global Business Ethics

Given the wide diversity of legal requirements and the continued existence of cultural differences and corruption, firms doing business abroad have a responsibility to develop guidelines and policies to guide their employees' ethical conduct.

ETHICAL IMPERIALISM OR ETHICAL RELATIVISM We learned in Chapter 7 about our "multiple ethical selves"—the idea that people are frequently willing to accept different rules for different contexts. When applied to the international business ethics environment, the concept becomes ethical relativism. "When in Rome, do as the Romans do" is the guiding slogan of ethical relativists, who claim that "no culture has a better ethics than any other"[58] and we shouldn't impose our standards on others. Tom Donaldson, a leading business ethicist and an expert in international business ethics, argues convincingly that ethical relativism must be rejected because, at the extreme, relativists would have to honor any practice that is accepted within another culture.[59] A pure ethical relativist would have to accept slave labor, the dumping of toxic wastes, and even murder if local customs called for those practices.

But Donaldson also rejects the opposite of ethical relativism—ethical imperialism.[60] Ethical imperialism assumes absolute truths that would require exactly the same standards and behavior in every culture. An absolutist would have to choose a single standard as the best for all situations. However, how would one choose between the American belief that individual liberty is a more important value than loyalty to a community and the Japanese belief that loyalty comes before liberty? Donaldson also points out that ethical imperialism can lead to disastrous mistakes. He offers the example of a large U.S. firm operating in China. When an employee was caught stealing, the manager followed company policy and turned the employee over to provincial authorities, who immediately executed the employee.

So how can companies help their employees to balance these extremes of ethical relativism and absolutism? First, Donaldson proposes that firms develop an "ethical threshold" for corporate behavior abroad based on a few core values—for example, the Golden Rule, respect for human dignity, respect for basic human rights, and good citizenship—that will guide its behavior everywhere.[61] These generalities then must be translated into more specific guidelines. For example, companies can respect human dignity by treating employees, customers, and suppliers as persons with intrinsic value and by creating safe products and a safe workplace. They can respect human rights by protecting employees' and customers' rights. And they can be good citizens by avoiding corruption and protecting the natural environment.

Some activities would not be allowed, because they cross the ethical threshold. Levi Strauss's global sourcing guidelines are a good example. They were adopted in 1992 to ensure that products were being produced in a manner consistent with the corporation's values. The first guideline bans the use of child labor. Others limit working hours and mandate safe working conditions and environmental responsibility. Implementing a company's standards, such as a ban on child labor, can be quite complicated, however. For example, Levi Strauss found that two contractors in Bangladesh used workers who appeared to be under the age of 14, the age set as reasonable by international standards. In analyzing the situation, the firm realized that there was no proof of age for these children and that the children contributed substantially to their families' income. Firing them might push them into more inhumane work such as begging or prostitution and create hardship for their families. To comply with Levi's standards, the contractor hired a physician who used growth charts to identify the underage children, and they were removed from the factory. The contractor continued to pay these children wages as if they were still working, and Levi Strauss paid for uniforms, tuition, and books so that they could attend school. At the age of 14, they would be rehired. The contractor also agreed not to hire additional underage workers. The contractor was willing to comply with Levi Strauss's standards in order to continue doing business with the firm.

But, adhering to standards higher than those of competitors increases costs. Contractors have to add emergency exits and staircases, improve ventilation or bathroom facilities, and install water treatment systems. These costs are passed along to the firm and, ultimately, to consumers. Management therefore must believe that decisions focused only on costs will not serve the company's long-term interests.[62]

Also, once a company decides which values it is going to uphold in an overseas environment, it has to decide how to actually make that happen. As an example, a number of European and American companies are learning the hard way about the potential damage to their brand images as they deal with the aftermath of the 2013 Rana Plaza building collapse in Bangladesh that killed more than 1,000 people in a factory that produced clothing for some well-known brands. The factory was located on floors that were added illegally (perhaps due to bribery) and workers were ordered to work despite their fears about cracks in the building. The minimum wage in Bangladesh is $38 per month, much less than in China and other countries. So, financial costs are low. But, in this case, the human cost was huge and one would think that a responsible company would want to avoid any unnecessary loss of human life.

As a pragmatic minimum, companies should assess whether the reputational risk of using factories in a particular locale is worth the savings. And, even if the cost-benefit analysis is favorable, where would an ethical analysis lead? It would certainly require that the firm know what the working conditions are. It would also require decisions about the company's responsibilities if it is going to do business there. In the aftermath of the Bangladesh factory collapse, some companies are joining with their competitors to set up systems designed to insure worker safety while others are deciding to go it alone. These are very complex issues requiring much deliberation. In other kinds of ethical situations, values may be in conflict, but cultural traditions do not violate any of the core human values. In those situations, Donaldson proposes that managers respect cultural traditions and take the context into account when deciding what is right and wrong.[63]

For example, gift giving is an important part of the Japanese culture. An absolutist might judge gift giving to be wrong. However, a corporate ethics code that respects local traditions would likely allow some forms of gift giving and receiving and would provide managers with specific guidance to help them differentiate between acceptable and unacceptable gift-giving situations. Gift giving does not violate a core value as long as there are limits on its scope and intention, and it remains within legal guidelines. For example, many firms allow employees to receive gifts of nominal value but require them to explain that the gift will be accepted on behalf of the organization and will be displayed for all employees to see or perhaps given to charity.

Similarly, many U.S. firms have rules against nepotism because they believe that the act of hiring and supervising one's family members presents an inappropriate conflict of interest. However, in cultures that have a deeper tradition of extended family and clan loyalty (collectivistic cultures), nepotism is not only approved, but expected. Companies are expected to hire employees' children, for example. Donaldson argues that although nepotism conflicts with Western concepts of equal employment opportunity, it is not necessarily wrong when viewed from the perspective of a culture that values family relationships and has high unemployment. Therefore it may be appropriate to hire family members as long as they are not in supervisory relationships with each other that would generate conflicts of interest.

Companies struggle to create codes and ethics management systems that are truly global or adaptable to the cultures in which they operate. In managing ethics across cultures, one area of challenge concerns hotlines for reporting misconduct. U.S. employees are often reluctant to report misconduct using such a reporting system because they fear negative consequences such as retaliation, but overseas employees are often even more reluctant to report. We suggested earlier that collectivists may find such systems too impersonal. In addition, in a number of countries (China, Germany, France, South Africa), whistleblowers are associated with historical horrors such as informants turning in their friends or family members. This has led individuals in these countries to resist the introduction of corporate reporting systems. And in countries with little job mobility, employees are likely to fear retaliation for questioning management decisions.

Beyond protecting employees from retaliation (as important in the United States as it is overseas), international business ethics experts recommend introducing help lines that are oriented more toward providing guidance (rather than reporting misconduct) so that employees can develop trust in the system and the people who run it. They also recommend tailoring the message about reporting to the particular culture and history, providing local resources for training, guidance, and reporting rather than a single headquarters system. Finally, they recommend involving senior international managers in the design of these systems so that they can be designed to fit the culture and local needs.[64]

Perhaps most important, organizations must take care to match their performance appraisal and reward systems for overseas employees to ethical goals. If ethical conduct is the goal, the organization must make it clear that the expatriate manager will not be punished, either explicitly or implicitly, for upholding the organization's ethical standards—even if it costs the organization business. Because it's difficult, if not impossible, to monitor expatriate managers or representatives' behavior from afar, organizations tend to focus on outcomes (the bottom line) to evaluate the expatriate's performance. For example, they set sales or production goals and evaluate performance in light of goal achievement. However, if the organization focuses only on outcomes and pays no attention to how those outcomes are achieved, the expatriate manager is likely to do the same, and ethical goals are more likely to be compromised.

A study found that individuals are more likely to report that their firm is involved in bribery when they perceive financial constraints and an intensely competitive business environment.[65] In such environments, it is even more important for the organization to recognize the ethical dilemmas employees are likely to face, openly acknowledge that lost business is a possibility if the employee rejects bribery requests, and reward employees for conducting business within ethical guidelines (or at least not punish them for doing so). Such a message was sent loudly and clearly in the case of the Lockheed Martin manager who received the first annual Chairman's Award for exemplary integrity. You may recall from Chapter 6, a manager who received an inappropriate "request for payment" from a foreign official not only rejected the request, but removed Lockheed Martin from the bidding process (walking away from an important contract), reported the problem to senior officials, and worked with both U.S. government officials and the foreign government to have the foreign official removed from the decision-making process. Instead of being punished for potentially losing an important contract, this manager was rewarded publicly by the chairman of the board.

By talking about aligning global codes and reward systems, we are essentially recommending that companies develop a global ethical culture that will guide employee behavior. They should first establish their core values and then take cultural differences into account in prescribing specific behavior in areas of cultural difference such as gift giving and nepotism.

In addition to providing guidance to employees through a code, a help line, and performance management, one U.S. executive who talked with us about these issues emphasized the importance of explaining to overseas business partners why you're required to behave in a particular way. Make it clear that this behavior is required by your home culture and laws and your company's values and code of conduct, and request your business partners' respect and cooperation. You are more likely to succeed if you are a large company with products that are particularly desirable. If so, you are in more of a position to dictate the terms of doing business. But, if you represent a small company with little leverage, you can expect to have more difficulty and you may want to think long and hard before getting involved if the culture is particularly corrupt.

THE ORGANIZATION IN A GLOBAL BUSINESS ENVIRONMENT

Although more small businesses are venturing into the global marketplace, large multinational corporations still represent much of international business, and the ethical expectations of them are often greater because of their size and visibility. These corporations face complex business ethics environments that vary widely from country to country. In addition to the stakeholders normally considered in any ethical business decision, the number of stakeholders grows to include host governments, foreign suppliers, agents, and other organizations. International law is often not particularly helpful in guiding business conduct, and it is often unclear whether a particular country's legal system has regulatory authority over global transactions.[66] Therefore a firm's own ethical standards become an important guide for its workers. Multinational corporations also face questions of legitimacy that may cause them to consider whether they should even involve themselves in a foreign culture. If they do decide to do business in a particular foreign environment, what are their responsibilities?

Deciding to Do Business in a Foreign Country

American businesses are aggressively pursuing foreign markets. They face increased competition in the global marketplace, thus requiring them to become cost effective in a variety of ways that include manufacturing goods abroad or buying from foreign suppliers who can often produce goods more cheaply.

THE CHALLENGE TO LEGITIMACY   Numerous ethical challenges accompany these forays into the international business environment. For example, in some environments, the very legitimacy of a company may be challenged by deciding to do business in a certain country. Particularly in developing countries, the company's motives may be questioned. For example, managerial lifestyles may be perceived as overly materialistic, paying local market wages may be viewed as exploitation, and expanding locally may be perceived as furthering control and dependence.[67]

Sometimes companies with good intentions get tripped up doing business overseas because they simply don't understand the perceptions and concerns of their overseas stakeholders. Consider the case of Monsanto and its promotion of genetically modified foods in Europe. The company developed these foods believing that they were good for the environment—they reduce pesticide use, increase crop yields, and promote efficient land use. Although the seeds are more expensive, yields are greater and farmers save on insecticides and herbicides. The company had experienced great success in the United States, easily winning regulatory approval for these products and increasing sales. Science was supportive, showing that genetically modified food was safe, and the World Health Organization agreed. Taking the products to Europe seemed the obvious thing to do.

However, the introduction of genetically modified foods in Europe was initially a disaster, and the company paid dearly for its failure to anticipate stakeholder reactions abroad. Fears about possible long-term health effects drew strong negative reactions and protests from a variety of vocal activist nongovernmental organizations (NGOs) such as Greenpeace, as well as individual critics including Prince Charles and Paul McCartney, who told the world to "say no to GMO" (genetically modified organisms). The European public supported the environmental movement's call to prohibit these products. Supermarkets banned the resulting products, and the European Union issued a moratorium on planting the seeds. For years, huge financial losses and a falling stock price were attributed to this negative stakeholder reaction and the company's failure to respond effectively. The situation has since turned around, in part because the company began to soften its stance and engage its critics more, including publishing formerly secret research in peer-reviewed journals where scientists could evaluate the work. Like other smart companies, Monsanto is now working with its critics, finding common ground and more acceptance of its products overseas. It also helped that the company began to focus on commodity products (corn, soybeans, cotton, canola) that are sold to other businesses rather than directly to the consumer and that none of the feared health disasters has yet occurred.[68]

What happened? First, Monsanto didn't understand the European environment and the fact that Europeans don't trust their regulators the way Americans do (or did).

Europe had recently experienced the "mad cow disease" crisis that raised questions about the adequacy of food safety regulation. Second, Monsanto didn't educate the European public or consult with activists in advance. Europeans heard about genetically modified foods first from Greenpeace, an environmental organization that opposed these products. The Europeans reacted with anger, believing that these products were being imposed upon them by a powerful American corporation.[69] Monsanto was initially tone deaf to these concerns, relying on the science rather than understanding and taking seriously Europeans' fears and concerns.

Differences in sociopolitical environments also raise a host of ethical questions. Should American companies invest in, or do business in, countries with corrupt public officials or companies that practice racial discrimination, allow gender discrimination, pollute the environment, or violate the human rights of their citizens through slave or child labor or inhumane working conditions? Does doing business in these countries or with these organizations tarnish a company's ethical reputation simply by association? Is it all right to do business in the country as long as the company avoids engaging in the unethical practices itself? Furthermore, is it all right to do business in a country if the company creates and sticks to its own standards regarding issues such as discrimination, pollution, or safety?

For example, should a company that manufactures children's sleepwear meet U.S. safety (fire hazard) standards when selling this product in countries that do not have such strict standards? Some firms routinely go beyond required local standards. But other firms take the absence of standards as license to behave unethically. For example, most developing countries require no health warnings on packages of cigarettes. As more and more restrictions have been placed on tobacco companies in the United States and other developed countries, firms such as Philip Morris have increased their marketing efforts in the developing world, often targeting women and young people in these efforts. This has been especially true since Philip Morris International (PMI) was spun off from its U.S. parent, Altria.

Companies should also consider consumers' concerns. Concerned citizens and organizations have put the plight of farmers in developing countries on the radar screen (see http://transfairusa.org). For example, they are promoting coffee that has earned the "fair trade" label, meaning that farmers who produced the beans were fairly compensated. Sales of fair trade coffee such as the Green Mountain brand have grown substantially in the last few years but remain a small percentage of the overall market. Increasingly, consumers say that corporate citizenship influences their buying habits. But the fair trade movement depends on people being willing to pay more for a product in order to feel good about not contributing to the misery of other human beings. The jury is still out on the long-term impact of such movements, but they do appear to be growing.[70]

Many firms are moved to reconsider their overseas ethical standards when media attention turns their way. For example, media attention to sweatshop conditions in overseas factories raised legitimacy questions about a number of large corporations. As globalization continues to expand and the world continues to shrink, companies that ignore working conditions in their own factories or in suppliers' factories risk their valuable reputations. In fact, one of the biggest changes in this arena involves companies' attention to ethical issues in their extended supply chains. Companies know they can no longer get away with saying that they didn't know what was going on or that they aren't responsible for what suppliers do.[71] Video cameras take consumers inside factories that for many years were out of sight and out of mind. And the Internet quickly spreads the news that often is then picked up by activist groups and media organizations.

In early 2013, Wal-Mart warned its global suppliers that they will be dropped if they are found to have subcontracted to factories that Wal-Mart has not authorized. This zero tolerance move came after a deadly fire at a factory in Bangladesh that was found to be manufacturing clothing for Wal-Mart without being authorized to do so. The fire brought increased public scrutiny on Wal-Mart and pressure to monitor supply chains much more closely and increase safety measures at suppliers' factories.[72]

When consumers learn about the working conditions, they demand change. But deciding how to handle issues such as labor conditions in foreign facilities, especially those that a company doesn't own, is not a simple matter. For example, consider the question of wages. Many well-intentioned protestors argue that U.S. firms should pay "first world" wages to employees in developing countries. But the developing countries themselves often oppose this stance because they know that their competitive advantage depends on the lower costs multinational companies can achieve by hiring their workers. So extending U.S. or European pay levels to these settings could result in shutting down factories, and that would hurt people rather than help them. Similarly, migrant workers in China have complained about codes that don't allow them to work as many hours as they would like. They want to work more so that they can save enough money to return to their villages.[73] Finally, child labor is an important source of income for many families in developing countries and can help keep families together as well as keep children from begging or resorting to prostitution. We are certainly not endorsing child labor or slave wages. But we do want to make clear that there are no easy answers.

Companies are increasingly aware that they need to evaluate ethical issues and risks before deciding to do business in a country or linking with a supplier or agent. Some companies, such as Hewlett-Packard, are developing supplier codes of conduct.[74] Other companies are combining forces with others in their industry to address common problems and reduce the cost of doing so. For example, Nike, Gap, Patagonia, and other companies and nonprofits have worked together to develop safety standards and an inspection system, and companies in the electronics industry have joined together to create an Electronic Industry Code of conduct.[75]

HISTORICAL EXAMPLE: DOING BUSINESS IN SOUTH AFRICA   Before South Africa dismantled its long-standing policies of strict racial segregation (apartheid) about two decades ago, the question of whether to do business in that country was a prominent ethical issue for multinational businesses. Some U.S. firms chose to stay out of South Africa completely during the apartheid years. Many companies felt pressured to do so by institutional investors, such as pension funds, that prohibited investment in companies doing business in South Africa. Others elected to do business there while adhering to the Sullivan Principles, a list of standards for U.S. multinationals doing business in South Africa that was drafted by Leon Sullivan, an African American minister. These principles called for integration of the races in work facilities, equal and fair employment practices, equal pay for equal work, training programs to prepare nonwhites for higher-level jobs, the movement of nonwhites into those jobs, and contribution to the quality of employees' life outside of work.[76]

Levi Strauss, as part of global training on ethics, taught managers how to use a decision tool called the principled reasoning approach. A cross-functional and multinational task force that met over several months used the approach to decide whether to enter the South African marketplace. Members conducted research on the history of apartheid, identified stakeholders, visited South Africa, and interviewed members of the government and community organizations. The task force recommended that it would be appropriate to enter the South African marketplace under certain conditions, including free elections.[77]

Such decisions can have long-term implications, however. In 2002, long after apartheid was dismantled, apartheid victims in South Africa began suing U.S.-based banks and other companies that conducted business in South Africa under the apartheid system. The lawsuits charge that the companies helped the South African government commit crimes against South African citizens. The lawsuits are based on a precedent established by lawsuits brought on behalf of Holocaust victims against Swiss companies, resulting in a $1.25 billion settlement. Similar lawsuits charge companies with liability for a number of human rights abuses in the developing world. For example, victim advocates claim that Unocal was aware that peasants were forced at gunpoint to help build a pipeline in Burma and that those who resisted were tortured or killed. Unocal denies the claim.[78] Whether or not the companies are "guilty," they are likely to be expending significant resources fighting such lawsuits for years.

HISTORICAL EXAMPLE: MARKETING INFANT FORMULA IN THE DEVELOPING WORLD Once engaged in business in a foreign country, companies must also consider whether practices that are perfectly acceptable at home are appropriate in the foreign environment. This is perhaps best exemplified in the now classic case of marketing infant formula in developing countries, particularly in the 1970s and early 1980s. The Swiss conglomerate Nestlé was singled out among companies that were engaging in practices that encouraged new mothers in these countries to give up breastfeeding and switch to formula.[79]

In addition to more routine advertising that inaccurately suggested that bottle-fed babies would be healthier, companies used so-called milk nurses to promote their products in maternity wards. These women, though dressed as nurses, were actually sales representatives who received a commission for selling formula.

Unfortunately, the switch to formula posed a serious health risk to the infants—for three reasons. First, the formula must be mixed with water, which is contaminated in many of these areas. Infants fed the formula were thus at high risk for infections and diarrhea. Second, mothers in these areas often cannot afford to continue buying formula. Therefore, they dilute it or substitute cheaper products that contribute to health problems such as malnourishment for their babies. Finally, and perhaps most important, women who give up breastfeeding cannot simply change their minds and return to it. After a short time, their own milk production diminishes, and they are no longer able to feed their babies themselves. They are forced to rely on formula. In response to organized protests and boycotts from numerous activist groups, the company finally agreed to alter its marketing practices.

Although some might argue that the marketing practices just described would be questionable even at home (given the known health benefits of breast milk), they would not as seriously compromise babies' health here as they would in a developing country because of the availability of clean water. Thus the very same practice could be considered ethical in one setting (assuming that consumers had solid information to inform their choice) but highly unethical in another.

CURRENT EXAMPLES: WHAT TO DO ABOUT HUMAN RIGHTS   Once a firm decides to do business in a developing country, human rights issues should be on the radar screen. Worldwide, companies seem to be converging to prohibit forced or child labor (especially bonded labor, in which small children are required to work to pay off family debts) and to address other issues such as worker safety. But a company that decides to hold itself accountable for protecting human rights in its overseas operations (including those of its suppliers) is taking on a tough task with no easy answers.

Nike has about 44,000 employees globally and many more who are employed by its suppliers in multiple countries to create sports and fitness footwear, apparel, equipment, and accessories for worldwide distribution. In the 1990s, the firm was the target of Internet and media campaigns, boycotts on college campuses, and protests outside its stores because of sweatshop conditions in suppliers' overseas factories. In 1998, the founder and CEO, Phil Knight, acknowledged the problem and decided to take it on. The company published its first corporate responsibility report in October 2001. In its discussion of the efforts it was taking to ameliorate current working conditions, the company criticized itself, acknowledging that work in its factories was hard, workers were sometimes harassed, and the company's monitoring system needed improvement.

The company continued to work at it, sending auditors to evaluate conditions and enforce the company code. In 2005, in the interest of full transparency, Nike released factory names and locations—and was the first in its industry to do so. It also brought in an MIT professor to assess its audit data. The results were disappointing. Most suppliers' factories had not improved, and some had even gotten worse. So, by itself, monitoring wasn't working. Along the same lines, a 2008 report in *Fortune* magazine highlighted a Malaysian T-shirt factory where, it seemed, little had changed. Migrant workers were housed in crowded, dirty conditions and had been required to turn over their passports until recruiting fees (subtracted from their wages) were paid off. But this time Nike responded quickly, admitting publicly that a serious breach of its conduct code had occurred. It reimbursed workers and paid to relocate them. It then held a meeting with representatives from 30 Malaysian contract factories to engage in tough talk about enforcing its standards. When the company drops a supplier, it recognizes that local jobs are lost, perhaps harming employees even more. The current CEO, Mark Parker, said "I'm proud of what we've accomplished, but we're still not where we need to be. This is a never-ending challenge." According to *Fortune*, Nike's slogan, "Just Do It," applies.[80]

In its ongoing attempts to address the labor problem, Nike has its social responsibility staff going beyond surface issues to search for the root causes of problems. In doing so, Nike learned that it had more leverage with long-term suppliers and suppliers that depended largely on Nike for their revenue. This meant that leverage was higher in the shoe business than in the apparel business, where the company tends to have shorter-term contracts. Nike is trying some unique approaches that completely change its outsourcing model. One goal is to convert suppliers to team-based, lean manufacturing that requires a higher-skilled labor force that the supplier will want to care for. Another is to avoid last-minute design changes that pressure suppliers toward violations like requiring excessive overtime. The company goal was to eliminate all excessive overtime in its suppliers' factories by 2011. Nike also aims to partner more with other brands to address these issues. In addition to efforts to fight labor abuses, *Fortune* reports that Nike has made big strides in sustainability, enlisting its shoe designers and challenging them to reduce waste and use greener materials. You can learn much more about Nike's efforts by reading its corporate social responsibility report online at www.nikebiz.com.

Research has highlighted model programs that companies have put into place over the past few years to respond to the challenges they recognize as resulting from the globalization process. For example, Reebok (now part of the Adidas group) implemented a program to ensure that Pakistani children are not involved in the manufacture of its soccer balls in Sialkot, Pakistan. Instead of having the panels stitched in villages (where children were often involved), the company set up factories where production could be monitored. The company also created a program that works toward placing children in schools so that they are kept out of the labor pool (see www.adidas-group .com). Sounds good, right? It is. But consider the complexities. These families have now lost the income that the children would have generated by working. Many firms are recognizing this challenge and are requiring suppliers who hire children not only to place them in educational programs but also to continue paying the youths their average daily wage while they are in school. Adidas has also been successful in doing this with its suppliers in Vietnam.[81]

Companies concerned about workplace conditions in their manufacturing facilities realize that they cannot solve these problems alone. For help, they can refer to the Universal Declaration of Human Rights and can get assistance from a number of organizations including the Fair Labor Association and Social Accountability International (SAI). A number of high-profile companies are members of the Fair Labor Association (FLA), including Adidas, American Eagle, H&M, New Balance, Patagonia, and Nike. By joining the association, companies subscribe to its code of conduct and commit to compliance with international labor standards in their supply chains. A large number of colleges and universities have also signed on with the FLA to promote fair working conditions in the production of collegiate apparel that bears their logo. They do this to ensure that their apparel is not being produced under sweatshop conditions. If you're a college student, check to see if your college or university is listed (www.fairlabor.org) and explore what is required of licensees.

Social Accountability International (see www.sa-intl.org was founded in 1997 to help organizations be socially accountable in the arena of workplace conditions (e.g., child labor, forced labor, health and safety, discrimination, etc.). The organization developed a standard called Social Accountability 8000 (SA8000) and a social auditing system for verifying compliance with these objective standards. The system, modeled after the well-known ISO 9000 quality initiative, was developed with input from an international advisory board that included experts from multiple sectors of society, including unions, businesses, and nongovernmental organizations. Its standards are based on shared norms regarding international human rights. Facilities can be "certified" as being in compliance with SA8000, meaning that the facility has been audited and found to conform to the standards.

CURRENT EXAMPLE: CLEANING UP THE JEWELRY BUSINESS Tiffany's, the upscale jewelry retailer, had been concerned about its supply chain since the late 1990s, when human rights groups accused the company of selling "blood diamonds" thought to be traded by African rebel groups to finance their civil wars. Turning its attention to gold, the company learned that attempting to ferret out where gold comes from is extremely difficult. It is mined in more than 60 countries in a very fragmented industry. Suppliers were simply unable to tell Tiffany where the gold was coming from, so the company decided to purchase all of its gold from a single mine. Tiffany's CEO didn't stop there. He has worked to bring activists and jewelers together, supported studies of mining practices, and expressed opposition to new mines in environmentally sensitive places. Two new organizations have emerged to help jewelers deal with the issue: the Responsible Jewelry Council and the Initiative for Responsible Mining Assurance.

The problem is more challenging for companies that don't produce their own jewelry. But they're getting on board too. For example, Wal-Mart is pressuring miners to follow strict environmental and social standards that can be verified, and the firm is tracking its gold through the supply chain with the help of a British company that specializes in supply chain traceability. Wal-Mart is beginning with modest goals but, according to Pam Mortensen, who is in charge of jewelry buying at Wal-Mart, "if we don't start somewhere, we won't get anywhere."[82]

Whatever the ethics or corporate social responsibility issue, companies large and small are finding that they must take responsibility for their extended supply chains and engage more with the links in the chain, including those they never would have interacted with before. In the last few years, safety of imported products (especially from China) has become a huge issue. In the United States, we've experienced pet food with deadly melamine, lead and cadmium-tainted toys, unsafe tires, contaminated seafood, antifreeze-laced toothpaste, and drywall that made houses inhabitable. The list goes on. Mattel was forced to recall almost a million lead-tainted toys in 2007.

Importers that care about their reputations can no longer afford to think about these as arms-length relationships. They certainly can't wait for someone to die before they act. They must be increasingly vigilant, including drawing up detailed contracts, monitoring suppliers (and their suppliers), and conducting testing on products before selling them.[83]

CURRENT EXAMPLE: HELP FOR THE DEVELOPING WORLD The World Bank estimates that nearly half the world's population survives (barely) on $2 per day or less. These people live at what is called "the bottom of the wealth pyramid," and their plight has proven difficult to overcome. Muhammad Yunus, a Bangladeshi and an economics professor, won the Nobel Peace Prize in 2006 for inventing the idea of using microcredit to spur economic development in a way that helps those at the base of the pyramid become self-sufficient. He also received the Presidential Medal of Freedom from Barack Obama in 2009 for being an international agent of change. The idea is to give small loans to entrepreneurs, especially the poorest women, for the purpose of starting small businesses. Yunus founded Grameen Bank in 1976 and got the idea started by lending $27 of his own money. The idea has been extraordinarily successful. There are now over 2,500 Grameen Bank branches in rural Bangladesh, over 8 million borrowers (96 percent of them women), a loan repayment rate of 90 percent (and that's without collateral), and a profitable bank that actually pays dividends. Borrowers join a five-member group that oversees the loan (although there is no joint liability). The idea has spread to many other developing countries. Companies such as Citigroup and organizations such as the Gates Foundation have gotten involved, and microlending is now a multibillion-dollar industry. For more information, go to www.grameen-info.org.

Building on his original idea, Yunus developed the notion of social business enterprise, an idea that combines corporate interests with microfinance and economic development. He enlisted Danone, the yogurt maker, to give it a try in Bangladesh. The company created a yogurt that was fortified to guard against malnutrition and was affordably priced (only 7 cents each). The factory depends on Grameen microborrowers, who buy cows to sell the factory milk and sell the yogurt door-to-door. Danone agreed to reinvest revenue and take only its initial cost of capital after three years. The enterprise employs many people, thus contributing enormously to the local economy. Organizations such as UNICEF see this as a wonderful way to improve nutrition in the developing world. Danone sees it as an opportunity to do good while exploring a sustainable business model for the future and a way to integrate social responsibility into the global business.[84]

Development of a Transcultural Corporate Ethic

Many businesspeople hope for the day when there will be wide agreement about appropriate business conduct in the global arena. Progress has been made in that direction through the efforts of government organizations, multinational companies, and private organizations interested in international business ethics. But the proliferation of these efforts just increases the complexity and the difficulty of deciding where to turn one's attention.

Movement toward "a transcultural corporate ethic"[85] has occurred as a result of a number of intergovernmental agreements reached during the last 50 years. These agreements set out normative guidelines for the business conduct of multinational corporations. The guidelines that emerge from these agreements cover the areas of employment practices and policies, consumer protection, environmental protection, political payments and involvement, and basic human rights and fundamental freedoms. They are based on four principles:

1. **The inviolability of national sovereignty.** Multinationals are expected to respect the "host country's economic and social development and its cultural and historical traditions."[86]

2. **Social equity.** Pay scales are expected to ensure equity between genders as well as racial and ethnic groups.

3. **Market integrity in business transactions.** Restrictions on political payments and bribes assume that these "inject non-market considerations into business transactions."[87]

4. **Human rights and fundamental freedoms.** This principle is based on belief in the inherent worth and dignity of every individual and the equality of rights of all human beings. However, this principle often competes with other principles, especially the first—national sovereignty. For example, South Africa's apartheid system was based on the denial of human rights to its black citizens, and women continue to be denied rights in many cultures and government systems.

As noted earlier, a number of efforts have also been under way to battle bribery and corruption on a global scale. Perhaps the most important is the Organization for Economic Cooperation and Development (OECD) Anti-Bribery Convention. Negotiators from 33 countries worked together to pass the convention in late 1997. Participating countries included members of the OECD (including nations of North America, Western Europe, and the industrialized democracies of the Pacific) plus Argentina, Brazil, Bulgaria, Chile, and the Slovak Republic. The convention requires signatories to make it a crime to bribe foreign public officials, and it includes the application of criminal penalties. In October, 2002, the OECD reported that 34 countries had already filed their "instrument of ratification" with the secretary-general of the OECD. By 2005, 36 countries had passed anti-bribery laws that make it a crime to bribe a foreign public official. Information about each country's efforts is available on the OECD website (www.oecd.org). An OECD report, also available on the website, cites the convention as "one of the most effective tools against foreign bribery." But the report recognizes that the credibility of the convention depends on rigorous monitoring of the legislation across countries to ensure that it is "adequate and effectively applied." Some argue that the treaty is weak because it does not require minimum penalties, does not ban gifts to political parties, and does not outlaw tax deductibility for bribes. However, it is clearly a step in the right direction.[88] The trend in many multinational companies is to prohibit all types of bribery, especially because laws are becoming more stringent (e.g., the UK Bribery Act). For example, British-based BP's policy exceeds the U.S. Foreign Corrupt Practices Act standard. The company considers small facilitating payments to be bribes and has a policy against paying them.[89] This approach certainly makes the rules clearer for employees and those seeking bribes.

The Organization of American States (OAS) has 35 members, which include all the independent republics of the Americas except Cuba. Most of these members signed the Inter-American Convention Against Corruption, which took force in 1997 (see www.oas.org). This binding treaty does not outlaw bribery, but it does require members to develop policies and practices that aim to reduce corruption.[90]

An important question remains: do these agreements influence multinationals to behave differently? Multinational corporations are not directly bound by these intergovernmental agreements. However, they are indirectly affected to the extent that countries enact laws requiring companies to comply. The agreements may also be contributing to a more informal type of compliance as they contribute to the development of accepted cross-cultural moral standards. The more multinationals become aware of these standards, the more likely they will be to comply.

Business leaders have also been working to develop their own worldwide corporate responsibility standards. The Caux Round Table, a group representing American, European, and Japanese multinationals, began meeting in Caux, Switzerland, in 1986. The group's mission was to focus attention on global corporate responsibility. They developed a set of standards for global business behavior that is based on two principles: human dignity and the Japanese concept of *kyosei*, "the ideal of living and working together for the common good to enable mutual prosperity." Although, again, the standards are not binding, it is hoped that businesses around the world will rely on them to develop their own standards.[91] (See www.cauxroundtable.org for more information about the group).

In an early 1999 speech at the World Economic Forum, UN Secretary-General Kofi Annan proposed the United Nations Global Compact (see www.unglobalcompact.org). He asked the leaders of multinational corporations to join this international initiative, along with UN agencies and other organizations interested in promoting global, values-based management. Annan suggested that an international framework that was built on internationally accepted principles could assist companies in their desire to practice voluntary corporate citizenship in a global economy. The initiative was formally launched in July 2000 in a meeting of senior executives from about 50 large corporations and other leaders from governments and civil society. The United Nations plays the role of convener and facilitator of dialogue and information sharing among these organizations. Membership is open to any organization that is serious about its commitment to the principles. In early 2013, the website (unglobalcompact.org) said that participants from over 7,000 businesses in 145 countries were involved (see www.unglobalcompact.org).[92] Interestingly, tobacco companies are discouraged from participation because of the negative health effects of tobacco.

The primary objective of the compact is to embed good corporate citizenship into corporate-management strategy and decision making and to complement regulatory approaches. The compact uses the power of transparency and dialogue to identify and disseminate good business practices based on ten shared principles in human rights, labor, the environment, and anti-corruption:

Human Rights:

1. Protection of internationally proclaimed human rights
2. Noncomplicity in human rights abuses
3. Support for freedom of association

Labor:

4. Elimination of forced and compulsory labor
5. Effective abolition of child labor
6. Elimination of employment and workplace discrimination

Environment:

7. Support for a precautionary approach to environmental challenges
8. Initiatives to promote greater environmental responsibility
9. Development and diffusion of environmentally friendly technologies

Anti-corruption:

10. Work against corruption

To participate in the compact, company CEOs send a letter of commitment to the United Nations secretary-general and agree to (1) take concrete steps within their organization to act on these principles, (2) share their experiences on the Global Compact website, and (3) advocate publicly for the Global Compact.

Another United Nations initiative, the United Nations Convention against Corruption, was signed in Mexico in December 2003 and took force in December 2005. Preventing corruption is an important goal of the convention. Countries that sign must work to increase transparency in elections and in public service. Public servants must be governed by codes of conduct and must be disciplined for misconduct. Countries also must criminalize various types of corruption, including bribery, money laundering, and embezzlement of public funds. Signatories also agree to cooperate with each other in anticorruption activities and to provide legal assistance on the return of assets.

Companies are taking these international agreements into account in designing codes of conduct for the twenty-first century. A group of Harvard researchers studied the business codes of multinational organizations (i.e., company codes and multinational efforts such as the Caux principles, the OECD guidelines, the UN Global

Compact, and the Global Reporting Initiative, among others) in an attempt to determine what it takes for these codes to meet what they called world-class standards. The researchers found that these codes address eight principles:

1. **Fiduciary principle.** This principle addresses managers' responsibility to act in the best interest of shareholders rather than themselves. Accordingly, codes prohibit behaviors such as conflicts of interest and self-dealing at the organization's expense.

2. **Property principle.** This principle addresses respect for property. Accordingly, codes prohibit behaviors such as theft (including theft of intellectual property) and waste.

3. **Reliability principle.** This principle addresses trust and promise-keeping behaviors that are required for cooperation to occur. Codes call for employees to abide by contracts, and they prohibit breaches of contract and trust.

4. **Transparency principle.** This principle addresses the importance of honesty and respect for truth and openness. Codes call for the accurate representation of information and prohibit behaviors such as misleading stakeholders (e.g., customers, suppliers, etc.).

5. **Dignity principle.** This principle addresses respect for people. Codes call for protection of people's health, safety, and privacy and prohibit human rights abuses.

6. **Fairness principle.** This principle addresses the fair distribution of rewards and burdens. Codes call for fair treatment (including ideas such as equal pay for equal work) and prohibit discrimination.

7. **Citizenship principle.** This principle addresses respect for the law, respect for "the commons" (shared resources, such as the natural environment), and contribution to society overall. Codes call for law-abiding behavior and contributions to society through behaviors such as care for the environment and philanthropy. Prohibited behaviors include bribery, despoiling the natural environment, and improper political activity.

8. **Responsiveness principle.** This principle calls for the organization's responsiveness to its stakeholders that are affected by a company's actions. This includes such behaviors as responding to stakeholder concerns and engaging with stakeholders such as suppliers.

The authors see these principles as representing an emerging consensus about a "core of global standards of conduct" being used by modern corporations to address concerns that arise when doing business in today's global business environment. They recommend that companies use the principles as a starting point for assessing their current code or for developing a new one. They also encourage firms to supplement these principles with material that has its source in the company's own unique values.[93]

CONCLUSION

From the individual's perspective, a foreign assignment is full of ethical challenges. Training and guidance, along with openness and flexibility, can go a long way toward preparing the expatriate manager to survive with integrity and sanity intact—and hopefully to enjoy the richness of the international business experience. Organizations can help their expatriate employees by developing a set of broad core values, as well as specific guidelines and support systems for ethical business practice at home and abroad. Multinational companies are gaining experience in managing these complex issues in a complex, transparent, but shrinking world. The expanding interest in business ethics and social responsibility and the development of international guidelines to guide business behavior across cultural boundaries will help level the playing field and contribute to making the international business experience richer and more satisfying. In the meantime, keeping up with all of the changes can be daunting. That's why we have provided information about a number of useful websites that can help you stay abreast of the complex and dynamic global business ethics environment.

DISCUSSION QUESTIONS

1. If you were going on your first overseas business assignment, what would you do to ensure that you were prepared to deal with ethical dilemmas you would face? What questions would you ask your superiors in preparation for the trip?

2. Your firm is expanding globally and is sending executives overseas for the first time. What will you do to be sure these individuals are prepared to deal with the ethical dilemmas they will face?

3. Imagine that someone from another culture asked you to provide information about business ethics when dealing with American managers. What would you say?

4. Talk with someone from another culture. Ask for information that would be helpful to you if you had to do business in their culture. What did you learn that you didn't know before? How might you behave differently because of what you know?

5. If you were planning to do business in a culture that was opposite from your own on the cultural dimensions of "power distance" and "individualism/collectivism," what challenges would you expect to face? How would you prepare?

6. Imagine yourself in a situation where you had to bribe someone or lose the deal. How would you think about it? What do you think you would do? Why? What would you hope for from your employer?

7. Assume the role of corporate decision maker in a decision about whether to do business in a particular foreign country in the developing world. What criteria will you establish for making the decision from an ethics and social responsibility perspective? Why are these the most important criteria? What information will you use to help you make the decision?

8. What are the costs and benefits of developing a transcultural corporate ethic? Whose responsibility should it be to develop such an ethic—governments, corporations, intergovernmental organizations, all of these?

9. Choose a multinational company. Study its website to see what you can learn about its approach to global business ethics and social responsibility.

10. If you had to create a global code of conduct for your company, what would you include? Which core values would you state? How would you treat behaviors such as gift giving and nepotism?

SHORT CASE

THE GIFT

You're an account executive with a multinational financial firm, and one of your biggest accounts is that of a shipping magnate in Greece. Several months after you've arranged very complex financing to build a new fleet of oil tankers for this customer, he asks if you and your wife would attend the christening of the first tanker. You, of course, agree to attend—it would be an insult to him if you didn't. When you arrive, he asks your wife to break the traditional champagne bottle over the bow of the tanker. Two weeks after the christening, your wife receives a package from your customer. In it is a gold bracelet with her initials and the date of the christening set in diamonds. To return the gift would insult your customer, but accepting it would clearly violate your company's policy. What should you do?

Case Questions

1. What kind of an ethical issue is this?

2. Why would it be against corporate policy to accept such a gift? Do you agree with the policy? Why or why not?

3. Put yourself in the "shoes" of each of the parties. How might they think about the issue?

4. Imagine that you are the corporate vice president in charge of business ethics and conduct for your firm. Would you be willing to change this policy? Why or why not?

CASE

SELLING MEDICAL ULTRASOUND TECHNOLOGY IN ASIA

by Linda Treviño and Alessandro Gubbini

A surprising ethical dilemma arose for a young engineer during his first business trip to Asia to work with customers of his company's ultrasound imaging technology. On the long airplane ride, Pat was dutifully reading a travel book to learn more about Korean and Chinese cultures when he was shocked to learn how ultrasound technologies were being used in these countries. A technology that he had always considered to be a way to help people by diagnosing disease was being commonly used to intentionally identify and terminate pregnancies when the fetus was female. As an engineer, Pat had been trained to be passionate about innovation and problem solving. He was used to thinking about these technologies as innovative high-tech solutions to serious health problems. He was also committed to developing higher-quality, more efficient, affordable devices so that they could be used more widely. It had never occurred to him that in some Asian cultures, where overpopulation combined with a strong patriarchal culture led to a preference for sons over daughters, this technology that he considered to be innovative, helpful, and supportive of people's well-being might be used to eliminate female lives.

As ultrasound technology has advanced and become more available, it has been used more widely in decisions to abort female fetuses in favor of sons. After some more research, Pat learned that this practice has become quite common in China, which controls population growth by allowing families to have only one child. In India, female children are more costly to families because the culture requires the family to bear the expenses of their daughters' weddings and dowries. By comparison, an ultrasound exam is a small expense even for these poor families. Pat was further surprised to learn that using ultrasound technology to identify fetus gender and abort the fetus based upon gender information is unlawful in most of these countries (for example, in India doctors are forbidden from disclosing the gender of fetuses). However, the enforcement of such laws is difficult and spotty, especially in clinics that are far away from cities and regulators. The problem is being exacerbated because many ultrasound machines are being sold on the second-hand market, thus making ultrasound more available and more affordable to these clinics. The increasing use of the technology to abort female fetuses is beginning to create a huge societal problem because males are outnumbering females, distorting nature's careful gender balance. There are estimates that more than 150 million women are "missing" from the world as a result of sex-selective abortions and female infanticide. That's equivalent to missing every woman in America! The 2001 Indian census demonstrated a huge drop in the number of young girls relative to boys (927 girls for every 1,000 boys compared to 945 to 1,000 a decade earlier), and the problem continues to worsen as the use of ultrasound technology increases. According to UNICEF, China now has only 832 girls for every 1,000 boys aged 0–4. Looking to the future as these children grow up, some have predicted increasing trafficking of women for prostitution and violent crime as young males compete for the smaller number of available females.

In thinking through what he had learned, Pat found himself considering the patients, the healthcare practitioners, and the healthcare industry as well as his company, other technology developers, and the broader cultures involved. Patients benefit from access to life-saving technologies that can identify diseases at an early stage so that they can be treated more successfully. But patients can also be harmed if, due to early identification of their child's gender, mothers feel forced into abortions against their will. In these cultures, many mothers apparently do feel compelled by cultural or family pressures to abort female fetuses. Medical practitioners benefit from the ability to do faster and more accurate diagnoses, but they too can be pressured to use these systems for unethical purposes. The industry and the developers (including Pat's company) certainly profit from the production and sale of more of these products. But the company and industry risk sullying their reputations if they are found responsible for selling these systems to unauthorized users for unlawful purposes. Imagine what the media could make of that story. According to a prestigious British medical journal, *The Lancet* (2006), the unlawful use of diagnostic ultrasound technologies is contributing to an estimated 1 million abortions of female fetuses every year. Yet, these diagnostic technologies still greatly benefit society worldwide in saving and improving the lives of many millions of patients.

How should Pat think about this? Do the benefits to society of the technology outweigh the harms? Even if they do, does the company want to be connected to a practice that many people find immoral and that is illegal in many countries? Pat found this practice particularly distasteful when looking at it from the perspective of the females who would not be born simply because of their gender. Pat wondered, "Is this practice fair to them? And aren't we all facilitating the practice by looking the other way? What would happen if such gender discrimination were globally accepted as normal practice? Could that ever be the right thing to do?" What would international health organizations such as the World Federation for Ultrasound in Medicine and Biology (WFUMB), which provides training and education to doctors worldwide, have to say about such practices? Pat wondered what his wife would think if she knew that his work involved this unexpected result? Would she expect him to do something? What is his individual responsibility here? What is his company's responsibility?

Because Pat felt so confused by what he had read, and he didn't fully understand the legal or cultural environment, he never mentioned the subject to his Asian clients. But it remained in the back of his mind. When he returned home, he kept thinking about it. There was no formal structure for him to surface the issue within the company, so he decided to discuss the subject with some trusted colleagues. He wondered whether they were aware of the issue and what they might think about it. Were they as bothered as he was? It turns out that they were as unaware of these practices as he had been. It also seemed more distant to them because they had not traveled to Asia as he had, and there was no agreement about what to do. Engineers tend to think about products only in technical terms—the potential for technical flaws and dangers that might harm patients. They rarely encounter the ultimate end users, and they're not trained to think about cultural implications.

As a Westerner, all of this was particularly hard for Pat to deal with. He was caught completely off guard. He asked himself: "What do I need to do, if anything? I'm scheduled to return to these countries to support our clients' use of our technology, so I won't be able to avoid the issue for long. It seems almost ridiculous that I became aware of this issue through a travel book. If it hadn't been for that book, I probably never would have thought about the issue at all. My company had not prepared me. It offered no special training on cultural or ethical issues for employees they send to work overseas. It seemed like the company's values of providing people with the opportunity for earlier diagnoses prevented us from exploring the potential misuse of our product. The company and industry focus on how to develop technologies to identify life-threatening conditions earlier, better, and faster. We like to think of ourselves and our technologies as saving lives, not risking them. The company's stated value is to provide healthcare solutions to patients worldwide. But, in this case, our technology was being used to both save and end lives. Do our values need to change? I think of our company as being good and ethical, but we were obviously unprepared in this case. We had not done our homework."

Even if the company wanted to do something, Pat wondered what they could do. The company is an original equipment manufacturer (OEM), meaning that it doesn't sell directly to the end users. Therefore the responsibility for putting these technologies into the wrong hands is widely dispersed across different manufacturers, distributors and local institutions. Pat also wondered whether and how the company could influence these different parties to take action even if it decided it was right to do so. On top of that, the company is in the United States, and these end users are halfway across the world.

Case Questions

1. Should Pat raise this issue with management? If so, what should he say?

2. What if he does raise the issue and the company does nothing? What should he do then, if anything?

3. Does this use of our technology breach a core value? Or is this a case where we should respect local cultural practice? Is there some compromise position in between?

4. Should the company be anticipating additional government regulation?

5. What is the risk to the company's reputation of doing nothing? Of doing something?

6. How might the company think about our responsibility from a supply-chain perspective? Might they learn anything from companies in other industries that have had to deal with this issue? For example, would it be appropriate to initiate a policy to engage with customers who certify that they will sell exclusively to authorized users? Even if the company did that, how could they be sure customers were complying?

7. Should the company also be educating and training employees and clients on ethical uses of our products? Or, would that be seen as ethical imperialism?

8. What should a sales representative do if he or she suspects that a client will be using the ultrasound equipment for sex-selective purposes?

9. The company provides service for these machines. Might that be a way to monitor use?

10. Can the company do anything to better understand the root cause of the problem and tackle that?

CASE

GOOGLE GOES TO CHINA

by Renee Flemish and Linda Treviño

Gu Ge (roughly translated as "harvesting song") is the name Google gave to the mainland Chinese version of its Internet search service. Mainland China boasts a huge and growing market of Internet users (the biggest in the world and now ahead of the United States). But China also has arguably the most sophisticated government censorship in the world. The same Chinese government that censors films and bans television programs and rock bands sanitizes search pages by systematically filtering out keywords, pictures, and news accounts. The government also records every keystroke, records sites that individuals surf, and searches for any material that government authorities find offensive. Guards are also posted at Internet cafes to ensure that no one is looking at banned content.

In 2006, Google decided that to retain access to China's huge and growing market of internet users (it then had 26 percent of the market, compared to 60 percent for Beijing-based rival Baidu.com), the company would cooperate with the Chinese government's demand to block Chinese customers' access to Internet sites that include information about topics the government deems off limits to its citizens—such as democracy, human rights, Tibet, Taiwanese independence, the meditation technique Falun Gong, or information about the Dalai Lama.[94] Searches either turn up "acceptable" information or no information and a message saying, "operation timed out."

Here are a few examples of "scrubbed" searches on Gu Ge:

Searches of "Tiananmen Square" produce some 400 photos, all depicting an empty square or one filled with tourists—whereas the same search on Google in the United States produces 22,000 photos, many of them of bloody protests. In 1989 Tiananmen Square was the site of student-led demonstrations against government corruption that culminated in a bloody standoff. Protestors defied orders to disperse, and tanks and infantry were sent in, subsequently killing 2,600 civilians and injuring another 7,000– 10,000. Widespread arrests followed and press coverage was strictly controlled.

Searches of "Falun Dafa" (also known as Falun Gong) find only a series of websites that condemn the practice—search on Google U.S., and you will learn that Falun Dafa is a system of New Age style meditation practiced by some 100 million members. It has been suppressed in China since 1999, when 10,000 members staged a peaceful meditational protest outside China's Central Appeal Office.

The Dalai Lama, often called "his Holiness," is considered by Tibetan Buddhists to be the current incarnation of Buddha, the latest in a lineage that dates back to 1391. However, searches of "Dalai Lama" produce only pictures of a young man that were taken before 1959 when China invaded and took over Tibet and the Dalai Lama was forced to flee to India, where he continues to lead the Tibetan government in exile. The Dalai Lama has been credited with preserving Tibetan culture and education and was awarded the Nobel Peace Prize in 1989 for his leadership of the global movement for a Free Tibet.

Google was criticized for its decision by U.S. Congress members, who accused the company of "decapitating the voice of dissidents in China," "enabling evil," and facilitating the oppression of Chinese citizens via "sickening collaboration" with Beijing. Google was also said to be violating the UN Declaration of Human Rights, which says, "Everyone shall have the right to hold opinions without interference" and "Everyone shall have the right to freedom of expression; this right shall include freedom to seek, receive, and impart information and ideas of all kinds. . . . " Some critics even introduced legislation that would require U.S. companies to locate their computer hardware outside China, create a code for all U.S. Internet companies doing business in repressive countries, curtail technology exports to countries with censorship policies, and create a State Department office of internet freedom.

Bloggers argued that Google had a "moral duty not to bow to China's wishes."[95] The Reporters Without Borders group said that Google's decision to "collaborate" with the Chinese government was a "real shame," and Amnesty International condemned Google's self-censorship policy. The Electronic Frontier Foundation argued that if companies are going to negotiate away users' rights, the companies should at least work together to form a code of practice.

On the other hand, the Chinese allege that they are no different from Western countries, like France and Germany, that restrict Nazi-related content. And company defenders say that these companies are helping to open up Chinese society in the long run.

GOOGLE'S POSITION IN 2006

- Despite admitting to compromising its values, Google maintained that the company would serve a more useful role in China through participation. Withdrawing the service would be "a greater evil," the company said.[96] Although the decision to go into China "involved a lot of hand-wringing and weighing the consequences of censoring results . . . providing some information to Chinese users is better than none at all."[97] The CEO called the choice a "difficult but principled decision."[98]

- Google's chief executive, Eric Schmidt, said that Google had a responsibility to abide by the law in every country where it does business.[99] "We had a choice to enter the country and follow the law, or we had a choice not to enter the country . . . I think it's arrogant for us to walk into a country where we are just beginning operations and tell that country how to run itself."

- The company decided to disclose censorship at the bottom of Web pages by saying, "In order to follow local laws, some search results are not displayed."[100] In addition, Google chat, e-mail, and blogs were not included in the company's service offering in China. Google did not wish to find itself in a position of having to turn over e-mail files to the government. (The company recently resisted U.S. government requests for data on what people were searching for).

GOOGLE'S STATED GOALS AND VALUES

"Never settle for the best." The perfect search engine would understand exactly what you mean and give back exactly what you want. . . .

Google's goal is to provide a much higher level of service to all those who seek information, whether they're at a desk in Boston, driving through Bonn, or strolling in Bangkok.

Following is a list of Google's stated goals and values:

1. Focus on the user and all else will follow. Google has refused to make any change that does not offer a benefit to the users who come to the site . . .

2. It's best to do one thing really, really well.

3. Fast is better than slow.

4. Democracy on the web works. Google works because it relies on the millions of individuals posting websites to determine which other sites offer content of value.

5. You don't need to be at your desk to need an answer. The world is increasingly mobile and unwilling to be constrained to a fixed location.

6. You can make money without doing evil.

7. There's always more information out there.

8. The need for information crosses all borders...Our mission is to facilitate access to information for the entire world.

9. You can be serious without a suit. Google's founders have often stated that the company is not serious about anything but search . . .

10. Great just isn't good enough. Always deliver more than expected.

HOW DO OTHER TECH COMPANIES COMPARE?

Here are a few examples of how other tech companies have handled similar issues:

- Yahoo! handed over e-mail files to the Chinese government to aid in the arrest of two "dissident" journalists who were using their e-mail system to spread news. The reporters are in a Chinese jail.

- MSN, acting on Chinese government orders, shut down a blog critical of local politicians. MSN has a clear policy (now) of taking down websites only when served with a legal order to do so, and of publicly stating why the site was taken down rather than merely deleting it.

- Cisco has been accused of helping the Chinese government build its censorship-heavy Internet system by providing the hardware to block Internet sites.

- MSN, Yahoo!, Cisco, and Google made a statement asking the U.S. government to pressure the Chinese to abandon its efforts to censor expression on the Internet.

■ Skype similarly agreed to filter phrases such as "Falun Gong" and "Dalai Lama."

RECENT DEVELOPMENTS

In January 2010, Google threatened to end its business in China. This was a potentially expensive decision to pull out of the world's largest and most rapidly growing Internet marketplace. Although Google has lost market share and remains a distant second to Baidu.com (China's own Internet search service, which is now estimated to have about 70 percent market share), estimates at the time said that a decision to leave China would mean passing up between $250 million and $600 million in revenue in 2010. That's a small chunk of the firm's $22 billion in total revenue. But Internet users in China were projected to grow rapidly and actually numbered over 500 million in early 2013 (and growing rapidly). The company would thus be deciding to forgo an enormous future market.

Google's decision was precipitated by the actions of sophisticated hackers, originating in China, when they broke into the e-mail accounts of Chinese human rights activists. At least 20 large companies in multiple sectors were affected. Google released a statement that linked the cyberattacks with government censorship, saying, "These attacks and the surveillance they have uncovered—combined with attempts of the past year to limit free speech on the Web—have led us to conclude that we should review the feasibility of our business operations in China."

The topic immediately increased traffic on Twitter. China began blocking Twitter in June 2009 along with Flickr (the photo editing site) and Microsoft's Bing (Internet search).[101]

Google said it would try to work with the Chinese government in arranging to conduct censorship-free searches, but that it was no longer willing to continue censoring results on Google.cn. If an agreement could not be reached, it would end Google.cn.

Given the financial loss to shareholders, some wondered whether the executives had the right to make this decision. Sergey Brin and Larry Page, Google's founders, have that right because Google has two classes of stock—and Page and Brin, who hold 58 percent of the stock, have veto power over everyone, including the company's CEO.

A National Public Radio report suggested that for Brin, misgivings about the company's original 2006 decision trace back to his family history. He was born in Russia, under Communist rule, and has strong negative reactions to governments with oppressive policies.[102]

In an interview with NPR on January 14, 2010, the firm's chief legal officer, David Drummond, defended Google's initial decision to accept some censorship. He said the company felt a responsibility to serve the Chinese market and felt that it could be a force for opening up that market. He noted that the company has been "a thorn in the government's side" since entering the market and has "pushed back at every opportunity."

Experts suggested that the company's response was a way of saying, "enough is enough." The company decided it could no longer protect the security of its users in China. The firm's new stance has been praised by human rights activists and Internet civil liberties specialists, one of whom said, "It helps realign Google's business with its ethos."[103] Another said, "No company should be forced to operate under government threat to its core values or to the rights and safety of its users."[104]

China's response was that firms doing business in China must obey its laws and it did not back down. In March 2010, while maintaining R&D work in China and a sales force, Google decided to close Google.cn and direct its Chinese users to its uncensored Hong Kong website, hoping to make uncensored information more available. When Hong Kong was set up by international treaty, China agreed to allow it to operate free from most Chinese laws. But Chinese users quickly reported that searches for politically sensitive information on the Hong Kong website produced blank pages.

In May 2012, Google began to inform users that certain search terms were being censored. The government responded by blocking Google for 24 hours and by increasing the censorship of gmail, Google's email service. This is in addition to the normal slowness of Google searches in China. The reason isn't clear, but in December 2012, Google stopped informing users about censorship. Every time Google has tried to fight censorship, the government has responded quickly and overwhelmingly, and it appears that Google may have given up trying.[105]

Case Questions

1. Why do you think so many American citizens and lawmakers reacted negatively to Google's decision in 2006?

2. Does the fact that Google is an Internet company change societal expectations of it regarding information openness?

3. Was Google facing an ethical dilemma (values in conflict) in 2006?

4. Analyze the dilemma from consequentialist, deontological, and virtue ethics perspectives (see Chapter 2). Based on your analysis, what do you think is the right thing to do? Do you agree with Google's CEO that the company made "a principled decision"? Why or why not?

5. Google's motto is "Don't Be Evil." What does that mean? And how does it apply in this situation? Is the company living up to its motto? Is it a good motto or would a more positive statement be better?

6. Consider Google's other values related to democracy, not doing evil, focusing on the user, providing information, and so on. Can Google do business in China and maintain these ideals? If so, how? If not, why not?

7. In defense of its 2006 decision, Google said that it complies with the law in countries where it does business. But the author of a book on IBM and the Holocaust says that IBM used the same defense in the 1930s when it provided Adolf Hitler with the tools to keep "the wheels of the Holocaust running on time." The author says, "[they] want to be good Americans in the U.S. and good collaborators in China. They want it both ways but there are certain things we must not do."[106] Do you agree with the company's stance? If so, what changed in 2010?

8. Google and other companies routinely comply with government rules to censor other types of material—especially pornography, but also hate speech and other moral matters such as sexual images in Islamic countries. Are some forms of censorship acceptable? If so, where and how would you draw the line?

9. Tom Donaldson rejects ethical relativism ("when in Rome") and ethical absolutism (insisting on exactly the same standards everywhere for every situation). Instead, he recommends that companies operating overseas adopt an ethical threshold based upon core values such as the Golden Rule and respect for human rights. Those must then be translated into specific guidelines. Do you think Google's 2006 operating standards were consistent or inconsistent with Donaldson's recommendations? If you were going to recommend a set of standards for Google, what would they say and why?

10. Every transcultural set of ethics standards for global business practice includes the principle of human rights. For example, the UN Global Compact says that companies should protect internationally proclaimed human rights and not be complicit in human rights abuses. The Caux Roundtable Principles state that businesses should contribute to human rights in the countries where they operate. Is Google's behavior consistent with these expectations? Do you agree that the company "negotiated away users' human rights" in 2006?

11. What about the company's decision to pull out of China in 2010? Do you agree with it? How might it affect other companies doing business in China? Does it change how you think about the company's original decision?

NOTES

1. P. Bhaskar-Shrinivas, D. Harrison, M. A. Shaffer, and D. M. Luk, "Input-Based and Time-Based Models of International Adjustment: Meta-analytic Evidence and Theoretical Extensions," *Academy of Management Journal* 48 (2005): 257.
2. Ibid.
3. K. J. Templer, C. Tay, and N. A. Chandrasekar, "Motivational Cultural Intelligence, Realistic Job Preview, Realistic Living Conditions Preview, and Cross-Cultural Adjustment," *Group and Organization Management* 31 (2006): 154–73.
4. J. S. Black and M. Mendenhall, "Cross-Cultural Training Effectiveness: A Review and a Theoretical Framework for Future Research," *Academy of Management Review* 15, no. 1 (1990): 113–36.
5. M. A. Shaffer and D. Harrison, "Expatriates' Psychological Withdrawal from International Assignments: Work, Nonwork, and Family Influences," *Personnel Psychology* 51 (1998): 87–118.
6. M. A. Shaffer, D. A. Harrison, K. M. Gilley, and D. M. Luk, "Struggling for Balance and Turbulence on International Assignments: Work-Family Conflict, Support, and Commitment," *Journal of Management* 27, no. 1 (2001): 99–121.
7. P. C. Earley, and S. Ang, *Cultural Intelligence: Individual Interactions across Cultures* (Stanford, CA: Stanford University Press, 2003).
8. P. C. Earley and E. Mosakowski, "Toward Cultural Intelligence: Turning Cultural Differences into a Workplace Advantage," *Academy of Management Executive* 18 (2004): 151–57.
9. K. J. Templer, C. Tay, and N. A. Chandrasekar, "Motivational Cultural Intelligence, Realistic Job Preview, Realistic Living Conditions Preview, and Cross-Cultural Adjustment," *Group and Organization Management* 31 (2006): 154–73.

10. N. Adler, *International Dimensions of Organizational Behavior* (Boston: PWS Kent, 1992).

11. P. Simon, *The Tongue-Tied American: Confronting the Foreign Language Crisis* (New York: Continuum Publishing, 1980).

12. H. C. Triandis, R. Brislin, and C. H. Hui, "Cross-Cultural Training across the Individualism-Collectivism Divide," *International Journal of Intercultural Relations* 12 (1988): 269–89.

13. G. Hofstede, *Culture's Consequences: International Differences in Work-Related Values* (Beverly Hills, CA: Sage, 1980).

14. Ibid.

15. N. Adler, *International Dimensions of Organizational Behavior* (Cincinnati, OH: South-Western College Publishing, 1997); S. J. Carroll and M. J. Gannon, *Ethical Dimensions of International Management* (Thousand Oaks, CA: Sage, 1997).

16. H. C. Triandis, R. Brislin, and C. H. Hui, "Cross-Cultural Training across the Individualism-Collectivism Divide," *International Journal of Intercultural Relations* 12 (1988): 269–89.

17. G. Weaver, "Ethics Management in Multinational Firms: Culture-Structure Contingencies," Paper presented at the Academy of Management meeting, Atlanta, Georgia, 1993.

18. H. C. Triandis, "A Theoretical Framework for the More Efficient Construction of Culture Assimilators," *International Journal of Intercultural Relations* 8 (1984): 301–30.

19. R. D. Albert, "Conceptual Framework for the Development and Evaluation of Cross-Cultural Orientation Programs," *International Journal of Intercultural Relations* 10 (1986): 197–213.

20. Ibid.

21. Ibid.

22. Ibid.

23. S. O. O'Grady and H. W. Lane, "The Psychic Distance Paradox," *Journal of International Business Studies* 27 (1996): 309–33.

24. T. Donaldson, "When in Rome, Do . . . What? International Business and Cultural Relativism," in *The Ethics of Business in a Global Economy*, ed. P. M. Minus (Boston: Kluwer, 1992), 67–78.

25. R. Cropanzano (ed.), *Justice in the Workplace: From Theory to Practice* (Mahwah, NJ: Erlbaum, 2001); K. Leung, "Some Determinants of Reaction to Procedural Models for Conflict Resolution: A Crossnational Study," *Journal of Personality and Social Psychology* 53 (1987): 898–908.

26. N. Adler, *International Dimensions of Organizational Behavior* (Cincinnati, OH: South-Western College Publishing, 1997)

27. Ibid., p. 219.

28. Ibid.

29. Ibid.

30. Ibid.

31. H. M. Tong and P. Welling, "What American Business Managers Should Know and Do about International Bribery," *Baylor Business Review*, November–December 1981, 8.

32. *Report to Congress: Impact of Foreign Corrupt Practices Act on U.S. Business*, March 4, 1981 (Washington, D.C.: U.S. Government Accounting Office, 1981).

33. J. Behrman, *Essays on Ethics in Business and the Professions* (Englewood Cliffs, NJ: Prentice-Hall, 1988); R. Grosse and D. Kujawa, *International Business* (Boston: Irwin, 1992); A. W. Singer, "Ethics: Are Standards Lower Overseas?" *Across the Board*, September 1991, 31–34 and Criminal Division of the U.S. Department of Justice and the Enforcement Division of the U.S. Securities and Exchange Commission. 2012. FCPA A Resource Guide to the U.S. Foreign Corrupt Practices Act. www.justice.gov/criminal/fraud/fcpa and www.sec.gov/spotlight/fcpa.shtml.

34. J. Nelson, "29 Countries Commit to Pact against Bribery," *Los Angeles Times*, November 21, 1997, 1.

35. A. Carroll, *Business and Society: Ethics and Stakeholder Management* (Cincinnati, OH: South-Western Publishing, 1989).

36. http://www.nytimes.com/2012/05/18/business/wal-mart-concedes-bribery-case-may-widen.html? pagewanted=all

37. A. Martin, "Wal-Mart Vows to Fix Its Controls," April 24, 2012, at http://www.nytimes.com/2012/04/25/business/wal-mart-says-it-is-tightening-internal-controls.html

38. C. Bowe, S. Davoudi, and S. Kirchgaesner, "J&J Acts to Push Its Reputation Back into Joint," *Financial Times*, February 15, 2007, 22.

39. J. A. Fadiman, "A Traveler's Guide to Gifts and Bribes," *Harvard Business Review*, July–August 1986, 122–34.

40. G. Koretz, "Bribes Can Cost the U.S. an Edge," *Businessweek*, April 15, 1996, 30.

41. Ibid.

42. M. Weinstein, R. Meyer, J. Clark, "The UK Bribery Act vs. the U.S. FCPA," April 22, 2011, at http://anticorruption.ethisphere.com/the-uk-bribery-act-vs-the-u-s-fcpa/

43. S. Schubert and T. C. Miller, "At Siemens, Bribery Was Just a Line Item," *New York Times*, December 21, 2008, www.nytimes.com.

44. N. Clark, "In Europe, Sharper Scrutiny of Ethical Standards," *New York Times*, May 7, 2008, C8.

45. R. Berenbeim, *Company Programs for Resisting Corrupt Practices: A Global Study*, Research Report 1279-00-RR (New York: The Conference Board, 2000).

46. J. G. Kaikat, G. M. Sullivan, J. M. Virgo, and K. S. Virgo, "The Price of International Business Morality: Twenty Years under the Foreign Corrupt Practices Act," *Journal of Business Ethics* 26 (2000): 213–22.

47. K. Schoenberger, "Hong Kong's Secret Weapon," *Fortune*, November 25, 1997, 141–42.

48. "The High Cost of International Bribery," *Business Finance*, January 7–8, 2007.

49. Transparency International, "Corruption Perception Index," Press Release, Berlin, July 31, 1997.

50. Ibid.

51. N. Onishi, "Making Honesty a Customer Policy in Indonesia Cafes," *New York Times*, June 16, 2009, A6.

52. J. A. Barach, "The Ethics of Hardball," *California Management Review* 27 (1985): 2.

53. K. Leung and K. Tong, "Justice across Cultures: A Three-Stage Model for Intercultural Negotiation," in *The Handbook of Negotiation and Culture* (Chap. 15), eds. M. J. Gelfand and J. M. Brett (Stanford, CA: Stanford Business Books, 2004).

54. D. Vogel, "The Globalization of Business Ethics: Why America Remains Distinctive," *California Management Review* (Fall 1992): 30–48.

55. J. Mahoney, "An International Look at Business Ethics: Britain," *Journal of Business Ethics* 9 (1990): 545–50.

56. L. Nash, "The New Realities of International Business Ethics," in *The Accountable Corporation*, eds. M. J. Epstein and K. O. Hanson (Westport, CT: Praeger, 2006).

57. M. Gunther, "Cops of the Global Village," *Fortune*, June 27, 2005, 158–66.

58. T. Donaldson, "When in Rome, Do . . . What? International Business and Cultural Relativism," in *The Ethics of Business in a Global Economy*, ed. P. M. Minus (Boston: Kluwer, 1992), 67–78.

59. T. Donaldson, "Values in Tension: Ethics Away from Home," *Harvard Business Review* (September–October 1996): 48–62.

60. Ibid.

61. Ibid.

62. R. Haas, "Ethics in the Trenches," *Across the Board*, May 1994, 12–13.

63. T. Donaldson, "Values in Tension: Ethics Away from Home," *Harvard Business Review* (September–October 1996): 48–62.

64. L. T. Martens and A. Kelleher, "A Global Perspective on Whistleblowing," *International Business Ethics Review* 7, no. 2 (2004); L. P. Hartman, D. R. Elm, T. J. Radin, and K. R. Pope, "Translating Corporate Culture around the World: A Cross-Cultural Analysis of Whistleblowing as an Example of How to Say and Do the Right Thing," *Politeiia* 25, no. 93 (2009): 255–72.

65. K. D. Martin, J. B. Cullen, J. L. Johnson, and K. P. Parboteeah, "Deciding to Bribe: A Cross-Level Analysis of Firm and Home Country Influences on Bribery Activity," *Academy of Management Journal* 50 (2007): 1401–22.

66. T. Dunfee and R. C. Holland, "Viable Ethical Standards for Global Corporations: A Glimpse of What Might Emerge," Unpublished paper (Philadelphia: Wharton School, 1993).

67. A. Carroll, *Business and Society: Ethics and Stakeholder Management* (Cincinnati, OH: South-Western Publishing, 1989).

68. B. Hindo, "Monsanto: Winning the Ground War," *Businessweek*, December 17, 2007, 35–41.

69. M. Skapinker, "How Monsanto Got Bruised in a Food Fight," *Financial Times*, March 8, 2002, 13.

70. R. Walker, "Brewed Awakening? Coffee Beans, Globalization and the Branding of Ethics," *New York Times Magazine*, June 6, 2004, 38.

71. D. Neef, *The Supply Chain Imperative: How to Ensure Ethical Behavior in Your Global Suppliers* (New York: AMACOM, 2004), http://www.hp.com/hpinfo/globalcitizenship/environment/pdf/supcode.pdf

72. A. D'Ionnocenzio, "Wal-Mart warns suppliers on measures," *Centre Daily Times*, January 23, 2013, B9.

73. M. Gunther, "Cops of the Global Village," *Fortune*, June 27, 2005, 158–66.

74. D. Neef, *The Supply Chain Imperative: How to Ensure Ethical Behavior in Your Global Suppliers* (New York: AMACOM, 2004), http://www.hp.com/hpinfo/globalcitizenship/environment/pdf/supcode.pdf

75. HP Electronic Industry Code of Conduct, Version 4.01, June 12, 2012, at http://www.hp.com/hpinfo/globalcitizenship/environment/pdf/supcode.pdf

76. A. Carroll, *Business and Society: Ethics and Stakeholder Management* (Cincinnati, OH: South-Western Publishing, 1989).

77. C. M. Solomon, "Put Your Ethics to a Global Test," *Personnel Journal*, January 1996, 66–74.

78. P. Magnusson, "Making a Federal Case Out of Overseas Abuses," *Businessweek*, November 25, 2002, 78.

79. J. E. Post, "Assessing the Nestle Boycott: Corporate Accountability and Human Rights," *California Management Review* (Winter 1985): 115–16.

80. E. Levenson, "Citizen Nike," *Fortune*, November 24, 2008, 165–70.

81. L. Hartman, "Innovative Solutions to the Global Labor Challenge," Presentation at the Ethics Officers Association meeting, Boston, October 2002, and personal communication.

82. M. Gunther, "Green Gold?" *Fortune*, September 15, 2008, 106–112.

83. J. Quittner, "The China Code," *Businessweek SmallBiz*, August–September 2007, 40–46.

84. S. Prasso, "Saving the World One Cup of Yogurt at a Time," *Fortune*, February 19, 2007, 97–101; C. Seelos and J. Mair, "Social Entrepreneurship: Creating New Business Models to Serve the Poor," *Business Horizons*, May–June 2005, 241–46.

85. W. C. Frederick, "The Moral Authority of Transnational Corporate Codes," *Journal of Business Ethics* 10 (1991): 165–77.

86. Ibid.

87. Ibid., p. 168.

88. "Report by the Committee on International Investment and Multinational Enterprise: Implementation of the Convention on Combating Bribery of Foreign Public Officials in International Business Transactions and the 1997 Recommendation" (Paris: OECD, 2002).

89. A. B. Baker, "Are Standards Becoming Standard Operating Procedures?" *International Business Ethics Review* 8, no. 1 (2005): 1, 3–7.

90. F. Coleman, "World Leaders Try to Ban Business Bribery," *USA Today*, November 24, 1997, 23B.

91. K. A. Getz, "International Instruments on Bribery and Corruption," Unpublished paper presented at the Conference on Global Codes of Conduct: An Idea Whose Time Has Come, South Bend, Indiana, University of Notre Dame, 1997.

92. "UN Global Compact Participants," United Nations Global Compact website: http://www.unglobalcompact.org/ParticipantsAndStakeholders/index.html

93. L. Paine, R. Deshpande, J. Margolis, and K. E. Bettcher, "Up to Code: Does Your Company's Conduct Meet World-Class Standards?" *Harvard Business Review* (December 2005): 1–12.

94. C. Chandler, "Inside the Great Firewall of China," *Fortune*, March 20, 2006, 149–58.

95. H. Bray, "Google China Censorship Fuels Calls for U.S. Boycott," *Knight Ridder Tribune Business News*, January 28, 2006, 1.

96. "Internet Giants Try to Find a Way to Live and Grow in China," *South China Morning Post*, February 7, 2006.

97. V. Kopytoff, "Google Defends Its China Policy: Decision to Comply with Government Censorship Was 'the Right One' says CEO," *San Francisco Chronicle*, April 13, 2006, C1.

98. J. Yardley, "Google Chief Rejects Putting Pressure on China," *New York Times*, April 13, 2006.

99. K. Chien, "Update 2: Google Sees Substantial Revenue Growth in China," *New York Times*, April 12, 2006.

100. H. W. French, "Google's China Problem," *New York Times Upfront*, April 3, 2006, 10–11.

101. B. Acohido and J. Swartz, "Censorship May Spur Google to Exit China," *USA Today*, January 13, 2010, B1.

102. "Google's Decision on China Traces Back to Founders," *NPR.org* (January 14, 2010), www.npr.org.

103. A. Jacobs, and M. Helft, "Google May End China Operation over Censorship," *New York Times*, January 13, 2010, 1, 3.

104. B. Acohido and J. Swartz, "Censorship May Spur Google to Exit China," *USA Today*, January 13, 2010, B1.

105. "Google in China. Mr. Kim, tear down that wall; Mr Xi, carry on," *The Economist*. January 11, 2013, at http://www.economist.com/blogs/analects/2013/01/google-china

106. Black. E. 2001 IBM and the Holocaust. Crown.

INDEX

Abbott Laboratories, 198, 370
ABC Insurance Company, 124
Abelson, R., 397n45
Abrahams, David, 353
Abu Ghraib prison scandal, 270
Ackerman, J. M., 107n34
Acohido, B., 445nn101, 104
Action, ethical, 84, 96–104
    Pinto Fires case, 96–100
Adams, Scott, 235
Adelphia Communications, 28, 91,
    207, 226, 351
Adidas group, 424
Adler, N., 442nn10, 15, 26
Adults' ethics, 16–19
Advantageous comparison, 85
Advertising, 367–372
1967 Age Discrimination in
    Employment Act, 117
Agle, B., 204n54
A.H. Robbins company, 226–228
AIDS epidemic, 54, 175, 305, 328–329
AIG Financial Products (AIGFP), 384
Akers, J. F., 25, 36n40
Albert, R. D., 442n19
Alcoa, 160–161
Alcohol abuse, 305
Alderson, Jim, 142–143
Alignment of ethical culture
    systems, 154–156
All the President's Men, 41
Allison, John, 321
Altruism, 22
Ambrose, M. L., 107nn25, 30
American Cast Iron Pipe Company
    (ACIPCO), 376
American Conference of Governmen-
    tal Industrial Hygienists, 374
American Eagle, 424
American Express, 172–174
American Institute of Certified Public
    Accountants (AICPA), 49–51,
    271
American International Group
    (AIG), 383–385
American Precision Components
    Inc., 208
American Psychological Association
    (APA), 47
Americans with Disabilities Act (ADA)
    of 1990, 117
Amgen, biotech company, 370
Andersen, Arthur, 15, 91, 129,
    186–187
Andersen, Ray, 332

Anderson, Gavin, 340
Anderson, Jenny, 147n8
Anderson, R. C., 348n41
Andreiuolo, P. A., 106n2
Andres, K. R., 69nn17, 19
Ang, S., 441n7
Angwin, J., 399n120
Annan, Kofi, 428
Anti-Bribery Convention (OECD), 427
Anti-Terrorism, Crime, and Security
    Act, 410
Apple Computer, 151, 320–321, 333,
    352
    iphone, 387
Arthur Andersen LLP, 28, 91, 129,
    186–187, 208, 253, 319, 351,
    354–356
Aspen Institute study, 11
2008 Aspen Institute study, 11
Assigned roles, 268–272
Astra Zeneca, 369–370
Attanuci, J., 107n22
Attitude of students, 10–11
Audience, analyzing, 217
    good soldiers, 217
    grenades, 217–218
    loose cannons, 217
Audit of ethical culture, 190
    questions for formal systems, 192
    questions for informal systems, 193
Auditing
    formal system, 192
    informal systems, 192
Augustine, Norman, 235, 334
Aupperle, K. E., 349n74
Austin, N. K., 249n12
Authority, 174
Authority, legitimate, 174, 275
Auto Center scandal, 281–284
Automatic ethical decision
    making, 92–93
Autonomous decision making, 82
Autonomous principled thinking and
    action, 81–83
Awareness, ethical, psychological
    approach to, 70–74
    euphemistic language use, 73
    language use, 72
    peers guidance in, 72

Bad apple theory, 14–15
Bad publicity, 26–27, 188, 306
Baker, A. B., 444n89
Bakker, Jim, 162
Ball, G. A., 286n22

Ball, G., 286n21, 315n7
Bandura, A., 108n38, 285n14
Bank of America, 9, 12, 29
Bank of England, 9
Banks, C., 286n28
Barach, J. A., 443n52
Barbaro, M., 347n26
Barboza, D., 347n9
Bardes, M., 203n40
Barnett, T., 106n13
Barrett, P.M., 348n35
Barrett, R. A., 202nn1, 8, 205nn91, 97,
    206n99, 285n2
Barrionuevo, A., 396n16
Barry, J., 286n30
Barsky, A., 285nn10, 12
Barstow, D., 398nn83–84
Bass, K., 106n13
Bate, R., 398n72
Bateman, T. S., 35n16
Batista, J., 206n104
Baucus, D., 348n57
Baucus, M. S., 348n57
Baxter Healthcare, 152
Bay of Pigs fiasco, 276
Bazelon, E., 68n6
Bazerman, B., 69n21
Bazerman, M., 108nn41, 44, 47, 50
Bazerman, M. H., 108nn40, 43
Beales, R., 399n109
Bear Stearns, 7
Bebeau, M., 69n16
Becke, H., 68n3
Beech-Nut Nutrition Corporation, 178
Beedles, W. L., 348n56
Behavior, ethical, 251–252
    managers rewarding, 262
    practical advice for managers, 252
    psychological approach to, 70–74
Behavioral consistency, 405
    assumption of, 405
    economics experiment, 22
Behrman, J., 442n33
Bell, Alexander Graham, 194
Belson, K., 349n67
Benevolence climate, 184–185
Benioff, M., 399n126
Benjamin, J. D., 349n75
Ben & Jerry's, 325
Berenbeim, R., 443n45
Berenson, A., 397n67
Berkeley Business school, 329
Berkowitz, B., 399n112
Berkshire Hathaway, 25, 138
Berney, K., 205n82

447

Bernstein, Carl, 41
Best Buy, 221
Best Practices Forum, 26
Bettcher, K. E., 444n93
Beyer, J. M., 205n75
Beyond Petroleum campaign, 163
Bhaskar-Shrinivas, P., 441n1
Bhopal disaster, 339
Big Company, 127, 216, 390–391
Big Pharma, 392
Big Oil Ltd, 314
Bing, Microsoft's, 439
Bird, F. B., 205nn81, 83
Black, E., 445n106
Black, J. S., 441n4
Blakeslee, S., 35n30
BMW, 365
Boatright, J. R., 395n10
Bonamici, K., 69n26
Booker, K., 398n102
Booklets, 222
Borden, M., 348n31
Borrowing cost reduction, 4
Borrus, A., 349n65
Boston's Bain & Company, 328
Bowe, C., 443n38
Bower, B., 108n55
Bowers, W. J., 204n49
Bowman, F. D., 106n1
Brady, F. N, 286n32
Bramati, I. E., 106n2
Braungart, Michael, 332
Bray, H., 444n95
Bribes
   Bribe Payers Index (BPI), 412
   dealing with, 408–413
   overt bribes, 123
   subtle bribes, 123–124
BRIC nations (Brazil, Russia, India,
      China), 10
Brislin, R., 442nn12, 16
Brochures, as communication
      channels, 221
Brockner, J., 315n9
Brooker, K., 35n18, 203nn16, 41, 37
Brown, G., 106n13
Brown, M., 203nn22, 24
Browne, John, 162
Browning, L., 350n91
Bruch, H., 347n24
Buck stops with managers, 307–309
   continually communicating
      standards, 308–309
   standards, 307–308
Buckingham, M., 315n1
Buffett, Warren, 25, 36n41
*Built to Last: Successful Habits of
      Visionary Companies*, 167
Burden of proof, 178
Bureaucracy, 174
Burger, J. M., 286n39
Burger, Jerry, 273
Burke, James, 160, 240
Burns, G., 348n55
Bush, George W., 4
Business ethics management, 2–36.
      See also Ethics
   future, 2–36. *See also* Cynicism
   MBA oath, 13

Business Ethics Network of Africa
      (BEN-Africa), 414
Business practices officers
      (BPOs), 244
Butterfield, K., 106n3, 205n80,
      348n48
Byham, W. C., 204n42
Byrne, J. A., 36n48, 148n15, 203n27,
      205n95, 249n4, 347nn21, 23,
      398n89
Byrne, John, 161

CalPERS, 335
Campus recruiting, 221–222
Caremark decision, 210
Carnegie, Andrew, 327
Carney, D., 148nn27, 32
Carney, J., 396n15
Carroll, A. B., 347n18, 349n74,
      442n35, 444nn67, 76
'Carrot and stick' approach, 208
Cascading, 233
Cases, 198–200, 345–346
   advertising, 391–393
   Bad to the Bone, 200–202
   clarifying your values, 62
   community, 394
   conflict of interest, 146, 390–391
   culture change at Texaco, 196–198
   customer confidence issue, 146–147
   employment basics, 314
   The Gift, 432
   Google goes to China, 436–441
   managing a diverse workforce, 314
   managing up and across, 314–315
   Merck and river blindness, 345
   Merck's ethical quandary, 345–346
   people issue, 146
   Pinto Fires case, 63–67, 96–100
   product safety, 391–393
   river blindness, 345
   Sears, Roebuck, and Co.: The Auto
      Center Scandal, 281–284
   selling medical ultrasound technol-
      ogy in Asia, 432–435
   shareholders, 393–394
   unethical culture in need of change,
      TAP pharmaceuticals, 198–199
   use of corporate resources issue, 147
   voicing your values, 145–146
   what's wrong with this
      picture?, 246–247
Casino industry, 372
Caterpillar, 333
Caux round table principles for
      business, 428–430
   general principles, 429, 441
   preamble, 440
   stakeholder principles, 442–444
      communities, 385
      competitors, 444
      customers, 442
      employees, 442–443
      owners/investors, 443
      suppliers, 443
Caveat emptor notion, 413
Celebrity endorsements, 228–229
Celgene, 55
CEO ethics, 25

Challenger space shuttle, 89–90,
      178–179, 275
Champy, J., 250n25
Chandler, C., 347n25, 444n94
Chandrasekar, N. A., 441nn3, 9
Channon, J., 36n32, 205n76
Character, 47, 56–57
Charles Schwab & Co., 357
Charan, R., 398n95
Cheating
   perception of peers and, 170
   pervasiveness of, 11
Cheevers, Owen, 265
Chemical dependencies, 305
Chemical Manufacturers
      Association, 339
Cherkasky, Michael, 359
Chevron, 320
Chien, K., 445n99
Child labor, 406, 415, 420–421, 423,
      425
Child, J., 36n44
Chlorofluorocarbons (CFCs), 331
Choi, J., 349n80
Chrysler, M., 397n51
Chu, J., 348n31
Cisco Systems, 330, 438
Citicorp, 8, 151–152, 164, 235
Citigroup, 7–9, 22, 152, 163–165,
      320, 336, 351–352, 356, 361,
      382–383
Citizenship principle, 430
Citrin, J. M., 160, 203n23
Civil Rights Act of 1964, 116–117, 120
Clare, David, 241
Clark, Dick, 229
Clark, J., 443n42
Clark, N., 443n44
Clinical trials, 200–201
Clinton, W. J., 106n6
Club Fed, 336
Cochran, P. L., 204nn46, 52, 249nn1, 9
Codes of conduct, 20, 28, 108n46, 156,
      168–170, 227–229, 410–411,
      429
   in communicating ethics, 229–235
Codes of ethics, 194
Codes, 168–170
Cognitive barriers, 83–91, 367
   consequences and, 88–89
   fact gathering and, 87–88
   gut reactions and, 92–93
   integrity and, 63, 72, 90–92
Cognitive moral development, 76–83
   autonomous principled thinking and
      action, 81
   Kohlberg's theory, 76–77
      conventional (level II), 78–79
      postconventional or principled, 78
      preconventional (level I), 77
      women and men difference,
         question of, 80
   looking up around, 81
   moral reasoning, principled levels
      of, 82
Cohen, J. D., 108n59
Coleman, A., 285n12
Coleman, F., 444n90
Coleman, Glen, 223

Coleman (camping equipment), 378
Collaterized debt obligations
    (CDOs), 384
Collective mental programming, 402
Collectivism, 403–404
Collins, James, 36n37, 167
Colvin, G., 34n1, 204n44, 348n53
Communicating ethics, 215–238.
        See also Multiple communica-
        tion channels
audience,
analyzing, 217
basic principles, 215–218
codes of conduct, 227–229
current status,
evaluating, 218–220
    communication channels
        existence, 219–220
    ethical dilemmas of employ-
        ees, 218–219
    policies communication, 219
ethics communication, interactive
        approaches to, 222–224
formal and informal communica-
        tions, aligning, 215
formal ethics communication
        channels, 220–222
formal systems to resolve questions
        and report ethical con-
        cerns, 235–238
informal systems to resolve
        questions and report ethical
        concerns, 235–238
mission or values statements,
        225–226
organizational policy, 226–227
prioritize policy, 227
relevant rules communication to
        people who need them, 227
reward system to reinforce ethics
        message, 238–239
Communicating senior management
        commitment to ethics, 229–235
ethics training programs, 231–232
local management in training,
        233–234
training existing employees,
        232–233
training new recruits, 232
Community, 394
ethics and, 385–388
Exxon, 385–388
Community ethics, 385–387
Compliance approaches, 241–242
Compliance officers, 211–212
Compliance programs, 156, 207–208,
        242
Computer Associates (CA), 188
Conduct, ethical, 18, 251–287.
        See also Managing for
        ethical conduct
Confidentiality, 127–128
Confirmation traps, 87–88
Conflicting roles, 271
Conflicts of interest, 122–126,
        354–367
costs, 125–126
description, 122–124
Enron, 358, 360

as an ethical problem, 125
fiduciary responsibilities, 129–130
friendship, 123
influence, 124
Johnson & Johnson, 362–364
kickbacks, 123
Marsh & McLennan (MMC),
        358–360
overt bribes, 123
pharmaceuticals, 367–372
privileged information, 124
subtle bribes, 123–124
Toyota, 364–367
ConocoPhillips, 333
Consequences, 88–89
consequences over time, 90
identifying, 54–55
    long-term versus short-term
        consequences, 55
    symbolic consequences, 55
reduced number of, 88
as risk, 89–90
for the self versus for others, 88
Consequentialist theories, 40
challenges in, 41–42
focus on duties, obligations, and
        principles, 42–46. *See also*
        Deontological theories
and principles approach, 45
Consumer ethics, 353–372. *See also*
        'Due care' theory
advertising, 367–372
conflicts of interest, 354–362
product safety, 362–367
Consumer Financial Protection Agency
        (CFPA), 341
Consumer Protection Act, 338
Consumers
ethics and, 353–372
    conflicts of interest, 354–355
    Enron, 355–358
    Johnson & Johnson, 362–364
    Marsh & McLennan
        (MMC), 358–362
    Pharmaceuticals, 367–372
    Toyota, 364–367
Continuous evaluation
        importance, 293
Control
of behavior, 18–19
illusion of, 89
Conway, E., 395n1
Cookie-cutter approach to
        ethics, 189
Cooking the books, 336
Cooper, Cynthia, 144
Corning, Dow, 155
Corporate Culture and Performance,
        229, 380
Corporate ethics committee, 214–215
Corporate ethics office, 211
Corporate guidelines development,
        414–418
Corporate resources use, 131–136
corporate reputation, 131
costs, 136
as an ethical problem, 136
financial resources, 134
providing honest information, 135

Corporate social responsibility
        (CSR), 26–27, 318–350
environmental sustainability,
        330–334
ethical reason for, 321
goodness, question of, 334–344
    benefit of a good reputation,
        334–335
    cost of government regulation,
        337–339
    cost of illegal conduct, 335–337
    investors reward, 335
and performance, research
        about, 339–342
    financial performance, 341
    'virtuous circle', 341
pragmatic approach to, 320
reason for, 318–325
    ethical reason for, 321
    pragmatic reason, 319–320
    strategic reason for, 322
    value chain activities, 323
socially responsible is the right thing
        to do, 342–344
stakeholder perspective on the
        firm, 319
strategic approach to, 322–323
triple bottom line, 330–334
types of, 325–329
    economic responsibilities,
        325–326
    ethical responsibilities, 326–327
    legal responsibilities, 326
    philanthropic responsibilities,
        327–329
Corporate soul-searching, 171
Corruption Perception Index
        (CPI), 411
Cost-benefit analysis, 102–102
Costco, 151
Costs, 299–300, 306
conflicts of interest, 125–126
of customer confidence issues,
        130–131
of discrimination, 116–117
of sexual harassment, 120–121
Covey, S. R, 36n43
*Cradle to Cradle: Remaking the Way
        We Make Things*, 332
Craig, S., 148n14
Credit default swaps (CDSs), 7, 358,
        384
Credit opinion, 7
Credo, 241
Criminal liability costs, 27
Cropanzano, R., 108n62, 442n25
Cross-cultural training. *See* Foreign
        business assignments; Global
        business environment
Cullen, J. B., 205n86, 443n65
Cultural approach to changing organi-
        zational ethics, 189–194
assumptions about people, 191
auditing formal system, 192
cultural systems view, 190–191
diagnosis, ethical culture audit,
        191–193
long-term view, 191
Cultural chameleons, 402

Cultural homogeneity, assumption of, 405–406
Cultural intelligence (CQ), 401
Cultural persistence, 187
Cultural systems approach, 189–194
Culture, 151
  ethical standards in different cultures, 413–414
  influencing behavior, 152–153
    internalization, 152–153
    socialization, 152–153
  negotiating across cultures, 407–408
  strong versus weak cultures, 151–152
Cummins Engine Company, 57
Customer confidence issues, 126–131
  confidentiality, 127–128
  costs, 130–131
  description, 126–130
  as an ethical problem, 130
  personal responsibility, 128
  special fiduciary responsibilities, 129–130
  telling the truth, 128–129
Cynicism, 9–14
  danger of, 10
  media fueling, 11–12
  moving beyond, 9–14
  September 11, 2001, 12
  students' cynical attitude towards business, 11

D'Ionnocenzio, A., 444n72
Danone, 426
Darley, J. M., 108n59, 287n43
Darlin, D., 106n7
Darnton, J., 106n5
Dash, E., 398n103
Davis, J., 249n16
Davis, K., 347n8
Davis, S. M., 204n66
Davoudi, S., 443n38
Deal, T. E., 202nn2, 4, 6, 205n73
DeAngelis, T., 249n14
Decision making, 20, 38–69, 177–178, 194. *See also* Individual ethical decision making
Decision making, psychological approach, 70–109
  ethical awareness and ethical judgment, 70–74
  Pinto Fires case, 96–100
    cost-benefit analysis, 102–104
    script processing, 101–102
  recognizing ethical nature of an issue, 72
    ethical/neutral language use, 72–73
    guidance from social environment, 72
    situations leading to harming others, 73
    toward ethical action, 96–104
Decision making, steps to, 51–58
  actions, creative thinking about (step 7), 57
  character and integrity, considering (step 6), 56–57

consequences, identifying (step 4), 54–55
  consequences of secrecy, 55
  long-term versus short-term consequences, 55
  symbolic consequences, 55
ethical issues, defining (step 2), 52–53
fact gathering (step 1), 51–52
obligations, identifying (step 5), 56–57
self gut, checking (step 8), 57–58
stakeholders, identifying (step 3), 53–54
'Deep Throat', 41
Defense Industry Initiative (DII) on Business Ethics and Conduct (DII), 26, 240–241, 228
Deferred prosecution agreement (DPA), 188
Defining ethics, 18
Dehghanpisheh, B., 286n30
Dehumanization, 86
Deindividuation, 268
Dell, 321
Denning, S., 203n38
Dent, E. B., 347n12
DeOliveira-Souza, R., 106n2
Deontological theories, 42–46
  challenge to, 45
  focus on duties, obligations, and principles, 42–46
  moral rules, 43–44
  veil of ignorance, 44, 53
Der Hovanesian, M., 398n101
Derry, R., 107n23
Descriptive approach, in decision making, 38
Deshpande, R., 444n93
Detert, J. R., 108nn39, 63
Developing world, marketing infant formula in, 422–423
Diagnosis of culture, 191–193
DIALOG coordinators, 243
Diffusing responsibility in organizations, 276–277. *See also* Organizations, responsibility diffused in
Dignity principle, 430
Dilbert cartoons, 235
Dilemmas, ethical, 38–39
  layoff, 39
  loyalty, 39
  truthfulness, 39
Dirty tricks, 407
Disciplinary procedures, 242
Discipline, 295–297
  effective ways to discipline employees, 296
  and rewards, 256–266
Disclosure rule, 55–56
Discrimination problem, 114–118
  costs, 116–117
  definition, 115
  as an ethical issue, 116
  lawsuits, 117
  valuing diversity, 117

Displacement of responsibility, 85
Distorting consequences, 85
Diverse workforce management, 300–306
  diversity, 301
  family and personal issues, 304–306
  harassment, 302–304
Dividing responsibility, diffusing responsibility by, 277–278
Division of responsibility, 277
Dodd-Frank Financial Regulation Legislation, 9
Dodd-Frank Wall Street Reform, 143, 338
Domini Social Index 400, 335
Donaldson, T., 397n43, 398n77, 442n24, 443nn58–59, 63
Dow Corning, 155–156
Dow Jones, 335
Dowie, M., 69n27
Downsizings, 298
Draffan, G., 396nn18, 38
Dreilinger, C., 315nn8, 11
Drug abuse, 305
Druyvesteyn, Kent, 19–20, 179, 183
Dryer, P., 148nn27, 32
'Due care' theory, 354, 367, 391, 394
  design, 354
  labeling, 354
  materials, 354
  notification, 354
  packaging, 354
  production, 354
  quality control, 354
  warnings, 354
Due diligence, 209, 411
Dugan, I. J., 148n16
Duhigg, C., 347n9
Duke Energy, 333
Dukerich, J., 107n29
Duncan, David, 129
Dunfee, T., 443n66
Dunkin, A., 148n22
Dunn, Patricia, 73
DuPont, 331–332
Durham, C. C., 285n11
Dwyer, P., 398n101

Earley, P. C., 441nn7–8
Ecology of Commerce, The, 332
Economic crisis, 126
Economic responsibilities, 325–326
Edelman Trust Barometer survey, 10
Eden, D., 285n13
Edmond, Kathleen, 221, 249n17
Edmondson, A., 108n63
Egoistic climates, 335
Eichenwald, K., 205n90
Eichler, A., 397n65
Eisenberg, N., 108nn56, 61
Elber, L., 35n14
Eli Lilly, 368–370
Elkind, P., 109n67, 286n23, 396nn26, 29, 32, 36
Elliott, V. S., 397n66
Elm, D. R., 107n29

Emotions in ethical decision
  making, 94–96
 anger and, 96
 philosophical dilemmas, 94
Employee engagement, 288–291
 drivers of, 290
  information sharing, 290
  involvement, 290
  line of sight, 290
  rewards and recognition, 290
 managers and, 288–291
 and productivity, 289
Employees and ethics, 372–380
 employee safety, 372
 Johns Manville company, 373
 Lincoln Electric company, 379–380
 Mcwane, Inc., 375–377
 Scott Paper company, 377–378
Employees awareness about right and
  wrong, 15–16
Employees care about ethics, 23–24
Enron, 28, 91, 49, 91, 253, 264, 351,
  354–358
 Enron's collapse in 2001, 2–3
 *Enron: The Smartest Guys in the
  Room*, 15
Environmental Protection Agency
  (EPA), 16, 385
Environmental sustainability,
  330–334
Equal Employment Opportunity
  Commission (EEOC), 117, 300
Escalation of commitment, 90
Eslinger, P. J., 106n2
Ethical awareness, 70–74
Ethical behavior
 reward for, 262
 roles supporting, 271–272
Ethical conduct management, 251–287
 behavior, 251–252
 Dennis Levine example, 255
 Kenneth Lay example, 253–256
 multiple ethical selves, 252–256
 obedience to authority, 272–275
 people fulfill assigned roles,
  268–272
  Abu Ghraib prison scandal, 270
  conflicting roles leading to
   unethical behavior, 271
  roles at work, 270–271
  Zimbardo prison experi-
   ment, 269–270
 responsibility diffused in organizations, 275–280. *See also
  individual entry*
 rewards and discipline, 256–266
Ethical culture, 153–156, 174. *See also*
  Multisystem ethical culture
  framework
 audit of, 190
 becoming, 187–189
 change, evaluation, 194
 change, intervention, 193–194
 developing and changing, 185–189
Ethical decision making, emotions
  in, 94–96
Ethical dilemmas, 38–39, 218–219
Ethical imperialism, 415–418

Ethical issues, recognizing and dealing
  with, 406–407
Ethical judgment, 70–74, 87–96
 cognitive biases getting on the
  way, 90–91
 solutions, 91
 facilitators of and barriers to, 87–96
  consequences, 88–89
  fact gathering, 87–88
  gut, 92–93
  unconscious biases, 93
Ethical leadership, 156–165
 ethically neutral or 'silent'
  leadership, 163–164
 executive leaders create culture,
  156–157
 hypocritical leadership, 162–163
 moral person/moral manager
  approach, 160
 unethical leadership, 161–162
Ethical problems of managers,
  288–315. *See also* Diverse
  workforce management;
  Manager as lens
 costs, 299–300, 306
 managers and employee engagement, 288–291. *See also under*
  Employee engagement
 managing the 'basics', 291–300
  discipline, 295–297
  hiring and work assign-
   ments, 291–292
  performance evaluation, 292–295.
   See also individual entry
  terminations, 297–299
 reasons for, 299, 306
Ethical problems of organizations,
  351–399
 costs, 388–389
 ethics and consumers, 353–372.
  See also under Consumers
 managing stakeholders, 352–353
 reasons for, 388
Ethical reason for CSR, 321
Ethical relativism, 415–418
Ethical responsibilities, 326–327
Ethics, 38–60, 372–380. *See also*
  Communicating ethics;
  Employees and ethics; Organizational culture, ethics as;
  Trust; Virtue ethics
 character and, 17
 and compliance officers, 211–213
  Ethics and Compliance Officer
   Association (ECOA), 211
  ethics infrastructure, 213–214
  ethics officer background, 213
  insiders versus outsiders,
   212–213
  Society for Corporate Compliance
   and Ethics (SCCE), 212
 'controlling' by organizations, 19
 defining, 18
 employees care about, 23–24
 ethical decision-making process, 20
 ethics game, 234
 ethics-related training and
  guidance, 406

executive leaders care about, 25
 importance of being ethical, 3,
  21–27
  behavioral economics
   experiment, 22
  motivation to be ethical, 22–23
  neuroscience, 23
  new imaging technologies, 23
 and the individual. *See* Individual
  ethical decision making
 industries care about, 26
 infrastructure, 213–214
 and law, relationship between, 21
 and legal compliance management, 207–250
  structuring, 208–215. *See also
  under* United States
 managers care about, 24–25
 program
  evaluating, 239–241
  globalizing, 242–244
  surveys, 240–241
 society cares about, 26–27
 supply chain and, 228–229
 teaching, question of, 14–19
  adults' ethics, 16–19
  bad apple theory, 14–15
  employees awareness about right
   and wrong, 15–16
  training business students in,
   importance, 17
  values or compliance
   approaches, 241–242
  values, importance of, 29–30
Ethics and Business Conduct Steering
  Committee, 214
Ethics and Compliance Officer
  Association (ECOA), 211
'Ethics Be A Star' contest, 233
Ethics game, 234–235
Ethics officers, 211–213
 backgrounds of, 213
 insiders *vs.* outsiders, 212–213
Ethics Resource Center's 2011
  National Business Ethics
  Survey, 12
Ethics training programs, 231–232
Etzioni, Amitai, 22, 35n28
Euphemistic language, 72–73
European Business Ethics Network
  (EBEN), 414
Evaluation
 ethical culture changing, 194
 ethics program, 239–241
  Johnson & Johnson's Credo
   survey, 240
  surveys, 240–241
'Everyone's doing it', 266
 people follow group norms,
  266–268
 pressure to go along, 267
 unethical behavior,
  rationalizing, 271
Excessive philanthropy, 341
Executive leaders
 care about ethics, 25
 create culture, 156–157
Existing employees, training, 232–233

Expatriate manager. *See* Foreign business assignments
External locus of control, 83–84
Externalities, 337
Exelon, 333
Exxon company, 385–388
Exxon *Valdez* oil spill, 334, 385–387

Facebook, 352
Fact gathering, 51–52, 87–88
Fadiman, J. A., 443n39
Fair Labor Association (FLA), 424
Fairness principle, 113, 430
  human resources issues and, 299
  measure, 114
    reciprocity, 115
  in organizational climate, 184–185
Fairness, 113–114, 184–185
False Claims Act, 142
Family issues, 304–306
Family, managing, 304–306
Farzad, R., 249n18
Father, Son & Co.; My Life at IBM and Beyond, 264
Federal Acquisition Regulation (FAR), 228
FedEx, 328
Felt, Mark, 41, 46–47
Fernando, C. S., 349n82
Ferrell, O. C., 395n8
Feuerstein, A., 342–343, 349n85
Fidelity Investments, 126
Fiduciary responsibilities, 125, 129–130
Film festivals, 233
Final Accounting:Ambition, Greed, and the Fall of Arthur Andersen, 186
Financial disaster of 2008, 4–9
  reasons for, 4–9
    borrowing cost reduced, 4
    credit-default swaps (CDS), 7
    'liar loans', 5–6
    mortgages, 'slicing and dicing' of, 6
    protection against financial calamity, failure in, 7–9
    real estate investment becoming a choice, 5
Financial resources, corporate, 134
Fine determination, under U.S. Sentencing Guidelines, 209, 247–249
Fineman, H., 349n63
Fionda, A. J., 107n34
Firing, 298
First Alert (smoke alarms), 378
First Boston Corporation, 6
First corporate ethics game, 234
Fisher, S., 205n79
Fishman, C., 348n31
Fiske, S. T., 106n4
Flickr, 439
Flirtations, 121
Flynn, J., 287n58
Focus on consequences. *See* Consequentialist theories

Focus on integrity. *See* Virtue ethics
Folger, R. G., 106n10, 108nn54, 57, 62, 64
Fombrun, C., 348n44
Ford Motor Company, 64–67, 100–101
Foreign business assignments. *See also* Global business environment
  behavioral consistency and, 405
  corporate guidelines and, 414–418
  cultural homogeneity and, 405–406
  difficulties of, 401
  ethical standard differences, 413–414
  ethics-related training, 406–413
  foreign language proficiency, 402
  individualism/collectivism, 403–404
  learning the culture, 402–404
  need for structure, training, guidance, 401–402
  negotiating across cultures, 407–408
  payoffs and bribes, 408–413
  power distance, 404
  recognizing ethical issues, 406–407
  selective perception and, 404–405
  similarity assumptions and, 406
Foreign Corrupt Practices Act (FCPA), 168, 408–411
Foreign country, doing business in, 419–426
  developing world, 422–423
  human rights issues, 423–425
  jewelry business, 425–426
  legitimacy challenge, 419–421
  South Africa, 421–422
Foreign language proficiency, 402
Forgery, 298
Formal and informal communications, aligning, 215
Formal cultural systems, 165–178. *See also* Informal cultural systems
  burden of proof, 178
  decision-making processes, 177–178
  new organizational structures, 175–176
  organizational authority structure, 174–177
    authority, 174
    responsibility, 174
  orientation and training programs, 170–171
  over-reliance on quantitative analysis, 177–178
  performance management systems, 171–174
  policies and codes, 168–170
  selection systems, 165–167
  structures to support reporting of problems, 176–177
  values and mission statements, 167–168
Formal ethics communication, multiple channels for, 220–222. *See also under* Communicating ethics
Formal ethics policies, 168
Formal system, auditing, 192

Forsyth, D. R., 106nn11–12
Foxconn, 320
Fraedrich, J., 395n8
Fragmentation of conscience, 278
Frank, H., 107n34
Frederick, W. C., 444n85
Freeman, E., 36n42, 347n2
Freeman, R. E., 395n6
Fremeth, A. R., 348n37
French, H. W., 445n100
Frieden, T., 35n4
Friedman, M., 347n19
Friendship, 123
Fritsche, D. J., 68n3
Frooman, J., 349n84
Fudging numbers, 135
Fujita, M., 35n16
Functional magnetic resonance imaging (fMRI), 23, 70
Fusaro, Peter, 389

Game jargon, in business dealings, 253
Gap, 421
Gary, E. R., 395n9
Gates, Bill, 36n41, 327
  Gates Foundation, 426
Gee, J. O., 108n64
Gellene, D., 287n55
Geller, A., 398n99
Gellerman, S., 204n68
Gelman, D., 315n15
Gender differences and cognitive moral development, 80–81
General Accounting Office (GAO), U.S. government's, 368
General Dynamics Corporation, 19, 183, 179, 211
General Electric, 25, 157, 331–333, 337
General Motors, 12, 95, 181, 353, 364
Genetically modified organisms (GMO), 419
Gentile, M. C., 35n25, 147n1
George, B., 147n2, 203n26
George, J., 349n68
Gesalman, A. B., 285n8
Getz, K. A., 444n91
Giacalone, R. A., 106n14
Gibson, D. G., 203nn30, 39, 204nn47, 58, 205nn70, 85
Gift giving, 413
Gilkey, R. 106n1
Gilley, K. M., 441n6
Gilligan, C., 107nn21–22, 80
Gillis, J., 347n26
Gimein, M., 398n97
Gioia, D., 100, 103, 109n71
Giving Voice to Values: How to Speak Your Mind When You Know What's Right, 232
'Giving Voice to Values' program, 111–116
Glass-Steagall Act, 8, 165
Glater, J. D., 147n12
GlaxoSmithKline, 143, 339, 369–371
Glazer, M. P., 204n63
Glazer, P. M., 204n63

Global business environment. *See also* Foreign business assignments; Transcultural corporate ethic, development
  challenge to legitimacy, 419–421
  decision to globalize, 400
  globalization, 400
  human rights example, 423–425
  marketing in developing world example, 422–423
  organization in, 418–430
  South Africa example, 421–422
  transcultural corporate ethics development, 426–430
Global business ethics, 414–418
  corporate guidelines and policies development for, 414–418
    ethical imperialism, 415–418
    ethical relativism, 415–418
  policies, development, 414–418
Global Compact, 428–429
Global Crossing, 382
Global environment
  ethics and social responsibility management in, 400–445.
    See also Individual expatriate manager
  organization in a, 418–431
Global Reporting Initiative, 430
Globalizing an ethics program, 242–244
  Ombudsman/DIALOG program, 243–244
Globalizing ethics program, 242–244
Goals, 258–259
  goal setting, 257
  reward systems and, 417
Gogus, C., 285n12
Goldberg, J., 109n75
Golden Rule, 43, 413
Goldman Sachs, 29, 358
Goldman, B., 108n62
Goldstein, M., 396n27
Goldstone, Steven F., 105
Good soldiers, 217–218
Goodman, E., 285n15
Goodman, Peter, S., 203n36
Google goes to China, 436–437
  Google's privacy policies and practices, 387–388
Gopal, A., 315n2
Gorenstein, N., 398n88
GovernanceMetrics International, 340
Government regulation, cost of, 337–339
Grameen Bank, 426
Grapevines, 216–217
Graves, S. B., 349n78
Graves, S. J., 349n73
Grease payments, 23
Green Company, 146, 246
Green Lab, 391
Greenbaum, R., 203n40
Greenberg, A. C., 204n65
Greenberg, J., 315n13
Greene, J. D., 108n59

Greening, D. W., 348n46
Greenspan, A., 4, 395n4
Grenades, 217–218
Groeger, L., 398n71
Groups
  diffusing responsibility in, 276–277
  norms, people following, 266–268
    pressure to go along, 267
    rationalizing unethical behavior, 266–267
Groupthink, 276–277
Grover, S., 286n33
Guinto, J., 203n17
Gunther, M., 203n20, 347n6, 443n57, 444nn73, 82
Gut, 92–93

Haas, R., 443n62
Hager, B., 36n38
Haidt, J., 108n53
Hakim, D., 396n37
Halper, J., 315n6
Hamilton, V. L., 204n61, 205n84, 286nn36, 38, 41, 287n49
Hammer, M., 250n25
Haney, C., 286n28
Harassment, 118–121, 302–304.
    See also Sexual harassment
  hostile work environment, 118
  Quid pro quo harassment, 118
Harenski, K., 106n1
Harned, P., 148nn28, 30
Harris Interactive company, 28
Harrison, D. A., 106n15, 204n48, 441nn5–6
Hartley, R. F., 399n114
Hartman, L. P., 203n24, 444n81
Hatfield, J. D., 349n74
Haunschild, P. R., 348n45, P., 349n59
Hawken, Paul, 332
Hay, R. D., 395n9
HealthSouth, 135
Hechinger, J., 148n14
Helft, M., 445n103
Help lines, 403, 417
Henle, C. A., 106n14
Henry, D., 349n65
Hensley, S., 398n73
Herman Miller, Inc. (HMI), 175
Heroes, 179–180
Heskett, J. L., 229, 249n19, 380, 398n94
Hess, C., 347n20
Hewlett-Packard (HP), 73, 332, 421
Hey, K., 347n20
Hindo, B., 444n68
Hippocratic Oath for Managers, A, 48–49
  accurate and transparent reporting, 49
  acting with integrity in the enterprise's interest, 48
  adherence to the law, 49
  balance multiple stakeholders' interests, 48
  professional development, 49
  respectful and unbiased decision making, 49

  responsibility to protect the profession, 49
  service to the public and society, 48
'*Hippocratic Oath for Managers, A*' article, 48. *See also under* Virtue ethics
Hiring, 291–292
Hirschfeld, S. J., 147n11
Hoffman W. M., 148n23
Hofstede, G., 442n13
Holland, R. C., 443n66
Home Depot, 320
Homogeneity within a culture, 405–406
Honda, 322
Honesty, importance, 311–312
Hong Kong Ethics Development Center, 411
Horatio Alger Award, 253
Hosenball, M., 286n30
Hostile work environment, 118
Hotz, R. L., 108n60
Housing investments, 5
Hui, C. H., 442nn12, 16
Human resources issues, 110, 131, 299
Human rights, 400, 415, 423–425, 427, 429, 441
Hurricane Katrina, 323, 338–329
Hypocritical leadership, 162–163

Iacocca, Lee, 257
IBM Corporation, 25, 151, 182, 188, 240, 264–265, 330, 340
Idealism, 75
Illusion of control, 89
Illusion of morality, 90
Illusion of optimism, 89
Illusion of superiority, 90
Immelt, Jeff, 158
Immelt, Jeffrey, 25
Imperialism, ethical, 415–418
Implicit Association Test (IAT), 93
In a Different Voice, 80
In Search of Excellence, 230
Incentives, 257
Inconvenient Truth, An, 334
Independent Commission Against Corruption (ICAC), 411
Indirect rewards and punishments, 260–262
Individual differences influencing ethical judgment and action, 74–86. *See also* Cognitive moral development
  decision-making style, 75–76
  idealism, 75
  relativism, 75
  ethical judgment and action relationship, 84
  locus of control, 83–84
  Machiavellianism, 84–85
  moral disengagement, 85–86
  universal ethical principles, 75
Individual ethical decision making, 38–60
  ethical dilemmas, 38–39
  practical preventive medicine, 58–59

Individual ethical decision making
(*Continued*)
doing homework, 58
snap decision, 59
prescriptive approaches to, 39–51
focus on consequences (consequentialist theories), 40
steps to, 51–58
character and integrity, considering (step six), 56–57
consequences, identifying
(step four), 54–55
creative thinking about potential
actions (step seven), 57
ethical issues, defining (step
two), 52–53
fact gathering (step one), 51–52
gut, checking (step eight),
57–58
obligations, identifying (step
five), 56
stakeholders, identifying
(step three), 53–54
veil of ignorance, 44
Individual expatriate manager,
401–418
behavioral consistency, assumption
of, 405
cultural homogeneity, assumption
of, 405–406
culture, learning about, 402–404
individualism/collectivism,
403–404
power distance, 404
foreign business assignments,
difficulties of, 401
foreign language proficiency, 402
power of selective perception,
recognizing, 404–405
similarity, assumption of, 406–413
ethical issues, recognizing and
dealing with, 406–407
ethical standards in different
cultures, 413–414
ethics-related training and
guidance, 406
negotiating across cultures,
407–408
payoffs and bribes, dealing
with, 408–413
structure, training, and guidance,
need for, 401–402
Individual responsibility, 174, 176
Individualism/collectivism, 403–404
Individuals care about ethics, 22–23
Individuals' common ethical
problems, 110–148
addressing, 110–148
blowing the whistle, 136–144
how to, 140–144
when to, 139–140
conflicts of interest, 122–126.
See also individual entry
corporate resources use, 131–136.
See also individual entry
customer confidence issues,
126–131. *See also individual
entry*

harassment, sexual and otherwise,
118–121
office romance, 121
people issues, 113–121
discrimination, 114–118
values, identifying and voicing,
111–113
Industries care about ethics, 26
Industries focus on ethics, 26–27
Influence, 124
Informal communications, 178–184,
215
language, 182–184
myths and stories, 181–182
norms, 180–181
rituals, 181
role models and heroes, 179–180
Informal cultural systems, 178–184
heroes, 179–180
heroes and role models, 179–180
language and, 182–184
mentoring, 179
myths, 181–182
norms, 180–181
rituals, 181
role models, 179–180
stories, 181–182
Informal systems, auditing, 192
Information processing, 101
Infrastructure, ethics, 213–214
Ingrassia, P., 397n53
Initial public offerings (IPOs), 163
Insiders versus outsiders, 212–213
'Instant experience' system, 222–224
Instructions, people following, 272–275
Milgram experiments, 273–274
Integrity, 56–57, 90–92
'The Integrity Minute', 233
Intellectual property, 71
Intentions, 46
Intentions, importance, 46
Inter-American Convention Against
Corruption, 428
Internal locus of control, 83–84
Internalization, 152–153
Internals, 84
Intervention and cultural change,
193–194
Investors, social responsibility
and, 335
Iran-Contra affair, 272
Isidore, C., 397n62
Isikoff, M., 349n63

Jackall, R., 204n59
Jacobs, A., 445n103
Janis, I., 287n44
Jefferson, Thomas, 56, 179
Jewelry business, 425–426
Johns Manville, 177, 373–374
asbestos products manufacturer, 374
renaming as Manville
Corporation, 374
Johnson & Johnson, 27, 160, 167, 226,
240, 340, 362–364, 366, 371,
392, 409
Tylenol poisoning, 362–363
LifeScan division, 364

Johnson, J. L., 443n65
Johnson, R. C., 107n34
Jones, R., 349n79
Jones, T. M., 106n8
JPMorgan Chase, 8–9, 29, 361
Judgment, ethical, 84
barriers to, 87–96
consequences, 88–89
as risk, 89–90
for self versus others, 88–89
facilitators of, 87–96
fact gathering, 87–88
psychological approach to, 70–74
reduced number of
consequences, 88
Jurkiewicz, C. L., 106n14

Kahn, R., 286n31
Kaikat, J. G., 443n46
Kant, Emmanuel, 43
Kanter, R. M., 204n60
Kaplan, J. M., 249n5
Karabell, Z., 348n29
Karpoff, J. M., 349n58
Katz, D., 286n31
Keillor, Garrison, 91
Kelleher, A., 443n64
Kelleher, Herb, 156–157
Kelly, K., 287nn52, 54
Kelly, M., 349n73
Kelman, H. C., 204n61, 205n84,
286nn36, 38, 41, 287n49
Kennedy, A. A., 202nn2, 4, 6,
205n73
Kentucky Fried Chicken (KFC), 320
Khurana, R., 69nn12–13, 25
Kickbacks, 123
Kidder, Rushworth M., 3, 34n2
Kiel, P., 399n104
Kilham, W., 287n48
Kilmann, R. H., 205n77
Kimberly-Clark Corporation, 377
Kimes, M., 206n109, 398n70
Kinder, Lydenberg, Domini
(KLD), 340
Kirchgaesner, S., 443n38
Kish-Gephart, J., 106n15, 107n37,
108n63, 204n48
Kleiman, C., 36n35
Knight, D., 285n11
Knox, A., 398n87
Kohlberg, L., 53, 107n16
Kohl's Department Stores, 330
Kopper, Matthew, 356
Kopytoff, V., 445n97
Koretz, G., 443n40
Kotter, J. P., 229, 249n19, 380, 398n94
Kramer, Mark R., 347n15, 348n38
Kratz, E. F., 347n17
Krauss, C., 399n115
Krell, Eric, 148n29
Kroll, Inc., 359
Kuenzi, M., 203n40
Kuttner, R., 349n60
Kyosei concept, 428

Labich, K., 36n39, 206n106, 349n71
Lane, H. W., 442n23

Language, 182–184, 400
  foreign language proficiency, 402
  and informal cultural systems,
    178–184
  decision-making using, 186
Larson, D. E., 69n18
Latane, B., 287n43
Laughlin, L., 399n109
Lavelle, J. J., 108n64
Lavery, John, 178
Law and ethics, relationship
    between, 21
Lawsuits, 117–118, 311, 327,
    355–356, 393, 422
Lay, Kenneth, 82, 253–256, 264
Layoffs, 12, 93, 127, 298–299, 377,
    384
Leadership, 156–165. *See also* Ethical
    leadership
Lederer, R., 285n7
Lee, D. S., 349n58
Legal compliance management,
    207–250. *See also* Communi-
    cating ethics
Legal responsibilities, 326
Legal standards, 21
Legislators role in financial calamity, 8
Legitimacy, challenge to, 419–421
Legitimate authority, 174–175, 275
Lehrer, J., 35n31, 108n58
Leo, J., 315n14
Leung, K., 443n53
Levenson, E., 444n80
Lever, J., 147n11
Levi Strauss, 327, 342, 415–416, 422
Levine, D. B., 255, 285n9,
    286n20
Levitt, A., 395n5, 396n19
Lewicki, R., 147n5
Lewis, M., 347n27
Li, J., 349n80
'Liar loans', 5–6, 73
Liberto, J., 395n3
LIBOR, 9
LiCari, Jerome, 178
Lim, P. J., 349n76
Lincoln Electric company, 379–380
Lind, E. A., 147n4
Liptak, A., 399n118
Little Company, 216, 390–391
LMCommit, 238
Local management in training,
    233–234
Locke, E. A., 285n11
Lockheed Martin, 212–213, 231
  ethics program, 222
  Mission Systems and Training
    (MST), 213
Lockheed Martin Corporation (global
    security), 181, 207, 212–214,
    222, 228–229, 231–233, 236,
    238, 241, 334, 418
Locus of control, 83–84
Loewenstein, G., 108nn46, 52
Logsdon, J. M., 286n32
Long-term consequences, 55
Long-term view, organizational
    culture, 191

Loomis, C., 203nn31–34
Loose cannons, 82, 217
Loyalty, 174
Ludington, John, 155
Luk, D. M., 441nn1, 6
Luthans, F., 206n101

Mac, Freddie, 5
Machiavelli, Niccolò, 84
Machiavellianism, 84–85
Madoff, Bernard L., 8
Mae, Fannie, 5
Magazines, 222
Magnusson, P., 444n78
Mahoney, J., 443n55
Malden Mills, 342–343
Malone, S., 350n89
Management focus on ethics, 18
Managers
  care about ethics, 24–25
  and employee engagement, 288–291.
    See also under Employee
    engagement
  are role models, 309–310
Manager as lens, 306–310. *See also*
    Ethical problems of managers
  buck stops with managers, 307–309
  continually communicating
    standards, 308–309
  managing up and across, 310–312
    honesty is rule one, 311–312
    standards go both ways,
      312
  standards, maintaining, 307–308
Managing ethics, 2–36, 207–250
  compliance officers, 211–213
    ethics officer background, 213
    insiders versus outsiders,
      212–213
    corporate ethics office, 211
  directions, 2–36
  ethics infrastructure, 213–214
  globalizing ethics program,
    242–244
  making ethics comprehensive and
    holistic, 211
  structuring, 208–215
    compliance program, 209
    corporate ethics programs
      in U.S., 208
    due diligence, 209
    U.S. Sentencing Commission
      in, 208–210
  values or compliance
    approaches, 242
Managing for ethical conduct,
    251–287
  advice for managers, 259–260
  discipline, 259–260, 265–266
  goals, 259–260
  group norms, 267–268
  obedience to authority, 275
  personal responsibility, 279–280
  rewards, 259–260
  behavior, 252
  Dennis Levine example, 255
  discipline, 256–266
  'everyone's doing it', 266

  goals combined with rewards
    encouraging unethical
    behavior, 258–259
  electronics appliance sales
    example, 258–259
  indirect rewards, 260–262
  instructions, people following,
    272–275
  Kenneth Lay example, 253–255
  managers rewarding ethical
    behavior, 262
  multiple ethical selves, 252–256
  obedience to authority at work, 275
  punishments, 260–262
  rewards, 256–266
  Tailhook example, 260–262
  Zimbardo prison experiment,
    269–270
Mann, L., 287n48
Manville, Johns, 326
Marcus, A. A., 348n37
Margolis, J. D., 348n28, 349n77,
    444n93
Marketing infant formula in developing
    world, 422–423
Markopolos, Harry, 8
Marsh & McLennan (MMC), 358–361
  Mercer HR Consulting, 360
  Putnam Funds, 359–361
Marshall, A., 286n17
Martens, L. T., 443n64
Martin, A., 442n37
Martin, G. S., 349n58
Martin, J., 205n78
Martin, K. D., 205n86, 443n65
Mason, E., 396nn25, 34
Massad, T. G., 399n111
Mayer, C., 398n88
Mayer, D., 147n2, 203n40
MBA oath, 13
McCabe, D. L., 35nn23–24, 204n50,
    348n48
McDonough, William, 332
McGeehan, P., 396n22
McGinn, D., 348n32
McGrane, V., 35n6
McGregor, J., 109n65
McLean, A. N., 147n2
McLean, B., 286n23
McNeil, D. G., 347n3
3M Corporation, 30
McPherson v. General Motors, 353
McWane, Inc., 375–377
McWhinney, W., 206n104
Media-fueled cynicism, 12
Media portrayal of business, 11–12
Medtronic, 161, 182
Melton, J., 348n50
Mendenhall, M., 441n4
Mentoring, 179
Mercedes Benz, 365
Mercer HR Consulting, 360
Merck & Co., Inc., 198, 225–226, 242,
    339, 345, 370
Merrill Lynch, 7, 22, 117, 336, 357,
    382
Messick, D. M., 69n21, 108nn41, 44,
    47, 50

Meyer, R., 443n42
Miceli, M. P., 206n102, 286n34
Microsoft, 352
Midlarski, E., 107n33
Milgram, S., 204n57, 286n37, 287n50
Milgram experiments, 273–275
Miller, Ross, 389
Miller, S. S., 250n27
Miller, T. C., 443n43
Milliken, Michael, 253
Millman, N., 147n10
Mills, Malden, 342–343
Minton, J. W., 147n5
Misalignment of rewards, 173
Mishel, L., 395n2
Misleading claims, 368
Mission or values statements, 225–226
Mitroff, I., 205n77
Mitsubishi Motor's, 121
Moll, J., 106n2
Monsanto case, 419–420
Montgomery, D. B., 348n47
Moore, J. M., 148n23
Moral Dimension, The, 22
Moral disengagement, 85–86
  advantageous comparison, 85
  categories, 85
    dehumanization, 86
    displacement of responsibility, 85
    moral justification, 85
  mechanisms, 85
Moral justification, 85
Moral muteness, 183
Moral person/moral manager
  approach, 160
Moral psychology research, 92
Moral reasoning, principled levels
  of, 82. *See also* Cognitive
  moral development
Moral rules, 43–44
'Moral sentiments', 3
Morgan Stanley, 9, 124
Morgenson, G., 286n25, 396n21, 399n105
Morris, B., 202n5, 205n71
Mortgages, 'slicing and dicing'
  of, 6
Mosakowski, E., 441n8
Motivations, 46
  to be ethical, 22–23
Mourao-Miranda, J., 106n2
Mozer, Paul, 381
MSN tech company, 438
Multiple communication channels,
  220–222
  for formal ethics communication,
    220–222
    booklets, 222
    brochures, 221
    campus recruiting, 221–222
    magazines, 222
    newsletters, 222
    orientation meetings and
      materials, 222
    social media, 220–221
    websites, 220
Multiple ethical selves, 252–256

Multiple stakeholders, 352–353
  primary, 353
  secondary, 353
Multisystem ethical culture frame-
    work, 153–156
  alignment of ethical culture
    systems, 154–156
    Dow Corning, 155–156
  formal systems, 153
  informal systems, 153
Munich Re, German reinsurance
  company, 331
Murphy, C., 69n26, 349n62
Murphy, E., 349n72
Murphy, P., 202n9, 203nn10, 12
Murr, A., 285n3
Murrell, A. J., 349n79
My Lai massacre 1968, 277–278
Myths and stories, 181–182

Nash, L., 69nn17, 19, 443n56
National Association of Securities
  Dealers (NASD), 126
National Business Ethics Survey, 12
National Highway Traffic Safety
  Administration (NHTSA), 65
National Whistleblower's Center, 144
'Natural rights', 43
Nature/Nurture debate, 15
Nazi war crimes, 272
Near, J. P., 206n102, 286n34
Neef, D., 444nn71, 74
Neff, T. J., 160, 203n23
'Negative rights', 43
Negotiating across cultures, 407–408
Nel, D., 204n51
Nelson, J., 204n62, 442n34
Nelson, Katherine, 151, 234
Nepotism, 418
Nestlé, 422
Neubaum, D. O., 107n30
Neuroscience, 23, 92
Neutral language use, 72–73
Neutral leadership, 163–164
New Balance, 424
New recruits, training, 232
Newsletters, 222
Nichols, J., 285n5
Nichols, M. L., 107n29
Nike, 170, 421, 423–424
Nixon, Richard, 404
Nocera, J., 399n116
Nohria, N., 69nn13, 25
Nongovernmental organizations
  (NGOs), 419
Nonprofit organizations, 132
Nonsteroidal anti-inflammatory drugs
  (NSAIDs), 392
Nord, W. R., 205n98
Norian, 200–201
Norian XR, 201
Norms, informal cultural systems,
  180–181
Norris, F., 398nn90–91
NOVA Award for Ethics, 231
Novartis, 330, 367
Nussbaum, B., 28, 36n45, 349n61
Nystrom, L. E., 108n59

O'Brien, K., 399n119
O'Connor, Kevin J., 244
O'Grady, S. O., 442n23
O'Neill, P., 160–161, 203n25
Obedience to authority, 272–275
  Milgram experiments, 273–274
  at work, 275
Obligations, identifying, 56
Occupational Safety and Health
  Administration (OSHA),
  372
Off the record conversations, 133
Office Depot, 320
Office romance, 121
Officer background, in ethics
  management, 213
Off-label marketing, 200–201
Ohnsman, A., 397n58
Ombudsman/DIALOG program,
  243–244
Ones, D. S., 249n14
Onishi, N., 443n51
Optimism, illusion of, 89
Organization for Economic Coopera-
  tion and Development
  (OECD), 427
Organization in a global business
  environment, 418–431
  business in a foreign country,
    deciding on, 419–426
    challenge to legitimacy,
      419–421
    help for the developing
      world, 426
    human rights, 423–425
    jewelry business, 425–426
    marketing infant formula in
      developing world, 422–423
  transcultural corporate ethic,
    development of, 426–430
Organization of American States
  (OAS), 428
Organizational authority structure,
  174–177
  authority, 174–175
  ethical culture, 174–175
  legitimate authority, 174
  new organizational structures,
    175–176
  reporting problems, structures to
    support, 176–177
  responsibility, 174–175
Organizational climates, 184–185
  benevolence, 184–185
  fairness, 184–185
  principles, 184–185
  rule-based climate, 185
  self-interest, 184–185
Organizational culture, ethics as,
  150–206. *See also* Ethical
  leadership; Formal cultural
  systems; Informal cultural
  systems
  organizational climates, 184–185
  benevolence, 184–185
  fairness, 184–185
  principles, 184–185
  self-interest, 184–185

Organizational ethics
  as culture, 151–153
  management, ethics of, 195
Organizational ethics, cultural
  approach to changing, 189–194
  assumptions about people, 191
  audit of ethical culture, 190
  changing evaluation, 194
  changing intervention, 193–194
  cultural systems view, 190–191
  ethical culture audit, 191–193
  long-term view, 191
  managing, 198
Organizational policy, in communicating ethics, 226–227
Organizational structure, 175–176
Organizations, ethical problems
  in, 14–15, 351–399. *See also*
    Conflicts of interest
  bad apples causing, question of,
    14–15
  consumers and ethics, 353–372.
    See also under Consumer ethics
  controlling employees, 19
  costs, 388–389
  managing stakeholders, 352–353
Organizations, responsibility diffused
  in, 85, 275–280
  by dividing responsibility, 277–278
  in groups, 276–277
  by psychological distance cre-
    ation, 278–279
Orientation programs, 194
  meetings and materials, 222
  and training programs, 170–171
Original equipment manufacturer
  (OEM), 435
Orlitzky, M., 349n75
Otis Elevator Company, 238–240
Ousley, O., 106n1
Overt bribes, 123

Page, K., 349n59
Paine, L., 444n93
Pandit, Vikram, 165
Parboteeah, K. P., 443n65
Parks, S. D., 35n25
Parnell, J. A., 347n12
Patagonia, 325, 421, 424
Paxil, 370–371
Payoffs, dealing with, 408–413
Peach, L., 68n2
Pear, R., 349n69, 397n64
Peck, M. S., 287n45
Peck, Scott, 277–278
Pellegrini, F., 148n24
People for the Ethical Treatment of
  Animals, 320
People issues, 113–121
  discrimination, 114–118
  harassment, sexual and otherwise,
    118–121. *See also* Sexual
    harassment
Performance evaluation, 292–295
  continuous evaluation
    importance, 293
  informal process of, 293
  practical problem with, 293

regular evaluations, 294
terminations for poor
  performance, 298
written assessment, 293
Performance management systems,
  171–174
  designing, 171–174
  dishonest or disrespectful
    behavior, 173
  rewards, 173
  that supports ethical conduct,
    designing, 171
Personal illnesses, 305
Personal issues, managing, 304–306
Personal responsibility, 128, 279–280
Peters, T. J., 206n103, 230, 250nn24
Petersen, M., 397nn44, 63
Pfizer, 210, 370–371
Pharmaceutical industry, 370–371
Pharmaceutical Research and
  Manufacturers of America
  (PhRMA), 339, 371
Pharmaceuticals, 367–371, *See also*
  Johnson & Johnson; Novartis
  Eli Lilly, 368
  Prilosec, 369
  Visudyne, 367–368
Philanthropic responsibilities, 327–329
Philip Morris International (PMI), 420
Pincus-Hartman, L., 203n22
Pinto fires case, 63–67, 96–102
  Corporate Milieu, 98–99
  cost-benefit analysis, 100–102
  personal aspect, 97–98
  script processing, 101–102
  Torch Passes to You, 99–100
Piper, T. R., 35n25
Pitt, L., 204n51
Plagiarism, 71
Playing field, 253
Plender, J., 399n124
PNM Resources, 333
PPG Industries, 138
Polartec products, 342–344
Policies, communication of, 219
Policy manuals, 58, 168, 226
Pollack, A., 397n69
Ponzi scheme, 8
Portable document format (PDF), 220
Porter, Eduardo, 147n6
Porter, M., 350n92
Porter, Michael E., 347n15, 348n38
Post, J. E., 444n79
Potential actions, thinking creatively
  about, 57
Powell, J. M., 250n26
Power distance, 404
'The Power of Dreams', 322
Power of selective perception, recog-
  nizing, 404–405
Practical preventive medicine, 58–60
  learning, 58
  snap decision, 59–60
Pragmatic reason for CSR, 319–320
Praise the Lord (PTL) ministry, 162
Prakash, A., 349n70
Prasso, S., 444n84
Pratt & Whitney jet engines, 207

Pregnancy Discrimination Act of
  1978, 117
Prejudice, 114, 291
Prentice, R. A., 108n51
Prescription drug risk, 371
Prescriptive approach
  in decision making, 38
  to ethical decision making, 39–51.
    See also under Decision
    making
Prevention, 132
PricewaterhouseCoopers (PwC), 126
Prilosec, 369
Primary stakeholders, 353
Prince, Chuck, 164–165
Prince, The, 84
Principle-based decisions, 81
Principles approach and consequences
  approach, 45
Principles, climate for, 184–185
Privacy, 127–128
Privileged information, 124
Procter & Gamble, 369
Product safety, 362–367
'Protect yourself' approach, 242
Property principle, 430
Propst, L. R., 107n35
Prospero, M. A., 348n31
Prozac Weekly, 368
Psychic distance paradox, 406
Psychological approach to decision
  making, 70–109
  cost-benefit analysis, 102–104
  emotions in, 94–96
  ethical awareness, 70–74
  ethical behavior, 74–86
  ethical judgment, 70–74
  individual differences, 74–86.
    See also individual entry
  integrity, thinking about, 90–92
  self gut, 92–93
  unconscious biases, 93
*Psychological Cost of Learning to Kill
  in War and Society, The*, 283
Psychological distance, responsibility
  diffused by creating, 278–279
Psychological warfare, 407
Punishments, 260–262
  administration of, 254
  indirect, 260–262
  indirect effects of, 263–264
  practical advice on, 265–266
Pure Food and Drug Act, 353
Putnam Funds, 359–361
Pygmalion effect, 260, 267

Quantitative analysis, over-reliance
  on, 177–178
Quid pro quo harassment, 118
Quittner, J., 444n83
Quorum Health Group, 142
Qwest, 338

Rachels, J., 68nn1, 5
Rainforest Action Network
  (RAN), 320–321
Ramus, C. A., 348n47
Rashbaum, W., 396n37

Rawls, J., 44, 68n4
Real estate investment, and financial disaster of 2008, 5
Reardon, K., 137, 148n18
Recruiting brochures, 221
Red Co, 147
Reebok Corporation, 424
Reed, John, 164–165
Reed, S., 398n101
Regulatory agencies role in financial calamity, 8
Regulatory backlash, 337
1973 Rehabilitation Act, 117
Reiss, S. A., 249n2
Relativism, ethical, 75
Relevant moral community, 47
Reliability principle, 430
Ren, L., 285n12
Reporting ethical concern systems, 234
Reputation, corporate, 131–134
Resolution of questions systems, 235–238
Resources, corporate, 131–136
Responsibility, 174–177
    diffused in organizations, 275–280.
        See also under Organizations
Responsive CSR, 323
Responsiveness principle, 430
Rest, J. R., 16, 35nn21–22, 107n28
Rest, M., 107nn17, 24
Reward system to reinforce ethics message, 238–239
    Full Spectrum Leadership, 238
    LMCommit, 238
    Model Personal Excellence, Integrity & Accountability, 238
Rewards and discipline, 256–266.
    See also Indirect rewards and punishments
    discipline role, 263–265
    goals, rewards, and discipline, 258–260
    importance, 256–257
    peoples' efforts, 257
Rhee, M., 348n45
Rice, D., 315nn8, 11
Richards, B., 398n93
Ricklees, R., 205n93
Rigas, John, 226
Rights concept, 43
    'natural rights', 43
    'negative rights', 43
Risk, consequences as, 89–90
Risling, G., 397n56
Rituals, in informal cultural systems, 181
Rivkin, J., 350n92
Road Less Traveled, The, 277
Robertson, D., 106n1
Role models, 179–180
Role-playing, 53
Roles, 268–272
    advice for managers, 272
    assigned, 268–272
    conflicting, 271
    practical advice on, 272

role readiness, 270
    supporting ethical behavior, 271–272
    at work, 270–271
Rommel, S., 106n10, 108nn54, 57
Rosenblatt, J., 399n121
Ross, I., 108n49
Rothracker, R., 148n25
Rotter, J. B., 107n32
Rule-based climate, 185
Ryan, M., 349n86
Ryan, O., 35n26

Sacks, D., 348n31
Safety, employee, 372–376
Sakano, T., 35n16
Salomon Brothers, 138, 381–383
Salvador, R., 203n40
Samuel, A., 148n17
Sandler O'Neill & Partners, 12
Sandroff, R., 36n34
Santoli, M., 397n46
Santoro, M. A., 287nn51, 53, 57
Saporito, B., 399nn106, 110
Sarbanes-Oxley Act (SOX), 143, 170, 337–338
Schawble, D., 147n9
Schein, E. H., 202n7, 203nn14, 19
Scherreik, S., 348n49
Schmidt, F., 249n14
Schmidt, M., 148n26, 397n68, 398n75
Schminke, M., 107nn25, 30
Schoenberger, K., 443n47
Schubert, S., 443n43
Schwartz, H., 204n66
Schwartz, N. D., 69n26
Schwartz, S. H., 286n42
Scott Paper company, 377–378
Script processing, 101–102
Sears, Roebuck, and Co., 281–284
Sears's wage policy, 283
Secondary stakeholders, 353
Secrecy, consequences of, 55
Secret, M., 397n69
Secure Bank, 314
Securities and Exchange Commission (SEC), 143, 351, 381
See, K., 285n10, 12
Seglin, J. L., 204n43, 350n90
Selection systems, formal cultural systems, 165–167
Selective perception, recognizing, 404–405
Self gut, 92–93
    automatic ethical decision making, 92
Self-interest climate, 184–185
Self-interest, 184–185
Self-love, 3
Sellers, P., 347n22
Sells, B., 398n78
Senior management
    communicating commitment to ethics, 229–235
    involvement in training, 233–234
Sentencing guidelines in managing ethics, 208–209
September 11, 2001 event, 12

Sewer, A., 203n18
Sexual harassment, 118–121
    costs, 120–121
    as an ethical issue, 120
    types, 118–119
        hostile work environment, 118–119
        Quid pro quo harassment, 118–119
Shaffer, J., 290, 315n3
Shaffer, M. A., 441nn1, 5–6
Shambora, J., 204n44
Shanley, M., 348n44
Shareholders, 393–394
    ethics and, 380–385
        American international group (AIG), 383–385
        Salomon Brothers, 381–383
Sharfman, M. P., 349n82
Sheppard, B., 147n5
Short-term consequences, in decision making, 54
Siehl, C., 205n78
Siemens, 410
Signature Brands (Mr. Coffee), 378
Sikorsky helicopters, 207
Silent leadership, 163–164
Silent Spring, 385
Silver-Greenberg, J., 35n5
Similarity, assumptions of, 406–413
Simmons, D. G., 249n13
Simon, P., 442n10
Sims, H. P. Jr., 286n21, 315n7
Sims, P., 147n2
Singer, N., 397n45
Siwek, S. E., 106n9
Sjoberg, G., 204n56
Skapinker, M., 444n69
Skinner, B. F., 19, 35n27
Skooglund, C., 24, 69n23, 223
Skype, 439
Sloan, A., 285n6
Smircich, L., 202n3
Smith, A. L., 249nn20, 23
Smith, Adam, 3, 34n3
Smith, C. W., 398n96
Smith, D. G., 348n56
Smith, P. H., 395n9
Snap decisions, 59
Snarey, J., 106n1
Social Accountability 8000 (SA8000), 425
Social Accountability International (SAI), 424
Social Investment Forum, 335
Social media, as communication channels, 220–221
Social responsibility, business and, 26–27
Socialization, 152–153
Socially responsible business, 334–344.
    See also Corporate social responsibility (CSR)
    excessive philanthropy, 341
    goodness of, 334–344
        benefit of a good reputation, 334–335
        investors, 335

government regulation, cost of, 337–339
illegal conduct, cost of, 335–337
research results, 339–342
as the right thing, 342–344
Society care about ethics, 26–27
Society for Corporate Compliance and Ethics (SCCE), 212
Society for the Prevention of Cruelty to Animals (SPCA), 132
Soeken, D. R., 148n31
Soeken, K. L., 148n31
Solomon, C. M., 444n77
Solomon, R. C., 68n8
Sommerville, R. B., 108n59
Sonnenfeld, J., 203n29
Sorkin, A. R., 348n52, 396n23
South Africa, doing business in, 421–422
Southwest Airlines, 156, 165, 180
Special fiduciary responsibilities, 129–130
Spillane, Michael, 343
'Spray and pray' program, 189
Stakeholders, 27, 40
identifying, 53–54
managing, 352–353
perspective on the firm, 319
primary stakeholders, 353
secondary stakeholders, 353
Standard & Poor rating agency, 7, 122
Standards
go both ways, 312
continually communicating standards, 308–309
maintaining, 307–308
Starbucks, 292, 320, 330
Staw, B. M., 108n49
Steiger, B., 69nn22, 24
Stewart, P., 286n19
Stolberg, S. G., 69n20
Stories, in informal cultural systems, 181–182
Strachan, J. L., 348n56
Strategic CSR analysis, 322–324
Strategic reason for CSR, 322
Streietfeld, D., 399n119
Structuring ethics management, 208–215
in United States, 208–215. See also under United States
Students' cynical attitude towards business, 11
Substance abuse, 305
Subtle bribes, 123–124
Sullivan, B. N., 349n59
Sullivan, G. M., 443n46
Sullivan, Paul, 148n13
Sunbeam, 378
Superiority, illusion of, 90
Supply chain, ethics and, 228–229
Surveys, 240–241
Johnson & Johnson's Credo survey, 240
Sustainability, environmental, 330–334
Sustainability Group Index, 335
Sustainable development, 330
Swainson, J. A., 205n94

Swanson, D., 347nn1, 11
Swartz, J., 445nn101, 104
Sweitzer, V. L., 108n39
Symbolic consequences, in decision making, 55
Synthes, 200–202
Syracuse, 213

Taco Bell, 320
Taibbi, M., 35n8
Tailhook scandal, 260–262
TAP Pharmaceuticals, 143, 198–199, 210
Task goal, 261
Tay, C., 441nn9, 93
Taylor, A., 397n60
Taylor, S. E., 106n4
Teaching business ethics, 14–19
bad apple theory, 14–15
controlling, 18–19
possibility of, 14–19
Teaching ethics, 18
Teal, T., 349n87
Templer, K. J., 441nn3, 9
Terminations, 297–299
Terminations, 297–299–303
Texas Instruments (TI), 25, 222
Thalidomide cases, 54–55
Theory of Moral Sentiments, The, 3
Thoma, S. J., 35n21, 107n28
Thomas, E., 285n3
Thomas, K., 148n26, 397n68, 398n75
Three hundred sixty degree (360x0030A;) feedback, 310
Tichy, N., 205n96
Tidwell, G., 203n28
Tiffany, 425
Tiger, L., 204n67
Tobacco industry, 372
Toffler, B. L., 186–187, 203n30, 39, 204n47, 58, 205nn70, 85, 87, 89, 285n1
Tommy Hilfiger, 343
Tong, H. M., 442n31
Tong, K., 443n53
Top management involvement in training, 233
Toshiba, 330
Touryalai, H., 35n7
Toyota, 364–367
Training
existing employees, 232–233
local management in, 233–234
model, ethics game, 234
new recruits, 232
Training and guidance, ethics-related, 406–413
American businesspeople, 409
bribes, 408
dealing with ethical issues, 406–407
Independent Commission Against Corruption (ICAC), 411
negotiating across cultures, 407–408
payoffs, 408
recognizing ethical issues, 406–407
Training programs, 170–171, 231–233
creating a dialogue, 232
existing employees, 232–233

local management in, 233–234
new recruits, 232
top management in, 233
training model, ethics game, 234–235
Transcultural corporate ethic, 426–430
development of, 426–430
principles, 427–430
Transcultural corporate ethic, development, 426–430
citizenship principle, 430
dignity principle, 430
fairness principle, 430
fiduciary principle, 430
Google, 436–441
human rights and fundamental freedoms, 427
inviolability of national sovereignty, 427
Japan, 428
Kyosei concept, 428
market integrity in, 427
principles, 428
property principle, 430
reliability principle, 430
responsiveness principle, 430
social equity, 427
transparency principle, 430
Transmitters and executants, 278
Transparency International (TI), 411–412
Treo, L., 315n7
Treviño, L. K., 35nn19, 23–24, 106nn3, 15, 107nn18, 27, 31, 108nn39, 63, 203nn22, 24, 30, 39, 204nn46–48, 50, 52, 54, 58, 205nn70, 80, 85, 249nn1, 9, 286nn21–22, 26, 35, 348n48
Triandis, H. C., 442nn12, 16, 18
Trice, H. M., 205n75
Triple bottom line, 330–334
Trust, 27–29. See also Ethics
Trust professions, 125
Truth in advertising, 126
Tsunami, 361, 328
Turban, D. B., 348n46
Turillo, C. J., 108n64
Twitter, 439
Tyco, 28, 336, 351
Tylenol poisoning, 160, 362–363
Tyler, T. R., 147n4
Type Co., 60

Ultimatum game, 23
Umphress, E. E., 108n64, 285nn10, 12
Unconscious biases, 93
Unethical behavior
conflicting roles leading to, 271
goals combined with rewards encouraging, 258–259
rationalizing, 266–267
Unethical culture, 186–187
Unethical leadership, 161–162
Union Carbide, 339
United Kingdom (UK), 410, 428
UK Bribery Act, 410, 428

United Nations Global Compact, 428
United States (U.S.)
  financial disaster of 2008, 4–9.
    See also individual entry
  structuring ethics management
    in, 208–215
    corporate ethics office, 211
    due diligence and effective
      compliance program,
      requirements for, 209
    ethics and compliance
      officers, 211–213
    making ethics comprehensive and
      holistic, 211
  U.S. Civil Rights Act of 1964,
    327
  U.S. Federal Sentencing Guide-
    lines, 208–211, 247–249
  U.S. Green Building Council, 332
  U.S. Sentencing Commission,
    155–156, 170, 208–211
United States v. Booker, 210
United Technologies (Otis elevators,
  Carrier air conditioners, Pratt &
  Whitney engines, Sikorsky
  helicopters), 207
United Technologies Corporation
  (UTC), 207, 220, 230, 238,
  240–244, 337
United Way, 253
Unsolicited mail, 368
Useem, J., 36n49, 69n26
Useem, M., 398n95
Utilitarianism, 40

Valdez, Exxon *Valdez* spill,
  385–387
Value chain activities, 323
Values, 29–30, 241–242
  definition, 29
  disciplinary procedures, 242
  importance of, 29–30
  and mission statements,
    167–168
  at organizational level, 30
  statements, 225–226
Valuing diversity, 117
Van Maanen, J., 202n7
Vaughan, T. R., 204n56
Veil of ignorance, 44, 53
Verizon, 167, 338
Versa Capital Management, 343
Verschoor, C., 349n72
Vickers, M., 203n35
Victor, B., 286nn26, 35
Virgo, J. M., 443n46
Virgo, K. S., 443n46

Virtue ethics, 46–51, 91
  character and, 47
  'A Hippocratic Oath for Managers'
    article, 48–49
    accurate and transparent
      reporting, 49
    acting with integrity in the enter-
      prise's interest, 48
    adherence to the law, 49
    balance multiple stakeholders'
      interests, 48
    professional development, 49
    respectful and unbiased decision
      making, 49
    responsibility to protect the
      profession, 49
    service to the public and
      society, 48
  intentions, 46
  in legal profession, 47
  motivations, 46
Vistica, G. L., 286n18
Visudyne, 367–368
Vlasic, B., 397nn49, 52, 61
Vogel, D., 414, 443n54
Voicing personal values, 111–113
Volkswagen, 95, 365
Vollrath, D. A., 107n29

Wachovia, 7
Waddock, S. A., 349
Walker, R., 444n70
Waller, D. C., 286n16
Wall Street traders, 7–8, 161
Wal-Mart, 26, 151, 170, 274, 282,
  328–332, 409, 421, 425
Walsh, J. P., 348n28, 349n77
Walter, F., 347n24
Wang, H., 349n80
Warren, E., 147n10
1972 Watergate break-in, 41, 46, 272
Waterman, R. H. Jr., 230, 250n24
Waters, J. A., 205nn72, 81, 83, 286n40
Watkins, Sherron, 81
Watson, R., 204n51
Watson, Thomas J., Jr., 264, 286n24
Wealth of Nations, 3
Weaver, G. R., 68n9, 69n15, 106n3,
  203nn30, 39, 204nn46–47, 52,
  54, 58, 205nn70, 80, 85,
  249nn1, 9, 442n17
Webber, R., 148n20
Weber, J., 107n19, 349n66
Weber, James, 77
Weber, M., 204n55
Websites, as communication
  channels, 220

Wee, H., 148n19
Weill, Sandy, 163
Weinstein, M., 443n42
Welch, Jack, 157
Welles, C., 204n69
Welling, P., 442n31
Werhane, P. H., 397n43, 398n77
Wesslund, P., 203n11
What Went Wrong at Enron, 389
Whistle-blowing activity, 136–144
  company's ethics officer or
    ombudsman, contacting, 141
  going outside the chain of com-
    mand, 141–142
  going outside the company, 142–144
  how to, 140–144
    approaching immediate
      manager, 140
    discussing with family, 140
    leaving the company, 144
    taking it to next level, 140
  when to, 139–140
Wilkins, A. L., 206n100
Williams, N., 204n56
Wilson, J. Q., 147n3
Winstar, 382
Women and men difference, question
  of, 80
Wood, D. J., 399n113
Wood, J. A., 35n11
Woodward, Bob, 41
Work assignments, 291–292
'The Work Ethic: An Exercise in
  Integrity' ethic game, 234
World Federation for Ultrasound in
  Medicine and Biology
  (WFUMB), 434
WorldCom, 28, 49, 135, 337, 351, 358,
  382
Wyeth Ayerst, 339

Xerox, 333
XYZ Drug Company, 127, 132

Yahoo! tech company, 438
Yardley, J., 445n98
Yavitz, Boris, 307
Youngblood, A., 35n19
Youngblood, S. A., 51, 107n18
Yum Brands company, 320

Zakariah, F., 35n9
Zellman, G., 147n11
Zemke, R., 36n36
Zimbardo prison experiment, 269–270
Zimbardo, P. G., 286nn27–29
Ziswesvaran, C., 249n14